50-

D1476345

Planetary Stock Trading

Bill Meridian

Cycles Research Publications

Copyright 1998 by Bill Meridian
All rights Reserved, including right of reproduction in whole or in part in any form.

Published by Cycles Research
666 5th Ave., #402
New York, NY 10103

Designed by M.B. Downing
Printed in the United States of America
ISBN: 0-9646030-0-4

Disclaimer: The techniques described in this book have been utilized successfully by the author. There is no guarantee of future success. No liability is assumed by the author for unsuccessful trades made through use of the methods described in this volume.

Price graphs: in this book are either courtesy of Yelton Fiscal or are from the Metastock Program from Equis International, 3950 South 700 East, Suite 100, Salt Lake City, Utah 84107, USA.

Contents

Money is always on the brain...if the brain is in reasonable order.

Samuel Colson

FOREWORD TO THE SECOND
EDITION

This book differs from the first in several respects. The changes were made to address suggestions from astrologers and booksellers. When it came time to reprint, I found that about 255 stocks no longer traded due to take-over or bankruptcy. In addition, about 150 stocks were so thin, that is they traded little volume or were of so little interest, that I decided to delete the chart wheels and simply list the birth data in an appendix in the back of the book. This enabled us to knock about 50 pages off of the original edition to make room for more analysis. Indeed, when I first published, I debated as to whether 500 or 1,000 was sufficient. After 3½ years, I have found that the first volume was too large; most buyers never used most of the charts. So this volume is more streamlined.

There are valuable additions to this book. First, more case studies and methodology has been added by request. The composition of the three Dow averages have been changed, so there are new first-trade charts for these indexes. In addition, horoscopes of the major exchanges and financial institutions have been included. From my USA database, charts of interesting new issues such as Netscape and Yahoo are in this book. I added the horoscopes of mutual funds.

In the first edition, I noted that stocks that had performed the best in the database tended to have the natal Sun in Taurus. I speculated that this may have been due to a tendency of underwriters to float stock in the spring. Since that time, I have obtained data about the number of stocks issued by season over the past 20 years. In fact, the second least number of new issues come to market at that time (least when the Sun is in Cancer).

Therefore, the fact that the best performers tend to have the Sun in Taurus is more significant than I would have imagined. Also, the first edition and this edition contain 32 charts for the Dow 30 because I included 3 charts for ATT for reasons explained in that section. I neglected to mention that I had found that the earliest ATT chart is the most sensitive to transits.

I have chosen to use the date of first trade, which is usually a day or two after the IPO. I do this because it is on this date that the active trading starts. Only large institutions can afford to be part of the IPO, and this is done through a negotiated price. All of the dates in the book were obtained from the NYSE. I use the last date that I consider to be important. For example, there is a earlier date for General Electric, but GE was then known as another company and

had a different ticker symbol. The story is similar for IBM which also re-incorporated on its 1924 first-trade date. It began trading on November 11, 1915 as another company. An extreme example is the old American Can (February 8, 1907) which sold its canning operations to enter the finance business as Primerica. Why would one use the date of first-trade when the operation, incorporation, company name, and the ticker symbol had changed? A canning company is very different from a finance operation. (This occurred as Neptune squared a stellium of planets in the incorporation chart.)

LSI Logic (LSI) entered the NYSE from NASDAQ, where it was LLSI (May 13, 1983). The new chart has many planets in the second decanate of Capricorn, different from its NASDAQ chart. LSI made ordinary chips, but then found a specialty, chips for SEGA Playstations. This made LSI into an ASIC (application-specific integrated circuit) company. As it turns out, all the ASIC stocks, (XLNX, ALTR, LLTC, LSCC) have concentrations of planets in Cap. LSI has become, and trades as, an ASIC and not a run-of-the-mill chip maker such as NSM and AMD. So the use of the latest listing date is proper in most cases, as it is here.

In some cases it is not proper, specifically where there is no great change in the company or the stock. In any event, I find that there is a shared degree area between all charts for a stock. For example, LSI has placements in cardinal signs in common with LLSI.

To answer your questions about specific stocks that have accumulated since I began the second edition, I include this data:

Travelers (TRV) used to trade as Travelers (TIC) on December 9, 1968.

America OnLine (AOL) used to trade on NASDAQ as AMER on March 19, 1992.

Genentech (GNE) used to trade on NASDAQ as GENE on Sept. 26, 1980.

Acuson (CAN) used to trade on NASDAQ as ACSN on September 16, 1986.

Nike (NKE) used to trade on NASDAQ as NIKE on November 28, 1980.

Seagate (SEG) used to trade on NASDAQ as SGAT on October 22, 1981.

Sensormatics (SRM) used to trade on NASDAQ as SNSR on December 1, 1970.

Silicon Graphics (SGI) used to trade on NASDAQ as SGIC on October 29, 1986.

Stratus Computer (SRA) used to trade on NASDAQ as STRA on June 1, 1979

Iomega (IOM) used to trade on NASDAQ as IOMG on July 7, 1983.

The file of earlier inactive trade dates is listed in the back of this book as an appendix. Also, through the generosity or Mr. Andy Pancholi of London, horoscopes of major British stocks are included.

Thank you for purchasing this second edition. It delivers greater value in a more compact form.

Development of the Work

This book is an offshoot of efforts that began in 1972. The author had completed his MBA at New York University. Reading all quantitative studies on the stock market led to the belief that irrational emotional waves ruled trend changes, not only in the marketplace, but in society as well. An NYU professor confirmed this conclusion. Then, it was noted that cycles from the Foundation for the Study of Cycles relating to stocks were similar in length to some astronomical cycles. Two years of basic astrology lessons followed, leading to these studies.

Early on, an experienced astrologer predicted that I would never have an inheritance. This seemed unlikely at the time because dad was a millionaire. He went broke shortly thereafter. I was impressed by the prediction and depressed by the event itself.

If astrology had predictive value, would it enable one to forecast the prospects for a company? The answer was yes; see the Equity Funding example later in this book. But, as the reader will see in the following pages, There is a big difference between the company and the stock. So, the dates that several stocks began trading were obtained, and horoscopes were cast. These horoscopes had a greater correlation to stock price movements than did the charts of incorporations. This was encouraging, but about 70% to 80% of the movement of any stock is related to overall market movements and not to the company itself. So, years of analysis of DJIA movements proved that there was a connection between planetary phenomena and market movements. However, the task was so time consuming that computerized research was the only answer. In 1977 and 1978, a program was designed to explore correlations between planets and prices. The software became feasible in the early 1980s when PCs became more powerful. I wrote a spreadsheet program in 1983 that enabled the user to plot cycles

generated from planetary positions and market data. This basic Cycles Projector became the heart of the AstroAnalyst program in the late 1980s.

Meanwhile, the number of first trade horoscopes approached 2,000. I utilized them as an aid in stock selection in various positions around Wall Street. Sifting through the batch was difficult. In 1989, the purchase of the Astrological Research Program (ARP) from Alphee Lavoie of AIR Software provided the solution. ARP read the hundreds of charts from the astrology program in which they resided within minutes. Then the charts could be quickly scanned for signs, aspects, midpoints, etc. This fortunate development greatly accelerated this research. Alphee and I then teamed up and combined this ARP scanning function, the first trade charts, horoscopes of highs and lows of various markets, and the Bayer and Bradley indicators into a new program called the Financial Trader. The latest release includes incorporation charts of US stocks and first trade charts from overseas markets. See Alphee.com to keep up with software developments.

This book makes available hundreds of first trade horoscopes to those who may not need or want to purchase the software. This is the only easily accessible source for this information. There is no yearbook or reference, and the exchanges are not obligated to divulge the information to those who are not associated with firms that are members of the exchanges. In fact, the NASDAQ has begun to charge for the data. I had to phone to obtain 4 or 5 dates per call over many years. In addition, the book was written as a guide to the analysis of the charts. Unfortunately, many good examples of the use of these charts from the late 1970s and the 1980s were not included because the files are in storage in the USA. Most of the case histories were actual purchases and sales of between 25,000 and 2,000,000 shares made in the author's capacity as a fund manager.

Bill Meridian ———————

> *27 April, 1998*
> *Abu Dhabi,*
> *United Arab Emirates*

Part 1: FIRST TRADE CHARTS

T hese horoscopes are set up for the date that an issue was listed on a given exchange. The time is that of the opening of trading for the exchange for that day. The New York Stock Exchange (NYSE) and the smaller bourses began trading at 10 AM until September 30,1985. Starting on that date, trading began at 9:30 AM. Subsequent horoscopes are set for this earlier time. The center for Wall Street action is the Big Apple, so all charts are set for New York City.

A bit of explanation about the history of a company and its shares will be helpful in understanding this concept.

1. First, a business opens its doors. Then, if it has not done so already, it incorporates.

2. If shares are sold to the public, the sale takes place through an underwriter.

3. The underwriter lines up buyers and then sells stock on the initial public offering (IPO) date. This puts a supply of stock in public and institutional hands.

4. About five business days later, the stock opens trading. A major new issue of a leading company may be listed directly on the NYSE, as Readers Digest was on February 15, 1990.

The two dates, IPO and first listing, occur close together. I have found the first trade date to be the more important of the two. Customarily, the chairman or president of the company will go to the floor of the exchange and make a token, personal purchase of 100 or 1,000 shares to kick off the trading. In the words of a NYSE official, trading begins "almost immediately." Thus, the choice of the 9:30 or 10:00 AM time for the charts is supported by fact.

Sources of First Trade Dates

The data was gathered from the various exchanges between 1974 and 1998. Data on the NYSE stocks was obtained from the research area of the Exchange. OTC dates are from the National Association of Securities Dealers (NASDAQ). Every effort has been made to ensure accuracy. The data bases were cleaned up before release. No liability is assumed on the part of the author from the use of this data. Because this information is generally available only to NYSE member firms, this valuable data base is your best source.

Organization of Your Data:

The data is arranged alphabetically in five sections:

1. DOW JONES INDUSTRIALS: The 30 stocks that make up the Dow Jones Industrial Average

2. DOW JONES TRANSPORT STOCKS: The 20 stocks that make up the Transport Average

3. DOW JONES UTILITY STOCKS: The 15 stocks that make up the Utility Average

4. S&P STOCKS: Other large-cap New York Stock Exchange stocks.

5. OTC: Over-the-counter or NASDAQ stocks.

As mentioned earlier, each chart is set for NYC at the time of the opening. The company name, ticker symbol, and industry group are listed for each. The Dow file contains more than 30 charts. AT&T has more than one date. The first is the listing date for the old AT&T. The second is the date on which the company reorganized. The third is the date upon which today's AT&T began trading after the forced divestiture of the regional companies.

In a few other cases, there are two charts for the same company, like Time-Warner (TWX). This company was the result of the merger of Time and Warner Communications. The first chart is that for the stock of the newly merged company. The second is that for the assignment of the ticker symbol "TWX." The NYSE considers the second date to be that of the first trade, even though the stock actually began trading on the earlier date. They are very close in time, but both charts are included. The story is the same for Kelly Services on the NASDAQ, and Marriott on the Big Board.

A few over-the-counter (OTC) stocks may show dates that precede the birth of the exchange itself. These dates are the first trades for the stocks on the over-the-counter market. They then joined the NASDAQ when it began operations at a later time.

This Data Is Also Available on Disk

Over 3000 first trade charts are in the Financial Trader program. This software was developed by Alphee Lavoie and myself and is available from AIR Software at 115 Caya

Ave., West Hartford, CT 06110. Phone: 860-232-6521. Fax: 860-233-6117. Website: www.alphee.com. It includes tools for screening the stocks in seconds.

Analyzing the Prospects for a Company

Rather than focus on one horoscope, we usually have a series of dates for any entity. As with countries and political groups, there is a progression of events. Each horoscope rules one facet of the over-all entity. For example, the chart of a country's constitution reflects national legal changes.

If you were fortunate enough to be present when the idea for the company popped into the founder's mind, then we could begin with an event chart. This would be like a chart of conception for a person. One of the next charts in the series might be one set up for the first day of operation. If you can locate the day that a business began, you have a good gauge of the pulse and flow of day-to-day business. The chart of incorporation tells us about the legal entity, the company. The future fundamental prospects of a business entity can be assessed from a set of these horoscopes. After reviewing all these charts, the astrologer will note that there are shared degree areas that are common to all the charts. These degree areas will be very important for the company's future. Most often, only the horoscope of incorporation is available. This will provide information about the company as a legal entity. It will give indications about the daily pulse of business, but not to the same degree as the chart set for the opening of the doors of the entity. The incorporation chart will reflect legal changes and takeovers better than the chart set for the opening of business. Usually, the first and last charts in the series are most important. For instance, the business opens up, it incorporates, it changes its name, it merges with another company and reincorporates. The first and last in the series will likely be most reflective of the current entity. I must note that name changes are also important. Many of today's best-known corporations began as something else. But today, they are commonly known by their most recent name.

Incorporation Charts

Incorporation dates are best obtained from the office of Secretary of State, Division of Corporate Records, in the state of incorporation. For tax and legal reasons, most incorporations in the US take place in Delaware. Records show that 60-65 percent of all companies that have stock listed on the NYSE are incorporated in this state. In Delaware, state law specifies that an exact time of incorpora-

tion must be stamped on the papers. According to officials there, the company is not a legal entity in the eyes of the state until that time. In other words, a company with an incorporation time of 10 AM did not exist under the laws of Delaware at 9:59 AM or before. This date and all subsequent dates involving legal changes such as name changes and re-incorporations can be found on the "certificate of long form of good standing". Further information is available from the Secretary's office in Dover.

In most other states, no time is stamped on the papers. The other state that I have had the most contact with is California, because of the large number of high tech companies there. Data is available from the Secretary of

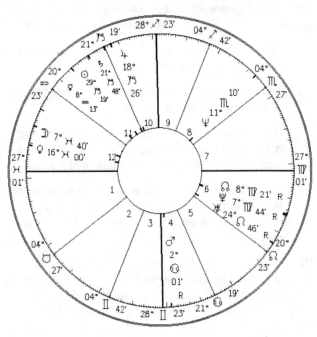

Chart # 1
Equity Funding Corp.
Jan 19, 1961 10:00 AM EST Dover DE

State's office in Sacramento. In this state, as best as can be determined, the corporation begins its existence at 12 midnight of the day of incorporation. I recommend the use of the natal angles in constructing the charts as well as a set of angles for the beginning of the business day, 9 AM. These horoscopes tell us about the fundamental and ongoing operations of the company. In short, if the chart is afflicted, the company faces a host of challenges. Takeovers, strikes, changes in management, the success of new product releases, *etc.*, are all reflected in this chart.

Even the physical appearance of the company can be seen. For example, timed charts of both Warner Communications and Paine Webber show Venus on the ASC. Both companies have extensive art collections. The latter's display adorns the ground floor atrium on New York City's 6th Avenue at 51st Street.

An Example

Examine horoscope *Chart #1*. If this were a person, would you trust this individual in a financial transaction? If this chart were that of an enterprise, would you invest in it? When this question is asked during lectures, 95 to 100 percent of the attendees turn thumbs down. They most frequently cite the Mercury square to Neptune in Scorpio in the 8th house.

Chart #2
Ray Dirks
Mar. 1, 1934, 0:05 AM CST, Ft. Wayne IN

This is a horoscope cast for the time and date of incorporation of the Equity Funding Corporation of America, one of the biggest Wall Street frauds of the 1970s. This insurance company was experiencing above average growth. They acquired other companies by using their insurance in force as collateral for loans. However, most of the insurance policies were fakes, existing only as phony computer entries.

The conspirators actually began to "kill" the bogus insureds and to collect the proceeds of the nonexistent policies! In addition to the long prison sentences that they received, they certainly deserved an award for audacity.

Ray Dirks, a NYC analyst, saw through the sham and punctured the Equity balloon. (His horoscope appears as *Chart #2*, data from him to the author.) The stock fell from the mid-30s to less than 5. The point is that a trained astrological eye could detect this fundamental flaw in the company while all the traditional analysts, except one, failed to do so utilizing the accepted tools of the trade. This case was one that greatly inspired my efforts in the early days.

Selecting Incorporation Times

While not the topic of this book, some readers may be interested in choosing times for incorporation astrologically. The state of Delaware will incorporate a company at a specific time. They require receipt of the chosen date at least two weeks in advance.

L. Edward Johndro followed two rules for choosing incorporation dates. He passed these on to Charles Jayne, and he occasionally mentioned more in his writings. The single most important factor was to identify the planet that ruled the type of business that was being launched. Then, the astrologer had to select a time when this planet would be strong in the sky. Johndro specified that a planet was strong when it was:

    1. conjunct or *opposite* a recent eclipse point
    2. stationary.

Note that these were the most important considerations; other factors, such as the aspects that the planet made at the time, were of secondary importance. Of course, if you have the choice of two horoscopes, and both show that the planet is strong, but one is better aspected than the other, select the one with the better aspects.

Point # 1 requires some discussion. Johndro was not specific about the term "recent eclipse point." In later writings, he clearly stated that eclipses began to have an effect *before* they occurred in time. So, one may look at upcoming eclipses, *i.e.*, eclipses that occur *after* the proposed incorporation date. Johndro stated that an eclipse was symbolic of a general event, happening, or idea. If another horoscope compared well to the eclipse chart, then the person represented by that chart would generally be favorably inclined toward the trend or event represented by the eclipse. So having the planet ruling a new business conjunct or opposite the eclipse point was to ensure that the venture was compatible with the current trends, in Johndro's view. In addition, Johndro greatly preferred solar eclipses. However, he would also work with a lunar eclipse if the solar eclipse dates were not workable.

There is a corollary to the first rule. Johndro also specified that one must look at the aspects made to the business-ruling planet at the time of the eclipse. Let's assume that an entrepreneur wants to incorporate a cosmetics company. Venus would be the likely ruler. We would attempt to find suitable days when Venus is conjunct or opposite the last or the next eclipse. If these dates did not fall in an acceptable period for the businessman, then we would have to look to the stations of Venus. If there was a station in our time frame, we would then look to the horoscopes of the nearest eclipses. Check the aspects that Venus makes within the eclipse horoscope. If we have a choice of two stations, then we would select the one station that is nearest the eclipse in which Venus is best positioned. Or, if we could not find a date on which either of Johndro's conditions could be met, we would have to resort to simple selection of the day upon which the ruling planet is best aspected. In this case, we would lean toward such a date that is nearer to a date of an eclipse with a well-aspected Venus. Incorporation dates near this type of eclipse would be preferable over those near to an eclipse that has an afflicted or unaspected Venus.

The second rule derives from the principle that the more slowly a body moves, the more powerful its effect is. I prefer direct stations over retrograde ones, but the principle is still valid. As an example, a start-up business in the technical analysis area failed in the 1960s. In the course of its business, a large mailing list of professional investors had been accumulated. The owner found a great demand for these names on Wall Street and went on to build a very profitable mailing list business. The company had been incorporated on the day of a direct Mercury station, February 28, 1968. Note that the business succeeded when management shifted to a Mercury-based business and away from technical analysis, which is more closely related to Uranus.

In 1985, I was asked to select a reincorporation date for a Memphis radio station that was to be acquired by a group of investors. Mercury was the planet that best represented the business. The solar eclipse of May 19, 1985 fell at 29 Taurus. Mercury would transit over this degree about 10 days later. May 31 was selected because Mercury was still conjunct the eclipse point, and had entered the sign of its rulership, Gemini. In addition, although Mercury made only a wide opposition to Pluto in the eclipse chart, the Winged Messenger did equal the Jupiter/Pluto midpoint, a favorable combination, fulfilling Johndro's corollary. The radio station did produce an above average return to the investors.

In the early 1980s, I was asked to select an incorporation date for a company that provided warranty protection for appliances. Saturn was selected as the planet most representative of the business. The dates of two Saturn stations were available; the planet was not near a recent eclipse point. The station date that had the better aspects to Saturn was chosen.

The astrologer's challenge lies first in the selection of the planet to match the business. Second, if the planet is an outer one and moves slowly, then it may not come close to an eclipse point within a reasonable amount of time. If that is the case, use the second rule; the stations of the planet, and the corollary to the first rule.

Incorporation
Versus First Trade Charts

Today, most researchers in this field utilize the incorporation chart to predict share price. This section has been included to answer questions that the reader may have about the use and relationship of these horoscopes. To make this comparison, we first need to back up and take a look at the theory of stock price movement and the conduct of research on Wall Street. Theoretically, an investor is willing to purchase a stock because he likes the prospects of the company in terms of earnings and dividends. The price he is willing to pay is primarily based upon:

1. The actual ongoing fundamentals of the company measured in earnings. This can be measured from incorporation charts.

2. His perception of the fundamentals of the company. Research by the Value Line Investment Survey has shown that large share price changes occur when a company reports earnings that are more than one standard deviation away from the mean estimate of earnings.

In other words, as long as the earnings fall into the range of estimated earnings on Wall Street, there is little price reaction. It is deviation from expectation that causes sudden movements. It is this perception that is reflected in the stock price that can be measured by the first trade chart.

We cannot leave this subject without some thoughts from my late friend and teacher, Charles A. Jayne. He did work on timed incorporation charts. He found that connections between the Moon, Jupiter, and Neptune in incorporation charts caused big upward moves in their share prices. The technique that was most powerful in this regard was secondary progression. If there was contact between secondary Jupiter to Neptune, or either to natal Moon, you have a winner. If an accurate time could be obtained, then the

continued on page 12

An Example —
Warner Communications

*Compare charts 3 and 4 against
the transits of December, 1982.
Which one indicated difficulty?*

These are the horoscopes of one of the Street's darlings in the 1982-1983 bull market. Warner rallied from 34 to 60 by December of 1983, but then was unable to rise further. Insiders were selling and volume soared. *Chart 3* depicts the first trade horoscope. Saturn opposed the Sun-Jupiter conjunction in the 10th house. Trading was halted, and opened up at 33 the next day. Warner did not bottom out until it hit $18 per share. Contrast the negative picture in the trade chart to the not-so-bad and relatively good incorporation horoscope, *Chart 4* (the data is from the state of Delaware, so the time is accurate).

Uranus is on the MC which could be interpreted as a change in public image, but there is also a favorable Jupiter return. The trade chart gave a more accurate signal of the subsequent stock price movement. It is important to remember that the incorporation chart reflected the fundamental operations of the company, which were still fairly sound. So why did Warner get hit so hard if the operations of the company did not begin to suffer until months later? The answer is because the expectations of investors were that earnings would be much higher in 6 to 12 months. This expectation was supporting the stock price. When it became apparent that sales of video games at the Atari division (note Saturn squaring Venus in Aquarius) would not be as good as expected, the air was let out of the balloon.

Patience paid off for the financial astrologer who kept his eye on this chart. The trine of transiting Uranus to that same Sun-Jupiter conjunction set Warner back into the spotlight in its 3-way takeover battle with *Time* in the spring of 1989. Note, in *Chart 5*, that *Time's* chart was stimulated by the same transit. In fact, *Time* began trading near the same date. Both stocks outperformed until *Time* bought Warner out in the autumn of the same year.

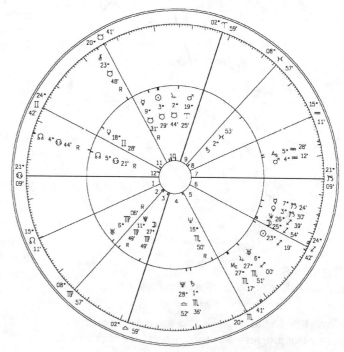

Chart #3

inside: Warner Communications first trade
April 23, 1964 10AM NYC, NY
outside: Transits for December, 1982

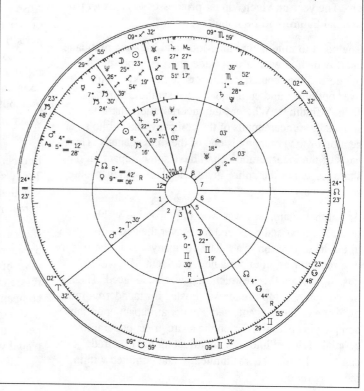

Chart #4

inside: Warner Communications incorporation
Dec. 31, 1971 10 AM, Dover, DE
outside: Transits for December, 1982

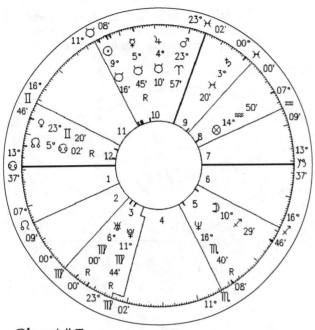

Chart #5
Time Inc. April 29, 1964 10 AM EDT NY, NY

MC was also an indicator. He also was quick to point out that an exact progressed-to-natal aspect between two outer planets in a natal chart was rare, happening about four or five times in a human lifetime. Because they are infrequent, they are very potent influences. For example, Jupiter and Saturn may be trine at birth, but slightly out of orb. The year in which Jupiter progresses to an exact trine to natal Saturn will be important.

The point to note is that the Moon and MC in a mundane chart, which is what a first trade chart is, represent the public and the reputation. Jupiter-Neptune symbolize over-optimism and euphoria. So the symbolism fits Jayne's findings. Whereas the incorporation chart describes the fundamentals of the company, the public's perception of the company is one of the fundamentals. Thus, parts of the incorporation chart have some impact on the share price, but the entire first trade chart relates to the share price.

As another example, I was working for Paine Webber when Pluto passed back and forth over the company's Sun in the incorporation chart. The company was in the midst of a reorganization under a new president. He was then ousted, and another restructuring was announced. Then, the company's top broker was busted for laundering money. None of these events had a material impact upon the company's operations or on the share price, but employees certainly felt it. Pluto was not affecting the first trade chart, so the impact was limited to and confined within the corporation.

Perception Versus Reality

A Harvard researcher conducted a study in the 1980s that drives this point home. He divided students into two groups. Both were given mythical $1 million portfolios to manage on a PC. They were fed price data on each stock. Additionally, one group received news items pertaining to the companies, while the other did not.

These news items were brief one-liners like notices of dividend increases or earnings reports. The items were deliberately skewed in tune with the price moves. Positive news accompanied price rises, while negative news followed price declines. When the test period was concluded, the portfolios of the "no-news" group had outperformed the "news" group, 27 versus 17 percent.

The added factor of the news releases tended to keep the students in stocks that should have been sold and kept them away from issues that were bottoming out. The students that outperformed based their decisions solely upon the price movements.

In this test, note how the subjects who received news were distracted from what was really going on (the share price) by the day-to-day operations of the company (the news). So if the price is not reflecting today's news, to what is it reacting?

Markets anticipate the future. The Wall Street word is "discount". Price changes are being made in anticipation of some future event. Studies by Ned Davis Research supports this phenomena. When aggregate earnings of the S&P companies are declining on a year-over-year basis, the stock market tends to rally. When the earnings of companies have risen strongly over the earnings for the previous year, the market tends to fall. The current news, or reported earnings in this case, was already anticipated and share price changed accordingly.

In other words, price has already discounted today's news. Today's price change is telling us a story about the future. It is this process that we attempt to measure with the horoscope of first trade.

It is certainly possible for the operations to be improving or deteriorating without the stock moving initially. But, most of the time, as we have seen, investors are buying on future expectations. The fundamental operations of the company are reflected by these charts: day of opening of business, incorporation, name change, *etc.* The future expectations or perceptions of the fundamentals of the company by investors that result in stock price movements, especially short-term, are reflected in the first trade charts.

The Over-all Market Versus the Individual Stock

Dr. B. King's Ph.D. dissertation determined that about 70 percent of the price movement of any individual security is associated with the over-all market. Only about 30 percent of the price action derives from activities of the company (like earnings or dividends) and its industry. In other words, in a bull market, *all* shares generally rise, and the reverse is true in a bear market. First trade charts are about the 30 percent of the price movement that is associated with the stock itself.

Over time - two or three years - increasingly positive conditions in an incorporation chart will generally result in a rising stock price, especially when coming out of a very afflicted period of poor planetary aspects. But most price movement can be anticipated with the trade horoscope.

Just remember, STP was one of the highest flying stocks on Wall Street in the '60s. There was and never has been a single shred of evidence that STP Oil Treatment did anything beneficial for the engine of an automobile. Yet, everyone believed it did, and bought the stock.

This type of crowd reaction is the type of energy that you are reading with the trade chart. The incorporation chart tells us what is actually happening in the company. The gap between the reality and the perception can be wide.

Combining the Effects of Both Horoscopes

So, there can be several different situations regarding a company and its share price. These situations can be reflected by the charts. If we have two horoscopes for each company, and each can be evaluated as well-aspected or poorly aspected, then we have four possible combinations:

1 - Well aspected horoscopes of both first trade and incorporation. Business is good and investors have a favorable view of the stock, which outperforms the averages. This is the type of situation that investors like best. It makes the most sense to the logical mind.

2 - Both charts are afflicted. This is the reverse of situation 1. Business is suffering, as is the share price. This is also logical to the average person.

3 - The chart of first trade appears favorable, while the incorporation is under stress. Business is not growing or there are some other fundamental difficulties, but the share price holds up or even rises. In this case, investors are looking past the company's current problems

to the future. They are buying the stock with the anticipation that the situation will clear up. This, and the next condition, are the most difficult for most to comprehend.

4 - The first-trade chart is afflicted, but the incorporation chart is not. Here, the basic business is sound, but Wall Street takes no notice. The share price languishes despite the positive fundamentals. Investors may simply not believe or understand the company's operations. Or, they may be anticipating a slowdown in the future, the reverse of situation 3. This was the case with Archer-Daniels Midland (ADM) in the spring and summer of 1994. The government mandated the use of ethanol as a gasoline replacement. ADM, ethanol producer, was to benefit from the decision, but the stock did not rally on the news.

If you are going to work with both charts, the best approach is to focus on shared degree areas. For example, IBM started trading with the Sun in Aquarius. It was also incorporated with the Sun in that sign. Therefore, aspects

---

Do's and Don'ts

No rules relating to any market are carved in stone, but the following guidelines will prove helpful.

1 - Select a small group of stocks to work with.

2 - Select horoscopes that make soft or positive connections to your own.

3 - Understand the concept of relative strength.

4 - Trade with the trend; the trend is your friend.

5 - Different groups of stocks have different characteristics.

6 - Confirm selections with technical analysis.

---

to Aquarius are important to IBM. And, of course, Aquarius is the sign that rules computers.

Note that the passage of Saturn through this sign coincided with Big Blue's slump. One reason that we felt the company and the stock had turned the corner was Saturn's transit out of this sign. Note that Saturn's last pass through late Aquarius occurred when the company's founder, Thomas J. Watson, died. This was symbolic of a Saturn passage over the Sun.

As this book was nearing completion, there was another good example of this principle when American Home Products began to buy American Cyanamid (ACY). See the ACY example, number 27, in the Case Studies section. ACY began trading on July 21, 1947 and was incorporated on July 22, 1907. Note that transiting Uranus was near the Sun positions in both horoscopes on August 2, 1994 when the bid was announced, and the stock jumped $30. It is not too surprising to see the Suns in the charts heavily aspected. The Sun (and the MC) symbolize the leader in mundane charts, and research demonstrates that about 60 to 65 percent of corporate presidents lose their positions when their companies are acquired.

Selection of a Working Stock Group

This book contains 1,000 charts. Choose a small group of perhaps 10 or 20. It is far better to concentrate your studies than to scatter your attention. Pick stocks in which you have always had an interest or in which you may have some knowledge of the industry.

Select Charts
Compatible with Your Own

As a junior analyst on Wall Street, I frequently called companies to speak to management. One day, after the phone rang for some time, an out-of-breath gentlemen answered. He introduced himself as the chairman, and we began a lively discussion and a fruitful relationship. My earnings estimates and share price projections were always very much on target. When the horoscope of incorporation was cast, I discovered that the company's Sun was conjunct my Moon and their Moon was conjunct my Sun. This powerful synastry explained the solid connection that began on that day. The chart of first trade also made favorable, though less dramatic contacts, to my planets.

In the summer of 1986, I purchased Horn and Hardart (no longer trading) on the Amex. The stock failed to move. We anticipated an over-all market pull-back, so Horn was sold at cost. The Dow then fell about 150 points...and Horn and Hardart ran from 13 to 19 in the midst of the decline. Mars in the horoscope of first trade opposed Mars in my natal chart. This stock and I were always at odds.

Novell, the computer network stock, was up for consideration. Despite some misgivings about the company, a position was taken for a fund. The stock appeared ready to move, but simply did not. What was particularly disturb-

ing was the strong price action of other equities in the same networking group. If a stock does not move after it has given buy signals, whether they are technical or planetary, back off. There is likely some bigger influence that is not yet apparent. The warning signs were heeded, and Novell was sold at a slight loss. The shares then fell an additional 45 percent. Novell (in the OTC or NASDAQ section) began trading on January 17,1985 with Pluto at 4 Scorpio 38. This is exactly opposite my Sun, 4 Taurus 38, symbolic of a strained relationship at best. That experience was enough to encourage me to look elsewhere in the industry.

I could go on, but you get the picture. Why invite difficulty by stepping into a stressful situation?

The Concept of Relative Strength

The performance of most fund managers is measured relative to the market. A benchmark, such as the S&P 500, is chosen, and the performance of a portfolio is compared to this average. If the S&P rises 5 percent and the portfolio is up 10 percent, then the manager has demonstrated sufficient relative strength (and he is employed for at least another quarter). If the market drops 10 percent, and the fund drops 3 percent, the manager has still outperformed even though he lost money.

This favorable interpretation may seem strange to some, but this is the way very large portfolios are measured. Funds that are over a billion dollars in market value present some unique difficulties. One may not be able to sell all the shares before an intermediate top. Thus, the manager may attempt to hedge by shorting options or futures on the S&P. But more often then not, the investment committee of any institution stipulates that the manager must remain in stocks to some degree, say 50 to 90 percent. There are some funds that must stay 100 percent in stocks at all times. Obviously, relative strength is an important concept for these folks.

The concept is important for the reader of this book. You may select a stock by the methods described herein, only to see the stock perform relatively, but not absolutely, well. The key point to remember is that about 70 percent of all movement in any share price is associated with the over-all market. Therefore, you must come up with some sort of an over-all market forecast first, a subject that is beyond the scope of this volume. If bullish, then one wants to find those charts that are aspected well. If bearish, one wants to go short and then should seek afflicted charts that will decline at a greater rate than the over-all market. The old saying is that the trend is your friend.

Trade with the Trend

It was once estimated that the investor's odds of making money by buying and holding stocks in a bull market were four-to-one in favor. In a bear market, one researcher reckoned that the odds were twenty-to-one against the investor who bought and held. Favorable planetary indications in a first trade chart may send the stock soaring in a bubbly bull market. The same indications in a bear market may only cause a brief uptick or interruption in an overall downtrend.

This may sound like a very large qualification, but history shows that the market rises most of the time. The DJIA has risen since the 1930s bottom, the 1974 low, the 1982 bottom, and the one in 1990. This is not to say that it will always rise, but the long side has been the best bet. Indeed, I know many investment professionals who have made a career by always being bullish. They only have to survive the brief discomforts of episodes like the 1987 and 1990 drops. Only a long and slow decline such as the 1972-1974 bear market will wipe these individuals out.

This rule also applies to industry groups. For example, the food stocks traded sideways for 25 years. I was a junior analyst following the industry in those days, and there was very little interest in this group. In the early 1980s, the companies began to benefit from 'disinflation' and the stocks took off. The group was a market leader for over a decade. It would have been very risky to short food stocks at the time. They were an excellent source for buy ideas. Thus I scanned first trade charts of food stocks for those that were best-aspected.

Different Groups of Stocks Are Different Critters

Standard & Poor's divides stocks into industry groups, as many as 90. Some brokerage houses make even finer distinctions. The important point is that these groups have their own trading patterns. Technology shares, such as software, are much more volatile than most other stocks. They make big moves to the upside as well as to the downside.

Stocks of more stable companies, such as consumer stocks like Procter and Gamble, rise more slowly but do not usually crash. Utilities and financial stocks like banks and insurance companies are very sensitive to changes in interest rates and are likely to be more affected by rate changes than are other equities.

If you have two stocks that share the same birthday, be aware that they will have similar patterns, but will move within the constraints of their industry groups. A very bearish configuration in the first trade chart of a utility may only send the stock down a couple of points whereas the same aspect could send a high-flying technology stock down by a much greater percentage. See the example of Archer Daniels Midland in the case studies section.

To draw one last analogy, an astrologer takes a reading of a client based upon age, sex, profession, *etc.*, and tailors their advice accordingly. For example, a Sun-Saturn hard aspect would have very different meanings for a 5-year old, a 35-year old, and a 75-year old.

Health might be a major issue in the two extreme cases, while the middle-aged person would more likely be concerned with career issues. The same applies to stocks. Technical analysis helps us to determine where in its lifecycle a stock is.

Use Technical Analysis to Confirm Selections

This section will be brief because this subject is fairly vast and there are many books that cover it. Technical methods tell us about the investor psychology that is driving the share price. There are many different tools and approaches based largely upon yesterday's data and useful only to the extent that they give clues about tomorrow. This is the major reason that I pursued astrology. It is based upon phenomena that is known to occur at a fixed point in the future.

Technical work does tell us what stage a stock is in. Here's an analogy. The therapist takes a life history to learn where the individual is. In the same fashion, we can determine the maturity of the market trend. If the trend is new, the equity is likely to remain in the trend for some time, a useful insight. If the trend is old, the probability of trend reversal grows as time marches on. With these stocks, therefore, a bearish astro signal must be given more weight.

For example, the tobacco stocks were lackluster in the 1970s. They then went on a tear for about a decade, making tops in 1993. Knowing that the trend had been in force for some time was a warning flag that bearish aspects to the first trade chart could lead to a much larger decline than these same aspects had caused in earlier years.

Arthur Merrill has calculated that the most frequent retracement of a prior trend is 50 percent. A 50 percent drop of the entire 1982-1993 run-up in a stock like Philip Morris would be quite significant.

Let's draw an analogy to reinforce this important principle. If one person jumps up and down on a diving board, there is little danger. If more people join in, one-by-one, the board weakens and breaks, and the divers go into the water. The number of people jumping up and down are symbolic of the number of bearish aspects. Lots of jumpers would be a concern to those watching. The last person is symbolic of the aspect or planetary effect that accompanies the break.

In a potentially bullish case, the reasoning goes like this: Assume that there is a stock that has dropped over many years, and has now begun to flatten out and form a base. As the base extends and the stock refuses to make new lows, even in the face of bearish hits from space, we must begin to give the positive or bullish contacts from the planets more weight. We begin to anticipate bigger up-moves when we see a good transit in the ephemeris.

Conversely, we would tend to play down or underweight the coming effect of bullish planets if the stock is smack in the middle of a very obvious and prolonged downtrend. In such a case, if we do not see the planetary causes of the price decline, we must assume that there is a cycle that is more powerful then the bullish contacts. Some strong negative cycles are overwhelming the positive ones. If one does not see the astrological cause of an event, it is attributable to the great undiscovered planet Bogus, an invention of Robert Hand's that conveniently accounts for all the happenings that astrologers cannot explain.

Basic to pattern recognition is the understanding of trendlines. One must connect a pair of low prices and draw a straight line. If the second low is higher than the first, we will have an uptrend. In the reverse situation, two prices with the second lower than the first defines a downtrend.

There are numerous variations on this theme, such as Gann lines, speed resistance lines, curved trendlines, *etc.* My chosen technique is the kitchen sink: put them all on the graph. A close bunching of trendlines generated by assorted theories represents solid support. A break of such a strong price area is important. A wide spread of such lines is mushy, like a swamp. A violation here would not be viewed so seriously. Trendlines will describe patterns of price formation. Certain patterns are associated with subsequent price movements. Few objective studies of the relationship between patterns and price have been conducted. Rather, theory has been developed by practice and handed down from past technicians.

An example is the triangle, a pattern in which two trendlines, one rising and the other declining, converge. Technicians recognize this as building momentum and as the prelude to a big move in one direction. However, will the move be up or down? The most accepted technical clue is that the price move will probably be in the same direction as the move prior to the beginning of the triangle. Here is where a competitive edge can be developed. Armed with the first trade chart, upcoming bullish configurations would not only suggest a direction, but also a time window for the beginning of the move.

The same applies to the breaking of a trendline. If a stock is very close to a line, its momentum waning and the first trade chart becoming afflicted, be alert for a trend breakdown. If the price reacts as predicted, then a continuation of more bearish aspects will likely ensure a continuation of the drop. Retrograde movement of the planets can prolong an aspect or cause it to repeat, creating this effect.

How would one anticipate a reversal back to the upside? Astrologically, look for a termination of the afflicting aspects, at least. Upcoming positive aspects would be a big plus. Technically, look for at least a 50 percent retracement of the previous upswing. Look for the price to stop falling at a new uptrend or support line. Look at momentum oscillators for an oversold reading.

The length of time needed for a stock to complete a price run is a sticky question. It can best be answered by looking at daily, weekly, and monthly graphs of price. Get the big picture first. If the monthly and weekly graphs point up, then downturns in price on the daily graph will likely be shallow and short-lived. If both the monthly and weekly prices have turned down, then daily upswings will probably be limited. Downdrafts will be sharp and prolonged. Price runs on a weekly graph can last for two to four months, as a rule of thumb. Remember, stock prices have historically risen, so the upmove is more common. And, as one of my professors said, most of the situations that you will meet will not be black and white; they will be gray; that is, many times, the graphs will conflict and give contradictory readings.

For example, the weekly and monthly price trends may clearly be down, but the daily may appear bullish. The most likely resolution of these seemingly contradictory readings may work out like this. Prices may rise very briefly and by a very limited amount. Or, the price may simply go sideways for a few days before resuming its downtrend. If both the weekly and daily trends were up, but the monthly still down, then price appreciation may last longer and be more pronounced. If all three point up, then there is the greatest harmony between the trio, and the trend is clearly up. Trading from the long side is favored. Bullish planetary signals will likely precede price accelerations or breakouts. If a downtrend is clearly evi-

Graphs courtesy of Equis International

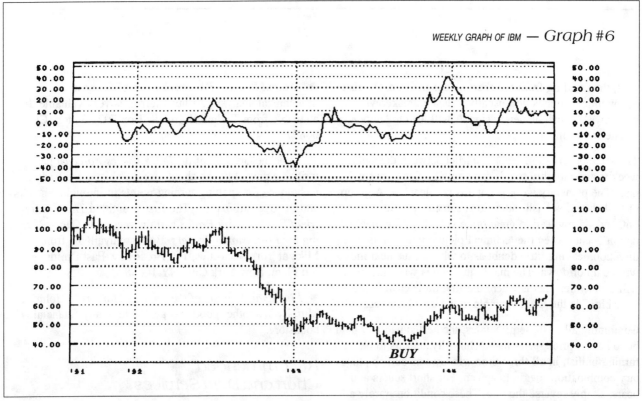

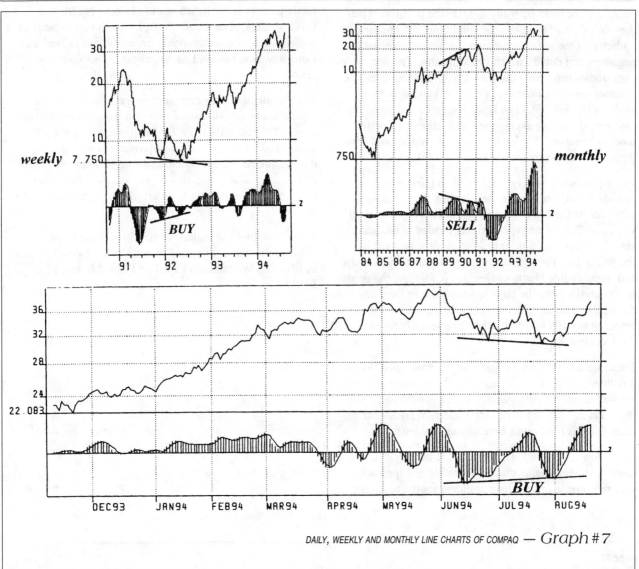

weekly 7.750

monthly

BUY

SELL

BUY

BUY

DAILY, WEEKLY AND MONTHLY LINE CHARTS OF COMPAQ — Graph #7

dent, then trading from the short side is advised. Bearish astronomical signals will usually indicate breakdowns to new lows. Bullish planetary signals will lead to temporary upside retracements.

The same observations about conflict between the daily, weekly, and monthly trends can apply to planetary signals. The planetary work is not always clear cut. A group of bullish and bearish indications can cancel each other out, and simply lead to great price volatility. The ideal situation occurs when the technical picture points in one direction, leaving little doubt as to whether the next move will be up or down. The major question is when the price will accelerate. This is where the first trade chart is most valuable. See the UAL example in the case histories.

Combining all of these principles, the best situation would be to have a price series that technically appears to be turning bullish in all three time windows as bullish planetary combinations begin to appear. For short sellers and bears, simply reverse the rule. These conditions rarely appear, and one must be ready to seize the initiative when they do. Most of the time, the conditions will appear contradictory. One must then weigh the positives versus the negatives and decide which predominates. The section on case studies provides examples. Preferred momentum oscillators are rate of change (*Graph #6*) and departure analysis (*Graph #7*). (The latter is calculaated by taking a five-period moving average and deducting a 15-period moving average. This quantity is then graphed as a three-period moving average. The result is a histogram).

In the preceding weekly graph of IBM (*Graph #6*), one can see the higher lows in the 12-week rate of change in 1993 versus the lower lows in price. This is a bullish divergence. This is the type of signal needed to confirm the astro-buy signal of Saturn making its final passage over the Sun in late 1993. *Graph #7* depicts the daily, weekly, and monthly line charts of Compaq (CPQ) and the departure analysis. Note the bullish divergence in the daily and the weekly graphs. The monthly graph gives a good example of the 1989-1990 bearish divergence before the 1991 decline.

There are several sound books that deserve study. Where possible, only reasonably-priced books are recommended. We will avoid the outrageously priced books containing the Great Secrets of the Hidden Masters Who Ascended from Atlantis (and don't have any money left).

● *How to Buy* and *When to Sell* are two separate volumes by Justin Mamis that are available in paperback at a very reasonable price. These are ideal for the beginner.

● *M and W Wave Patterns* by one of the best researchers in technical analysis, Arthur Merrill, is very valuable. It is available from Technical Trends, Box 792, Wilton, Ct. 06897.

● Michael Jenkins of the *Stock Cycles Forecast* has written a pair of books about more sophisticated trading techniques for spotting turning points in individual stocks and the over-all market. The first is entitled *The Geometry of Stock Market Profits* and the second is *Chart Reading for Professional Traders*. Both are available from Mike at York Securities, 160 Broadway, East Building, 3rd Floor, New York City, NY 10038.

● *Financial Analysis of the Futures Markets* by John Murphy is another good text available in any financial bookstore.

Recommended Chart and Data Services

Daily Graphs is published weekly in both NYSE and OTC editions. These daily high, low, and close charts of individual stocks are available from William O'Neil and Company, Box 66919, Los Angeles, CA 90066-0919, USA.

The Financial Trader computer program will read the stock files of the *Metastock* program from Equis International, 3950 South 700 East, First Floor, Salt Lake City Utah 84107, USA. *Metastock* provides a wealth of standard technical indicators and charting techniques. The *Financial Trader* program will pull the data from *Metastock* and enable the user to insert planetary data into the graph.

Metastock does not include data, which must be purchased separately. I use and recommend the data services of CSI, 200 W. Palmetto Park Road, Boca Raton, FL 33432.

Part 2: INTERPRETATION
of the NATAL FIRST TRADE HOROSCOPE

As one might guess, very dynamic first trade horo—scopes represent stocks that are very active. That is, they have very high average daily volume and frequently show up on the most active list. The media typically comments on these stocks in the evening business report. The charts of these stocks usually have planets in cardinal signs and planets on angles. Planets usually cluster around the MC.

For example, the April 23,1964 chart for the old Warner Communications had Mars in Aries in the 10th, along with a Sun-Jupiter-Mercury conjunction in early Taurus. In addition, the Moon was opposite the MC. Thus, both lights were prominent with six planets angular.

Software giant Microsoft has Mars at 22 Sag within four minutes of natal Uranus. This conjunction is square the 23 Pisces Sun with a maximum orb of 24 minutes. This is the sign of a very dynamic stock. In fact, MSFT's 11th-house Sun is closely sesquiquadrate Pluto in the 8th. This chart resembles that of the fallen hardware giant, IBM. Big Blue's Moon-Jupiter-Uranus T-square is a very dy-namic configuration. This is what made IBM an outper-former over many years.

Walmart (WMT) is another fine example of an active, closely watched, and profitable stock. It has Venus on the MC and Uranus on the ASC. The Sun is conjunct Mars, semisquare Venus, trine Jupiter, and square Neptune. The orb for the Sun-Neptune and Sun-Venus aspects are less then a degree. These are very dynamic combinations.

Because a time of 9:30 or 10 AM is used, the Sun is al-ways in the same relative house position. Since Mercury and Venus can never be more about 28 and 48 degrees from the Sun respectively, these planets also tend to be found at the top of the chart. Very active stocks tend to have some close connection of the MC and Venus, usually the conjunction. The symbolism is obvious. An individual with this type of connection would be popular or would have an appealing reputation.

Interpretation of the Planets in the First Trade Horoscope

The Sun- As always, the Sun is a vital point in the chart. A Sun that is afflicted by transit will usually depress pric-es, especially if the Sun is poorly placed natally. If the Sun is in hard aspect to Uranus, the stock will tend to fluctu-ate, especially if it is in a volatile group like technology. Cancer is the Sun sign most frequently found in the horo-scopes of first trade. However, Taurus is the Sun sign most frequently found in charts of stocks that outperform the market. Cancer and Sagittarius are the most frequent Sun signs of stocks that underperform the market. A prominent natal Sun usually denotes a stock that is nota-ble. That is, it has many shareholders and is widely com-mented on in the media. Contacts to Jupiter will add to the "reputation" of the stock. Connections between natal Sun and Pluto symbolize a powerful mover on the ex-change. Its price fluctuations effect whole industries, as Microsoft does. It may either be a company that acquires others or one that may itself be merged.

The Moon- The Moon in mundane charts has traditional-ly represented the public. It is important because it can represent the public's feelings about or perceptions of a stock. Transits to the Moon can cause erratic trading pat-terns. Natal charts with Moon-Uranus contacts cause ir-regular price movements while Saturn-Moon connections tend to bring stability. Taurus Moons, like Taurus Suns, are found in the charts of strong stocks while Scorpio Moons predominate with weak stocks.

Mercury — Mercury has an effect similar to that of the Moon. A prominent Mercury attracts much mention in the press. Rumors may move the stock. Good transits to the natal Mercury can bring favorable rulings from the courts or the government. Indeed, a Jupiter hit to Mercury heralded a favorable court ruling for Advanced Micro De-vices *vs.* Intel, as we will see in the case histories. Taurus and Gemini are the natal signs associated with outper-forming stocks while Sagittarius is frequent with the un-derperformers.

Venus — Venus enhances the marketability of shares. As with people, the stock's popularity is enhanced. Apple Computer has a Venus-Uranus conjunction on the MC. Scorpio Venus turns up frequently with strong shares while Capricorn and Aquarius show up with a slightly greater than average probability in the horoscopes of underperforming equities. Transiting hits to natal Venus can signal stock moves resulting from agreements or mergers.

Mars — Needless to say, Mars adds energy to the trading of a stock. A well-aspected natal Mars will give rise to well-defined up and down trends. Mars in hard aspect to Uranus brings erratic and choppy moves–very tough to trade. A very afflicted Mars may simply cause listless and dull trading. Gemini Mars is symbolic of outperformers while Virgo is symbolic of the underperformers.

Jupiter — As one might guess from Jupiter's symbolism, this can be the planet of the bull. A well-aspected Jupiter will likely lead to good relative performance. The strong stocks tended to have the Greater Benefic in Aries or Pisces. Their weaker counterparts have Jupiter in Aquarius. Generally speaking, transits from Jupiter to the natal chart are positive, but will not be long lasting. In order to generate a sustained move, Jupiter must be moving slowly or must aspect a group of natal planets. Having both effects is best. See the example of Goodyear in the Case Studies section. Jupiter contacting Uranus can bring big moves up and down. Most biotech companies began trading in 1983 when these two planets were conjunct in the sky. This group of stocks has certainly been a speculator's dream. Saturn's transit over the biotech's Jupiter-Uranus conjunction terminated the price run and sent the group's price run into a tailspin in the later 1980s.

Saturn — As with Jupiter, Saturn's basic nature tells all: this is a bearish or depressing influence. A prominent natal Saturn will usually hold the share price back over time. A well-aspected Saturn can be a stabilizing influence. Staid and steady "old reliables" will have such an aspect. Going back to the Warner Communications example, Saturn passing opposite the natal Sun-Jupiter conjunction dropped the shares hard.

Uranus — If you like volatility, look for horoscopes with a strong Uranus. Uranus on the MC of Apple Computer is a fine example. Hard natal aspects to the lights and angles will cause choppy patterns and very sudden price movements. Stations of transiting Uranus are one of the best movers of share prices, next to eclipses. A station of Uranus in 1985 square the Sun of the old industrial stock, Kidde, occurred on the day of the takeover of the company, sending the share price 50 percent higher. See the UAL example in the Case Studies section. Hard transiting aspects can bring big moves up or down, depending upon other conditions in the chart and the natal position of the planets aspected. Poorly aspected natal planets to Uranus will usually cause a fall.

Neptune — Stocks that are considered inflation hedges, like gold, oils, or natural resource stocks will usually have a strong Neptune. Deceptive price movements and fakeouts are common. The stock may break to the upside, in technical terms, and then change course to the downside. See Delta Airlines in the following section. By transit, soft aspects from stationary Neptune are most frequently bullish.

Pluto — Natal Pluto tells us about mergers or very substantial price moves. A prominent Pluto indicates that these events are likely during the trading life of the stock. A weak Pluto would point to the reverse. Pluto is frequently strong by transit during merger or takeover attempts. Very big and prolonged price declines or rises can begin with a Pluto hit. See the Novell and Mediavision examples as case histories. Also, see Kemper. This stock took off due to a takeover bid when Jupiter stationed on natal Pluto. The outermost planet has a "make or break" effect.

Lunar Node — The Node can be significant during mergers or major agreements that impact the stock price.

The Angles — The MC and ASC are very sensitive and bear close watching. Planets on the angles take on greater strength. Aspects to them and to the angles will lead to larger price moves. See the UAL example. The progressed angles are also important. See the Gerber example.

The Uranian Planets — These points originated in the Hamburg School of astrology with Alfred Witte. He and Freiderich Sieggrun hypothesized the existence of eight planets beyond Pluto. (In the 1980s, an independent researcher who analyzed data sent back by deep space probes found evidence of eight large cold-temperature bodies beyond Pluto.)

I have used this system for many years, and some of the Uranian planets, also known as the Trans-Neptunian planets (or TNPs), do contribute to the analysis. Apollon tends to have a bullish effect. Pop this into the chart of UAL (at 0 Libra 53) in the case histories, and the rally in the stock becomes more understandable. Hades has a bearish effect, while Admetos has a restricting or deadening influence. Vulcanus tends to move stocks up.

An Odd Digression

Horoscopes of incorporation show what the company does, but the chart of the first trade sometimes eerily gives the same or a better indication. For example, Alfin Fragrances (May 8,1986 on the Amex) makes sexy perfumes. The first trade horoscope has Mars and Venus conjunct in

Leo on the MC. Apple Computer has Venus and Uranus conjunct on the MC, and they were the first to popularize the PC, especially the user-friendly aspect of the computer interface.

Let's go back to Microsoft. Not only were the planets an indication of the trading activity of the shares, the group also reflects its boss's management and marketing style: Sun-Pluto-Mars-Uranus.

Compaq, the number-one PC maker at this moment, began trading with the Sun 16 minutes of arc from Uranus, the planet that rules computing. This conjunction is sextile Jupiter in Aquarius. Thus, Jupiter and Uranus are not only in aspect, but are in mutual reception.

In early 1994, we awaited the outcome of Intel's lawsuit versus Advanced Micro Devices. Jupiter's station on AMD's Mercury in the first trade chart was the indication of a favorable ruling. The incorporation chart did not reflect the outcome as clearly. Perhaps this effect is created by public attention. That is, the charts reflect the fundamental issues that investors feel are relevant to the share price.

Finding the Winners

This section explains what qualities to look for in a natal chart. These rules were developed in two ways. The first was simple observation. Experience over the years has taught that certain signs, aspects, *etc.* are associated with price appreciation while others are associated with price declines.

The second method was rigorous testing. First, the stocks in this book were loaded into a portfolio reporting system. Their price performance was then measured over different time periods. This presented some difficulties. First, most data bases do not carry daily price data back more then a few years, due to the cost of maintenance. Fortunately, a decade of price data was available. Second, with the large number of takeovers and mergers over the last decade, many issues simply do not have a long trading history. The farther back one goes, fewer stocks were trading. To deal with this second obstacle, several tests were run. Performance was measured going back ten, five, and two years. The 10-year study did not provide enough stocks to fill the sample, so the best and worst from the other stud-

Bullish and Bearish Planetary Combinations by Transit

The best learning procedure is to choose several stocks and follow their price movements in relation to the activity in the horoscope. But there are some combinations that stand out as generally being associated with rising and with falling prices.

Bullish contacts:	Bearish contacts:
Sun-Venus	Saturn-Sun
Jupiter-Sun	Saturn-Venus
Jupiter-Mercury	Saturn-Jupiter
Jupiter-Venus	Saturn-Uranus
Jupiter-Jupiter	Saturn-Neptune
Jupiter-Uranus	Saturn-Pluto
Jupiter-Neptune	Saturn to the angles or Nodes
Jupiter-Pluto	Uranus-Pluto
Jupiter to the angles	Neptune-Pluto
Uranus-Venus	Pluto to the angles or Nodes
Uranus to the angles	Eclipses to Saturn and Pluto
Neptune-Sun	
Neptune-Venus	
Eclipses to Jupiter, Neptune, Uranus, and angles	

The Pluto combinations frequently show up in takeovers, as we will see in the Case Studies section.

ies were tapped as sources to give one batch of winners and one of losers. To qualify as a winner, the stock had to outperform the S&P 500. The reverse qualification was true for the other end of the spectrum.

These two batches of horoscopes were then screened for outstanding qualities. The pair of groups were compared to each other and to all 700 NYSE stocks. For example, the next section notes that outperforming stocks tend to have the Sun in Taurus. This group showed 17 percent of the charts with this Sun placement versus 8.2 percent for the whole NYSE group and 7 percent for the group of underperformers.

The results of all tests follow. Although the asteroids are not included in the horoscopes in this book (the charts were too small), I have placed them in every chart since studying with Eleanor Bach in New York in the 1970s.

Prominent Aspects

The two batches of horoscopes were scanned again to determine which aspects stood out. The aspects within

Significant placements for outperformers were:

Ceres: Leo	*Pallas:* Capricorn
Juno: Cancer	*Vesta:* Gemini

Significant placements for underperformers were:

Ceres: Scorpio	*Pallas:* Libra
Juno: Aries	*Vesta:* Cancer

each cell are listed in order of strength with the strongest on top. MC stands for midheaven; ASC represents ascendant. An entry that lists three planets means that either of the first two planets aspecting the third will produce the listed result. Thus: Mars, Uranus-Sun under "square" means that *both* Mars-Sun and Uranus-Sun squares were frequent in the charts of underperformers. The frequency was the same for both squares.

An entry of 'NM' means that there was no meaningful result. In these cases, the planets were simply evenly distributed by sign, not giving any useful reading. Some as-

Prominent Natal Signs

The following table lists the signs most frequently occupied by the planets and angles in the horoscopes of the equities that outperformed and underperformed the S&P over time.

natal factor	bullish	bearish
Sun	Taurus	Sagittarius and Capricorn
Moon	Taurus	Scorpio
Mercury	Taurus and Gemini	Cancer
Venus	Scorpio	Capricorn and Aquarius
Mars	Gemini	Virgo
Jupiter	Aries and Pisces	Aquarius
***Saturn	Scorpio	Scorpio
*Uranus	Sagittarius	Sagittarius
*Neptune	Capricorn	Sagittarius
*Pluto	Scorpio	Libra
*Lunar Node	Pisces	Aquarius
**MC	Aries	Aquarius
**ASC	Cancer	Aquarius

*These findings are presented for informational purposes. The high readings in certain signs are most likely due to the slow movement of the outer planets.

**The readings on the angles need to be placed in context. Because stocks begin trading in the morning in New York, the Aries-Cancer result may be more due to a seasonal tendency to float new issues at certain times of the year. For example, stocks are usually strong in the spring and at year end. They are usually weak in the fall. So underwriters may time new issues to take advantage of this seasonal tendency. Because the Sun is in Virgo-Libra in the fall, we likely see fewer midheavens running from Leo through Libra in first trade charts. Indeed, these signs do show up infrequently on the midheavens of outperforming stocks. On the other hand, the angles of charts set for morning during the spring season do dominate the outperformers.

***Saturn in Scorpio was significant for both the outperformers and the underperformers. We can conclude that Saturn in this sign makes stocks move both up and down.

ASPECT (ORB)	BULLISH	BEARISH
Conjunction (6)	Jupiter-Uranus	Venus-MC* Sun-Mercury** Venus-Jupiter Venus-Mars
Semisextile (3)	NM	NM
Semisquare (3)	Venus-Mars	Mercury-Venus Sun-Neptune Moon-Jupiter
Sextile (4)	Mars-Node Moon-ASC Moon-Jupiter	Venus-Neptune Moon-Mars
Square (6)	Mars-MC Uranus-MC	Venus-Neptune Saturn,Node-Moon Mars, Uranus-Sun
Trine (4)	Mercury-Pluto Uranus-Node	Sun-Pluto
Sesquiquadrate (3)	Venus-Uranus	Venus-Saturn Venus-Pluto
Quincunx (3)	Moon-Uranus	NM
Opposition (6)	Pluto-Node Uranus-Node Mercury-Vertex	Saturn-Neptune Mars-Uranus

*Actually, Venus-MC conjunctions are prominent in both the charts of bulls and bears. They are more significant in the latter group, turning up with greater frequency. Further testing showed that the magnitude of the increases in the outperforming stocks was much greater than the magnitude of the declines in the underperformers.

**Sun-Mercury conjunctions occur frequently. The aspect is listed here because it occurs 50% more often in the horoscopes of underperforming stocks versus the outperformers.

pects were excluded from the listing even though they turned up frequently. These were angles that were simply in force for a very long period, like Uranus or Neptune to Pluto. These results were not meaningful. Also excluded were aspects, like Sun to the MC, that were caused by the fixed starting time of the charts.

Due to the morning start time, the Sun is in the 11th house in 94 percent of the charts. This creates many semisextile and semisquare aspects from the Sun to the MC. In these cases, the frequency of the aspect in the bullish group was compared to that in the bearish one to see if there was a great discrepancy, which there was not. These comments also apply to Mercury, Venus, and the angles. More explanatory notes follow the table.

Other Aspects

Other less popular aspects were tested: 40, 72, 75, 105, 144, and 165 degrees. The only ones that were prominent were: Mars 75 degrees to Uranus for the outperformers, and Mercury and Jupiter 40 degrees to Pluto for the outperformers. The two groups tended to have the following aspects by declination:

Natal Midpoints

NATAL FACTOR	BULLS	BEARS
Sun	Uranus/Pluto	Jupiter/Saturn
Moon	Sun/Saturn Moon/Pluto Sun/Jupiter Moon/Venus	ASC/MC Uranus/Pluto Jupiter/ASC
Mercury	Moon/Saturn	Sun/Jupiter Sun/Node
Venus	Moon/ASC Uranus/MC	Jupiter/Pluto Mercury/Venus
Mars	Mercury/Saturn	Mars/Node Mercury/Venus
Jupiter	Mercury/Pluto Venus/Pluto Neptune/MC	Node/MC
Saturn	Uranus/Pluto Jupiter/Node Venus/ASC	Venus/Node Pluto/Node
Uranus	Neptune/Pluto	Sun/Moon Moon/Neptune Venus/Neptune
Neptune	Venus/Mars Saturn/Neptune	Pluto/ASC Mercury/Venus
Pluto	Moon/Venus	Venus/Pluto
Lunar Node	NM	Mars/Node Mercury/Venus
ASC	Jupiter/Node	Uranus/MC
MC	Mercury/Pluto	NM

NM=Not meaningful

Outperformers:

Parallels: Jupiter-Uranus
Contraparallels: Neptune-Saturn, Jupiter-ASC, Mars-Saturn, Uranus-ASC, Saturn-ASC, Venus-Saturn

Underperformers:

Parallels: Mars-MC, Sun-Node, Mercury-MC, Jupiter-Node.
Contraparallels: Jupiter-Neptune

Multiple Configurations

The charts were also scanned for multiple conjunctions, grand trines, T-squares, and grand squares. There was no meaningful difference in the frequency of these configurations. There was a difference in the planets that made up some of these aspects:

Outperformers tended not to have Mars involved in multiple conjunctions when compared to the underperformers. Outperformers tended to have the Moon involved in T-squares more frequently then did the underperformers. Underperformers tended to have Mars, Jupiter, and Neptune involved in T-squares more frequently then did the out-performers.

Going one step further, the scan was set to detect Marc Edmund Jones type temperament patterns. The outperformers had many more "locomotive" and "lame duck" formations then did the underperformers. The underperformers had a greater tendency to be "open square" charts.

Prominent Midpoints

The two groups of horoscopes were then scanned again to determine if any midpoints were important. The *Financial Trader* program was asked to cull the midpoints that were in 8th-harmonic aspect to the natal factors within a one degree orb. (The 8th harmonic means any division of the 360 degree circle by eight: 45 degrees, 90, 135, 180.) The best book on the subject is *Dial Detective* by Maria K. Simms, published by ACS in San Diego. The results are listed in the table on this page.

Other Considerations:

Retrogrades and Lunar Phases

Retrograde planets were also examined. Underperforming stocks tended to have retrogrades more often then did the outperformers. Specifically, Mars, Saturn, and Pluto were retrograde more often in the charts of the lagging stocks. The lunar phase was also researched. A third of the outperformers began trading at the Full Moon or in the next, the disseminating, phase. The other prominent phase was the first quarter in which 15 percent of the bulls began trading. Turning to the underperformers, most (20 percent) began trading in the third quarter. The second most prominent phase was the New Moon (18 percent).

Significant Natal Features of Stocks

Over the years, 310 stocks that were in the files were bought out, merged, or were taken private. This group was scanned to determine how the natal horoscopes might differ from the norm. The configuration is mentioned only if it stood out from the group of horoscopes of NYSE stocks that are still actively traded.

Stocks of aquired companies were most likely to have the Sun in Gemini, Venus in Scorpio, and Jupiter in either Pisces or Sagittarius. Leo was the most frequent ASC. Almost two-thirds of the group began trading at the New Moon or in the two following phases: crescent or first quarter. The most frequent aspects were Jupiter in hard aspect to Pluto (especially, the 135-degree angle), Pluto to the Node (the quincunx was frequent), Jupiter-MC, Saturn-Neptune, and Mercury-Mars. The most frequent natal planetary pictures (in the eighth harmonic) were:

Moon/Uranus=Sun	Jupiter/Saturn=Moon
Saturn/Node=Venus	Mercury/Saturn=Mars
Jupiter/Uranus=Saturn	Pluto/Node=Uranus
Jupiter/Node=Neptune	Saturn/Neptune=Node
Mars/Pluto=ASC	Jupiter/Pluto=MC

Scanning for multiple conjunctions of three or more planets, these charts showed a tendency to have fewer such groupings then did the entire group on NYSE stocks (32 *vs* 53 percent).

Heliocentric Analysis

To leave no stone unturned, heliocentric or Sun-centered astrology was employed in the natal analysis. For those who are unfamiliar with this type of work, we will review some of the more important considerations:

1. Because the Sun is at the center of the chart, no Sun appears in the horoscope. Instead, the Earth appears in a zodiacal position that is directly opposite to that of the Sun in a tropical chart of the same stock. So if the Sun is at 3 Capricorn in a geocentric chart, the Earth will be at 3 Cancer in a heliocentric chart.

2. In a geocentric chart, Mercury and Venus can be no farther then 28 and 48 degrees from the Sun. In a helio chart, Mercury and Venus can be at any angu-

lar separation from the Earth. So you will see Earth-Mercury or Venus aspects, such as an opposition or trine, that are not possible with the Sun and the same planets in a geo chart.

3. The Moon does not appear in a helio chart. It is in the same position as the Earth.

Prominent Natal Signs

NATAL FACTOR	BULLISH	BEARISH
Earth	Scorpio	Gemini & Capricorn
Mercury	Virgo	NM
Venus	Pisces & Gemini	Aquarius
Mars	Virgo	Leo
Jupiter	Aries	Aquarius & Scorpio
Saturn	Scorpio & Taurus	Cancer
*Uranus	Scorpio	Scorpio
*Neptune	Sagittarius & Libra	Sagittarius
*Pluto	Scorpio	Libra

* The readings on the outer planets are presented for informational purposes only. They are probably not significant.
NM=Not meaningful

Prominent Natal Aspects

ASPECT (ORB)	BULLISH	BEARISH
Conjunction (6)	Jupiter-Uranus Sun-Mars, Uranus Mer.-Mars, Saturn	Sun-Saturn Venus-Mars Mars-Neptune
Semisextile (3)	Venus-Jupiter	Mars-Saturn
Semisquare (3)	Jupiter-Neptune	Mercury-Mars Mercury-Venus
Sextile (4)	Venus-Neptune	Mars-Pluto
Square (6)	Mars-Saturn	Mercury-Pluto
Trine (4)	NM	NM
Sesquiquadrate (3)	Venus-Saturn	Mars-Jupiter
Quincunx (3)	NM	Mars-Neptune
Opposition (6)	Jupiter-Saturn	Saturn-Neptune

Our *Financial Trader* program enables the user to switch from geo to helio horoscopes very easily.

Multiple Configurations

The charts were also scanned for multiple conjunctions, grand trines, T-squares, and grand squares. The bulls had more multiple conjunctions then did the bears, but the percentage was not significantly different from the sample of all charts. Outperformers had significantly more T-squares then had the underperformers and the entire sample of charts.

There was a difference in the planets that made up some of these aspects:

● Outperformers tended to have Mars and Jupiter involved in T-squares when compared to the underperformers.

● Underperformers tended to have Venus involved in T-squares more frequently then did the outperformers.

Prominent Natal Midpoints

NATAL FACTOR	BULLS	BEARS
Earth	Jupiter/Uranus	Venus/Jupiter
Mercury	Sun/Jupiter	Venus/Uranus
Venus	Saturn/Pluto	Saturn/Uranus
Mars	Jupiter/Uranus	Venus/Mars
Jupiter	NM	Sun/Jupiter Venus/Mars
Saturn	Mercury/Uranus	Jupiter/Saturn
Uranus	Saturn/Uranus	Jupiter/Saturn
Neptune	Saturn/Neptune Venus/Pluto Sun/Mercury	Mercury/Neptune
Pluto	NM	Saturn/Uranus

NM=Not meaningful

Predictive Techniques

In order of strength, from the most powerful to the least, practice indicates that these phenomena are the ones to watch when working with first trade charts:

● Solar eclipses
● Uranus stations
● Lunar eclipses
● Jupiter stations
● Neptune stations
● Pluto stations
● Major aspects between outer planets
● Mars stations
● Venus stations

Charles Jayne taught that eclipses are the most powerful effect in astrology. Always watch the effect of eclipses on the horoscopes in this book. A basic tenet of astrology is that the slower a planet moves, the greater its strength. Outer planets are the slowest, and they have their greatest strength when they go stationary, either retrograde or direct. After spending over 20 years in astrology, I can say that one can come up with a reasonably good forecast by simply observing the eclipses and the stations. Take these points from an ephemeris or a computer program and search for hits to the first trade charts. See Case Study 32 as a fine example of the power of eclipses and Uranus stations. This type of forecasting involves factors that are external to the horoscope. There are, of course, techniques that are specific to each chart, like solar arcs or progressions.

Directions and Progressions

The transit and eclipse screen will target many movers, but methods that are individual to the specific chart are sometimes important. Examine directions and progressions individually for each stock. This can be a lot of work. I recommend screening first for eclipse and station hits to the charts. Then apply directions and progressions to the stocks that have been culled by the screening method. This will save a lot of time and prevent you from going bonkers.

Secondary progressions deserve special consideration. One might theorize that secondaries would be vital in describing long periods of outperformance by individual stocks, but this has not consistently been the case. Further research may clarify the issue. Secondaries should be checked after stocks have come up for a final and serious consideration as purchase or sale candidates. See *Case Study 13*, Gerber.

Rudhyar's progressed lunation cycle is a very strong influence. This cycle bottoms when the progressed Moon is conjunct the progressed Sun. Its peak occurs when the two are opposite, about 14 years later. There is a general background tendency for stocks to rise from the new to the full point in the cycle. The aspects made at the extremes in the cycle add to the analysis. IBM, case 4, demonstrates this, as well as some other key principles.

The progressed Sun can be important. Waste Management (WMX) topped in February, 1992 when its progressed Sun semisquared Pluto. Its big 1984-1990 1000 percent price run slowed in late 1989 when the progressed full Moon occurred. The aspect of the progressed Sun plus transits were sufficient to send the shares down almost 40 percent from 1992 to 1994. Note how no single technique coincided with these big moves. It was the combined effect of the techniques.

Eclipses

Eclipses were Charles Jayne's specialty for 50 years. They are, in his opinion, the single most powerful influence in astrology. Eclipses conjunct or opposite a planet or an angle are the potent hits. The orb is five degrees. For a square from an eclipse to be effective, the orb must be small, three degrees or less. The effects of eclipses can reinforce each other. One eclipse can be roughly opposite its predecessor. In this case, Jayne and his contemporaries found that the effect was most likely to fall between the two eclipses. See Mediavision in Case Studies.

The effect, in terms of whether to expect a bear or bull move, largely depends upon the configuration of the point being eclipsed. Is this point well or poorly situated in the chart?

To answer this question, one must go beyond aspects and sign placement. The midpoint structure is very significant. If the midpoints equaling the natal point are well-placed, then the net result of energization of that point will likely be positive. If the midpoint structure is an incompatible one, then the effect of an eclipse or strong transit will likely depress the share price.

For example, an eclipse falls on Jupiter in the horoscopes of two different equities. In the first, natal Jupiter lies on the Sun/Uranus and the Venus/MC midpoints.

These are harmonious combinations that will probably lead to higher prices. In the second chart, natal Jupiter equals Saturn/Pluto and Uranus/Saturn. These are conflicting energies leading to lower prices. See *Case Studies 23 and 24.*

Natal Eclipses

The natal eclipse return can be most potent. This information is derived from the my studies in mundane astrology. Work on my upcoming *The Predictive Power of Eclipse Paths,* was put aside to complete this book. Johndro and Jayne worked with eclipses that fell nearest birth, either before or after the date. The eclipsed degrees tend to stay hot or active. Aspected planets take on a more energized nature. I have found that important events always occur if these degrees are eclipsed again. For example, North Korea came into existence in 1948, a year in which there were eclipses at 18 Taurus and 9 Scorpio. Dramatic events unfolded in 1994 when the US confronted that country over its nuclear capabilities and Kim Il Sung died. In 1994, there were again eclipses at these two degrees.

This technique can also be helpful when choosing a stock. American Cyanamid (*Case number 27*) is an example. ACY began trading in 1947, so its natal eclipse points were hit in 1993, and natal Jupiter was hit by the eclipse in the spring of 1994. These signals were enough to attract attention. I delved a bit further. The stock leaped 50 percent in the summer of 1994 on a takeover bid from American Home Products.

A more complete analysis of natal eclipses will appear in my upcoming book on eclipse paths.

The Saturn Cycle

The Saturn cycle in personal natal charts is well known. I learned the technique from Marc Robertson in the 1970s. One cycle is defined by the ascent of Saturn from the IC or the bottom of the chart up to the MC. This usually describes a cycle during which the career fortunes are rising. There is a tendency for stock to rise during this 14-year period. In particular, there is a tendency for the share price to peak or culminate when Saturn passes over the MC. The 1993-1994 takeover attempt of Paramount and the breakdown in Paramount are good examples (see Case Studies, 16 and 17).

Heliocentric Transits

The application of helio work can best be explained by an example. Go to an ephemeris and look at the geo Jupiter-Saturn oppositions from 1989 to 1991. There were five. If you add right ascension, there were five more. But, *heliocentrically*, there was one! This type of action usually describes a multiple top or bottom in a market.

For instance, an uptrend ends near the first opposition. This short-term pullback ends on the second, when prices change course to the upside, and so on. This back-and-forth action can trace out what technicians call a distributional top like a head and shoulders or triple top. The last aspect in the series usually strikes the telling blow, as the final Saturn-Pluto square did to the DJIA in early 1994. In first trade charts, helio hits can be as important as geo contacts. See the Bausch and Lomb case study, #26.

New Ways to Analyze the Charts:
The "Time Tunnel" and "The Alphee Twist" —

These concepts are so new that you will not find them in any books. These are Alphee Lavoie's latest innovations, and they are included in the *Financial Trader* and *Star Trax 8000* programs. The Time Tunnel is essentially a circular graphic ephemeris. The natal planets of any chart are expressed as straight lines from the edge of the circle to the center. The curved lines in various colors represent the transiting planets. The intersection of these lines with the natal straight lines are aspects of the transits to the natal charts. The type of aspect or contact is determined by the harmonic chosen. For example, if you select a 4th harmonic, then all the contacts or crossovers in the Time Tunnel will be either squares, semisquares, oppositions, conjunctions, *etc.* If the 6th harmonic is chosen, the line intersections will be multiples of 60 degrees: the sextile,

trine family of aspects. With this new tool, one can see a year's transits, progressions or directions at a glance. By pressing the arrow keys, you can move a black concentric circle from the outer circumference of the Tunneld to the precise day represented by the intersection of lines on the screen. For example, a curved red transit line that represents Mars intersects a yellow line representing the Sun. This means that there is a 4th harmonic contact or aspect between the pair on that day. Fourth harmonic means 0, 90, 180, or 270 (360 degrees divided by 4). If this intersection also crosses a straight black line, then there is also a 4th-harmonic aspect to a planet in the natal chart. If the colored line curves back and moves in the opposite direction, then the planet has gone stationary, a very powerful indication.

No, the *Alphee Twist* is not a new dance craze. The concept utilizes the Time Tunnel. But the Twist employs tertiary progressions. Secondary progressions, a more common technique, count each day after birth as a year. According to theory, the planets in the 10th day after birth describe conditions in the 10th year of life. These progressions are very slow and describe gradual change in conditions. Tertiaries employ the same theory, but this theory counts the days after birth in a very different way. Assume that there are 13 new moons in the 365 days after your birth. Then the 13 days after your birth equal 1 year. In other words, instead of one day equals one year, the number of new moons in the year after birth equals oneyear.

The *Twist* draws the direct tertiary progressions of any chart as spiral lines from the center to the edge of the concentric circle. It simultaneously draws the converse tertiaries for the same chart. Direct means that we go forward in time after birth, say 100 months. Converse tertiary progressions go back 100 months *before* the date of birth. Definitions aside, Alphee has found that the intersection of two of the tertiary lines, especially with a straight line representing a natal planet, makes things happen in the horoscopes of individuals. The Twist can be a very valuable forecasting tool.

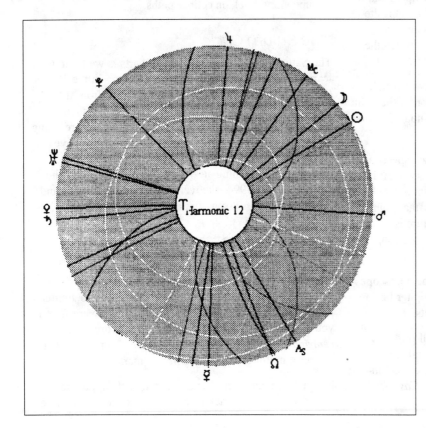

part 3: CASE STUDIES

and now for some action...

1- *Delta's Dive*

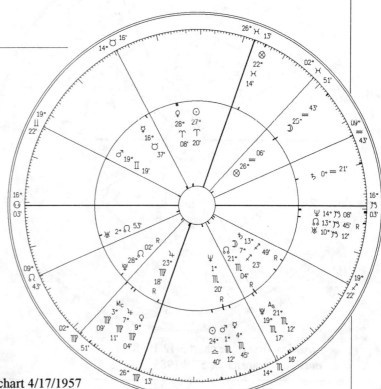

One picture is worth ten thousand words, so here we go. Delta Airlines (DAL) began trading on April 17, 1957. In 1991, the stock had a rough ride as Saturn moved back and forth in early Aquarius, squaring natal Neptune and opposing natal Uranus. In late October, this bearish combination was triggered by transiting Mars on DAL's natal Neptune square transiting Saturn and natal Uranus (Chart 1). Graph 1 shows the sharp break in the stock. These harsh angles were a sign to either avoid the shares or to go short. Also, note the natal Uranus-Neptune square. This is typical of speculative shares that gyrate very widely, such as airlines. Also, the strong Neptune hints at the relation between moves in oil prices, (a major cost factor for air carriers) and movements in their stocks.

inside: first trade chart 4/17/1957
outside: transits for 10/18/1991

2 · Katy's Collapse

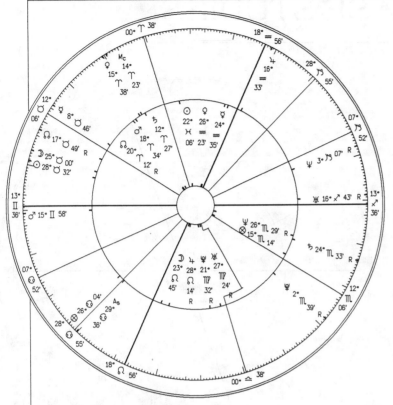

inside: first trade chart 3/12/1968
outside: transits for 5/19/1985

Katy Industries (KT) had rallied from 11 to 33 by May of 1985 (Graph 2). Then the eclipse at 29 Taurus opposed transiting Saturn at 25 Scorpio, which was also near the degree of the previous Saturn station in late Scorpio. KT's trading was halted by the Big Board at 33 and re-opened at 22, a 33 percent drop in one day. The stock eventually bottomed in the 13-15 area. Note that the combination in the sky at 29 of fixed degrees hit KT's fixed T-cross of Venus-Mercury-Neptune-Moon-Jupiter (Chart 2). Quite a hit.

This example is an illustration of several principles. Note that the combination in space that brought the stock down was a strong combination: eclipse, Saturn stationary point, and transiting Saturn. Also note that the natal configuration that was afflicted contained five planets. In this case, Jupiter passing over the MC was not nearly powerful enough to offset the bearish effects. In you had only considered the Jupiter transit, you might have bought it near the top.

There is an interesting addendum to this case. A trader who was born on September 29, 1941 subsequently consulted with me. He was very concerned with a big hit that he had taken. The stock was KT, and he was one of the largest shareholders. The same planets that collapsed the stock were hitting his Saturn-Uranus conjunction in late Taurus-early Gemini.

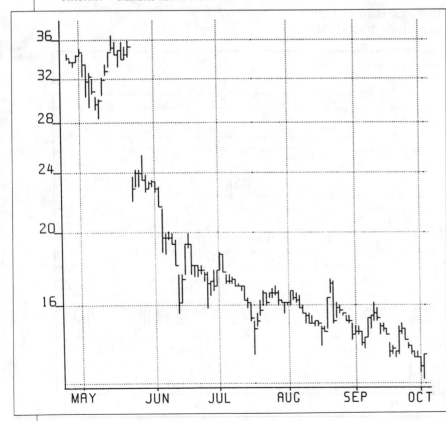

STK moves up almost as rapidly as it moves down. The Jupiter-Uranus opposition of 1989 was on the natal Moon and widely trine the MC. STK began to move up in the summer of 1989. The shares re-accelerated in January when the second Jupiter-Uranus opposition at 6 Cancer-Capricorn was closely sextile and trine the 6 Taurus MC. The stock rallied from the 17-18 area in January 1990 to a high of 35 prior to the July, 1990 market top. The July 22 eclipse at 29 Cancer fell at the top of the 1990 upmove. Those charts that were hit directly by the eclipse fell the most. Chart 3 reveals that the eclipse squared STK's Uranus as the stock fell 10 points - 35 percent, in a single day (Graph 3). These contacts, plus the extremely overbought condition of the stock were a bright red warning flag.

Now let's move forward to the summer of 1991 when the solar eclipse at 18 Cancer fell on the STK Saturn. This was the high point for 1991; STK fell from 50 to the high 30s. In December 1991, a lunar eclipse fell on the Moon, and STK made a huge run from 40 to 78. It was quickly ended by a solar eclipse widely opposite Saturn in January. The ensuing decline probably would have been ordinary, but the Uranus-Neptune conjunction began its long opposition to the STK Saturn at 18 Cancer. Remember, the combination of these three planets is bearish. Note the severe 75 percent decline that followed throughout the year. The long opposition was the signal to avoid STK in 1992.

More recently, a computer scan utilizing the Financial Trader program picked STK as a potential winner for the month of November, 1993. Uranus was passing over Jupiter in the STK first-trade chart. The stock ral-

Storage Technology - 3

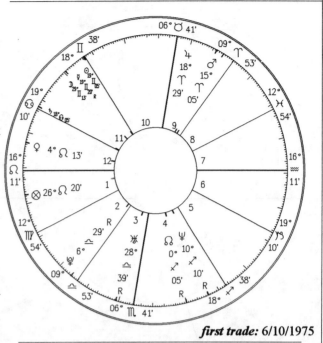

first trade: 6/10/1975

lied 19.3 percent during the month of November versus a 1.5 percent drop in the S&P. STK is an excellent trading stock, very sensitive to its horoscope.

This is an example that is worthy of close study. Note how a number of principles were demonstrated. All of the significant turns in the share price were marked by eclipses, stations, or outer-planet combinations. Also note that the stock was always at an overbought or oversold extreme when the planets heralded a turning point.

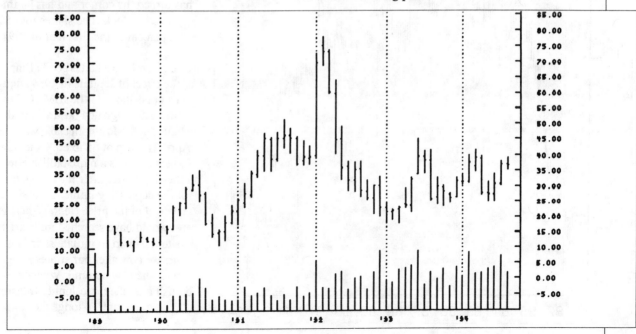

4 - IBM

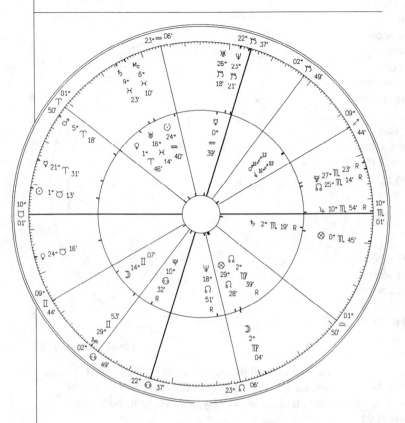

inside: first trade chart 2/14/1924 *outside:* transits for 4/21/1994

Chart 4 and Graph 4 tell an interesting story that demonstrates several key points. The power of a strong transit to an important natal axis was seen on the all-time top day, August 31,1987 with the share price at $165. Saturn was conjunct the dynamic combination of a Mars-Jupiter conjunction square Uranus. Next, in February of 1989, IBM had its progressed Full Moon, which also was conjunct progressed Saturn. Then transiting Saturn entered Aquarius, the sign that rules computers, in February of 1991 and remained there until January of 1994. Also, Saturn had passed over the MC and was descending in the chart. The monthly price graph shows the decline. IBM finally began to rise after Saturn passed over the first trade chart's Sun.

It is interesting to note that the company adopted its current name on February 14,1924 with the Sun at 25 Aquarius. Name changes are important and have much the same effect as incorporation horoscopes. Thus, the orbit of Saturn through these degrees combined with the square from Pluto to deliver a double whammy.

The confirmation of this degree area as sensitive was confirmed by the death of IBM's founder, Tom Watson, during the transit. Now that Saturn has left Aquarius, it appears that IBM has turned the corner and has an improved outlook. The shares rose 50 percent in the first half of 1994.

More recently, we had a good glimpse of the effect of Jupiter. In 1994, Jupiter's oppositions to the IBM 10 Taurus ASC signaled upsurges in the share price. Most noticeable was the April 21 jump of $5 to $6. Note how Jupiter now has a more bullish effect on the share price after the dissipation of the depressing influences and the reversal of the price trend. Whereas we would have searched for bearish hits to the chart to initiate short positions, we now alter our strategy to go with the new uptrend. We look for bullish hits like these Jupiter transits to "go long" the stock.

The Friendly Skies of United - 5

UAL, Chart 5, blasted off on a run from 60 to 85 on April 1,1987. Note that this was the very day that Uranus turned stationary retrograde opposite the MC, square the ascendant, Pluto, Moon, and opposite Venus. The addition of the Uranian planet Apollon at 1 Libra increased the bullish potential of the natal planetary grouping. Graph 5 tells the price story.

At first glance, one may wonder why a rally would have been expected in view of the hard aspects made by the station. The answer here lies in the compatibility of Uranus with the natal planets and the technical picture. Uranus in combination with Pluto can be interpreted as "sudden change in financial position." The two angles plus Moon, Venus, and Apollon add a benign flavor.

Second, the technical reading was one of a stock that was about to rise. UAL had been going sideways, building a base, while the rest of the market was strong. The technical oscillators were oversold, and the picture was one of a pile of dry leaves. The Uranus station was the flame.

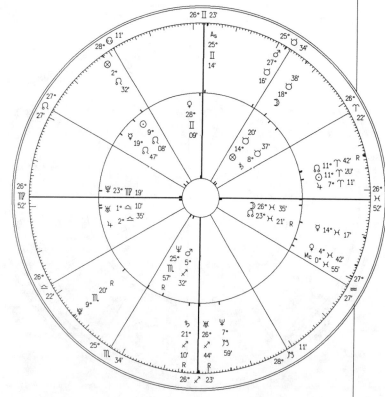

inside: first trade chart 8/16/1969 *outside:* transits for 4/01/1987

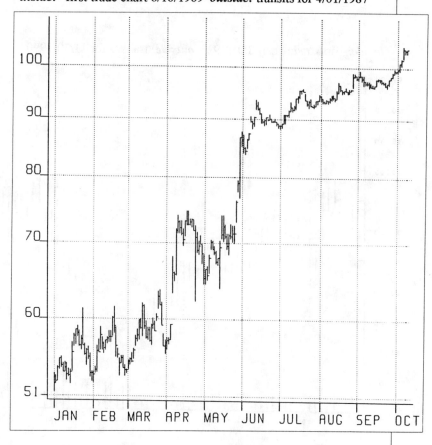

6 · In the Driver's Seat with Goodyear

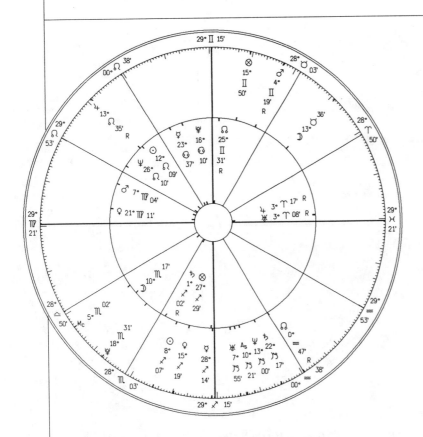

Chart 6 represents Goodyear (GT). On November 30, 1990 Jupiter went stationary on the Sun of the chart. It went direct in the spring of 1991, trining GT's Jupiter, Uranus, and Saturn. Graph 6 reveals how accurately this picked the bottom. This is a very good example of how to work with Jupiter. Note that not only did the GT chart catch the station, but it also aspected an entire grouping of planets. Its forward movement made a long slow series of trines to the natal chart. This is the best type of hit from the Great Benefic.

inside: first trade chart 8/05/1927 ***outside:*** transits for 11/30/1990

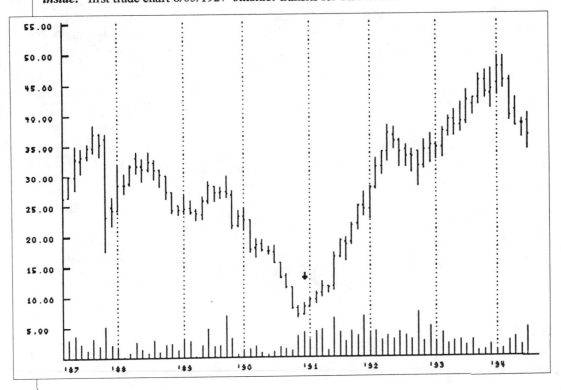

Jupiter went retrograde on January 28, 1993 on the Libran Sun and Moon (Chart 7). See weekly Graph 7 and note the sudden jump up over the $30 price level. Jupiter remained retrograde until it went direct on June 2 at 5 Libra, sextile the natal Jupiter. But note the big run-up in the previous month of May. There was a solar eclipse in that month at zero Gemini, exactly square Venus at zero Virgo. The best part of a hit from a Jupiter station is that, if an aspect is made, it lasts long and there is a repeat hit as the planet moves forward. Compare this with the Goodyear example. All good things come to an end. The retrograde station of Pluto square the MC in the first quarter of 1994 topped the run. As Pluto moves forward, it will square the MC again, and then begin to square Venus and Mars. This stock subsequently fell to 30.

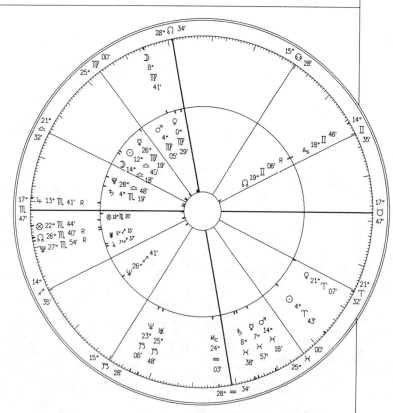

inside: first trade chart 10/06/1983 *outside:* transits for 3/25/1994

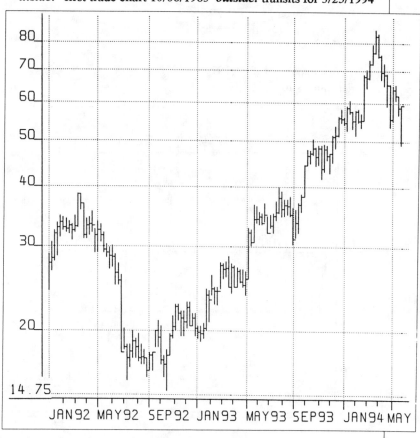

8· Advanced Micro Beats Intel

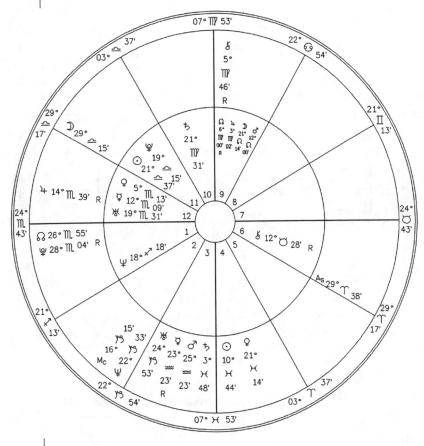

Advanced Micro Devices (AMD) was being sued by Intel.. The entire semi-conductor group had been very strong, but AMD's progress had been restrained by the prospect of losing the suit.

Note that Jupiter turned retrograde on March 1, 1994. The station was conjunct the Mercury in AMD's first trade chart (*Chart 8*). AMD won the suit 11 days later and the stock jumped 50 percent (*Graph 8*).

This configuration was the deciding factor determining the decision to be long in the stock.

inside: first trade chart 10/15/1979
outside: transits for 3/01/1994

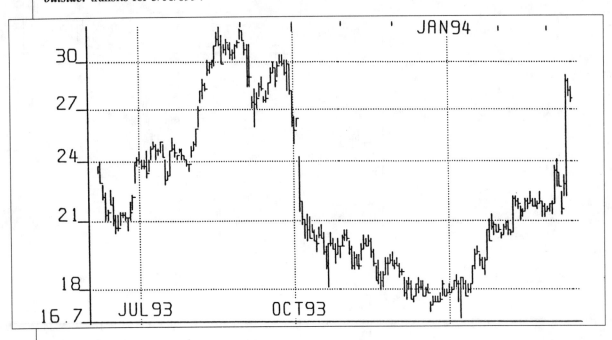

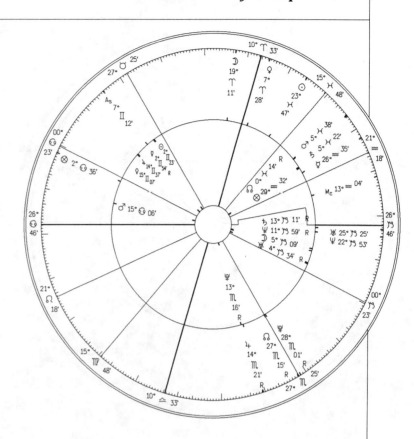

The same Jupiter station was conjunct the Pluto of Kemper (KEM), (Chart 9) the financial services company. A takeover of KEM was announced on March 14 leading to a 40 percent rise (Graph 9). This is a good example of the significance of Pluto in acquisitions.

Note how the bullish effect of the Jupiter station was modified by the natal planet that it conjoined. The station on Mercury led to a favorable court decision for AMD while Jupiter on Pluto led to a buy-out for KEM.

inside: first trade chart 5/23/1989 *outside:* transits for 3/14/1994

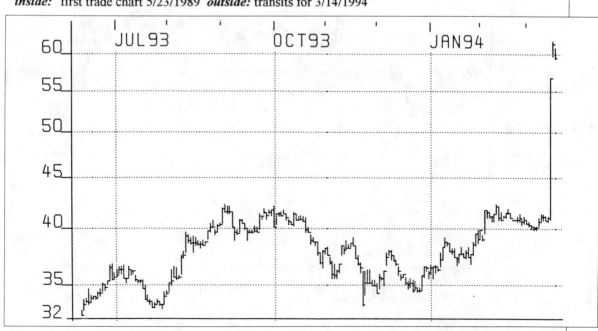

10 - Taking a Bath in Great Lakes

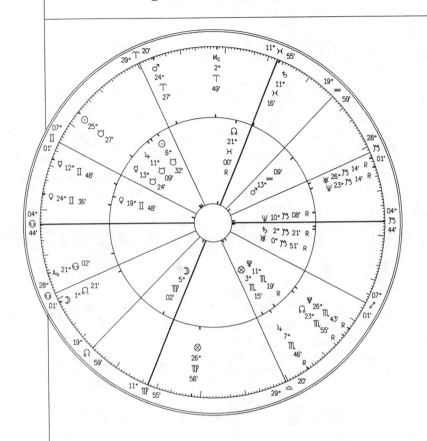

This stock, Great Lakes Chemical, (Graph 10) was already in decline when transiting Saturn reached the MC while the planet was semisquare transiting Uranus (Chart 10). The last break in April led to a waterfall decline. Again, we see the sensitivity of the angles.

inside: first trade chart 4/26/1988 *outside:* transits for 5/16/1994

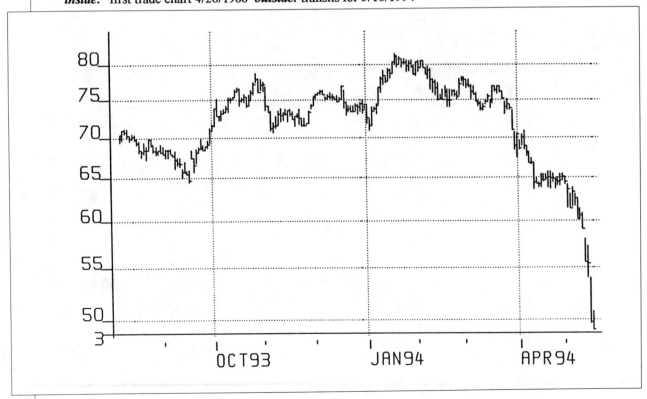

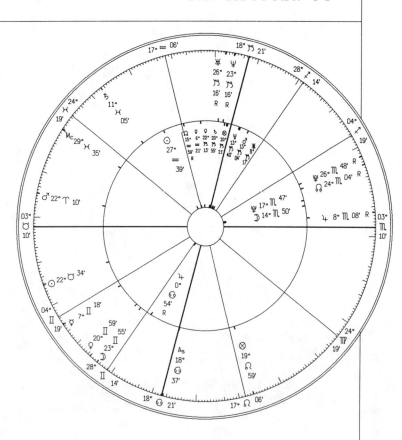

As mentioned under the description of the planets, Pluto's effect is dramatic and final. Cisco had a great run as a premier networking stock. Pluto was almost exactly square Cisco's Sun when the stock broke. (Graph 11 and Chart 11).

inside: first trade chart 2/16/1990 *outside:* transits for 5/13/1994

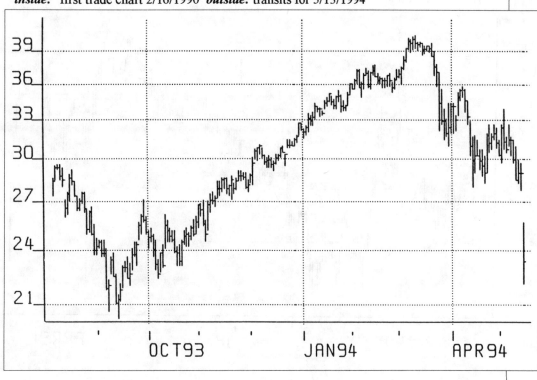

12-Neptune Hits Xilinx

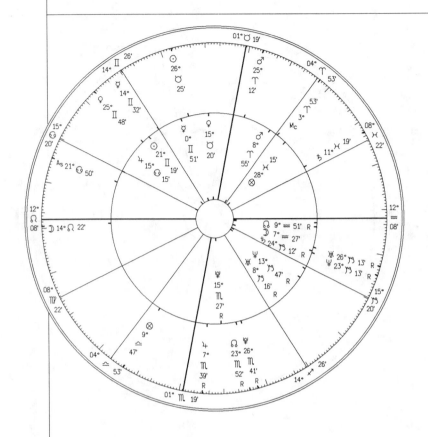

This volatile semiconductor stock began to trend down when Uranus passed over natal Saturn (Chart 12). The big break came when Neptune reached Saturn, a deflationary combination. See Graph 12.

inside: first trade chart 6/12/1990 *outside:* transits for 5/17/1994

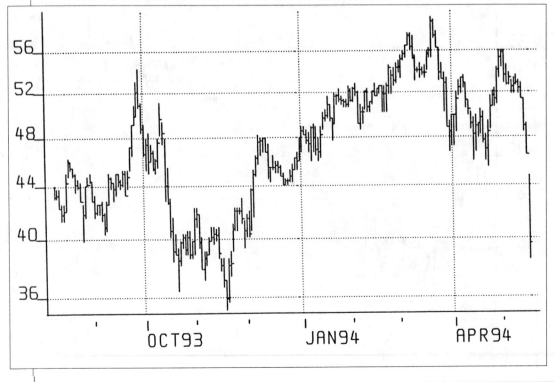

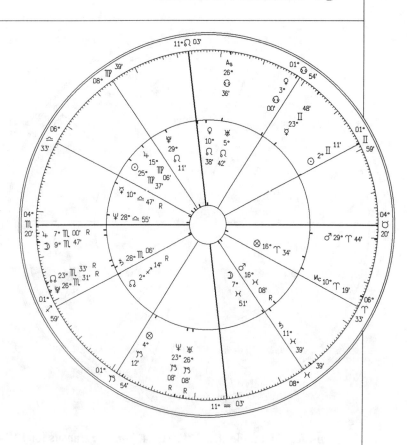

Gerber, the baby food company, was the target of a European buy-out on May 23 of 1994. The lunar eclipse of May 24 was conjunct the progressed ASC at 2 Sagittarius. This is a good example of the importance of the angles, even when they are progressed. See Graph and Chart 13.

inside: first trade chart 9/18/1956 ***outside:*** transits for 5/23/1994

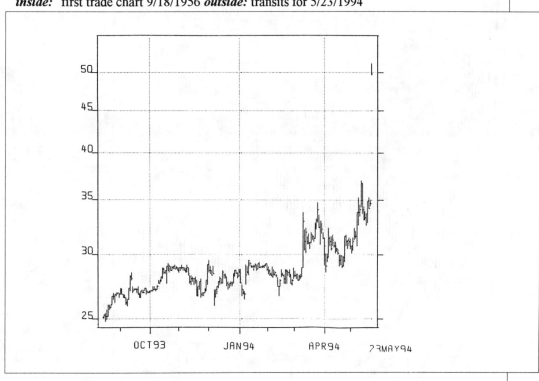

14 - The Power of Eclipses: Archer Daniels Midland

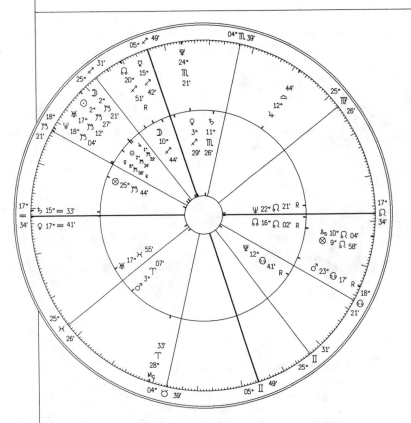

On December 24,1992, a solar eclipse at 2 Capricorn fell on the Sun-Jupiter conjunction in the first trade chart. The graph is a weekly one, depicting the 30 percent rise in price in the six months prior to the eclipse. The stock topped a couple of weeks later. Note how this point in January 1993 was a significant high. This may not seem to be a big move, given the nature of the planets involved. (See item number 5 under Do's and Don'ts on page 13.) But ADM is not a big mover. This is the stock of a slow-growth agricultural company that does well during inflationary times.

inside: first trade chart 12/24/1924 *outside:* transits for 12/24/1992

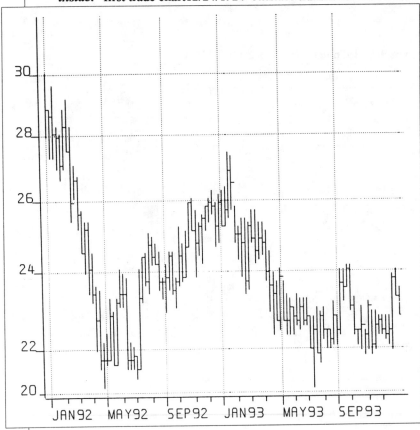

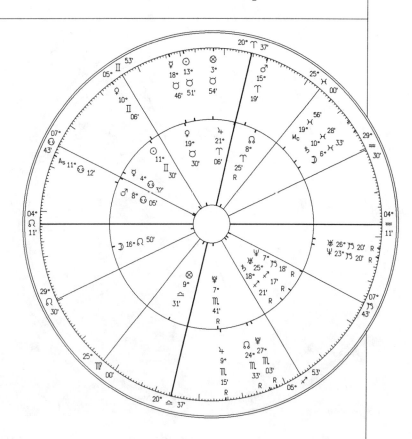

WMB decided to sell off assets, a deal that would net millions in cash. The shares jumped 25 percent in a day. The May 10 solar eclipse was conjunct Venus. Remember that Venus is frequently representative of a deal or agreement. But how do you know whether this would be bullish? Note that Jupiter was conjunct Pluto making favorable aspects to Mars and Jupiter.

inside: first trade chart 6/02/1987 ***outside:*** transits for 5/4/1994

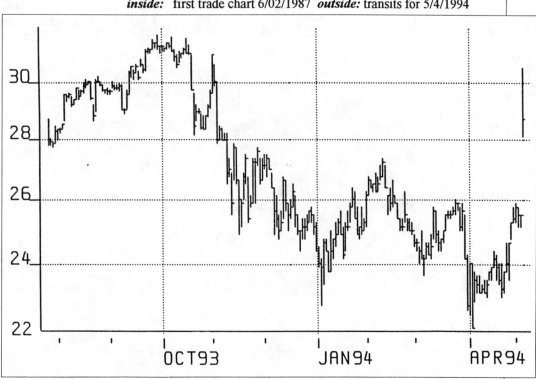

16 - The Big Top in Paramount

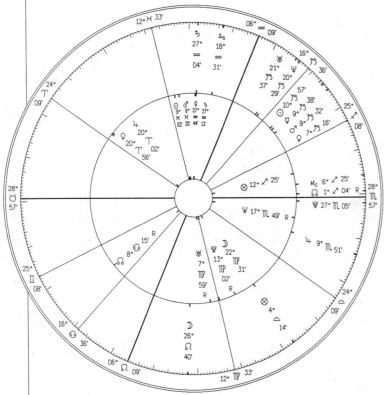

inside: first trade chart 2/28/1964 *outside:* transits for 1/01/1994

This was a takeover target in 1993. Saturn sailing over the top of the chart and toward four planets in the 10th house in 1994 was the first sign that the price rise was soon to end. Also note that Saturn would also be opposite Uranus and Pluto on the IC. The approaching transit of Pluto opposite the ASC was also a contributing factor.

In fact, the natal Sun is on the Uranus/Pluto midpoint, an axis that is known for drastic changes in financial position. Graph 16 depicts the tremendous price break. This is a good example of a hard hit to a very unstable axis. If the Sun had been better positioned, the price decline would not have been as severe.

This is an important example. Midpoint structures to a natal point are vital in determining the effect that a transit might have. The same transit may hit the same planet in different charts, but the effects can differ. The effects usually differ in terms of magnitude.

The Rise and Fall of Philip Morris -17

Chart 17 is that of Philip Morris. This was one of the stellar performers of the 1982-1994 bull market. Saturn was rising toward the MC. Eventually, it would oppose Neptune, cross the MC, and run over four planets in the 10th house. Saturn's station in June of 1994 was square natal Uranus. This transit put an end to MO's long price run..

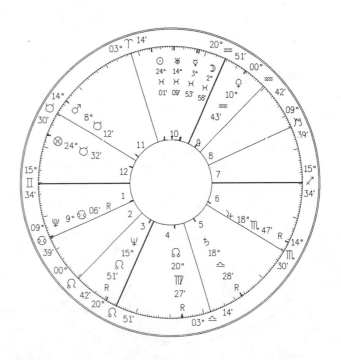

first trade chart 3/15/1923

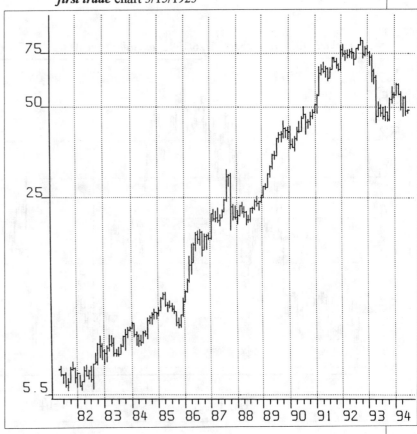

18 · Broderbund's Rollercoaster Ride

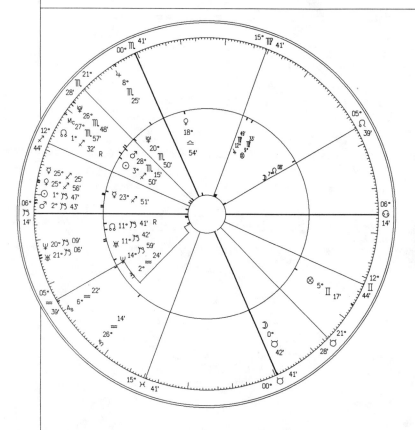

BROD was the target of a bid from Electronic Arts (ERTS). The shares ran up, and then the deal fell through. First, note that the November 1993 solar eclipse fell on the natal Pluto and the lunar eclipse widely opposed the Sun. In the period following the eclipses, when the deal was being finalized, the hard aspects that transiting Pluto was to make were a sign that all was not well. Pluto conjoined Mars and then semisquared both Uranus and the Node. The deal was called off. Chart 18 and Graph 18 tell the story.

inside: first trade chart 11/26/1991 *outside:* transits for 12/23/1993

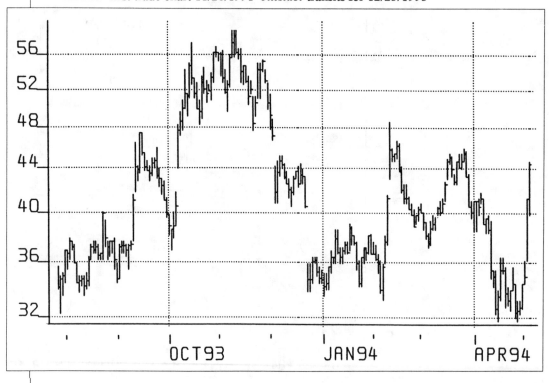

This was a high-flying new issue in the software industry. The solar eclipse of May 10, 1994 was precisely square the natal Sun and Saturn, and disappointing earnings collapsed the stock. The pattern of the stock price gave a hint as to the direction of the next move, whenever it came. The stock had broken a pair of uptrend lines, failed to penetrate its February high, and then made two lower highs, all bearish signals. The eclipse hitting the Sun was the sign of a big move to come. Note that the closeness of the square is related to the size of the move.

Again, we see the importance of midpoints here. The eclipse squared the Suns in other first trade charts, so why did it have such a strong effect in this case and not in the others? The answer lies in the midpoint structure that equals the Sun. It is an unstable one: Venus/Saturn=Aries/ Pluto= Midheaven (MC), Mars/Aries= Node/Uranus, Neptune, ASC. This notation is read as follows: The Sun equals the midpoint of Saturn and Venus. It is also on the Mars/MC and the Aries/ MC midpoints, and so on. The term "equals"

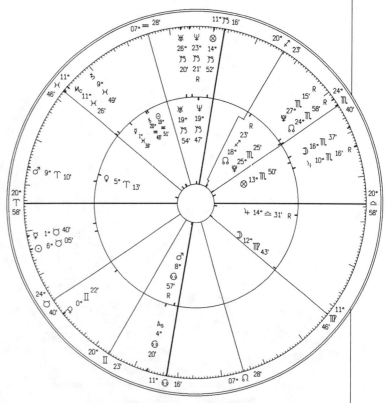

means that the Sun is in a 0, 45, 90, 135, or 180-degree aspect to all the midpoints listed above. This type of structure is called a planetary picture. Its flavor is negative due to the contrary nature of the planets involved. This is a very important point that can explain the difference in reaction when similar points in different horoscopes are hit by the same planet or eclipse.

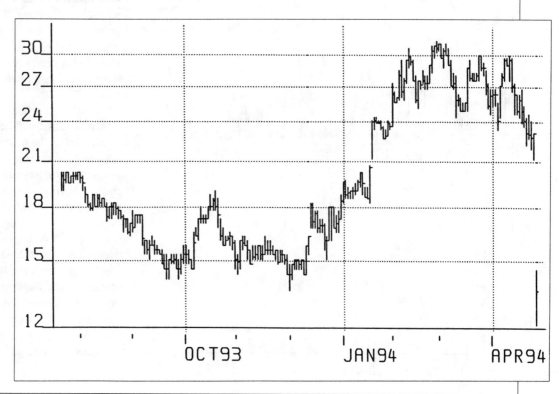

20 - The Setting of Sun Microsystems

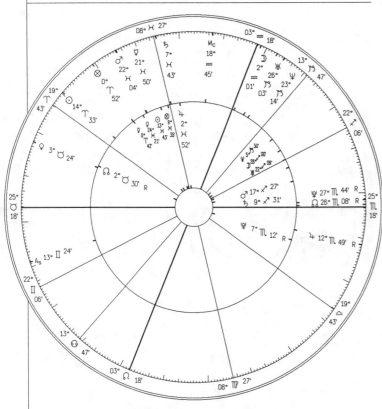

inside: first trade chart 3/04/1986 *outside:* transits for 4/04/1994

I first looked at this stock in 1992. There were two reasons to avoid Sun. First, the workstation business, Sun's main line, did not look prosperous. Second, Saturn had already passed over the MC. Remember, this is an important cycle. Once Saturn exited Aquarius, it would run over the three planets in Pisces: Jupiter, the Sun, and Venus. It would also square four planets in Sagittarius. Given these aspects and the sideways-to-down trading range in the share price, there was little to get excited about from the standpoint of the investor seeking consistent share appreciation over a two-to-three-year time horizon. There were ample opportunities for traders, however. SUNW made some very sharp moves when the Scorpio-Taurus eclipses of 1993-1994 hit the ASC and Pluto.

This is an important example. Shorter-term influences can push the stock up, but the long Saturn transit put on a ceiling. Note that the March, 1994 Jupiter station trined the Sun in SUNW's first trade chart. The stock ran up and then croaked. In such cases, upside resistance will probably not be penetrated. The share price has to climb a steep grade. When it reaches the top, Saturn pours olive oil on the slope, and further appreciation is unlikely.

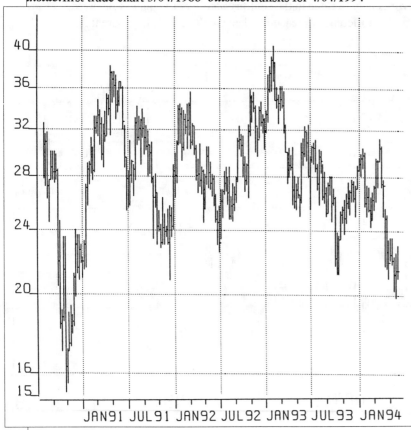

If you were seeking a longer-term investment, this stock would not be on your list. As a trading vehicle, it would be of interest. The important point is that you must first decide what your goal is, and then devise a strategy for reaching it. This is where most investment plans go astray.

There is also a second important lesson here that will become more significant in the next section. Suppose you screened the OTC stock horoscopes for any charts that had their Suns trined by the Jupiter station at 14 Scorpio in March of 1994. The *Financial Trader* program would have selected SUNW due to the solar position at 14 Pisces. True, the Sun was being trined, but the computer screen did not show you the adverse influence of Saturn. A second computer screen would show Saturn hits. This would have provided a list of stocks to avoid, sell, or sell short.

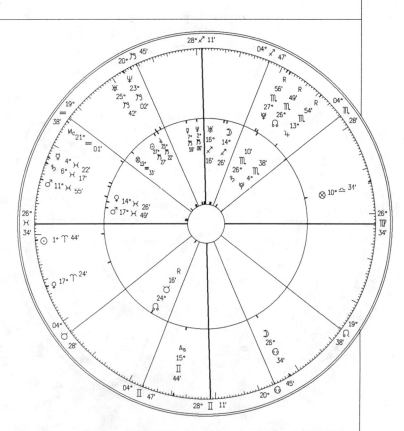

Novell, the top computer networking stock, had made a great run from three to the mid-30s by 1993. The danger signal was the approach of Pluto to oppose the Node and conjoin Saturn. This is an example of how Pluto can lead to major trend changes, in this case a 50 percent decline.

inside: first trade chart 1/17/1985 ***outside:*** transits for 3/22/1994

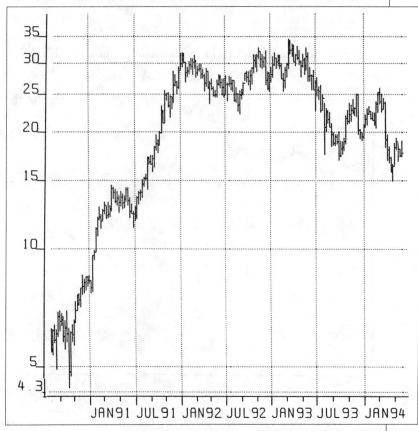

22 - Pluto Breaks Mediavision

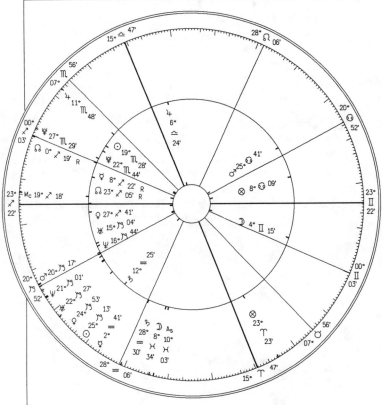

This was a hot new issue in 1992. MVIS was a maker of computer sound cards and was Creative Technology's biggest competitor. The stock was pitched hard by Wall Street, but we did not bite. The November 1993 solar eclipse was conjunct Pluto, and the May 1994 eclipse was opposite the Sun and Pluto. Management had cooked the books, set up a secret warehouse to hide returned merchandise, and had taken their girlfriends on jet trips. The FBI and SEC moved in. Graph 22 depicts the stock's collapse. This is another illustration of the power of eclipses, and the total 'all or nothing' effect of Pluto. Again, note the tendency for the manifestation to occur between a pair of eclipses that conjoin and oppose a planet. MVIS filed for Chapter 11 in July of 1994.

inside: first trade chart 11/11/1992 *outside:* transits for 1/15/1994

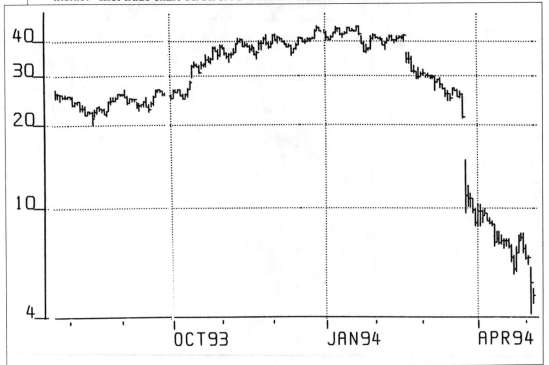

The Importance of Midpoint Structures: Computer Associates · 23

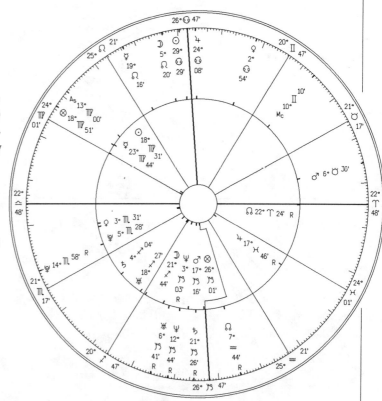

Computer Associates (CA) had fallen 50 percent from its 1989 high. It began to rally at the 10-11 area in late 1989 until it broke 16 in July of 1990. The solar eclipse of July 22, 1990 at 29 Cancer was on CA's MC. First, CA was technically overextended. Second, a strong hit usually heralds a trend change. Third, the natal condition of the MC was not favorable: MC= Mars/Pluto= Sun, Uranus, Jupiter/Saturn. These are not harmonious combinations and were a hint at what the effect of the eclipse was to be. The stock stopped trading at 16 and re-opened at 10 an hour later. It dipped as low as the 5-6 area before bottoming out. Elliott wavers may note that the 1982-1987 advance seems to have a five-wave pattern. The 1989 drop looks like an A wave while the 1990 rally appears to be a B wave. The 1990 collapse had all the earmarks of a final C wave.

inside: first trade chart 9/11/1986 *outside:* transits for 7/22/1990

24 · Microsoft

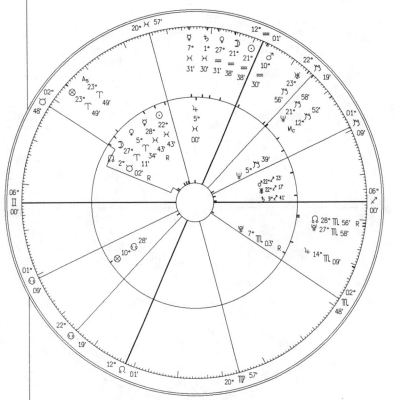

Graph 24 depicts the summer 1993 bottom and the spring, 1994 acceleration in MSFT. At the bottom, Uranus and Neptune were semisquare natal Jupiter. Pluto also trined the Sun. Alone, these aspects would not have been sufficient to raise the share price; together, and in absence of any harsh aspects, this was a bullish signal. The stock took off in the first quarter of 1994 as the over-all market experienced its first 10 percent correction in over three years. In February, Uranus and Neptune were trine the Sun. Jupiter had passed over natal Pluto and was going to retrograde back over it again during the spring and summer. On the Jupiter station in August, the government ended its investigation quite leniently. The November, 1994 solar eclipse conjoined Pluto, leading to the Intuit acquisition and the refusal of a federal judge to accept the August agreement.

inside: first trade chart 3/13/1986 *outside:* transits for 2/10/1994

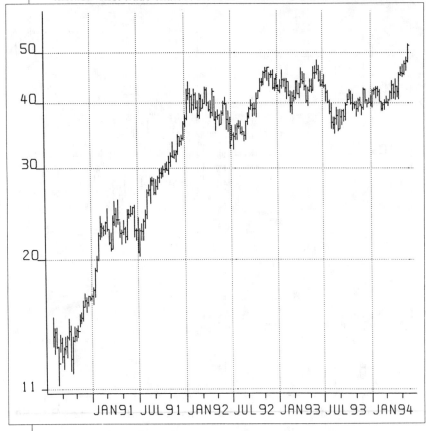

Digital Equipment was up there with IBM before the PC-downsizing wave engulfed the mainframe group. DEC's difficulties were reflected in the horoscope of first trade. Pluto first ran over all the Libra planets in the 9th house and then steamrolled the Scorpio planets in the 10th. The big top near 200 occurred in late 1987 when Pluto began to run over Venus and the MC. Pluto then squared Saturn and the Node. Progressed Sun moved into orb of a sesquiquadrate to natal Saturn in 1992. The late 1993 and early 1994 solar eclipses hit the natal Jupiter-Saturn opposition. This is a good illustration of the types of heavy hits needed to reverse a big uptrend. Note the combination of outer planet transits, secondary progressions, and solar eclipses. Each of these hits alone would not likely have been sufficient; but the combination was very powerful. Also of interest is the incorporation date of August 23, 1957. As Pluto enters Sagittarius in 1995, it will square the natal Sun-Pluto conjunction at zero Virgo. This is indicative of a major restructuring. Given the weakened condition of the company at this time, DEC will likely emerge as a very different company.

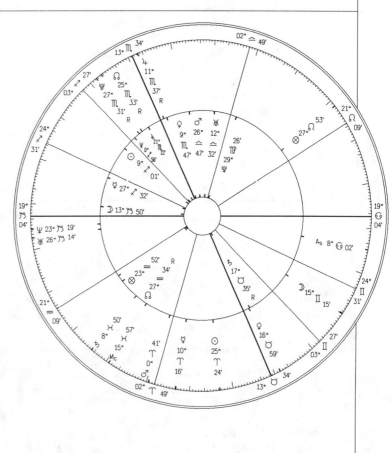

inside: first trade chart 12/01/1970 *outside:* transits for 4/15/1994

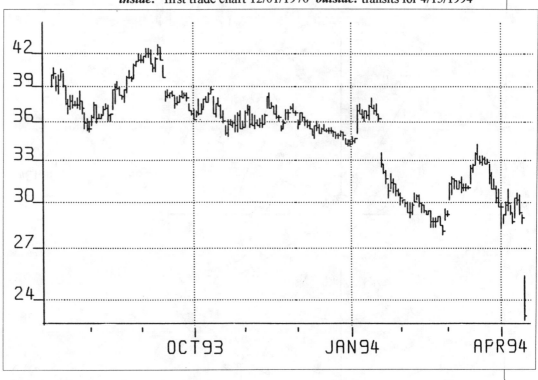

26 · The Value of Heliocentric Analysis: Bausch & Lomb

BOL declined about 25 percent in the spring of 1994. The shares peaked in late January and gapped down on June 3. Geo Saturn, Uranus, and Neptune were in hard aspect to natal Uranus and Neptune. Heliocentrically, the aspects were closer to timing the breakdown. See Chart numbers 26, 26A, and 26B.

above: Geocentric-A
below: Heliocentric-B
inside: first trade chart 12/17/1973
outside: transits for 6/03/1994

The Takeover of American Cyanamid and Natal Eclipses · 27

Graph 27 and Charts 27A and 27B describe the action. ACY jumped 50 percent when AHP announced a hostile takeover on August 2, 1994. Note that Uranus, and eventually Neptune, will transit the Sun in both the horoscopes of first trade and incorporation (Chart 27B set for July 22, 1907 in Maine, time unknown).

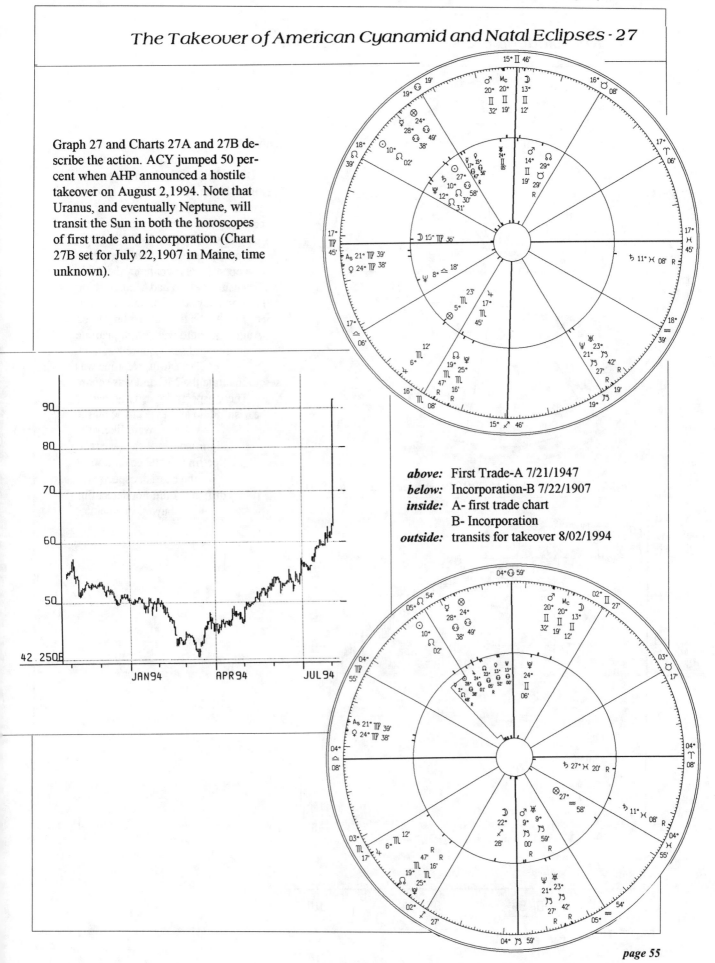

above: First Trade-A 7/21/1947
below: Incorporation-B 7/22/1907
inside: A- first trade chart
      B- Incorporation
outside: transits for takeover 8/02/1994

28 · Knowledgeware's Decline and Buyout

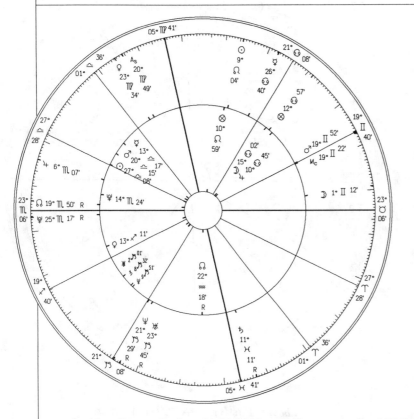

inside: first trade chart 10/20/1989 *outside:* transits for 8/01/1994

This software company's stock had just recovered from a multi-year tumble. In December, 1993, the stock peaked again. It broke down completely when it was revealed that some of the company's accounts receivable were suspect. KNOW hit a low of 2 1/4 in July. Note the previous pair of eclipses were opposite and conjunct the ASC. Too, transiting Pluto had been crossing it. The company was then taken over at about $7. At the time of the buyout on August 1, Pluto was sesquiquadrate Jupiter and semisquare Neptune. Transiting Neptune was sesquiquadrate the MC and was square Mars. These aspects are usually read as bearish. Pluto and the eclipse on the ASC were likely the significators of the takeover. Spotting the takeover amidst the bearish aspects was difficult. I did not detect this buyout in advance.

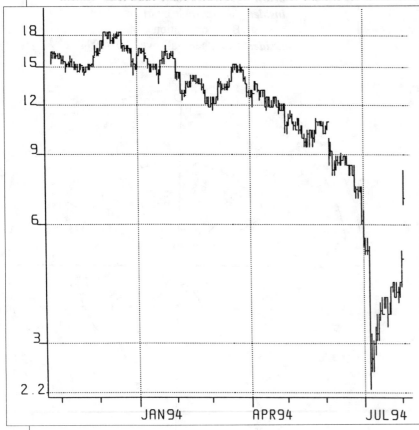

Policy Management Systems: A Very Afflicted Horoscope - 29

Policy Management (PMS) was sailing along as an institutional darling when the stock fell 50 percent on April 6,1993. The upcoming eclipse in May, 1993 at 0 Gemini was on the MC of this chart. A second red warning flag was the upcoming hard aspects of Saturn and then Pluto to the MC. Closer analysis reveals a host of afflictions: Saturn in hard aspect to Neptune; Uranus and Neptune conjunct Saturn and opposite the natal Jupiter, being ignited by transiting Mars. This is a good example of a clear-cut call. There were no offsetting positive aspects.

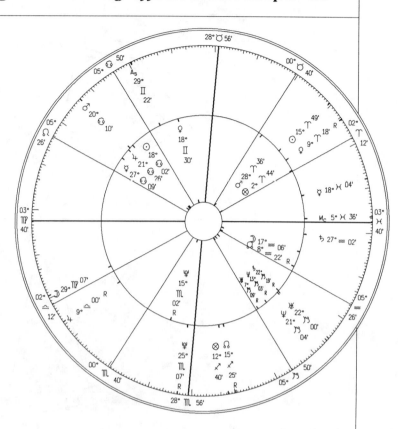

inside: first trade chart 7/10/1990 *outside:* transits for 4/06/1993

30 - The Takeover of NCR

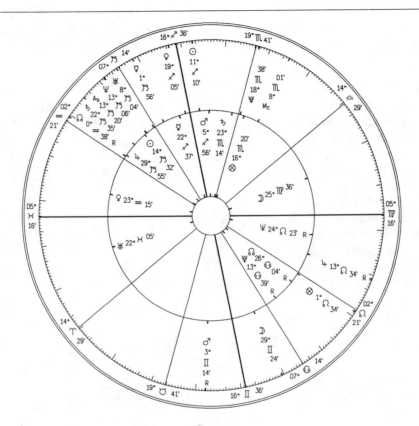

inside: first trade chart 1/05/1926 *outside:* transits for 12/03/1990

NCR was bought by ATT on December 3, 1990. The first trade Chart, number 30, is not included in the chart collection because it is no longer a public company. First, the solar eclipses of July, 1990 and January, 1991 were opposite and conjunct natal Jupiter. Note that the acquisition occurred between the two eclipses. Turning to transits, Neptune was within a degree and a half of the Sun and was opposite Pluto. The Node was passing over natal Jupiter. Helio Pluto was conjunct Saturn within a degree.

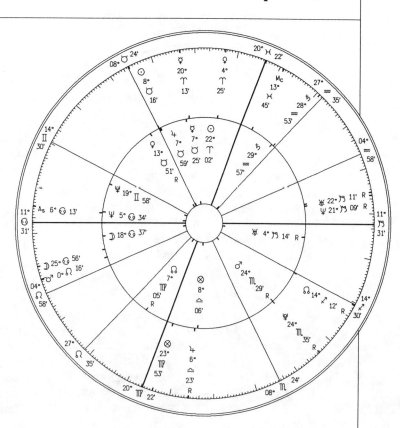

In April of 1993, Eastman Kodak made a lower high, an indication that the stock was losing momentum. But there were further indications. The May 21, 1993 eclipse was square Saturn within one degree. Transiting Saturn was conjunct natal Saturn. Uranus and Neptune were both in hard aspect to the Sun and the Node. And Pluto was passing over Mars. The negative aspects far outweighed the positive.

inside: first trade chart 4/12/1905 *outside:* transits for 4/28/1993

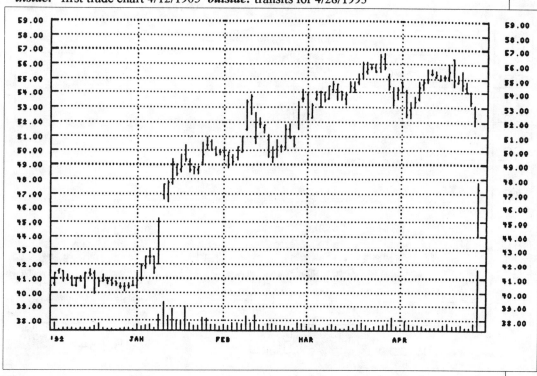

32 - The Grumman Acquisition

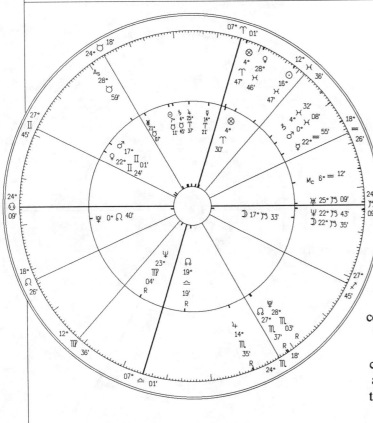

Grumman (GQ) was bought out on March 7,1994 for about 50 percent over its share price. The eclipses of November, 1993 and May, 1994 were opposite and conjunct natal Uranus, respectively. Transiting Uranus and Neptune were opposite the ASC and trine natal Neptune. Past the date of the takeover, Jupiter was to go direct opposite natal Saturn in July, and the eclipses of late 1994 and early 1995 were opposite and conjunct the Sun.

With all this activity, this stock was on the watch list. The big price run was anticipated late in the year, due to the eclipses hitting the Sun. So what sent the shares up prior to expectations? The answer was likely the action of Uranus. First, the eclipses had energized natal Uranus. Then transiting Uranus was slowing down, getting ready to go stationary in late April. Its opposition to the Asc. and close square to Jupiter were the key determinants. There was a short-term clue that led to this conclusion. Note the position of the Moon, March 7- almost 23 Capricorn. As astrologers know, the Moon frequently is the timer that ignites bigger configurations. When a stock moves unexpectedly and you are searching for the planetary cause, the transiting Moon will frequently point to the larger configuration. Remember, Uranus stations and eclipses are two of the most powerful influences. This is a good example of their power.

inside: first trade chart 4/27/1940 *outside:* transits for 3/07/1994

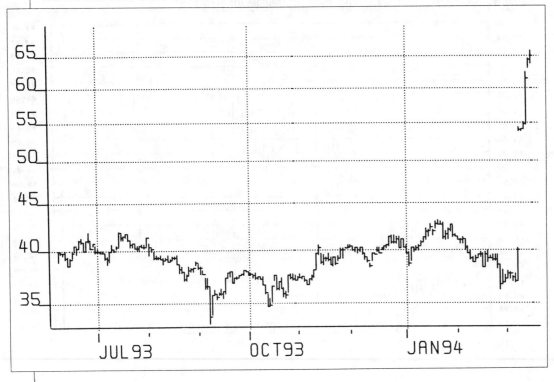

The Rise and Fall of Symantec - 33

SYMC was a high-flying software stock. Jupiter in Cancer was a beneficial influence in 1990, and the stock soared. The January 4, 1992 solar eclipse at 14 Capricorn was close enough to the chart's Saturn-Neptune conjunction to warrant concern, particularly after a big price run-up. With the beneficial influence of Jupiter past, the stock trended down after the eclipse. The July, 1992 eclipse at 9 Cancer was opposite the same Saturn-Neptune. Then the heavy and adverse hits from Pluto came in like storm clouds: square to the Moon and semisquare Saturn and Neptune. When the dust cleared, SYMC had fallen from 51 to 7.

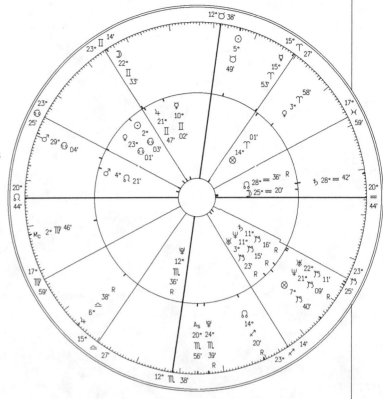

Note this important sequence:
1 - The stock runs up sharply.
2 - The beneficial planetary contacts fade away.
3 - The first really adverse contacts terminate the move.
4 - The addition of strong and long-lasting af- flictions crumples the stock..

What conditions would be necessary to move the stock up again? First, we would need to see a basing period. This is a long period of back-and-forth movement in a narrow price range that resembles a flat base. Then, some positive aspects must appear. As these aspects come in, trading volume should pick up and the price should begin to rally. The first signs of upside price movement are a confirmation that the analysis is correct. If the bull- ish contacts will continue with few ad- verse ones, then it is likely we have found a winner.

Borland, another software stock, plunged from 85 to 8. This was not surprising for two reasons. First, Bor- land was in the same industry and subject to the same influences, in this case, the introduction of Windows from Microsoft. More interesting is the first trade date of Borland, Decem- ber 19,1989. Most of the outer planet afflictions that sank SYMC also hit BORL.

inside: first trade chart 6/23/1989 *outside:* transits for 4/25/1993

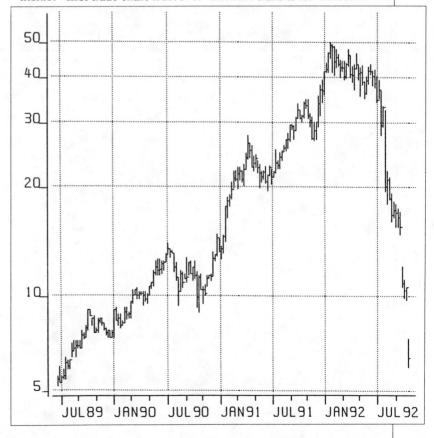

Computerized Stock Selection
and Portfolio Management

O nce chart patterns that fit one's requirements are isolated, you must identify horoscopes that fit the mold. The *Financial Trader* features a scanner that enables the user to screen hundreds of charts instantly. For example, stocks with the Sun in Taurus usually outperform the averages. The Research module of the program can easily find stock charts with certain planetary positions, aspects, midpoints, *etc.*

For example, when looking ahead to 1993 and 1994, the sequence of eclipses in Taurus-Scorpio and the passage of Jupiter into Scorpio were noted. Any stock that began trading in the last decade must have natal Pluto in Scorpio. In addition, there was the series of Jupiter-Saturn oppositions in Cancer-Capricorn in 1989-1990. (One financial astrologer predicted that this relatively benign grouping of Jupiter opposite Saturn and Neptune in late 1989 would collapse the market and the national financial structure, which it did not.) Therefore, in 1994, transiting Jupiter would have to conjoin natal Pluto, trine natal Jupiter, and sextile Saturn, Uranus, and Neptune in the horoscopes of any stock that began trading in 1989-1990. These are all favorable aspects, and the influence of the eclipses was an added kicker. Stratus Computer, Chart 1 on page 66, is an example.

One can also test stock groups to find the common elements within a group. For example, we could separate a group that has outperformed or underperformed the market over a given time period. The *Wall Street Journal* prints a daily list of the biggest gainers and losers every day. *Barrons* does the same for the week and for each quarter. *Value Line* also has winners and losers for the previous 13 weeks.

But the most valuable function is the ability to easily identify charts that are being activated by upcoming transits, stations, or eclipses. This module enables us to scan all the charts to see which ones are being activated by an upcoming event. Select the degree of the January 4, 1992 solar eclipse at 13 Capricorn 51. Remember, this eclipse was also conjunct transiting Uranus. Select conjunctions only and a 4 degree orb applying and separating. The Scanner is asked only to look for conjunctions to Jupiter in the trade charts. Within seconds, 700 NYSE charts were scanned. The performance of the group 90 days later is listed in the table below.

Separating the Wheat From the Chaff

Question: Why did UIS outperform the others? Why was there such a difference between the top and bottom of the list, if the eclipse hit them all in the same way? The answer, again, lies in the natal configuration of the point

Computerized Selection of
1/4/1992 Solar Eclipse Conjunct Jupiter Charts

STOCK, TICKER	PRICE 1/3/92	PRICE 4/1/92	% CHANGE
Unisys UIS	4.625	9.875	113.5%
Louisiana Pacific LPX	30.417	40.917	34.5
Outboard Marine OM	19.875	22.625	13.8
Perkin Elmer PKN	29.75	32.375	8.8
First Bank System FBS	24.5	26.5	8.2
TCBY Enterprise TBY	5.5	5.125	-6.8
Home Depot HD	46.417	42.917	-7.5
British Telecomm BTY	62.875	55.	-12.5

Average % Change	+19.0
Change in S&P 500	-3.6
Change in DJIA	+1.5
Change in NASDAQ	-0.4

Note that the average appreciation in the portfolio exceeded that of 3 different market indice, and outperformance is the name of the game. Also, Unisys was not only the top performer on our list, it was the top performer in the S&P 500 in the first quarter of 1992.

that is energized. Jupiter in the UIS chart, by aspect, is sextile Jupiter, semisextile Uranus, and quincunx Pluto. All of the other charts have a Jupiter that has similar soft aspects, or, they are relatively unaspected. But experience has demonstrated that the midpoint structures hold the answer.

The UIS Jupiter equals
    = Mercury/Node,Venus,
    = Neptune/Venus,Node
    = Sun/Mars=Saturn/Uranus.

The last combination is not a bullish one, but it is a bit out of orb and overshadowed by the more positive groupings. (In the Uranian system, the bullish influence of Vulcanus and Apollon adds to the bullish flavor of the Jupiter axis).

The LPX Jupiter also has a positive midpoint structure
    Jupiter= Node= Mars/Neptune=
    Venus/Ascendant= Moon/Venus.
Again, the addition of the Uranian planets makes the axis even more attractive.

OM, the number three performer on the list, also has a favorable Jupiter axis. But, the Sun, Uranus/ Neptune, Saturn picture creeps in along with a pair of positive pictures. The saving grace here is that the Saturn is slightly out of our one-degree orb, thereby weakening its influence.

PKN and FBS both have fairly favorable Jupiter axes, but the bottom three on the list do not:

TCBY
    Jupiter= Saturn/Uranus= Venus/Pluto

HD
    Jupiter= Venus/Mars= Uranus, Midheaven/Saturn

BTY
  Jupiter= Ascendant, Venus/Saturn= Midheaven/Uranus

The addition of Saturn and Uranus to these Jupiter axes, with no or few offsetting bullish pictures, made the difference. So the eclipse-Uranus that hit the Jupiter in these charts also set off the negative planetary pictures, thereby restraining the otherwise bullish effect of the Greater Benefic.

The next step in our screening process would have been to investigate the other influences affecting the charts. In the case of BTY, we see that transiting Pluto was conjunct natal Saturn within less than a half of one degree, a negative influence. HD is less clear cut. Saturn had recently finished squaring the Sun and Mercury, and was on its way toward a square of its own natal place. Saturn in Aquarius would square five TBY natal planets on its transit through this sign, which should have been enough to warn the analyst or trader off. By contrast, transiting Uranus was also sextiling natal Saturn as it passed over natal Jupiter.There were few easy aspects to offset the harsh aspects. LPX, number two on the list, began trading with the natal Node conjunct natal Jupiter, so both were hit by Uranus and the eclipse. With no hard aspects at the time of the eclipse, the effect here was much more beneficial then in most of the cases.

Recall the example of Sun Microsystems in the Case Studies section. Again, the purpose of screening is to screen. That is, screening saves time by eliminating the issues that do not meet our requirements. It does not guarantee a list of winners. If a screen of the most bearish planetary configurations were run, some of the same stocks that pop up on the bullish list might also appear on the bearish list. These runs are not mutually exclusive. After screening for some criteria, one must screen again to identify the best in the list.

One more analogy may help to clarify an important point. Have you ever had a mixture of both easy and difficult aspects to your horoscope? In a basic astrology class given by Charles Jayne, we young students asked what happened in such cases. Did the positive and negative cancel out? No, answered Charles. He gave an example of such a chart. A woman was driving down a country road, and a deer ran in front of her car. The deer was killed, the car went out of control and was wrecked, and the woman walked away without a scratch. The latter event was the result of the positive aspects.

So a first trade chart can have both bullish and bearish influences. The screen can provide a list of one or the other. The task then remains to analyze each chart to weed out the best of the best. You may come up with a pair of stocks that appear attractive in terms of transits. However, the secondary progressions or the natal structure in one horoscope may cause some doubt or concern. Drop this stock in favor of the other. In the case histories section, STK was earlier noted for having a well-positioned natal Jupiter. This was one factor that would have led us to lean toward this stock over the others in the screen.

Important distiguishing factors such as this have been mentioned several times thus far. Let us summarize these vital points here.

Important Factors to Consider in Chart Selection

1. Carefully check the natal condition of the planet that is being energized in the chart. Does it make soft or hard natal aspects? More importantly, does it make compatible or incompatible midpoints? See the Storage Tek example in Case Studies.

2. Assume that bullish stocks are being sought. Once a screen for hits from transiting planets has been run, check to see if there are also adverse aspects being made to the chart. If there are, eliminate these stocks from consideration. Now check other predictive techniques that are unique to the individual charts, such as secondary progressions, tertiaries, solar arcs, *etc.* Again, drop any charts that do not meet your requirements. After having separated the wheat from the chaff, we have a list of buy (or sell) candidates.

3. Remember from Do's and Don'ts (page 13): different types of stocks have different share-price characteristics. Just as boxers are classified according to weight, stocks are broken down into categories. Assume you want to screen for maximum share price movement and you boil your choices down to ten equities. If the screen picks up five fast-moving technology stocks in a good technology market, focus on those issues. If the screen also kicked out a utility and a food stock, not as likely to make a big move as are the tech issues, these stocks would be bypassed. By the same token, remember that gold stocks move primarily with the price of bullion. Financial shares move with interest rates, oil stocks with the price of the commodity, and so on. If we were looking for the best oil or utility share, we would separate these charts into like groups and select the best of the lot. In this fashion, you could then search for the best or worst potential performer within a given group during a certain time period.

Thus, the researcher saves time by narrowing the field of study. Many portfolio managers typically screen databases of financial information or stock price data to find those stocks that meet certain standards. These standards are typically determined by examining the features of past winners. By the same method, the author reviews the horoscopes of past outperformers and searches for these qualities in first trade charts.

The next screen was presented at the World Conference of Astro-Economics in San Francisco in the fall of 1993 as stocks that had the potential to outperform in November, 1993. This is a list of all first trade charts that had Jupiter transit over natal Uranus or natal Jupiter in that month. Note that the group's performance exceeded that of three market indices. In particular, the *Financial Trader* picked Storage Tek (STK), which was the leader of the group.

Once again, a screen can only screen. Once it has done its job, the list of stocks must be analyzed individually. STK would have likely passed the next test; its natal Uranus is well-placed by aspect and by midpoint. There were few hard aspects that would have offset the beneficial ones. On the other end of the list, ESY has an afflicted natal Uranus. It is in hard aspect to the Sun and Mars. BLY's Uranus is in hard aspect to Mars, Saturn, and Neptune. So, when transiting Uranus lit up the natal planet in these charts, it also activated the difficult aspects, thereby restraining the share price.

Jupiter-Uranus combinations work well. Jupiter conjoining the Sun usually brings a fall in the share price into the aspect, and a rise in the period after the aspect. Mars passing through a sign can be a useful indicator. Its passage will usually (75% of the time) lift the price of any security that has its Sun in the same sign. Jupiter's orbit

FT Charts with Jupiter Transiting Natal Uranus or Jupiter in Nov. 1993

STOCK	PRICE 11/1/1993	PRICE 12/1/1993	% CHANGE
StorageTek STK	26.5	31.625	+19.3
Airborne Freight ABF	30.5	33.125	+8.6
Potlatch PCH	44.5	47.0	+5.6
Grainger GGW	55.0	56.875	+3.4
Limited LTD	21.25	21.375	+0.6
Norfolk & Southern NSC	67.0	67.25	+0.4
Rollins REN	5.5	5.5	0.0
Zenith ZE	7.625	7.375	-3.3
Bally BLY	9.875	9.375	-5.1
E Systems ESY	46.25	41.625	-10.0

Average % Change	**+2.0**
Change in S&P	-1.5
Change in DJIA	+0.1
Change in NASDAQ	-1.3

through a sign has a similar effect, but the magnitude of the price rise is greater. However, the transiting Sun will not have the same beneficial effect. Transiting Jupiter conjunct Neptune has a mildly bullish effect, but with much less consistency than Jupiter and Uranus.

The best course is to select a small group and to trace past price history versus the transits. As seen in the previous section, big price moves come from major league hits to a chart. One or two bullish contacts will have only a mild effect.

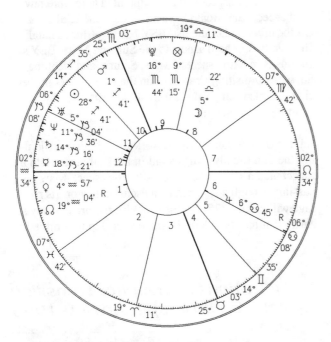

Chart 1: Stratus Computer

12/20/1989 NYC 9:30 AM EST

The *Financial Trader* program can be utilized to perform the types of screens outlined above. This procedure can be used to see which charts are being hit by a planet.

Assume that Saturn is advancing 4 degrees in 1 month.

- Select Saturn and the desired aspects.

- Then choose to scan all planets in the natal chart of each stock horoscope.

- Assume that Saturn begins the month at 4 Aquarius, so we go to *Aspects* to a *Selected Point* and type in the starting zodiacal position.

-Then choose an orb of 4 degrees, applying only. This instructs the program to start at 4 and then look ahead 4 more degrees to 8 Aquarius, the distance that Saturn will travel that month.

Easier than looking through an ephemeris and then wading through all the charts!

Completing The Analysis

Please look at this screening method as a step in a process. While the preceding analysis is impressive, most stock picking is done by a series screening processes. Incorporation horoscopes can be checked, especially if the investment is longer term. And let's not ignore technical analysis of the price graphs. Any stock that popped up on our list should be screened technically. Thus, if the stock is very oversold and giving technical buy signals from MACD, RSI, or other indicators, it would stand out as a choice over other shares on our list that are not in the same technical condition.

One last and important repetition:

If the planets in a trade chart are not compatible with your birth chart, pass the stock up and find one that is more friendly.

While doing this type of screening, one frequently finds a single stock showing up on more than one list. Let's assume a stock passed our Jupiter scan but also was selected by a scan of transiting Saturn to natal Neptune. In this case, it has both very bullish and very bearish aspects. The result will likely be an erratic trading range as one aspect offsets the other. Thus, we would pass up the issues on our bullish lists that also have bearish configurations. In other words, we are screening just as a prospector sifts for gold.

THE FUTURE OF FINANCIAL ASTROLOGY

AS LONG AS THERE ARE FREE MARKETS

In 1974, a financial astrologer could not even gain a spot as a speaker at an astrology conference. There was little interest. I felt that this type of work would become popular in 10 years. Now, 20 years later, major financial institutions purchase my software. An analyst from a European bank wanted to order a program. He made a presentation to his superior, explaining that he felt that this type of approach might be helpful. His boss approved the purchase. This was unheard of in the early 1980s.

A reader of a European astrology journal wrote to the magazine, asking what mundane astrology had accomplished. He asked where the books of the great predictions were. Because I have been working in this area, I replied that my investigations suggest that little effort had been made. It is a subject that is talked about, but little is actually done. Indeed, there was little remuneration to be gained, and all the work had been done slowly by hand.

Today's practitioner has access to PCs and software that have propelled research efforts ahead by light years. Judging by attendance at recent conferences, interest has grown. The past two decades were the covered wagon days. We are moving ahead into the jet age. The future of financial and mundane astrology appears to be bright and exciting.

A New Tool in the Works

As this book is being completed, Alphee and I have developed a new and valuable tool. This module will weight transiting hits to the first trade charts. So, for example, the passage of Jupiter over the Sun might be a +10 while Saturn's passage over the same point might be assigned a -10.

The user selects the time period and the group of stocks to be scanned, and this upcoming addition to the Financial Trader will produce a bar chart of all the stocks in the group for the time period selected. Bars extending into positive territory on the graph represent a high number of positive influences to that first trade chart for that day. Bars extending into minus territory represent charts that are receiving a large number of stressful, and potentially bearish, hits.

As long as there are free markets - that is how long this and any predictive market techniques will work. Free markets, called capitalism by detractors, are the enemy of dishonest politicians everywhere. Markets are ruled by Neptune. They are like mirrors in that they reflect the society. And what individual wants his image reflected in that mirror as he goes about his darkest deeds? For example, if consumers did not demand illicit drugs or prostitution, then there would be no suppliers. The market is only the intermediary between the buyer and the seller.

Markets react adversely to practices that are detrimental to the economy. For example, politicians like to spend money and inflate the currency to pay for the bill. They "inflate" by pushing more money into the system then the system needs or demands. In other words, the supply of money greatly exceeds the need. This caused the big speculations in the 1920s, 1970s, and the 1980s. The sudden reversal of this procedure caused the depression of the 1930s. The rise in the prices of gold and real estate in the 1970s was only a symptom of this practice, and not a cause. The underlying cause was the inflation of the currency by the Federal Reserve, a process that eventually enriches a few at the expense of the many, despite the claims of the liberal establishment. To the extent that a free market lifts the veil to reveal what is going on to those who know how to read the signs, the establishment dislikes the free market. They will make every attempt to discredit and control it. In the 1930s, gold owners were criminals. When the pound fell out of the ERM in the 1990s, the blame was placed upon "speculators who attacked the currency" and not upon those who mismanaged the currency so much that Sterling owners decided to sell their holdings.

The bottom line is that a market is made up of the collective wants and needs of the people. If restrictions are placed upon it, then restrictions are placed upon individual freedom. Economic and political freedom go hand in hand. It is truly remarkable that New Agers and activists do not grasp this simple truth. They claim to support the common man while promoting programs that require more inflation, taxes, and regulations, the very source of most economic problems. Every tariff, tax, regulation, *etc.,* moves us away from the freedom that built the country and toward socialism. It is only one small step from that point to complete totalitarianism, and this will put an end to free markets. How close are we? These quotes answer the question:

"Whoever refuses to obey the general will shall be constrained to do so by the entire body politic, which is only another way of saying that his fellows shall force him to be free." -Jean Jacques Rousseau *The Social Contract* (1762)

"While we can't use the 'S' word (socialism) *too effectively in American politics, we have found that, in the greatest tradition of American advertising, the word* "economic democracy" *sells. You can take it door to door like Fuller Brushes, and the doors will not be slammed in your face."*
-Derek Shearer, long-time friend and economic advisor to Bill Clinton. From *The New Social Contract* (1983)

Methodology

THE STOP-AND-REVERSE METHOD

This method was developed from a client reading that was done in New York in the late 1970s. The fellow was having a dreadful run of money management at a major bank. Saturn had been running over a bunch of his planets in the fifth house. He was at the end of his rope, but Saturn was nearing the end of this transit. In fact, Jupiter was entering a new sign and was about to station trine the first of his planets in the fifth. This, of course, was about to bring a very extreme shift in his trading from negative to positive. The difficulty was that he had become so risk-averse that he was unable to believe that his luck was about to change. It took a great deal of coaching plus a couple of successful trades before he began committing large amounts of capital to the market again. His confidence returned and he said, "I barely saved my job."

Astrologers are probably familiar with such situations. It happens with stocks as well as with people and can lead to dramatic profits if detected early and handled properly. These are situations where a stock nosedives and then reverses to the upside or vice-versa. Here is an example.

Cisco (CSCO) had a great 1996. See *chart 1* and *graph 1*. The primary reason that I stayed optimistic was due to Jupiter transiting over CSCO's planets in Capricorn. In situations like this, the effect of Jupiter usually causes acceleration in the appreciation of the share price. When Jupiter leaves the sign, the stock returns to a more normal rate

Feb 16, 1990 Cisco Systems — Chart 1

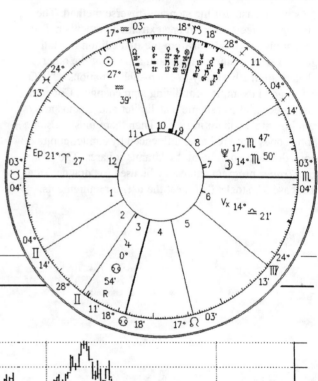

Cisco Systems — **Graph 1**

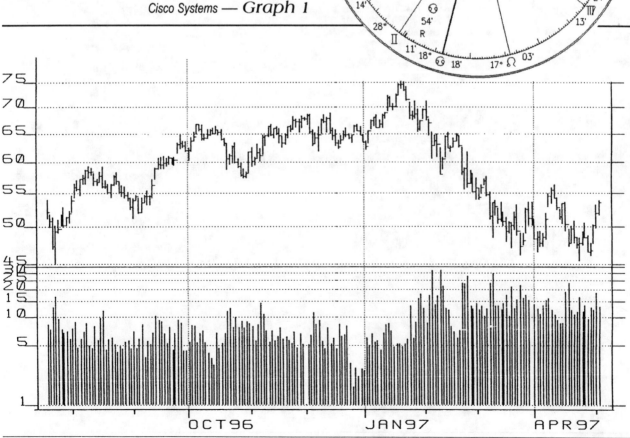

of change. When the horoscope is afflicted, as was the chart of my trader friend, returns are below the historical norm. In 1996, Saturn entered Aries, which is a cardinal sign that squares Capricorn. So, any planet in early Cap that had enjoyed a conjunction from transiting Jupiter was now catching a square from Saturn. This is what hit CSCO in 1997 as Jupiter's expansive influence waned and Saturn's squares began to hit. CSCO fell almost 50 percent in the first quarter after enjoying a great upmove in 1996.

This is the basis for the stop-and-reverse method. The planetary effects go from one extreme to the other. The case study on Goodyear from the first edition is another good example. Sign changes and aspects of the outer planets are the best way to catch such situations. CSCO was a good example of utilizing sign changes. Concerning aspects, let us assume that Jupiter and Uranus are coming into a square in space. Then there must be some horoscopes that are being influenced by Jupiter conjunctions that will soon be hit by Uranus squares. The *Financial Trader* program can easily be used to "dragnet" the database for stocks that meet the user's requirements.

Super Search is Super for First Trade Horoscopes

Super Search is one of the greatest features of the *Financial Trader*. Most programs have a one-level search. That is, it can find all Mercury retrograde dates. Super Search can perform multi-level searches. It can find all Mercury retrogrades when the Sun is in Cancer or Mars is in Gemini. The same module can be used to do multi-level searches of batches of horoscopes in a file. Let us assume that Jupiter will be in Aries and that Mars will be in Taurus. We want to locate all first-trade charts that have the Sun in Aries and the Moon in Taurus. This can be done by performing a two-level search of the first-trade database. Many levels can be searched, and the program does accept "and-or" commands, such as find charts with Moon square Jupiter *and-or* Venus square Uranus. This is a great time-saver. In addition, one can run transit searches of selected planets to thousands of charts. The aspect hits are generated chronologically.

THE EARNINGS ANNOUNCEMENT METHOD

Companies report earnings four times per year. Most are on a calendar year basis. That is, the financial reporting period coincides with the calendar year, beginning on January 1 and ending on December 31. The first quarter ends on March 31, and earnings are usually released in the second or third week in April. The same timing applies to the quarters ending on June 30, September 30, and December 31. The type of fiscal year and reporting dates can be obtained from the company's investor relations department, your broker, or a *ValueLine* information sheet. Academic studies have demonstrated that share prices become more volatile around earnings reporting time.

This is understandable since the reported figures could be a positive or a negative surprise. Services such as IBES collect

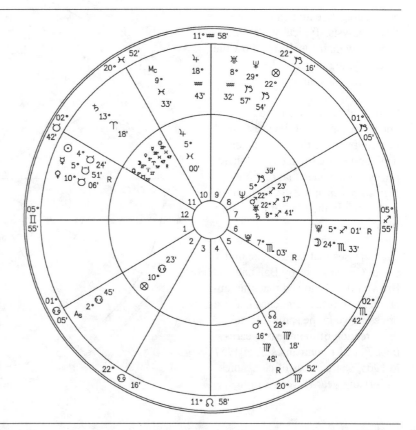

inside: MSFT Mar. 13, 1986
outside: Earnings surprise, Apr. 24, 1997

Microsofts earnings were way over estimates and the stock leaped in 97 — **Chart 2**

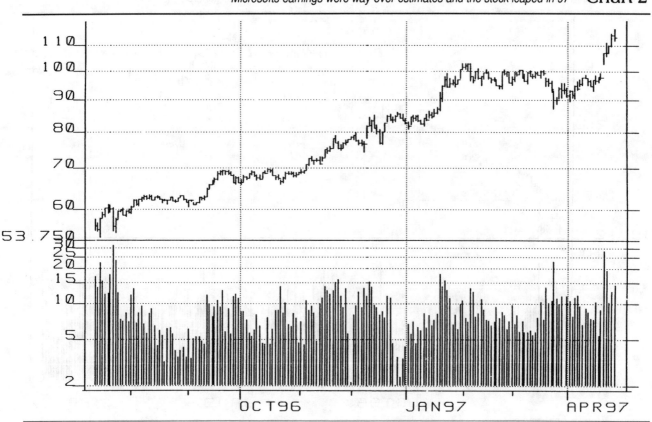

and aggregate earnings estimates from analysts. Typically, a report will show how many analysts follow the company, the range of their estimates, the median and the mean.

Studies have demonstrated that reported earnings that deviate from the median by more than one standard deviation cause big moves in share prices. Companies that report earnings surprises are listed in *Barrons* each week in the Market Laboratory section.

There is one more notion about earnings releases that needs to be understood. One analysis by Ball and Brown (1968) showed that after annual earnings are announced, share prices move in the same direction as the direction of the released earnings. For 261 companies from 1957 to 1965, share prices of companies with rising year-to-year earnings

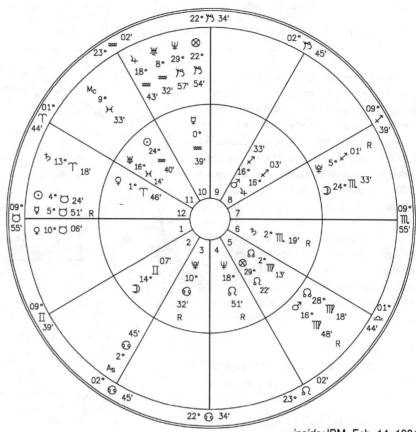

inside: IBM Feb. 14, 1924
outside: Earnings surprise, Apr. 24, 1997

Chart 3 — *IBM earnings report triggers Mars-Jupiter-Uranus T-square, sending stock sharply higher in 1997*

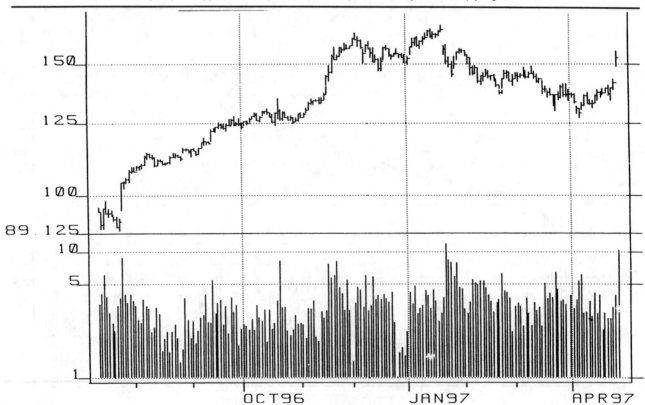

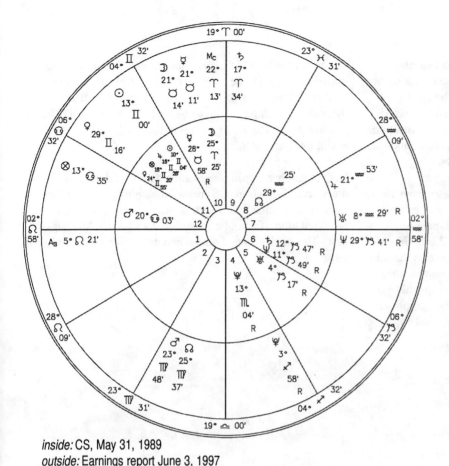

inside: CS, May 31, 1989
outside: Earnings report June 3, 1997

increased by 7.3 percent in the year before, but rose by 2.4 percent annually in the next quarter. Note that the bulk of the rise occurs *before* the earnings release.

Knowing that stocks make bigger moves around the time of their earnings announcements, I always pay greater attention to the first-trade chart at that time. Generally, an exceptionally well-aspected horoscope leads to a move up in response to the announcement. A poorly-aspected chart leads to a downmove. Remember that the report may not be that bad, but it is interpreted by traders as being negative. Sometimes, a company beats its estimate, but the stock falls. In such cases, the traders and investors were expecting the company to exceed the estimates by an even greater margin. The opposite case, in which earnings are down but not down by as much as Wall Street expects, can send the stock up.

Cabletron stock plunged at earnings announcement when Saturn approached natal MC — **Chart 4**

It is important to remember that the reported earnings must be measured against expectations. The condition of the first-trade chart at the time will show the reaction in the marketplace. A horoscope that is neutrally aspected describes a situation in which there will be little reaction. That is, the announcement was already expected, and the share price has already adjusted to the news.

In the examples below, we will see some cases from 1997. In the first, Microsoft's earnings were way over estimates and the stock leaped. Note that transiting Jupiter and Uranus were straddling the midheaven (*Chart 2* and *Graph 2*). In fact, the transiting midpoint was almost on the midheaven. If this were the chart of a person who was about to make an announcement, what kind of news would you anticipate? Because this is a mundane entity, I emphasize the MC, Sun, and Moon more than the other bodies.

The next case is IBM (*Chart 3* and *Graph 3*). Big Blue reported earnings in late April. Note that the Mars station on April 27 at 16 Virgo 44. The station touched off IBM's dynamic Mars-Jupiter-Uranus t-square at 16 mutable. The positive report led to the gap up in the stock. It happened again, one year later.

Here is another earnings announcement that did not go down well. Cabletron (CS) released earnings at about the same time. Notice that Saturn is near the natal midheaven. What kind of a public reception does Saturn-MC suggest? The stock plunged on the bad news. See *Chart* and *Graph 4*.

INDUSTRY PLANETS

The next horoscope (*Chart 5*) and price graph (*Graph 5*) are that of Micron (MU), a semiconductor company. The Jupiter station of September 4, 1996 fell on Uranus in the first trade chart. The stock had bottomed with the rest of the market in mid-July. It had made one low then and made a second low on the day of the station. Note how the volume jumped and continued to rise.

There are other stocks that caught similar aspects from Jupiter, but these shares did not rise so much. The reason is Uranus rules or is related to the technology industry. A food stock or a cosmetic stock will not respond with the same strength because they are ruled by different industry planets. So, whenever looking at a first-trade or incorporation chart, give an extra measure of strength to the planet that rules the industry.

Knowing which planet rules which industry can sometimes be simple and other times can be very difficult. Because Venus is associated with beauty, this planet rules the cosmetics group. Mercury rules transportation and communication.

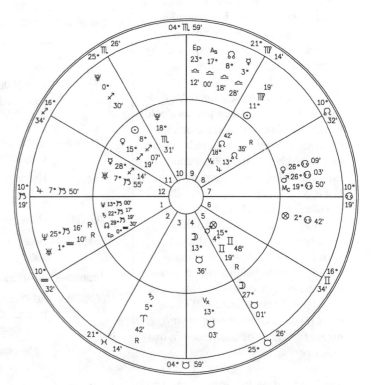

inside: Micron, Nov. 30, 1990
outside: Jupiter Sta., Sept. 3, 1996

Jupiter stationed on Micron's Uranus in Sept. 1996 — **Chart #5**

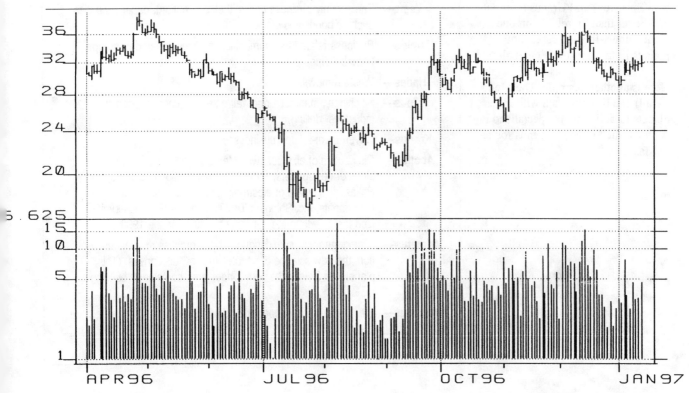

New industries are a bit more difficult because we have had much less experience with them. Biotechnology is ruled by Pluto, and perhaps a bit by Neptune in some cases.

For example, a biotech company that focuses exclusively on allergies would be ruled by both Pluto and Neptune. One that worked on the immune system would be ruled by Pluto and the asteroid Pallas. This brings us to the last level of complexity, asteroids and Uranian planets. These bodies have proved valid in my work, so they must be utilized. Before I studied with Eleanor Bach who first introduced the asteroids to astrology, I associated many Ceres-ruled matters to the Moon. I was to learn that Ceres rules food, so Ceres is an industry planet for stocks of companies in that industry.

The key to using this method can lie in combining the meanings of planets to arrive at an exact description of the business. Electronic Arts makes computer games. This can be described by Venus (fun) and Uranus (computers) better than by relying on one planet alone. In such cases, both planets in the first-trade chart should be given an extra measure of weight. Here is another example. The Moon (retail) can be combined with other planets to derive more specialized industries, such as Moon-Venus for retail fashion.

Here is a list of bodies and their industries. In selecting industries, I tried to stick close to the 90 Standard and Poors industry groups, but I included other basic types of businesses. It is not meant to be complete. Feel free to expand it.

Moon—	Retail. (Generally, a strong Moon is required for any walk-in type of business that relies upon walk-in business and public recognition.)
Sun—	Gold.
Mercury—	Communication, short-distance travel, telecommunication, telephone, footwear, trucking.
Venus—	Recreation, cosmetics, fashion, leisure, beverages (soft drink).
Mars—	Construction, sports, defense.
Jupiter—	Publishing, travel, gambling, consumer goods sector.
Saturn—	Real estate, regulated industries such as utilities, capital goods sector.
Uranus—	Most technology such as computers, aviation.
Neptune—	Advertising, chemicals, some entertainment businesses, marine activities such as off-shore drilling, natural gas, oil, photography, tobacco, alcoholic beverages.
Pluto—	Biotechnology, financial businesses such as mergers, insurance, and brokerage.
Ceres—	Food, nursing homes.
Pallas—	Computer programming, the immune system, precision instruments.
Juno—	Hospitality, hotels.
Vesta—	The security business (locks, theft prevention), paper securities such as bonds and stocks.
Cupido—	Business related to communities, business related to groups, homebuilding.
Hades—	Waste removal.
Zeus—	Machinery, manufacturing, railroads, automobiles, heavy industries, drilling.
Kronos—	Government-related businesses.
Apollon—	Distribution of all types: with Mercury- distribution of magazines or newspapers, with Venus- distribution of clothes, with Pallas, distribution of electronic gadgets and precision instruments, etc. Shipping. (Apollon square Vulcanus symbolized the growth in the networking industry in the 1990s)
Admetus—	Mining, geology, semiconductors, the process of miniaturization, the new science of nanotechnology, disk drives. (This planet with Zeus rules semiconductors), containers, building materials.
Vulcanus—	Steel, aluminum, copper and other metals.
Poseidon—	Education.

Planetary Portfolios

One screening method that I have successfully utilized involves Jupiter. This planet is traditionally associated with expansion and optimism. Its passage over natal planets in the first trade chart usually lifts the price of the stock. Jupiter transits through one sign of the zodiac in about one year. *The Financial Trader* program can be set to find all the horoscopes that have four or more points in a given sign.

This means that the chart had to have a total of four or more of the following in Scorpio: planets, angles (the midheaven and ascendant), plus the Moon's Node. For example, a 1994 scan of the 600 NASDAQ horoscopes in the database yielded 29 stocks that began trading with four or more points in Scorpio.

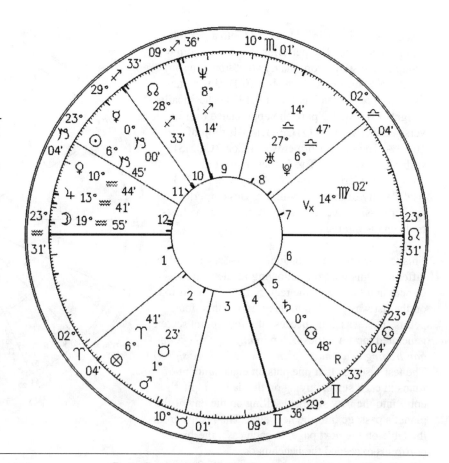

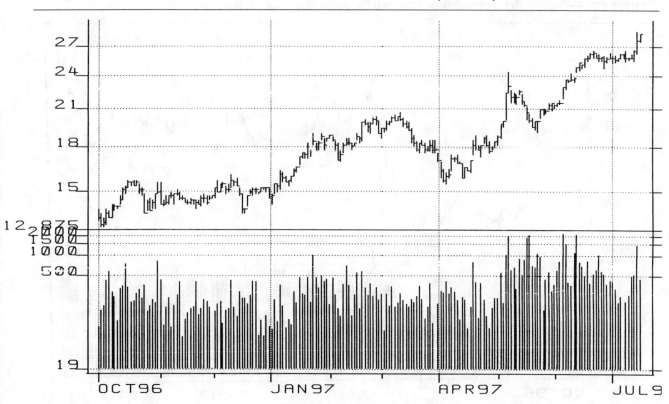

Data General, Jupiter in Aquarius choice — **Chart #6**

Once this list is generated, it is fed into a portfolio reporting system. The performance of the Scorpio group is measured from the day that transiting Jupiter enters Scorpio on November 10,1993 until the day that it leaves on December 9,1994. The equally-weighted NASDAQ portfolio appreciated by 12.63% versus the NASDAQ OTC Industrials drop of 10.59%. The top performer was 3 Com (COMS) with a 148.3% gain. The Jupiter dragnet also scooped up Gartner Group (GART) with a 132.3% rise. Twenty of the twenty-nine issues outperformed. Jupiter passing over the Scorpio points in the first-trade charts did the job.

This test was repeated for Jupiter's passage through different signs with the following results. (In the Cancer and Leo tests, the requirement for inclusion on the list was lowered to three, rather than four, points. This was done because the four-point screen generated too few stocks. *Apparently, few stocks began trading when many planets were in these signs.*) The test assumes that one puts an equal amount of funds in each stock, buying on the day of Jupiter's entry into the new sign and selling on the day of the planet's passage into the next sign. The results are in the table on the next page. In each case, the Jupiter portfolios exceeded the benchmark.

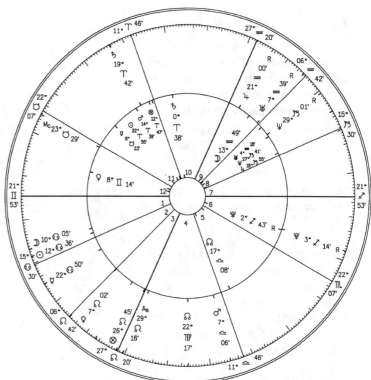

inside: Yahoo, Apr. 12, 1996
outside: Breakout, July 14, 1997

Chart #7 — *Yahoo, Aquarian planets activated by Jupiter and Uranus transits*

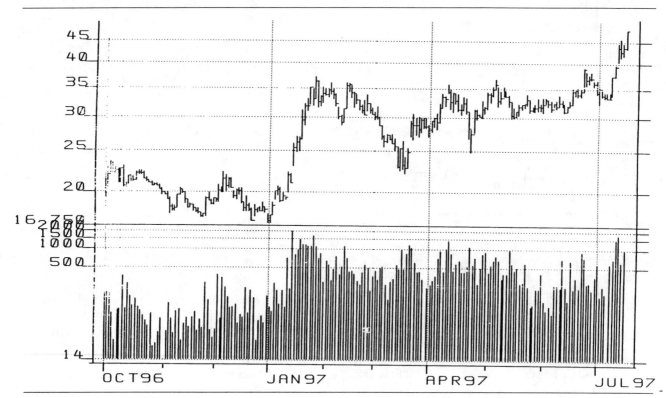

In analyzing the results, one must realize that the effect of the planets are not mutually exclusive. That is, simply because Jupiter is beneficially contacting the planets in a given chart, this does not immunize the rest of the chart from the negative influences of bearish planets. And, the charts may receive other bullish effects from planets besides Jupiter. In the first case, the Jupiter effect is mitigated or negated due to the bearish influences. In the second case, the bullish influence is magnified.

The Scorpio and Sagittarius portfolios are good examples. The above-average results from the Scorpio group were partly attributable to the favorable aspects from Uranus and Neptune in Capricorn, 60 degrees away. With the Sag stocks, Saturn in Pisces squared planets in Sagittarius, offsetting the positive effects of Jupiter and pushing the portfolio's performance closer to the benchmark. The

same can be said for the Cap portfolio. As Saturn crept up into Aries, it began to square Capricorn, thereby offsetting the beneficial effect of Jupiter's transit through that sign. In these latter cases, it requires a bit of fancier footwork and stock-switching to avoid the Saturn square.

The important point is that the groups should outperform their respective indices by the time Jupiter exits the sign of transit. *Charts 6* and *7* show a pair of successes thus far in 1997 from the Aquarius screening process. These were Data General (DGN) and Yahoo (YHOO). Note the grouping of planets in Aquarius in both horoscopes. Jupiter, and eventually Uranus, will conjoin these natal planets. The point is that these transits usually continue to provide the energy for continued outperformance versus the S&P through the rest of Jupiter's stay in a sign.

It is also important to remember that these are raw screens. That is, one then has to separate the wheat from the chaff. We must eliminate those charts that are very afflicted by other factors. If this test is passed, then look at the "internal" astrology. These are the progressions and the directions that are specific to the individual horoscope itself. Then, I look at the industry that the company is in. Being in a group that is out of favor is like running a race with one leg tied to a rock. Better to own a strong stock in a strong group then a strong stock in a weak group. Finally I go to the technical outlook: is the stock giving technical buy signals? And last, I analyze the fundamentals and the corporate chart. Avoid those charts that make difficult aspects to your own. Experience has proven that one will have a difficult time with such stocks.

JUPITER NASDAQ PORTFOLIOS

PORTFOLIO	Buy Date	Sell Date	% Change–Portfolio	% Change–NASDAQ
Cancer 3	7/28/89	8/17/90	-.36	-4.42
Leo 3	8/17/90	9/12/91	+59.78	+39.08
Virgo 4	9/12/91	10/9/92	+30.85	+3.53
Libra 4	10/9/92	11/10/93	+97.69	+33.01
Scorpio 4	11/10/93	12/9/94	+12.63	-10.59
Sag 4	12/30/94	12/28/95	+35.22	+26.58
Cap 4	12/29/95	1/22/97	+ 7.68	+ 6.33
Aqua 4	1/22/97	2/4/98	+14.41	+7.47

INDUSTRY FORECASTS

The question of how to astrologically analyze industry groups has often arisen. I have used two methods. The first simply identifies parts of the zodiac that are astrologically sensitive for a given group of stocks or companies. The second relies upon locating a base chart for the industry.

Shared Degree Areas

The first method can be demonstrated by the growth of the biotechnology industry. Genentech was one of the first companies, but the industry really began to grow with the Jupiter-Uranus conjunction of 1983. Many companies were founded, and their stocks were floated at that time. They all have a Jupiter-Uranus conjunction in their incorporation and first-trade horoscopes. Many of these companies are gone today, acquired by big pharmaceutical concerns. We can use one of the biggest, Amgen, as a base (*Chart 8*).

When a planet passes through the first decanate of Sagittarius, it conjoins this 1983 Jupiter-Uranus conjunction. In 1985-1986, when Saturn passed over, the entire biotech group underperformed the

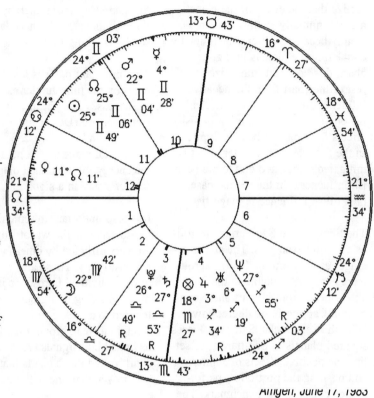

Amgen, June 17, 1983

Chart #8 — *Amgen and the bio industry*

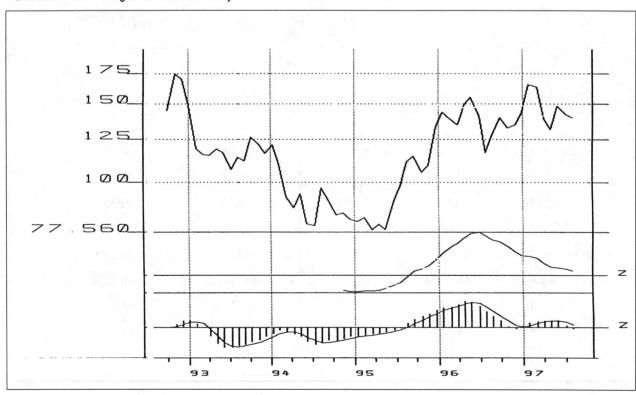

Chart #9 — *Arpanet First Call -the internet industry*

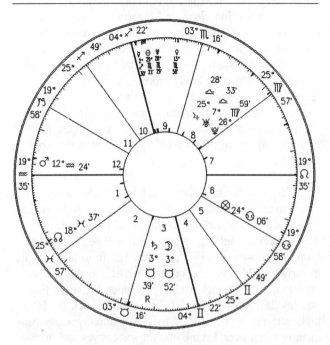

Nov. 21, 1969, 00 PM, PST Los Angeles CA

market. In December of 1994, when Jupiter was preparing to enter these degrees, I analyzed *Graph 8* of the biotech group. Note that the group was oversold and beginning to give buy signals. I was able to anticipate this low many months in advance with the knowledge of this degree area.

Let us digress for a moment. The art of this type of work lies in this example. The technical graph is bullish. The first-trade horoscope is about to be ignited. A check with a fundamental analyst who is trained in this field was positive. All three disciplines were giving buy signals. I can produce other technical graphs that looked like the biotech group at that time, but this was one of the few that fulfilled its technical promise by taking off. *Whether this was a group or an individual stock, the difference between this and the others that did not move higher was the bullish first-trade chart. This provides one with an advantage over those who only employ technical methods.*

Obviously, we are relying on two traditional astrological methods: shared degree area and orb. When I was a basic student, John Townley said that shared degree area was the most important consideration in synastry. And, the

Let us look at the technology group as a second example.

IBM, Microsoft, Compaq, and Oracle are leaders in their fields. The first-trade charts all have some very close and dynamic aspects as laid out in this table.

IBM:	Mars= 16 Sag 33	Jupiter= 16 Sag 03	Uranus= 16 Pisces 14
	Moon= 14 Gemini 07		
Microsoft:	Sun= 22 Pisces 43	Mars= 22 Sag 23	Uranus= 22 Sag 17
Compaq:	Sun= 18 Sag 29	Uranus= 18 Sag 13	
Oracle:	Sun= 21 Pisces 43	Mars= 21 Sag 50	Uranus= 22 Sag 16

These stocks and the over-all market topped with the solar eclipse of March 9,1997 at 18 Pisces 31. The Mars station of April 27,1997 at 16 Virgo 44 occurred as these stocks hit lows and suddenly jumped into new uptrends. The Jupiter passage in April 1998 sent the stocks up. Watch the Jupiter and Mercury stations at 17 Pisces in November 1998. It is easy to see how activity at 16 to 22 mutable would effect all of the horoscopes. By working with horoscopes from the same industry, one will see how the stocks are tied together in this fashion. The Venus-Jupiter conjunction in these degrees in Pisces in April of 1998 sent all of these stocks higher.

closer the orb, the greater the energy. In the technology example, we saw both principles at work. The best procedure is to take the leading stocks in an industry and put them around the same wheel. Then look for the shared degree areas. Here is another example: an analysis of the 30 DJIA stocks reveals that six of the stocks have the Sun between 9 mutable 58 and 12 mutable 10. Planetary activity at this degree hits all of the Suns in these charts in the fourth harmonic.

Industry Foundation Horoscopes

If one can isolate the birth moment of an industry, the resultant chart will prove useful. For example, one might use the date of the first nuclear reaction as the birth of the nuclear industry. There are horoscopes for the Wright Brothers first flight at Kittyhawk and for the first successful oil-well gusher at Spindletop. Here is a more recent example – the internet. This article first appeared in the *ISAR Journal.*

The first plans for the internet were laid in 1969. Four sites were to be linked to the computer at UCLA, making a system that was then called the Arpanet. In a recent magazine interview, one witness recalled that they were in the computer center at UCLA at around mid-day as the first message was transmitted on November 21,1969.

The Sun-Neptune-Mercury conjunction in the ninth suggests an ethereal expansion of the higher mind. The Sun-Pluto sextile symbolizes the emergence of electronic commerce via the net. This probably also represents talk at the UN of a "world tax," beginning with a levy on electronic transactions. The Scorpio location of Sun, Venus, and Neptune plus the close Venus-Mars square, the Venus-Pluto semisquare, and Venus/Uranus=Jupiter immediately brought to mind the pornography controversy.

It is interesting to note that the internet began in 1969, the same year that men walked on the Moon. We heard about that event immediately, but not this one. As Pluto moved over the Sun-Neptune-Mercury conjunction, interest in the net exploded. Also note that transiting Uranus has been trine the late-Virgo Pluto. This creates a planetary picture of transiting Uranus/natal Pluto= natal Sun – Neptune. This picture likely represents the growth in interest in internet commerce and the accompanying issues such as security against fraud. It may also herald government regulation, the bane of most free enterprises. As the midpoint advanced in 1995-1996, we heard more about these issues.

Experience demonstrates that such horoscopes serve as a "base chart" in mundane work. Subsequent developments will lead to "modifier" charts, observed Charles Jayne. This creates shared degree areas that will be sensitive to transits, eclipses, etc. This area may run from late Scorpio to early mutable degrees for the internet. One new issue on the NASDAQ stock exchange, Uunet, began trading on May 25,1995 with the Sun at 3 Gemini, near the IC of this chart and opposite Mercury. The company was subsequently taken over. I think that the executives and original backers would score this as a success. Favorable synastry between the Uunet chart and the internet chart was an indication. The addition of horoscopes of companies and natal charts for pioneering internet individuals will denote sensitive zodiacal degrees for this new and exciting industry.

MARKET ANALYSIS
for ASTROLOGERS

Profitable use of the charts in this book requires the employment of market, or technical, analysis. Many readers of the first edition requested more explanation. I can only give the basics that I employ here. As mentioned in the first edition, the books by John Murphy and Martin Pring are good basic works, while the two books by Mike Jenkins contain good advanced material.

Here is a good analogy to begin with. If you have ever interpreted a natal chart for a person, then you must have taken into account the age and circumstances of the individual. For example, a Saturn-to-Sun transit would probably be interpreted quite differently depending upon the person's age. The manifestations would vary from a 5-year old to a 25-year old, to a 75-year old. The child is unlikely to have a problem with the boss at the office. In the two extreme cases, health may be the big issue. With the 25-year old, career considerations would likely be paramount.

In a similar fashion, one must judge the condition of a stock in the market. It has been said that it is "a market of stocks and not a stock market." So, if the market has been falling while a given stock has been moving sideways,

then the stock has actually been strong, relative to the market (relative strength was introduced in the first edition). There are numerous ways to look at a stock, so I shall limit the discussion to a few. Not all techniques work all of the time. It depends what type of market we are in. As one of my superiors once said, "Tell me what is going to happen in five years, and I'll give you the right investment strategy." The trick is in having at least some inkling as to what will happen. I do this by combining the technical price action and the fundamental story.

Typically, the relationship between the fundamental goings-on within the company and the share price works like this. The company is rolling along, increasing earnings by 10 percent per year. Assume that the average company is earning 15 percent. Logically, the stock should not do as well as the stocks of companies that are earning a better return. Then the management embarks on a new strategy (usually at a time when the horoscope of incorporation is well-aspected). The strategy pays off and earnings rise.

The stock begins to rise (usually at a time when the horoscope of first trade becomes better-aspected). The stock

Rate of Change (ROC) indicator and price, Compaq — **Graph #1**

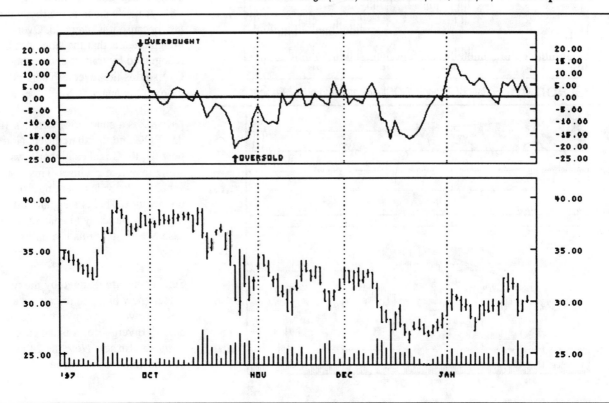

frequently turns up before the improving results are evident. I do not know whether this is due to people who have knowledge of the internal workings of the company or whether investors are psychic. Anyway, the investor who looks at the price graph must ask himself if the hints at a forthcoming rally are actually reflective of a turnaround in the company or not. A short-term trader does not care; he will sell quickly when he realizes a profit. How does one recognize the trends?

Three Basic Tools

The three main barometers that I employ are momentum, relative strength, and pattern recognition. Sentiment is also important, but that will be bit difficult for you to measure. I am in touch with brokers and analysts all day long. I see their latest opinions. At extremes, sentiment is usually wrong. That is, in-

vestors are too bearish at bottoms and too bullish at tops. My favorite situation is when a stock is starting to give buy signals after a period of decline, but the experts are still bearish. At tops, you will probably have to go to Yellowstone National Park to find a bear. Anyway, perhaps you can glean the prevailing opinion on a stock from the media, the internet, *etc.* Let's move on to the indicators that can be quantified more readily.

Momentum

This refers to the rate of change of a share price. The simplest such measure is a rate-of-change oscillator (ROC). Look at *Graph 1.* The indicator is simply the price on the previous day less the price 10 days earlier. The zero line is the point of equilibrium.

At zero, the price on a given day is unchanged from the price 10 days earlier. If the price is below the zero line, it is said to be *oversold.* If it is above the zero line, it is termed *overbought.* One does not automatically sell because a stock is overbought or buy because it is oversold. Overbought means that the stock has been recognized by traders and pushed up. Oversold is the reverse. There is more to the analysis.

Graph 2 is a chart of Motorola's 10-day ROC and the share price. Note how the ROC makes higher lows while the price declines. This is a divergence. Price is diverging from momentum. This is a signal that the trend may be ready to change. In this case, we say that this is a bullish divergence.

Sell signals are denoted by the reverse – new highs in price plus a series of lower highs in momentum, a bearish divergence as is the case in *Graph 3,* Texaco. Note the 24 percent decline that followed.

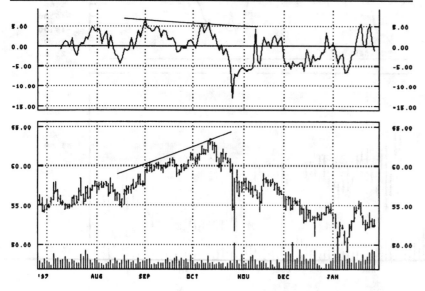

Graph #2 — *Rate of Change (ROC) indicator and price, Motorola*

Graph #3 — *Rate of Change (ROC) indicator and price, Texaco*

The ROC is the simplest type of indicator; there are many. Most are some combination of moving averages. I always use ROC because I have found that it is one of the most sensitive. Departure analysis is also valuable.

Departure analysis creates a histogram out of moving averages. Testing has demonstrated that there is a combination that works best with stocks: a five-period *moving average* (MA) minus a five-period MA, expressed as a three-period MA. In other words, take the MA of the price over five days and deduct the MA over 15 days. Then take this difference and plot it as a three-day MA.

Graph 4 depicts this indicator on a monthly (using monthly MAs instead of daily) graph for Xilinx. Note how the price made a higher high (top strip) while departure histogram made a lower high (middle strip). *Graph 5* shows the 50 percent decline that followed.

This is another *divergence*. One average (or indicator) diverges from the other. In this case, the divergence is a bearish one. This represents a situation in which selling is increasing, even as the average hits a new high.

This particular divergence is between price and momentum. Prices are continuing to rise, but the rate of ascent is lessening. As we will see, divergence can occur between price and a number of different indicators.

Graph 6 depicts a bullish divergence. In this case, the stock is falling, making a series of lower lows on a daily basis. But momentum is making a series of higher highs. This means that buyers are coming in as the price falls. In most cases, the buyers will soon overcome the sellers, and then prices will begin a period of ascent.

Departure Analysis, Xilinx — Graph #4

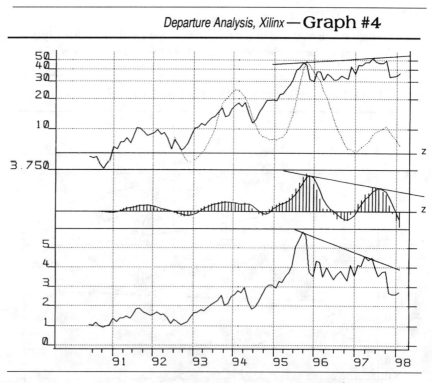

Daily Bar Chart, Xilinx — Graph #5

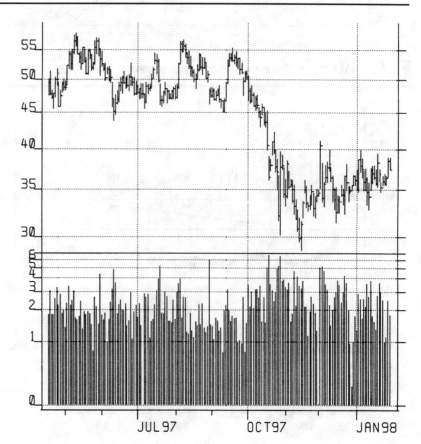

Relative Strength

This concept was introduced in the first edition, but requires further explanation. As we know, the *relative strength* is simply the share price divided by

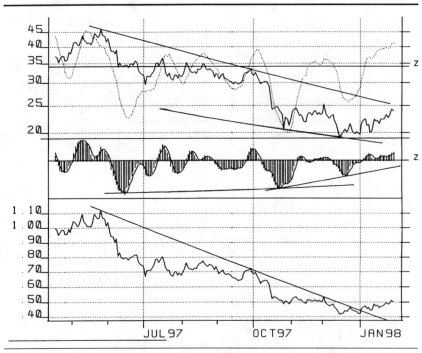

Graph #6 —*Departure analysis, LSI Logic Corp.*

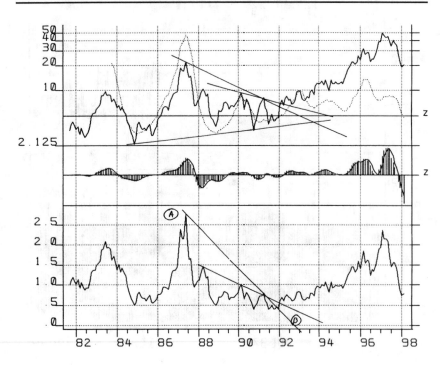

Graph #7 —*Price, momentum & relative strength, Seagate*

some index, such as the S&P 500. If IBM's relative strength line is moving sideways, then the stock is moving with the same trend as the market. If IBM's line is rising, then it is exceeding or outperforming the index against which it is being measured. If falling, then IBM is not going up with the market. This is what I call "profitless prosperity." In 1997, many stocks rose in absolute terms, but were not keeping pace with the market. In fact, only 10 percent of all mutual funds in the USA outperformed the market in 1997. Half of the Standard & Poors 500 gain was attributable to only 25 stocks! Unless you had these stocks in your portfolio, you probably underperformed. Late in a bull market, it is typical for fewer and fewer stocks to lead the market. Breadth (the number of advancing stocks less the number of declining stocks) narrows. This is a sign of the late stages of an advance. So, in the latter part of a bull market, the relative strength of any stock should assume increasing importance in the stock selection process.

Here's how important it can be. I have run studies of portfolios in the following way. Take any portfolio of stocks and eliminate all issues that have had weak relative strength over the previous six or 12 months (the test results are the same no matter which time period is used). I have found that this process cuts about 55 to 60 percent of the stocks out of the portfolio. In the next 12 months, results are usually improved by 5 to 8 percent. It is amazing that most fund managers do not utilize this simple tool.

Relative strength frequently signals trend changes before the absolute price moves. In *Graph 7,* look at the bottom strip. This is the relative strength of Seagate versus the S&P.

Note that the relative strength trend at line A-B was reversed to the upside in late 1991, prior to the reversal by the absolute price trend in the top strip of the graph. Look back at the daily graph of LSI, # 6. You see the same phenomenon at work. Look for relative changes in trend as early warning signals to reversals in absolute price trend.

Relative strength has another use. It, like momentum, can be used to confirm new highs or new lows in a price trend. Go back to *Graph 4* of Xilinx. Note how the relative strength in the bottom strip failed to make a new high with price. Thus, relative price was in line with momentum above in giving a sell signal.

Pattern Recognition

This is probably the best-known technical methodology. Price movements trace out patterns. These formations represent market psychology. Technical work attempts to assess what the impact of fundamental news is upon any price series.

The bible of technical work is *Technical Analysis of Stock Trends* by Edwards and Magee. This is pretty heavy reading. I cannot cover the subject in depth here, but can give you a good idea of the basics.

Trendlines are constructed by drawing a line across a series of lows or highs. These lines represent a psychological barrier, the breaking of which signals a change in trend or psychology. There are two important rules to remember. First, the longer that a trendline has been in force, the stronger it is. Second, the more horizontal the trendline is, the stronger it is. The breaking of trendlines of this type are more significant than the breaking of shorter or more steep trendlines. Exhibit A is *Graph 8*.

This is the graph of the price of the S&P Food industry. This is a group chart; that is, it represents the combined prices of many stocks of food companies. Note how it stayed in a big rectangle for 25 years. I was a food analyst in the late 1970s when no one was interested in these stocks. Who would want to buy into a group that had essentially gone sideways for 25 years? The breakout to the upside was followed by 13 years of relative outperformance versus the S&P. A very old and very horizontal trendline had been broken and you can see how far the stocks rallied, from an index of 80 to over 1000.

This means that the average food stock increased by 13 times in value over 15 years. Stocks of good companies rose by more. *A breakout on a longer-term graph is extremely significant and is worth 100 breakouts on a daily graph and 50 breakouts on a weekly graph. These do not happen that often.* Remember that once you have determined if a given market or a group is in a bull market, the odds of picking a stock that will rise are 4-to-1 in your favor. In a bear market, the odds are against you by 20-to-1.

Let's turn to sentiment for a moment. During that 13-year rally, most investors refused to believe what the market was telling them. Whenever I recommended these stocks, I was told that they were dull companies or that they had al-

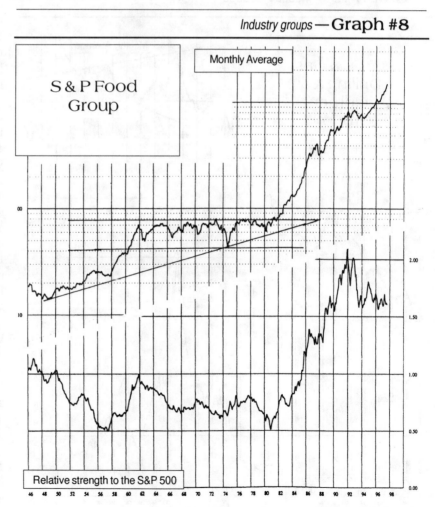

Industry groups — **Graph #8**

page 87

ready risen too much. Yes, they were dull companies, but they were exciting stocks. Bull markets, whether they be in the overall market or in industry groups, usually climb a "wall of worry." That is, investors refuse to believe the rally that they are witnessing. They expect it to end any day. They continually spout a series of bearish fundamental stories. What they miss is the fact that the market has probably already discounted the bad news, and is rallying on good news to come. They put the cart before the horse, failing to see that their fundamental facts are considered to be old news by the market itself.

There is another lesson to be learned here. Look at the relative strength line below the price line. Note that it stopped going up in late 1991. Since that time, the absolute price has resumed its advance, but it is not advancing as much as the S&P. This is profitless prosperity. It is like swimming upstream or trying to walk up the down escalator.

There is more to be gleaned from this graph. First, the sideways movement of the average over those many years is a consolidation or a base. Think of these areas as energy accumulators. Potential is being built up, waiting to be re-

leased. *The bigger the base, the bigger the move after the breakout.* I always keep my eyes on these big consolidations. When I first learned this concept, I looked around for the biggest, flattest base that could be found. It was gold in 1967. If I mentioned gold as an investment, I would be told that the price was regulated, it was not a good idea, etc. As we know, the price was deregulated and gold soared. The breakout from the base was right and the opinions were wrong.

Take another look at the graph. Note that there is a rising trendline drawn below the pair of horizontal and parallel lines. The top parallel line and the rising trendline trace out an ascending triangle. This type of formation is usually followed by a resumption of the previous uptrend. This type of pattern has been very common in this bull market. We see another type of triangle pattern, the symmetrical triangle in *Graph 9* of the S&P Oil and Gas Drilling and Equipment industry. Note the descending and the ascending lines that trace out a 20-year formation. This breakout is still in force and will likely last for years to come, probably into the latter part of the next decade. These types of triangles are less reliable than the ascending ones. The trend that was in force usually resumes after the completion of the triangle. Also note the long relative strength downtrend that has been reversed to the upside.

Let's take a look at one more long-term graph. #10 is that of the S&P Paper and Forest Product group. Look at the relative strength; it has been falling since 1957! As one wise man once said, only a fool or the federal government would buy this.

The wedge patterns have also been very common in the 1990s. *Graph 11* is that of Telecommunications A

Graph #9 —*Industry Groups*

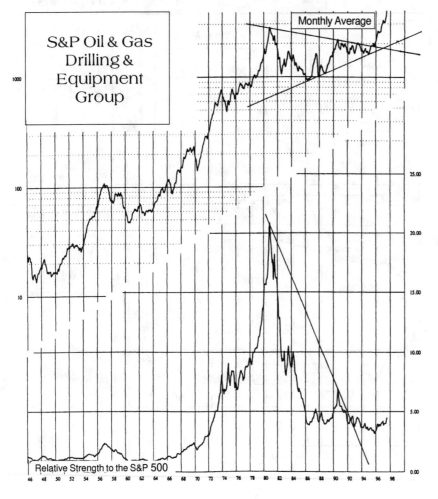

S&P Oil & Gas Drilling & Equipment Group

Monthly Average

Relative Strength to the S&P 500

(TCOMA). Note the pair of converging lines that form the falling wedge. This is a sign of an impending reversal. Selling is drying up as the stock falls. This will be confirmed by a rate-of-change oscillator that will show a series of higher lows. TCOMA went on to $41. A rising wedge is the reverse: two converging lines rising, a sign of selling.

Also note the gap in the share price. Gaps are caused by imbalances in demand. That is, the demand for shares is so great that the price has to be raised substantially. This leaves a gap between the high price of the previous day and the opening price of the next day. Old technical lore from the 1960s and earlier stated that "gaps are always filled." This means that the price comes back and closes the gap. This has not been true in the 1990s. A stock that gaps up usually keeps right on moving up. I have bought many stocks that have gapped up, and a very high percentage have gone on to outperform.

Graph 12 is a fine example. Comcast gapped up from 18 to 21. Many would look at this chart and feel that they had missed the move. As you can see, the stock rose another 50%. There are generally three types of gaps — breakaway, continuation, or exhaustion. The first is the type depicted in the graph. These occur at the beginning of an upmove or a downmove. Continuation gaps occur at the midway point in a move. These are generally useful in determining how much further the stock may go. Exhaustion gaps occur at the end of a move. In the summer of 1995, Microsoft gapped up to 50. That gap marked the top day, and a 20 percent drop followed. Do not mistake the exhaustion gap for the breakaway gap.

The number of waves up or down is another important indicator of highs

or lows. Going back to the TCOMA graph, note that the stock came down in three waves. Wave one was down; wave two was up; and wave three was down. This roughly corresponds with the Elliott Wave. The last wave is usually quite steep, accompanied by high volume. Gaps down are common at this point. The news is usually at its most pessimistic. A stock will usually move up in five waves, the odd-numbered ones being up and the even-numbered ones being the downwaves or the retracements.

Go back and look at *Graph 4*. XLNX roughly made five waves up from 1990 to 1997 before it fell. Waves #1 , #3, and #5 are up; waves #2 and #4 are down. Concerning waves #2 and #4, there is alternation. One wave is usually a sharp drop while the other is mild or a sideways move.

For example
- A stock ends a decline and moves up in a wave #1. The sentiment and the news about the stock are still negative and most investors ignore the rise.

- The stock pulls back in a wave #2, or say it just moves sideways.

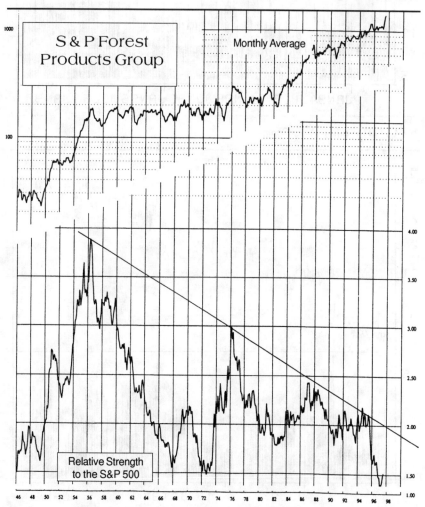

Industry Groups — **Graph #10**

page 89

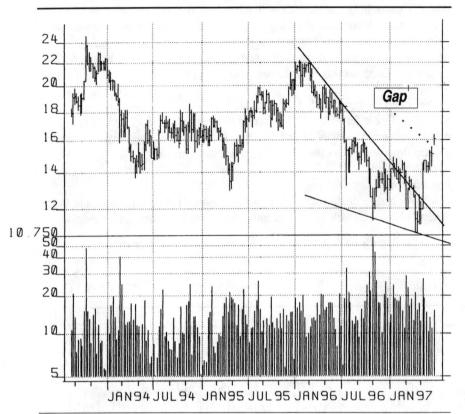

Graph #11 —*Telecommunications A*

Gap

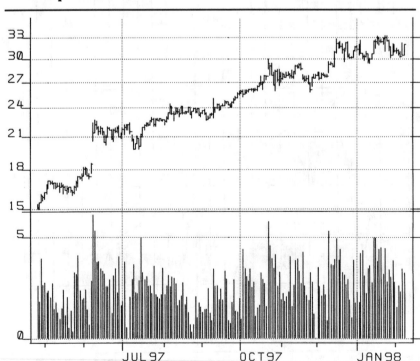

Graph #12 —*Comcast*

• Then the price accelerates in a wave #3. This move is usually the strongest and typically dispels most of the doubts about the company as positive news begins to break.

• Wave #4 is a sharp pullback, thus it alternates with the wave 2 correction which was mild. But wave #4 is brushed aside by investors. Unlike wave #2, the news is good and any drop is seen as an opportunity to buy more.

• Wave #5 hits new highs. All the news is great, and here is where you must watch for bearish non-confirmations.

The first wave down, call it 'A', is greeted like wave #4; it is seen as another opportunity to buy more shares. When the stock moves up ("B" wave), investors feel that they were right to add to their holdings. So when wave "B" fails, and the stock collapses dramatically, bewildered and disappointed investors give up and dump the stock at any price.

This is usually the biggest drop, and it occurs on heavy volume. The Oracle graph depicts a clear "C" wave drop. These rules are not carved in stone, but you will see them in action in the case studies section.

If a stock pulls back in an ongoing uptrend, the most frequent pullback is 50 percent. In other words, a stock rallies from 10 to 50. A pullback to 30 would be normal in an ongoing move up. The work of Arthur Merrill confirms that the most frequent retracement is 50 percent. I think that a one-third retracement is the second most frequent. It is especially helpful if the retracement level is also a support line. This would create stronger support.

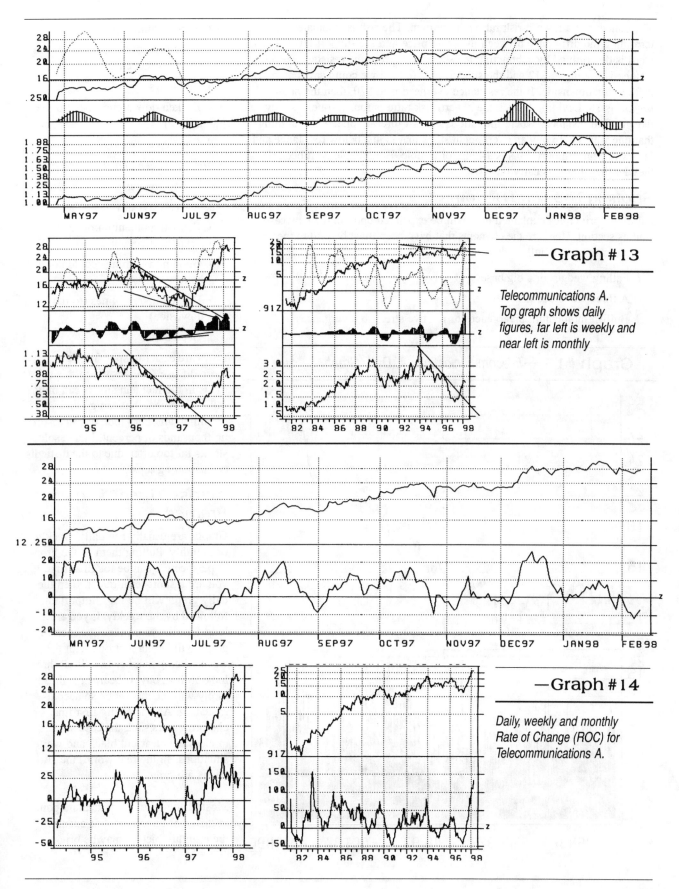

—Graph #13

*Telecommunications A.
Top graph shows daily
figures, far left is weekly and
near left is monthly*

—Graph #14

*Daily, weekly and monthly
Rate of Change (ROC) for
Telecommunications A.*

The concept of a reward-risk ratio is important. The risk is calculated by determining the difference between the share price and the support level. The reward is determined by subtracting the share price from the resistance level. If a stock is trading at $12 and the support is $10, then we could say that the *risk* is $2 to the downside. If the resistance overhead is at $20, then the potential *reward* is $8. Dividing 8 by 2, the reward-risk ratio is four-to-one. Usually, one likes to find instances where the ratio is at least three-to-one. The last thing that one wants is to buy an overbought stock that is just below resistance and far away from support. This is asking for trouble. But, people do it because they let their feelings carry them away.

Spotting Tops and Bottoms

All of the principles explained here will be expanded upon in the new case studies section. Here are the elements that have been most helpful to me in finding lows in this bull market:

1. Falling wedges or a big base

2. A three-wave decline

3. Bullish momentum divergences or relative strength divergences

4. High volume

5. A 50 percent retracement of the previous move up

6. Bad news

7. Broken downtrend lines (to the upside)

8. Gaps up

Highs have been characterized by:

1. Rising wedges

2. A five-wave advance

3. Bearish momentum or relative strength divergences

4. Good news– things could not be better

5. Broken uptrend lines (to the downside)

6. Gaps down

Lows are easier to spot. Tops are more diffuse. The answer to this riddle is in the fact that stocks can only fall 100 percent, but can go up by an unlimited amount– look at Microsoft, up thousands of percent. I have sold stocks far too often due to the difficulty in spotting tops.

Across Three Time Frames

Graphs are usually run daily, weekly, or monthly. Putting them in the proper perspective can be tough at first. If you are a short-term trader, then the daily graph will be most important, followed by the weekly. If you are a long-term investor, then the monthly graph will be number one with the weekly being number two. If all three look bullish, buy. If bearish, sell. But rarely will the market be so accommodating. As one of my first financial professors said, the case studies in class are clear-cut black and white situations. In the real world, the situations are gray.

Most of the time, the indicators point in different directions. For example, the monthly picture may be bright,

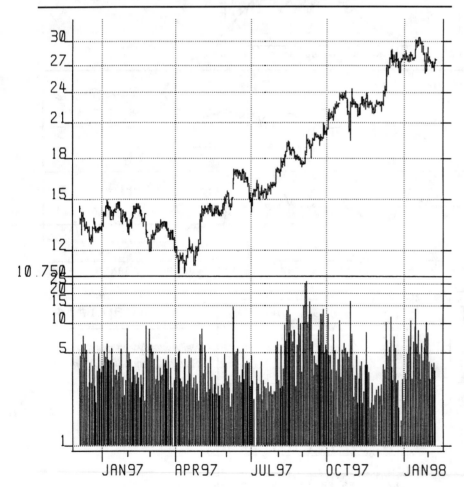

Graph #15 —*Telecommunications A, Daily Graph*

but the daily and weekly are not. This usually reflects a stock that is in the process of making a longer-term base, but is simply not ready to take off yet. The stock may rally a bit, fall back, rally again, and so on until the daily, weekly, and monthly pictures align. A bullish short-term picture in the daily graph likely indicates an imminent rally in an over-all downtrend. Once the bullish picture in the daily graph dissipates by becoming overbought, the bearish-looking weekly and monthly picture takes over and the decline resumes.

A longer-term low like the one described in the first case will usually occur under a cloud of negative sentiment. The news is bad and frustrated investors sell the stock, tired of waiting for a turnaround. At a high, all the news is usually good. Investors are pleased with their holdings, and think of adding more shares to their portfolios. As the prices fall, investors think that the pullback is a normal one in a longer-term bull market. As the decline wears on, shareholders surrender their high expectations and sell the stock. This creates the next bottom.

Graph 13 is a three-up chart. There is one daily graph (top), one weekly graph (left), and one monthly graph (right). The top strip is the closing price and a smoothed moving average. The middle strip is the departure analysis, and the bottom strip is the relative strength versus the S&P. The second set of graphs (14) is a three-up set depicting price and rate of change (ROC). The daily chart shows 12-day ROC while the weekly shows 12-week ROC and the monthly shows 12-month ROC. *Graph 15* is the daily bar chart. Here's how to approach it.

First, we see that the weekly pattern form 1996 into 1997 was a falling wedge. Below that, we see that the de-

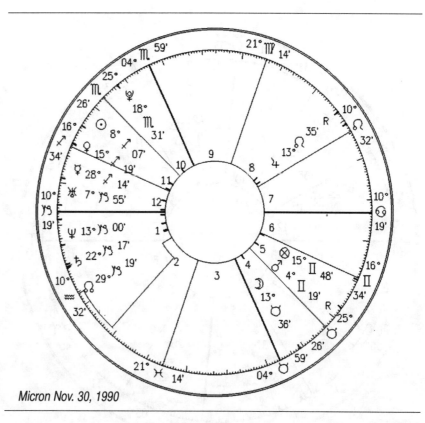

Micron Nov. 30, 1990

Micron Tech., horoscope and price graph — **Graph #16**

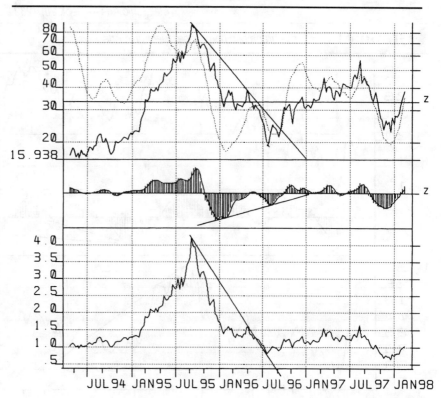

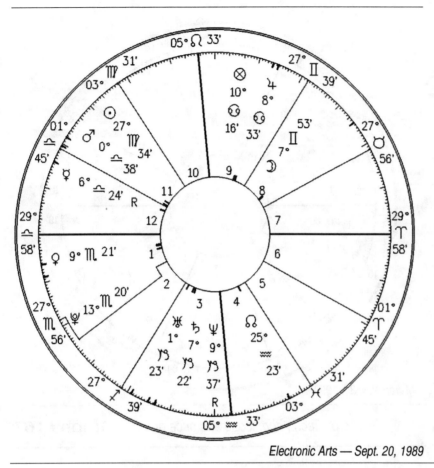

Electronic Arts — Sept. 20, 1989

parture analysis reveals higher lows, a bullish sign. Third, note how the relative strength (RS) line reversed its downtrend in the first quarter of 1997. Three constructive developments. Let's move on to the monthly graph. Note that the stock was very oversold on a longer-term basis in early 1997, an indication of low risk. The stock had been battered down by 50 percent from its 1996 high. The weekly and the monthly ROC charts both show a very oversold condition, confirming the departure analysis. *Graph 15* shows a big jump up in late April. (See how the last decline from February into the April low was a three-step fall?) Then there is a gap up in May. Now go back to the monthly graph #13. See how a 3-year old downtrend line was broken to the upside in late 1997. This was a late but confirming sign of TCOMA's recovery to new highs. At this time, the stock is very overbought both weekly and monthly. The daily momentum oscillator shows a lower high, a bearish, but minor, divergence from price. The stock has not risen in five

Graph #17 — *Price graph and horoscope, Electronic Arts*

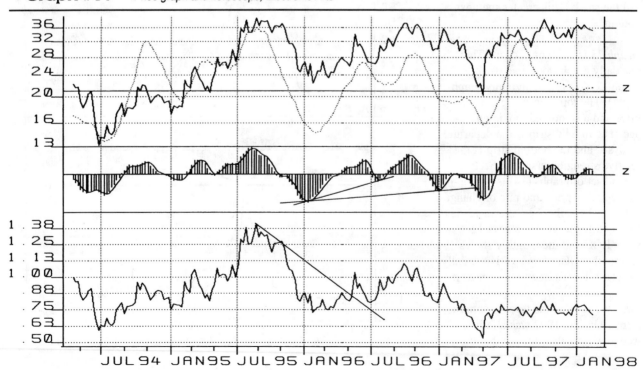

waves; there is only one. So it appears that TCOMA has arrived at its first resting or consolidation phase from its bottom. This pullback or sideways consolidation will likely be followed by another rally (wave #3), another pullback (#4), and a final run up (#5). It is at this point that we would anticipate a longer-term top. Here is where long-term investors would sell. Shorter-term traders would sell now.

At times, the three graphs point in three different directions. When there is doubt, stay out. Just look at another stock. Why play with fire?

Putting It All Together

The difficulty is in the application of these principles. The indicators are like an orchestra. At any point, a few play a solo. The trick is in anticipating which ones to rely upon. Seldom will the market be so accommodating as to supply all of the signals and then wait for you to buy it. The marketplace is extremely competitive and others are looking for some of the same signs. When these signs begin to appear, investors begin to act.

The next step in the process is knowing when to act. If you wait for all of these indicators to be in place, it is like arriving at the station a minute after the train has pulled out. One must decide at what point one will act. This is where the astro edge comes in.

The Astro Edge
Combining the Technical and Planetary Tools

Graph 16 is the weekly graph of Micron Technology (MU) and *Graph 17* is that of Electronic Arts (ERTS) over the same time period. First note that MU shows higher lows in weekly momentum, a buy signal. Now note that ERTS is giving the same type of signal. Most technicians would be pressed to choose between the two.

The horoscopes of first trade of both stocks follow. Note that on September 4, Jupiter stationed on Uranus in the first trade chart of MU. This is a bullish combination, especially so because Uranus has rule over technology. See how MU then doubled from the station into July. ERTS went down and then sideways over the same period. **This is the astro edge!** Any technical analyst can find stocks that look bullish, but he must then sort out the wheat from the chaff. With the first trade chart, one has a big advantage. In fact, this is the very process that I went through in buying MU. In the horoscope of ERTS, Jupiter stationed on Saturn, which is okay but not as good as station-

ing on Uranus in the chart of a tech stock. In addition, the station was near my ascendant and exactly trine my Venus in Taurus. So all the ingredients for success were present.

It does not always work out this way. At times, the planets will not make good contacts to our personal charts, or not all of the contacts to the first-trade chart will be positive, or not all of the technicals will line up, etc. What one does in those situations is dependent upon the amount of risk that one is willing to assume. If you hold your requirements for a buy candidate high, then you will generate fewer stocks. If you loosen them, then you will have more buy ideas, but greater risk. Let's look at it from another viewpoint. If an astrologer does a scan of the first-trade charts, he will come up with a list of acceptable candidates. A technical analysis will then be helpful in choosing the best stocks. The technical picture represents the sum total of all influences on the first-trade horoscope. Let's say that there is an unknown planet influencing the chart. We may miss that influence in the horoscope, but the price action will tell us what the results are. If you think that the horoscope of a stock looks bullish, but the price falls, there is something that you are missing. In that case, listen to the share price.

Case Studies: Edition Two

Edition #1 contained 33 case studies. Readers indicated that they found these most helpful and wanted more such analyses, so we've added 20 cases. Many of the technical techniques discussed earlier will be incorporated.

34—Oracle's Collapse

inside: **Oracle, Mar 12, 1986**
outside: **Crash, Dec. 9, 1997**

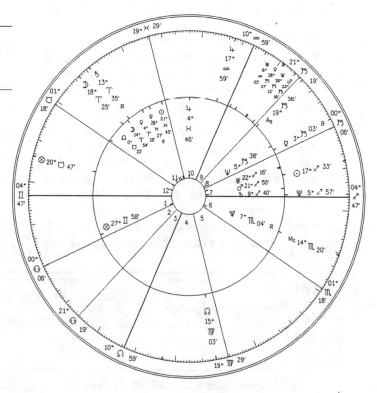

This is an extremely interesting case for several reasons. First, Alphee Lavoie told me that he was anticipating a fall in December to be followed by a rally. In the bar chart below, we see that the stock fell over 25 percent on December 9 as Saturn passed over the Moon.

A closer look shows that transiting Saturn was conjunct transiting Moon that morning before the opening in New York. In fact, the conjunction was a very powerful type that falls under a broad heading of linear configurations. Charles Jayne found that these "planetary eclipses" were much more powerful than regular conjunctions or oppositions.

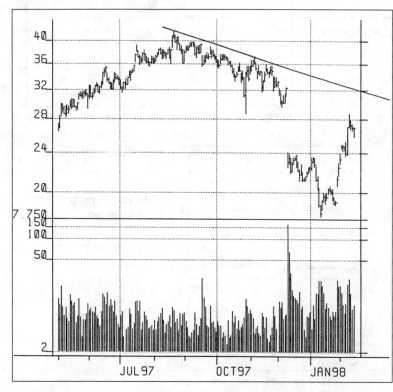

This occurs when planets were either conjunct or opposite in longitude *and* were in the same latitude. In this situation, one could draw a straight line through the planets and the Sun. That is, they "lined up", as the planets did in the movies 2001 and 2010. A linear configuration involving the Moon is specifically termed an occultation. It is denoted in an ephemeris by a conjunction or opposition circle symbol that has been darkened or filled in as an eclipse symbol is.

Let's look at the technical picture.

Look at the 3-up graph on the next page. Remember, the daily picture is on top, the weekly picture is to the lower left, and the monthly picture is to the lower right. First, the weekly graph shows that relative strength (RS) did not make a new high with the price, a bearish non-confirmation or divergence. Also, the RS had been falling since August; this stock was not doing as well as the averages. Second, note that the momentum oscillator in the center strip was over-bought both weekly and monthly. Then the daily picture turned weak in August. See how the momentum hit a lower high in late August and could barely stay above the zero line into the fall? This stock was like a weak link waiting to be snapped.

After the quick collapse, the technology-laden NASDAQ index began to give buy signals. ORCL also began to give daily and weekly buy signals. Let's see how the technical picture had brightened and the astrology sent ORCL up again. First, the daily graph shows a 3-wave decline. Next, note how the downtrend lines were broken to the upside, led by the relative strength (RS) line. Third, the stock was very

oversold as reflected by the momentum oscillator in the center strip in the month of December. The monthly oscillator had just become oversold, not enough to say that there was a new long-term advance coming, but enough to conclude that the downside risk was limited. Here is where the regular technical trader's analysis stops, and here is where astrology adds value.

On January 28 the New Moon at 8 Aquarius was conjunct Uranus at 9 Aquarius, near enough to Oracle's 11 Aquarius midheaven. In addition, Mars was passing over the natal Jupiter. Now go back to the daily bar graph and see how the stock gapped up, proof of the effect of the lunation and a sign that Oracle had reversed to the upside.

How far would it rise? Well, probably at least to the 28-32 area, just below where I have drawn a downtrend line.

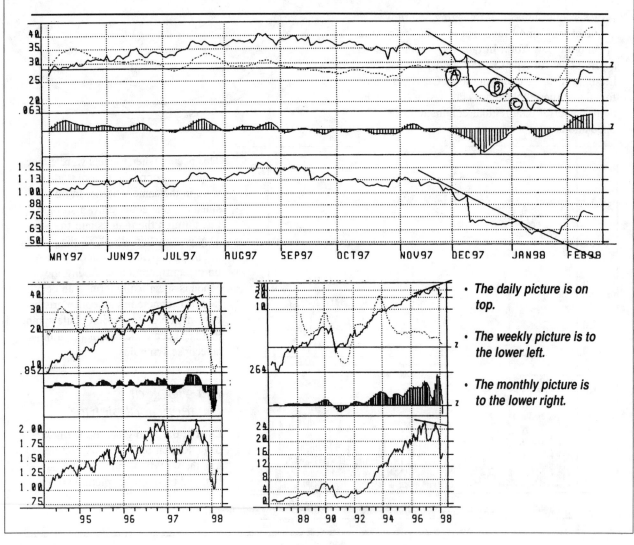

- *The daily picture is on top.*

- *The weekly picture is to the lower left.*

- *The monthly picture is to the lower right.*

35— The New Moon and NASDAQ

The NASDAQ is the average of the over-the-counter market. Most stocks in the average are technology stocks, and not surprisingly, this average began when the Sun was in Aquarius.

The graph shows the 10-day ROC in the top strip and the average in the bottom strip. The ROC is making higher lows as the average makes lower lows-a bullish divergence. Uranus is the industry planet for tech stocks in general, and the previously mentioned New Moon in Aquarius conjunct Uranus occurred on January 28. See how the NASDAQ gapped up at the arrow on the lower graph on that day.

Not only did it gap up, but the lunation propelled it through the overhead resistance line. Knowing it was an industry planet and that the lunation would hit on that day was the key to anticipating the breakout.

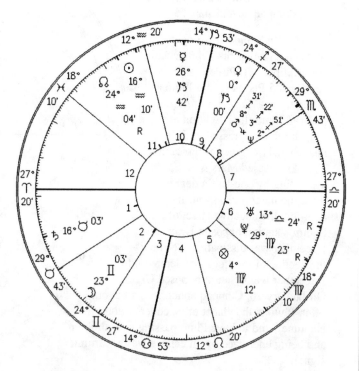

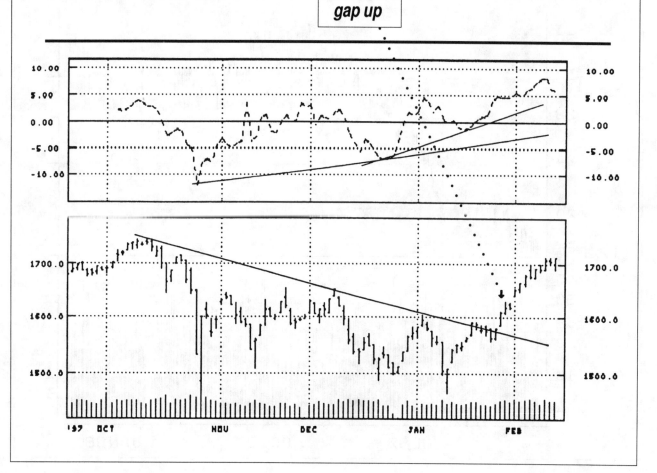

gap up

36—Compaq Buys Digital

inside: **Digital, Dec. 1, 1970**
outside: **Compaq buyout, Jan. 26, 1998**

In early 1998, most astrologers were anticipating the February 26 solar eclipse at 8 Pisces conjunct Jupiter at 5 Pisces square Pluto at 8 Sagittarius. This configuration tied right into the DEC Sun at 9 Sag and the progressed midheaven at 11 degrees of the same sign. Progressed Mars was separating by one-half a degree from the natal midheaven. In addition, the negative effect of Saturn's station opposite Uranus in December was dissipating. See how the decline of the stock accelerated into December while Saturn opposed Uranus? On January 26, Compaq announced a buyout offer. Pluto is the planet of takeovers (with Neptune), and to have Pluto passing over the Sun and being energized by an eclipse was a warning signal.

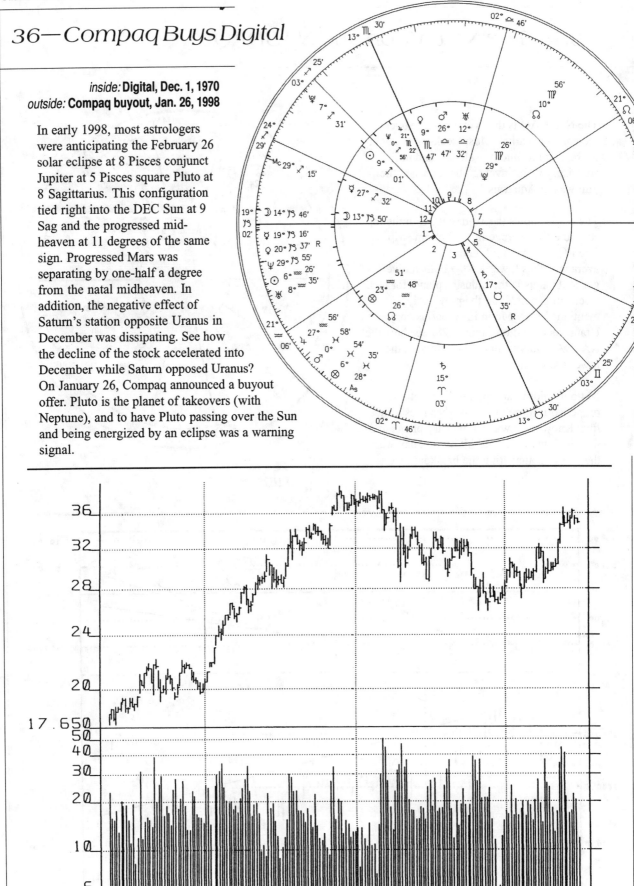

First Data's Fall —37

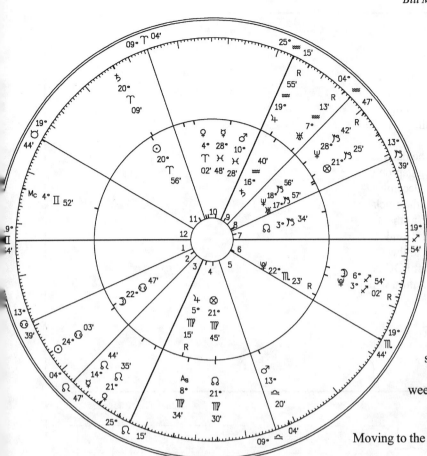

inside: **First Data, Apr. 10, 1992**
outside: **Top, July 16, 1997**

FDC rose from the April low into July. Saturn was to make a station on the Sun and square the Moon in the first days of August.

First let's look at the rally from April to July on the bar graph. There were two well-defined upmoves. The third was a weak one that lasted only a few days in mid-July. The stock then fell 50 percent.

The 3-up graphs *(shown on the next page)* were flashing many warning signs. First, we see that FDC had dipped and then rallied to a new high. Looking at the monthly and the weekly high, we see that the RS had not reached new highs with price, a bearish divergence.

Moving to the weekly chart, momentum was registering

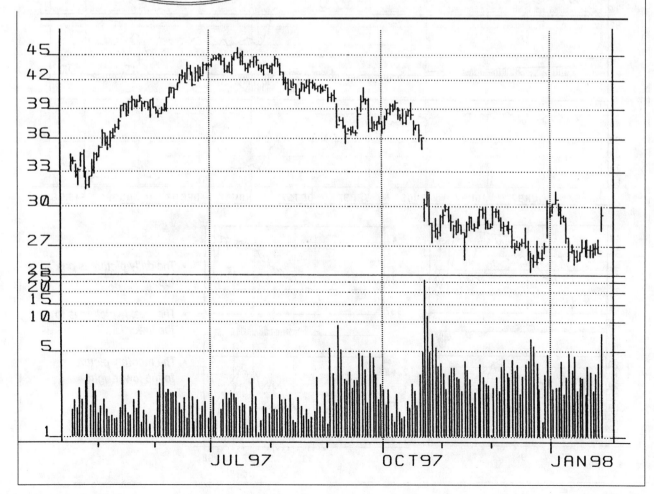

overbought. Moving up to the daily chart, the daily momentum oscillator was making lower highs from May into July. So this stock was ripe for a fall.

Let's analyze the new rally. Going back to the daily bar chart, there is a 3-step decline with a big gap on heavy volume in October. The low came in December. Jupiter passed over the midheaven, and the stock gapped up in late January 1998. Going back to the 3-up charts, FDC was very oversold both weekly and monthly. This signifies that any positive hit to the horoscope would send the share price up. But FDC is not likely completely out of the woods yet. Saturn will pass over the Sun again.

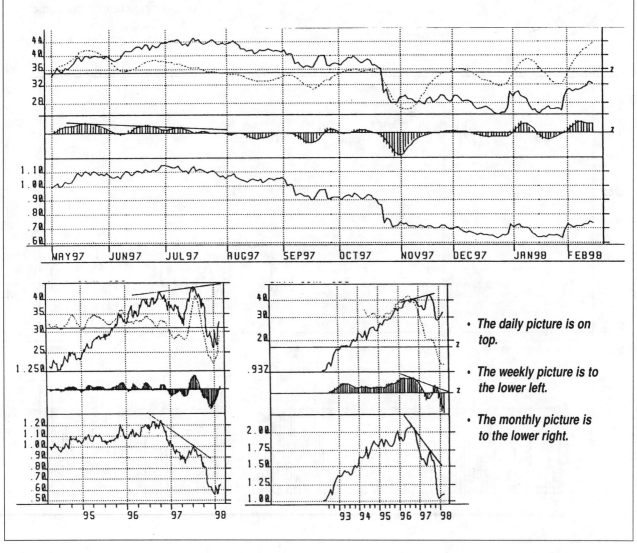

- **The daily picture is on top.**

- **The weekly picture is to the lower left.**

- **The monthly picture is to the lower right.**

38 — Lowes Bottom

inside: **Lowes, Dec. 19, 1979**
outside: **Bottom, Sept. 2, 1997**

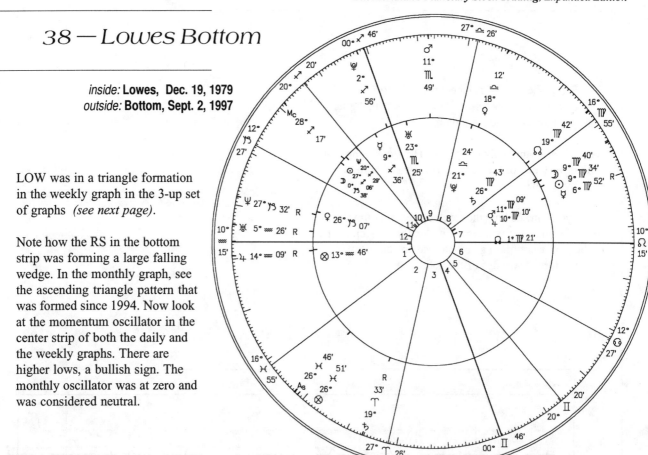

LOW was in a triangle formation in the weekly graph in the 3-up set of graphs *(see next page)*.

Note how the RS in the bottom strip was forming a large falling wedge. In the monthly graph, see the ascending triangle pattern that was formed since 1994. Now look at the momentum oscillator in the center strip of both the daily and the weekly graphs. There are higher lows, a bullish sign. The monthly oscillator was at zero and was considered neutral.

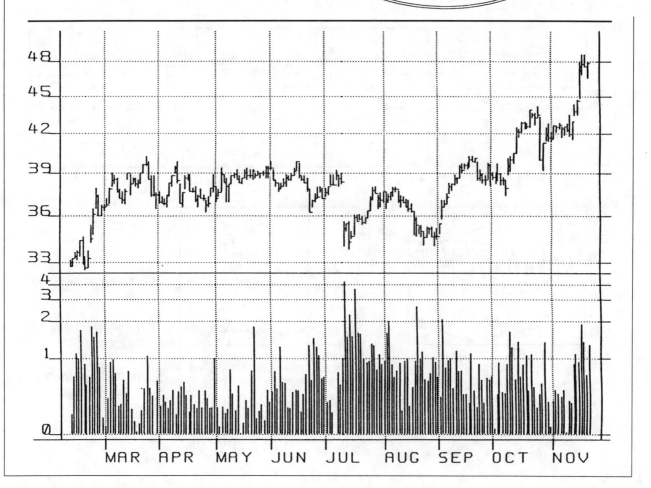

The September 1,1997 solar eclipse at 10 Virgo was conjunct the natal Mars-Jupiter conjunction. Jupiter was passing over the ascendant.

Now refer to the daily bar graph. The stock gapped up on the very day of the eclipse. How was that for a confirmation?

Now you can see how the stock busted out of the triangles that it was trapped in. Again, the technical indicators were hinting at what was to come, but we had the foreknowledge of the eclipse.

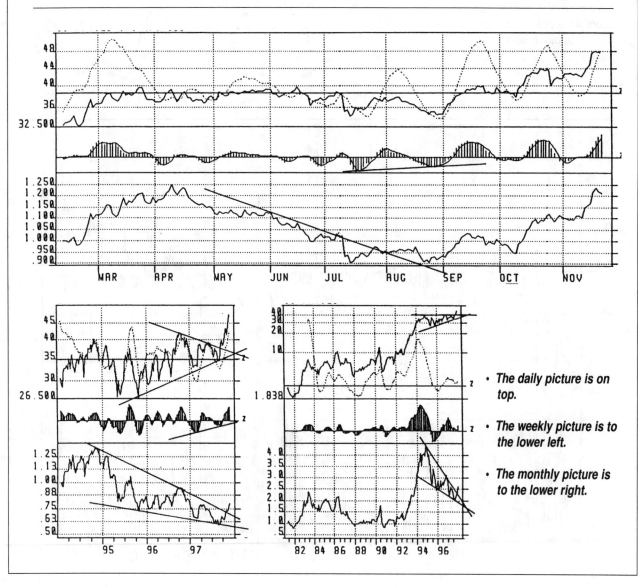

- *The daily picture is on top.*

- *The weekly picture is to the lower left.*

- *The monthly picture is to the lower right.*

If You Like Volatility, You'll Love Silicon Graphics—39

inside: **Silicon Graphics, Feb 6, 1990**
outside: **Crash , Oct. 6, 1997**

I had to include this great
horoscope.

Look at the 6 planets in Capricorn and the 2 in Cancer with a
Cap midheaven and an Aries
ascendant.

With Saturn in Aries, it is no
wonder that SGI took such hard
knocks in 1997.

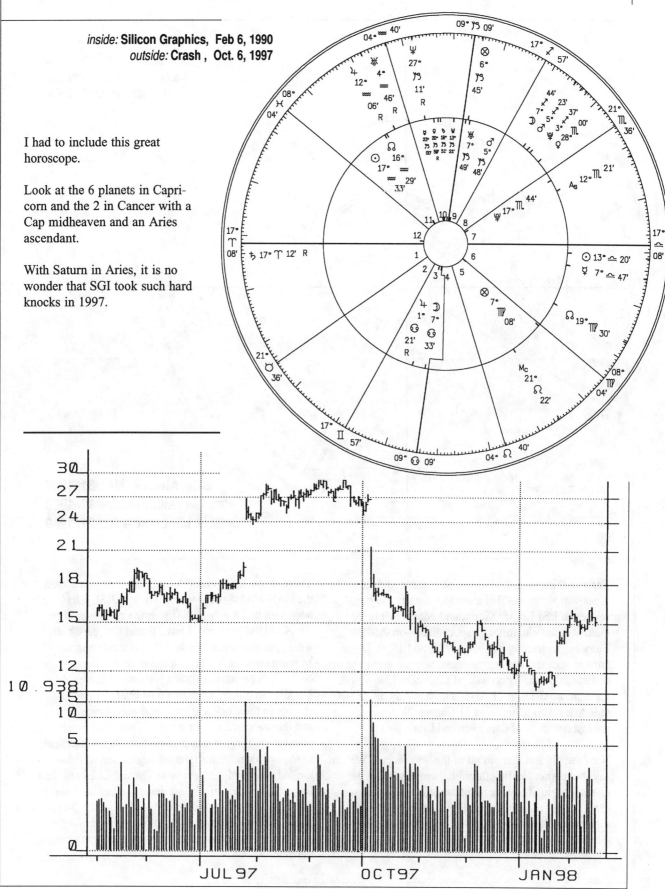

40 — A Case in Shared Degree Areas

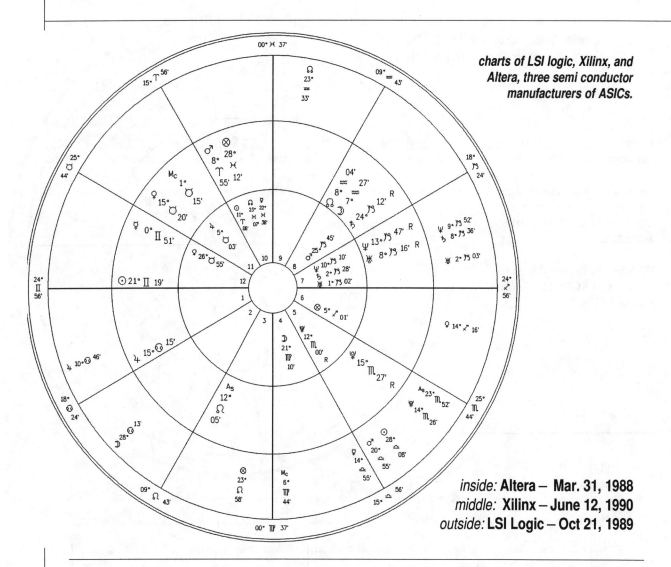

charts of LSI logic, Xilinx, and Altera, three semi conductor manufacturers of ASICs.

inside: **Altera – Mar. 31, 1988**
middle: **Xilinx – June 12, 1990**
outside: **LSI Logic – Oct 21, 1989**

Early in this book, the importance of shared degree areas was stressed. This tri-wheel depicts the horoscopes of LSI Logic, Xilinx, and Altera. All three make semiconductors of a specialized sort-ASICs. They began trading in 1988, 1989, and 1990. It is not hard to spot the hot degree areas. See the grouping of planets in the first decanate of Capricorn? Now note the Sun of ALTR at 11 Aries and the Mars of XLNX at 9 Aries. LSI's Jupiter is 11 Cancer. Now search for the last decanate of Capricorn and Libra.

Note the planets there in all of the horoscopes. We can say that planets sailing through these degrees will effect the trio. They are in the same industry, and we can see why the stocks would be subject to the same influences. Saturn in Aries was difficult for these stocks.

There is one more observation. LSI used to trade on the NASDAQ with the ticker symbol LLSI. It has been said that the "right" first-trade chart would be the NASDAQ version. I have found that they both work, but the newer one has the greatest weight. Moving onto the NYSE is a big event for most companies because it does attract more shareholder interest. So it does warrant a new chart as a new change in the stock's growth and acceptance. But just think about it for a moment: if the stock were about to go through a big step, doesn't it make sense to expect connections (shared degree areas) between the old chart and the new one? The old LLSI also has important planets in the last degree of cardinal signs. The new LSI began trading on Oct. 21, 1989. Note that as LSI transformed itself into an ASIC maker, it just happened to change its first-trade chart to match the other ASICS.

Quantum's Leap —41

inside: **Quantum, Dec. 10, 1982**
outside: **Crash, Dec. 11, 1997**

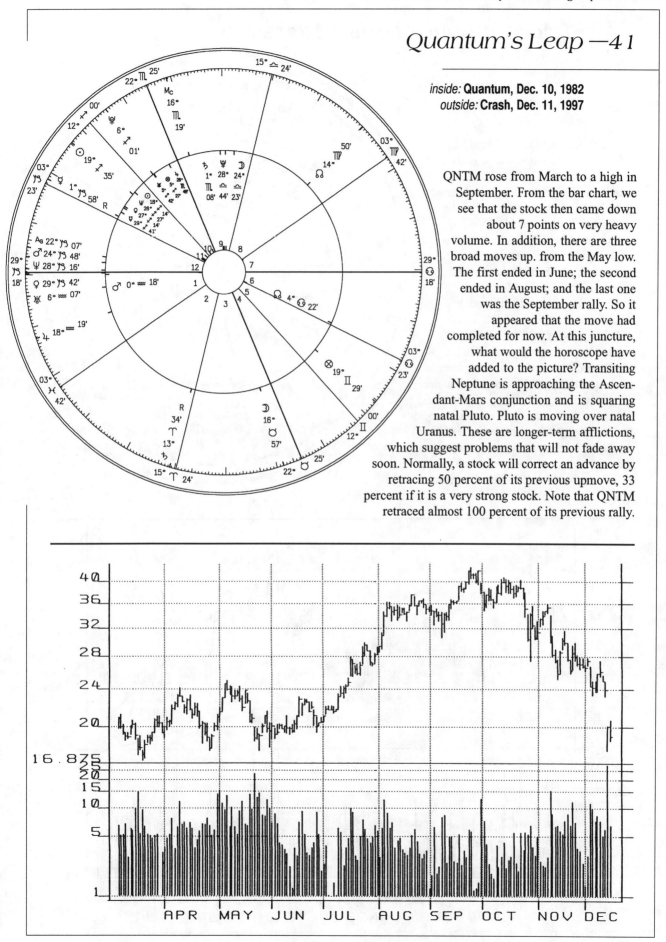

QNTM rose from March to a high in September. From the bar chart, we see that the stock then came down about 7 points on very heavy volume. In addition, there are three broad moves up. from the May low. The first ended in June; the second ended in August; and the last one was the September rally. So it appeared that the move had completed for now. At this juncture, what would the horoscope have added to the picture? Transiting Neptune is approaching the Ascendant-Mars conjunction and is squaring natal Pluto. Pluto is moving over natal Uranus. These are longer-term afflictions, which suggest problems that will not fade away soon. Normally, a stock will correct an advance by retracing 50 percent of its previous upmove, 33 percent if it is a very strong stock. Note that QNTM retraced almost 100 percent of its previous rally.

42 —Telecommunications A Revisited

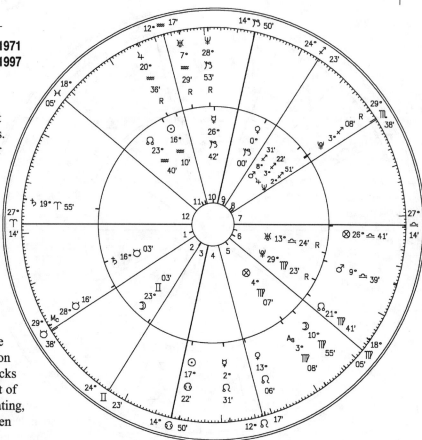

inside: **TCOMA, Feb. 5, 1971**
outside: **Gap Up, June 9, 1997**

In the section on technical analysis, TCOMA was given as a case study. But astrology was omitted from the analysis. The horoscope shows why I had greater faith in the stock than the technicals warranted. This is a cable TV company and the Sun is in Aquarius. With Jupiter heading toward the Sun and the Node, sextiling Jupiter and Mars, and trining the Moon and Uranus, it appeared that the stock would rally for most of 1997, which it did. The passage of Pluto off of the Jupiter-Neptune conjunction lifted a cloud off of the stock, too. Remember, Pluto usually represents matters that are pervasive or beyond control. Competition from satellite TV had sent all of the stocks in the industry down; this was the effect of the Pluto. With this conjunction dissipating, the prospects brightened, especially when Bill Gates put $1 billion into ComCast.

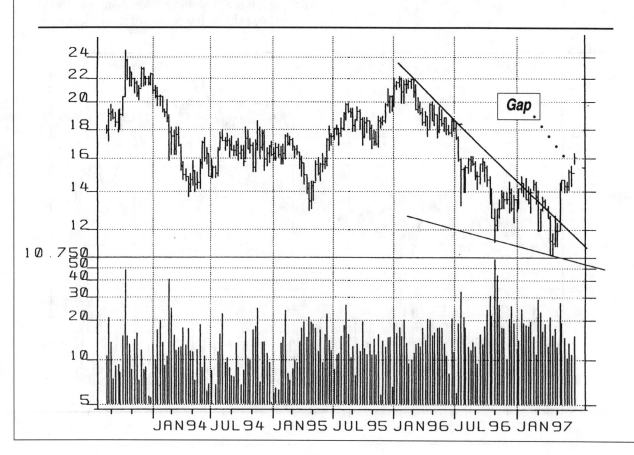

Compaq's 1997 Rally —43

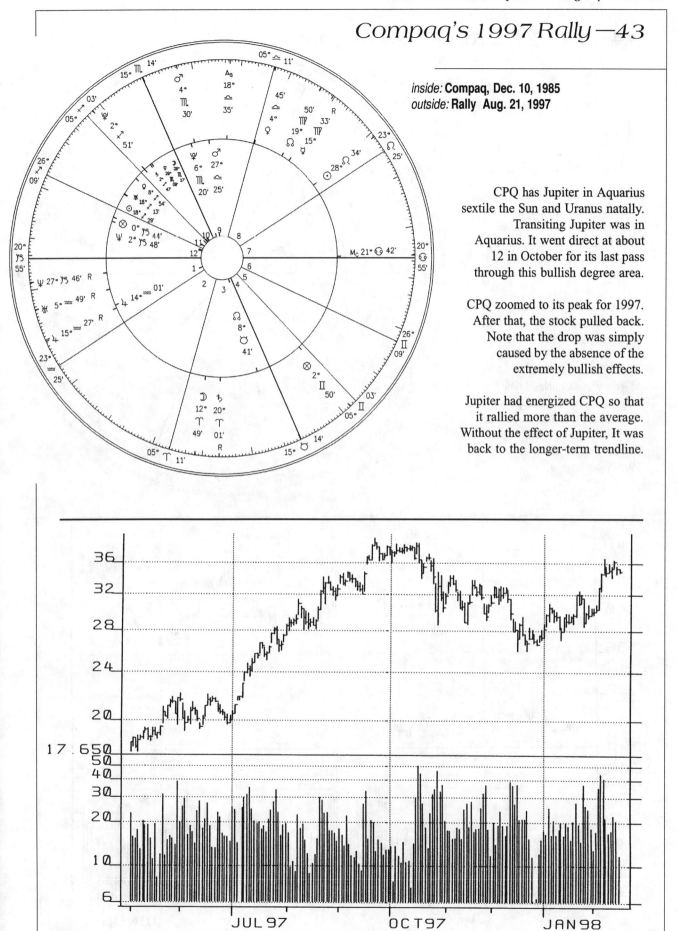

inside: **Compaq, Dec. 10, 1985**
outside: **Rally Aug. 21, 1997**

CPQ has Jupiter in Aquarius sextile the Sun and Uranus natally. Transiting Jupiter was in Aquarius. It went direct at about 12 in October for its last pass through this bullish degree area.

CPQ zoomed to its peak for 1997. After that, the stock pulled back. Note that the drop was simply caused by the absence of the extremely bullish effects.

Jupiter had energized CPQ so that it rallied more than the average. Without the effect of Jupiter, It was back to the longer-term trendline.

44— *Bergen Brunswig's Buyout*

inside: **BBC, Dec. 16, 1993**
outside: **Buyout, Sept. 25, 1997**

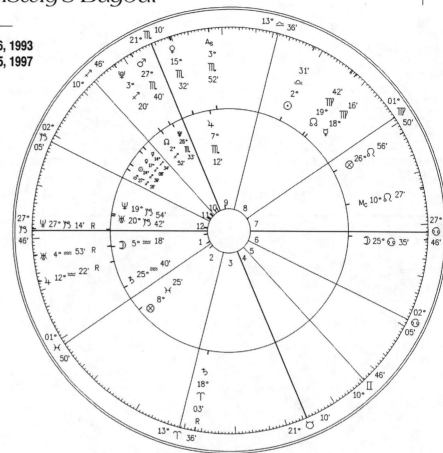

BBC had transiting Pluto passing over the Node. I find that this pair, as well as Neptune, are usually active in buyouts. In August of 1997, BBC shares jumped.

This case is a good example of eclipse activation. Note that the solar eclipse earlier in the year was at 18 Pisces, in the same axis as the first-trade Venus and Mercury. As Charles Jayne taught, the subsequent passage of the transiting Lunar Node over the eclipse point will re-ignite the degree. See the Node at 19 mutable?

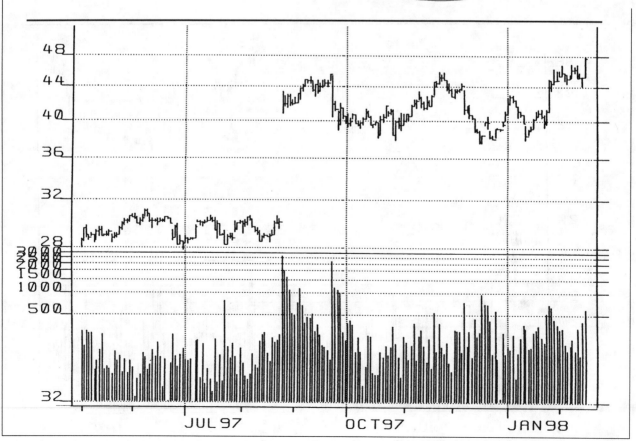

Barnett Banks Buyout — 45

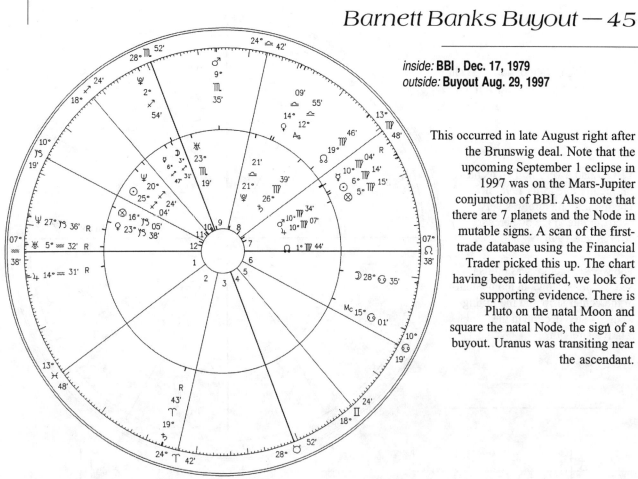

inside: BBI , Dec. 17, 1979
outside: Buyout Aug. 29, 1997

This occurred in late August right after the Brunswig deal. Note that the upcoming September 1 eclipse in 1997 was on the Mars-Jupiter conjunction of BBI. Also note that there are 7 planets and the Node in mutable signs. A scan of the first-trade database using the Financial Trader picked this up. The chart having been identified, we look for supporting evidence. There is Pluto on the natal Moon and square the natal Node, the sign of a buyout. Uranus was transiting near the ascendant.

Try this exercise.

Following are the dates of incorporation for the bank according to Standard and Poors:

1 – January 1,1930 in
    Tallahassee, Fla.

2 – Reincorporation on
    September 23,1969 in the
    same place

3 – Name change on
    April 24,1987.

Except for the eclipse squaring Jupiter in the 1930 chart, you will not find any more accurate indications than those in the first-trade chart.

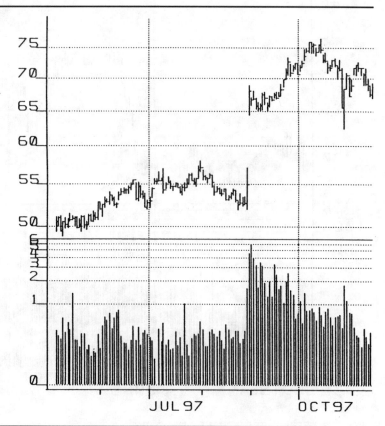

46 — *Yahoo!*

inside: **Yahoo, Apr. 12, 1996**
outside: **Breakout, July 14, 1997**

YHOO had a very limited technical picture due to its 1996 birth. The monthly picture was very oversold due to the 50 percent drop in late 1996.

The weekly picture was bullish. See the higher lows in momentum in the center strip and the falling wedge 3-step decline in the relative strength?

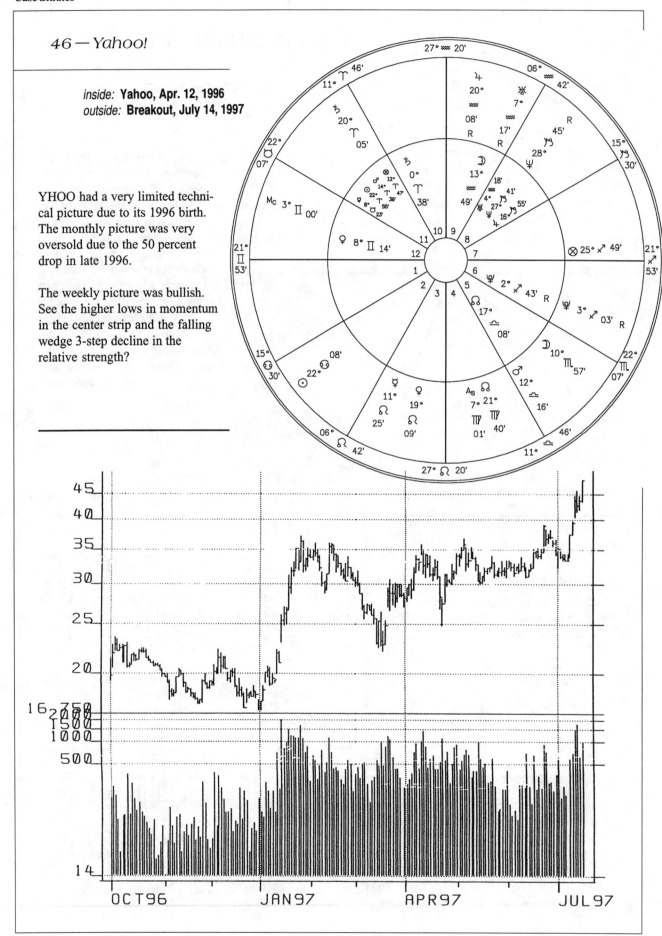

I was hesitant because there was such limited monthly information. The first-trade chart supplied the necessary signals. Jupiter in Aquarius would pass over Uranus (ruling planet for tech stocks), the Moon, and the Midheaven. It would make positive aspects to the Sun, Venus, Pluto, and the ascendant.

It was fortunate that Saturn would not reach the degree of the Sun until 1998. This stock was one of the best performers in the software group in 1997.

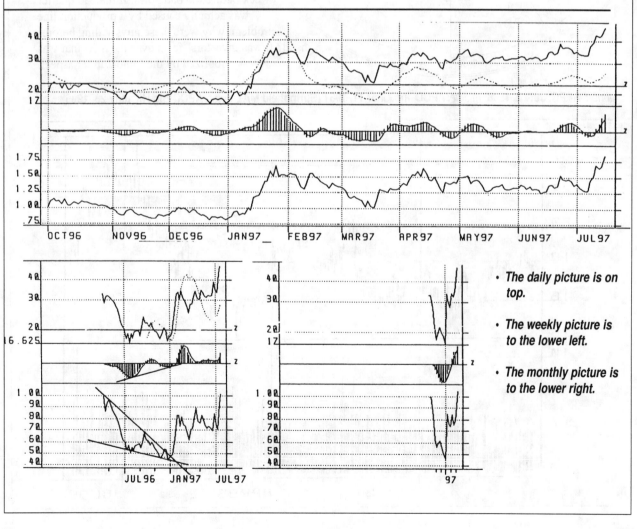

- **The daily picture is on top.**

- **The weekly picture is to the lower left.**

- **The monthly picture is to the lower right.**

47— *Confirmation from Incorporation Charts*

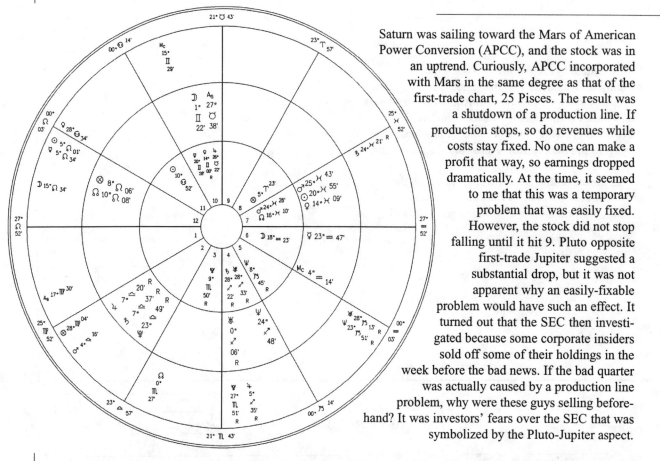

Saturn was sailing toward the Mars of American Power Conversion (APCC), and the stock was in an uptrend. Curiously, APCC incorporated with Mars in the same degree as that of the first-trade chart, 25 Pisces. The result was a shutdown of a production line. If production stops, so do revenues while costs stay fixed. No one can make a profit that way, so earnings dropped dramatically. At the time, it seemed to me that this was a temporary problem that was easily fixed. However, the stock did not stop falling until it hit 9. Pluto opposite first-trade Jupiter suggested a substantial drop, but it was not apparent why an easily-fixable problem would have such an effect. It turned out that the SEC then investigated because some corporate insiders sold off some of their holdings in the week before the bad news. If the bad quarter was actually caused by a production line problem, why were these guys selling beforehand? It was investors' fears over the SEC that was symbolized by the Pluto-Jupiter aspect.

inner: **APPC, July 2, 1988** *middle:* **APCC Inc., Mar 11, 1981 (Springfield MA)**, *outer:* **APCC Big Hit July 28, 1995**

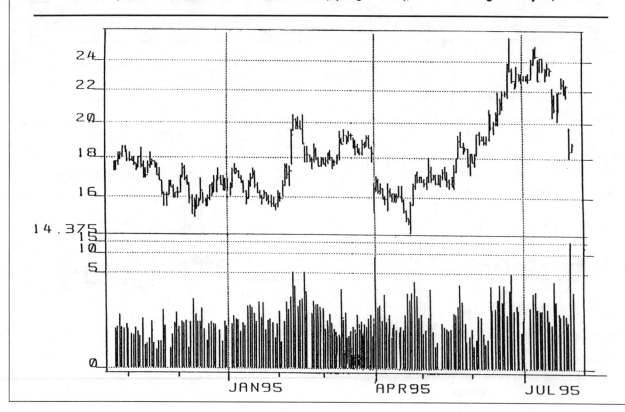

The Connrail Takeover —48

CRR's chart was picked up by a *Financial Trader* scan for the September 26, 1996 lunar eclipse at 4 Aries. It was conjunct the Sun-Jupiter conjunction. The only danger was Saturn retrograding 3 degrees away from the Sun. However, exact hits and applying aspects are the strongest.

That is, a planet that is less than a degree away from another is exponentially stronger than one that is, say, 2 degrees away. The power goes up on a curve as the conjunction gets closer, hits a peak, and then the energy falls away dramatically. So the eclipse was only a degree away while Saturn was 3 degrees away, and Saturn was moving backwards.

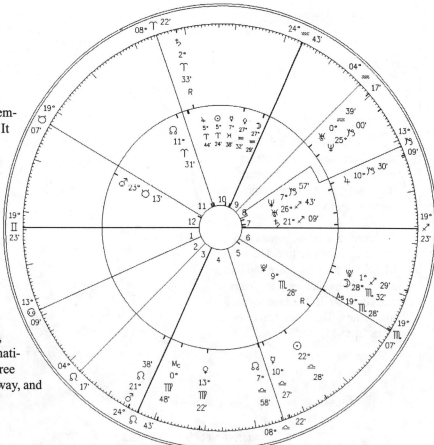

inside: **Connrail, Mar. 26, 1987**
outside: **Buyout, Oct. 15, 1996**

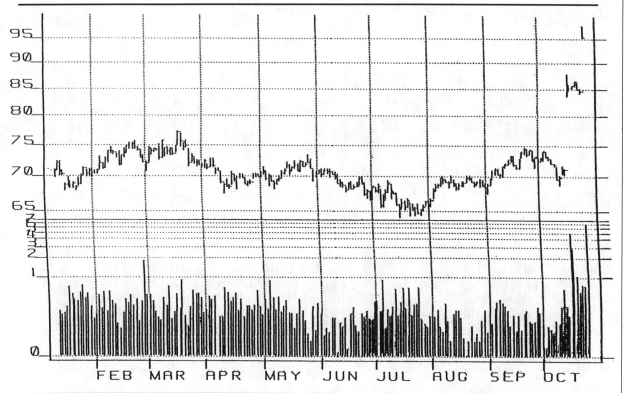

49 — Antec's Crash

I had to include this little-known stock because I heard a conference call on a Friday in which the brokers were trying to push this one on us.

I clicked this on the screen and saw the bearish picture. On Monday, Saturn opposed the Sun and made hard aspects to Venus and Mars while Neptune squared natal Mars. The stock collapsed from 24 to 15.

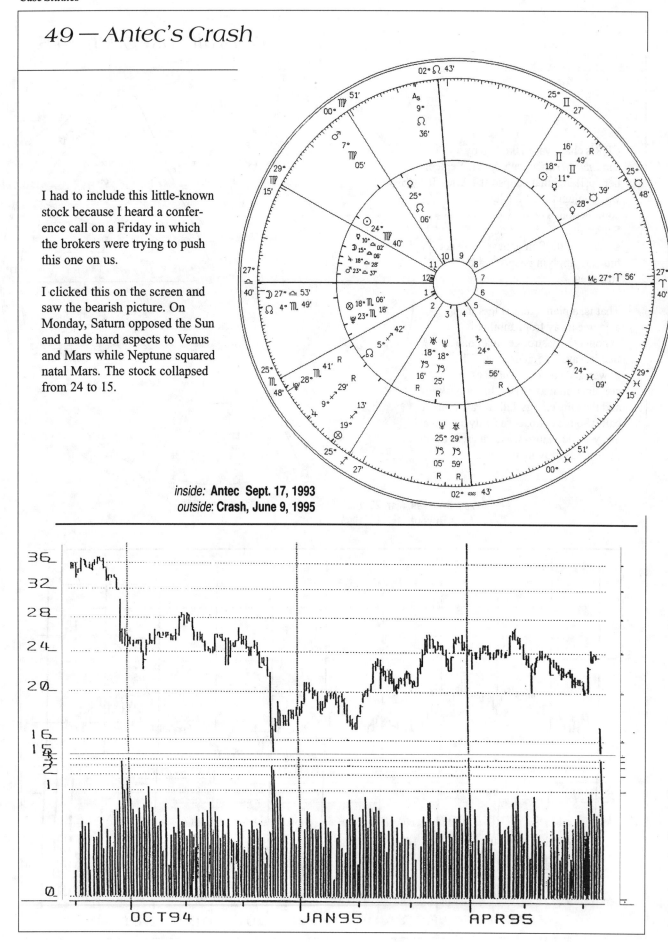

inside: **Antec Sept. 17, 1993**
outside: **Crash, June 9, 1995**

The Microsoft–Intuit Deal — 50

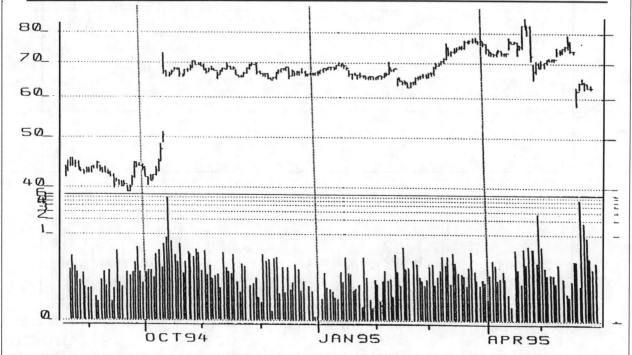

inside: **Intuit, Mar 12, 1993**
middle: **Microsoft, Mar. 13, 1986**
outer: **Deal's Off, May 25, 1995**

Microsoft made a bid to buy Intuit in the fall of 1994. In the summer of 1994, I had looked ahead and successfully predicted that MSFT would make a large takeover and/or would somehow provoke the government again. They had just managed to get the Justice Department off of their back, so everyone assumed that they would keep a low profile for a while. But the upcoming fall solar eclipse on the natal Pluto suggested otherwise.

When the deal was first announced, I looked ahead again and concluded that the spring 1995 eclipse opposite MSFT's Pluto would make or break the deal. Eclipse pairs frequently work this way. Further analysis detected Saturn moving over MSFT's Sun, and wait a minute, INTU's Sun also. A double hit. The government stopped the deal and INTU collapsed. Take a good look at INTU's bar chart, and you will see how the stock took off at the fall eclipse and fell after the spring eclipse. Just for fun, I went to great and loud lengths at meetings beforehand about my expectations for this deal. It was amusing to watch the faces at investment committee meetings after the predictions came true.

51 — Medpartner Needs a Doctor

inside: **MDM, Feb 22, 1996**
outside: **Crash Jan. 9, 1998**

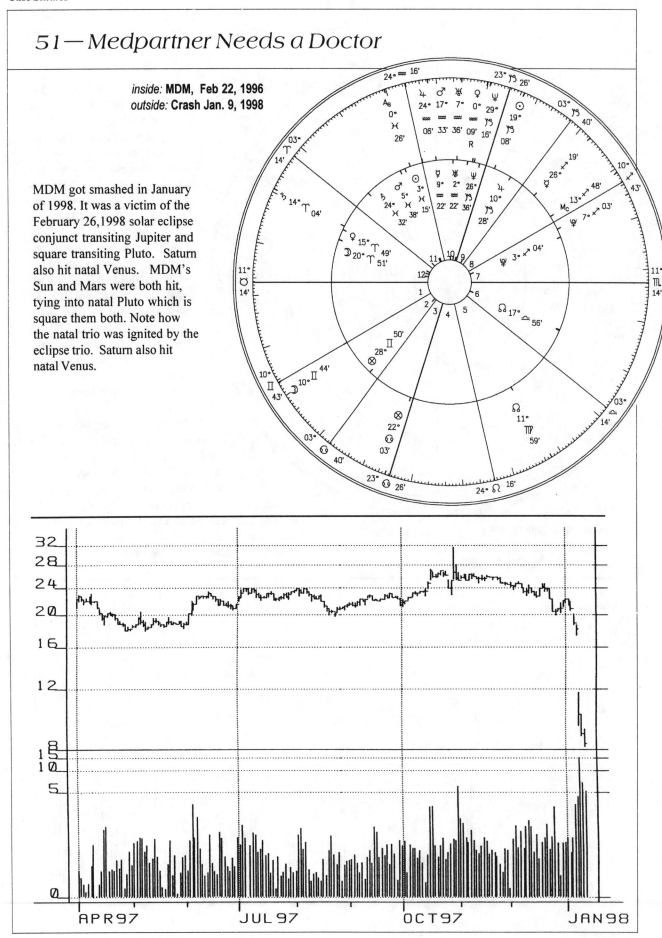

MDM got smashed in January of 1998. It was a victim of the February 26,1998 solar eclipse conjunct transiting Jupiter and square transiting Pluto. Saturn also hit natal Venus. MDM's Sun and Mars were both hit, tying into natal Pluto which is square them both. Note how the natal trio was ignited by the eclipse trio. Saturn also hit natal Venus.

The Kingworld Deal Folds —52

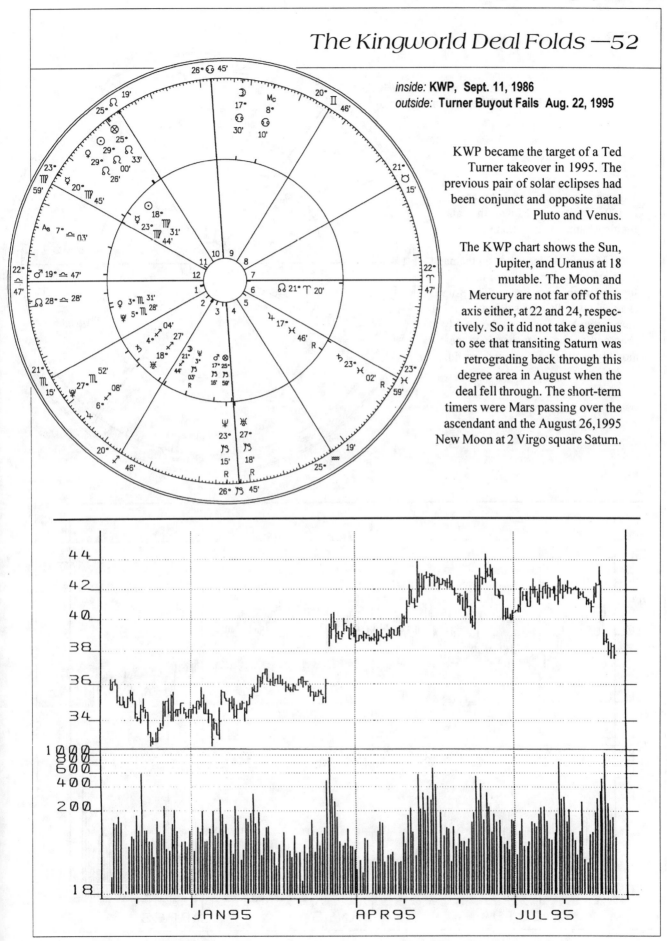

inside: **KWP, Sept. 11, 1986**
outside: **Turner Buyout Fails Aug. 22, 1995**

KWP became the target of a Ted Turner takeover in 1995. The previous pair of solar eclipses had been conjunct and opposite natal Pluto and Venus.

The KWP chart shows the Sun, Jupiter, and Uranus at 18 mutable. The Moon and Mercury are not far off of this axis either, at 22 and 24, respectively. So it did not take a genius to see that transiting Saturn was retrograding back through this degree area in August when the deal fell through. The short-term timers were Mars passing over the ascendant and the August 26,1995 New Moon at 2 Virgo square Saturn.

53 — *Goodbye, Lotus*

inside: **Lotus, Oct. 6, 1983**
outside: **IBM Takeover June 5, 1995**

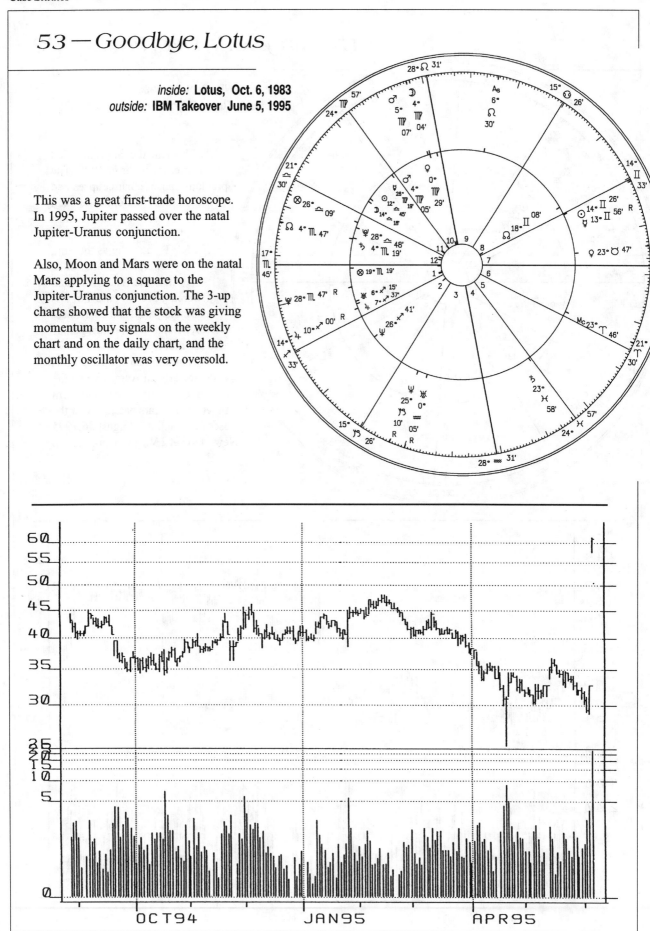

This was a great first-trade horoscope. In 1995, Jupiter passed over the natal Jupiter-Uranus conjunction.

Also, Moon and Mars were on the natal Mars applying to a square to the Jupiter-Uranus conjunction. The 3-up charts showed that the stock was giving momentum buy signals on the weekly chart and on the daily chart, and the monthly oscillator was very oversold.

We also see a falling wedge on the weekly graph and the 3-wave decline. With the stock being so sold out, and the first-trade chart so bullish (Jupiter to Jupiter-Uranus), the signs of appreciation due to the IBM takeover were apparent.

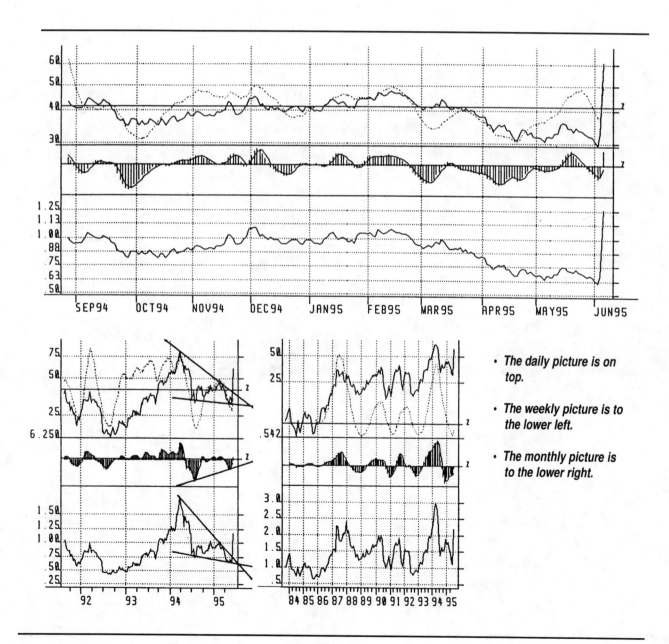

- *The daily picture is on top.*

- *The weekly picture is to the lower left.*

- *The monthly picture is to the lower right.*

The Future Gets Even Brighter

A s this second edition was going to press, Financial Trader 3 in Windows was completed. This program is simply the most powerful financial astrology software ever created. And I should know, having been around in the early days of *AstroAnalyst*.

There is so much to FT3 that you should go to the website, Alphee.com, to see all the of the tools that apply to both the overall market and to individual stocks. Here we will look at some of the new features that apply to first-trade charts:

Multiple-level Super Search

Scan hundreds of horoscopes and determine which will have transiting Saturn square the Sun while transiting Jupiter makes favorable aspects all year.

Efficiency Tester

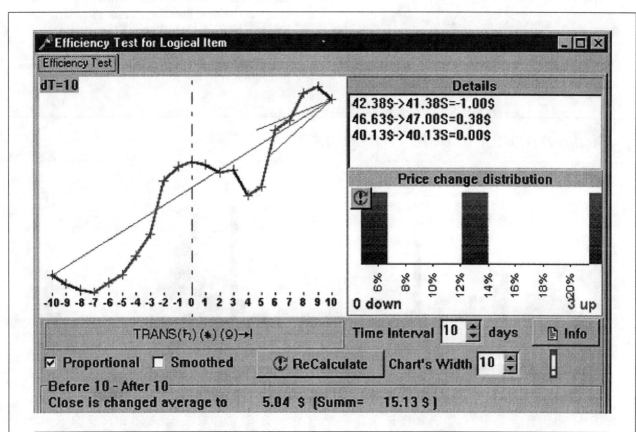

This is the most powerful financial astrology tool ever developed. The new efficiency tester (ET) will quantify market movements around any planetary phenomena. Here we see Sun-Mercury conjunctions in Aries versus a price series.

The ET will tell you how many times the market rose and fell around that configuration and will compute the magnitude of the moves. This can be done for transit-to-transit or for transit-to-natal, such as hits to first-trade charts.

Bradley Barometer

This graph shows the regular Bradley techniques indicating key turning points (October 28, 1997 and July 17, 1998).

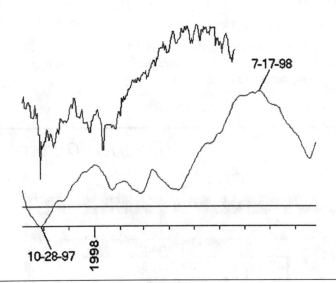

The media has featured the use of the Bradley barometer by well-known market analysts several times in the last year. More recently, it predicted the July 1998 market top. AIR Software was the first to computerize Bradley in the 1980s.

Our very advanced Bradley is completely user-adjustable. It can be used to compute models for transit-to-transit or to natal charts. The new Financial Trader Pro will have an artificial intelligence feature that will automatically optimize the weights for any aspect for any given market and project prices out into the future.

Sign-Aspect-Cycle Analysis

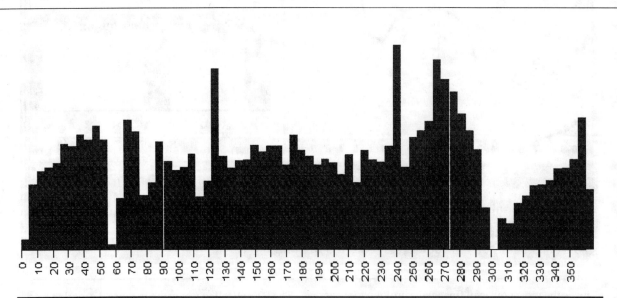

The following graph depicts the power of one of our new modules. It shows the Venus-Mars synodic cycle in terms of right ascension versus the Swiss Franc. Note how the Franc has tended to top at 120 and 240 degrees and bottom at 60 and 300 degrees. You can graphically see how any planetary cycle through signs or relative to any other body affects any market.

32
DOW

First Trade Charts

1. ALCOA-AA   **Aluminum**
June 11, 1951   NYC   10:0:0 AM EDT
40N45'00"   2:20:36 ST   74W00'23"

2. ALLIED SIGNAL-ALD   **Conglomerate**
Sep. 19, 1985   NYC   10:0:0 AM EDT
40N45'00"   8:57:53 ST   74W00'23"

3. AMERICAN EXPRESS-AXP   **Financial Services**
May 18, 1977   NYC   10:0:0 AM EDT
40N45'00"   0:48:45 ST   74W00'23"

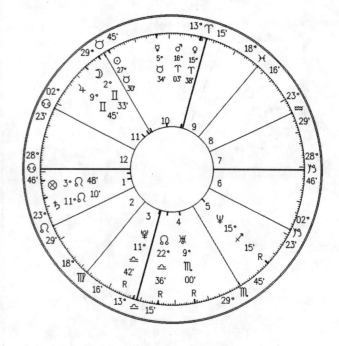

4. ATT-T (NEW) *Telephone*
Feb. 15, 1984   NYC   10:0:0 EST
40N45'00"   19:43:28 ST   74W00'23"

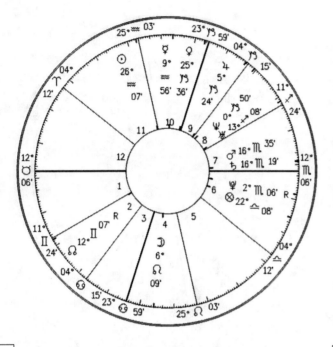

5. ATT-T (OLD) *Telephone*
Sep. 4, 1901   NYC   10:0:0 AM EST
40N45'00"   8:56:19 ST   74W00'23"

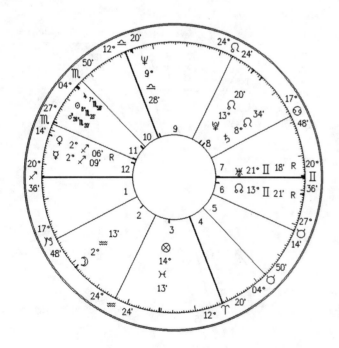

6. ATT-T (REORGANIZATION) *Telephone*
Nov. 1, 1946   NYC   10:0:0 AM EST
40N45'00"   12:45:23 ST   74W00'23"

7. BOEING-BA *Airplanes*
Sep. 4, 1935   NYC   10:0:0 AM EDT
40N45'00"   7:55:14 ST   74W00'23"

8. CATERPILLAR-CAT   *Machinery*
Dec. 2, 1929   NYC   10:0:0 AM EST
40N45'00"   14:48:04 ST   74W00'23"

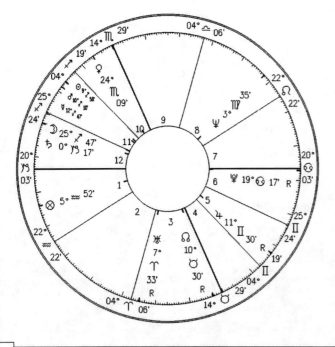

9. CHEVRON-CHV   *Oil International*
June 24, 1961   NYC   10:0:0 AM EDT
40N45'00"   3:14:08 ST   74W00'23"

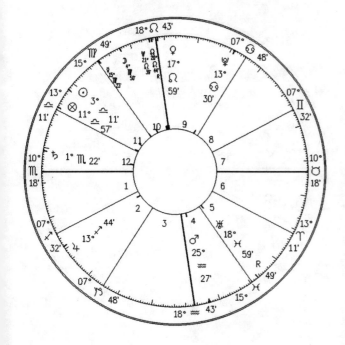

10. COCA COLA-KO   *Beverages*
Sep. 26, 1924   NYC   10:0:0 AM EDT
40N45'00"   9:24:35 ST   74W00'23"

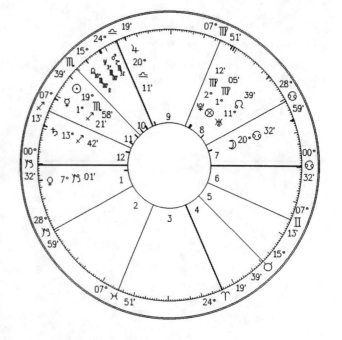

11. DISNEY-DIS   *Entertainment*
Nov. 12, 1957   NYC   10:0:0 AM EST
40N45'00"   13:30:05 ST   74W00'23"

12. DUPONT-DD   *Chemicals*
May 25, 1922   NYC   10:0:0 AM EDT
40N45'00"   1:13:40 ST   74W00'23"

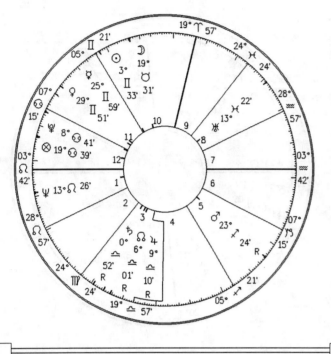

13. EASTMAN KODAK-EK   *Misc.*
Apr. 12, 1905   NYC   10:0:0 AM EST
40N45'00"   23:24:46 ST   74W00'23"

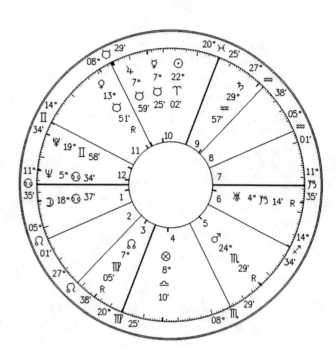

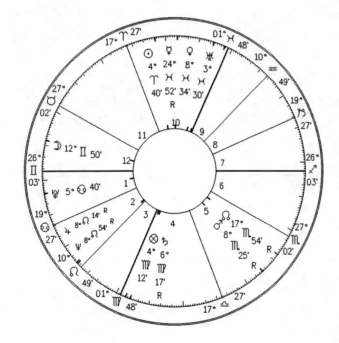

14. EXXON-XON   *Oil International*
Mar. 25, 1920   NYC   10:0:0 AM EST
40N45'00"   22:15:15 ST   74W00'23"

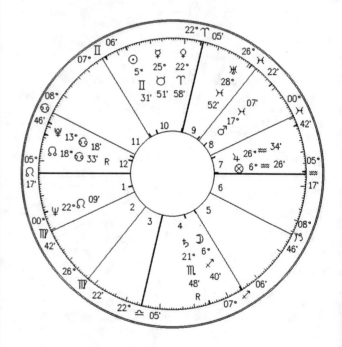

15. GENERAL ELECTRIC-GE   *Electric Equipment*
May 27, 1926   NYC   10:0:0 AM EDT
40N45'00"   1:21:41 ST   74W00'23"

16. GENERAL MOTORS-GM   Auto
Dec. 20, 1916   NYC   10:0:0 AM EST
40N45'00"   15:59:38 ST   74W00'23"

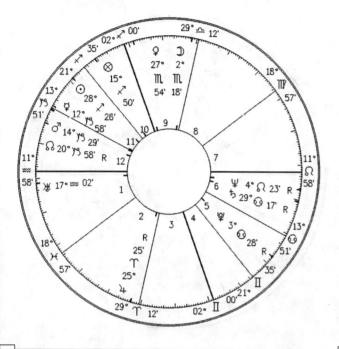

17. GOODYEAR-GT   Auto Parts
Aug. 5, 1927   NYC   10:0:0 AM EDT
40N45'00"   5:56:43 ST   74W00'23"

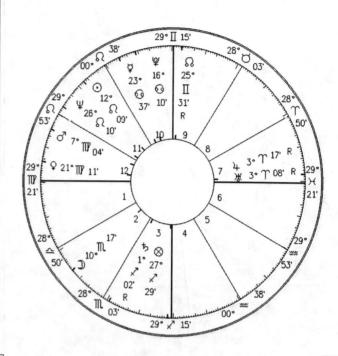

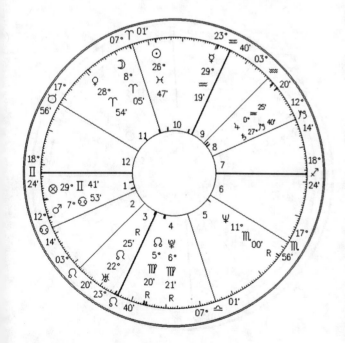

18. HEWLETT PACKARD-HWP   Computers
Mar. 17, 1961   NYC   10:0:0 AM EST
40N45'00"   21:43:59 ST   74W00'23"

19. IBM-IBM* Computers
Feb. 14, 1924   NYC   10:0:0 AM EST
40N45'00"   19:37:40 ST   74W00'23"

20. INTERNATIONAL PAPER-IP   Forest Products
June 23, 1941   NYC   10:0:0 AM EDT
40N45'00"   3:09:35 ST   74W00'23"

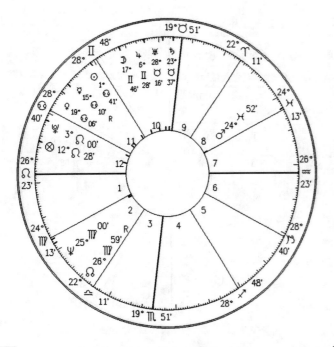

21. J.P. MORGAN-JPM   Banks
Apr. 1, 1969   NYC   10:0:0 AM EST
40N45'00"   22:43:22 ST   74W00'23"

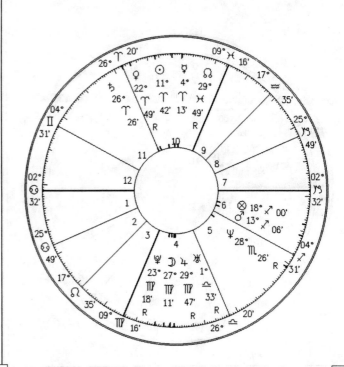

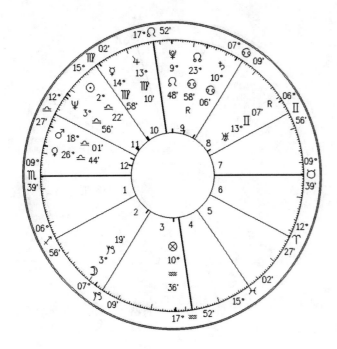

22. JOHNSON & JOHNSON-JNJ   Drugs
Sep. 25, 1944   NYC   10:0:0 AM EWT
40N45'00"   9:21:16 ST   74W00'23"

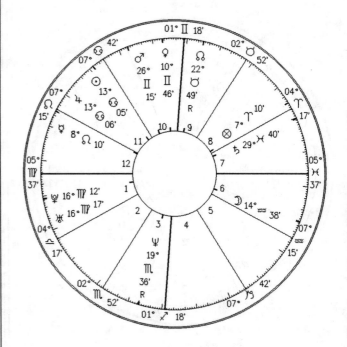

23. MCDONALDS-MCD   Restaurants
July 5, 1966   NYC   10:0:0 AM EDT
40N45'00"   3:56:41 ST   74W00'23"

24. MERCK-MRK *Drugs*
May 15, 1946   NYC   10:0:0 AM EDT
40N45'00"   0:34:59 ST   74W00'23"

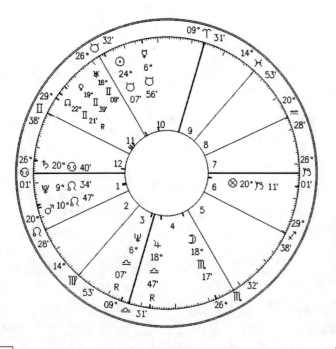

25. MINN. MINING & MAN.-MMM *Misc.*
Jan. 14, 1946   NYC   10:0:0 AM EST
40N45'00"   17:38:43 ST   74W00'23"

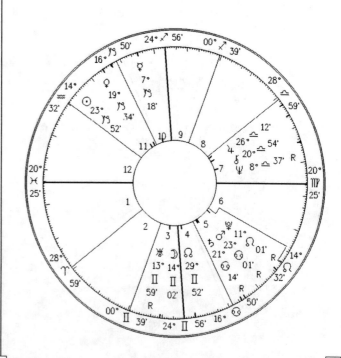

26. PHILIP MORRIS-MO *Tobacco*
Mar. 15, 1923   NYC   10:0:0 AM EST
40N45'00"   21:32:58 ST   74W00'23"

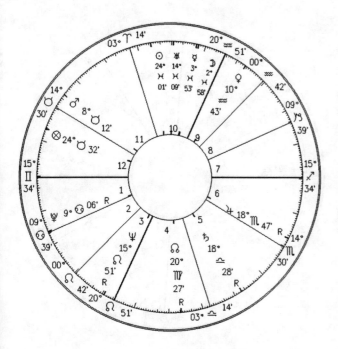

27. PROCTER & GAMBLE-PG *Household Products*
Sep. 12, 1929   NYC   10:0:0 AM EDT
40N45'00"   8:28:34 ST   74W00'23"

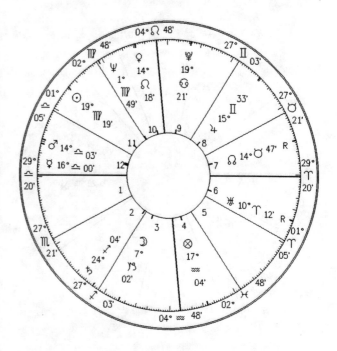

28. SEARS ROEBUCK-S   Retail
Mar. 3, 1910   NYC   10:0:0 AM EST
40N45'00"   20:46:14 ST   74W00'23"

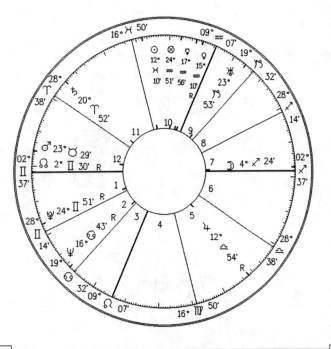

29. TRAVELERS-TRV   Insurance
May 11, 1988   NYC   9:30:0 AM EDT
40N45'00"   23:52:12 ST   74W00'23"

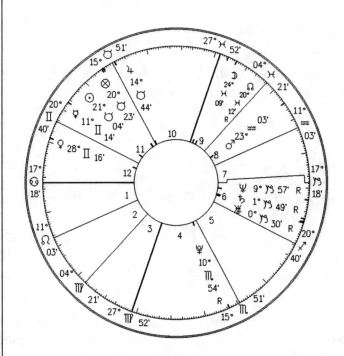

30. UNION CARBIDE-UK   Chemical
Mar. 1, 1926   NYC   10:0:0 AM EST
40N45'00"   20:38:51 ST   74W00'23"

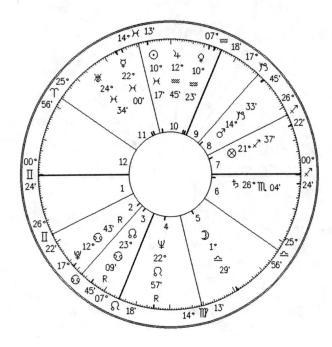

31. UNITED TECHNOLOGIES-UTX   Aerospace
Sep. 5, 1934   NYC   10:0:0 AM EDT
40N45'00"   8:00:08 ST   74W00'23"

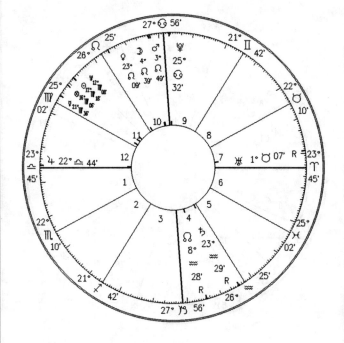

32. WALMART-WMT *Retail*
Aug. 25, 1972   NYC   10:0:0 AM EDT
40N45'00"   7:19:54 ST   74W00'23"

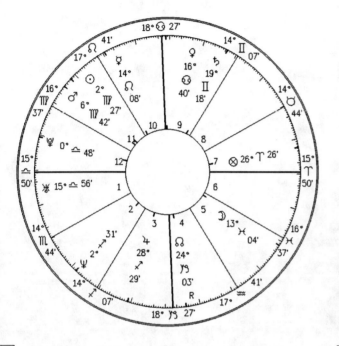

20
DJTA
First Trade Charts

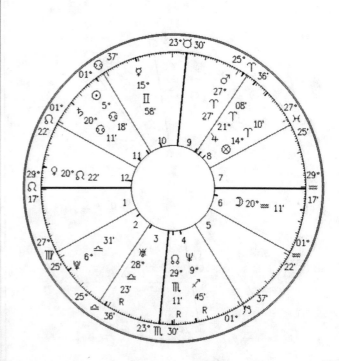

1. AIRBORNE FREIGHT-ABF   Air Freight
June 27, 1975   NYC   10:0:0 AM EDT
40N45'00"   3:24:26 ST   74W00'23"

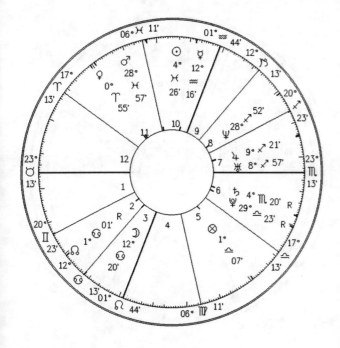

2. ALASKA AIR-ALK   Airlines
Feb. 23, 1983   NYC   10:0:0 AM EST
40N45'00"   20:15:57 ST   74W00'23"

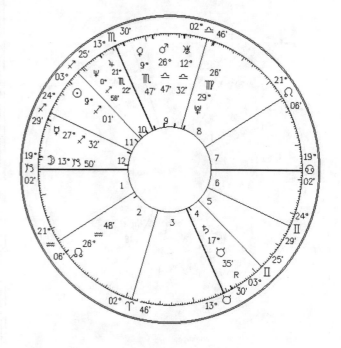

3. ALEXANDER & BALDWIN-ALEX   Shipping
Dec. 1, 1970   NYC   10:00 AM EST
40N45'00   14:44:13 ST   74W00'23

4. AMR-AMR *Airlines*
June 10, 1939   NYC   10:0:0 AM EDT
40N45'00"   2:16:18 ST   74W00'23"

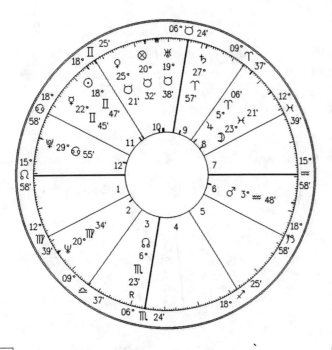

5. BURLINGTON NORTHERN-BNI *Railroad*
Mar. 30, 1970   NYC   10:0:0 AM EST
40N45'00"   22:34:32 ST   74W00'23"

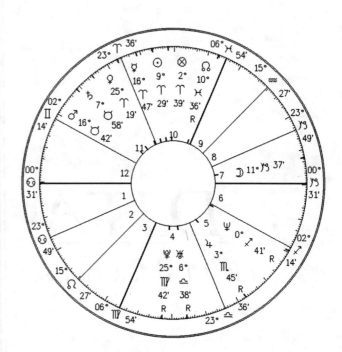

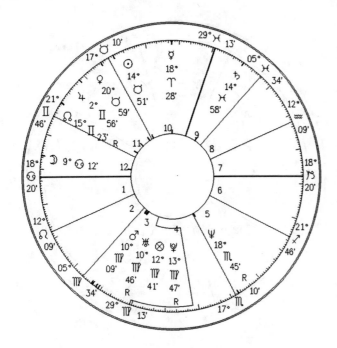

6. CONSOLIDATED FREIGH.-CNF *Trucking*
May 5, 1965   NYC   10:0:0 AM EDT
40N45'00"   23:57:08 ST   74W00'23"

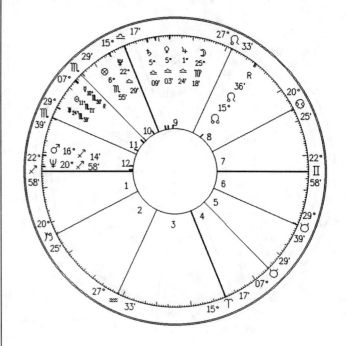

7. CSX CORP.-CSX *Railroad*
Nov. 3, 1980   NYC   10:0:0 AM EST
40N45'00"   12:56:18 ST   74W00'23"

8. DELTA-DAL   Airlines
Apr. 17, 1957   NYC   10:0:0 AM EST
40N45'00"   23:46:05 ST   74W00'23"

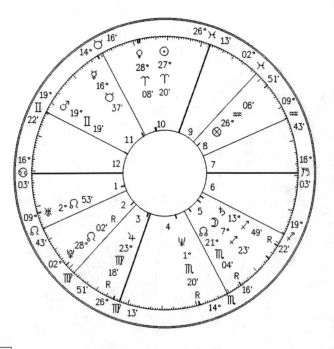

9. FDX CORP-FDX   Air Freight
Dec. 28, 1978   NYC   10:0:0 AM EST
40N45'00"   16:31:06 ST   74W00'23"

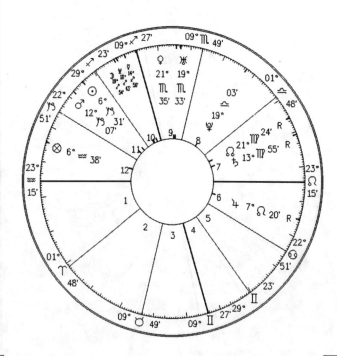

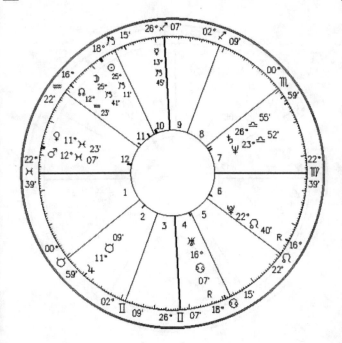

10. GATX-GMT   Railroad
Jan. 15, 1953   NYC   10:00:0 AM EST
40N45'00"   17:43:03 ST   74W00'23"

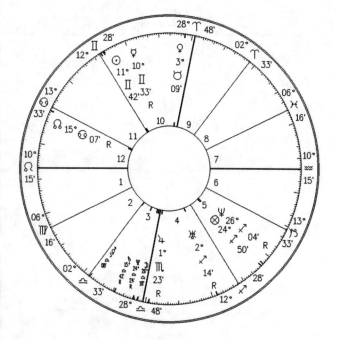

11. NORFOLK & SOUTHERN-NSC   Railroad
June 2, 1982   NYC   10:0:0 AM EDT
40N45'00"   1:47:04 ST   74W00'23"

12 ROADWAY SERVICES-ROAD   Trucking
Feb. 5, 1972   NYC   10:0:0 AM EST
40N45'00"   19:03:40 ST   74W00'23"

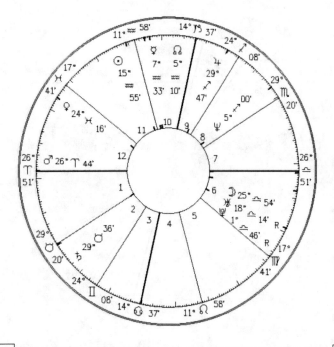

13 RYDER-R   Trucking
Sept. 19, 1960   NYC   10:0:0 AM EDT
40N45'00"   8:58:06 ST   74W00'23"

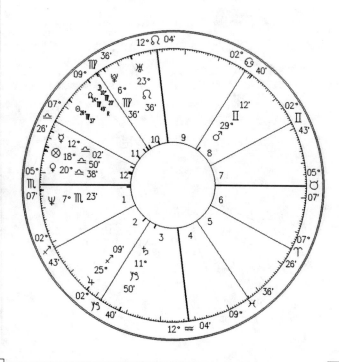

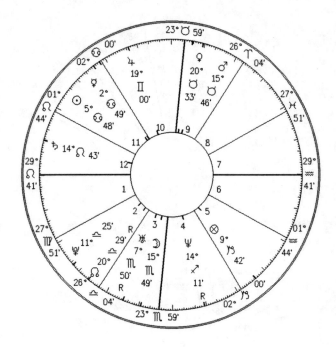

14. SOUTHWEST AIR-LUV   Airlines
June 27, 1977   NYC   10:0:0 AM EDT
40N45'00"   3:26:28 ST   74W00'23"

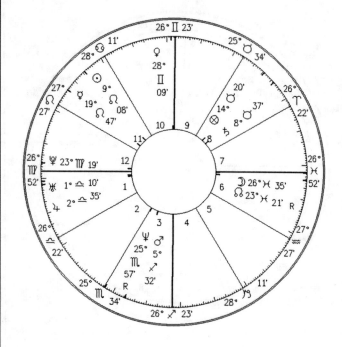

15. UAL CORP.-UAL   Airlines
Aug. 1, 1969   NYC   10:0:0 AM EDT
40N45'00"   5:44:12 ST   74W00'23"

16. UNION PACIFIC-UNP   Railroad
June 20, 1969   NYC   10:0:0 AM EDT
40N45'00"   2:58:37 ST   74W00'23"

18. US AIRWAYS GROUP-U   Airlines
Feb. 1, 1983   NYC   10:0:0 AM EST
40N45'00"   18:49:00 ST   74W00'23"

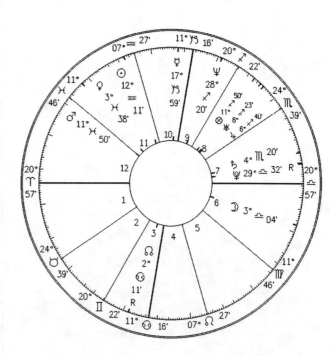

18. US FREIGHTWAYS-USFC   Trucking
Feb. 1 3, 1992   NYC   9:30:0 AM EST
40N45'00"   16:56:40 ST   74W00'23"

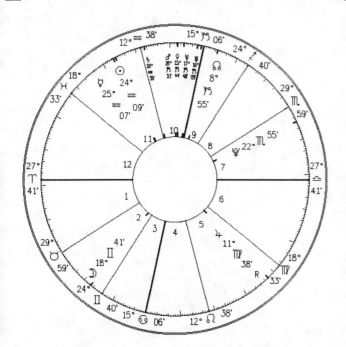

19. XTRA-XTR   Trucking
Jan. 3, 1977   NYC   10:0:0 AM EST
40N45'00"   16:56:40 ST   74W00'23"

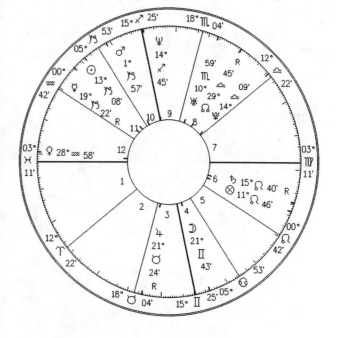

20. YELLOW FREIGHT-YELL   *Trucking*
Feb. 5, 1972   NYC   10:0:0 AM EST
40N45'00"   19:03:40 ST   74W00'23"

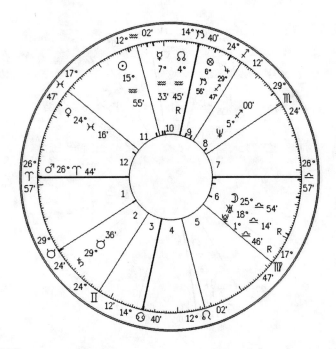

15
DJUA
First Trade Charts

1. AMERICAN ELEC. POWER-AEP *Utility*
Sep. 1, 1949   NYC   10:0:0 AM EDT
40N45'00"   7:45:35 ST 74W00'23"

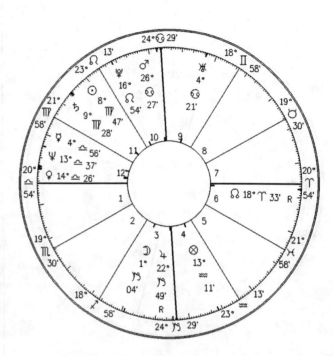

2. COLUMBIA GAS-CG *Utility*
May 1, 1948   NYC   10:0:0 AM EDT
40N45'00"   23:41:49 ST   74W00'23"

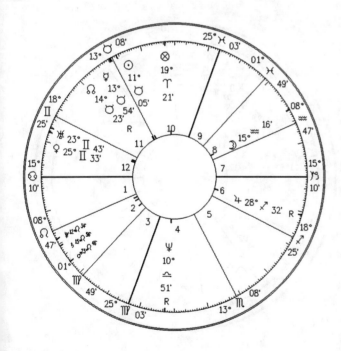

3. CONSOLIDATED EDISON-ED *Utility*
June 21, 1948   NYC   10:0:0 AM EDT
40N45'00"   3:02:40 ST   74W00'23"

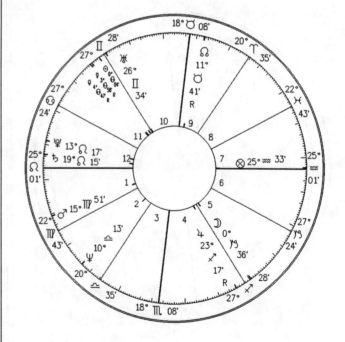

4. CONSOLIDATED NAT.GAS-CNG *Utility*
Oct. 27, 1943   NYC   10:0:0 AM EWT
40N45'00"   11:24:13 ST   74W00'23"

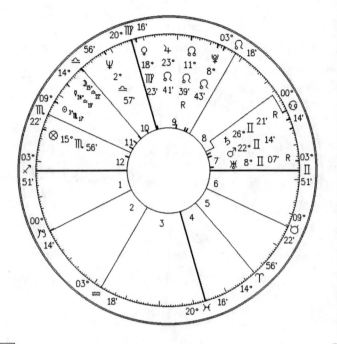

5. DUKE POWER-DUK *Utility*
June 16, 1964   NYC   10:0:0 AM EDT
40N45'00"   2:43:29 ST   74W00'23"

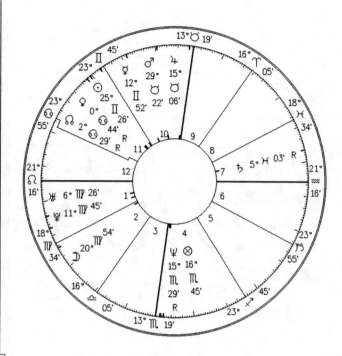

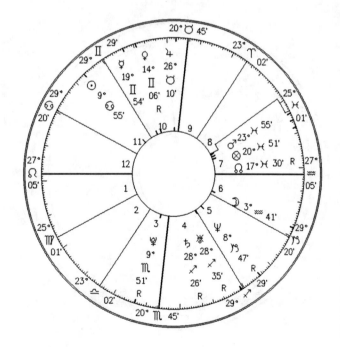

6. EDISON INTERNAT.-EIX *Utility*
July 1, 1988   NYC   9:30:0 AM EDT
40N45'00"   3:13:16 ST   74W00'23"

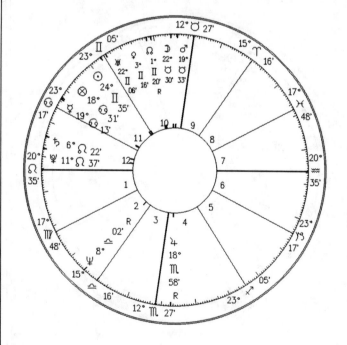

7. ENRON-ENE *Utility*
June 16, 1947   NYC   10:0:0 AM EDT
40N45'00"   2:40:00 ST   74W00'23"

8. HOUSTON INDUSTRIES-HOU   *Utility*
Jan. 17, 1977   NYC   10:0:0 AM EST
40N45'00"   17:51:38 ST   74W00'23"

9. PECO ENERGY-PE   *Utility*
July 15, 1949   NYC   10:0:0 AM EDT
40N45'00"   4:36:22 ST   74W00'23"

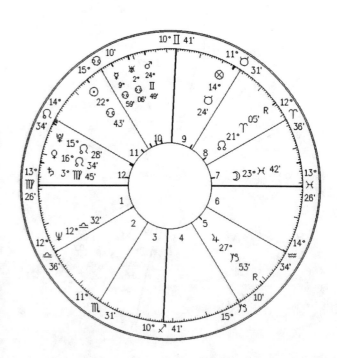

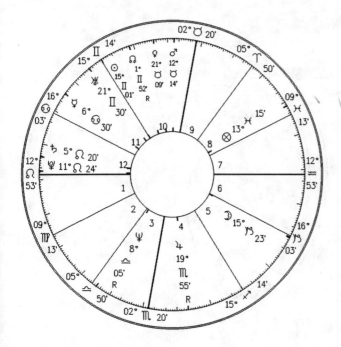

10. PG & E CORP.-PCG   *Utility*
June 6, 1947   NYC   10:0:0 AM EDT
40N45'00"   2:00:34 ST   74W00'23"

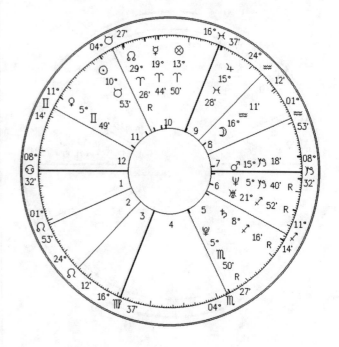

11. PUBLIC SERVICE ENT.-PEG   *Utility*
May 1, 1986   NYC   9:30:0 AM EDT
40N45'00"   23:10:43 ST   74W00'23"

12. SOUTHERN CO.-SO   *Utility*
Oct. 4, 1949   NYC   10:0:0 AM EST
40N45'00"   10:55:53 ST   74W00'23"

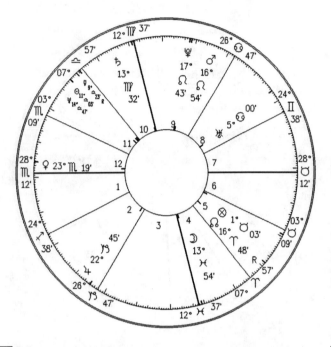

13. TEXAS UTILITIES-TXU   *Utility*
Feb. 13, 1951   NYC   10:0:0 AM EST
40N45'00"   19:35:21 ST   74W00'23"

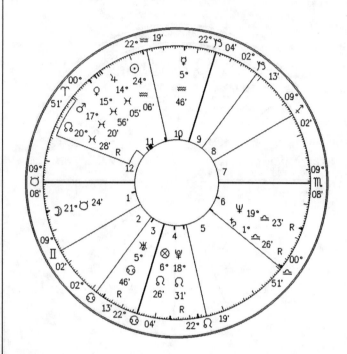

14. UNICOM CORP.-UCM   *Utility*
Nov. 5, 1952   NYC   10:0:0 AM EST
40N45'00"   13:03:07 ST   74W00'23"

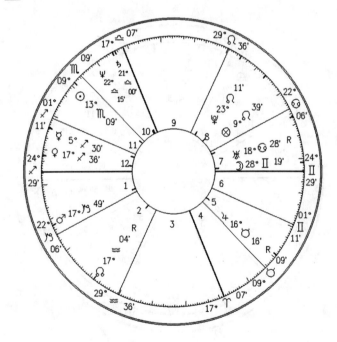

15. WILLIAMS COS.-WMB   *Utility*
June 2, 1987   NYC   9:30:0 AM EDT
40N45'00"   1:15:55 ST   74W00'23"

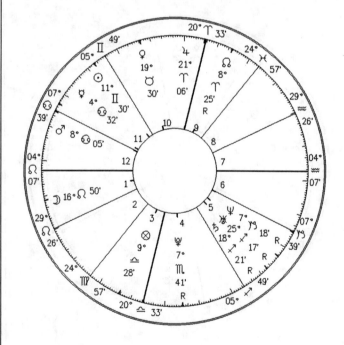

382 NYSE

First Trade Charts

1. ABBOTT LABS-ABT **Medical Supplies**
Mar.1, 1937   NYC   10:0:0 AM EST
40N45'00   20:40:10 ST   74W00'23

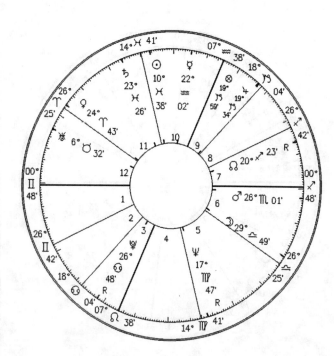

2. ACUSON-ACN **Medical Equip.**
Oct. 14, 1988   NYC   9:30 AM EDT
40N45'00   10:07:27 ST   74W00'23

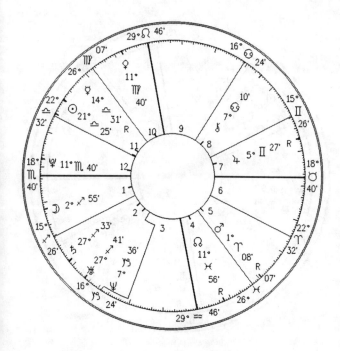

3. ADVANCED MICRO DEV.-AMD **Semiconductors**
Oct. 15, 1979   NYC   10:00 AM EDT
40N45'00   10:38:14 ST   74W00'23

4. AETNA-AET *Insurance*
Sep. 24, 1968 NYC 10:00 AM EDT
40N45'00 9:18:03 ST 74W00'23"

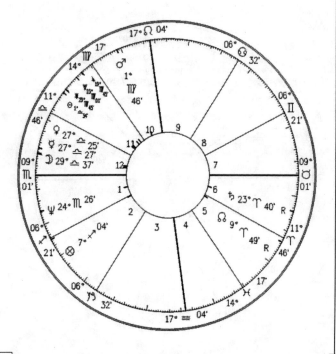

5. AHMANSON-AHM *Insurance*
May 23, 1985 NYC 10:00 AM EDT
40N45'00 1:08:43 ST 74W00'23

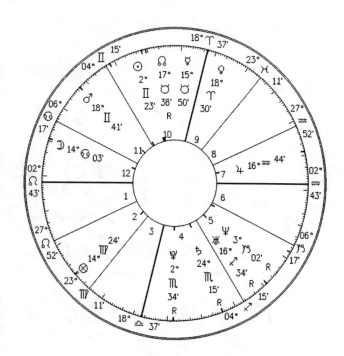

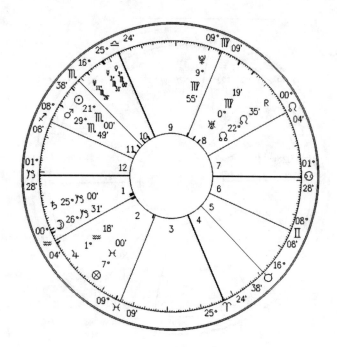

6. AIR PRODUCTS-APD *Chemicals*
Nov. 13, 1961 NYC 10:00 AM EST
40N45'00 13:34:09 ST 74W00'23

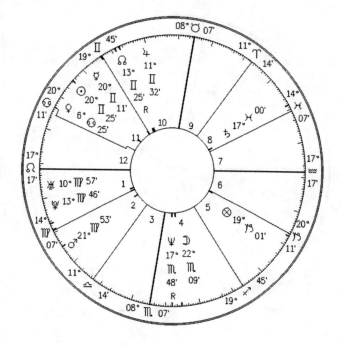

7. ALBERTO CULVER-ACV *Cosmetics*
June 11, 1965 NYC 10:00 AM EDT
40N45'00 2:23:00 ST 74W00'23

8. ALBERTSONS-ABS *Retail Food*
Feb. 10, 1970   NYC   10:00 AM EST
40N45'00   19:25:17 ST   74W00'23

9. ALCAN-AL *Aluminum*
May31, 1950   NYC   10:00 AM EDT
40N45'00   1:38:12 ST   74W00'23

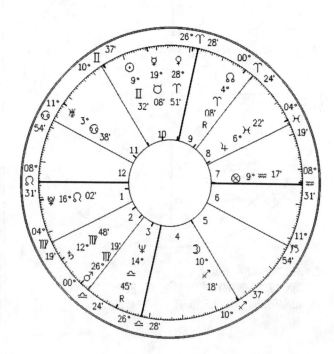

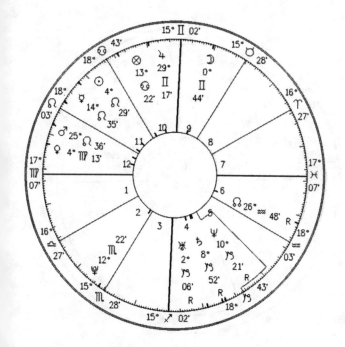

10. ALLERGAN-AGN *Drugs*
July 27, 1989   NYC   9:30 AM EDT
40N45'00   4:55:01 ST   74W00'23

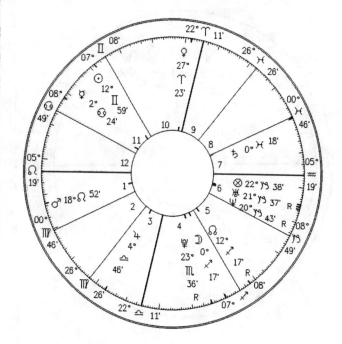

11. ALLSTATE-ALL *Insurance*
June 3, 1993   NYC   9:30 AM EDT
40N45'00"   1:22:01 ST   74W00'23

12. ALLTEL-AT *Telephone*
Jan. 18, 1965 NYC   10:00 AM EST
40N45'00   17:55:26 ST   74W00'23

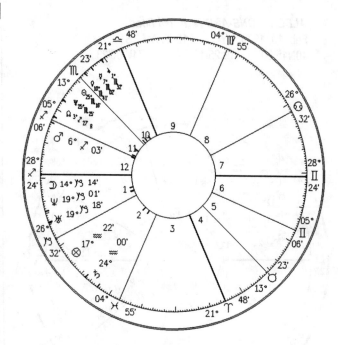

13. ALUMAX-AMX *Metals*
Nov. 17, 1993 NYC   9:30 AM EST
40N45'00"   13:20:36 ST   74W00'23

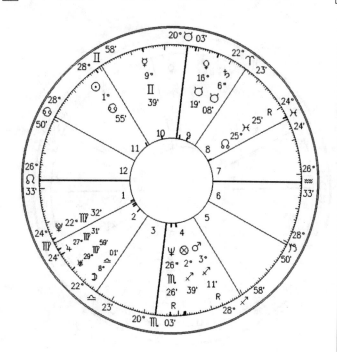

14. AMERADA HESS-AHC *Oil*
June 23, 1969 NYC   10:00 AM EDT
40N45'00   3:10:27 ST   74W00'23

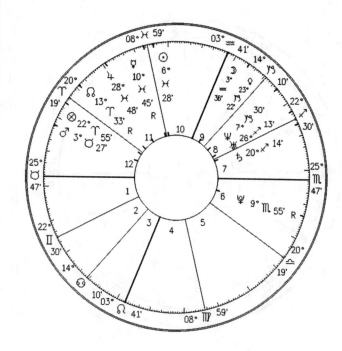

15. AMERICAN BARRICK-ABX *Gold*
Feb. 25, 1987 NYC   10:00 AM EST
40N45'00   20:23:58 ST   74W00'23

16. AMERICAN GENERAL-AGC *Insurance*
July 1, 1980   NYC   10:00 AM EDT
40N45'00   3:43:18 ST   74W00'23

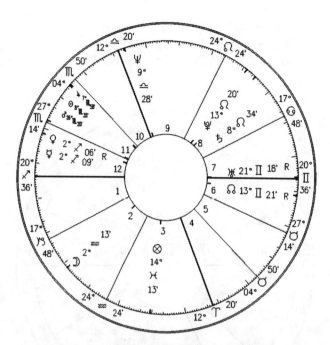

17. AMERICAN HOME PRODS.-AHP   **Drugs**
Nov. 1, 1946   NYC   10:00 AM EST
40N45'00   12:45:23 ST   74W00'23

18. AMERICAN INT. GROUP-AIG   *Insurance*
Oct. 10, 1984 NYC   10:00 AM EDT
40N45'00   10:21:38 ST   74W00'23

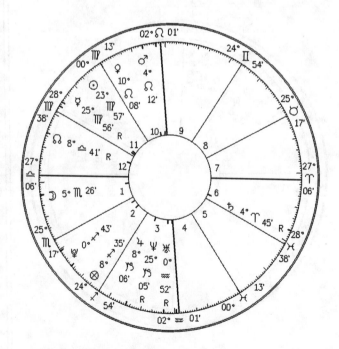

19. AMERICAN ONLINE – AOL   *Internet*
Sept 16, 1996 NYC   9:30 AM EDT
40N45'00   8:17:06 ST   74W00'23

20. AMERICAN STORES-ASC   *Retail*
Mar. 15, 1971   NYC   10:00 AM EST
40N45'00   21:34:26 ST   74W00'23

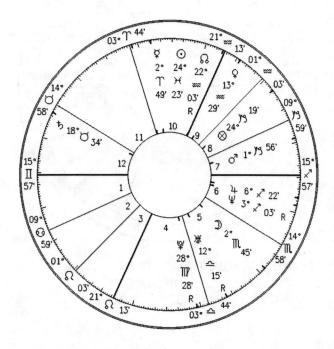

21. AMERICAN WASTE SERV.-AW *Waste Management*
Oct. 4, 1990   NYC   9:30 AM EDT
40N45'00   9:26:07 ST   74W00'23

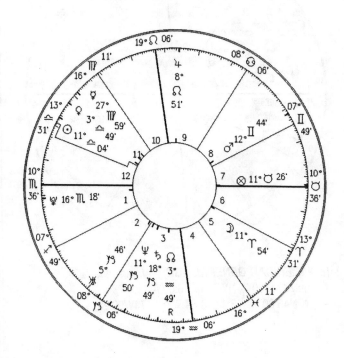

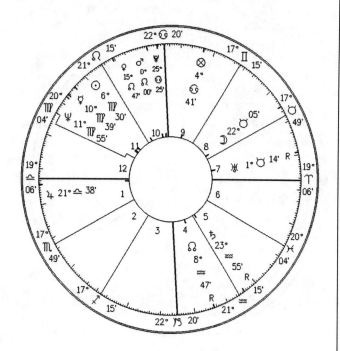

22. AMOCO-AN   *Oil*
Aug. 30, 1934   NYC   10:00 AM EDT
40N45'00   7:36:28 ST   74W00'23

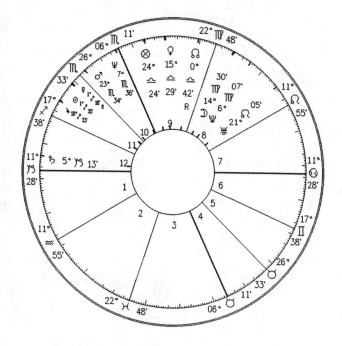

23. AMP-AMP   *Electric Components*
Nov. 24, 1959   NYC   10:00 AM EST
40N45'00   14:15:29 ST   74W00'23

24. ANADARKO PET.-APC Oil
Oct. 1, 1986 NYC 9:30 AM EDT
40N45'00 9:14:09 ST 74W00'23

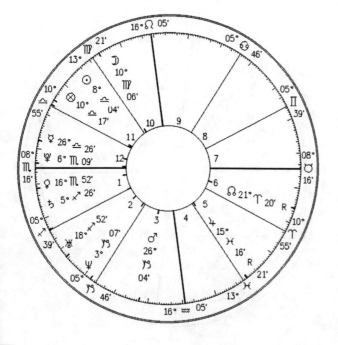

25. ANALOG DEVICES-ADI Semiconductors
Apr. 3, 1979 NYC 10:00 AM EST
40N45'00 22:49:24 ST 74W00'23

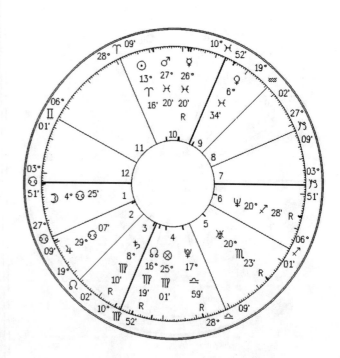

26. ANHEUSER BUSCH-BUD Beverages
Apr. 18, 1980 NYC 10:00 AM EST
40N45'00 23:51:43 ST 74W00'23

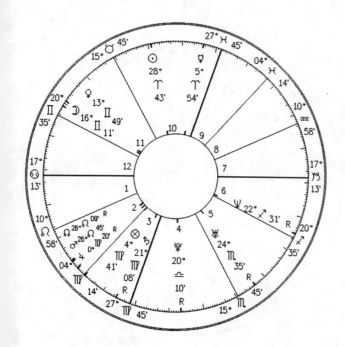

27. APACHE-APA Oil
Feb. 24, 1981 NYC 10:00 AM EST
40N45'00 20:21:48 ST 74W00'23

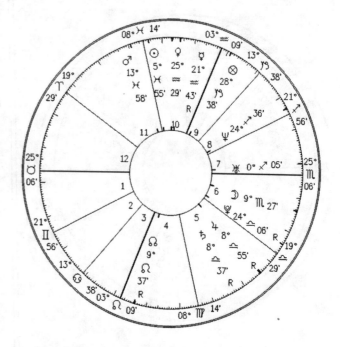

28. ARCHER DANIELS-ADM   *Food*
Dec. 24, 1924   NYC   10:00 AM EST
40N45'00   16:15:39 ST   74W00'23

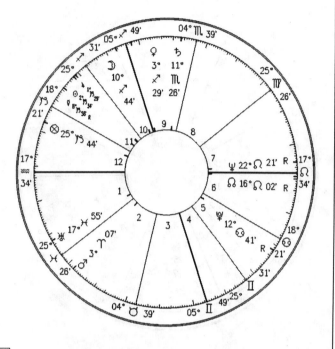

29. ARCO CHEMICAL-RCM   *Chemicals*
Oct. 5, 1987   NYC   9:30 AM EDT
40N45'00   9:28:58 ST   74W00'23

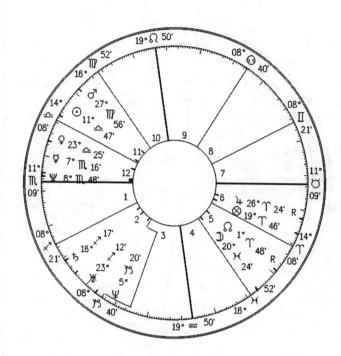

30. ASA-ASA   *Gold*
Dec. 8, 1958   NYC   10:00 AM EST
40N45'00   15:11:38 ST   74W00'23

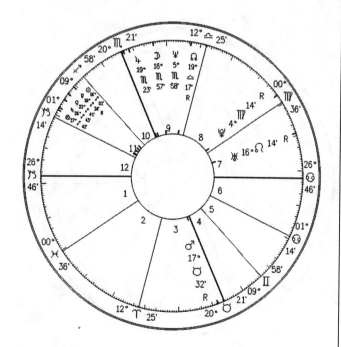

31. ASARCO-AR *Metals*
Feb. 11, 1916   NYC   10:00 AM EST
40N45'00   19:25:36 ST   74W00'23

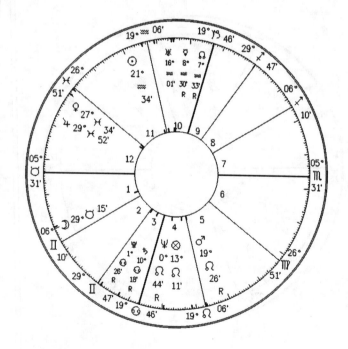

32. ASHLAND OIL-ASH *Oil*
May 8, 1950   NYC   10:00 AM EST
40N45'00   0:07:19 ST   74W00'23

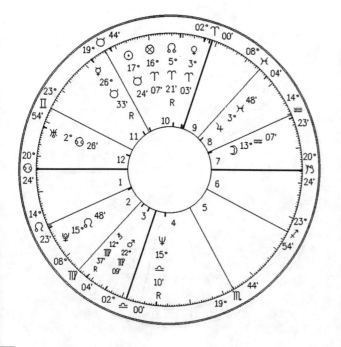

33. ATLANTIC RICHFIELD-ARC *Oil*
Feb. 13, 1920 NYC   10:00 AM EST
40N45'00   19:33:36 ST   74W00'23

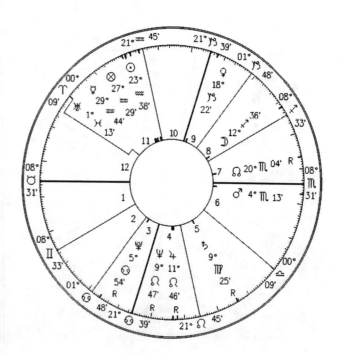

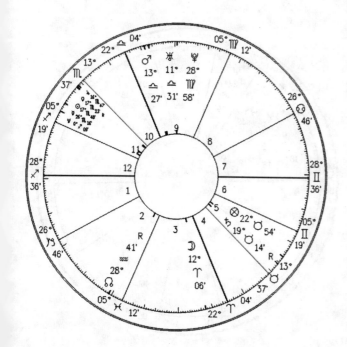

34. AUTO. DATA PROCESS.-AUD *Software*
Nov. 10, 1970 NYC   10:00 AM EST
40N45'00   13:21:37 ST   74W00'23

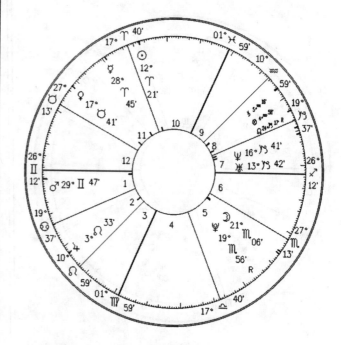

35. AUTOZONE-AZO *Retail*
Apr.2, 1991   NYC   9:30 AM EST
40N45'00   22:15:56 ST   74W00'23

36. AVERY-DENNISON-AVY **Packaging**
Oct. 17, 1990   NYC   9:30 AM EDT
40N45'00   10:17:22 ST   74W00'23

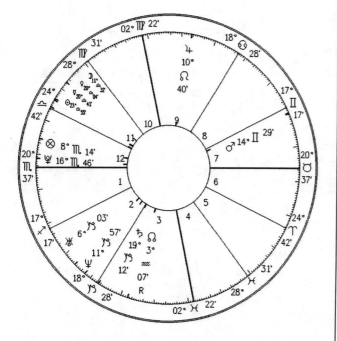

37. AVNET-AVT **Connectors**
Dec. 30, 1960   NYC   10:00 AM EST
40N45'00   16:40:11 ST   74W00'23

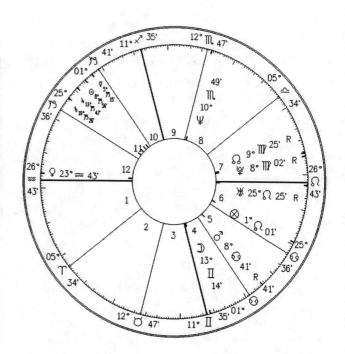

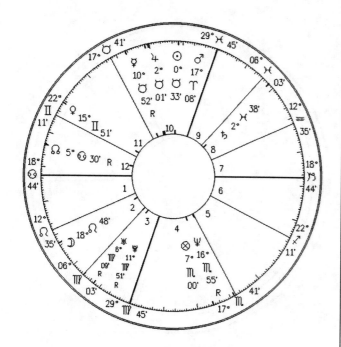

38. AVON PRODUCTS-AVP **Cosmetics**
Apr. 20, 1964   NYC   10:00 AM EST
40N45'00   23:59:07 ST   74W00'23

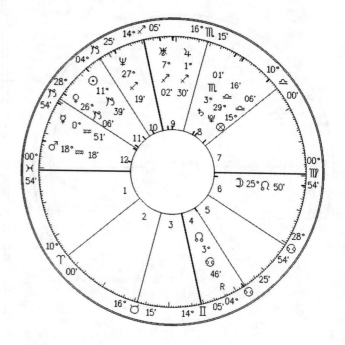

39. BABY BELL COS. **Telephone**
Jan. 2, 1983   NYC   10:00 AM EST
40N45'00   16:50:56 ST   74W00'23

40. BAKER HUGHES-BHI *Oil & Gas*
Apr. 6, 1987   NYC   9:30 AM EDT
40N45'00   21:31:25 ST   74W00'23

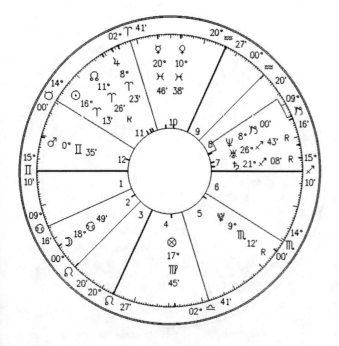

41. BALL CORP.-BLL   *Packaging*
Dec. 17, 1973 NYC   10:00 AM EST
40N45'00   15:48:34 ST   74W00'23

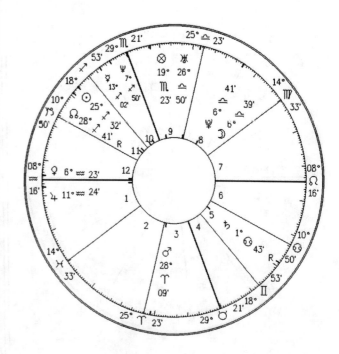

42. BANC ONE-ONE   *Banks*
Sep. 29, 1983 NYC   9:30 AM EDT
40N45'00   9:05:12 ST   74W00'23

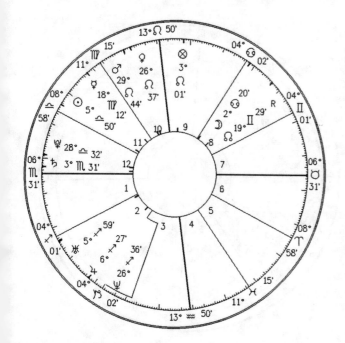

43. BANK OF BOSTON-BKB   *Banks*
Jan. 6, 1971   NYC   10:00 AM EST
40N45'00   17:06:21 ST   74W00'23

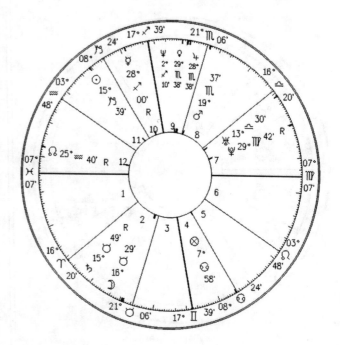

44. BANKAMERICA-BAC Banks
June 28, 1976 NYC   10:00 AM EDT
40N45'00   3:31:21 ST   74W00'23

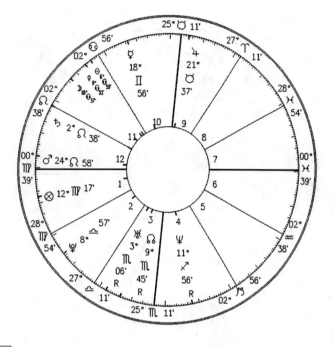

45. BANKERS TRUST-BT Banks
May 16, 1969 NYC   10:00 AM EDT
40N45'00   0:40:37 ST   74W00'23

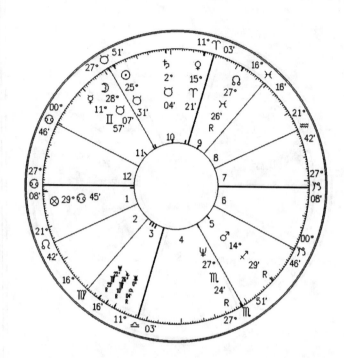

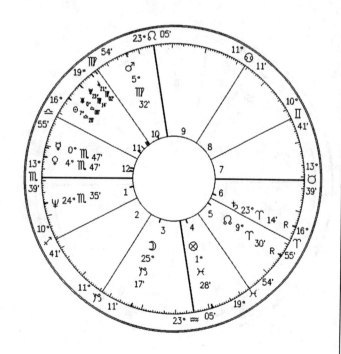

46. BARD-BCR Drugs
Sep. 30, 1968 NYC   10:00 AM EDT
40N45'00   9:41:43 ST   74W00'23

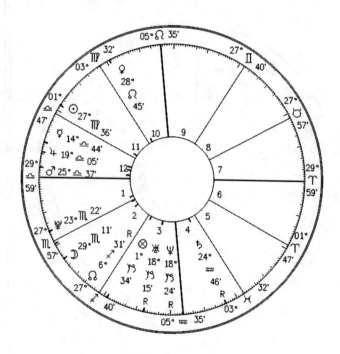

47. BARNES & NOBLE-BKS   Retail
Sep. 20, 1993 NYC   9:30 AM EDT
40N45'00"   8:31:46 ST   74W00'23

48. BARNETT BANKS- BBI   **Banks**
Dec. 17, 1979   NYC   10:00 AM EST
40N45'00   15:46:47 ST   74W00'23

49. BAXTER TRAVENOL-BAX   *Medical Supplies*
May 15, 1961   NYC   10:00 AM EDT
40N45'00   0:36:26 ST   74W00'23

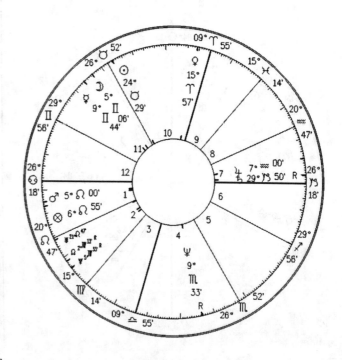

50. BEAR STEARNS-BSC   **Brokerage**
Oct. 29, 1985   NYC   9:30:00 EST
40N45'00   14:48:21 ST   74W00'23

51. BECTON DICKINSON-BDX   *Medical Supplies*
Sep. 25, 1963   NYC   10:00 AM EDT
40N45'00   9:18:53 ST   74W00'23

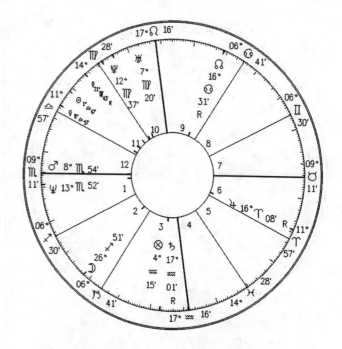

52. BENEFICIAL CORP.-BNL   *Finance*
Aug. 10, 1933   NYC   10:00 AM EDT
40N45'00   6:18:35 ST   74W00'23

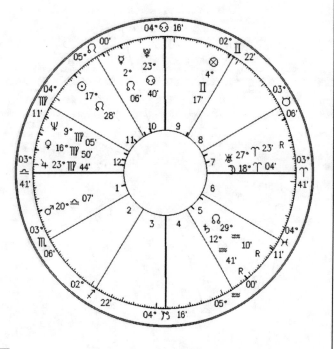

53. BEST BUY-BBY   *Retail*
July 20, 1987   NYC   9:30 AM EDT
40N45'00   4:25:24 ST   74W00'23

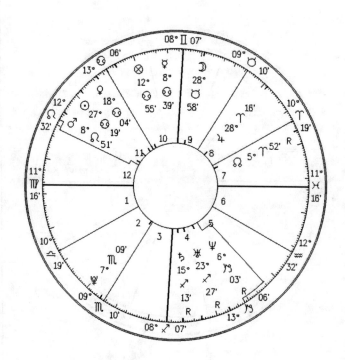

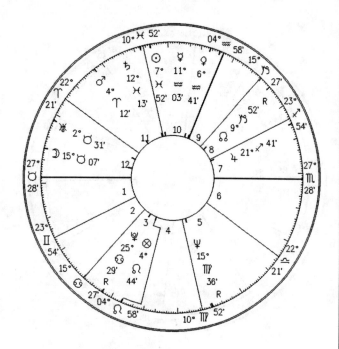

54. BETHLEHEM STEEL-BS   *Steel*
Feb. 27, 1936   NYC   10:00 AM EST
40N45'00   20:29:18 ST   74W00'23

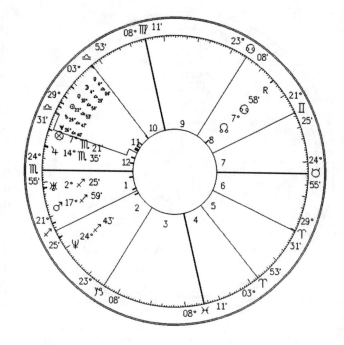

55. BEVERLY ENTERPRISES-BEV   *Real Estate*
Oct. 15, 1982   NYC   10:00 AM EDT
40N45'00   10:39:19 ST   74W00'23

56. BLACK & DECKER-BDK Home Furn., Appl.
Nov. 9, 1936   NYC   10:00 AM EST
40N45'00   13:18:36 ST   74W00'23

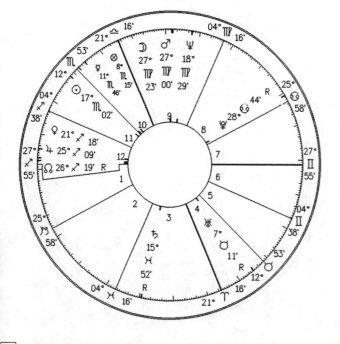

57. BOISE CASCADE-BCC Paper, Forest Prod.
June 2, 1965   NYC   10:00 AM EDT
40N45'00   1:47:31 ST   74W00'23

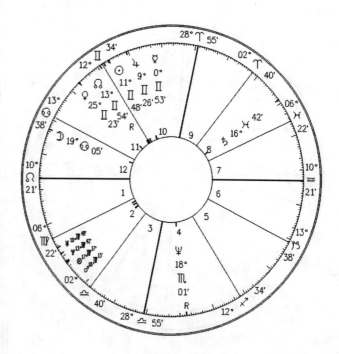

58. BOSTON SCIENTIFIC-BSX Medical Equip.
May 19, 1992   NYC   9:30 AM EDT
40N45'00   0:24:04 ST   74W00'23

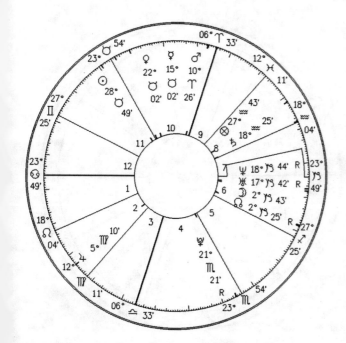

59. BRIGGS & STRATTON-BGG Industrial
July 5, 1929   NYC   10:00 AM EDT
40N45'00   3:56:31 ST   74W00'23

60. BRISTOL MYERS-BMY **Drugs**
Sep. 8, 1933 NYC 10:00 AM EDT
40N45'00 8:12:55 ST 74W00'23

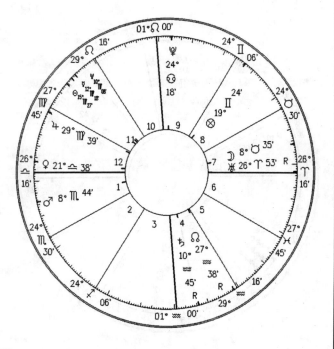

61. BRITISH PETROLEUM-BP **Oil**
Mar. 23, 1970 NYC 10:00 AM EST
40N45'00 22:06:44 ST 74W00'23

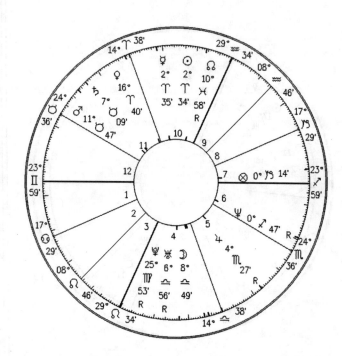

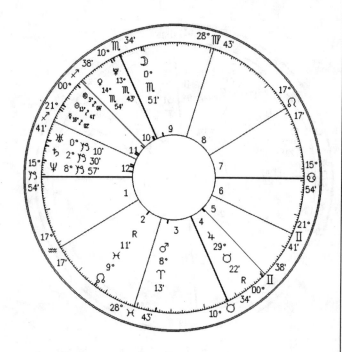

62. BRITISH STEEL –BST Steel
Dec. 5, 1988 NYC 9:30 AM EST
40N45'00 14:32:37 ST 74W00'23

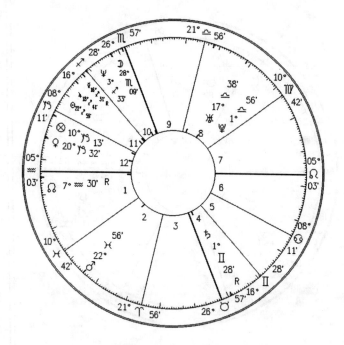

63. BROWNING FERRIS-BFI **Waste Mgmt.**
Dec. 15, 1971 NYC 10:00 AM EST
40N45'00 15:38:39 ST 74W00'23

64. BRUNSWICK-BC *Recreation*
Jan. 15, 1925 NYC 10:00 AM EST
40N45'00 17:42:23 ST 74W00'23

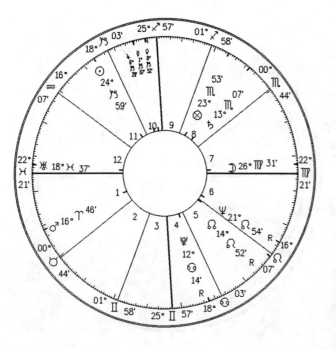

65. CABLE & WIRELESS-CWP *Telecom.*
Sep. 27, 1989 NYC 9:30 AM EDT
40N45'00 8:59:28 ST 74W00'23

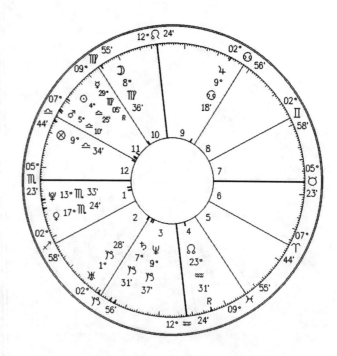

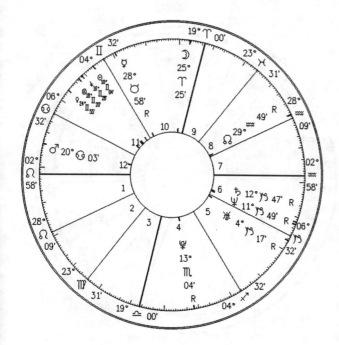

66. CABLETRON-CS *Computer Net.*
Aug. 31, 1989 NYC 9:30 AM EDT
40N45'00 7:13:01 ST 74W00'23

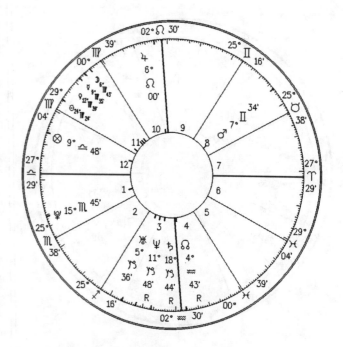

67. CADENCE DESIGN-CDN *Software*
Sep. 17, 1990 NYC 9:30 AM EDT
40N45'00 8:19:05 ST 74W00'23

68. CALGON-CCC   **Chemicals**
June 21, 1991   NYC   9:30 AM EDT
40N45'00   2:31:11 ST   74W00'23

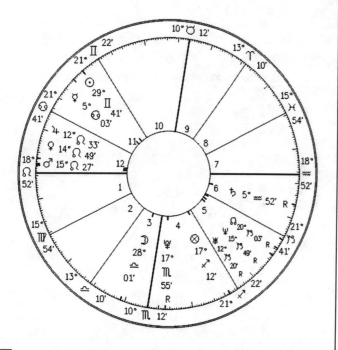

69. CALLOWAY GOLF-ELY **Recreation**
Feb. 27, 1992   NYC   9:30 AM EST
40N45'00   20:00:56 ST   74W00'23

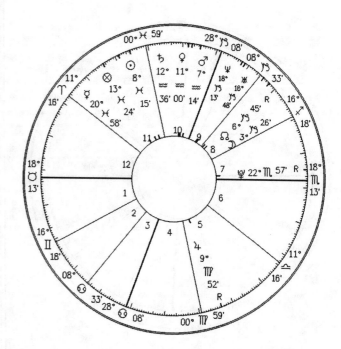

70. CAMPBELL RED LAKE-CCH   **Gold**
Apr. 11, 1955   NYC   10:00 AM EST
40N45'00   23:20:24 ST   74W00'23

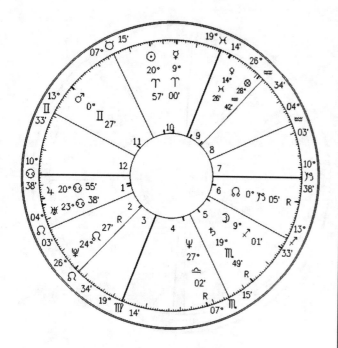

71. CAMPBELL SOUP-CPB   **Food**
Dec. 13, 1954   NYC   10:00 AM EST
40N45'00   15:31:14 ST   74W00'23

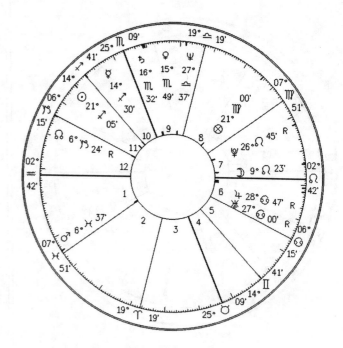

72. CARTER WALLACE-CAR   **Drugs**
Oct. 22, 1957   NYC   10:00 AM EDT
40N45'00   11:07:08 ST   74W00'23

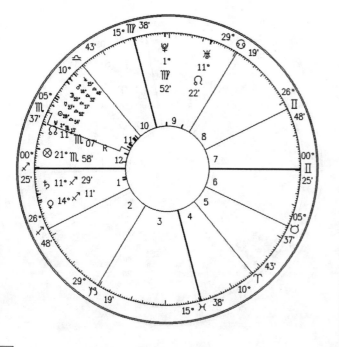

73. CENTEX-CTX   **Homebuilding**
Dec. 28, 1971   NYC   10:00 AM EST
40N45'00   16:29:54 ST   74W00'23

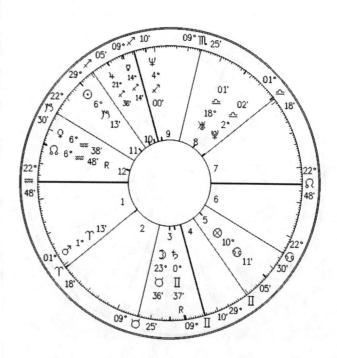

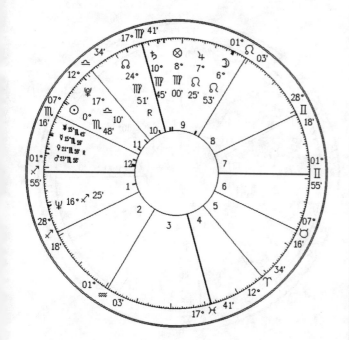

74. CENTURY TELEPHONE-CTL   **Telephone**
Oct. 24, 1978   NYC   10:00 AM EDT
40N45'00   11:14:40 ST   74W00'23

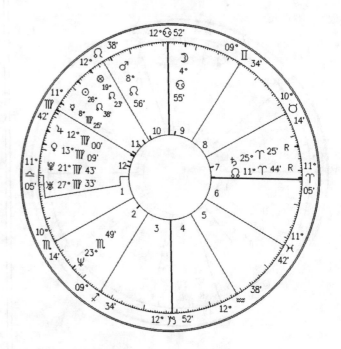

75. CERIDIAN-CEN   **Computer Ser**
Aug. 19, 1968   NYC   10:00 AM EST
40N45'00   6:55:55 ST   74W00'23

76. CHAMPION INT.-CHA **Paper, Forest Prod.**
Nov. 28, 1940 NYC   10:00 AM EST
40N45'00   14:33:38 ST   74W00'23

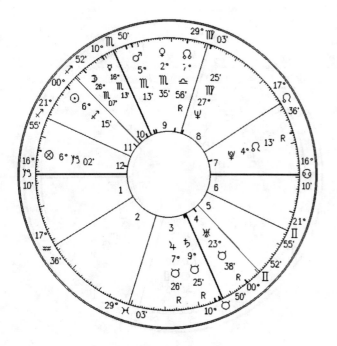

77. CHASE MANHATTAN-CMB **Banks**
June 5, 1969 NYC   10:00 AM EDT
40N45'00   1:59:29 ST   74W00'23

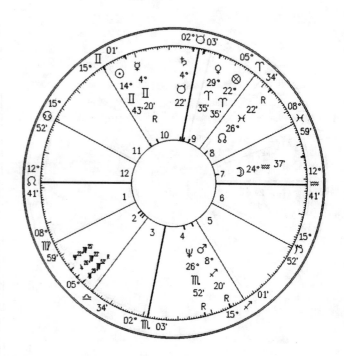

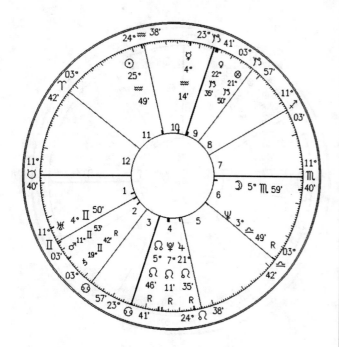

78. CHESAPEAKE-CSK **Paper, Forest Prod.**
Feb. 15, 1944 NYC   10:00 AM EST
40N45'00   19:42:14 ST   74W00'23

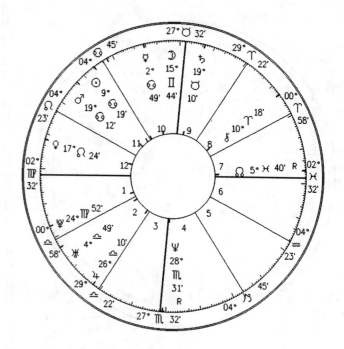

79. CHIQUITA BRANDS-CQB **Food**
July 1, 1970   NYC   10:00 AM EDT
40N45'00   3:41:02 ST   74W00'23

80. CHRYSLER-C   **Autos**
July 7, 1925   NYC   10:00 AM EDT
40N45'00   4:04:17 ST   74W00'23

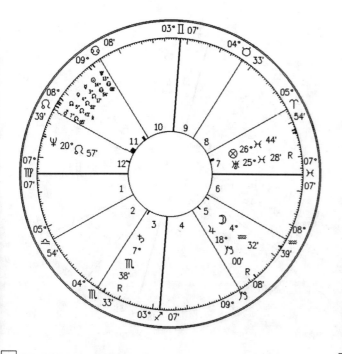

81. CHUBB-CB   **Insurance**
Feb. 29, 1984   NYC   10:00 AM EST
40N45'00   20:38:39 ST   74W00'23

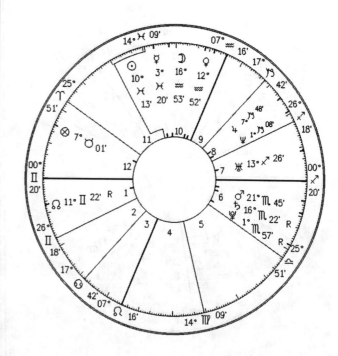

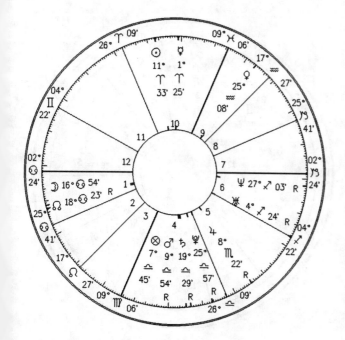

82. CIGNA-CI   **Insurance**
Apr. 1, 1982   NYC   10:00 AM EST
40N45'00   22:42:47 ST   74W00'23

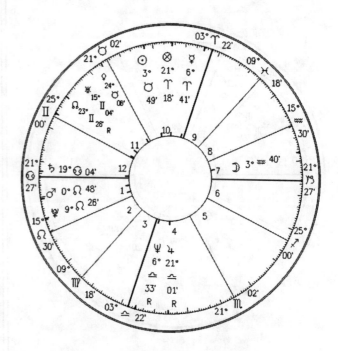

83. CINCINNATI MILACRON-CMZ   **Machinery**
Apr. 24, 1946   NYC   10:00 AM EST
40N45'00   0:12:21 ST   74W00'23

84. CIRCUIT CITY-CC   **Retail**
June 21, 1984   NYC   9:30 AM EDT
40N45'00"   2:33:42 ST   74W00'23

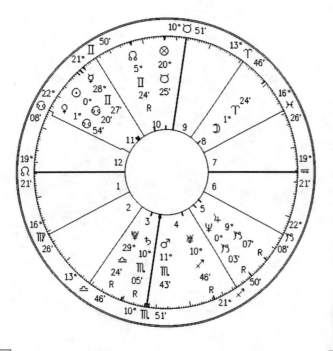

85. CIRCUS CIRCUS-CIR   **Gambling**
Oct. 25, 1983   NYC   10:00 AM EDT
40N45'00   11:17:47 ST   74W00'23

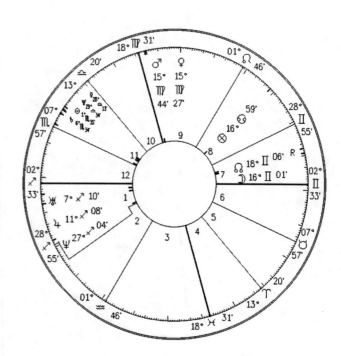

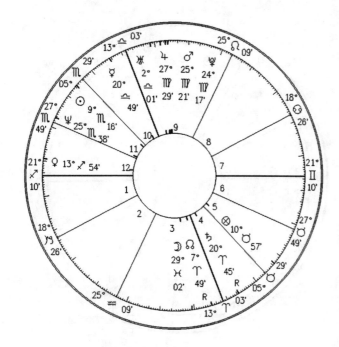

86. CITICORP-CCI   **Banks**
Nov. 1, 1968   NYC   10:00 AM EST
40N45'00   12:48:02 ST   74W00'23

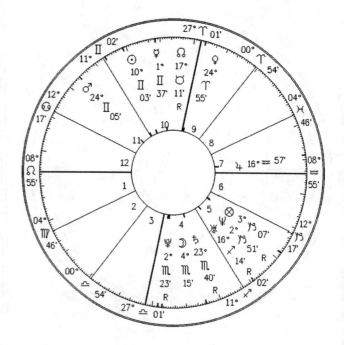

87. CLAIRES STORES-CLE   **Retail**
May 31, 1985   NYC   10:00 AM EDT
40N45'00   1:40:15 ST   74W00'23

88. CLAYTON HOMES-CMH **Homebuilding**
Dec. 19, 1984 NYC 10:00 AM EST
40N45'00 15:57:47 ST 74W00'23

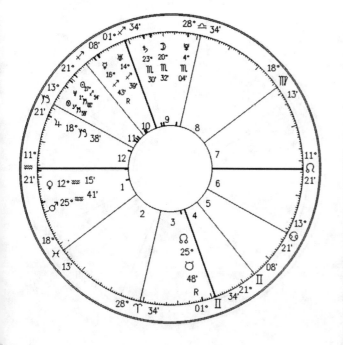

89. CLOROX-CLX **Household Prod.**
Oct. 1, 1968 NYC 10:00 AM EDT
40N45'00 9:45:39 ST 74W00'23

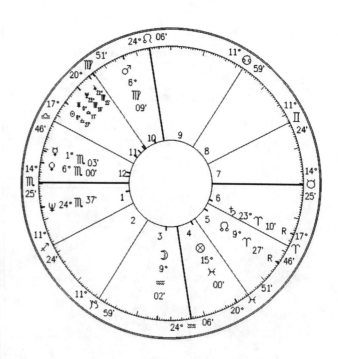

90. COCA COLA ENT.-CCE **Beverage**
Nov. 21, 1986 NYC 9:30 AM EST
40N45'00 13:35:24 ST 74W00'23

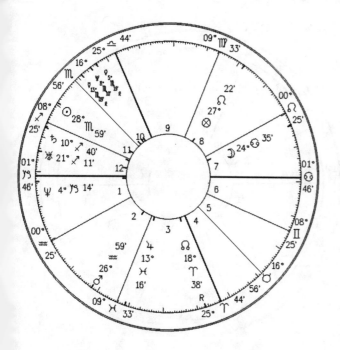

91. COLGATE-CL Household Prod.
Jan. 9, 1951 NYC 10:00 AM EST
40N45'00 17:17:33 ST 74W00'23

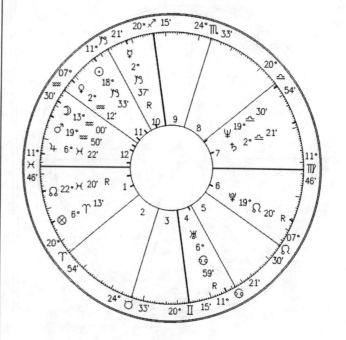

92. COLTEC-COT *Aerospace*
Mar. 24, 1992 NYC 9:30 AM EST
40N45'00 21:43:27 ST 74W00'23

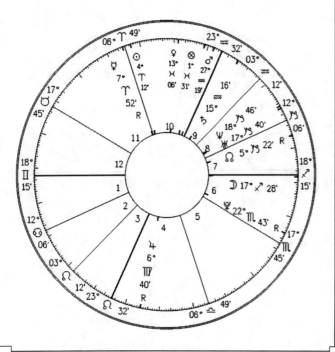

93. COMPAQ-CPQ *Computers*
Dec. 10, 1985 NYC 9:30 AM EST
40N45'00 14:51:15 ST 74W00'23

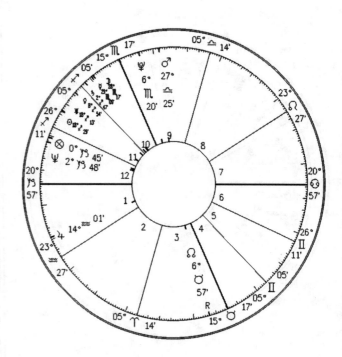

94. COMPUTER ASSOCIATES-CA *Software*
Sep. 11, 1986 NYC 9:30 AM EDT
40N45'00 7:55:18 ST 74W00'23

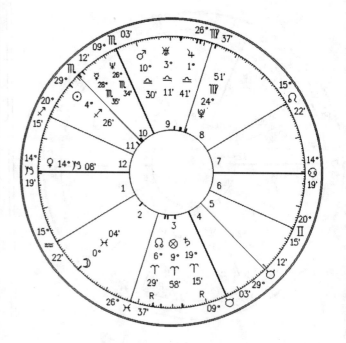

95. COMPUTER SCI.CORP.-CSC *Software*
Nov. 26, 1968 NYC 10:00 AM EST
40N45'00 14:26:36 ST 74W00'23

96. COMPUTER TASK GROUP-TSK **Software**
Feb. 26, 1987 NYC 9:30 AM EST
40N45'00 19:57:49 ST 74W00'23

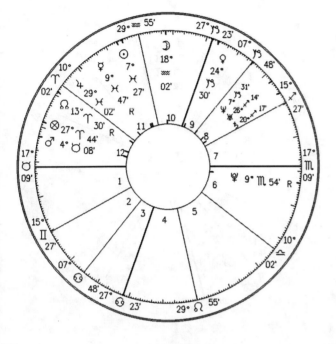

97. COMSAT-CQ **Telecom.**
Sep. 8, 1964 NYC 10:00 AM EDT
40N45'00 8:14:51 ST 74W00'23

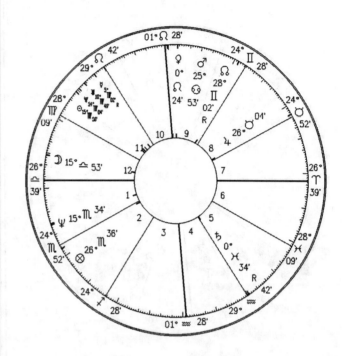

98. CONAGRA-CAG **Food**
Jan. 12, 1976 NYC 10:00 AM EST
40N45'00 17:29:10 ST 74W00'23

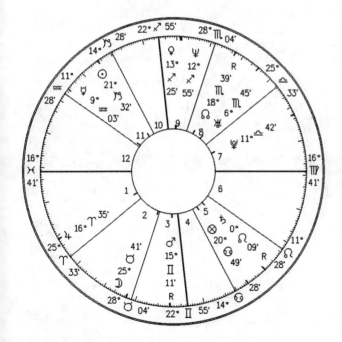

99. CONSECO-CNC **Insurance**
Sep. 24, 1986 NYC 9:30 AM EDT
40N45'00 8:46:34 ST 74W00'23

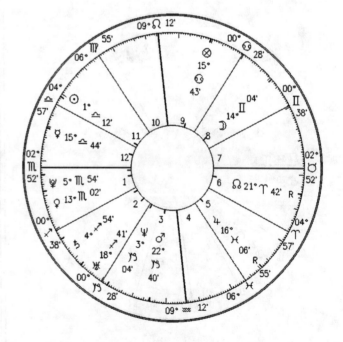

100. COOPER IND.-CBE *Industrial*
Feb. 11, 1944 NYC   10:00 AM EWT
40N45'00   18:26:18 ST   74W00'23

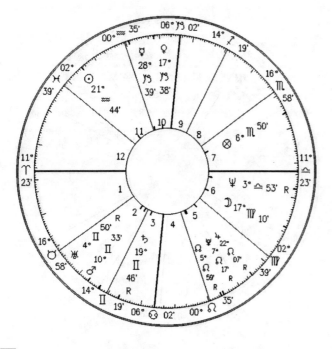

101. CORNING GLASS-GLW *Industrial*
May 21, 1945 NYC   10:00 AM EDT
40N45'00   0:59:36 ST   74W00'23

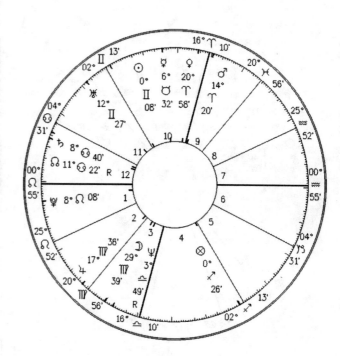

102. COUNTRYWIDE CREDIT-CCR *Financial Ser.*
Feb. 6, 1987 NYC   9:30 AM EST
40N45'00   18:38:58 ST   74W00'23

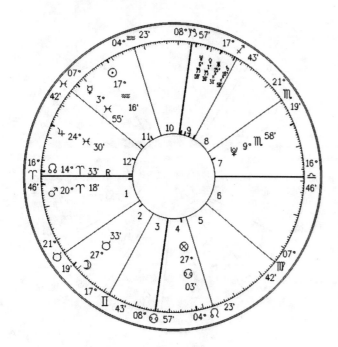

103. CPC INTERNATINAL-CPC *Food*
Oct. 1, 1958 NYC   10:00 AM EDT
40N45'00   9:43:23 ST   74W00'23

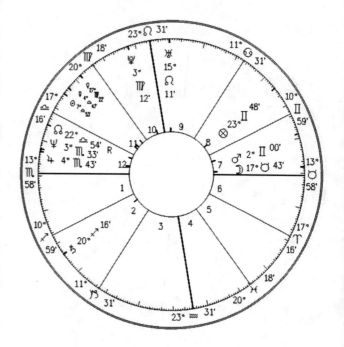

104. CRANE-CR   *Industrial*
Oct. 26, 1936   NYC   10:00 AM EST
40N45'00   12:23:24 ST   74W00'23

105. CROWN CORK & SEAL-CCK   *Packaging*
May 9, 1929   NYC   10:00 AM EDT
40N45'00   0:11:48 ST   74W00'23

106. CUMMINS ENGINE-CUM   *Industrial*
Sep. 10, 1964   NYC   10:00 AM EDT
40N45'00   8:22:44 ST   74W00'23

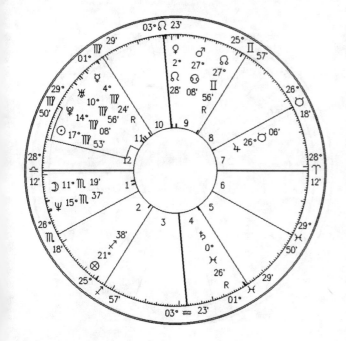

107. CYPRESS SEMICNDTR-CY   *Semiconductors*
Oct. 17, 1988   NYC   9:30 AM EDT
40N45'00   10:19:16 ST   74W00'23

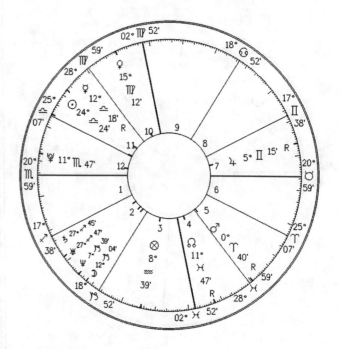

108. DANA-DCN *Auto Parts*
Mar. 18, 1949 NYC 10:00 AM EST
40N45'00 21:47:34 ST 74W00'23

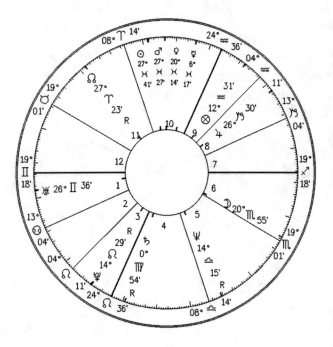

109. DATA GENERAL-DGN *Computers*
Dec. 28, 1973 NYC 10:00 AM EST
40N45'00 16:31:56 ST 74W00'23

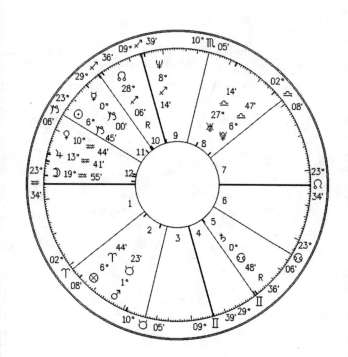

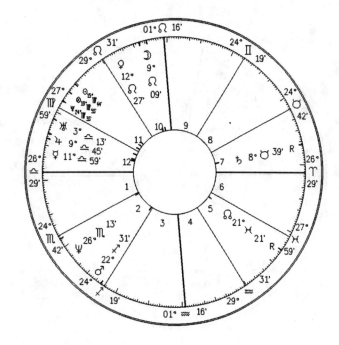

110. DAYTON HUDSON-DH *Retail*
Sep. 8, 1969 NYC 10:00 AM EDT
40N45'00 8:14:01 ST 74W00'23

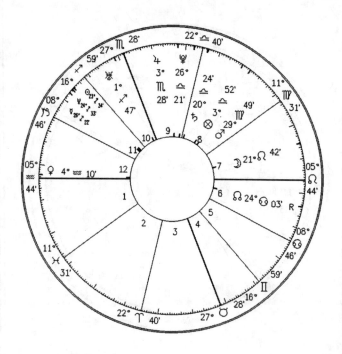

111. DEAN FOODS-DF *Food*
Dec. 15, 1981 NYC 10:00 AM EST
40N45'00 15:40:44 ST 74W00'23

112. DEERE-DE   Machinery
June 29, 1933 NYC   10:00 AM EDT
40N45'00   3:32:59 ST   74W00'23

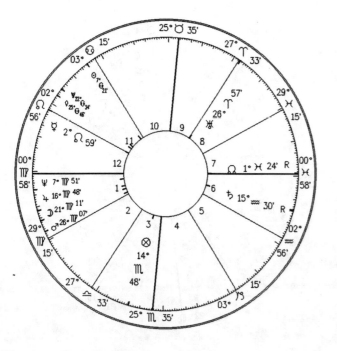

113. DESTEC-ENG   Engineering
Mar. 15, 1991 NYC   9:30 AM EST
40N45'00   21:04:58 ST   74W00'23

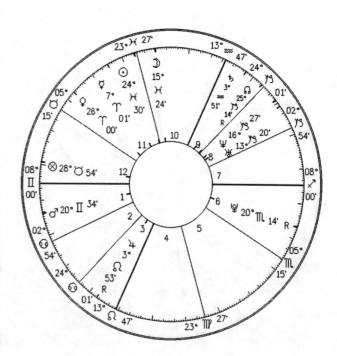

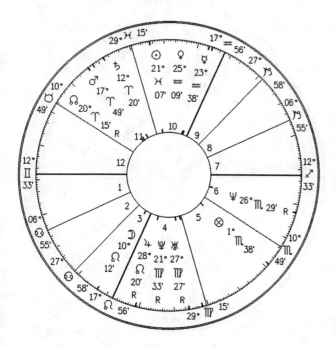

114. DEXTER-DEX   Chemicals
Mar. 11, 1968 NYC   10:00 AM EST
40N45'00   21:21:32 ST   74W00'23

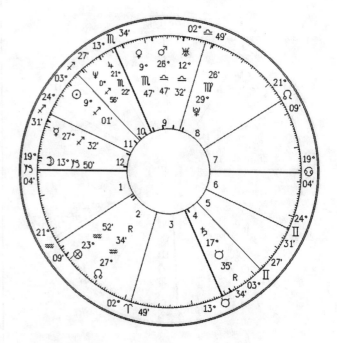

115. DIGITAL EQUIPMENT-DEC   Computers
Dec. 1, 1970 NYC   10:00 AM EST
40N45'00   14:44:25 ST   74W00'23

116. DILLARD DEPT. STORES-DDS　*Retail*
　　June 23, 1989　NYC　　9:30 AM EDT
　　40N45'00　　2:40:59 ST　　74W00'23

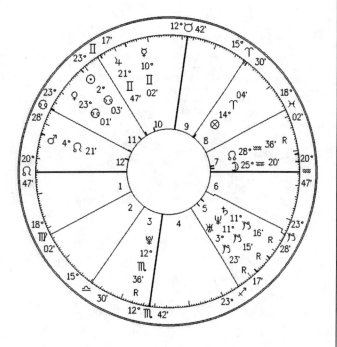

117. DOW CHEMICAL-DOW　　*Chemicals*
　　June 26, 1937　NYC　　10:00 AM EDT
　　40N45'00　　3:21:17 ST　　74W00'23

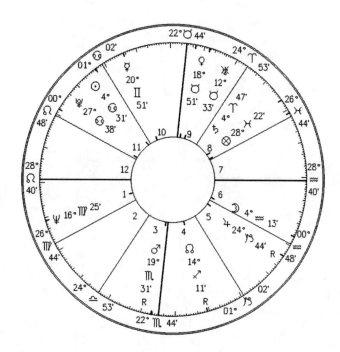

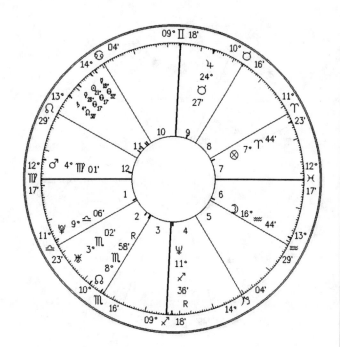

118. DOW JONES-DJ　　*Publishing*
　　July 13, 1976　NYC　　10:00 AM EDT
　　40N45'00　　4:30:30 ST　　74W00'23

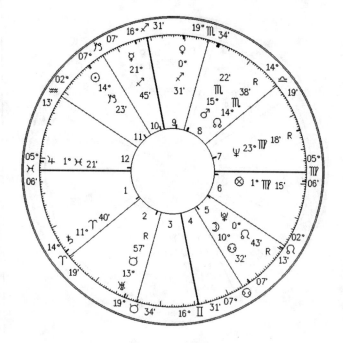

119. DRESSER IND.-DI　　*Oil Machinery*
　　Jan. 5, 1939　NYC　　10:00 AM EST
　　40N45'00　　17:01:25 ST　　74W00'23

120. DUN & BRADSTREET-DNB   *Publishing*
June 1, 1973   NYC   10:00 AM EDT
40N45'00   1:43:50 ST   74W00'23

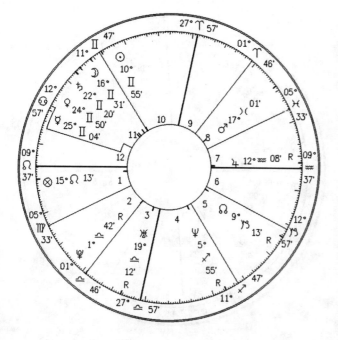

121. EASTMAN CHEMICAL-EMN   *Chemical*
Jan. 3, 1994   NYC   9:30 AM EST
40N45'00"   16:25:54 ST   74W00'23

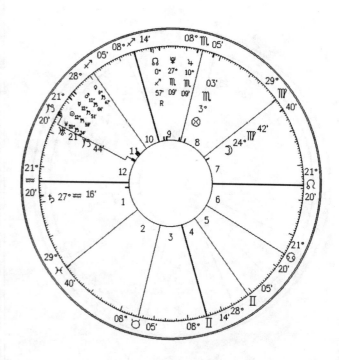

122. ECHLIN-ECH   *Autoparts*
Mar. 4.1963   NYC   10:00 AM EST
40N45'00   50:50:37 ST   74W00'23

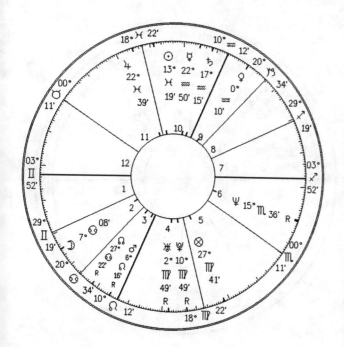

123. EG&G-EGG   *Scientific Equip.*
July 6, 1965   NYC   10:00 AM EDT
40N45'00   4:01:34 ST   74W00'23

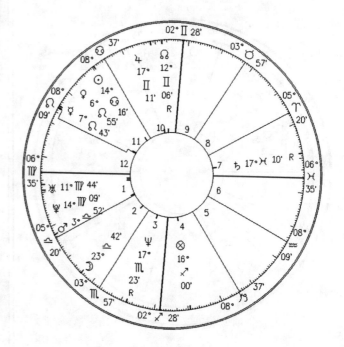

124. EL PASO NAT. GAS-EPG   Nat. Gas Util.
Mar. 13, 1992   NYC   9:30 AM EST
40N45'00   21:00:04 ST   74W00'23

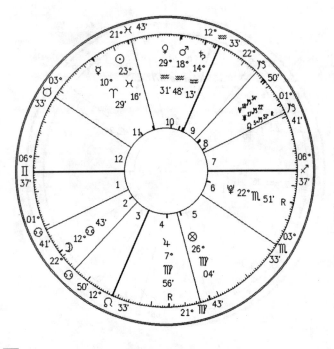

125. ELI LILLY-LLY   Drugs
July 9, 1970   NYC   10:00 AM EDT
40N45'00   4:12:34 ST   74W00'23

126. EMC CORP.-EMC   Computer Equip.
Mar. 22, 1988   NYC   9:30 AM EST
40N45'00   21:35:26 ST   74W00'23

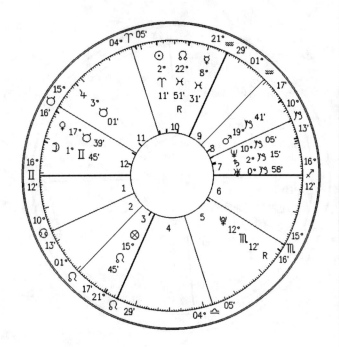

127. EMERSON ELECTRIC-EMR   Electric Equip.
Sep. 5, 1944   NYC   10:00 AM EDT
40N45'00   8:02:25 ST   74W00'23

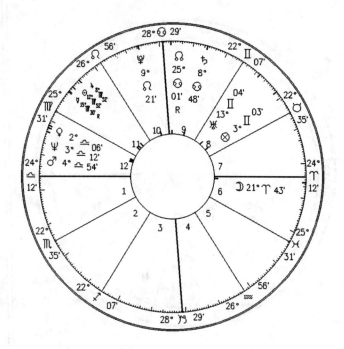

128. ENGELHARD-EC   **Metals**
  May 21, 1981   NYC   10:00 AM EDT
  40N45'00   1:00:42 ST   74W00'23

129. ENRON LIQUID GAS-ENP   **Nat. Gas**
  July 30, 1992   NYC   9:30 AM EDT
  40N45'00   5:07:56 ST   74W00'23

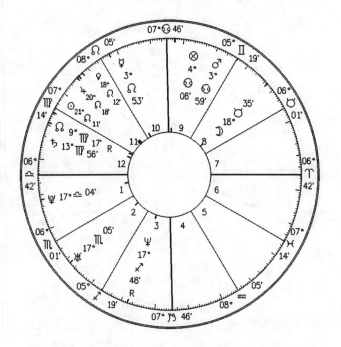

130. EQUITABLE COS.-EQ   **Insurance**
  July 17, 1992   NYC   9:30 AM EDT
  40N45'00   4:16:41 ST   74W00'23

131. FAMILY DOLLAR STORES-FDO   **Retail**
  Aug. 14, 1979   NYC   10:00 AM EDT
  40N45'00   6:33:48 ST   74W00'23

132. FEDERATED-FD   Retail
Feb. 6, 1992   NYC   9:30 AM EST
40N45'00   18:38:08 ST   74W00'23

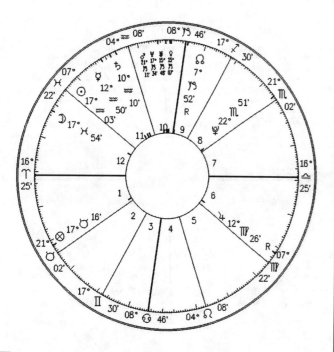

133. FERRO-FOE   Chemical
Nov. 1, 1939   NYC   10:00 AM EST
40N45'00   12:44:11 ST   74W00'23

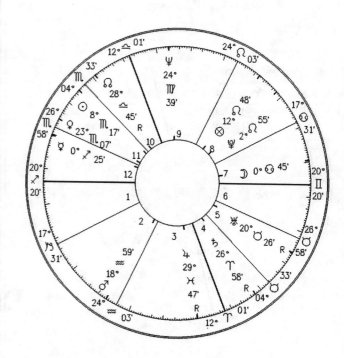

134. FIRST BANK SYSTEM-FBS   Bank
May 7, 1984   NYC   10:00 AM EDT
40N45'00   0:06:35 ST   74W00'23

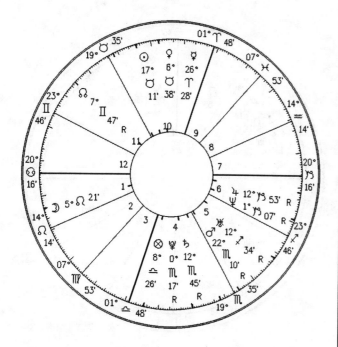

135. FIRST DATA-FDC   Software
Apr. 10, 1992   NYC   9:30 AM EDT
40N45'00   21:50:18 ST   74W00'23

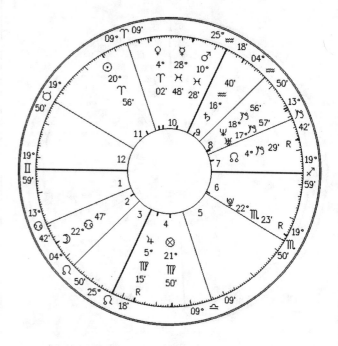

136. FIRSTAR-FSR   **Bank**
Sep. 13, 1971   NYC   10:00 AM EDT
40N45'00   8:31:49 ST   74W00'23

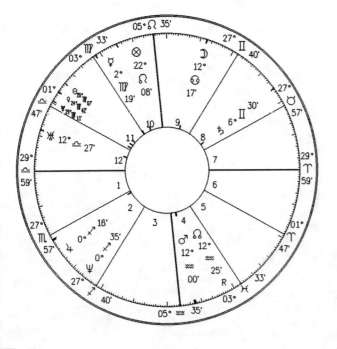

137. FLEETWOOD-FLE   **Recreation**
Nov. 13, 1970   NYC   10:00 AM EST
40N45'00   13:33:27 ST   74W00'23

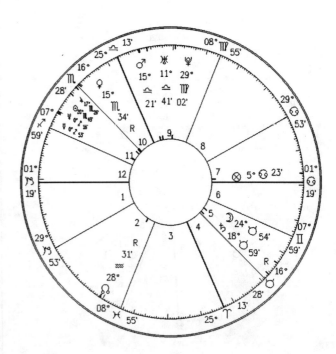

138. FMC-FMC   **Machinery**
May 29, 1986   NYC   9:30 AM EDT
40N45'00   1:01:20 ST   74W00'23

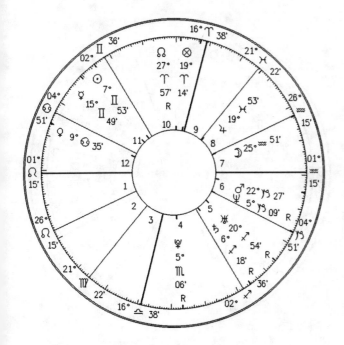

139. FORD-F   **Auto**
Mar. 7, 1956   NYC   10:00 AM EST
40N45'00   21:05:24 ST   74W00'23

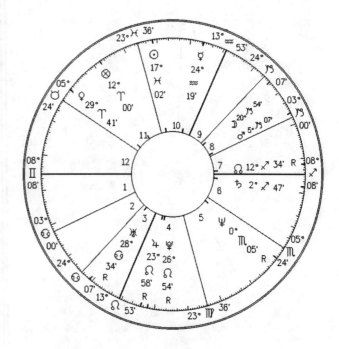

140. FORTUNE BRANDS #1   **(American Brands)**
Jan 24, 1920   NYC   10:00 AM EST
40N45'00   18:14:33 ST   74W00'23

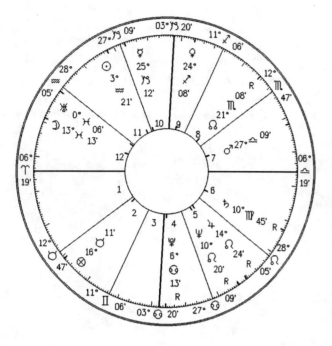

141. FORTUNE BRANDS #2 FO
Jan 2, 1986   NYC   10:00 AM EST
40N45'00   16:21:44 ST   74W00'23

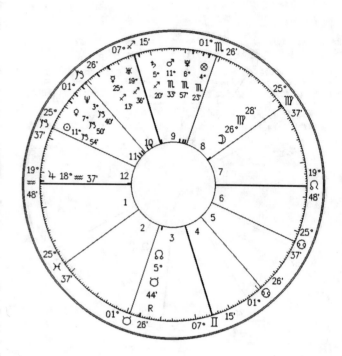

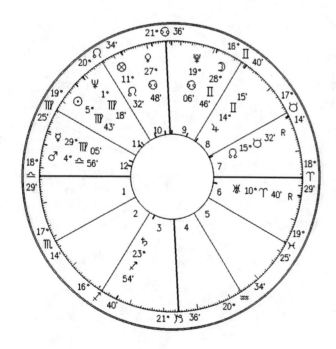

142. FOSTER WHEELER-FWC   **Construction**
Aug. 29, 1929   NYC   10:00 AM EDT
40N45'00   7:33:22 ST   74W00'23

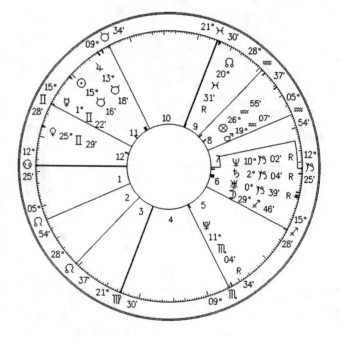

143. FREEPORT MCMORAN-FCX   **Gold**
May 5, 1988   NYC   9:30 AM EDT
40N45'00   23:28:45 ST   74W00'23

144. GANNETT-GCI   *Publishing*
May 18, 1972   NYC   10:00 AM EDT
40N45'00   0:49:35 ST   74W00'23

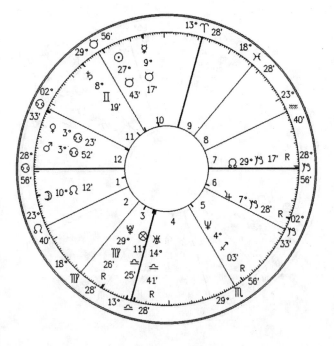

145. GAP STORES-GPS   *Retail*
July 30, 1976   NYC   10:00 AM EDT
40N45'00   5:37:31 ST   74W00'23

146. GATEWAY - GTW   *Computers*
May 22, 1997   NYC   10:00 AM EST
40N45'00   0:34:52ST   74W00'23

147. GENCORP-GY   *Aerospace*
Apr. 3, 1952   NYC   10:00 AM EST
40N45'00   22:51:43 ST   74W00'23

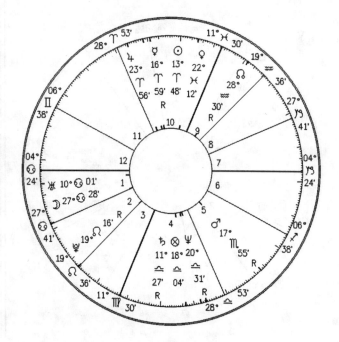

148. GENENTECH-GNE *Biotech*
Mar. 2, 1988   NYC   9:30 AM EST
40N45'00   20:16:35 ST   74W00'23

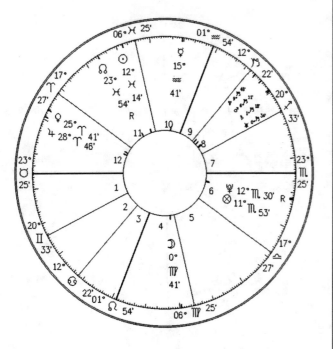

149. GENERAL DYNAMICS-GD *Aerospace*
Apr. 25, 1952   NYC   10:00 AM EST
40N45'00   0:18:27 ST   74W00'23

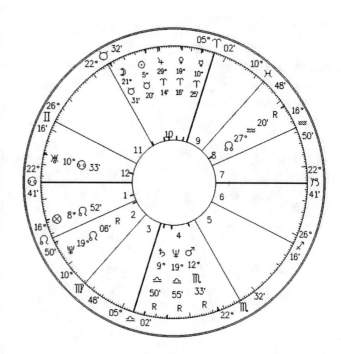

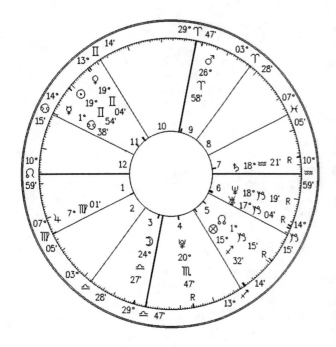

150. GENERAL INSTRUMENT-GIC *Electric Equip.*
June 10, 1992 NYC   9:30 AM EDT
40N45'00   1:50:48 ST   74W00'23

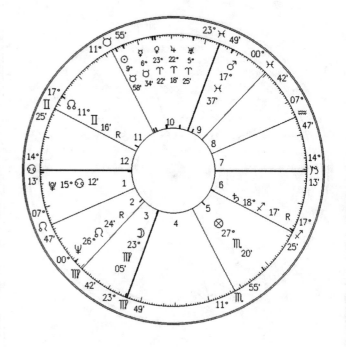

151. GENERAL MILLS-GIS *Food*
Apr. 30, 1928   NYC   10:00 AM EDT
40N45'00   23:37:16 ST   74W00'23

152. GENESIS HEALTH CARE-GHV *Health Care*
Jan. 20, 1993 NYC 9:30 AM EST
40N45'00" 17:33:53 ST 74W00'23

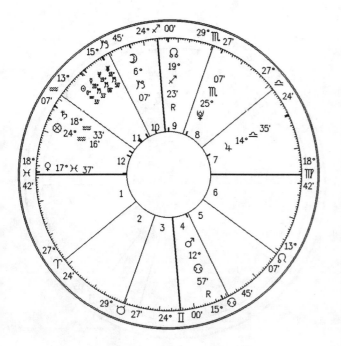

153. GENUINE PARTS-GPC *Auto Parts*
Aug. 20, 1968 NYC 10:00 AM EDT
40N45'00 7:00:04 ST 74W00'23

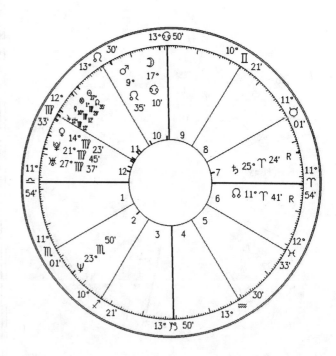

154. GEORGIA GULF-GGC *Chemical*
Nov. 2, 1987 NYC 9:30 AM EST
40N45'00 12:19:32 ST 74W00'23

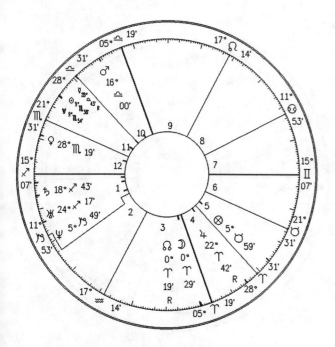

155. GEORGIA PACIFIC-GP *Paper, Forest Prod.*
Feb. 7, 1949 NYC 10:00 AM EST
40N45'00 19:13:48 ST 74W00'23

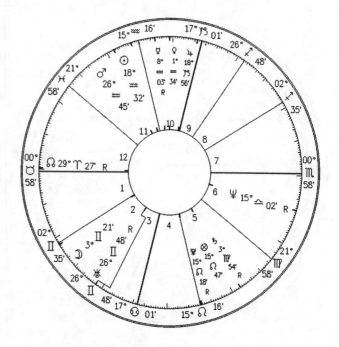

156. GILLETTE-GS — Cosmetics
Sep. 29, 1927 NYC 10:00 AM EST
40N45'00 10:33:43 ST 74W00'23

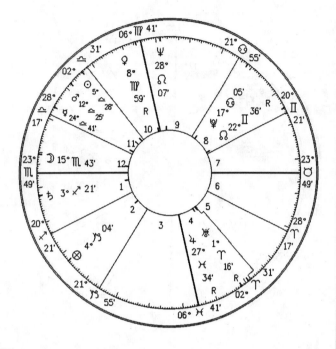

157. GLENFED-GLN — Financial Ser.
Jan. 2, 1986 NYC 9:30 AM EST
40N45'00 16:21:56 ST 74W00'23

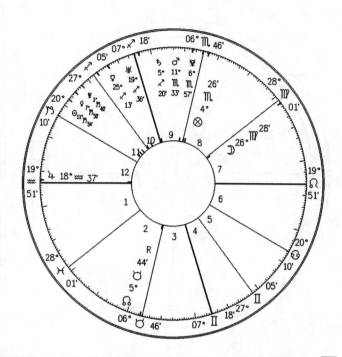

158. GLOBAL MARINE-GLM — Oil Drilling
Nov. 29, 1967 NYC 10:00 AM EST
40N45'00 14:35:27 ST 74W00'23

159. GOODRICH-GR — Chemicals
Oct. 31, 1950 NYC 10:00 AM EST
40N45'00 12:41:34 ST 74W00'23

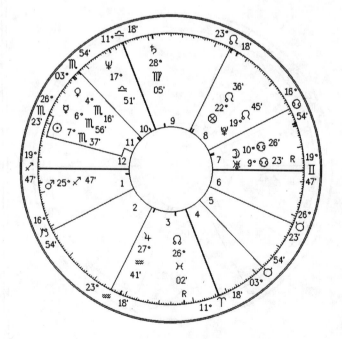

160. GRAINGER-GWW *Electric Equip.*
July 29, 1975 NYC   10:00 AM EDT
40N45'00   5:30:35 ST   74W00'23

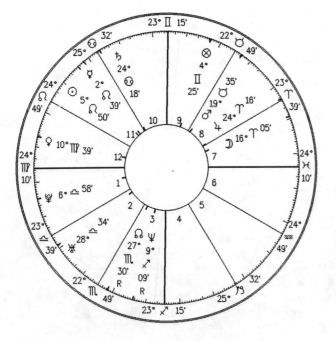

161. GREAT ATLANTIC & PA.-GAP *Retail Food*
Dec. 15, 1958 NYC   10:00 AM EST
40N45'00   15:39:14 ST   74W00'23

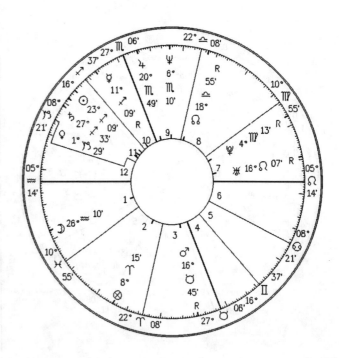

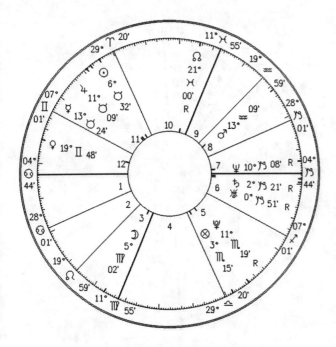

162. GREAT LAKES CHEMICAL-GLK *Chemicals*
Apr. 26, 1988 NYC   9:30 AM EDT
40N45'00   22:53:16 ST   74W00'23

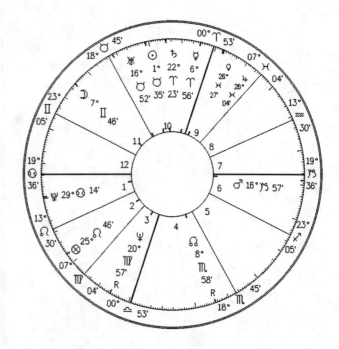

163. GTE-GTE *Telephone*
Apr. 22, 1939 NYC   10:00 AM EST
40N45'00   0:03:16 ST   74W00'23

164. HAEMONETICS-HAE   Medical Equip.
May 10, 1991   NYC   9:30 AM EDT
40N45'00   23:45:36 ST   74W00'23

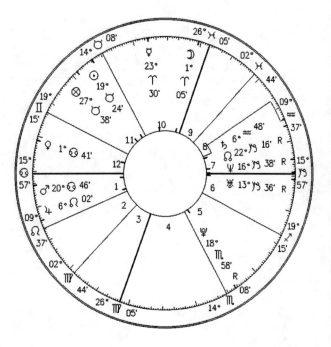

165. HALLIBURTON-HAL   Oilfield Machinery
Sep. 15, 1948   NYC   10:00 AM EDT
40N45'00   8:41:58 ST   74W00'23

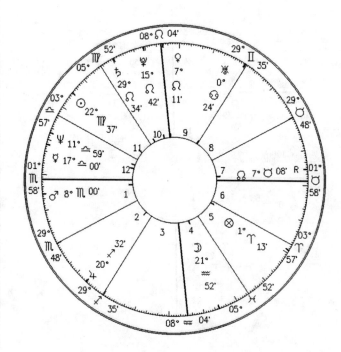

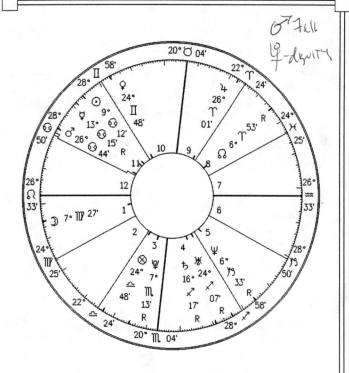

166. HARLEY DAVIDSON-HDI   Recreation
July 1, 1987   NYC   9:30 AM EDT
40N45'00   3:10:29 ST   74W00'23

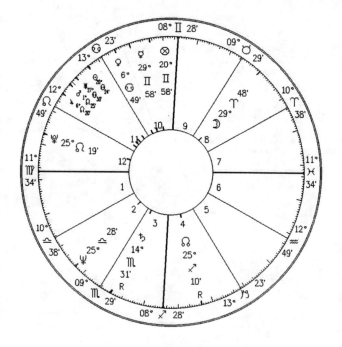

167. HARRIS-HRS   Electric Equip.
July 13, 1955   NYC   10:00 AM EDT
40N45'00   4:26:53 ST   74W00'23

168. HEINZ-HNZ *Food*
Nov. 27, 1946 NYC 10:00 AM EST
40N45'00 14:27:54 ST 74W00'23

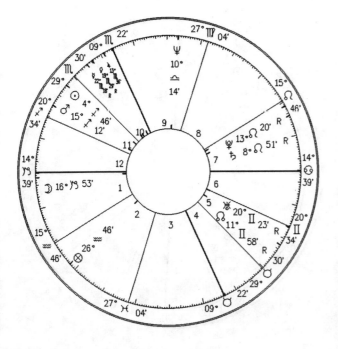

169. HERCULES-HPC *Chemicals*
July 11, 1929 NYC 10:00 AM EDT
40N45'00 4:20:11 ST 74W00'23

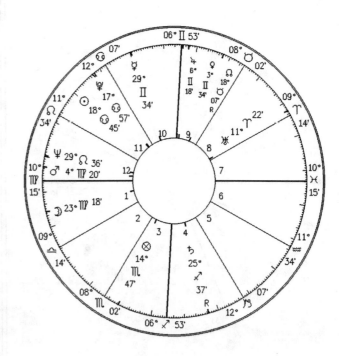

170. HERSHEY-HSY *Food*
Sep. 19, 1947 NYC 10:00 AM EDT
40N45'00 8:54:44 ST 74W00'23

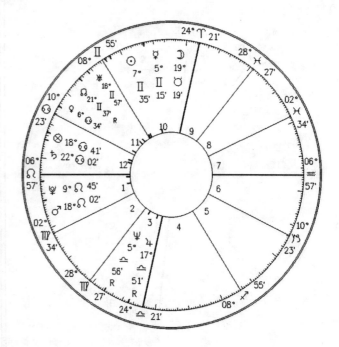

171. HILTON HOTELS-HLT *Hotel*
May 29, 1946 NYC 10:00 AM EDT
40N45'00 1:30:11 ST 74W00'23

172. HOME DEPOT-HD   *Retail*
Apr. 19, 1984   NYC   10:00 AM EDT
40N45'00   22:55:37 ST   74W00'23

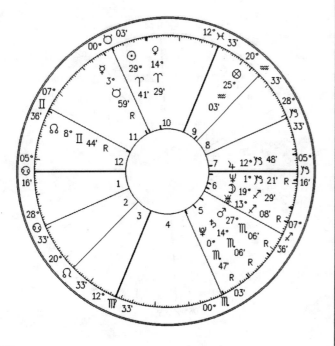

173. HOMESTAKE-HM   *Gold*
Jan. 16, 1879   NYC   10:00 AM LMT   40N45'00
17:42:40 ST   74W00'23

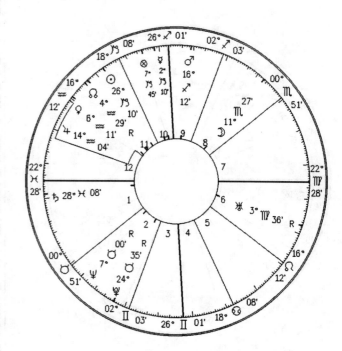

174. HONEYWELL-HON   *Computers*
Sep. 19, 1929   NYC   10:00 AM EDT
40N45'00   8:56:10 ST   74W00'23

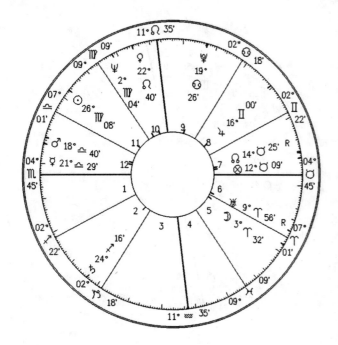

175. HOUSEHOLD INTER.-HI   *Financial Ser.*
Dec. 17, 1936   NYC   10:00 AM EST
40N45'00   15:48:25 ST   74W00'23

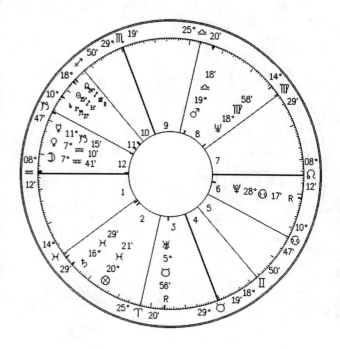

176. HUMANA-HUM   *Health Care*
May 18, 1971   NYC   10:00 AM EDT
40N45'00   0:46:36 ST   74W00'23

177. ILLINOIS TOOL WORKS-ITW   *Industrial*
Mar. 13, 1973   NYC   10:00 AM EST
40N45'00   21:28:35 ST   74W00'23

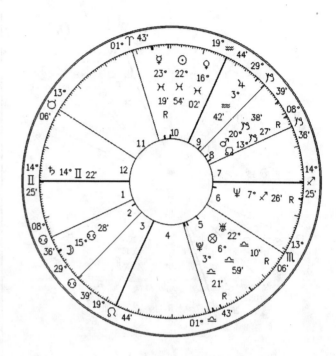

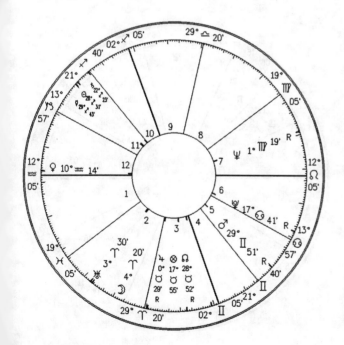

178. INCO-N   *Metals*
Dec. 20, 1928   NYC   10:00 AM EST
40N45'00   16:00:00 ST   74W00'23

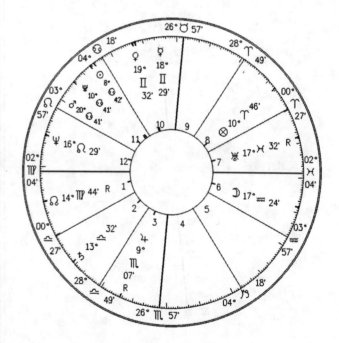

179. INGERSOLL RAND-IR   *Industrial*
July 1, 1923   NYC   10:00 AM EDT
40N45'00   3:38:36 ST   74W00'23

180. INLAND STEEL-IAD   **Steel**
Apr. 18, 1923   NYC   10:00 AM EST
40N45'00   23:47:00 ST   74W00'23

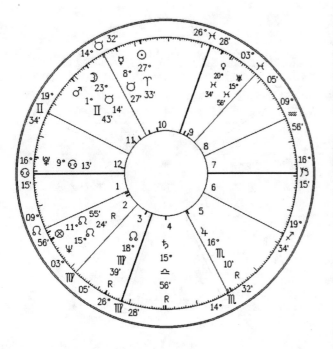

181. INT. FLAVORS & FRAG.-IFF   **Cosmetics**
Mar. 2, 1964   NYC   10:00 AM EST
40N45'00   20:45:56 ST   74W00'23

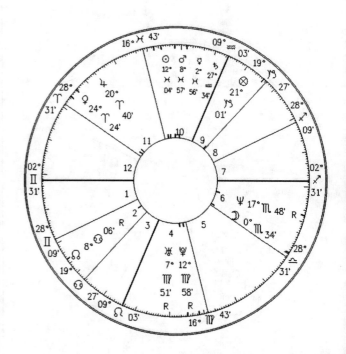

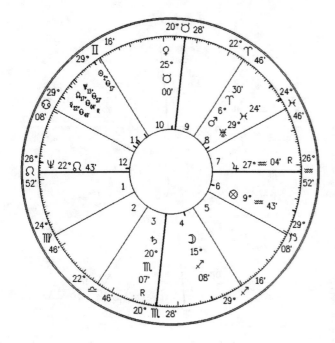

182. INTERLAKE-IK   **Steel**
June 24, 1926   NYC   10:00 AM EDT
40N45'00   3:12:05 ST   74W00'23

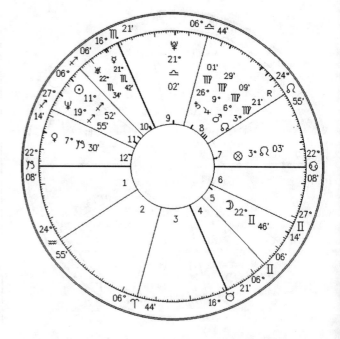

183. INTERN. RECTIFIER-IRF   **Semiconductor**
Dec. 4, 1979   NYC   10:00 AM EST
40N45'00   14:55:32 ST   74W00'23

184. IOMEGA-IOM   *Computer Peripherals*
Nov. 11, 1996   NYC   10:00 AM EST
40N45'00   12:58:03 ST   74W00'23

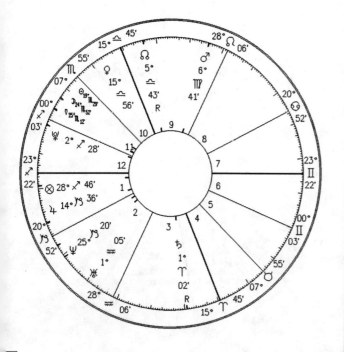

185. ITT-ITT   *Conglomerate*
Dec. 31, 1983   NYC   10:00 AM EST
40N45'00   16:42:06 ST   74W00'23

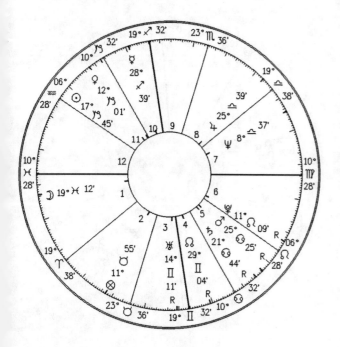

186. J.C. PENNEY-JCP   *Retail*
Jan. 8, 1946   NYC   10:00 AM EST
40N45'00   17:14:27 ST   74W00'23

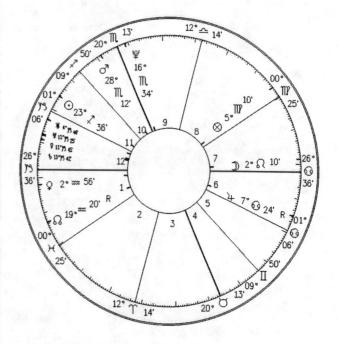

187. JACOBS ENGINEERING-JEC   *Engineering*
Dec. 15, 1989   NYC   9:30 AM EST
40N45'00   15:11:06 ST   74W00'23

188. JAMES RIVER-JR Paper, Forest Prod.
Jan. 29, 1980 NYC 10:00 AM EST
40N45'00 18:36:19 ST 74W00'23

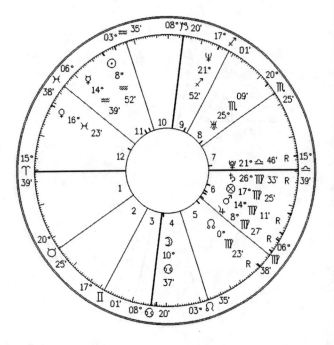

189. JEFFERSON PILOT-JP Insurance
June 9, 1969 NYC 10:00 AM EDT
40N45'00 2:15:15 ST 74W00'23

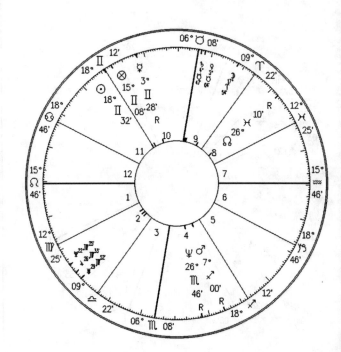

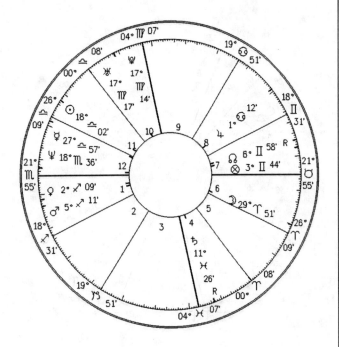

190. JOHNSON CONTROLS-JCI Industrial
Oct. 11, 1965 NYC 10:00 AM EDT
40N45'00 10:24:00 ST 74W00'23

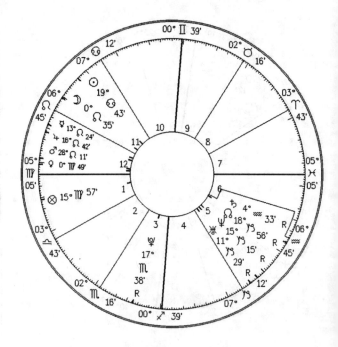

191. KAISER ALUMINUM-KLU Aluminum
July 12, 1991 NYC 9:30 AM EDT
40N45'00 3:53:59 ST 74W00'23

192. KANEB SERVICES-KAB   Oil Machinery
Jan. 28, 1976 NYC   10:00 AM EST
40N45'00   18:32:15 ST   74W00'23

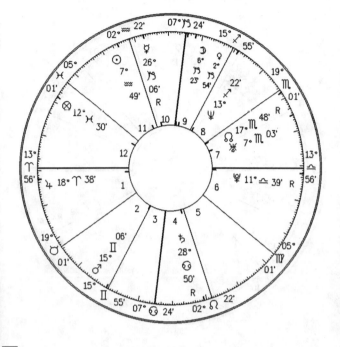

193. KATY IND.-KT   Machinery
Mar. 12, 1968 NYC   10:00 AM EST
40N45'00   21:25:28 ST   74W00'23

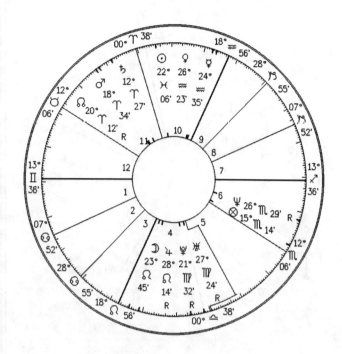

194. KAUFMAN & BROAD-KBH   Home Building
May 29, 1969 NYC   10:00 AM EDT
40N45'00   1:31:53 ST   74W00'23

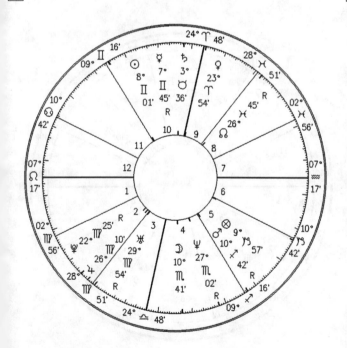

195. KELLOGG-K   Food
May 12, 1959 NYC   10:00 AM EDT
40N45'00   0:22:34 ST   74W00'23

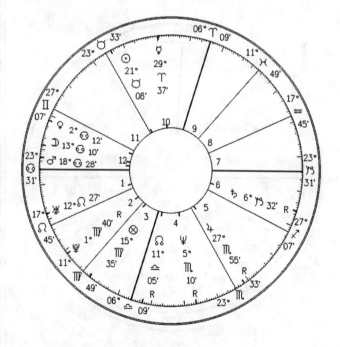

196. KEY CORP.-KEY *Banks*
May 27, 1983   NYC   10:00 AM EDT
40N45'00"   1:22:14 ST   74W00'23

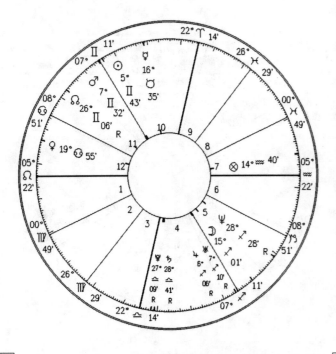

197. KIMBERLY CLARK-KMB *Paper, Forest Prod.*
May 9, 1929   NYC   10:00 AM EDT
40N45'00   0:11:48 ST   74W00'23

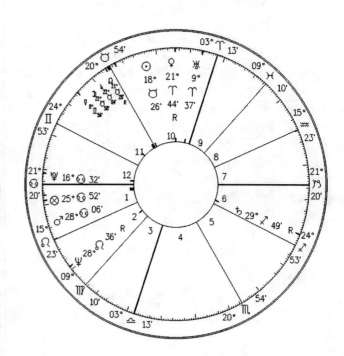

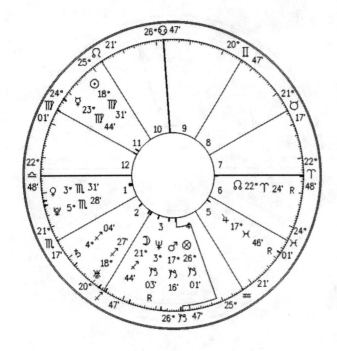

198. KING WORLD PROD.-KWP *Entertainment*
Sep. 11, 1986   NYC   9:30 AM EDT
40N45'00   7:55:18 ST   74W00'23

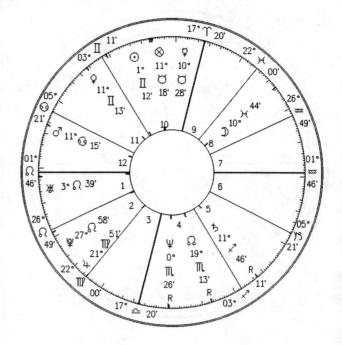

199. KLM ROYAL DUTCH-KLM *Oil*
May 22, 1957   NYC   10:00 AM EDT
40N45'00   1:03:55 ST   74W00'23

200. KMART-KM   **Retail**
May 23, 1918 NYC   10:00 AM EDT
40N45'00   1:05:40 ST   74W00'23

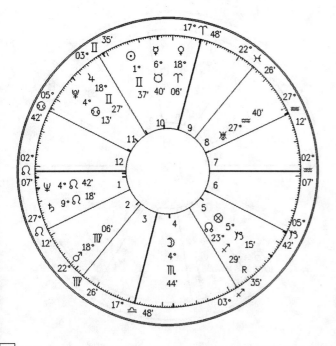

201. KROGER-KR   **Retail Food**
Dec. 18, 1979 NYC   10:00 AM EST
40N45'00   15:50:43 ST   74W00'23

202. L.A. GEAR-LA   **Shoes**
Feb. 13, 1989 NYC   9:30 AM EST
40N45'00   19:08:36 ST   74W00'23

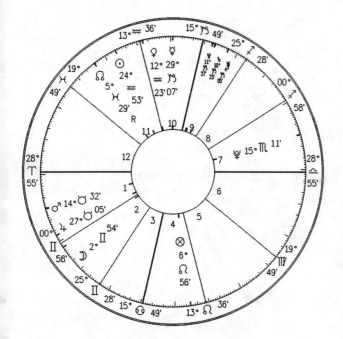

203. LAKELAND PIPELINE-LHP   **Oil Pipeline**
Dec. 20, 1991 NYC   9:30 AM EST
40N45'00   15:28:54 ST   74W00'23

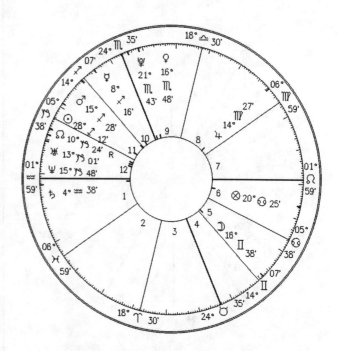

204. LAMSON & SESSIONS-LMS *Industrial*
Jan. 29, 1968 NYC   10:00 AM EST
40N45'00   18:35:57 ST   74W00'23

205. LIMITED-LTD   *Retail*
June 10, 1982 NYC   10:00 AM EDT
40N45'00   2:18:36 ST   74W00'23

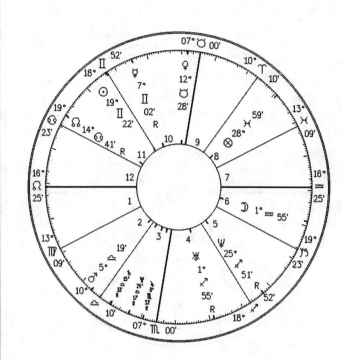

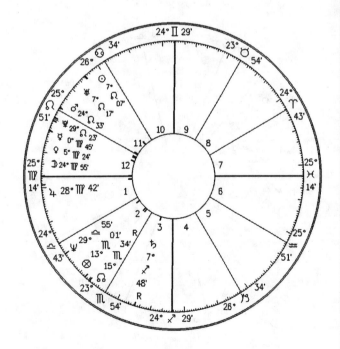

206. LITTON IND.-LIT   *Aerospace*
July 30, 1957 NYC   10:00 AM EDT
40N45'00   5:35:57 ST   74W00'23

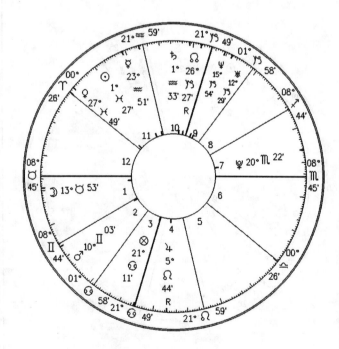

207. LIZ CLAIBORNE-LIZ   *Apparel*
Feb. 20, 1991 NYC   9:30 AM EST
40N45'00   19:34:18 ST   74W00'23

208. LOCKHEED MARTIN #1   *Aerospace*
Oct. 11, 1961   NYC   9:30 AM EST
40N45'00   10:23:41 ST   74W00'23

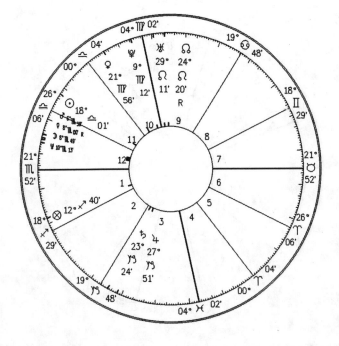

209. LOCKHEED MARTIN #2-LMT   *Aerospace*
Mar. 15, 1995   NYC   9:30 AM EST
40N45'00   21:08:50 ST   74W00'23

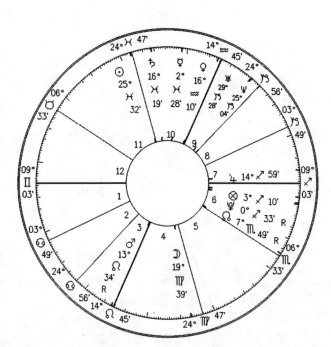

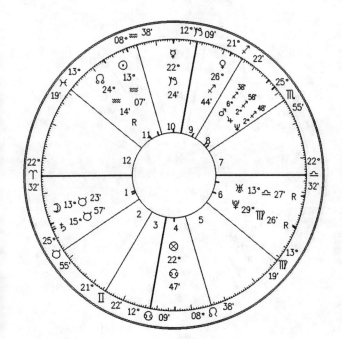

210. LOEWS-LTR   *Tobacco*
Feb. 2, 1971   NYC   10:0:0 AM EST
40N45'00"   18:52:48 ST   74W00'23"

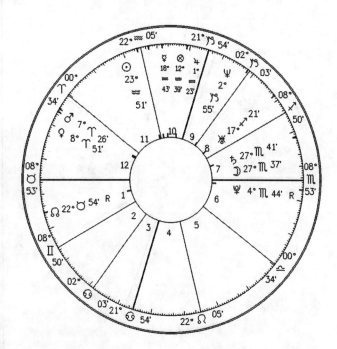

211. LOGICON-LGN   *Electrical Equip.*
Feb. 12, 1985   NYC   10:0:0 AM EST
40N45'00"   19:34:37 ST   74W00'23"

212. LORAL SPACE & COMM-LOR **Telecom Equip.**
May 7, 1996 NYC 9:30 AM EDT
40N45'00" 23:36:41 ST 74W00'23"

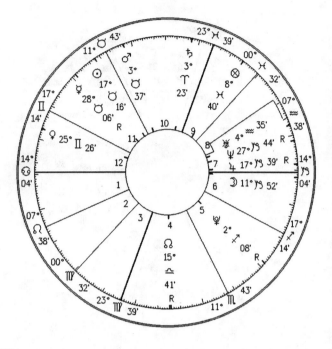

213. LOUISIANA PACIFIC-LPX **Forest Products**
Dec. 27, 1972 NYC 10:0:0 AM EST
40N45'00" 16:28:57 ST 74W00'23"

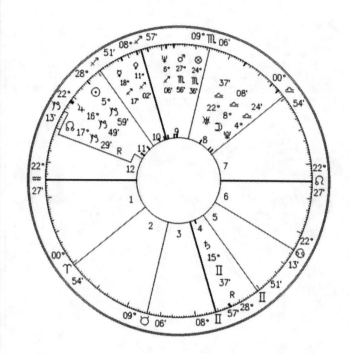

214. LOWES-LOW **Building Materials**
Dec. 19, 1979 NYC 10:0:0 AM EST
40N45'00" 15:54:40 ST 74W00'23"

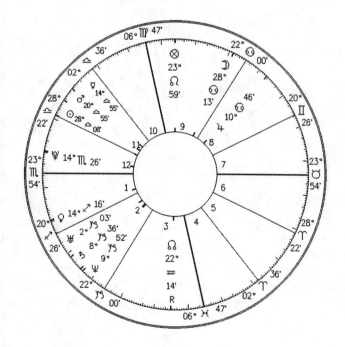

215. LSI LOGIC-LSI **Semiconductors**
Oct. 21, 1989 NYC 9:30:0 AM EDT
40N45'00" 10:34:05 ST 74W00'23"

216. LTV-LTV   **Steel**
Sep. 23, 1960   NYC   10:0:0 AM EDT
40N45'00"   9:13:52 ST   74W00'23"

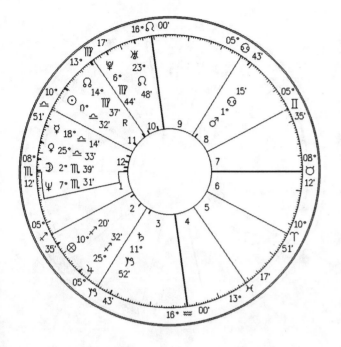

217. LUCENT TECH-LU   **Telecom equip**
Apr. 4, 1996   NYC   9:30 AM EST
40N45'00   22:26:44 ST   74W00'23

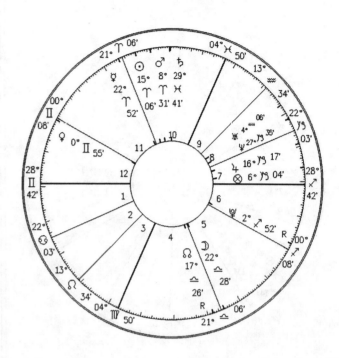

218. MAPCO-MDA   **Oil**
Aug. 10, 1966   NYC   10:0:0 AM EDT
40N45'00"   6:18:37 ST   74W00'23"

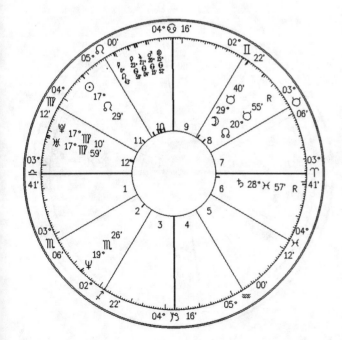

219. MARRIOTT INT.-MAR   **Hotels**
Oct. 11, 1993   NYC   9:30:0 AM EST
40N45'00""   10:54:43 ST   74W00'23"

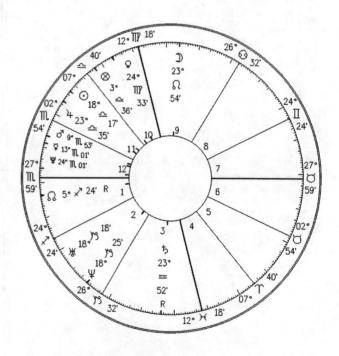

220. MARRIOTT-MHS **Hotels**
Aug. 26, 1968 NYC 10:0:0 AM EDT
40N45'00" 7:23:43 ST 74W00'23"

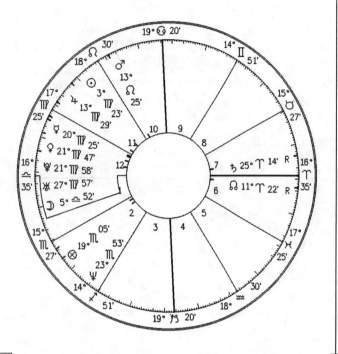

221. MARTECH-MUS **Pollution Control**
Feb. 13, 1991 NYC 9:30:0 AM EST
40N45'00"" 19:06:28 ST 74W00'23"

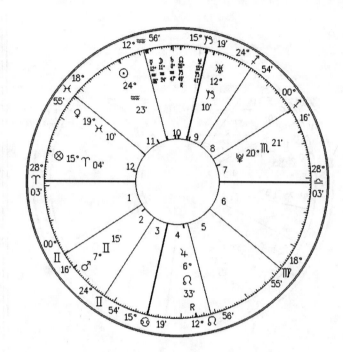

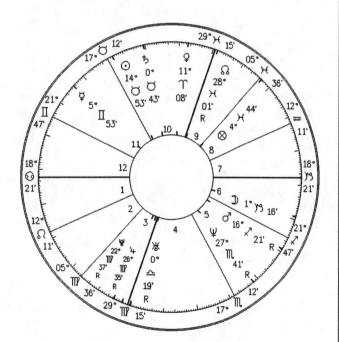

222. MASCO-MAS **Building Materials**
May 5, 1969 NYC 10:0:0 AM EDT
40N45'00" 23:57:15 ST 74W00'23"

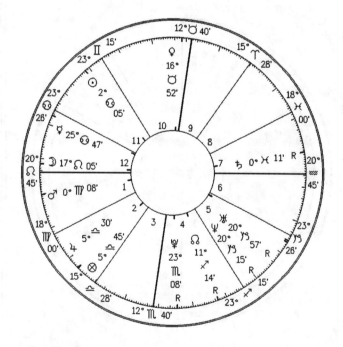

223. MASOTECH-MSX **Oilfield Machinery**
June 23, 1993 NYC 9:30:0 AM EDT
40N45'00"" 2:40:52 ST 74W00'23"

224. MATTEL-MAT — *Recreation*
June 3, 1968 NYC 10:0:0 AM EDT
40N45'00" 1:52:33 ST 74W00'23"

225. MAYTAG-MYG — *Household Furniture & Appliances*
Aug. 20, 1958 NYC 10:0:0 AM EDT
40N45'00" 6:57:47 ST 74W00'23"

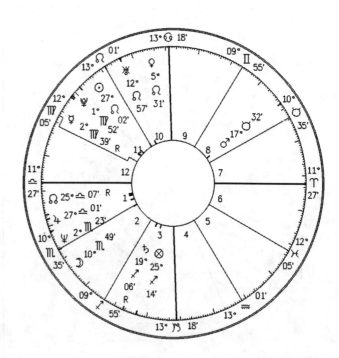

226. MBNA CORP.-KRB — *Financial Services*
Jan. 23, 1991 NYC 9:30:0 AM EST
40N45'00" 17:43:54 ST 74W00'23"

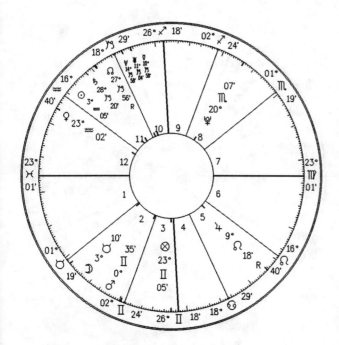

227. MCDERMOTT-MDR — *Oilfield Services*
Nov. 29, 1982 NYC 10:0:0 AM EST
40N45'00" 14:36:54 ST 74W00'23"

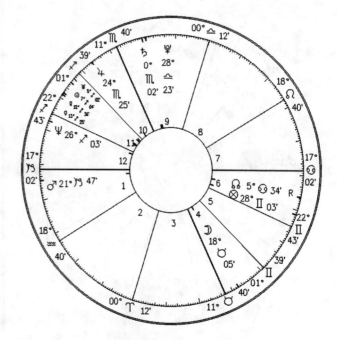

228. MCDONNELL DOUGLAS-MD   Aerospace
Mar. 31, 1959 NYC   10:0:0 AM EST
40N45'00"   22:37:09 ST   74W00'23"

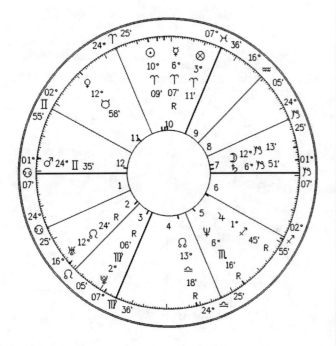

229. MCGRAW HILL-MHP   Publishing
Feb. 14, 1929 NYC   10:0:0 AM EST
40N45'00"   19:40:47 ST   74W00'23"

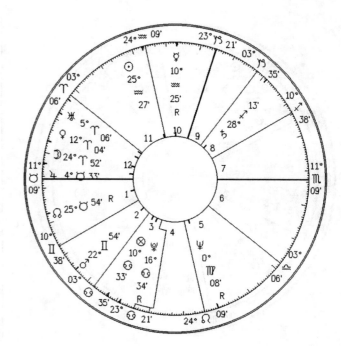

230. MEAD-MEA   Forest Products
Dec. 20, 1935 NYC   10:0:0 AM EST
40N45'00"   15:57:15 ST   74W00'23"

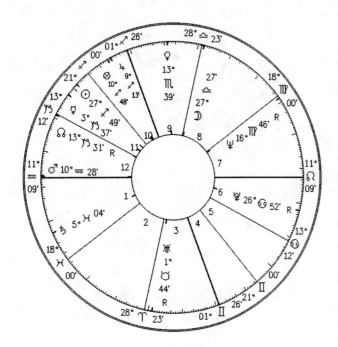

231. MEDTRONIC-MDT   Medical Equipment
Nov. 21, 1977 NYC   10:0:0 AM EST
40N45'00"   14:06:11 ST   74W00'23"

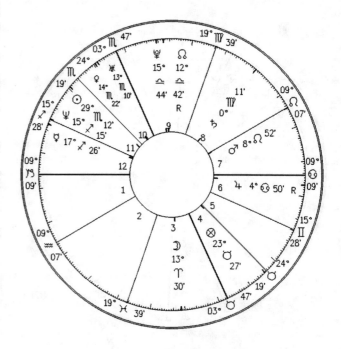

232. MELLON-MEL   **Bank**
Sep. 30, 1984 NYC   10:0:0 AM EDT
40N45'00"   9:42:12 ST   74W00'23"

233. MERCANTILE STORES-MST   **Retail**
July 1, 1946 NYC   10:0:0 AM EDT
40N45'00"   3:40:17 ST   74W00'23"

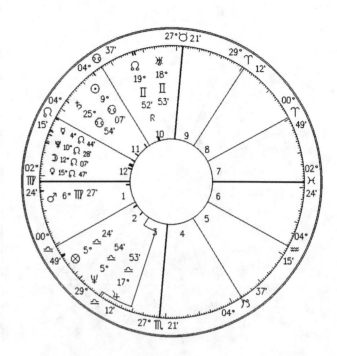

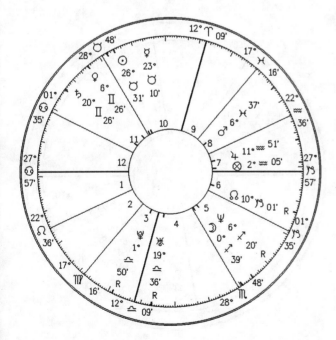

234. MERRILL LYNCH-MER   **Brokerage**
May 17, 1973 NYC   10:0:0 AM EDT
40N45'00"   0:44:41 ST   74W00'23"

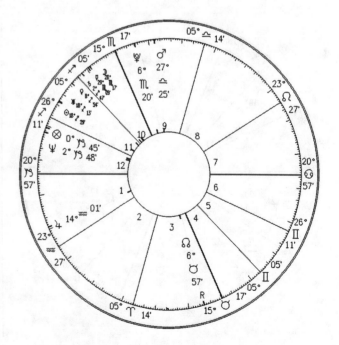

235. MESA-MXP   **Oil**
Dec. 10, 1985 NYC   9:30:0 AM EST
40N45'00"   14:51:15 ST   74W00'23"

236. MICRON TECH.-MU   *Computer Equip.*
Nov. 30, 1990 NYC   9:30:0 AM EST
40N45'00"   14:11:00 ST   74W00'23"

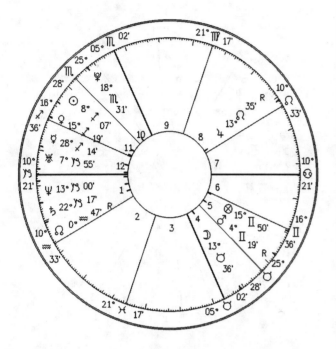

237. MILLIPORE-MIL   *Technology*
Dec. 23, 1987 NYC   9:30:0 AM EST
40N45'00"   15:40:36 ST   74W00'23"

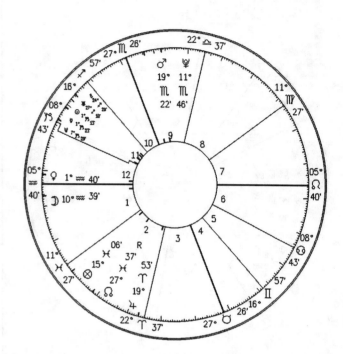

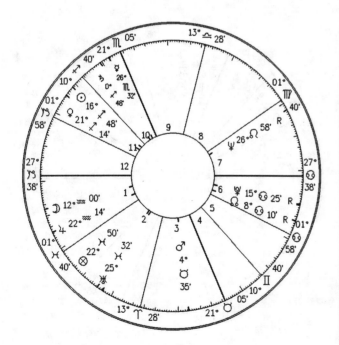

238. MOBIL-MOB   *Oil*
Dec. 9, 1926 NYC   10:0:0 AM EST
40N45'00"   15:14:36 ST   74W00'23"

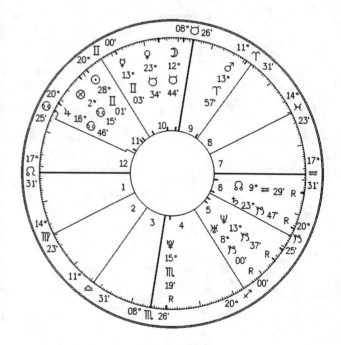

239. MOLECULAR BIOSYSTEMS-MB   *Biotech*
June 19, 1990 NYC   9:30:0 AM EDT
40N45'00"   2:24:15 ST   74W00'23"

240. MONSANTO-MTC **Chemicals**
June 1, 1933 NYC   10:0:0 AM EDT
40N45'00"   1:42:36 ST   74W00'23"

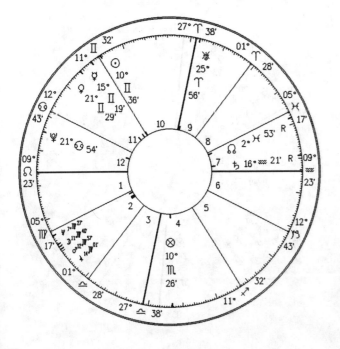

241. MORGAN STANLEY INDIA-IIF **Brokers**
Feb. 18, 1994 NYC   9:30 AM EST
40N45'00   19:27:16 ST   74W00'23

242. MORGAN STANLEY-MS **Brokers**
Mar. 21, 1986 NYC   9:30 AM EST
40N45'00   21:29:16 ST   74W00'23

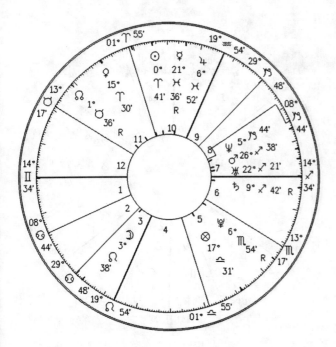

243. MOTOROLA-MOT **Semiconductors**
May 20, 1946 NYC   10:0:0 AM EDT
40N45'00"   0:54:42 ST   74W00'23"

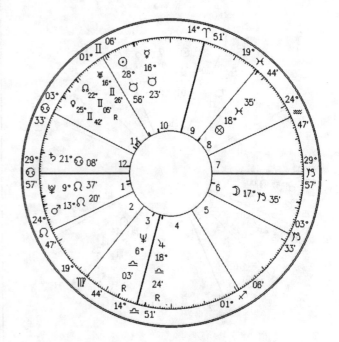

244. MYLAN LABS-MYL   *Drugs*
Apr. 14, 1986   NYC   10:0:0 AM EST
40N45'00"   23:34:10 ST   74W00'23"

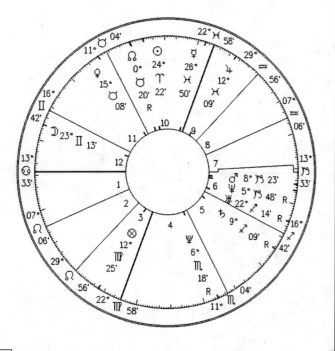

245. NAT. INTERGROUP-NII   *Consumer Products*
Sep. 13, 1983   NYC   10:0:0 AM EDT
40N45'00"   8:32:12 ST   74W00'23"

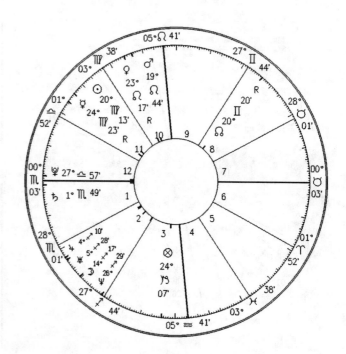

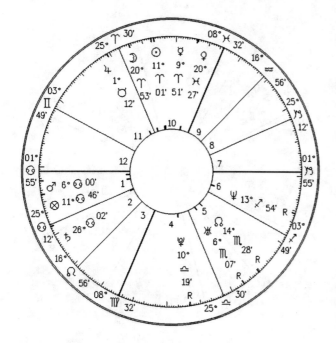

246. NAT. MEDICAL ENTER.-NME   *Health Care*
Mar. 31, 1976   NYC   10:0:0 AM EST
40N45'00"   22:40:38 ST   74W00'23"

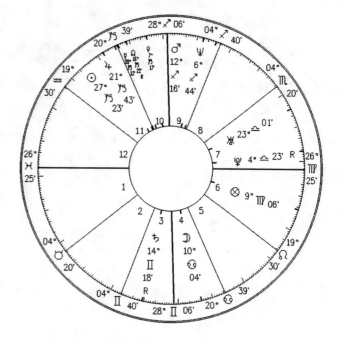

247. NATIONAL SEMI.-NSM   *Semiconductors*
Jan. 17, 1973   NYC   10:0:0 AM EST
40N45'00"   17:51:45 ST   74W00'23"

248. NATIONS BANK-NB   Bank
June 5, 1979   NYC   10:00 AM EDT
40N45'00   1:57:37 ST   74W00'23

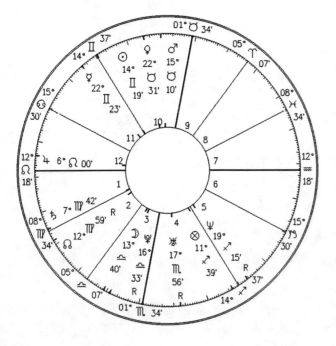

249. NAVISTAR-NAV   Autoparts
Feb. 20, 1986   NYC   9:30:0 AM EST
40N45'00"   19:35:07 ST   74W00'23"

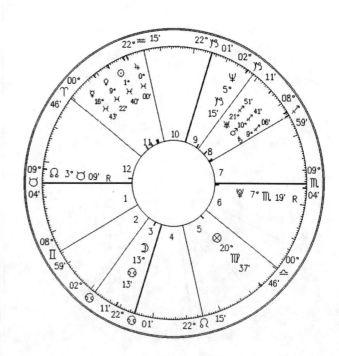

250. NETWORK SYSTEMS-NWK   Computer Equip
June 12, 1989 NYC   9:30:0 AM EDT
40N45'00"   1:57:36 ST   74W00'23"

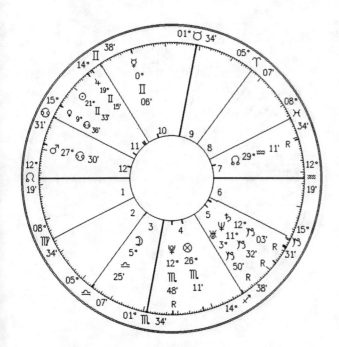

251. NEWBRIDGE NETWORKS-NN   Telecom Equip.
Sept. 14, 1944 NYC   9:30 AM EDT
40N45'00   8:07:11 ST   74W00'23

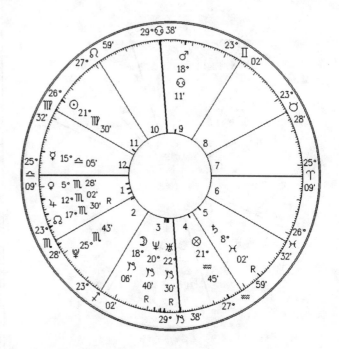

252. NEWMONT GOLD-NGC   *Gold*
June 24, 1986 NYC   9:30:0 AM EDT
40N45'00"   2:43:50 ST   74W00'23"

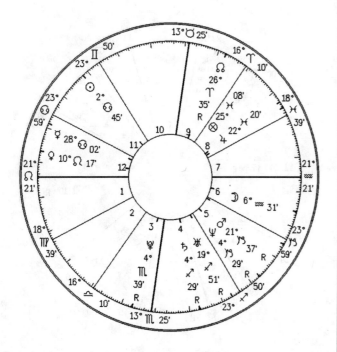

253. NEWMONT MINING-NEM   *Gold*
Jan. 27, 1940 NYC   10:0:0 AM EST
40N45'00"   18:27:12 ST   74W00'23"

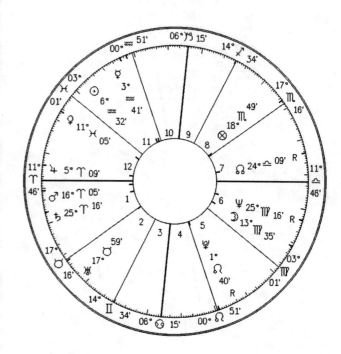

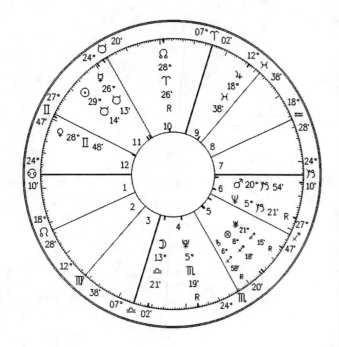

254. NEWS CORP.-NWS   *Publishing*
May 20, 1986 NYC   9:30:0 AM EDT
40N45'00"   0:25:51 ST   74W00'23"

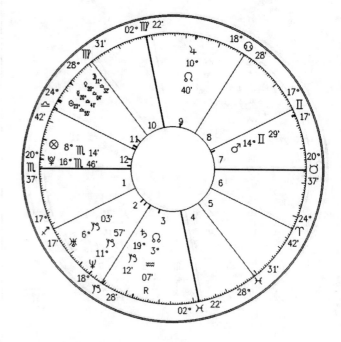

255. NIKE-NKE   *Shoes*
Oct. 17, 1990 NYC   9:30:0 AM EDT
40N45'00"   10:17:22 ST   74W00'23"

256. NORTH FORK BANCORP-NFB *Banks*
Mar. 7, 1990   NYC   9:30:0 AM EST
40N45'00"   20:34:23 ST   74W00'23"

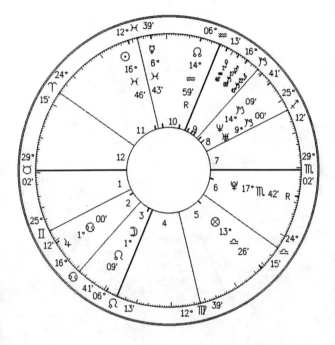

257. NORTHERN TELECOM-NT   *Telecommunications*
Nov. 10, 1975 NYC   10:0:0 AM EST
40N45'00"   13:20:47 ST   74W00'23"

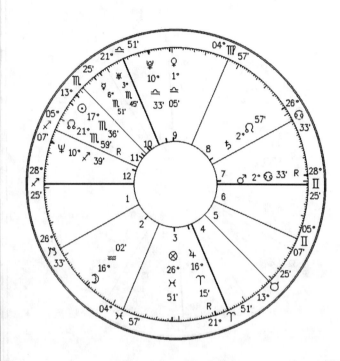

258. NORTHROP-NOC   *Aerospace*
June 19, 1985 NYC   10:0:0 AM EDT
40N45'00"   2:55:10 ST   74W00'23"

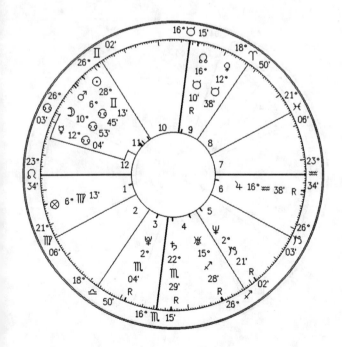

259. NORWEST CORP.-NOB   *Banking*
May 2, 1983   NYC   10:0:0 AM EDT
40N45'00"   23:43:53 ST   74W00'23"

260. NUCOR-NUE   Steel
July 12, 1972   NYC   10:0:0 AM EDT
40N45'00"   4:26:26 ST   74W00'23"

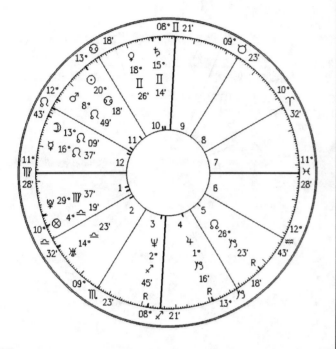

261. OCCIDENTAL PETROL.-OXY   Oil
Mar. 3, 1964   NYC   10:0:0 AM EST
40N45'00"   20:49:52 ST   74W00'23"

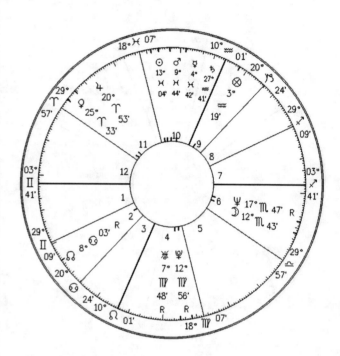

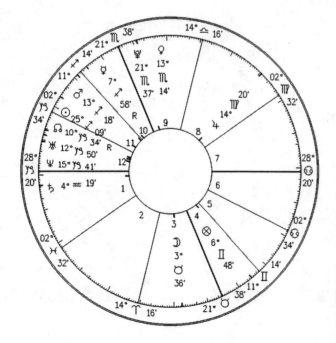

262. OCEAN ENGINEERING-OII   Oilfield Services
Dec. 17, 1991   NYC   9:30:0 AM EST
40N45'00""   15:16:51 ST   74W00'23"

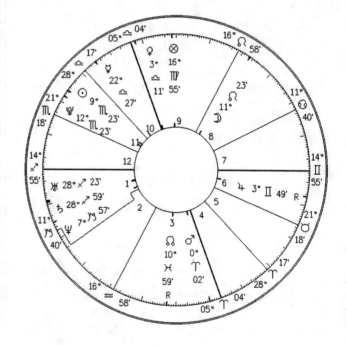

263. ORYX ENERGY-ORX   Oil
Nov. 1, 1988   NYC   9:30:0 AM EST
40N45'00"   12:18:34 ST   74W00'23"

264. OUTBOARD MARINE-OM   *Recreation*
Jan. 25, 1937   NYC   10:0:0 AM EST
40N45'00"   18:22:11 ST   74W00'23"

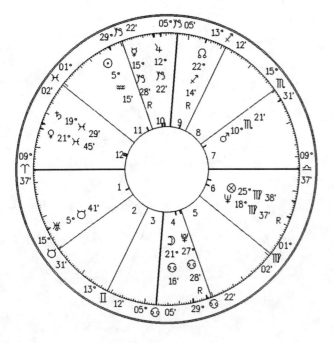

265. OWENS ILLINOIS-OI   *Chemicals*
Dec. 4, 1991   NYC   9:30:0 AM EST
40N45'00"   14:25:49 ST   74W00'23"

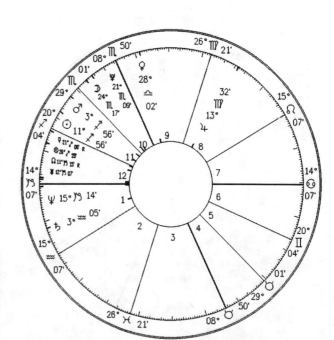

266. PAINE WEBBER-PWJ   *Brokerage*
Feb. 1, 1974   NYC   10:0:0 AM EDT
40N45'00"   17:49:46 ST   74W00'23"

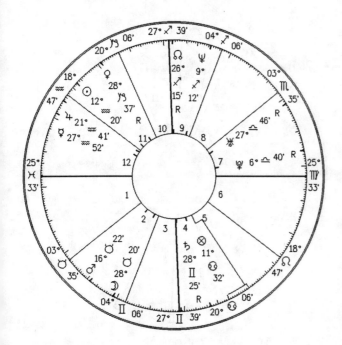

267. PARKER HANNIFIN-PH   *Industrial*
Dec. 9, 1964   NYC   10:0:0 AM EST
40N45'00"   15:17:44 ST   74W00'23"

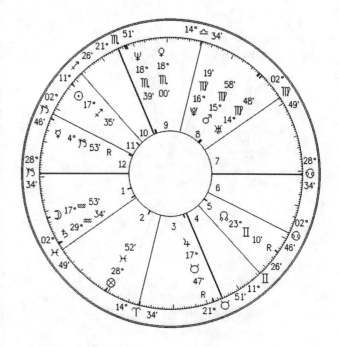

268. PENNZOIL-PZL   *Oil*
   Apr. 1, 1968   NYC   10:0:0 AM EST
   40N45'00"   22:44:20 ST   74W00'23"

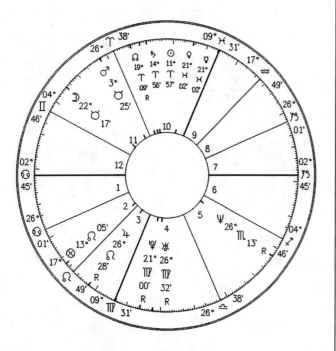

269. PEPSICO-PEP   *Beverages*
   Dec. 18, 1919   NYC   10:0:0 AM EST
   40N45'00"   15:48:53 ST   74W00'23"

270. PERKIN ELMER-PKN   *Computer Equip.*
   Dec. 13, 1960   NYC   10:0:0 AM EST
   40N45'00"   15:33:23 ST   74W00'23"

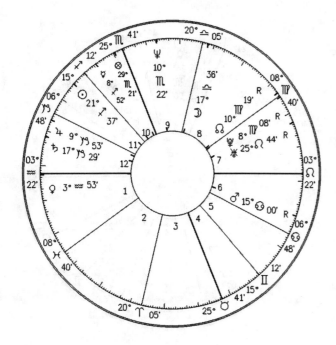

271. PFIZER-PFE   *Drugs*
   Jan. 17, 1944   NYC   10:0:0 AM EST
   40N45'00"   17:47:54 ST   74W00'23"

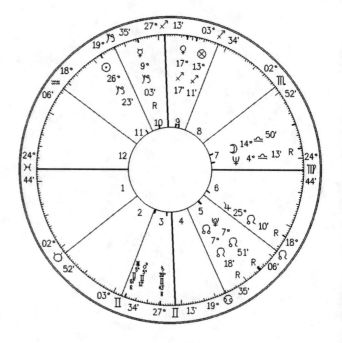

272. PHARMACIA UPJOHN-PNU   *Drugs*
Nov. 3, 1995   NYC   9:30 AM EST
40N45'00   12:23:31 ST   74W00'23

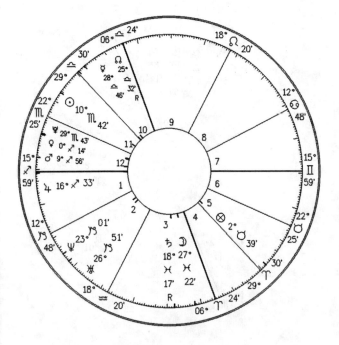

273. PHELPS DODGE-PD   *Metals*
May 9, 1929   NYC   10:0:0 AM EDT
40N45'00"   0:11:48 ST   74W00'23"

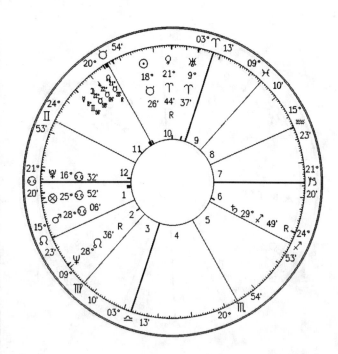

274. PHILLIPS PETROLEUM-P   *Oil*
Aug. 4, 1950   NYC   10:0:0 AM EDT
40N45'00"   5:54:28 ST   74W00'23"

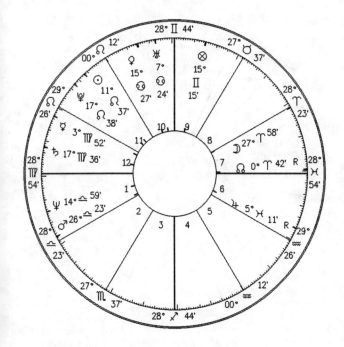

275. PIONEER FINAN.-PFS   *Insurance*
May 16, 1990   NYC   9:30:0 AM EDT
40N45'00""   0:09:59 ST   74W00'23"

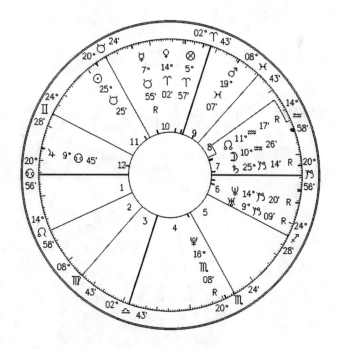

276. PITTSTON-PCO   *Coal*
Jan. 23, 1930   NYC   10:0:0 AM EST
40N45'00"   18:13:05 ST   74W00'23"

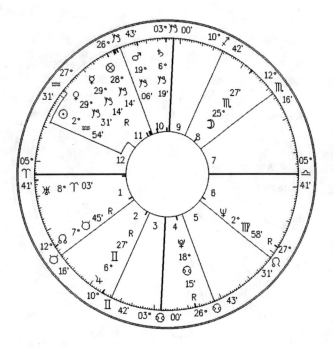

277. PLANT CORP –PLN   *Machinery*
Apr. 25, 1992   NYC   9:30 AM EST
40N45'00   22:49:15 ST   74W00'23

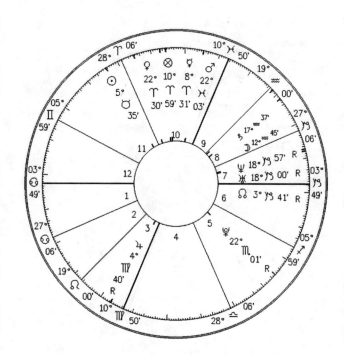

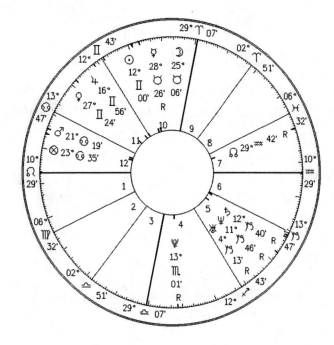

278. PLUM CREEK TIMBER-PCL   *Forest Products*
June 2, 1989   NYC   10:0:0 AM EDT
40N45'00"   1:48:16 ST   74W00'23"

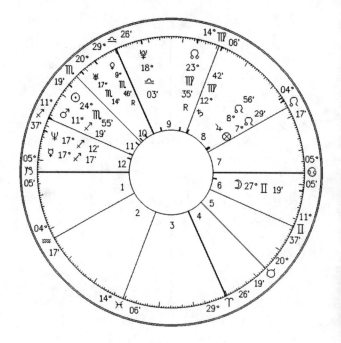

279. POGO PRODUCING-PPP   *Oil*
Nov. 17, 1978   NYC   10:0:0 AM EST
40N45'00"   13:49:28 ST   74W00'23"

280. POLAROID-PRD **Recreation**
Nov. 4, 1957 NYC 10:0:0 AM EST
40N45'00" 12:58:33 ST 74W00'23"

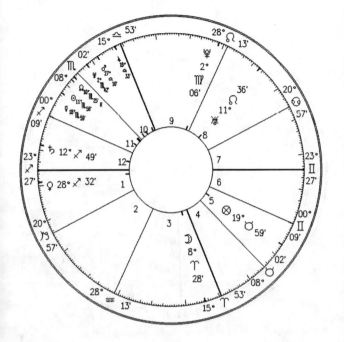

281. POLICY MANAGE.SYSTEM-PMS **Software**
July 10, 1990 NYC 9:30:0 AM EDT
40N45'00" 3:47:03 ST 74W00'23"

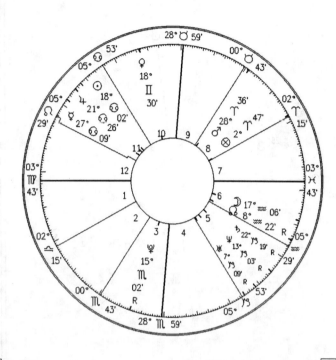

282. POTLATCH-PCH **Forest Products**
Dec. 15, 1969 NYC 10:0:0 AM EST
40N45'00" 15:40:34 ST 74W00'23"

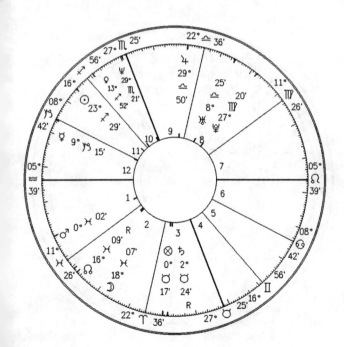

283. PPG IND.-PPG **Chemicals**
Dec. 17, 1945 NYC 10:0:0 AM EST
40N45'00" 15:47:42 ST 74W00'23"

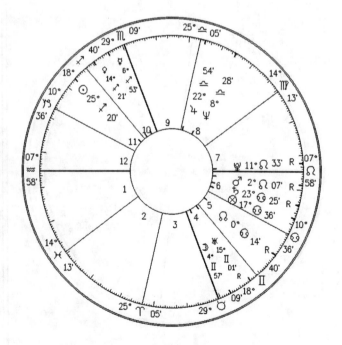

284. PRAXAIR-PX **Chemicals**
June 24, 1992 NYC 9:30:0 AM EDT
40N45'00" 2:46:00 ST 74W00'23"

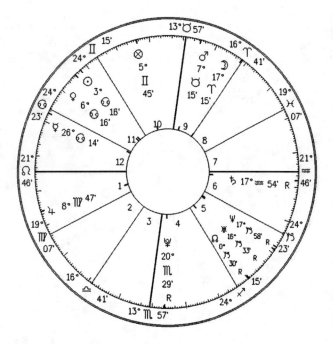

285. QUAKER OATS-OAT **Food**
Jan. 22, 1951 NYC 10:0:0 AM EST
40N45'00" 18:08:48 ST 74W00'23"

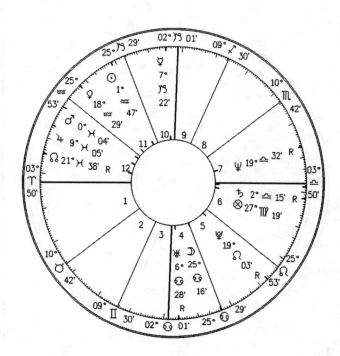

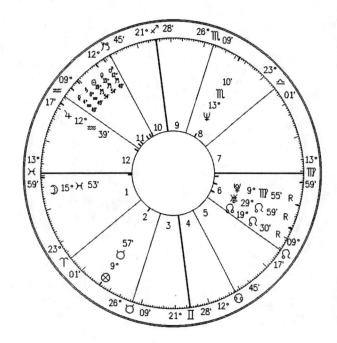

286. RALSTON PURINA-RAL **Food**
Jan. 10, 1962 NYC 10:0:0 AM EST
40N45'00" 17:22:49 ST 74W00'23"

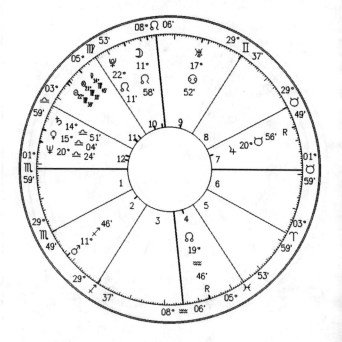

287. RAYTHEON-RTN **Aerospace**
Sep. 15, 1952 NYC 10:0:0 AM EDT
40N45'00" 8:42:05 ST 74W00'23"

288. READERS DIGEST-RDA   *Publishing*
Feb. 15, 1990 NYC   9:30:0 AM EST
40N45'00"   19:15:32 ST   74W00'23"

289. REEBOK-RBK   *Shoes*
Dec. 3, 1986 NYC   9:30:0 AM EST
40N45'00"   14:22:42 ST   74W00'23"

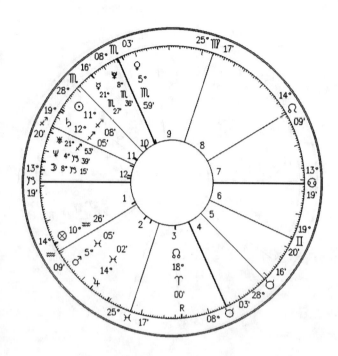

290. REYNOLDS METALS-RLM   *Metals*
Mar. 3, 1959 NYC   10:0:0 AM EST
40N45'00"   20:46:45 ST   74W00'23"

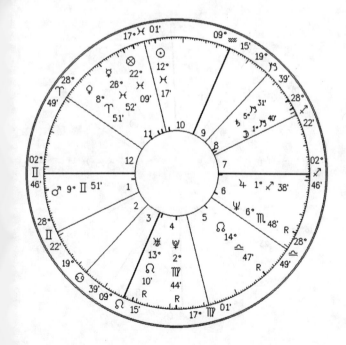

291. REYNOLDS+REYNOLDS-REY   *Office Equipment*
Jan. 26, 1989 NYC   9:30:0 AM EST
40N45'00"   17:57:38 ST   74W00'23"

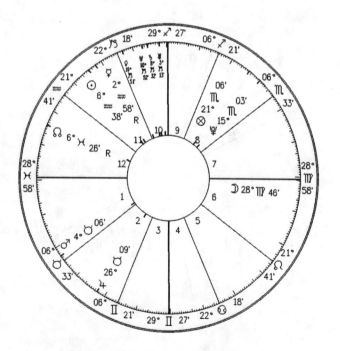

292. RITE AID-RAD　　**Retail**
Jan. 26, 1970　NYC　　10:0:0 AM EST
40N45'00"　　18:26:09 ST　　74W00'23"

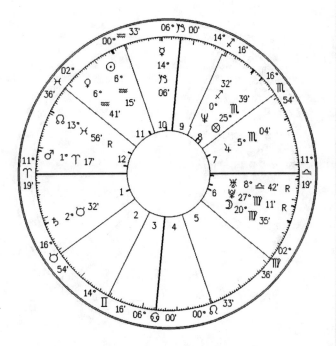

293. RJR NABISCO-RN　　**Tobacco**
Feb. 1, 1991　NYC　　9:30:0 AM EST
40N45'00"　　18:19:23 ST　　74W00'23"

294. ROWAN COS.-RDC　　**Oilfield Services**
Dec. 18, 1975　NYC　　10:0:0 AM EST
40N45'00"　　15:50:36 ST　　74W00'23"

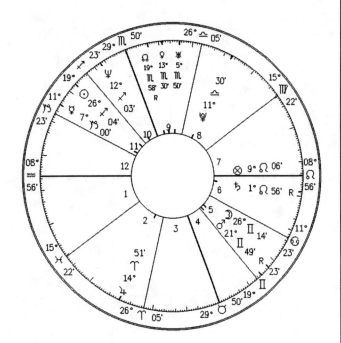

295. ROYAL DUTCH-RD　　**Oil**
July 20, 1954　NYC　　10:0:0 AM EDT
40N45'00"　　4:55:27 ST　　74W00'23"

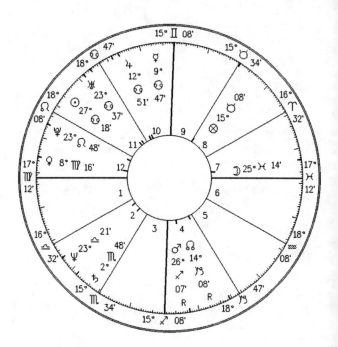

32

3342

222444

23243

296. RUBBERMAID-RBD   Consumer Products
June 22, 1959 NYC   10:0:0 AM EDT
40N45'00"   3:04:13 ST   74W00'23"

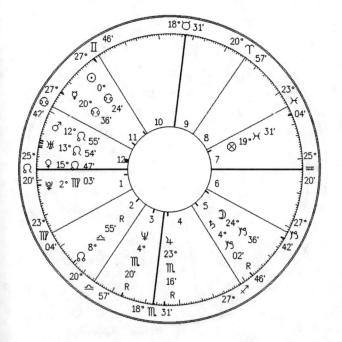

297. SALOMON BROS.-SB   Brokerage
Sep. 7, 1960 NYC   10:0:0 AM EDT
40N45'00"   8:10:47 ST   74W00'23"

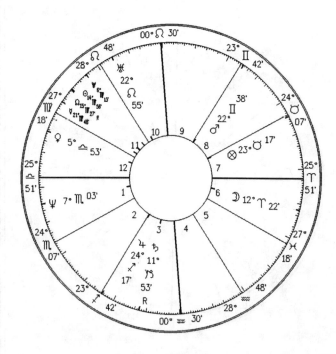

298. SANTA FE PACIFIC-SFL   Oil Pipeline
Dec. 13, 1988 NYC   9:30:0 AM EST
40N45'00"   15:04:10 ST   74W00'23"

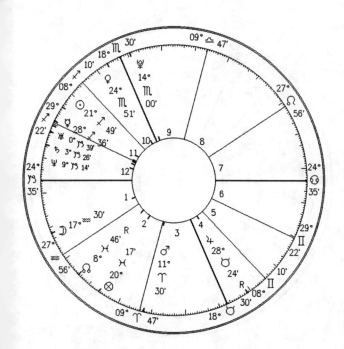

299. SARA LEE-SLE   Foods
July 10, 1951 NYC   10:0:0 AM EDT
40N45'00"   4:14:56 ST   74W00'23"

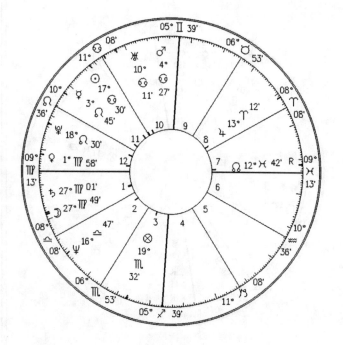

300. SCHERING PLOUGH-SGP   **Drugs**
Jan. 18, 1971 NYC   10:0:0 AM EST
40N45'00"   17:53:39 ST   74W00'23"

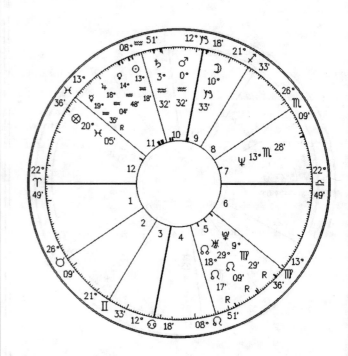

301. SCHLUMBERGER-SLB   **Oilfield Services**
Feb. 2, 1962 NYC   10:0:0 AM EST
40N45'00"   18:53:30 ST   74W00'23"

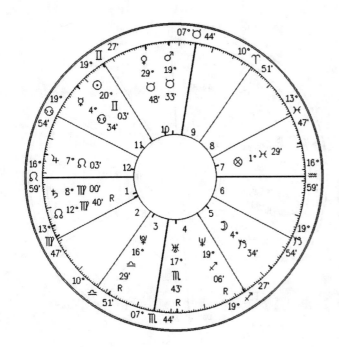

302. SCIENTIFIC ATLANTA-SFA   **Technology**
June 11, 1979 NYC   10:0:0 AM EDT
40N45'00"   2:21:28 ST   74W00'23"

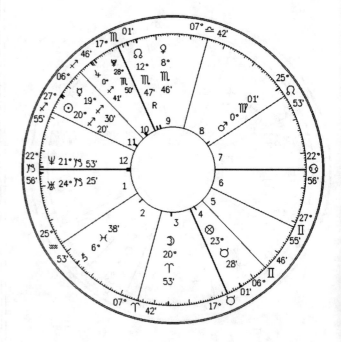

303. SEAGATE TECHNOLOGY-SEG **Computer Peripherals**
Dec 12, 1994 NYC   9:30 AM EST
40N45'00   14:58:14 ST   74W00'23

304. SEAGRAM-VO　　**Beverages**
Dec. 2, 1935　NYC　　10:0:0 AM EST
40N45'00"　　14:46:17 ST　　74W00'23"

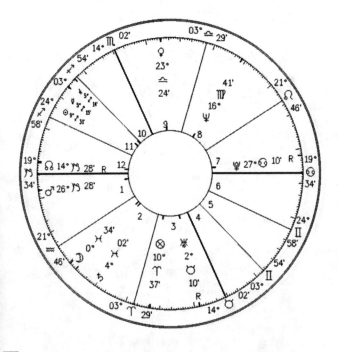

305. SENSORMATICS-SRM　**Technology**
May 16, 1991　NYC　　9:30:0 AM EDT
40N45'00"　　0:09:15 ST　　74W00'23"

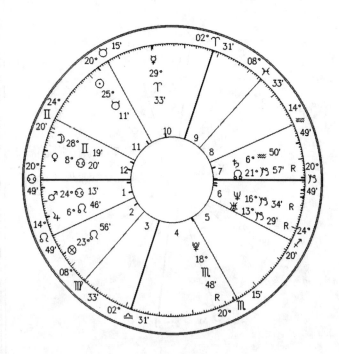

306. SHOPKO-SKO　　**Retail**
Oct. 8, 1991　NYC　　9:30:0 AM EDT
40N45'00"　　9:40:55 ST　　74W00'23"

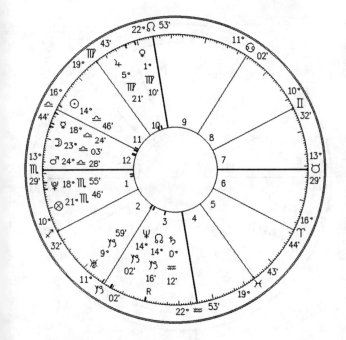

307. SILICON GRAPHICS-SGI　　**Computer Graphics**
Feb. 6, 1990　NYC　　9:30 AM EST
40N45'00　　1839:51　74W00'23

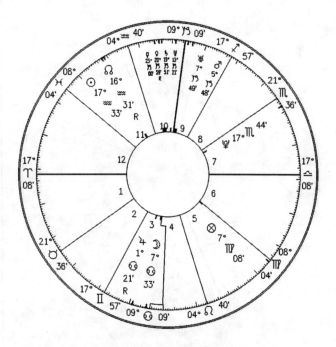

308. SKYLINE-SKY   *Recreation*
Jan. 10, 1969 NYC   10:0:0 AM EST
40N45'00"   17:24:01 ST   74W00'23"

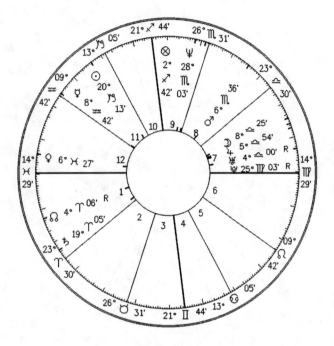

309. SMITH INTERNAT.-SII   *Oilfield Services*
Feb. 26, 1968 NYC   10:0:0 AM EST
40N45'00"   20:26:20 ST   74W00'23"

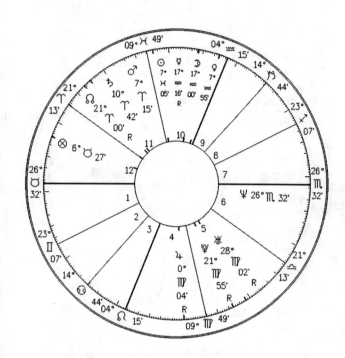

310. SNAP ON TOOLS-SNA   *Industrial*
Feb. 27, 1978 NYC   10:0:0 AM EST
40N45'00"   20:32:33 ST   74W00'23"

311. SPRINT-FON   *Telecommunications*
Apr. 10, 1963 NYC   10:0:0 AM EST
40N45'00"   23:16:42 ST   74W00'23"

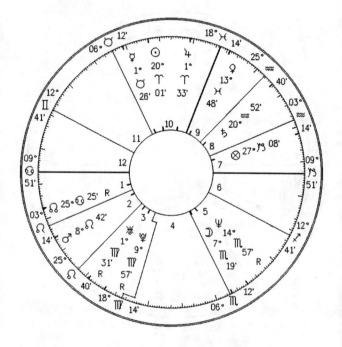

312. STERLING SOFTWARE-SSW   Software
  Mar. 28, 1990 NYC   9:30 AM EST
  40N45'00   21:56:59 ST   74W00'23

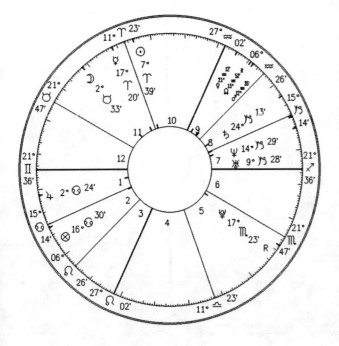

313. STORAGE TECHNOLOGY-STK Computer Equip.
  June 10, 1975 NYC   10:0:0 AM EDT
  40N45'00"   2:17:24 ST   74W00'23"

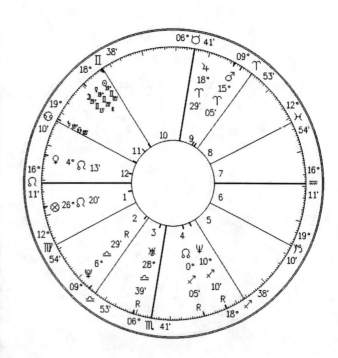

314. STRATUS COMPUTER-SRA   Computers
  Dec. 20, 1989 NYC   9:30:0 AM EST
  40N45'00"   15:30:48 ST   74W00'23"

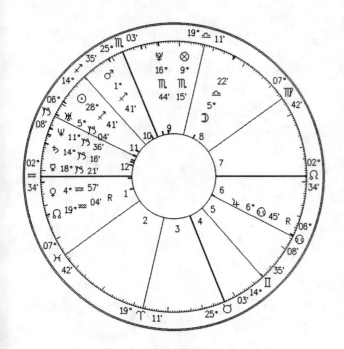

315. SUN CO.-SUN   Oil
  Oct. 1, 1971 NYC   10:0:0 AM EST
  40N45'00"   10:42:57 ST   74W00'23"

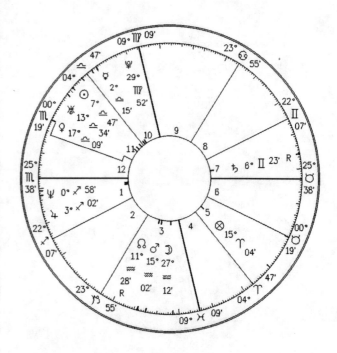

316. SUNDSTRAND-SNS   *Aerospace*
Dec. 2, 1966   NYC   10:0:0 AM EST
40N45'00"   14:48:14 ST   74W00'23"

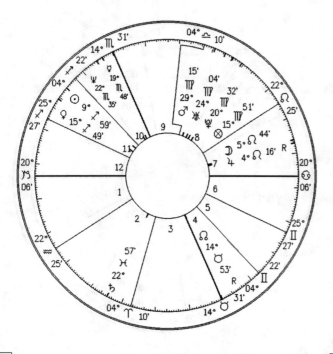

317. SYMBOL TECHNOLOGY-SBL   *Technology*
Jan. 28, 1988   NYC   9:30:0 AM EST
40N45'00"   18:02:32 ST   74W00'23"

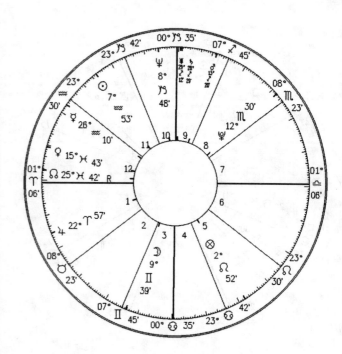

318. TAMBRANDS-TMB   *Personal Care*
June 1, 1994   NYC   10:00 AM EDT
40N45'00   1:44:57 ST   74W00'23

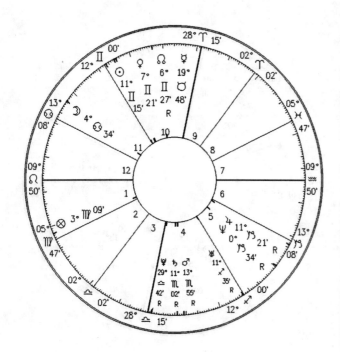

319. TANDEM-TDM   *Computers*
Apr. 7, 1987   NYC   9:30:0 AM EDT
40N45'00"   21:35:22 ST   74W00'23"

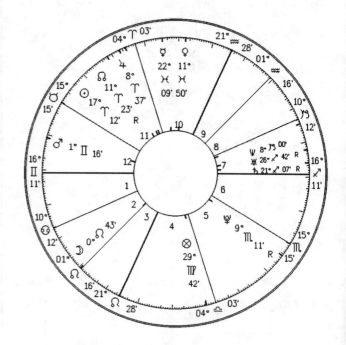

320. TANDY-TAN **Retail**
Feb. 28, 1968 NYC 10:0:0 AM EST
40N45'00" 20:34:13 ST 74W00'23"

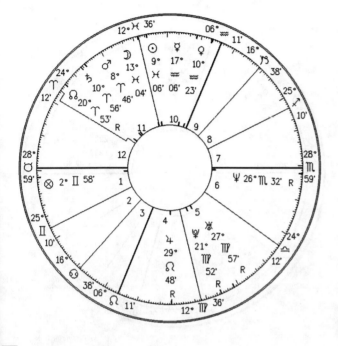

321. TCBY-TBY **Retail Food**
May 10, 1984 NYC 10:0:0 AM EDT
40N45'00" 0:18:25 ST 74W00'23"

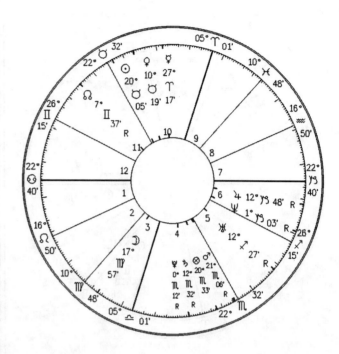

322. TEKTRONIX-TEK **Technology**
Jan. 10, 1964 NYC 10:0:0 AM EST
40N45'00" 17:20:55 ST 74W00'23"

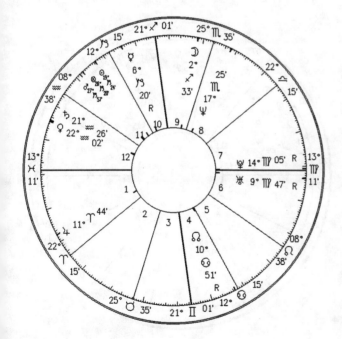

323. TELEPHONE DE MEXICO-TMX **Telephone**
May 14, 1991 NYC 9:30:0 AM EDT
40N45'00" 0:01:22 ST 74W00'23"

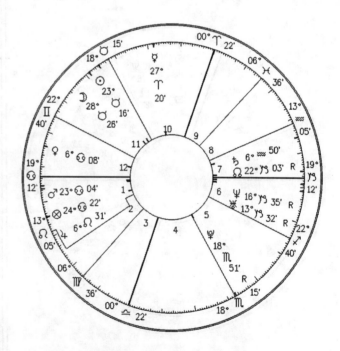

324. TEMPLE INLAND-TIN *Packaging*
Dec. 19, 1983 NYC   10:0:0 AM EST
40N45'00"   15:54:47 ST   74W00'23"

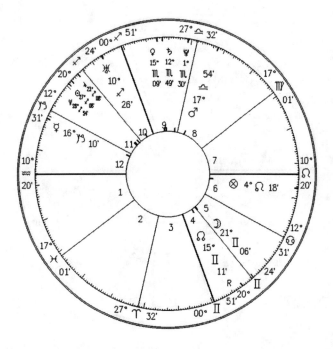

325. TENNECO-TEN   *Nat. Gas Pipeline*
Dec. 28, 1967 NYC   10:0:0 AM EST
40N45'00"   16:29:47 ST   74W00'23"

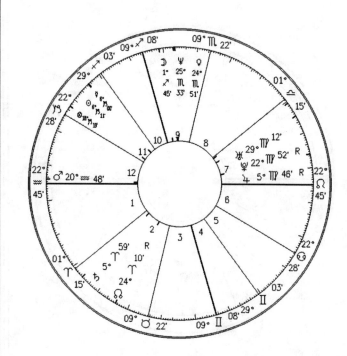

326. TEXACO-TX *Oil*
Oct. 28, 1926 NYC   10:00 AM EST
40N45'00   12:29:00 ST   74W00'23

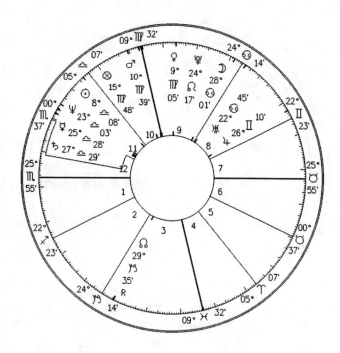

327. TEXAS INSTRUMENTS-TXN   *Semiconductors*
Oct. 1, 1953 NYC   10:0:0 AM EST
40N45'00"   10:44:22 ST   74W00'23"

328. TEXTRON-TXT **Aerospace**
Dec. 22, 1947 NYC 10:0:0 AM EST
40N45'00" 16:05:31 ST 74W00'23"

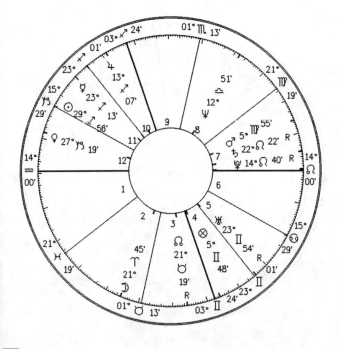

329. THOMAS & BETTS-TNB **Electric Equipment**
Sep. 27, 1962 NYC 10:0:0 AM EDT
40N45'00" 9:27:44 ST 74W00'23"

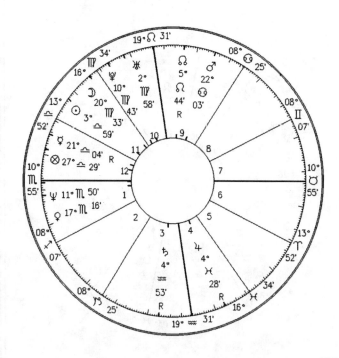

330. TIFFANY-TIF **Retail**
May 5, 1987 NYC 9:30:0 AM EDT
40N45'00" 23:25:45 ST 74W00'23"

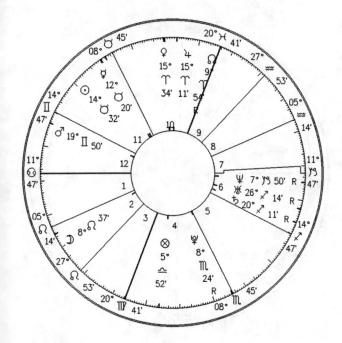

331. TIME WARNER-TWX **Entertainment**
Dec. 11, 1989 NYC 9:30:0 AM EST
40N45'00" 14:55:19 ST 74W00'23"

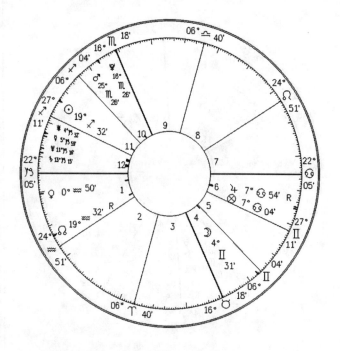

332. TIMKEN-TKR *Industrial*
Sep. 26, 1922 NYC   10:0:0 AM EST
40N45'00"   10:22:43 ST   74W00'23"

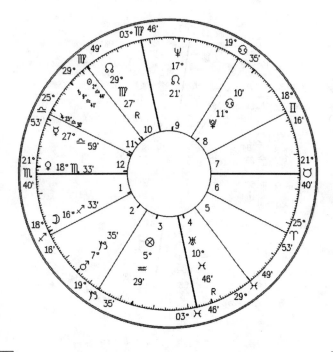

333. TJX COS.-TJX   **Retail**
June 25, 1987 NYC   9:30:0 AM EDT
40N45'00"   2:46:50 ST   74W00'23"

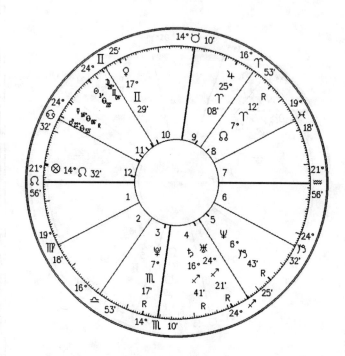

334. TOLL BROS.-TOL   **Home Building**
July 16, 1986 NYC   9:30:0 AM EDT
40N45'00"   4:10:35 ST   74W00'23"

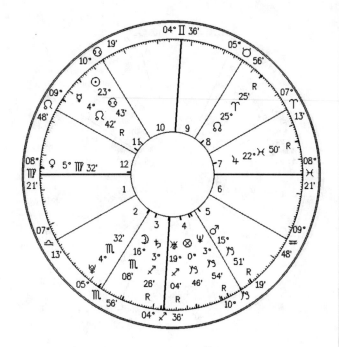

335. TOOTSIE ROLL-TR   **Food**
Aug 19, 1946 NYC   10:00 AM EDT
40N45'00   6:53:17 ST   74W00'23

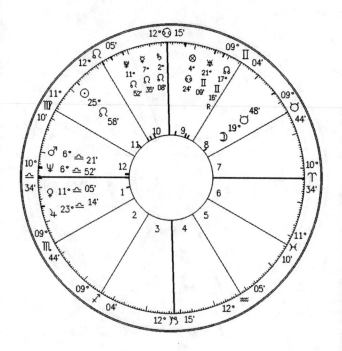

336. TOSCO-TOS *Oil*
Jan. 30, 1980 NYC 10:00 AM EST
40N45'00 18:40:03 ST 74W00'23

337. TOTAL-TOT *Oil*
Oct. 28, 1991 NYC 9:30:0 AM EST
40N45'00" 11:59:56 ST 74W00'23"

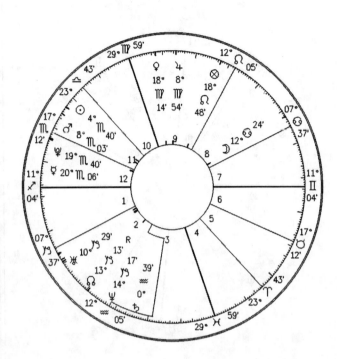

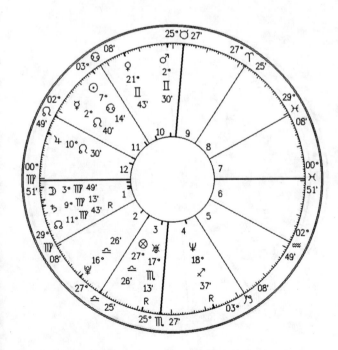

338. TOYS R US-TOY *Recreation*
June 29, 1979 NYC 10:0:0 AM EDT
40N45'00" 3:32:26 ST 74W00'23"

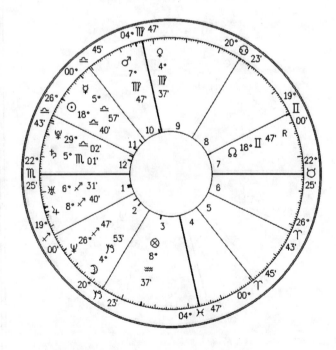

339. TRIBUNE-TRB *Publishing*
Oct. 12, 1983 NYC 10:0:0 AM EDT
40N45'00" 10:26:32 ST 74W00'23"

340. TRITON ENERGY-OIL   Oil
Sep. 15, 1982 NYC   10:0:0 AM EDT
40N45'00"   8:41:02 ST   74W00'23"

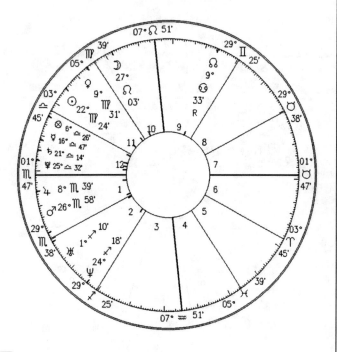

341. TRW-TRW   Aerospace
Feb. 14, 1930 NYC   10:0:0 AM EST
40N45'00"   19:39:50 ST   74W00'23"

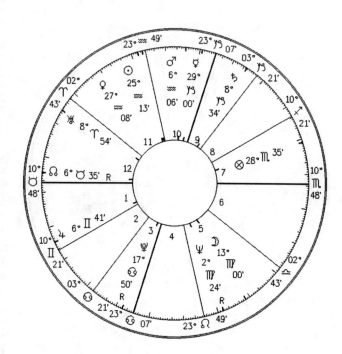

342. TULTEX-TTX   Apparel
May 21, 1985 NYC   10:0:0 AM EDT
40N45'00"   1:00:50 ST   74W00'23"

343. U.S. HOME-UH   Homebuilding
July 6, 1971 NYC   10:0:0 AM EDT
40N45'00"   3:59:47 ST   74W00'23"

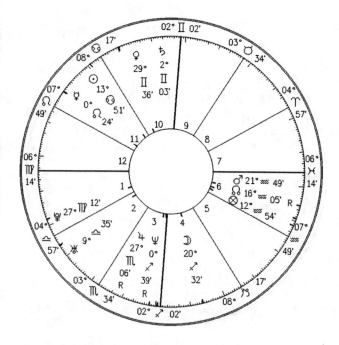

344. U.S. SURGICAL-USS **Medical Equipment**
Dec. 9, 1987 NYC   9:30:0 AM EST
40N45'00"   14:45:24 ST   74W00'23"

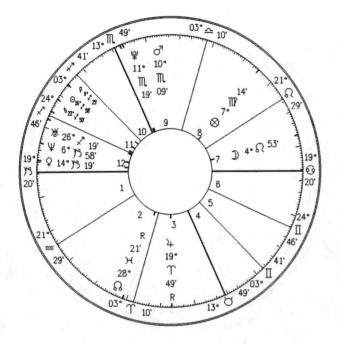

345. U.S. WEST-USW **Telephone**
Jan. 2, 1984 NYC   10:0:0 AM EST
40N45'00"   16:49:59 ST   74W00'23"

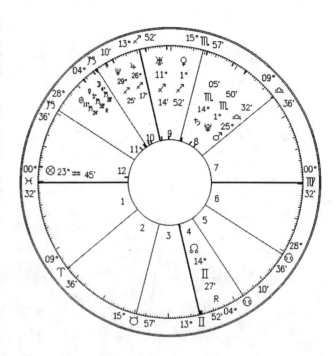

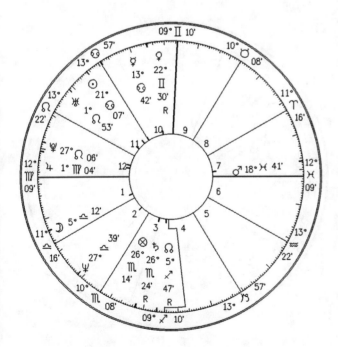

346. UNION CAMP PRODUCTS- UCC **Paper Products**
July 13, 1956 NYC   10:0:0 AM EDT
40N45'00"   4:29:53 ST   74W00'23"

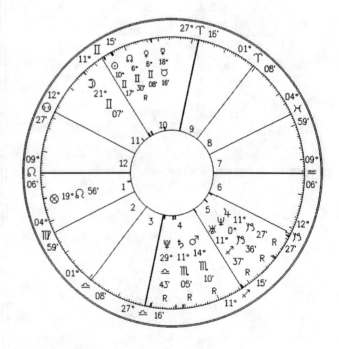

347. UNISYS-UIS **Computers**
May 31, 1984 NYC   10:0:0 AM EDT
40N45'00"   1:41:13 ST   74W00'23"

348. UNITED HEALTH-UNH   **Health Care**
Oct. 10, 1991   NYC   9:30:0 AM EDT
40N45'00"   9:48:49 ST   74W00'23"

349. UNIVERSAL FOODS-UFC   **Foods**
Nov. 15, 1979   NYC   10:0:0 AM EST
40N45'00"   13:40:37 ST   74W00'23"

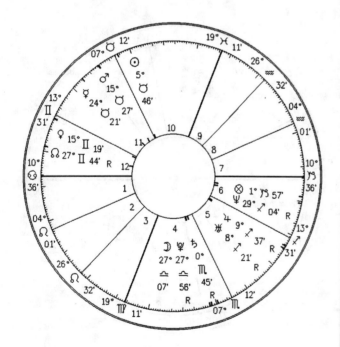

350. UNOCAL-UCL   **Oil**
Apr. 26, 1983   NYC   10:0:0 AM EDT
40N45'00"   23:20:14 ST   74W00'23"

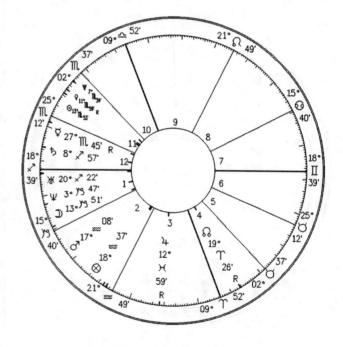

351. UNUM CORP.-UNM   **Insurance**
Nov. 6, 1986   NYC   9:30:0 AM EST
40N45'00"   12:36:15 ST   74W00'23"

352. USF&G-FG **Insurance**
Oct. 1, 1981   NYC   10:0:0 AM EST
40N45'00"   10:45:14 ST   74W00'23"

353. USG CORP.-USG **Building Materials**
Jan. 2, 1985   NYC   10:0:0 AM EST
40N45'00"   16:52:58 ST   74W00'23"

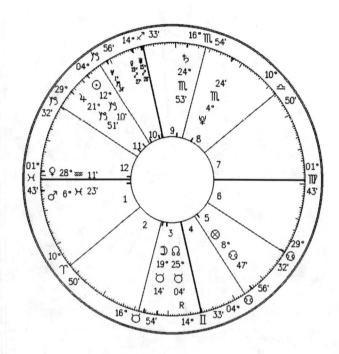

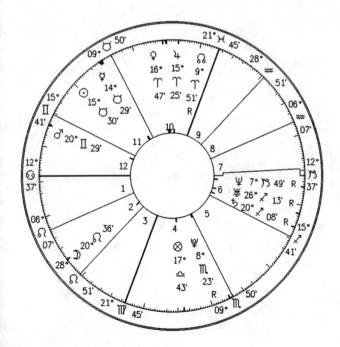

354. UST-UST **Tobacco**
May 6, 1987   NYC   9:30:0 AM EDT
40N45'00"   23:29:42 ST   74W00'23"

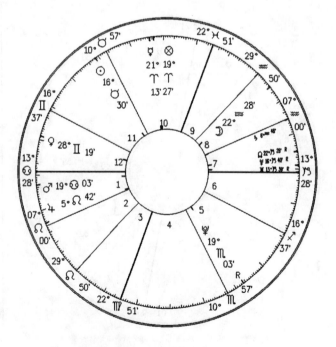

355. USX MARATHON-MRO **Oil**
May 7, 1991   NYC   9:30:0 AM EDT
40N45'00"   23:33:46 ST   74W00'23"

356. USX-X   **Steel**
July 9, 1986   NYC   9:30:0 AM EDT
40N45'00"   3:42:59 ST   74W00'23"

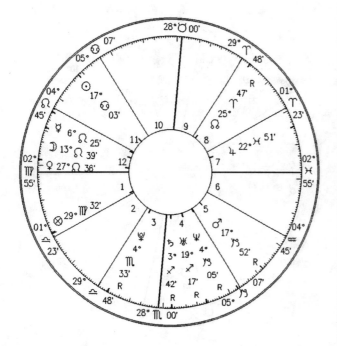

357. VALASSIS COMMUN.-VCI   **Commercial Services**
Mar. 11, 1992   NYC   9:30:0 AM EST
40N45'00""   20:51:58 ST   74W00'23"

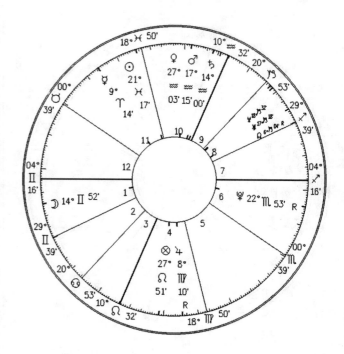

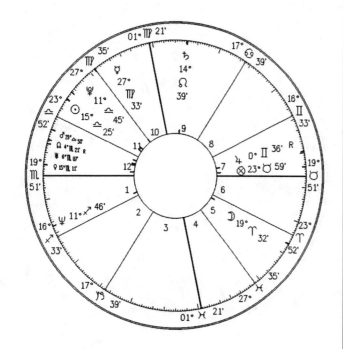

358. VARIAN-VAR   **Technology**
Oct. 8, 1976   NYC   10:0:0 AM EDT
40N45'00"   10:13:30 ST   74W00'23"

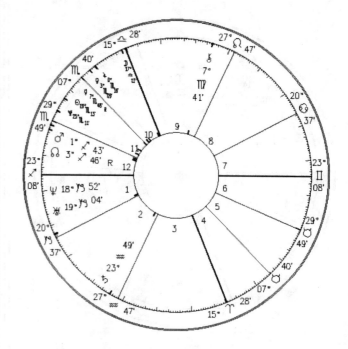

359. VESTA INSURANCE-VTA   **Insurance**
Nov. 11, 1993   NYC   9:30:0 AM EST
40N45'00""   13:00:53 ST   74W00'23"

360. W.R. GRACE-GRA **Chemicals**
Feb. 27, 1953 NYC   10:0:0 AM EST
40N45'00" 20:32:46 ST   74W00'23"

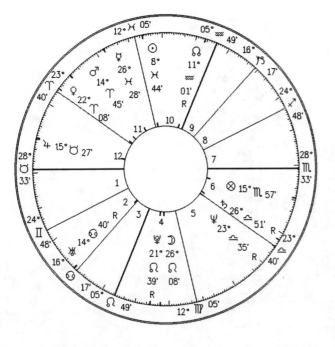

361. WABAN-WBN **Retail**
June 15, 1989 NYC   9:30:0 AM EDT
40N45'00" 2:09:26 ST   74W00'23"

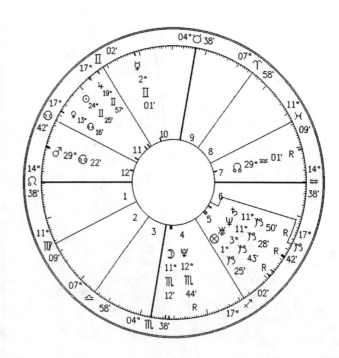

362. WALGREEN-WAG **Retail**
Dec. 16, 1952 NYC   10:0:0 AM EST
40N45'00" 15:44:58 ST   74W00'23"

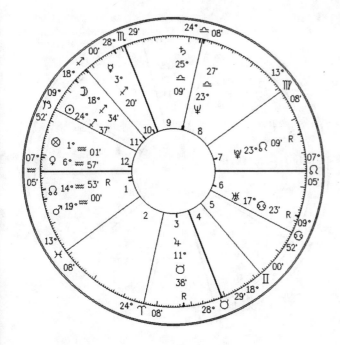

363. WARNACO-WAC **Apparel**
Oct. 11, 1991 NYC   9:30:0 AM EST
40N45'00" 12:55:08 ST   74W00'23"

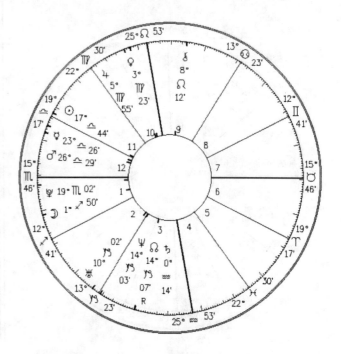

364. WARNER LAMBERT-WLA   **Drugs**
June 18, 1951 NYC   10:0:0 AM EDT
40N45'00"   2:48:12 ST   74W00'23"

365. WASTE MANAGEMENT-WMX   **Waste Management**
Oct. 25, 1973 NYC   10:0:0 AM EDT
40N45'00""   11:19:13 ST   74W00'23"

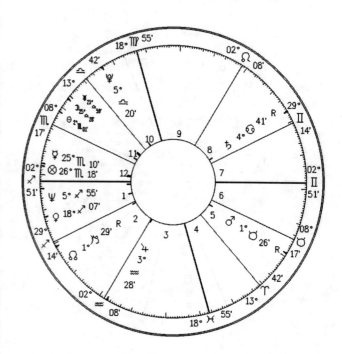

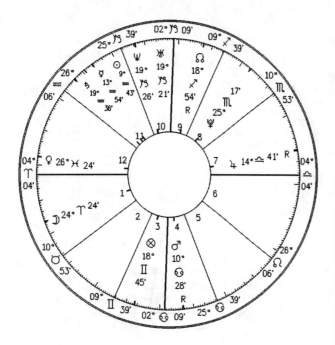

366. WELLPOINT HEALTH-WLP   **Health Care**
Jan. 29, 1993 NYC   9:30:0 AM EST
40N45'00""   18:09:22 ST   74W00'23"

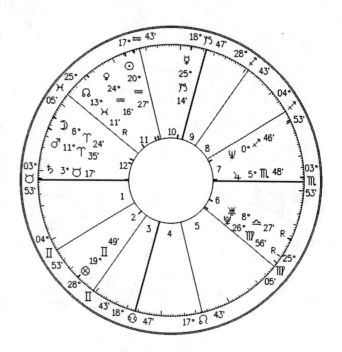

367. WELLS FARGO-WFC   **Banks**
Feb. 9, 1970 NYC   10:0:0 AM EST
40N45'00"   19:21:21 ST   74W00'23"

368. WENDYS-WEN **Restaurants**
May 27, 1981 NYC   10:0:0 AM EDT
40N45'00"   1:24:22 ST   74W00'23"

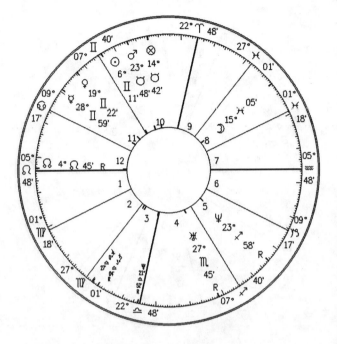

369. WESTERN DIGITAL-WDC **Computer Equipment**
Feb. 5, 1991 NYC   9:30:0 AM EST
40N45'00"   18:35:09 ST   74W00'23"

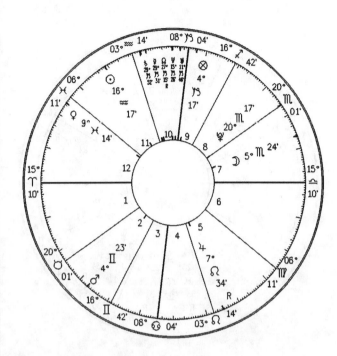

370. WESTERN GAS RESOURCE-WGR **Nat. Gas Pipeline**
Dec. 8, 1989 NYC   9:30:0 AM EST
40N45'00"   14:43:30 ST   74W00'23"

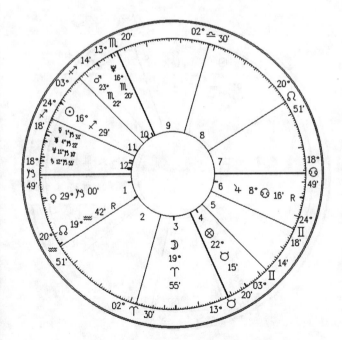

371. WESTINGHOUSE-WX **Electrical Equip.**
May 11, 1945 NYC   10.00 AM EDT
40N45'00"   0:20:10 ST   74W00'23"

372. WESTVACO-W **Forest Products**
Nov. 22, 1939 NYC 10:0:0 AM EST
40N45'00" 14:06:59 ST 74W00'23"

373. WEYERHAUSER-WY **Forest Products**
Dec. 6, 1963 NYC 10:0:0 AM EST
40N45'00" 15:02:55 ST 74W00'23"

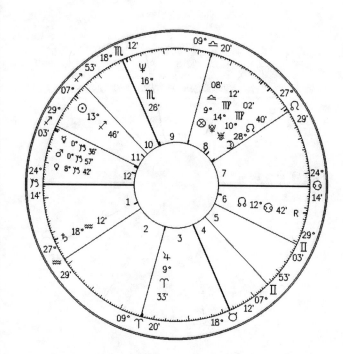

374. WHIRLPOOL-WHR **Home Furnishings, Appliances**
Sep. 13, 1955 NYC 10:0:0 AM EDT
40N45'00" 8:31:20 ST 74W00'23"

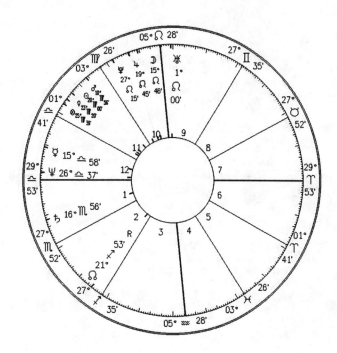

375. WINN-DIXIE-WIN **Retail Food**
Feb. 18, 1952 NYC 10:0:0 AM EST
40N45'00" 19:54:18 ST 74W00'23"

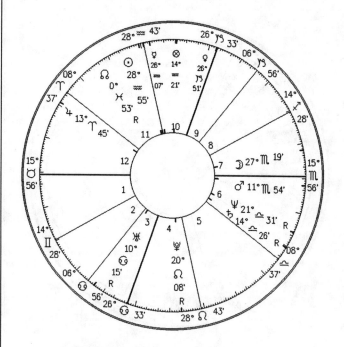

376. WMS INDUSTRIES-WMS   *Recreation*
Feb. 11, 1982   NYC   10:0:0 AM EST
40N45'00"   19:29:36 ST   74W00'23"

377. WOLVERINE TUBE-WLV   *Industrial*
Aug. 13, 1993   NYC   9:30:0 AM EDT
40N45'00""   6:01:57 ST   74W00'23"

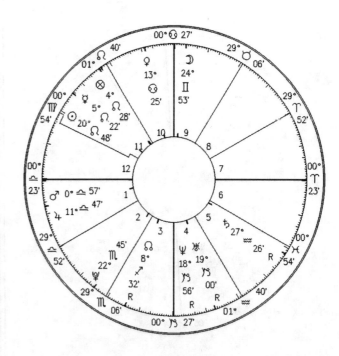

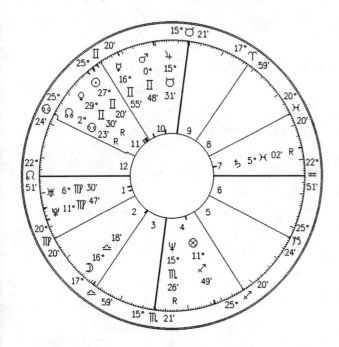

378. WOOLWORTH-Z   *Retail*
June 18,1964   NYC   10:00 AM EDT
40N45'00   2:15:34 ST   74W00'23

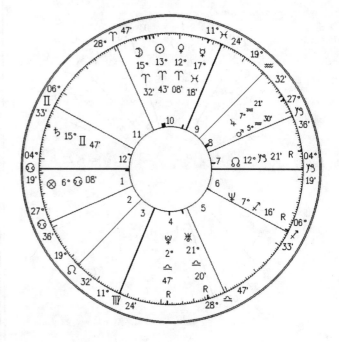

379. WRIGLEY-WWY   *Food*
Apr. 3, 1973   NYC   10:0:0 AM EST
40N45'00"   22:51:23 ST   74W00'23"

380. XEROX-XRX   *Office equipment*
July 11, 1962   NYC   10:0:0 AM EDT
40N45'00"   4:20:12 ST   74W00'23"

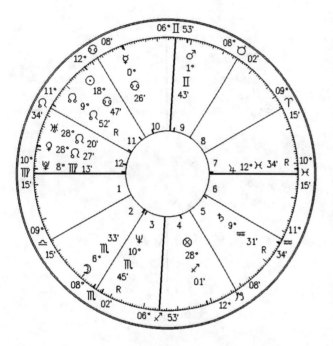

381. ZENITH ELECTRONICS-ZE   *Electronics*
Apr. 1, 1958   NYC   10:0:0 AM EST
40N45'00"   22:42:03 ST   74W00'23"

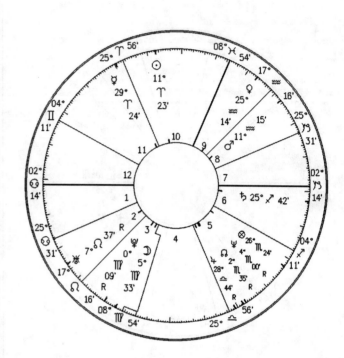

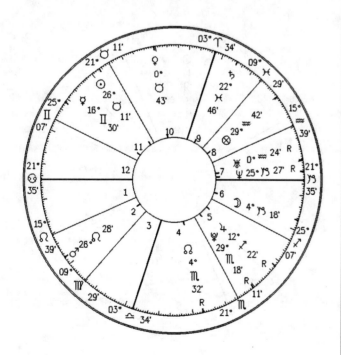

382. ZILOG-ZLG   *Semiconductors*
May 17, 1995   NYC   9:30 AM EDT
40N45'00   0:13:07 ST   74W00'23

201
OTC

First Trade Charts

1. **3 COM-COMS** *Semiconductors*
Mar. 21, 1984   NYC   10:0:0 AM EST
40N45'00"   22:01:27 ST   74W00'23"

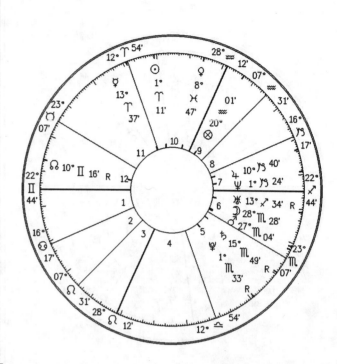

2. **3DO-THDO** *Entertainment*
May 4, 1993   NYC   9:30:0 AM EDT
40N45'00"   23:23:45 ST   74W00'23"

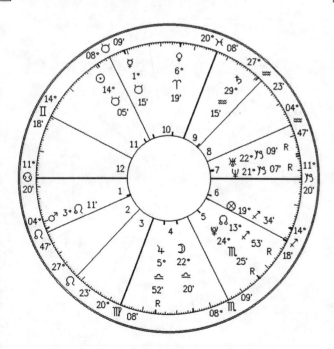

3. **ABAXIS-ABAX** *Medical Equipment*
Jan. 23, 1992   NYC   9:30:0 AM EST
40N45'00"   17:42:43 ST   74W00'23"

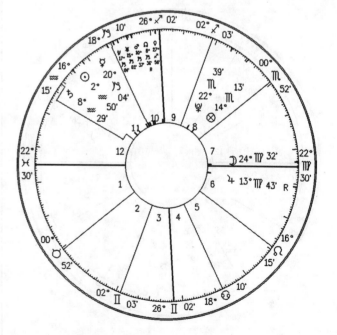

4. ACCLAIM-AKLM   Software
June 22, 1988   NYC   9:30:0 AM EDT
40N45'00"   2:37:46 ST   74W00'23"

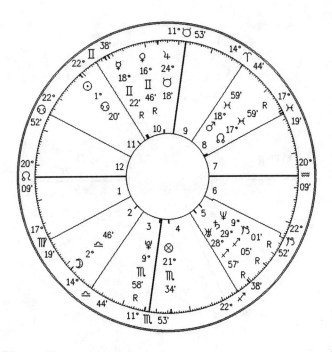

5. ADAPTEC-ADPT   Computer Equip
June 11, 1986   NYC   9:30:0 AM EDT
40N45'00"   1:52:35 ST   74W00'23"

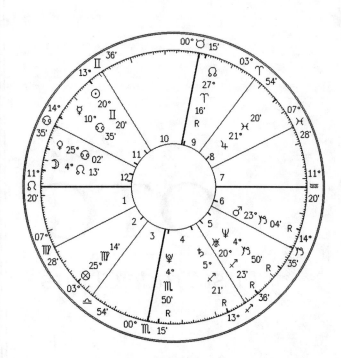

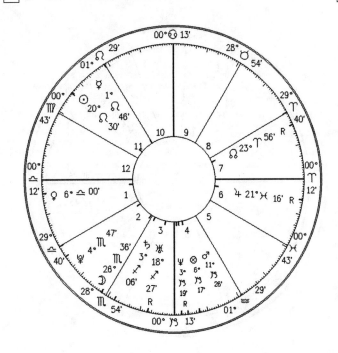

6. ADOBE-ADBE   Software
Aug. 13, 1986   NYC   9:30:0 AM EDT
40N45'00"   6:00:58 ST   74W00'23"

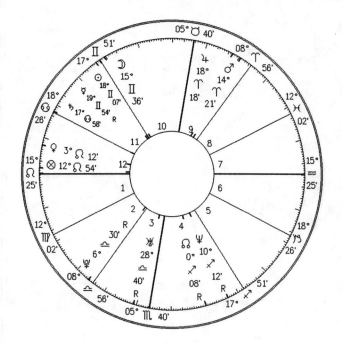

7. ADOLPH COORS-ACCOB   Beverage
June 9, 1975   NYC   10:0:0 AM EDT
40N45'00"   2:13:28 ST   74W00'23"

8. ADVANCED LOGIC RES.-AALR   Computers
Apr. 12, 1990   NYC   9:30:0 AM EDT
40N45'00"   21:56:09 ST   74W00'23"

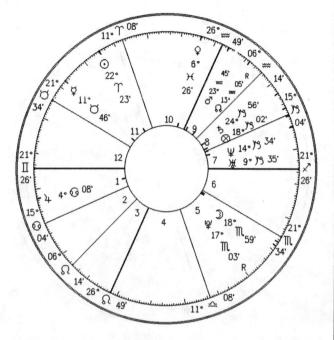

9. ADVANTAGE BANCORP-AADV   Banks
Mar. 24, 1992   NYC   9:30:0 AM EST
40N45'00"   21:43:27 ST   74W00'23"

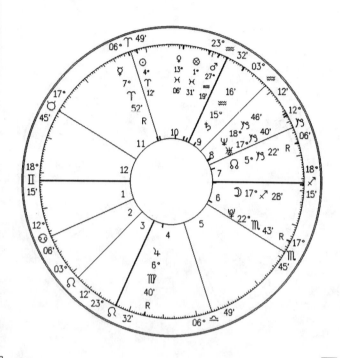

10. ALBANK FINANCIAL-ALBK   Banks
Apr. 1, 1992   NYC   9:30:0 AM EST
40N45'00"   22:14:59 ST   74W00'23"

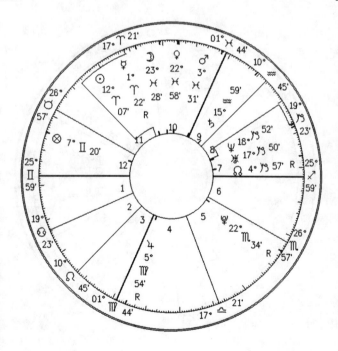

11. ALPHA MICRO SYSTEMS-ALMI   Computer
June 17, 1981   NYC   10:0:0 AM EDT
40N45'00"   0:07:16 ST   74W00'23"

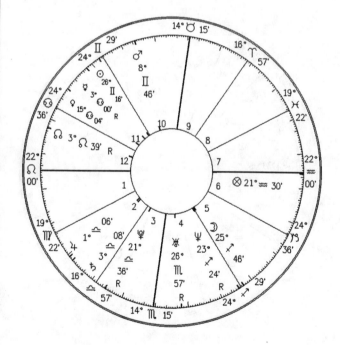

12. ALTERA-ALTR *Semiconductors*
Mar. 31, 1988   NYC   9:30:0 AM EST
40N45'00"   22:10:42 ST   74W00'23"

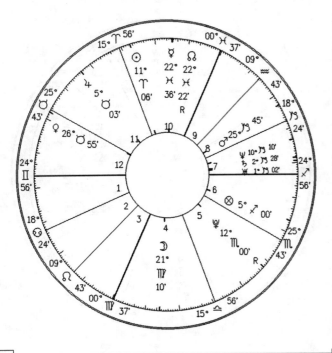

13. AMAZON-AMZN *Electronic Commerce*
May 15, 1997   NYC   9:30:0 AM EDT
40N45'00"   0:07:16 ST   74W00'23"

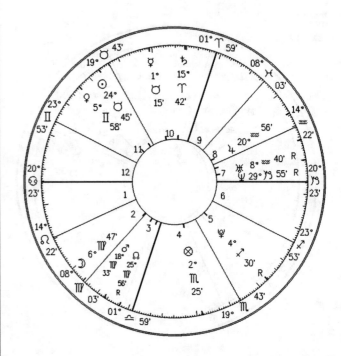

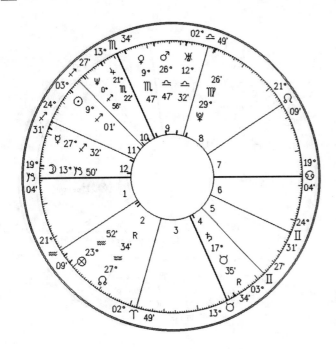

14. AMERICAN GREETINGS-AGREA *Consumer Prod.*
Dec. 1, 1970   NYC   10:0:0 AM EST
40N45'00"   14:44:25 ST   74W00'23"

15. AMERICAN POWER CONV-APCC *Computer Equip*
July 2, 1988   NYC   9:30:0 AM EDT
40N45'00"   3:17:25 ST   74W00'23"

16. AMGEN-AMGN   **Biotech**
June 17, 1983   NYC   10:0:0 AM EDT
40N45'00"   2:45:15 ST   74W00'23"

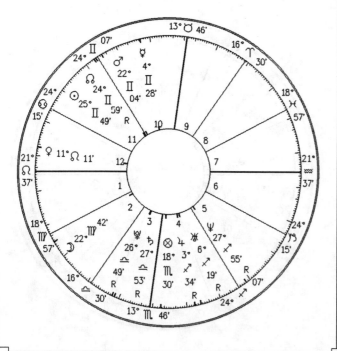

17. ANCHOR BANCSHARES-ABCW   **Banks**
July 16, 1992   NYC   9:30:0 AM EDT
40N45'00"   4:12:44 ST   74W00'23"

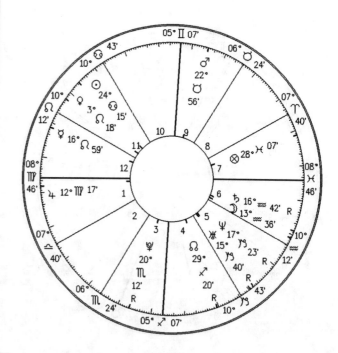

18. ANDREW CORP.-ANDW   **Telecom**
June 18, 1980   NYC   10:0:0 AM EDT
40N45'00"   2:52:03 ST   74W00'23"

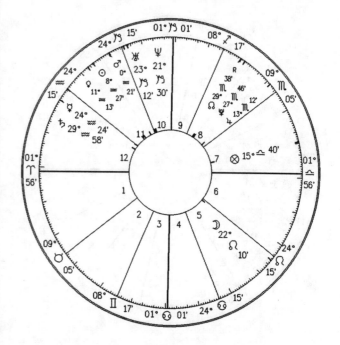

19. ANESTA CORP.-NSTA   **Drugs**
Jan. 28, 1994   NYC   9:30:0 AM EST
40N45'00"   18:04:28 ST   74W00'23"

20. APPLE COMP.-AAPL   *Computers*
Dec. 12, 1980   NYC   10:0:0 AM EST
40N45'00"   15:30:03 ST   74W00'23"

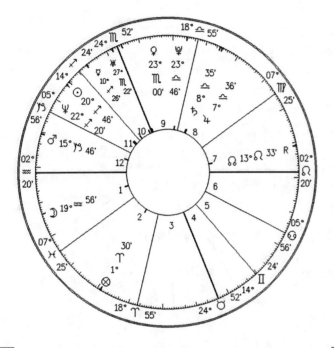

21. APPLE SOUTH-APSO   *Restaurants*
Nov. 21, 1991   NYC   9:30:0 AM EST
40N45'00"   13:34:34 ST   74W00'23"

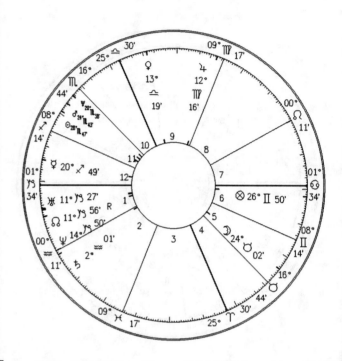

22. APPLIED MATERIALS-AMAT   *Semiconductors*
Oct. 12, 1972   NYC   10:0:0 AM EDT
40N45'00"   10:28:57 ST   74W00'23"

23. ARROW IND.-ARRO   *Medical Equipment*
June 9, 1992   NYC   9:30:0 AM EDT
40N45'00"   1:46:51 ST   74W00'23"

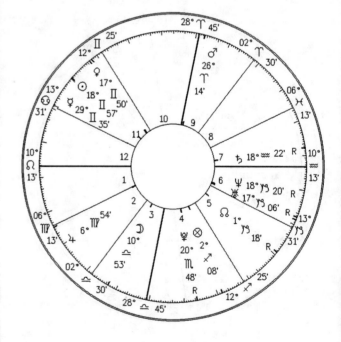

24. ASCEND COMMUNS.-ASND *Local Networks*
May 16, 1994   NYC   9:30:0 AM EDT
40N45'00"   0:10:08 ST   74W00'23"

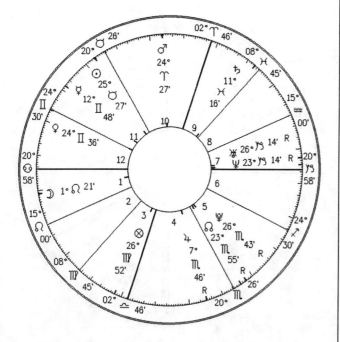

25. AST RESEARCH-ASTA *Computers*
Dec. 20, 1984   NYC   10:0:0 AM EST
40N45'00"   16:01:43 ST   74W00'23"

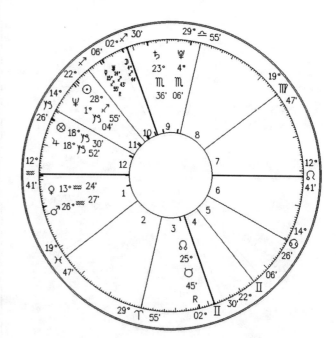

26. ATLANTIC COAST AIR-ACAI *Airline*
July 22, 1993   NYC   9:30:0 AM EDT
40N45'00"   4:35:13 ST   74W00'23"

27. AUSPEX-ASPX *Computers*
May 12, 1993   NYC   9:30:0 AM EDT
40N45'00"   23:55:17 ST   74W00'23"

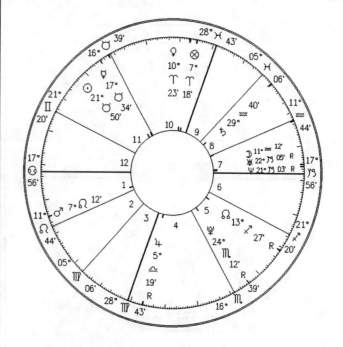

28. AVID TECHNOLOGY-AVID   Consumer Products
Mar. 12, 1993   NYC   9:30:0 AM EST
40N45'00"   20:54:57 ST   74W00'23"

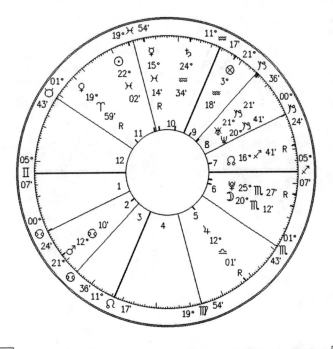

29. BANYAN SYSTEMS-BNYN   Software
Aug. 7, 1992   NYC   9:30:0 AM EDT
40N45'00"   5:39:15 ST   74W00'23"

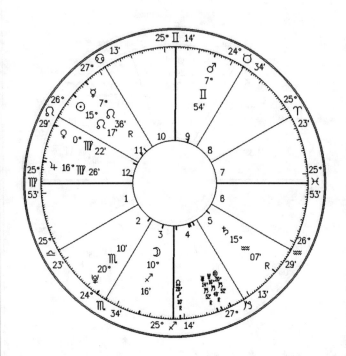

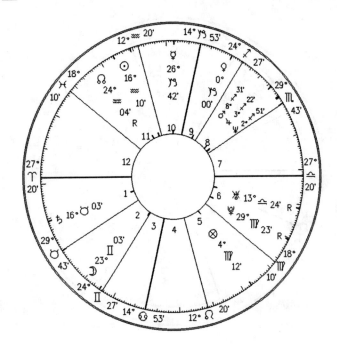

30. BASSETT FURNITURE-BSET   Household Furn.
Feb. 5, 1971   NYC   10:0:0 AM EST
40N45'00"   19:04:37 ST   74W00'23"

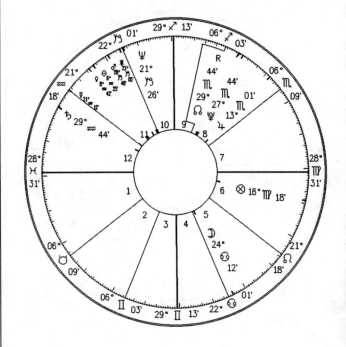

31. BATTERY TECH.-BTIOF   Industrial
Jan. 26, 1994   NYC   9:30:0 AM EST
40N45'00"   17:56:35 ST   74W00'23"

32. BED, BATH & BEYOND-BBBY   Retail
June 5, 1992   NYC   9:30:0 AM EDT
40N45'00"   1:31:05 ST   74W00'23"

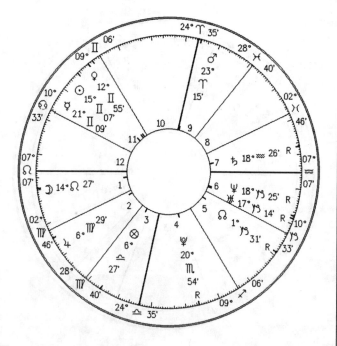

33. BELL SPORTS-BSPT   Recreation
Apr. 9, 1992   NYC   9:30:0 AM EDT
40N45'00"   21:46:22 ST   74W00'23"

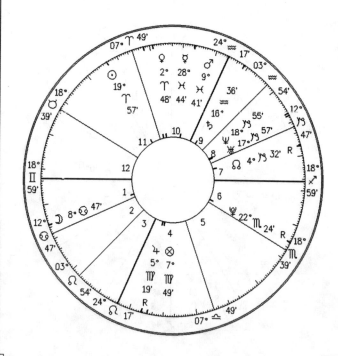

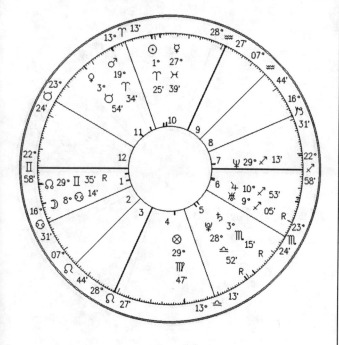

34. BIOGEN-BGEN   Biotech
Mar. 22, 1983   NYC   10:0:0 AM EST
40N45'00"   22:02:24 ST   74W00'23"

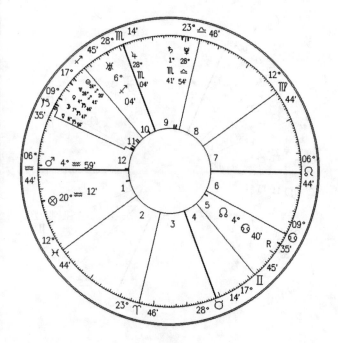

35. BIOMET-BMET   Biotech
Dec. 16, 1982   NYC   10:0:0 AM EST
40N45'00"   15:43:55 ST   74W00'23"

36. BMC SOFTWARE-BMCS   Software
Aug. 12, 1988   NYC   9:30:0 AM EDT
40N45'00"   5:58:50 ST   74W00'23"

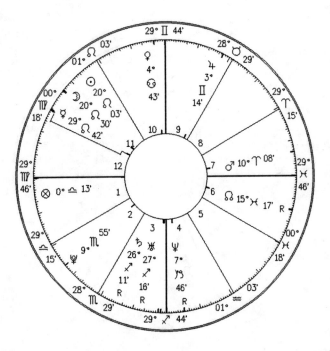

37. BOSTON CHICKEN-BOST   Restaurant
Nov. 8, 1993   NYC   9:30:0 AM EST
40N45'00"   12:45:07 ST   74W00'23"

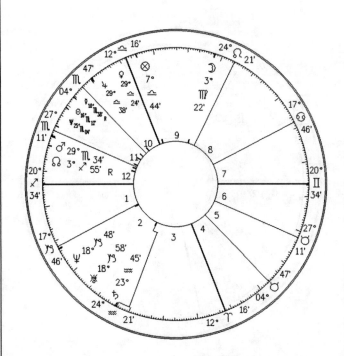

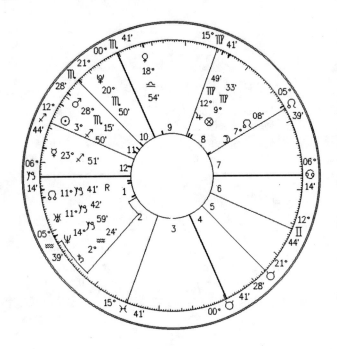

38. BRODERBUND-BROD   Software
Nov. 26, 1991   NYC   9:30:0 AM EST
40N45'00"   13:54:17 ST   74W00'23"

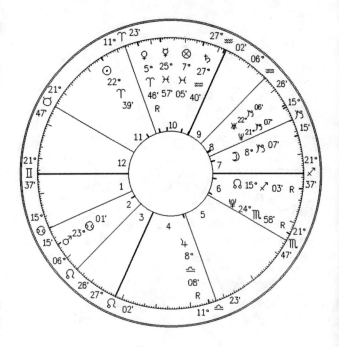

39. CAMBRIDGE TECH.-CATP   Software
Apr. 12, 1993   NYC   9:30:0 AM EDT
40N45'00"   21:57:00 ST   74W00'23"

40. CE SOFTWARE-CESH   *Software*
Oct. 16, 1990   NYC   9:30:0 AM EDT
40N45'00"   10:13:25 ST   74W00'23"

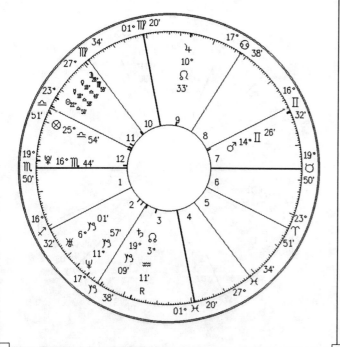

41. CELESTIAL SEASONS-CTEA   *Food*
July 7, 1993   NYC   9:30:0 AM EDT
40N45'00"   3:36:04 ST   74W00'23"

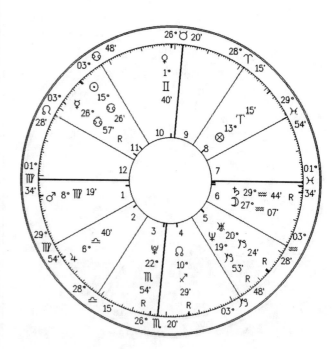

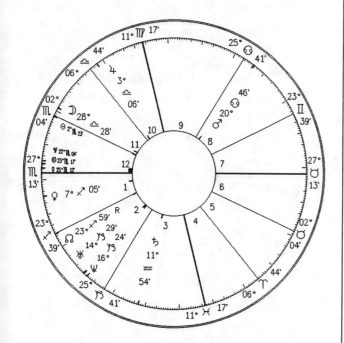

42. CENFED FINANCIAL-CENF   *Banks*
Oct. 25, 1992   NYC   9:30:0 AM EDT
40N45'00"   10:50:56 ST   74W00'23"

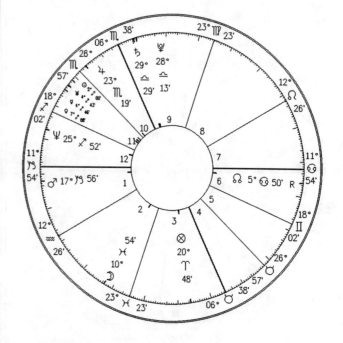

43. CENTOCOR-CNTO   *Biotech*
Nov. 24, 1982   NYC   10:0:0 AM EST
40N45'00"   14:17:11 ST   74W00'23"

44. CHARMING SHOPS-CHRS **Retail**
July 6, 1981 NYC 10:0:0 AM EDT
40N45'00" 4:02:04 ST 74W00'23"

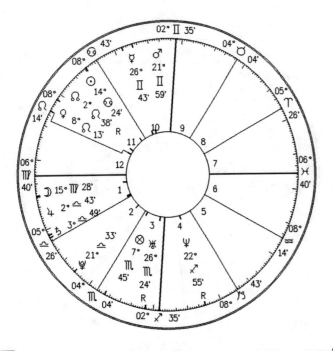

45. CHECKERS DRIVE IN-CHKR **Restaurant**
Nov. 15, 1991 NYC 9:30:0 AM EST
40N45'00" 13:10:54 ST 74W00'23"

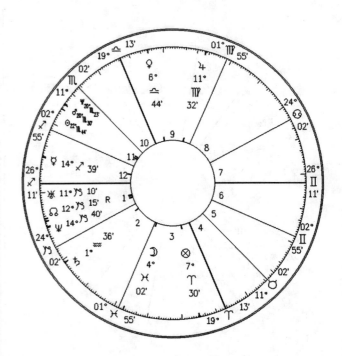

46. CHECKFREE-CKFR **Electronic Commerce**
Sep. 28, 1995 NYC 9:30:0 AM EDT
40N45'00" 9:01:25 ST 74W00'23"

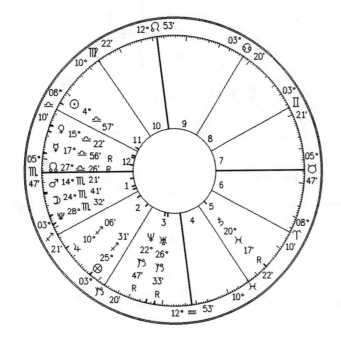

47. CHIPS & TECHNOLOG.-CHPS **Semiconductors**
Oct. 8, 1986 NYC 9:30:0 AM EDT
40N45'00" 9:41:45 ST 74W00'23"

48. CHIRON-CHIR   Biotech
Aug. 2, 1983   NYC   10:0:0 AM EDT
40N45'00"   5:46:24 ST   74W00'23"

49. CIRRUS LOGIC-CRUS   Semiconductors
June 9, 1989   NYC   9:30:0 AM EDT
40N45'00"   1:45:47 ST   74W00'23"

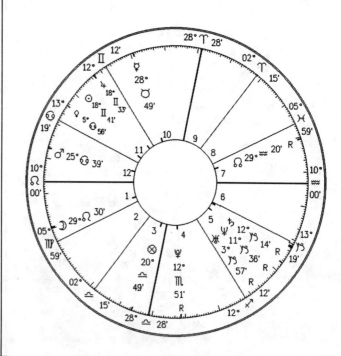

50. CISCO SYSTEMS-CSCO   Networks
Feb. 16, 1990   NYC   9:30:0 AM EST
40N45'00"   19:19:29 ST   74W00'23"

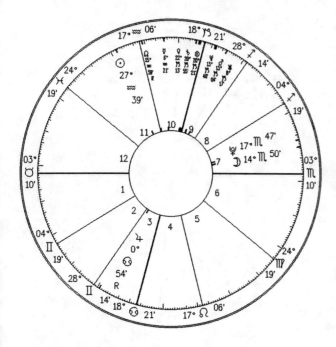

51. CITIFED BANCORP-CTZN   Banks
Jan. 23, 1992   NYC   9:30:0 AM EST
40N45'00"   17:42:57 ST   74W00'23"

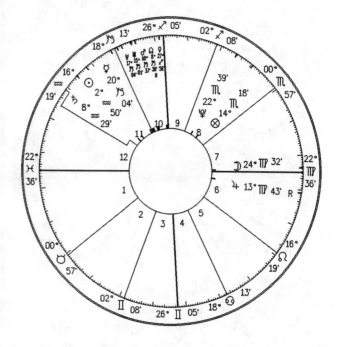

52. COGNEX-CGNX   Technology
July 20, 1989   NYC   9:30:0 AM EDT
40N45'00"   4:27:12 ST   74W00'23"

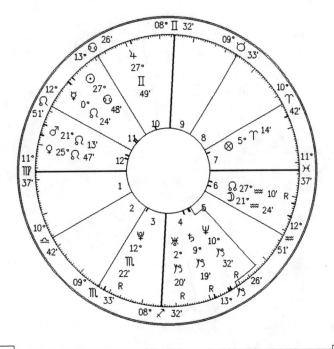

53. COLLAGEN-CGEN   Biotech
Nov. 2, 1981   NYC   10:0:0 AM EST
40N45'00"   12:51:24 ST   74W00'23"

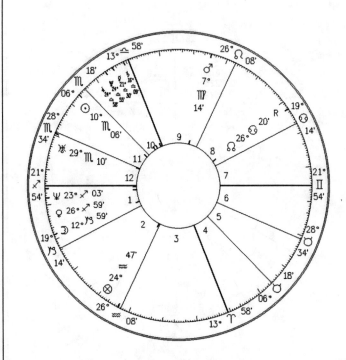

54. COMCAST CORP.-CMCSA   Telecom
July 11, 1972   NYC   10:0:0 AM EDT
40N45'00"   4:22:29 ST   74W00'23"

55. COMMONWEALTH BANK-CMSB   Banks
Jan. 21, 1994   NYC   9:30:0 AM EST
40N45'00"   17:36:52 ST   74W00'23"

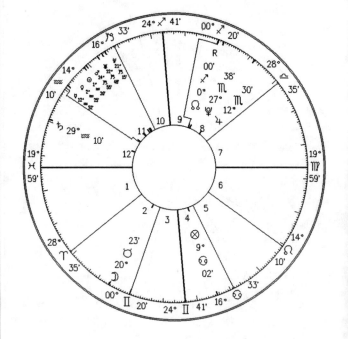

56. COPLEY PHARM.-CPLY   **Drugs**
Oct. 14, 1992   NYC   9:30:0 AM EDT
40N45'00"   10:07:20 ST   74W00'23"

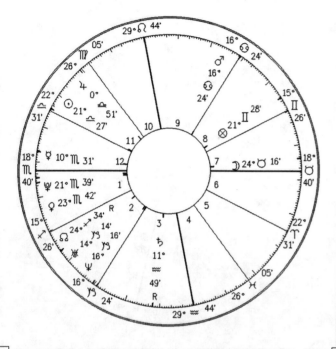

57. COR PHARMACEUTICALS-CORR   **Drugs**
June 27, 1991   NYC   9:30:0 AM EDT
40N45'00"   2:54:38 ST   74W00'23"

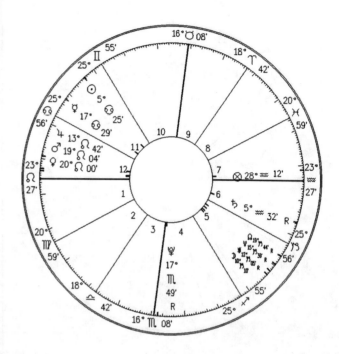

58. CREATIVE TECHNOL.-CREAF   **Computer Equip.**
Aug. 4, 1992   NYC   9:30:0 AM EDT
40N45'00"   5:27:39 ST   74W00'23"

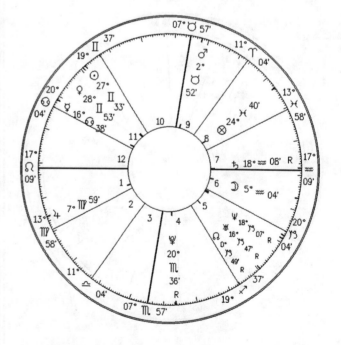

59. CROSSCOM-XCOM   **Software**
June 18, 1992   NYC   9:30:0 AM EDT
40N45'00"   2:22:20 ST   74W00'23"

60. CYBERCASH-CYCH *Electronic Commerce*
Feb. 15, 1996 NYC 9:30:0 AM EST
40N45'00" 19:13:33 ST 74W00'23"

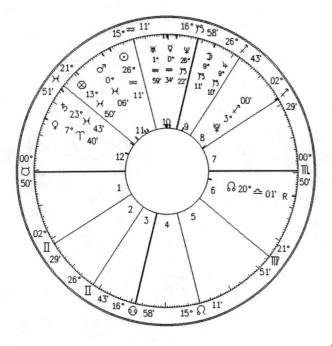

61. CYBERMEDIA-CYBR *Software*
Oct. 23, 1996 NYC 9:30:0 AM EDT
40N45'00" 10:42:58 ST 74W00'23"

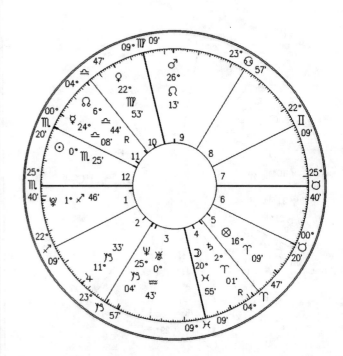

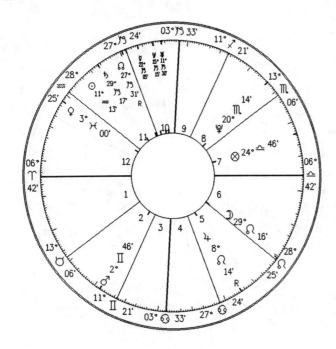

62. CYGNUS-CYGN *Biotech*
Jan. 31, 1991 NYC 9:30:0 AM EST
40N45'00" 18:15:26 ST 74W00'23"

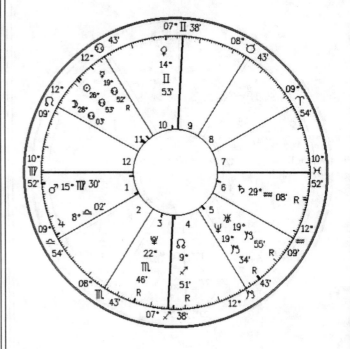

63. CYRIX-CYRX *Semiconductors*
July 19, 1993 NYC 9:30:0 AM EDT
40N45'00" 4:23:23 ST 74W00'23"

64. CYRK-CYRK *Commercial Ser.*
July 8, 1993   NYC   9:30:0 AM EDT
40N45'00"   3:40:01 ST   74W00'23"

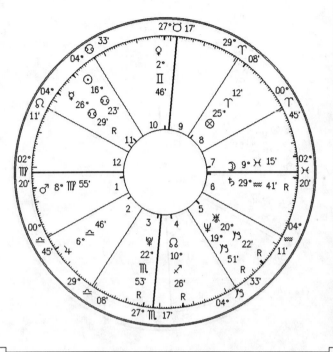

65. DATA RESEARCH-DRAI *Technology*
July 1, 1992   NYC   9:30:0 AM EDT
40N45'00"   3:13:36 ST   74W00'23"

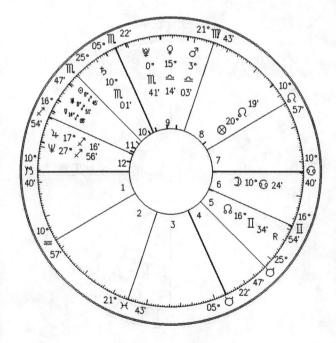

66. DELCHAMPS-DLCH *Retail Food*
Nov. 23, 1983   NYC   10:0:0 AM EST
40N45'00"   14:12:17 ST   74W00'23"

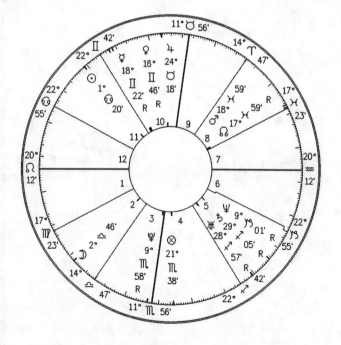

67. DELL COMPUTER-DELL *Computers*
June 22, 1988   NYC   9:30:0 AM EDT
40N45'00"   2:37:59 ST   74W00'23"

68. DIGITAL LINK-DLNK   Telecom Equip.
Feb. 1, 1994   NYC   9:30:0 AM EST
40N45'00"   18:20:14 ST   74W00'23"

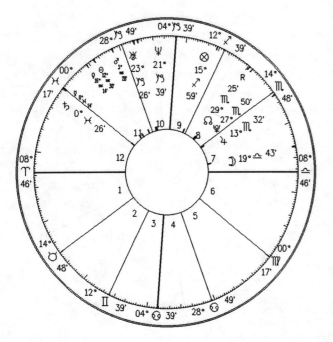

69. DSC COMMUNICATIONS-DIGI   Telecom. Equip.
July 10, 1980   NYC   10:0:0 AM EDT
40N45'00"   4:18:47 ST   74W00'23"

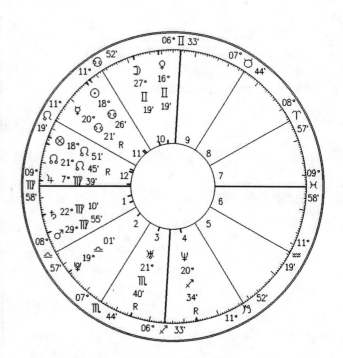

70. DSP COMMUNICATIONS-DSPC   Semiconductors
Mar. 7, 1995   NYC   9:30:0 AM EST
40N45'00"   20:33:21 ST   74W00'23"

71. ETRADE-EGRP   Electronic Commerce
Aug. 16, 1996   NYC   9:30:0 AM EDT
40N45'00"   6:14:53 ST   74W00'23"

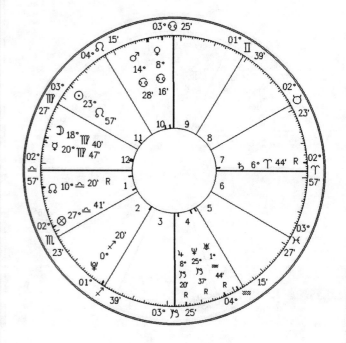

72. ELECTROGLAS-EGLS *Semiconductors*
July 25, 1993   NYC   9:30:0 AM EDT
40N45'00"   4:47:02 ST   74W00'23"

73. ELECTRONIC ARTS-ERTS *Software*
Sep. 20, 1989   NYC   9:30:0 AM EDT
40N45'00"   8:31:52 ST   74W00'23"

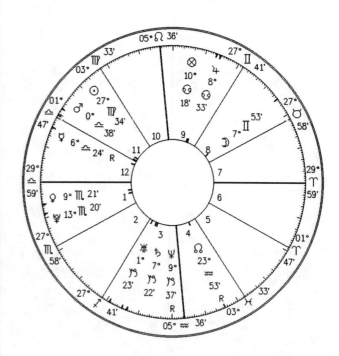

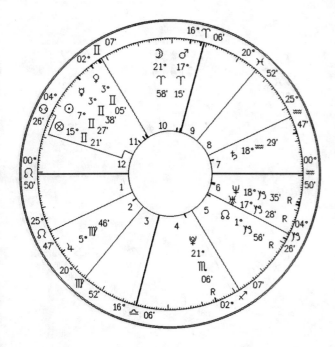

74. FINISH LINE-FINL *Retail*
May 28, 1992   NYC   9:30:0 AM EDT
40N45'00"   0:59:19 ST   74W00'23"

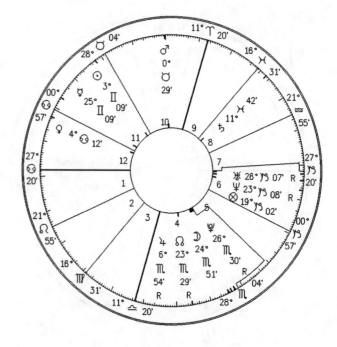

75. FORE SYSTEMS-FORE *Local Networks*
May 24, 1994   NYC   9:30:0 AM EDT
40N45'00"   0:41:40 ST   74W00'23"

76. GENERAL NUTRITION-GNCI   Retail Food
Jan. 25, 1993   NYC   9:30:0 AM EST
40N45'00"   17:53:36 ST   74W00'23"

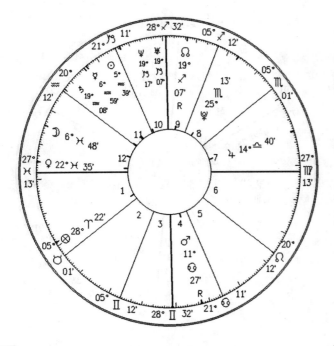

77. GLENAYRE-GEMS   Telecom Equip.
Nov. 12, 1992   NYC   9:30:0 AM EST
40N45'00"   13:01:52 ST   74W00'23"

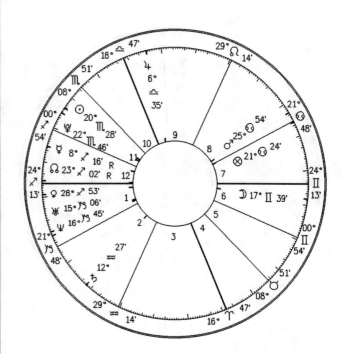

78. GLOBAL IND.-GLBL   Oilfield Services
Feb. 11, 1993   NYC   9:30:0 AM EST
40N45'00"   19:00:37 ST   74W00'23"

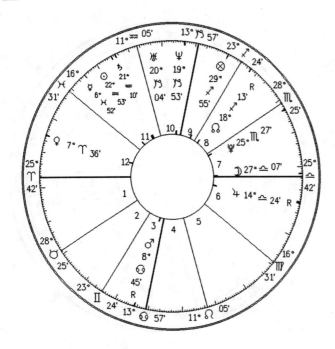

79. HEALTH MNGMT.-HMSY   Health Care
Feb. 6, 1991   NYC   9:30:0 AM EST
40N45'00"   18:38:52 ST   74W00'23"

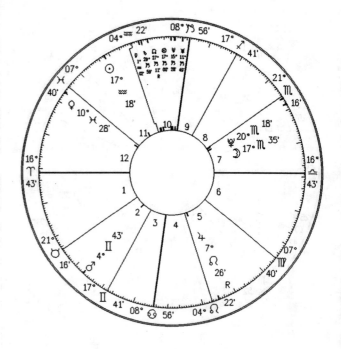

80. HELEN OF TROY-HELE *Cosmetics*
July 6, 1976　　NYC　　10:0:0 AM EDT
40N45'00"　　4:02:54 ST　　74W00'23"

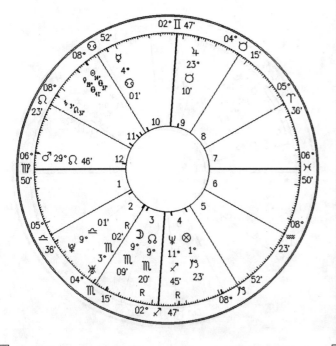

81. HERBALIFE-HERB *Consumer Prod.*
July 7, 1987　　NYC　　9:30:0 AM EDT
40N45'00"　　3:34:08 ST　　74W00'23"

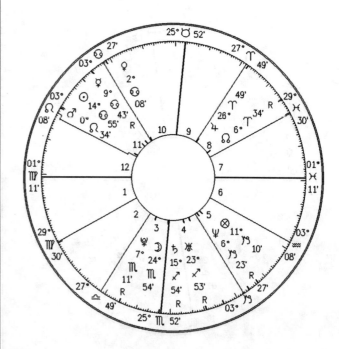

82. HOLLYWOOD ENT.-HLYW *Retail*
July 16, 1993　　NYC　　9:30:0 AM EDT
40N45'00"　　4:11:33 ST　　74W00'23"

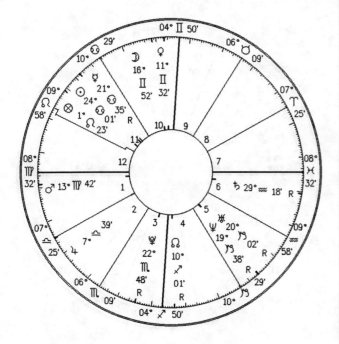

83. HUTCHINSON TECH.-HTCH *Computer Equip.*
Aug. 15, 1985　　NYC　　10:0:0 AM EDT
40N45'00"　　6:39:40 ST　　74W00'23"

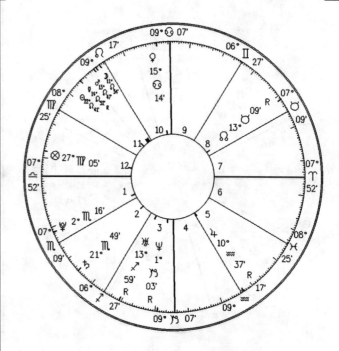

84. IDEXX LABS-IDXX   *Medical Prod.*
June 21, 1991   NYC   9:30:0 AM EDT
40N45'00"   2:31:11 ST   74W00'23"

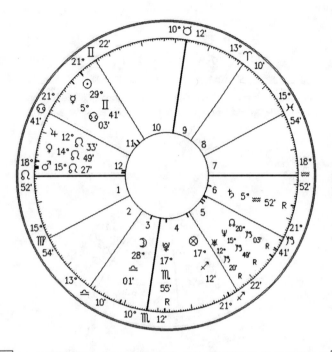

85. IGEN,INC.-IGEN   *Medical Equip.*
Feb. 3, 1994   NYC   9:30:0 AM EST
40N45'00"   18:28:07 ST   74W00'23"

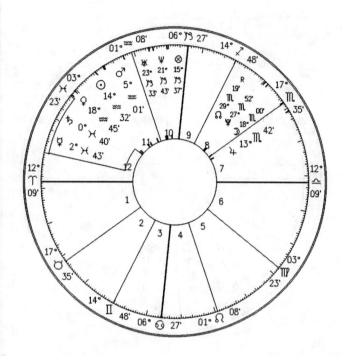

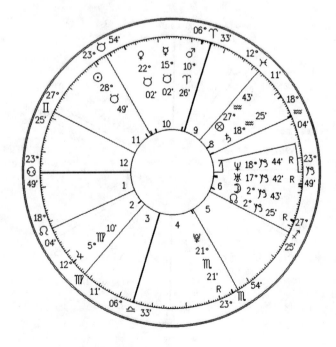

86. IMPERIAL CREDIT-ICII   *Financial Services*
May 19, 1992   NYC   9:30:0 AM EDT
40N45'00"   0:24:04 ST   74W00'23"

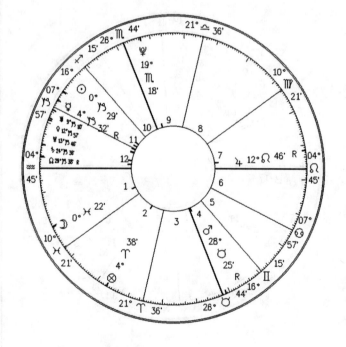

87. IN FOCUS SYSTEMS-INFS   *Computer Equip.*
Dec. 22, 1990   NYC   9:30:0 AM EST
40N45'00"   15:37:44 ST   74W00'23"

88. INFORMIX-IFMX *Software*
Sep. 24, 1986   NYC   9:30:0 AM EDT
40N45'00"   8:46:22 ST   74W00'23"

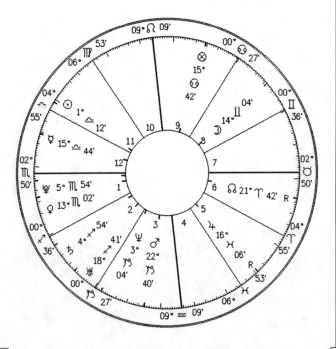

89. INTEGRATED CIRCUITS-ICST *Semiconductors*
June 20, 1991   NYC   9:30:0 AM EDT
40N45'00"   2:27:01 ST   74W00'23"

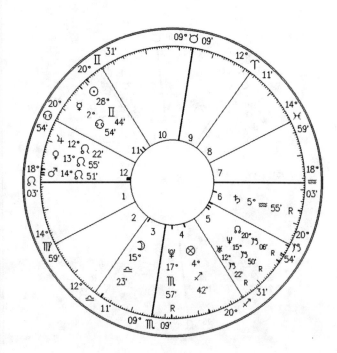

90. INTEGRATED DEVICES-IDTI *Semiconductors*
Feb. 17, 1984   NYC   10:0:0 AM EST
40N45'00"   19:51:07 ST   74W00'23"

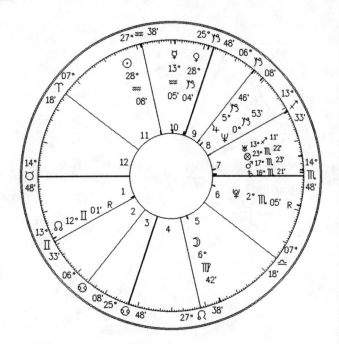

91. INTEL-INTC *Semiconductors*
Aug. 7, 1981   NYC   10:0:0 AM EDT
40N45'00"   6:08:14 ST   74W00'23"

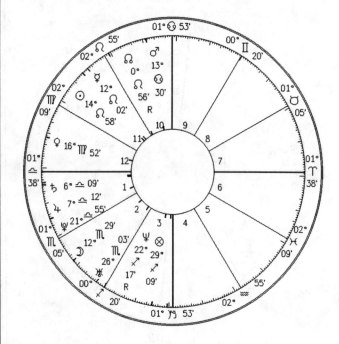

92. INTELLIGENT ELEC.-INEL   *Retail*
June 30, 1987   NYC   9:30:0 AM EDT
40N45'00"   3:06:33 ST   74W00'23"

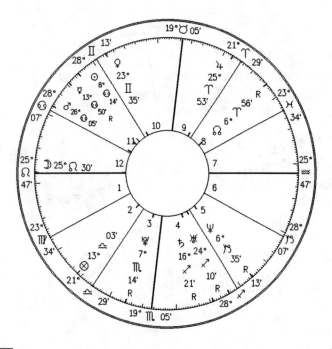

93. INTER. DAIRY QUEEN-INDQA   *Retail Food*
Feb. 20, 1986   NYC   9:30:0 AM EST
40N45'00"   19:35:07 ST   74W00'23"

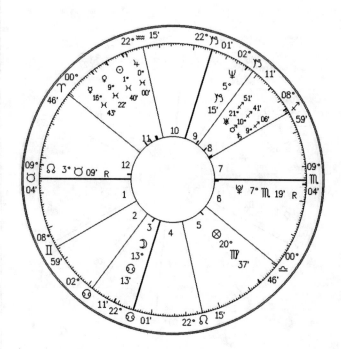

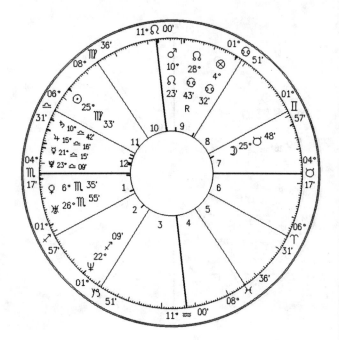

94. INTERGRAPH-INGR   *Computers*
Sep. 18, 1981   NYC   10:0:0 AM EDT
40N45'00"   8:53:49 ST   74W00'23"

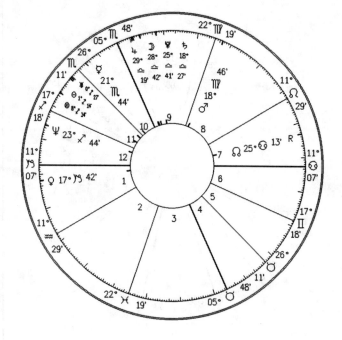

95. INTERN. TOTALIZATOR-ITSI   *Electronics*
Nov. 23, 1981   NYC   10:0:0 AM EST
40N45'00"   14:13:58 ST   74W00'23"

96. INTERVOICE-INTV   Electronics
May 8, 1985   NYC   10:0:0 AM EDT
40N45'00"   0:09:35 ST   74W00'23"

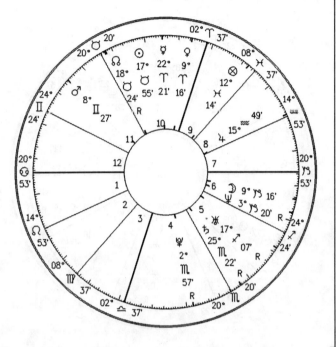

97. INTUIT-INTU   Software
Mar. 12, 1993   NYC   9:30:0 AM EST
40N45'00"   20:54:59 ST   74W00'23"

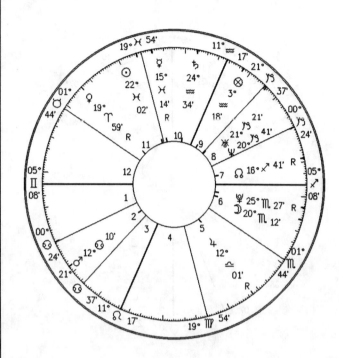

98. J.B. HUNT TRANSPORT-JBHT   Trucking
Nov. 22, 1983   NYC   10:0:0 AM EST
40N45'00"   14:08:20 ST   74W00'23"

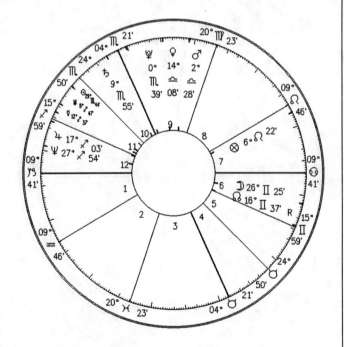

99. JACKSON HEWITT-JTAX   Misc.
Jan. 21, 1994   NYC   9:30:0 AM EST
40N45'00"   17:36:52 ST   74W00'23"

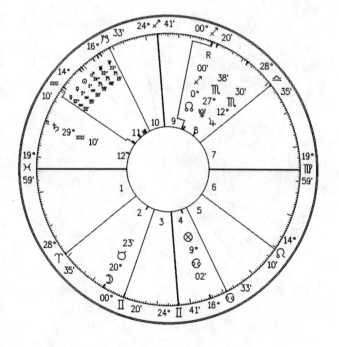

100. JAMESON INNS-JAMS   *Real Estate*
Jan. 27, 1994   NYC   9:30:0 AM EST
40N45'00"   18:00:31 ST   74W00'23"

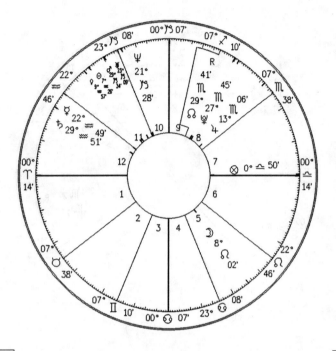

101. JETFORM-FORMF   *Software*
Apr. 21, 1993   NYC   9:30:0 AM EDT
40N45'00"   22:32:29 ST   74W00'23"

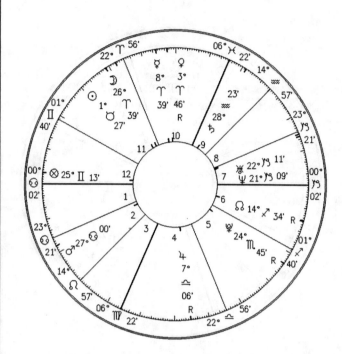

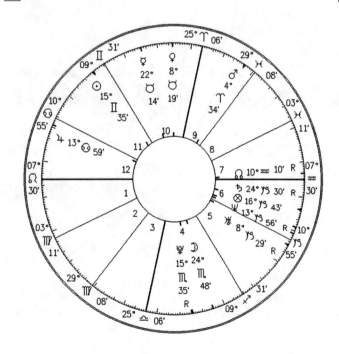

102. K SWISS-KSWS   *Shoes*
June 6, 1990   NYC   9:30:0 AM EDT
40N45'00"   1:33:00 ST   74W00'23"

103. KELLY SERVICES #1   *Commercial Ser.*
Sep. 18, 1981   NYC   10:0:0 AM EDT
40N45'00"   8:53:49 ST   74W00'23"

104. KELLY SERVICES #2-KELYA   *Commercial Ser.*
July 24, 1984   NYC   10:0:0 AM EDT
40N45'00"   5:14:07 ST   74W00'23"

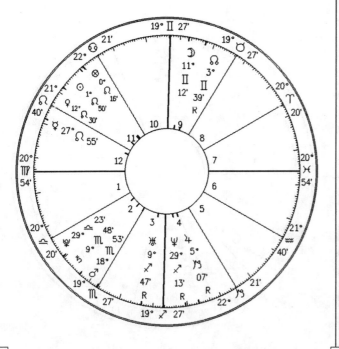

105. KLA INSTRUMENTS-KLAC   *Semiconductor Equip.*
Oct. 8, 1980   NYC   10:0:0 AM EDT
40N45'00"   10:13:25 ST   74W00'23"

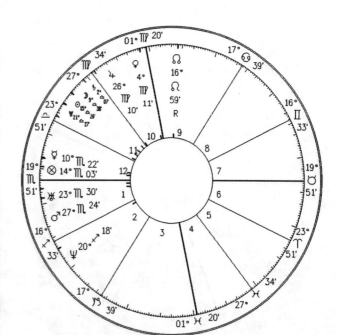

106. KOMAG-KMAG   *Computer Equip*
May 28, 1987   NYC   9:30:0 AM EDT
40N45'00"   0:56:26 ST   74W00'23"

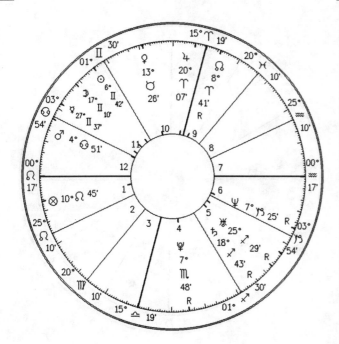

107. KURZWEIL APP.INT.-KURZ   *Technology*
Aug. 17, 1993   NYC   9:30:0 AM EDT
40N45'00"   6:17:43 ST   74W00'23"

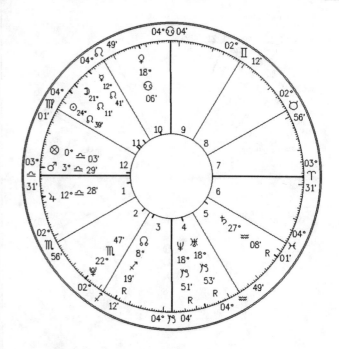

108. LAM RESEARCH-LRCX *Semiconductor*
May 4, 1984   NYC   9:30:0 AM EDT
40N45'00"   23:24:27 ST   74W00'23"

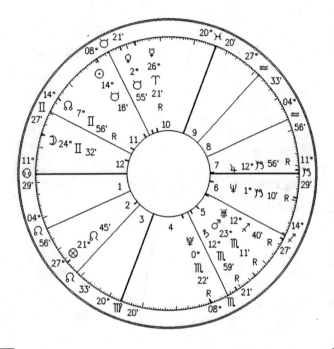

109. LANDSTAR SYSTEM-LSTR *Trucking*
Mar. 5, 1993   NYC   9:30:0 AM EST
40N45'00"   20:27:21 ST   74W00'23"

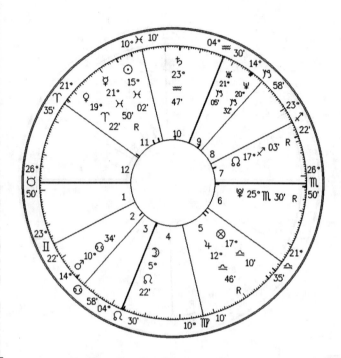

110. LATTICE SEMI-LSCC *Semiconductor*
Nov. 9, 1989   NYC   9:30:0 AM EST
40N45'00"   12:49:10 ST   74W00'23"

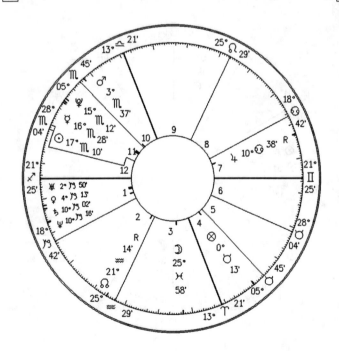

111. LEVEL ONE COMMUN.-LEVL *Electronics*
Aug. 20, 1993   NYC   9:30:0 AM EDT
40N45'00"   6:29:33 ST   74W00'23"

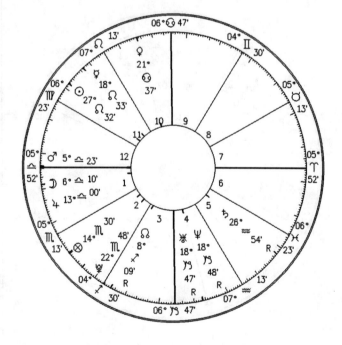

112. LIFELINE SYSTEM-LIFE *Medical Equipment*
Feb. 2, 1984   NYC   10:0:0 AM EST
40N45'00"   18:52:12 ST   74W00'23"

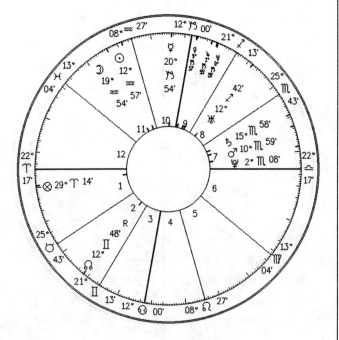

113. LINCARE-LNCR   *Health Care*
Mar. 19, 1992   NYC   9:30:0 AM EST
40N45'00"   21:23:44 ST   74W00'23"

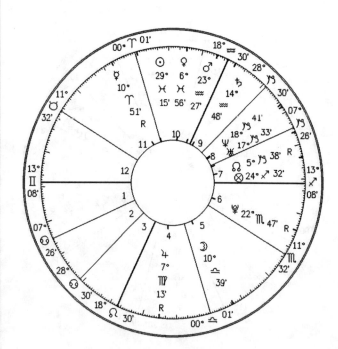

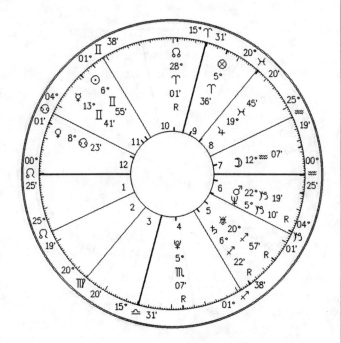

114. LINEAR TECH.-LLTC   *Semiconductor*
May 28, 1986   NYC   9:30:0 AM EDT
40N45'00"   0:57:10 ST   74W00'23"

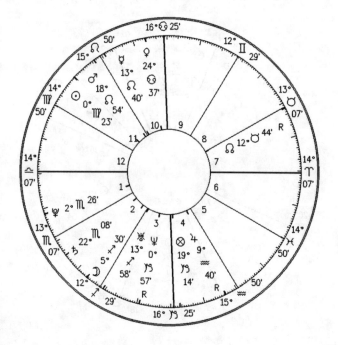

115. LO-JACK-LOJN   *Industrial*
Aug. 23, 1985   NYC   10:0:0 AM EDT
40N45'00"   7:11:12 ST   74W00'23"

116. LONE STAR STEAKHOUSE.-STAR **Restaurant**
Mar. 12, 1992   NYC   9:30:0 AM EST
40N45'00"   20:56:08 ST   74W00'23"

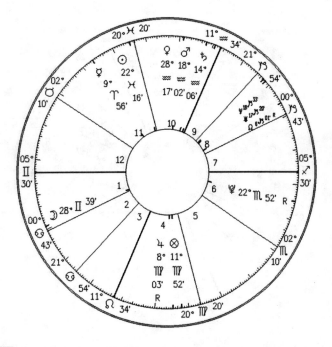

117. LUNAR CORP.-LUNR **Medical Equip.**
Aug. 14, 1990   NYC   9:30:0 AM EDT
40N45'00"   6:05:02 ST   74W00'23"

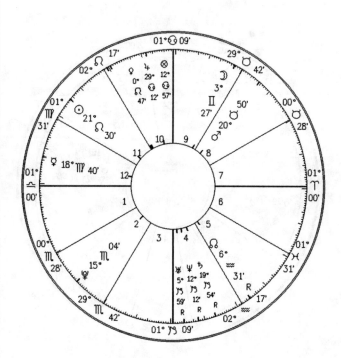

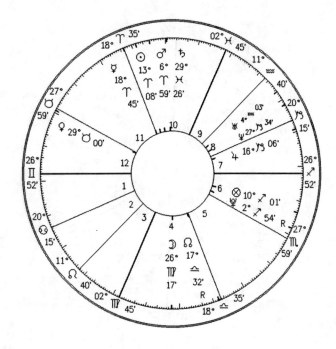

118. LYCOS-LCOS **Software**
Apr. 2, 1996   NYC   9:30:0 AM EST
40N45'00"   22:18:51 ST   74W00'23"

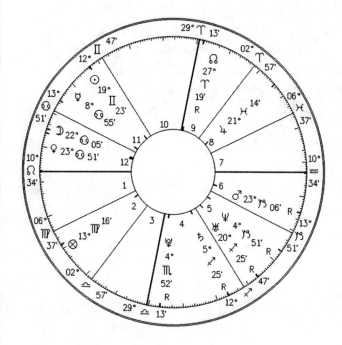

119. MAIL BOXES-MAIL **Commercial Ser.**
June 10, 1986   NYC   9:30:0 AM EDT
40N45'00"   1:48:39 ST   74W00'23"

120. MANGUISTICS-MANU *Software*
Aug. 13, 1993   NYC   9:30:0 AM EDT
40N45'00"   6:01:57 ST   74W00'23"

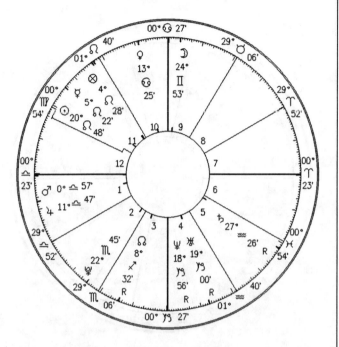

121. MAPINFO-MAPS *Software*
Feb. 1, 1994   NYC   9:30:0 AM EST
40N45'00"   18:20:14 ST   74W00'23"

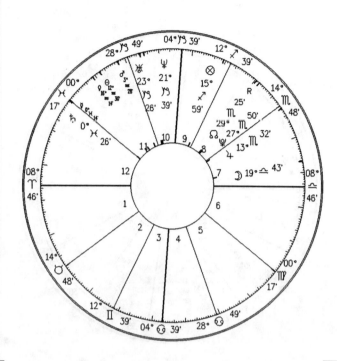

122. MATHSOFT-MATH *Software*
Feb. 4, 1993   NYC   9:30:0 AM EST
40N45'00"   18:33:01 ST   74W00'23"

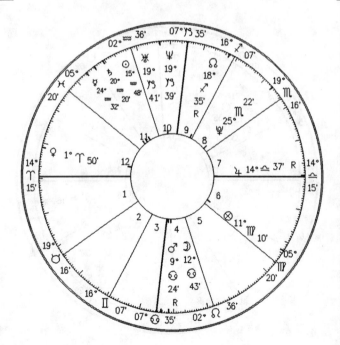

123. MAXIM-MXIM *Semiconductors*
Feb. 29, 1988   NYC   9:30:0 AM EST
40N45'00"   20:08:42 ST   74W00'23"

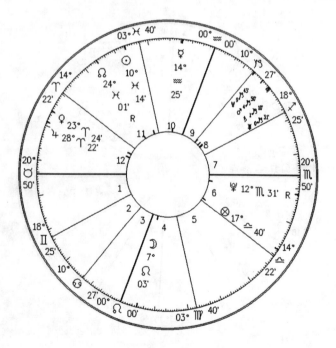

124. MCAFEE ASSOCIATES-MCAF   Software
Oct. 6, 1992   NYC   9:30:0 AM EDT
40N45'00"   9:35:50 ST   74W00'23"

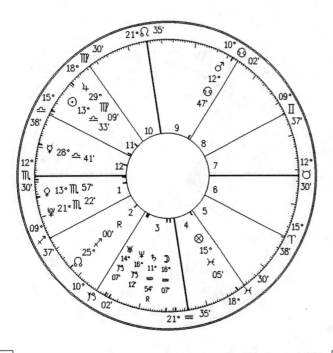

125. MCI COMMUNICATIONS-MCIC   Telecom
Jan. 1, 1978   NYC   10:0:0 AM EST
40N45'00"   16:47:50 ST   74W00'23"

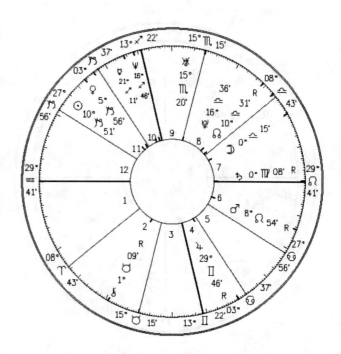

126. MENTOR CORP-MNTR   Computers
Aug. 31, 1977   NYC   10:0:0 AM EDT
40N45'00"   7:42:44 ST   74W00'23"

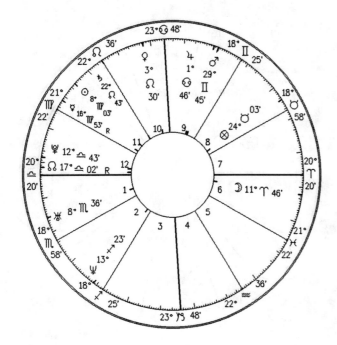

127. METROCALL-MCLL   Telecom
July 16, 1993   NYC   9:30:0 AM EDT
40N45'00"   4:11:33 ST   74W00'23"

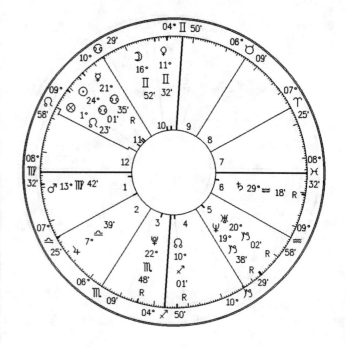

128. MICROCHIP-MCHP   **Semiconductors**
Mar. 19, 1993   NYC   9:30:0 AM EST
40N45'00"   21:22:33 ST   74W00'23"

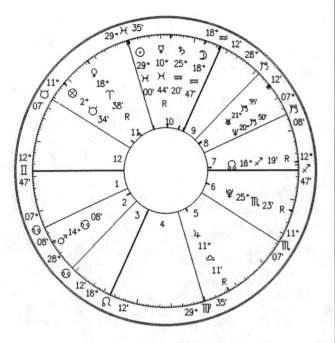

129. MICROSOFT-MSFT   **Software**
Mar. 13, 1986   NYC   9:30:0 AM EST
40N45'00"   20:57:43 ST   74W00'23"

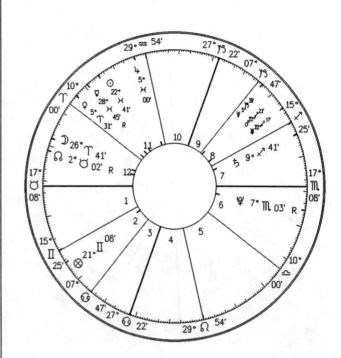

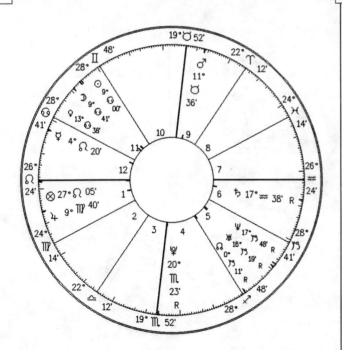

130. MICROTOUCH SYSTEMS-MTSI   **Computer Equip.**
June 30, 1992   NYC   9:30:0 AM EDT
40N45'00"   3:09:39 ST   74W00'23"

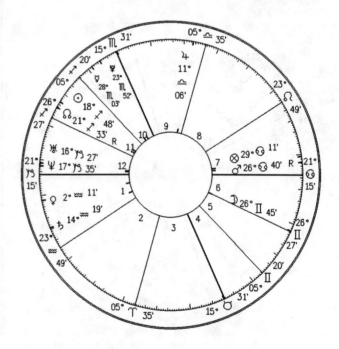

131. MICROWAREHOUSE-MWHS   **Retail**
Dec. 10, 1992   NYC   9:30:0 AM EST
40N45'00"   14:52:14 ST   74W00'23"

132. MOLEX-MOLXA　　*Electrical Equip.*
July 26, 1990　　NYC　　9:30:0 AM EDT
40N45'00"　　4:50:08 ST　　74W00'23"

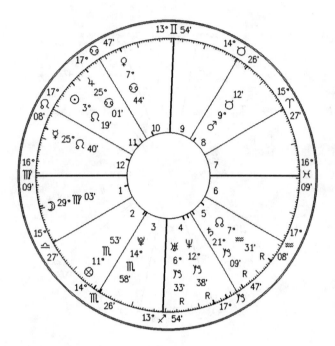

133. NAM TAI ELECT.-NTAIF　　*Electronics*
Mar. 28, 1988　　NYC　　9:30:0 AM EST
40N45'00"　　21:59:05 ST　　74W00'23"

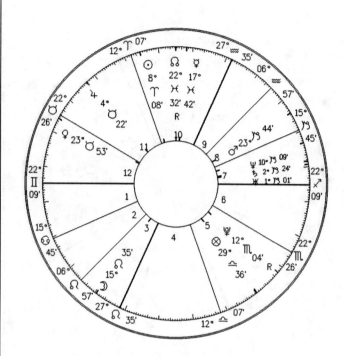

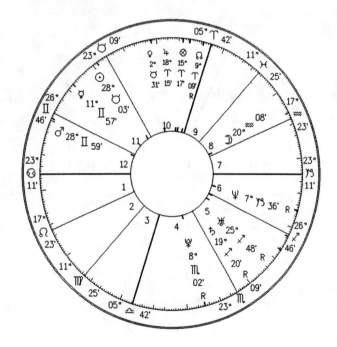

134. NELLCOR-NELL　　*Medical Equipment*
May 19, 1987　　NYC　　9:30:0 AM EDT
40N45'00"　　0:20:57 ST　　74W00'23"

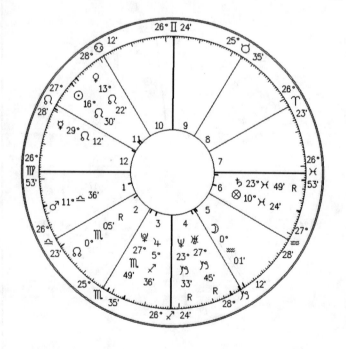

135. NETSCAPE-NSCP　　*Software*
Aug. 9, 1995　　NYC　　9:30:0 AM EDT
40N45'00"　　5:44:18 ST　　74W00'23"

136. NETWORK COMP.DEVICE-NCDI *Networks*
June 5, 1992   NYC   9:30:0 AM EDT
40N45'00"   1:30:52 ST   74W00'23"

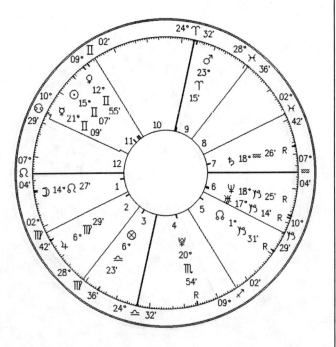

137. NORDSTROM-NOBE   *Retail*
Aug. 9, 1971   NYC   10:0:0 AM EDT
40N45'00"   6:13:50 ST   74W00'23"

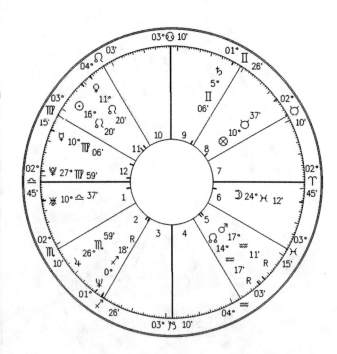

138. NOVELL-NOVL   *Networks*
Jan. 17, 1985   NYC   10:0:0 AM EST
40N45'00"   17:52:07 ST   74W00'23"

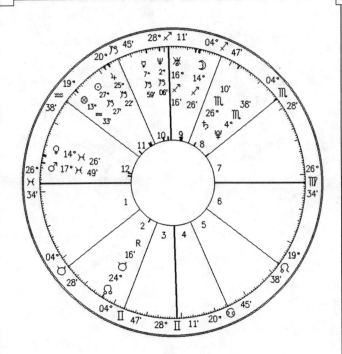

139. NOVELLUS-NVLS   *Semiconductors*
Aug. 11, 1988   NYC   9:30:0 AM EDT
40N45'00"   5:55:07 ST   74W00'23"

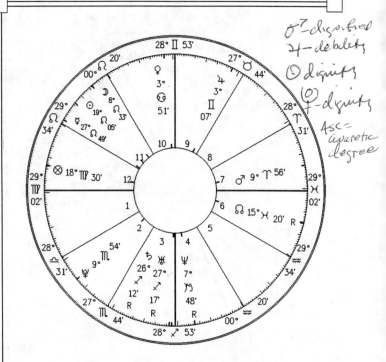

140. OFFSHORE LOGISTICS-OLOG   Oilfield Ser.
Dec. 1, 1971   NYC   10:0:0 AM EST
40N45'00"   14:43:27 ST   74W00'23"

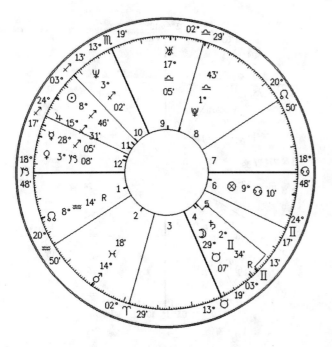

141. ONCOGENE-ONCS   Health Care
Apr. 3, 1986   NYC   9:30:0 AM EST
40N45'00"   22:20:29 ST   74W00'23"

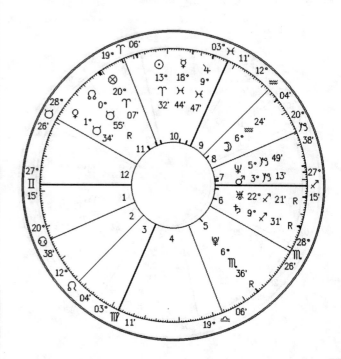

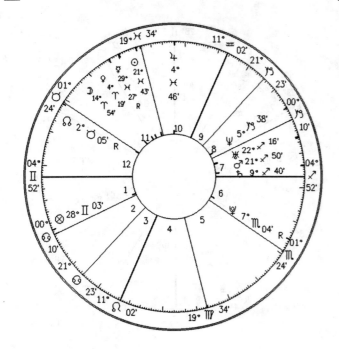

142. ORACLE SYSTEMS-ORCL   Software
Mar. 12, 1986   NYC   9:30:0 AM EST
40N45'00"   20:53:59 ST   74W00'23"

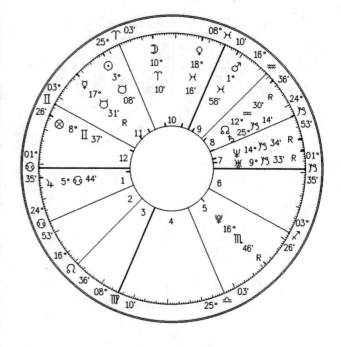

143. ORBITAL SCIENCES-ORBI   Aerospace
Apr. 23, 1990   NYC   9:30:0 AM EDT
40N45'00"   22:39:18 ST   74W00'23"

144. OREGON METAL.-OREM   *Metals*
June 12, 1974   NYC   10:0:0 AM EDT
40N45'00"   2:26:15 ST   74W00'23"

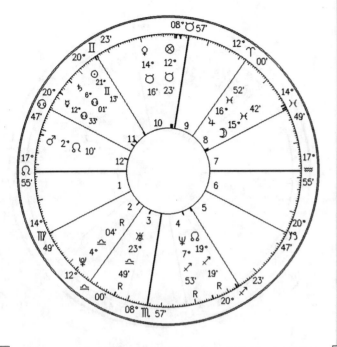

145. OSHGOSH B'GOSH-GOSHA   *Apparel*
May 2, 1985   NYC   10:0:0 AM EDT
40N45'00"   23:45:55 ST   74W00'23"

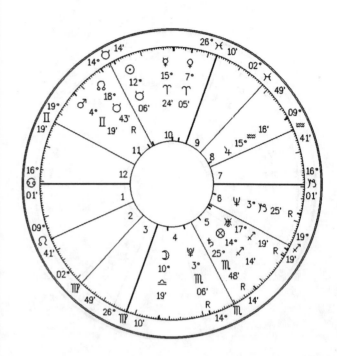

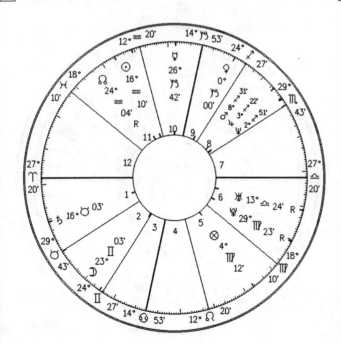

146. PACCAR-PCAR   *Autos*
Feb. 5, 1971   NYC   10:0:0 AM EST
40N45'00"   19:04:37 ST   74W00'23"

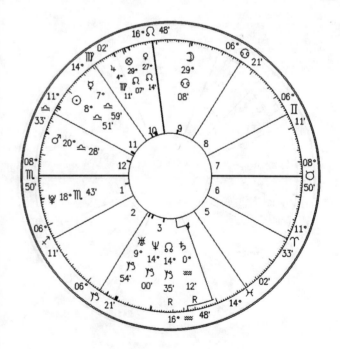

147. PAGING NETWORK-PAGE   *Telecom*
Oct. 2, 1991   NYC   9:30:0 AM EDT
40N45'00"   9:17:03 ST   74W00'23"

148. PARAMETRIC-PMTC   *Software*
Dec. 8, 1989   NYC   9:30:0 AM EST
40N45'00"   14:43:30 ST   74W00'23"

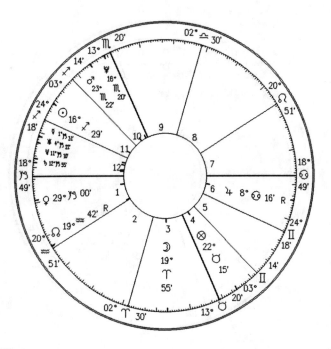

149. PARCPLACE-PARQ   *Software*
Feb. 11, 1994   NYC   9:30:0 AM EST
40N45'00"   18:59:40 ST   74W00'23"

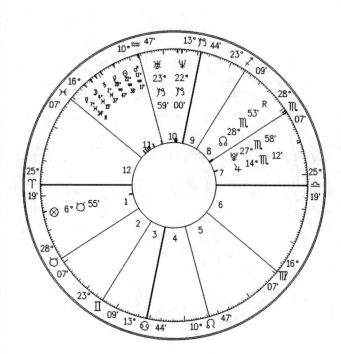

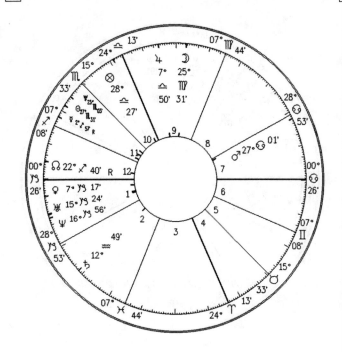

150. PEOPLESOFT-PSFT   *Software*
Nov. 19, 1992   NYC   9:30:0 AM EST
40N45'00"   13:29:40 ST   74W00'23"

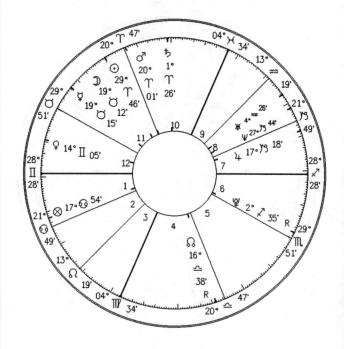

151. PLANET HOLLYWOOD-PHII   *Restaurants*
Apr. 19, 1996   NYC   9:30:0 AM EDT
40N45'00"   22:25:43 ST   74W00'23"

152. PLATINUM SOFTWARE-PSQL Software
Oct. 22, 1992   NYC   9:30:0 AM EDT
40N45'00"   10:38:53 ST   74W00'23"

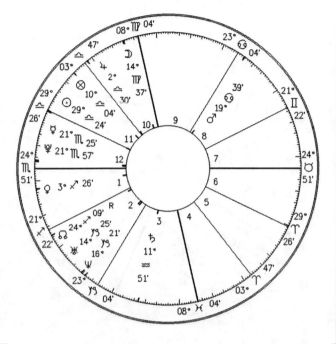

153. POOL ENERGY SVCS.-PESC   Oilfield Services
Apr. 17, 1990   NYC   9:30:0 AM EDT
40N45'00"   22:15:52 ST   74W00'23"

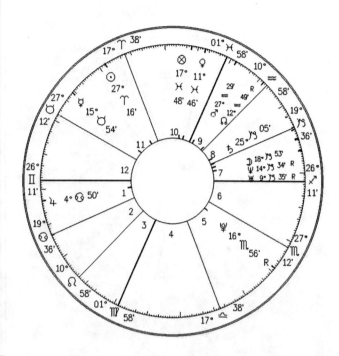

154. PROGRESS SOFTWARE-PRGS   Software
July 30, 1991   NYC   9:30:0 AM EDT
40N45'00"   5:04:57 ST   74W00'23"

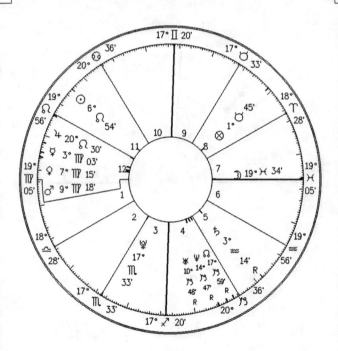

155. PURE TECH.-PURT   Waste Mgmt.
Mar. 22, 1989   NYC   9:30:0 AM EST
40N45'00"   21:34:29 ST   74W00'23"

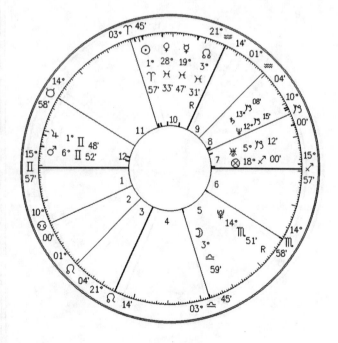

156. QLOGIC-QLGC Software
Feb. 28, 1994   NYC   9:30:0 AM EST
40N45'00"   20:06:41 ST   74W00'23"

157. QUALCOMM-QCOM   Telecom. Equip
Dec. 13, 1991   NYC   9:30:0 AM EST
40N45'00"   15:01:06 ST   74W00'23"

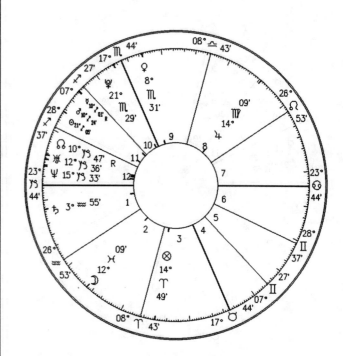

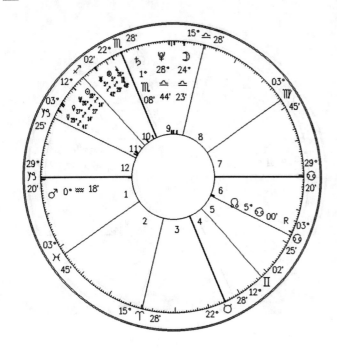

158. QUANTUM-QNTM   Computer Equip.
Dec. 10, 1982   NYC   10:0:0 AM EST
40N45'00"   15:20:16 ST   74W00'23"

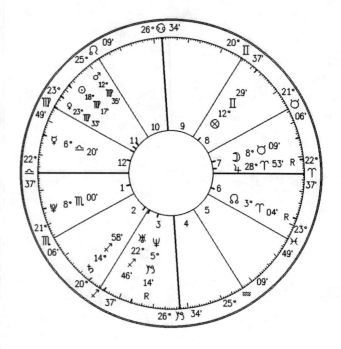

159. RAINBOW TECH.-RNBO   Software
Sep. 11, 1987   NYC   9:30:0 AM EDT
40N45'00"   7:54:21 ST   74W00'23"

160. REMEDY-RMDY   Software
Mar. 17, 1995   NYC   9:30:0 AM EST
40N45'00"   21:12:47 ST   74W00'23"

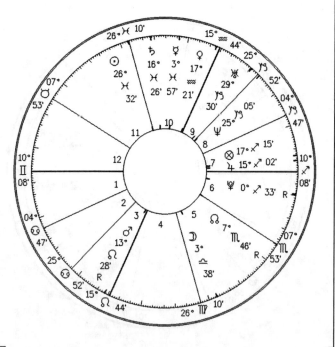

161. REPLIGEN-RGEN   Biotech.
Apr. 29, 1986   NYC   9:30:0 AM EDT
40N45'00"   23:03:03 ST   74W00'23"

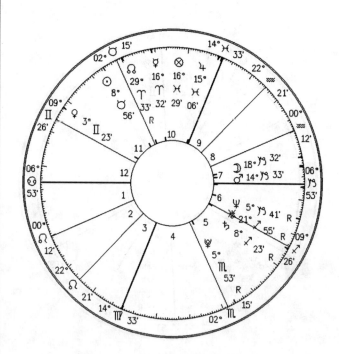

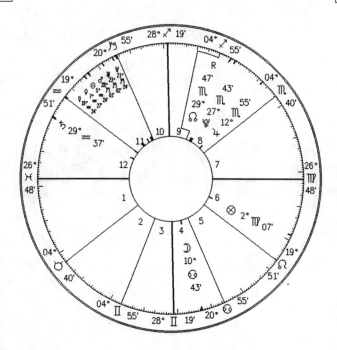

162. RICHEY ELECTRONICS-RCHY   Electronics
Jan. 25, 1994   NYC   9:30:0 AM EST
40N45'00"   17:52:38 ST   74W00'23"

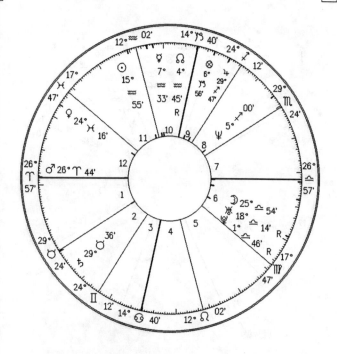

163. ROADWAY SERVICES-ROAD   Trucking
Feb. 5, 1972   NYC   10:0:0 AM EST
40N45'00"   19:03:40 ST   74W00'23"

164. RYAN STEAK HOUSE-RYAN   Restaurant
July 13, 1982   NYC   10:0:0 AM EDT
40N45'00"   4:28:43 ST   74W00'23"

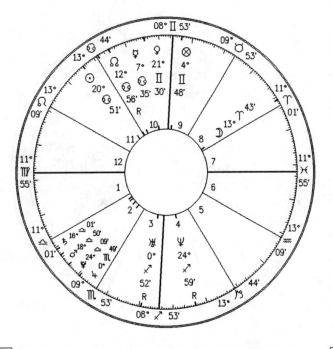

165. S-THREE-SIII   Software
Mar. 5, 1993   NYC   9:30:0 AM EST
40N45'00"   22:04:54 ST   74W00'23"

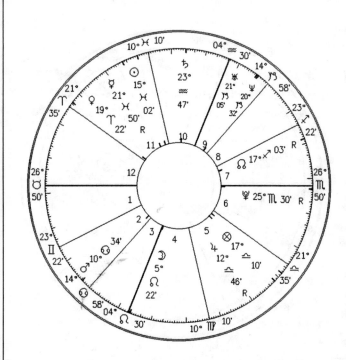

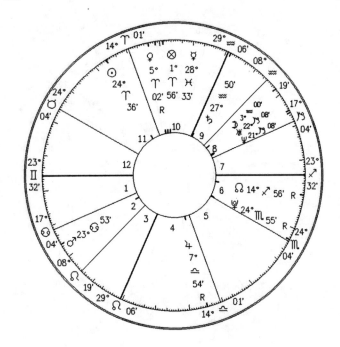

166. SANMINA-SANM   Electronics
Apr. 14, 1993   NYC   9:30:0 AM EDT
40N45'00"   22:04:54 ST   74W00'23"

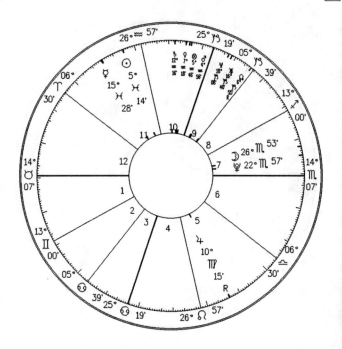

167. SCHOLASTIC-SCHL   Publishing
Feb. 24, 1992   NYC   9:30:0 AM EST
40N45'00"   19:49:06 ST   74W00'23"

168. SECURITY DYNAMICS-SDTI   *PC Peripheral Equip.*
Dec. 14, 1994   NYC   9:30:0 AM EST
40N45'00"   15:06:07 ST   74W00'23"

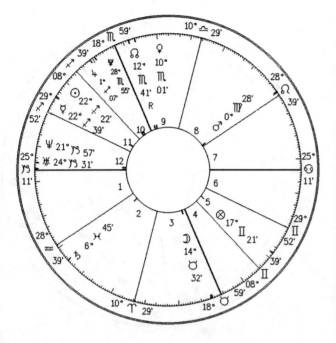

169. SEILER POLLUTION-SEPC   *Pollution Control*
Feb. 3, 1994   NYC   9:30:0 AM EST
40N45'00"   18:28:07 ST   74W00'23"

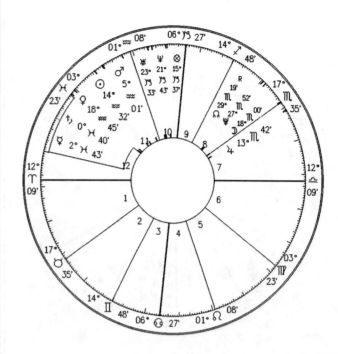

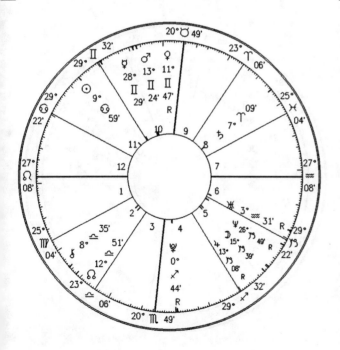

170. SIEBEL SYSTEMS-SEBL   *Software*
July 01, 1996   NYC   9:30 AM EDT
40N45'00"   3:07:42 ST   74W00'23"

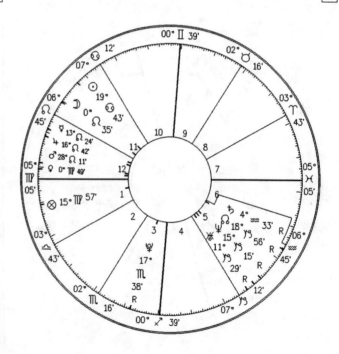

171. SOFTWARE SPECTRUM-SSPE   *Software*
July 12, 1991   NYC   9:30:0 AM EDT
40N45'00"   3:53:59 ST   74W00'23"

172. SPECIAL DEVICE-SDII   *Aerospace*
   Aug. 8, 1991   NYC   9:30:0 AM EDT
   40N45'00"   5:40:26 ST   74W00'23"

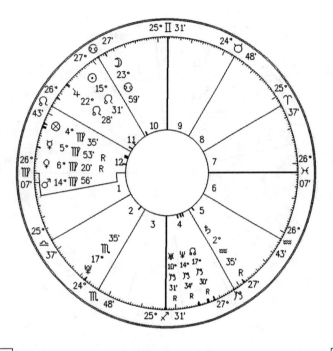

173. SPYGLASS-SPYG   *Software*
   June 27, 1995   NYC   9:30:0 AM EDT
   40N45'00"   2:54:46 ST   74W00'23"

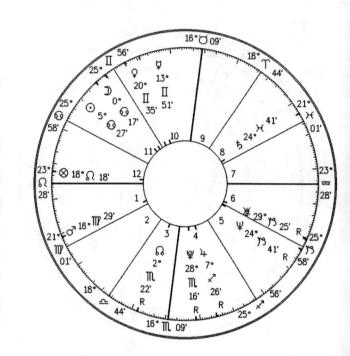

174. STATE OF THE ART-SOTA   *Software*
   May 23, 1991   NYC   9:30:0 AM EDT
   40N45'00"   0:36:37 ST   74W00'23"

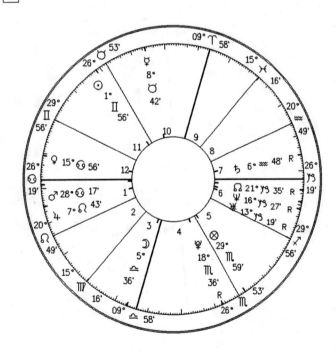

175. SUN MICROSYSTEMS-SUNW   *Computers*
   Mar. 4, 1986   NYC   9:30:0 AM EST
   40N45'00"   20:22:26 ST   74W00'23"

176. SYBASE-SYBS *Software*
Aug. 8, 1991   NYC   9:30:0 AM EDT
40N45'00"   5:40:26 ST   74W00'23"

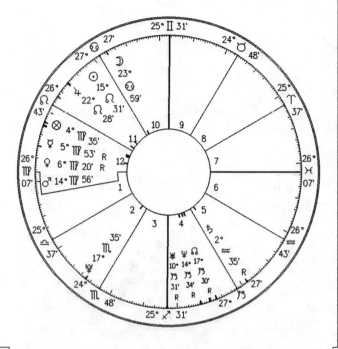

177. SYMANTEC-SYMC *Software*
June 23, 1989   NYC   9:30:0 AM EDT
40N45'00"   2:40:45 ST   74W00'23"

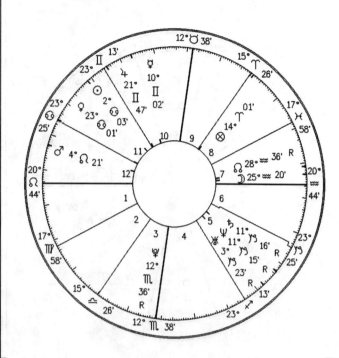

178. SYMBOLLON-SYMBA *Biotech*
Jan. 20, 1994   NYC   9:30:0 AM EST
40N45'00"   17:32:55 ST   74W00'23"

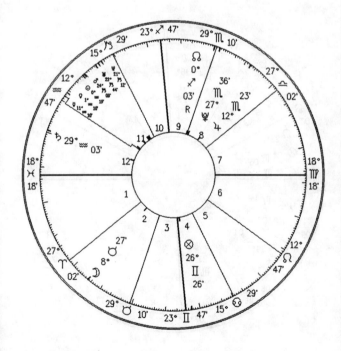

179. SYQUEST TECHNOLOGY-SYQT *Computer Equip.*
Dec. 19, 1991   NYC   9:30:0 AM EST
40N45'00"   15:24:57 ST   74W00'23"

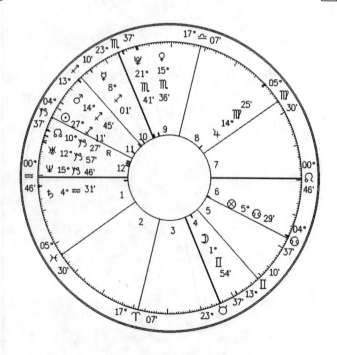

180. TELCO SYSTEMS-TELC   *Telecom Equip.*
Feb. 15, 1984   NYC   10:0:0 AM EST
40N45'00"   19:43:28 ST   74W00'23"

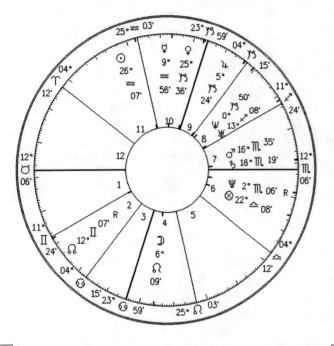

181. TELECOM LIBERTY-LBTYA   *Radio, TV*
Aug. 15, 1995   NYC   9:30:0 AM EDT
40N45'00"   6:07:57 ST   74W00'23"

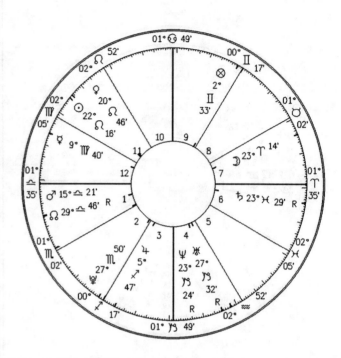

182. TELECOMMUNICATIONS. A-TCOMA   *Cable TV*
Feb. 5, 1971   NYC   10:0:0 AM EST
40N45'00"   19:04:24 ST   74W00'23"

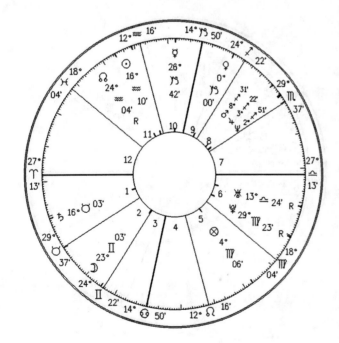

183. TELLABS-TLAB   *Telecom Equip*
July 11, 1980   NYC   10:0:0 AM EDT
40N45'00"   4:22:32 ST   74W00'23"

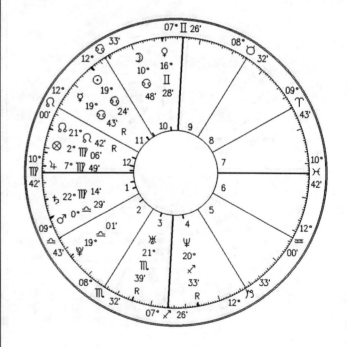

184. TRICORD SYSTEMS-TRCD   Networks
Mar. 19, 1993   NYC   9:30:0 AM EST
40N45'00"   21:22:33 ST   74W00'23"

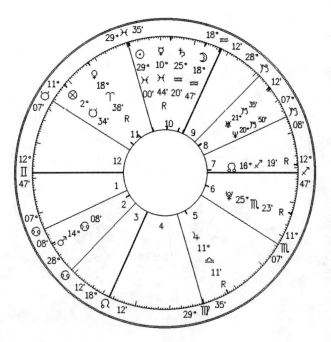

185. TRIMBLE NAVIG.-TRMB   Scientific Equipment
July 23, 1990   NYC   9:30:0 AM EDT
40N45'00"   4:38:18 ST   74W00'23"

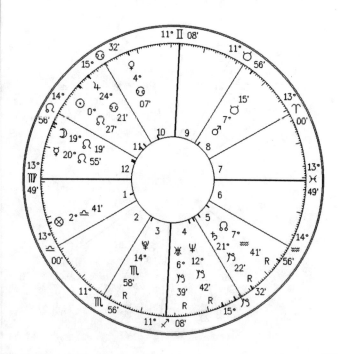

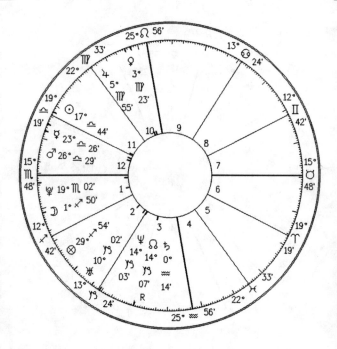

186. U.S. ROBOTICS-USRX   Computer Equip.
Oct. 11, 1991   NYC   9:30:0 AM EDT
40N45'00"   9:52:45 ST   74W00'23"

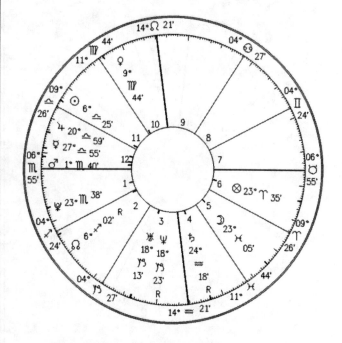

187. ULTRATECH STEPPER-UTEK   Semiconductors
Sep. 29, 1993   NYC   9:30:0 AM EDT
40N45'00"   9:07:15 ST   74W00'23"

188. US WATS-USWI   *Telecom.*
Jan. 21, 1994   NYC   9:30:0 AM EST
40N45'00"   17:36:52 ST   74W00'23"

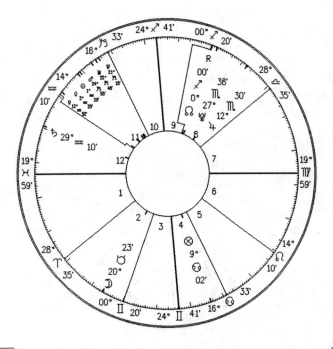

189. VALUJET-VJET   *Airline*
June 28, 1994   NYC   9:30:0 AM EDT
40N45'00"   2:59:39 ST   74W00'23"

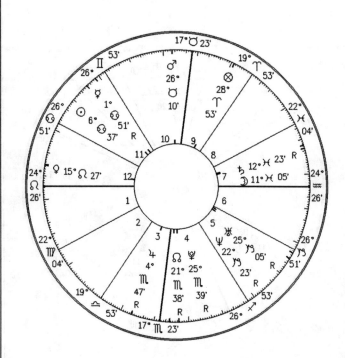

190. VENGOLD-VENGF   *Gold*
Jan. 18, 1994   NYC   9:30:0 AM EST
40N45'00"   17:25:04 ST   74W00'23"

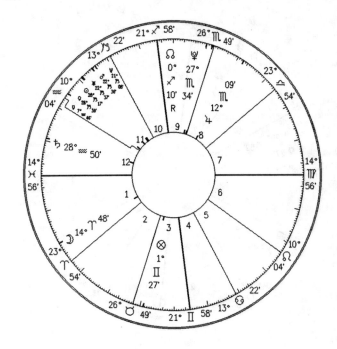

191. WALL DATA-WALL   *Software*
Mar. 16, 1993   NYC   9:30:0 AM EST
40N45'00"   21:10:45 ST   74W00'23"

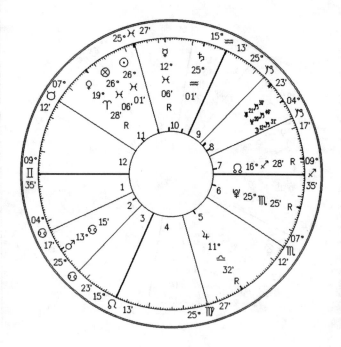

192. WARRANTECH-WTEC *Commercial Ser.*
Dec. 26, 1986   NYC   9:30:0 AM EST
40N45'00"   15:53:23 ST   74W00'23"

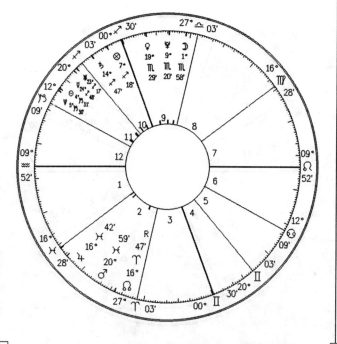

193. WONDERWARE-WNDR *Software*
July 23, 1993   NYC   9:30:0 AM EDT
40N45'00"   4:39:09 ST   74W00'23"

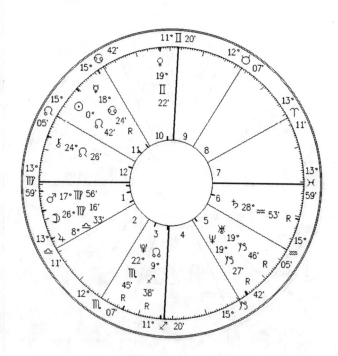

194. WORTHINGTON IND.-WTHG *Steel*
Oct. 19, 1971   NYC   10:0:0 AM EDT
40N45'00"   10:53:45 ST   74W00'23"

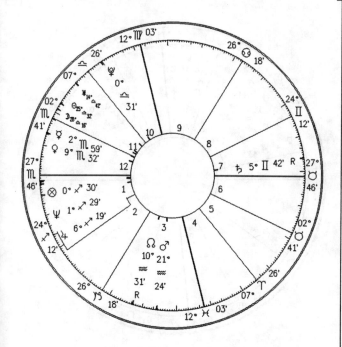

195. XILINX-XLNX *Semiconductors*
June 12, 1990   NYC   9:30:0 AM EDT
40N45'00"   1:56:39 ST   74W00'23"

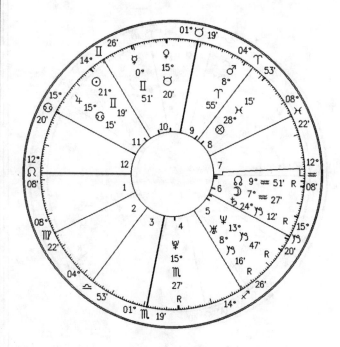

196. XIRCOM-XIRC *Local Networks*
Mar. 31, 1992   NYC   9:30:0 AM EST
40N45'00"   22:10:50 ST   74W00'23"

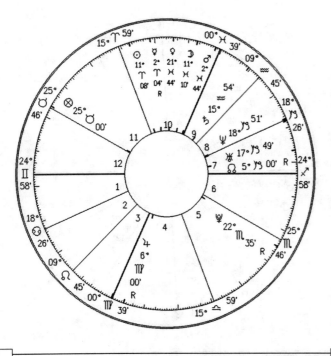

197. YAHOO-YHOO *Software*
Apr. 12, 1996   NYC   9:30:0 AM EDT
40N45'00"   21:58:07 ST   74W00'23"

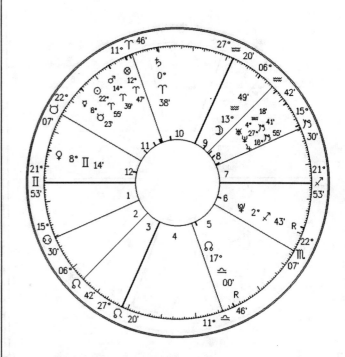

198. YELLOW FREIGHT-YELL *Trucking*
Feb. 5, 1972   NYC   10:0:0 AM EST
40N45'00"   19:03:40 ST   74W00'23"

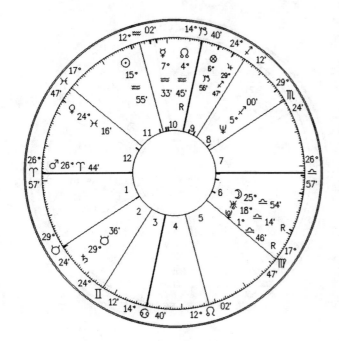

199. YOUTH SERVICES-YSII *Misc.*
Feb. 3, 1994   NYC   9:30:0 AM EST
40N45'00"   18:28:07 ST   74W00'23"

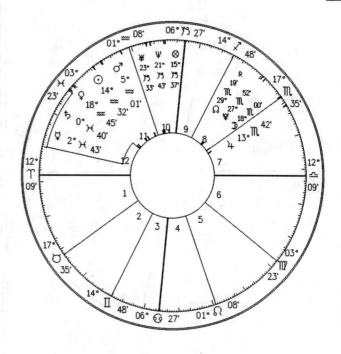

200. ZEBRA TECHNOLOGIES-ZBRA *Optical Recognition*
Aug. 15, 1991   NYC   9:30:0 AM EDT
40N45'00"   6:07:49 ST   74W00'23"

201. MCI WORLDCOM- *Communications*
Sep 15, 1993   NYC   9:30:0 AM EDT
40N45'00"   9:0832 ST   74W00'23"

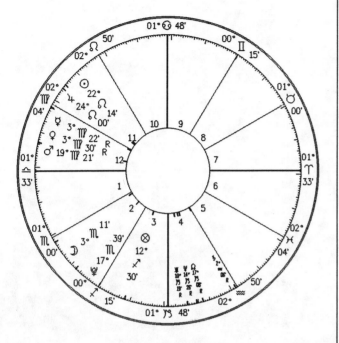

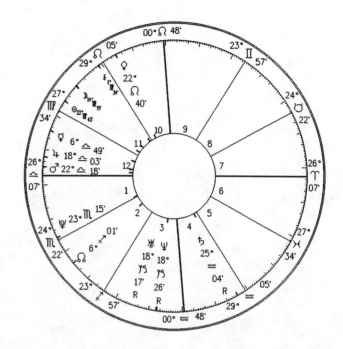

MUTUAL FUNDS

The dates utilized in this section are the inception dates of the funds. The definition of this date is the day upon which the fund became available to the public. This date may differ from the commencement of operations.

The commencement of operations is the date that the seed money was injected into the fund, the first date upon which the fund could buy stocks, and the first date upon which the net asset value is determined.

This date may be the same or it may be up to ten days earlier than the inception date. Fidelity utilizes this date as both the inception and the commencement date.

The inception date has no legal meaning; the commencement date does. I look at the inception date as being the equivalent to the first-trade date. It is the first day upon which the public can buy the fund. Some funds listed January 1 as the date. Most people that I know are recovering from New Year's Eve on the first. These funds are not listed. It is difficult to see how these dates could be meaningful because businesses and goverments are closed. In addition to employing the usual predictive techniques, there is one other regarding mutual funds. Most fund prospectuses will list the date upon which the current manager took control. Compare a chart for that date with the inception date. If the synastry is unfavorable, look for another fund. In 1997, Fidelity's software fund was turned over to a woman while transiting Saturn was afflicting the female planets in the fund chart. Six months later, the fund had underperformed and the manager was replaced.

Also, you will notice that some funds have the same date, which suggests that they will perform in line with each other. This is especially true of the Fidelity sector funds. Remember the section about industry planets. A horoscope for a gold fund will react more to the planets and sign that rule gold and inflation, such as the Sun, Leo, and Jupiter-Neptune, than will a fund begun the same day but for a different industry.

Mutual Funds

1. AIM GROWTH A-AGWFX
Dec. 4, 1967   NYC   10:0:0 AM EST
40N45'00"   14:54:57 ST   74W00'23"

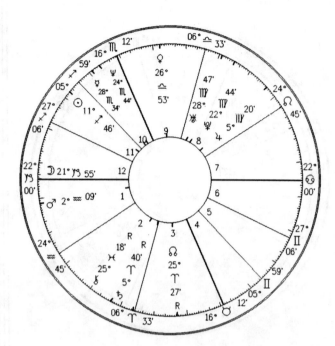

2. ALLIANCE CAPITAL-CHCLX
May 1, 1938   NYC   10:0:0 AM EDT
40N45'00"   23:39:21 ST   74W00'23"

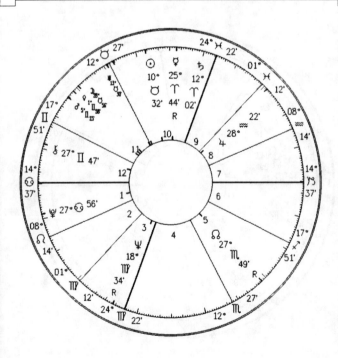

3. AMCAP-AMCAPX
May 1, 1967   NYC   10:0:0 AM EDT
40N45'00"   14:19:58 ST   74W00'23"

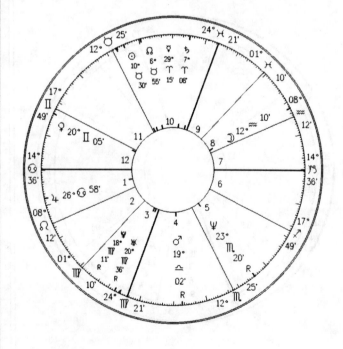

4. AMERICAN CENTURY 20th-TWCVX
Nov. 25, 1983   NYC   10:0:0 AM EST
40N45'00"   13:28:32 ST   74W00'23"

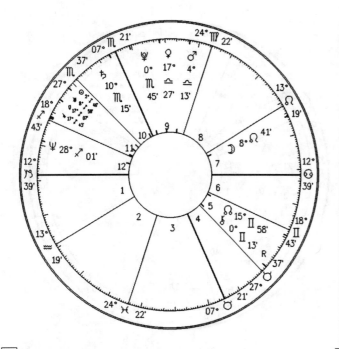

5. AMERICAN CENTURY-TWCIX
Oct. 31, 1958   NYC   10:0:0 AM EST
40N45'00"   12:41:37 ST   74W00'23"

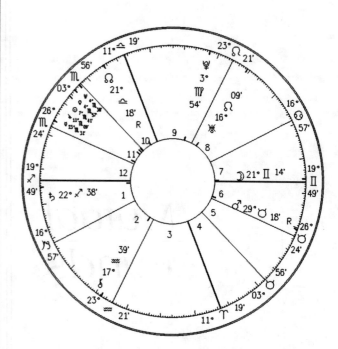

6. AMERICAN MUTUAL-AMRMX
Feb. 21, 1950   NYC   10:0:0 AM EST
40N45'00"   20:07:50 ST   74W00'23"

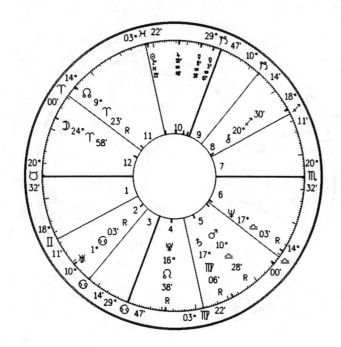

7. BABSON GROWTH-BABSX
June 8, 1959   NYC   10:0:0 AM EDT
40N45'00"   2:08:49 ST   74W00'23"

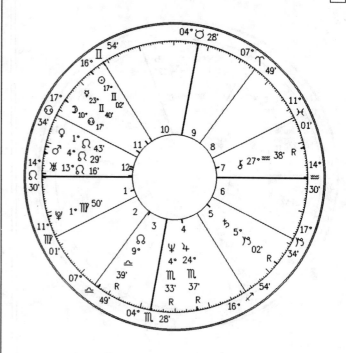

8. BABSON VALUE-BVALX
Dec. 21, 1984   NYC   10:0:0 AM EST
40N45'00"   16:05:28 ST   74W00'23"

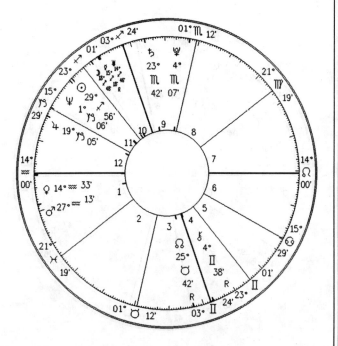

9. BRANDYWINE BLUE-BLUEX
Jan. 10, 1991   NYC   9:30:0 AM EST
40N45'00"   16:52:27 ST   74W00'23"

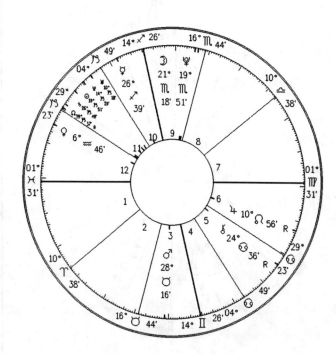

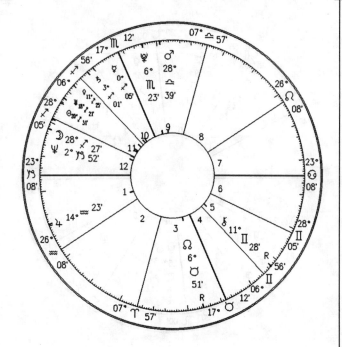

10. BRANDYWINE-BRWIX
Dec. 12, 1985   NYC   9:30:0 AM EST
40N45'00"   14:58:57 ST   74W00'23"

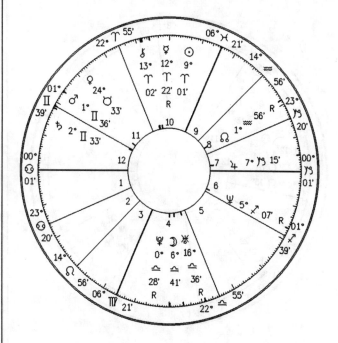

11. DREYFUS 3RD CENT.-DRTHX
Mar. 29, 1972   NYC   10:0:0 AM EST
40N45'00"   22:32:25 ST   74W00'23"

12. DREYFUS APPREC.-DGAGX
Jan. 18, 1984   NYC   10:0:0 AM EST
40N45'00"   17:52:52 ST   74W00'23"

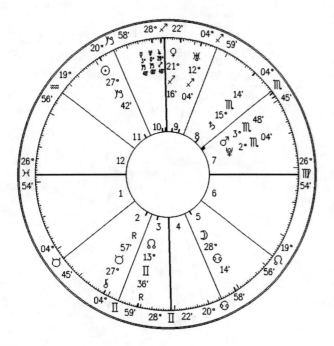

13. DREYFUS GROWTH-DREQX
Feb. 4, 1972   NYC   10:0:0 AM EST
40N45'00"   18:59:31 ST   74W00'23"

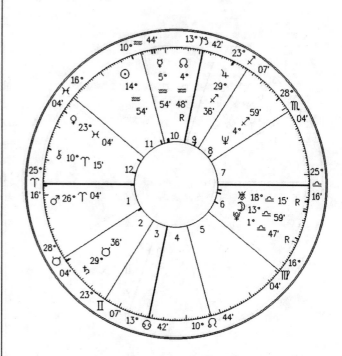

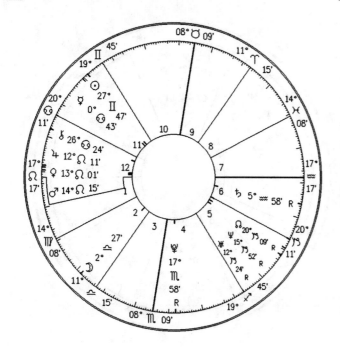

14. DREYFUS MIDCAP-PESPX
June 19, 1991   NYC   9:30:0 AM EDT
40N45'00"   2:23:06 ST   74W00'23"

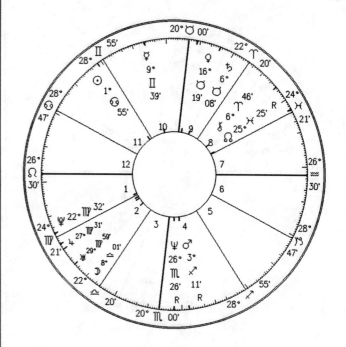

15. DREYFUS PREMIER A-DRLEX
June 23, 1969   NYC   10:0:0 AM EDT
40N45'00"   3:10:15 ST   74W00'23"

16. DREYFUS-DREVX
May 24, 1951   NYC   10:0:0 AM EDT
40N45'00"   1:09:26 ST   74W00'23"

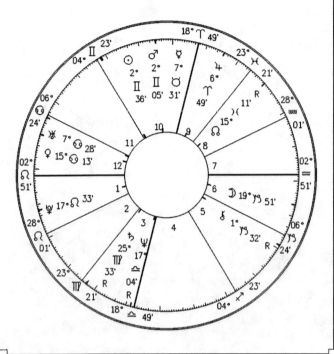

17. EVERGREEN Y-EVGRX
Oct. 01, 1971   NYC   10:0:0 AM EST
40N45'00"   17:49:53 ST   74W00'23"

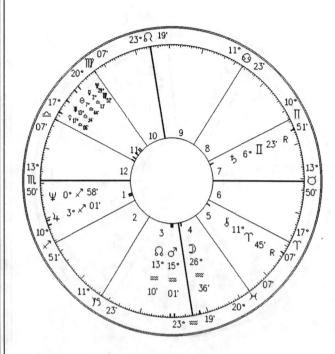

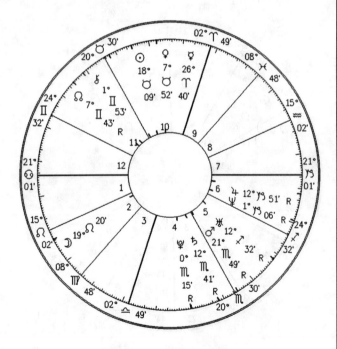

18. FIDEL.AEROSPACE-FSDAX
May 8, 1984   NYC   10:0:0 AM EDT
40N45'00"   0:10:20 ST   74W00'23"

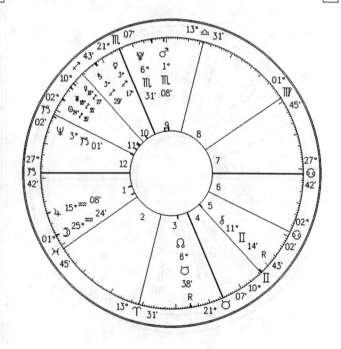

19. FIDEL.AIR TRANSP.-FSAIX
Dec. 16, 1985   NYC   9:30:0 AM EST
40N45'00"   15:14:43 ST   74W00'23"

20. FIDEL.AUTO-FSAVX
June 30, 1986   NYC   9:30:0 AM EDT
40N45'00"   3:07:18 ST   74W00'23"

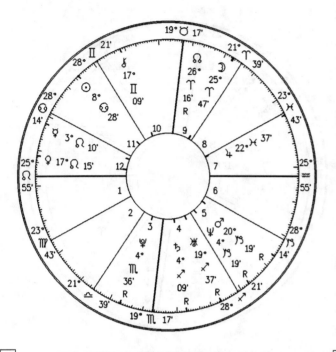

21. FIDEL.BIOTECH-FBIOX
Dec. 16, 1985   NYC   9:30:0 AM EST
40N45'00"   15:14:43 ST   74W00'23"

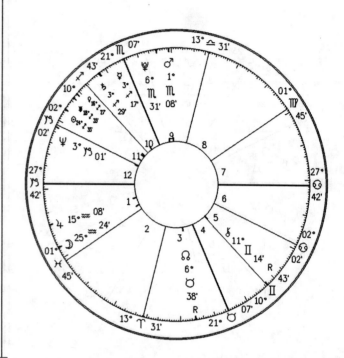

22. FIDEL.BLUE CHIP-FBGRX
Dec. 31, 1987   NYC   9:30:0 AM EST
40N45'00"   16:11:57 ST   74W00'23"

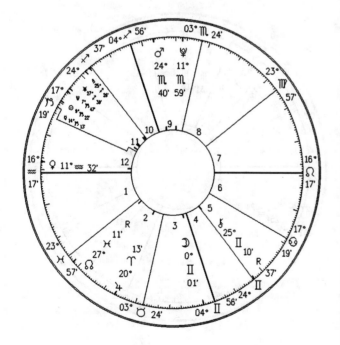

23. FIDEL.BROKERAGE-FSLBX
July 29, 1985   NYC   10:0:0 AM EDT
40N45'00"   5:32:40 ST   74W00'23"

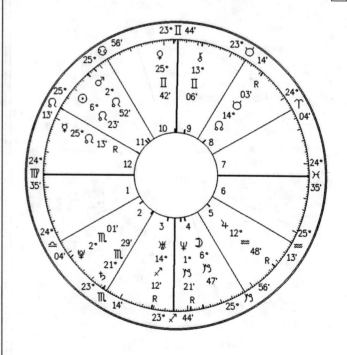

24. FIDEL.CHEMICALS-FSCHX
July 29, 1985   NYC   10:0:0 AM EDT
40N45'00"   5:32:40 ST   74W00'23"

25. FIDEL.COMMUNICAT.-FSDCX
June 29, 1990   NYC   9:30:0 AM EDT
40N45'00"   3:03:29 ST   74W00'23"

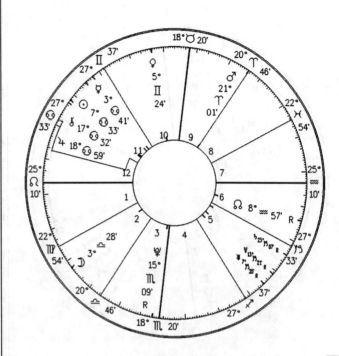

26. FIDEL.COMPUTER-FDCPX
July 29, 1985   NYC   10:0:0 AM EDT
40N45'00"   5:32:40 ST   74W00'23"

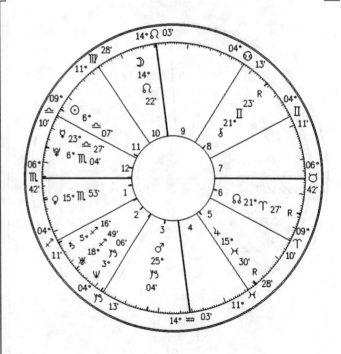

27. FIDEL.CONSTRUCTION-FSHOX
Sep. 29, 1986   NYC   9:30:0 AM EDT
40N45'00"   9:06:04 ST   74W00'23"

28. FIDEL.CONSUMER-FSCPX
June 29, 1990   NYC   9:30:0 AM EDT
40N45'00"   3:03:29 ST   74W00'23"

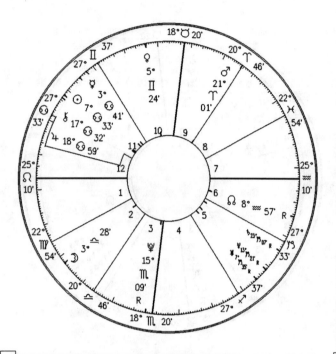

29. FIDEL.CYCLICAL-FCYCF
Mar. 3, 1997   NYC   9:30:0 AM EST
40N45'00"   20:19:37 ST   74W00'23"

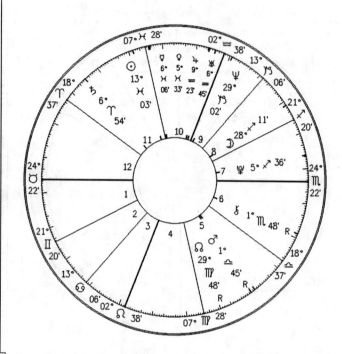

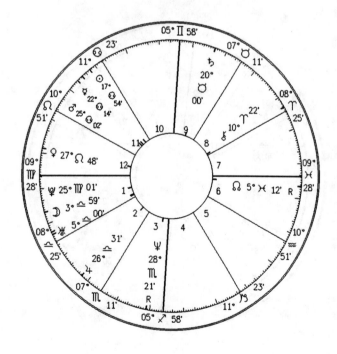

30. FIDEL.DESTINY1-FDESX
July 10, 1970   NYC   10:0:0 AM EDT
40N45'00"   4:16:19 ST   74W00'23"

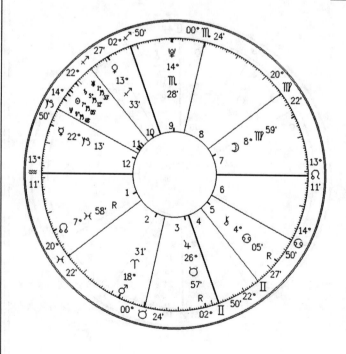

31. FIDEL.DISCIPLINED-FDEQX
Dec. 28, 1988   NYC   9:30:0 AM EST
40N45'00"   16:03:06 ST   74W00'23"

32. FIDEL.ELECTRONICS-FSELX
July 29, 1985   NYC   10:0:0 AM EDT
40N45'00"   5:32:40 ST   74W00'23"

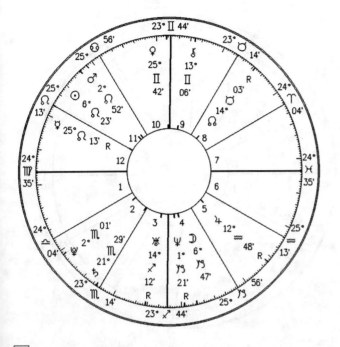

33. FIDEL.EMERGING GR.-FDEGX
Dec. 28, 1990   NYC   9:30:0 AM EST
40N45'00"   16:01:12 ST   74W00'23"

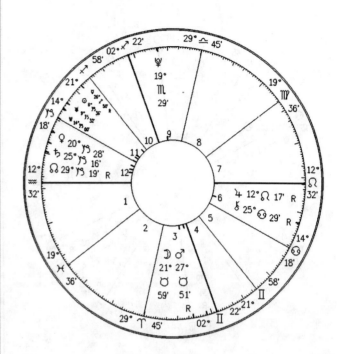

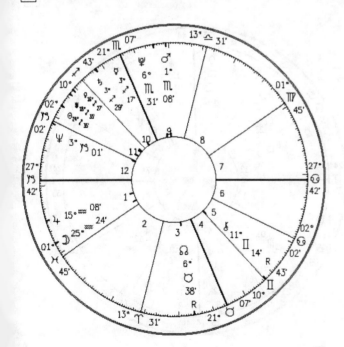

34. FIDEL.ENERGY SERV.-FSESX
Dec. 16, 1985   NYC   9:30:0 AM EST
40N45'00"   15:14:43 ST   74W00'23"

35. FIDEL.ENERGY-FSENX
July 14, 1981   NYC   10:0:0 AM EDT
40N45'00"   4:33:24 ST   74W00'23"

36. FIDEL.ENVIRONMENT-FSLEX
June 29, 1989   NYC   9:30:0 AM EDT
40N45'00"   3:04:26 ST   74W00'23"

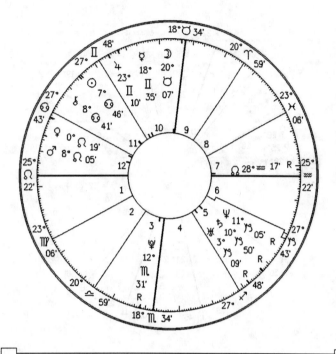

37. FIDEL.FIFTY-FFTYX
Sep. 17, 1993   NYC   9:30:0 AM EDT
40N45'00"   8:19:58 ST   74W00'23"

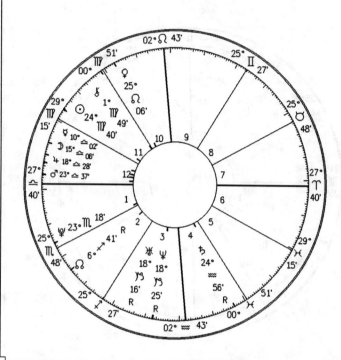

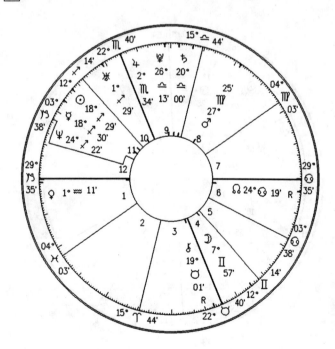

38. FIDEL.FINANCIAL-FIDSX
Dec. 10, 1981   NYC   10:0:0 AM EST
40N45'00"   15:21:01 ST   74W00'23"

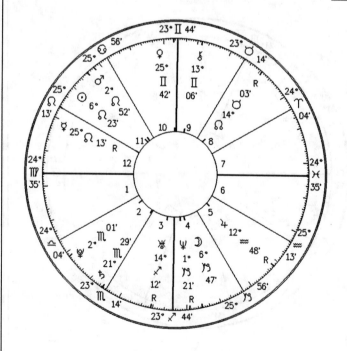

39. FIDEL.FOOD & AGR.-FDFAX
July 29, 1985   NYC   10:0:0 AM EDT
40N45'00"   5:32:40 ST   74W00'23"

40. FIDEL.FOREST PRDS.-FSPFX
June 30, 1986   NYC   9:30:0 AM EDT
40N45'00"   3:07:18 ST   74W00'23"

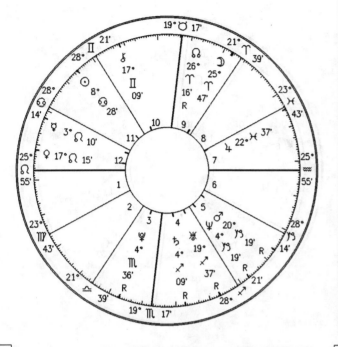

41. FIDEL. GROWTH CO.-FDGRX
Jan. 17, 1983   NYC   10:0:0 AM EST
40N45'00"   17:49:53 ST   74W00'23"

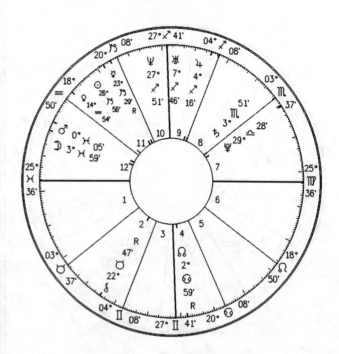

42. FIDEL.HEALTH CARE-FSPHX
July 14, 1981   NYC   10:0:0 AM EDT
40N45'00"   4:33:24 ST   74W00'23"

43. FIDEL.HOME FINANCE-FSVLX
Dec. 16, 1985   NYC   9:30:0 AM EST
40N45'00"   15:14:43 ST   74W00'23"

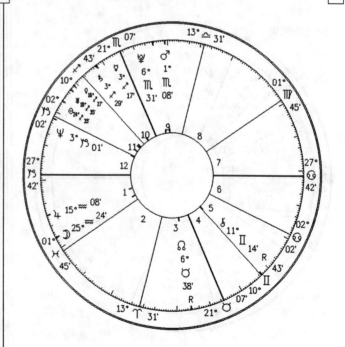

44. FIDEL.INDUS.EQUIP.-FSCGX
Sep. 29, 1986   NYC   9:30:0 AM EDT
40N45'00"   9:06:04 ST   74W00'23"

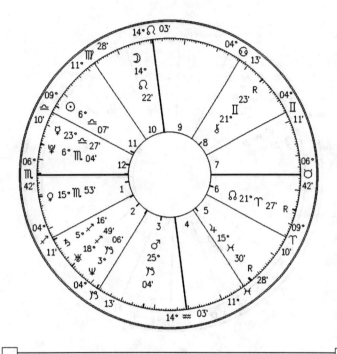

45. FIDEL.INDUS.MATER.-FSDPX
Sep. 29, 1986   NYC   9:30:0 AM EDT
40N45'00"   9:06:04 ST   74W00'23"

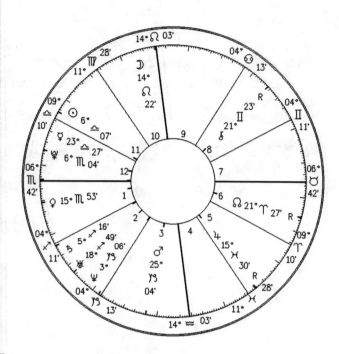

46. FIDEL.INSURANCE-FSPCX
Dec. 16, 1985   NYC   9:30:0 AM EST
40N45'00"   15:14:43 ST   74W00'23"

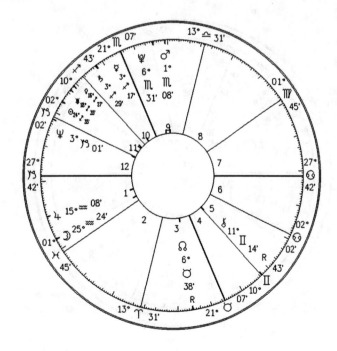

47. FIDEL.LARGE CAP-FLCSX
June 22, 1995   NYC   9:30:0 AM EDT
40N45'00"   2:35:03 ST   74W00'23"

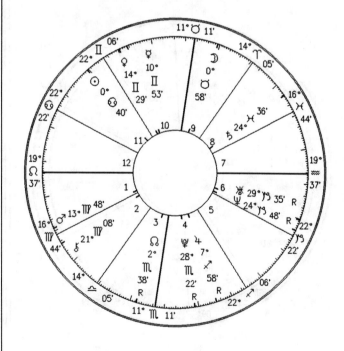

48. FIDEL.LEISURE-FDLSX
May 8, 1984   NYC   9:30:0 AM EDT
40N45'00"   23:40:15 ST   74W00'23"

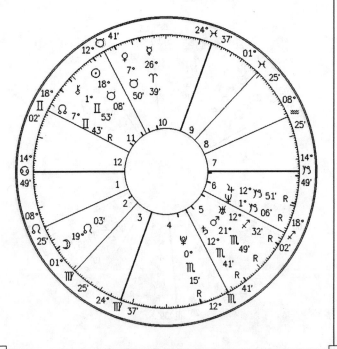

49. FIDEL.MAGELLAN-FMAGX
May 2, 1963   NYC   10:0:0 AM EDT
40N45'00"   23:43:04 ST   74W00'23"

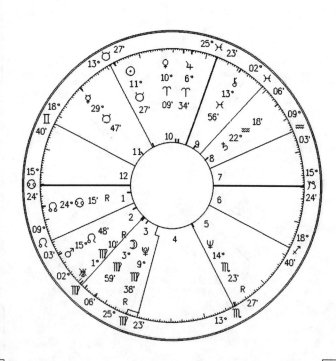

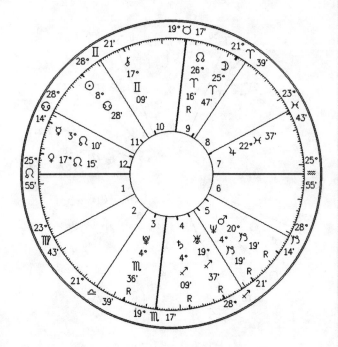

50. FIDEL.MEDICAL-FSHCX
June 30, 1986 NYC   9:30:0 AM EDT
40N45'00"   3:07:18 ST   74W00'23"

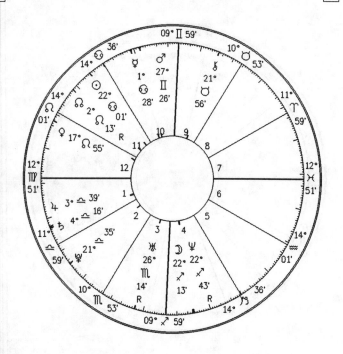

51. FIDEL.METALS-FDPMX
July 14, 1981 NYC   10:0:0 AM EDT
40N45'00"   4:33:24 ST   74W00'23"

52. FIDEL.MID-CAP-FMCSX
Mar. 29, 1994   NYC   9:30:0 AM EST
40N45'00"   22:01:03 ST   74W00'23"

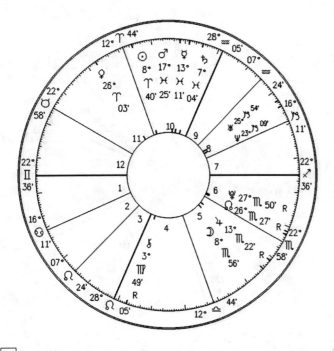

53. FIDEL.MULTIMEDIA-FBMPX
June 30, 1986   NYC   10:0:0 AM EDT
40N45'00"   3:37:23 ST   74W00'23"

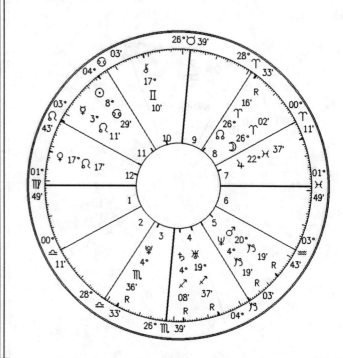

54. FIDEL.NAT.RESOURCE-FNATF
Mar. 3, 1997   NYC   9:30:0 AM EST
40N45'00"   20:19:37 ST   74W00'23"

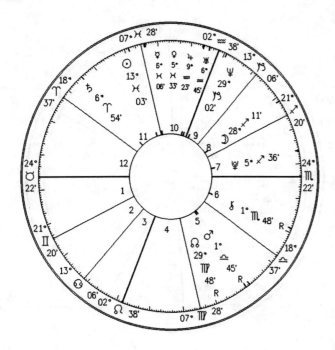

55. FIDEL.NATURAL GAS-FSNGX
Apr. 21, 1993   NYC   9:30:0 AM EDT
40N45'00"   22:32:31 ST   74W00'23"

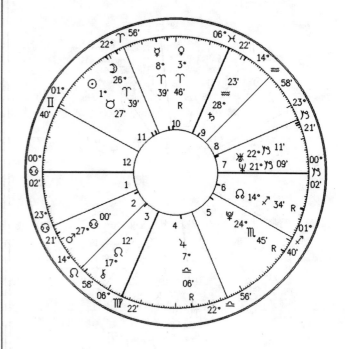

56. FIDEL.NEW MILLEN.-FMILX
Dec. 28, 1992   NYC   9:30:0 AM EST
40N45'00"   16:03:14 ST   74W00'23"

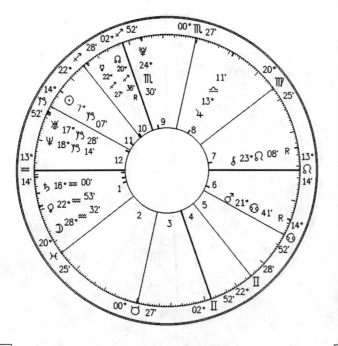

57. FIDEL.REGION.BANKS-FSRBX
June 30, 1986   NYC   9:30:0 AM EDT
40N45'00"   3:07:18 ST   74W00'23"

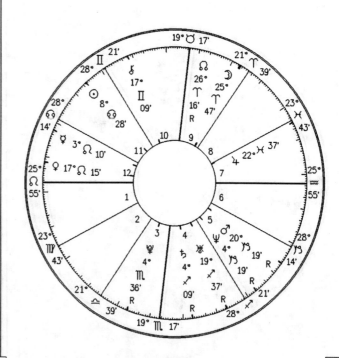

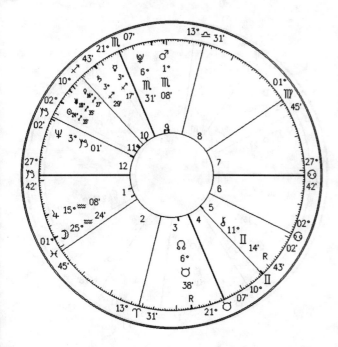

58.   FIDEL.RETAIL-FSRPX
Dec. 16, 1985   NYC   9:30:0 AM EST
40N45'00"   15:14:43 ST   74W00'23"

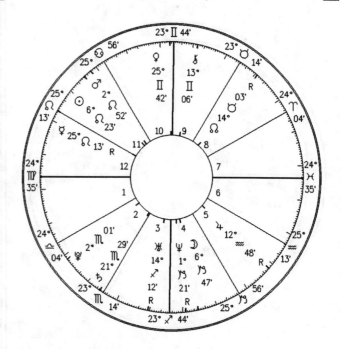

59.   FIDEL.SOFTWARE-FSCSX
July 29, 1985   NYC   10:0:0 AM EDT
40N45'00"   5:32:40 ST   74W00'23"

60. FIDEL.STOCK SELECT-FDSSX
Sep. 28, 1990   NYC   9:30:0 AM EDT
40N45'00"   9:02:15 ST   74W00'23"

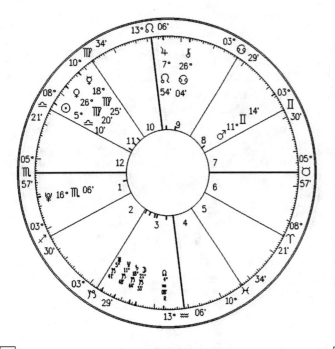

61. FIDEL.TECHNOLOGY-FSPTX
July 14, 1981   NYC   10:0:0 AM EDT
40N45'00"   4:33:24 ST   74W00'23"

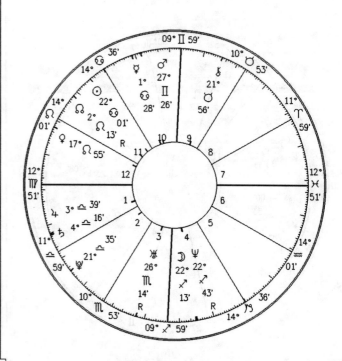

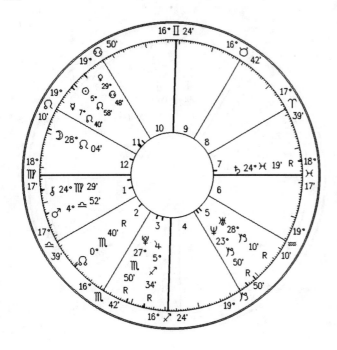

62. FIDEL.TELELCOM-FSTCX
July 29, 1995   NYC   9:30:0 AM EDT
40N45'00"   5:00:55 ST   74W00'23"

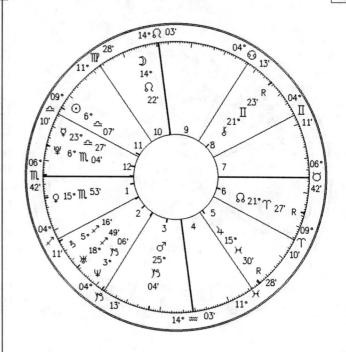

63. FIDEL.TRANSPORTAT.-FSRFX
Sep. 29, 1986   NYC   9:30:0 AM EDT
40N45'00"   9:06:04 ST   74W00'23"

64. FIDEL.UTILITIES-FSUTX
Dec. 10, 1981   NYC   10:0:0 AM EST
40N45'00"   15:21:01 ST   74W00'23"

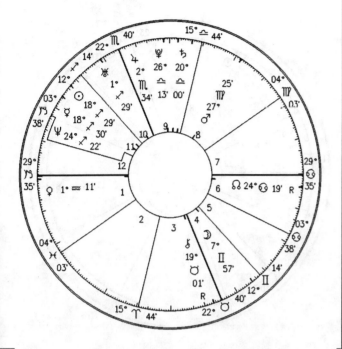

65. FIDELITY CAP.APPRE-FDCAX
Nov. 26, 1986   NYC   9:30:0 AM EST
40N45'00"   13:54:54 ST   74W00'23"

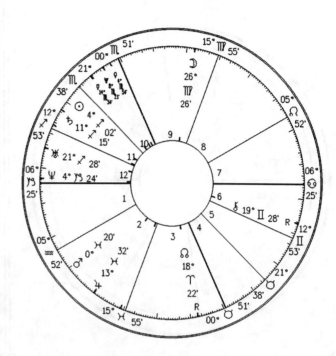

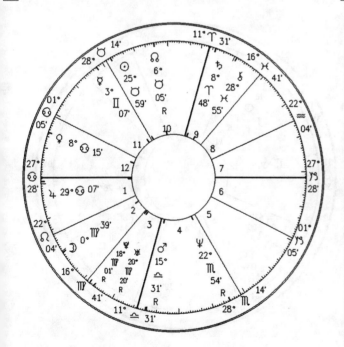

66. FIDELITY CONTRAFUN-FCNTX
May 17, 1967   NYC   10:0:0 AM EDT
40N45'00"   0:42:20 ST   74W00'23"

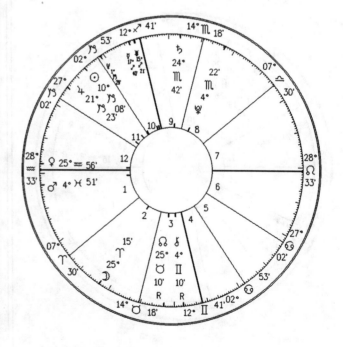

67. FIDELITY OTC-FOCPX
Dec. 31, 1984   NYC   10:0:0 AM EST
40N45'00"   16:44:53 ST   74W00'23"

68. FIDELITY TREND-FTRNX
June 16, 1958   NYC   10:0:0 AM EDT
40N45'00"   2:41:19 ST   74W00'23"

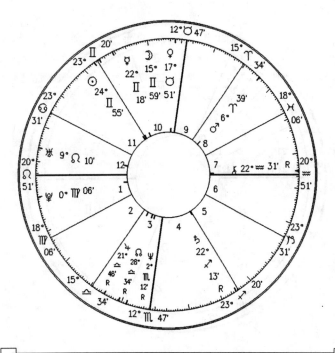

69. FIDELITY-FFIDX
Apr. 30, 1930   NYC   10:0:0 AM EDT
40N45'00"   23:35:09 ST   74W00'23"

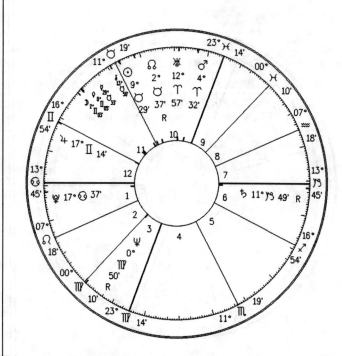

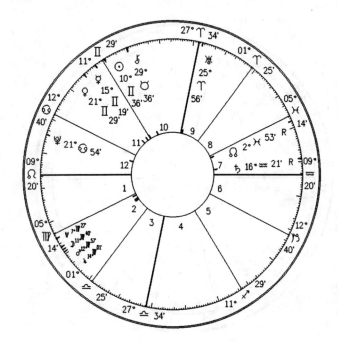

70. FRANKLIN EQUITY1-FKREX
June 1, 1933   NYC   10:0:0 AM EDT
40N45'00"   1:42:24 ST   74W00'23"

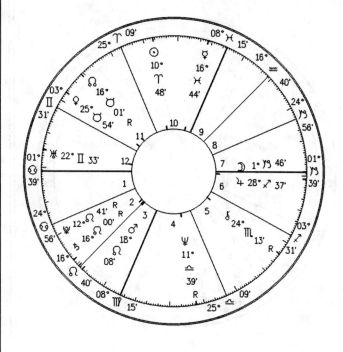

71. FRANKLIN GROWTH1-FKGRX
Mar. 31, 1948   NYC   10:0:0 AM EST
40N45'00"   22:39:34 ST   74W00'23"

72. GABELLI ASSET-GABAX
Mar. 3, 1986   NYC   9:30:0 AM EST
40N45'00"   20:18:18 ST   74W00'23"

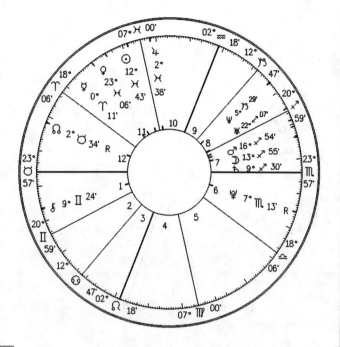

73. GABELLI GROWTH-GABGX
Apr. 10, 1987   NYC   9:30:0 AM EDT
40N45'00"   21:47:00 ST   74W00'23"

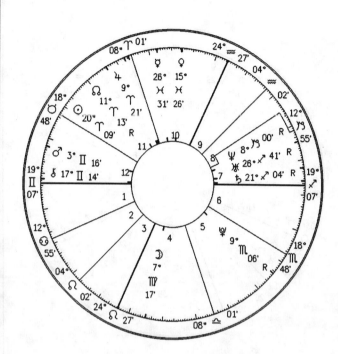

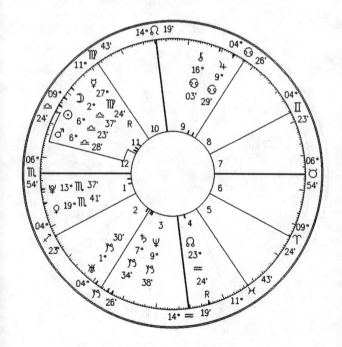

74. GABELLI VALUE-GABVX
Sep. 29, 1989   NYC   9:30:0 AM EDT
40N45'00"   9:07:09 ST   74W00'23"

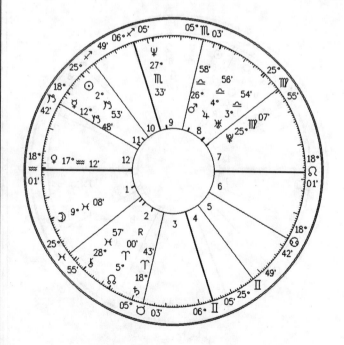

75. J.HANCOCK GROWTH-JHNGX
Dec. 24, 1968   NYC   10:0:0 AM EST
40N45'00"   16:16:48 ST   74W00'23"

76. JANUS MERCURY-JAMRX
May 3, 1993   NYC   9:30:0 AM EDT
40N45'00"   23:19:50 ST   74W00'23"

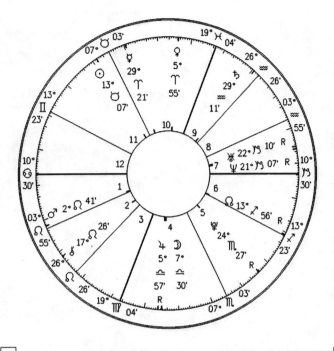

77. JANUS OLYMPUS-JAOLX
Dec. 29, 1995   NYC   9:30:0 AM EST
40N45'00"   16:04:18 ST   74W00'23"

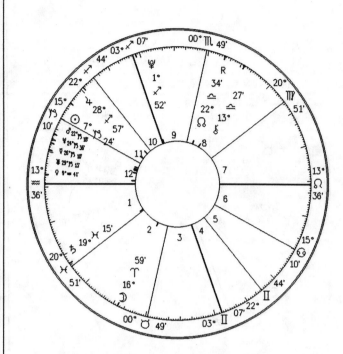

78. JANUS TWENTY-JAVLX
Apr. 26, 1985   NYC   10:0:0 AM EDT
40N45'00"   23:22:04 ST   74W00'23"

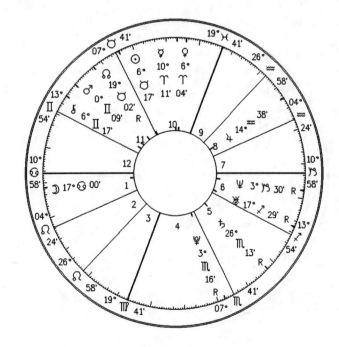

79. JANUS-JANSX
Feb. 27, 1970   NYC   10:0:0 AM EST
40N45'00"   20:32:07 ST   74W00'23"

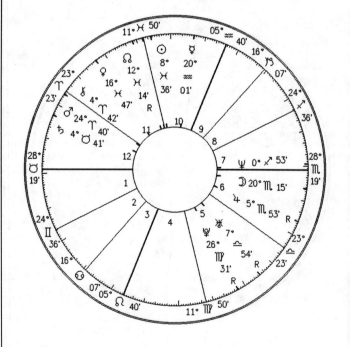

80. KEMPER GROWTH A-KRAGX
Apr. 4, 1966   NYC   10:0:0 AM EST
40N45'00"   22:53:55 ST   74W00'23"

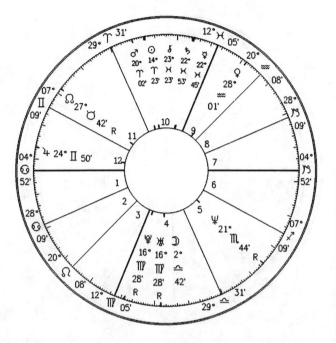

81. KEMPER STRATEGIC-KKTWX
Sep. 11, 1935   NYC   10:0:0 AM EDT
40N45'00"   8:22:38 ST   74W00'23"

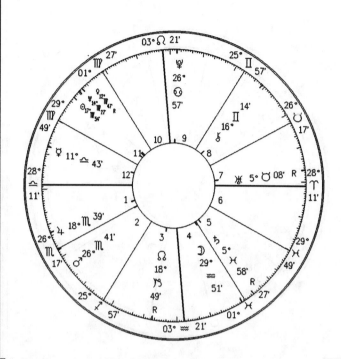

82. OPPEN. GROWTH A-OPPSX
Mar. 15, 1973   NYC   10:0:0 AM EST
40N45'00"   21:36:16 ST   74W00'23"

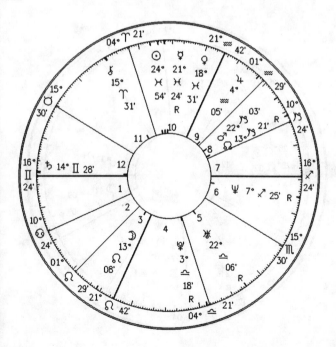

83. OPPEN. CAPITAL A-OPTFX
Jan. 22, 1981   NYC   10:0:0 AM EST
40N45'00"   18:11:30 ST   74W00'23"

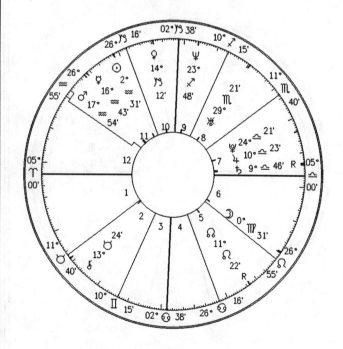

84. PIONEER GROWTH A-MOMGX
Jan. 2, 1969   NYC   10:0:0 AM EST
40N45'00"   16:52:17 ST   74W00'23"

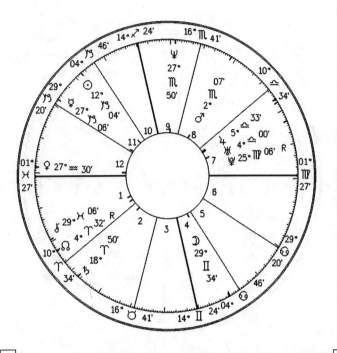

85. PUTNAM CAPITAL A-PCAPX
Aug. 5, 1993   NYC   9:30:0 AM EDT
40N45'00"   5:30:26 ST   74W00'23"

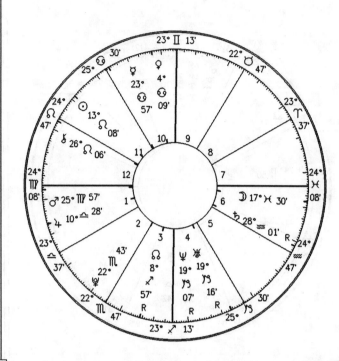

86. RYDEX OTC-RYOCX
Feb. 14, 1994   NYC   9:30:0 AM EST
40N45'00"   19:11:31 ST   74W00'23"

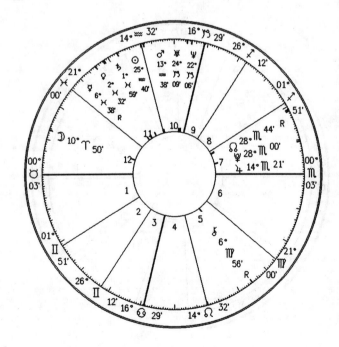

87. SCUDDER LARGE CO.-SCDUX
June 26, 1956   NYC   10:0:0 AM EDT
40N45'00"   3:22:39 ST   74W00'23"

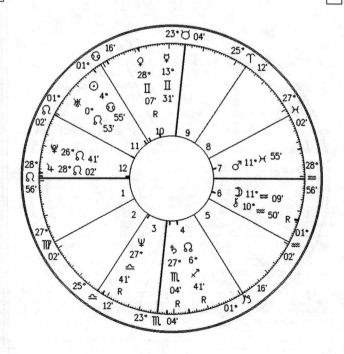

88. SELIGMAN GROWTH A-SGRFX
Jan. 26, 1937   NYC   10:0:0 AM EST
40N45'00"   18:25:55 ST   74W00'23"

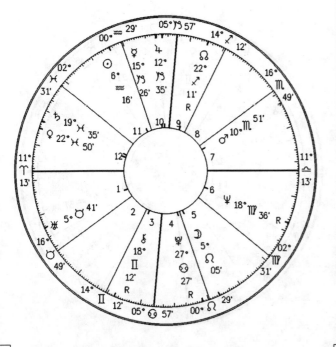

89. STEIN ROE GROWTH-SRFSX
July 1, 1958   NYC   10:0:0 AM EDT
40N45'00"   3:40:28 ST   74W00'23"

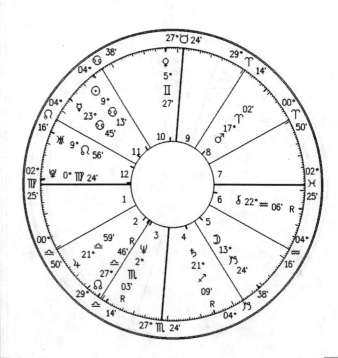

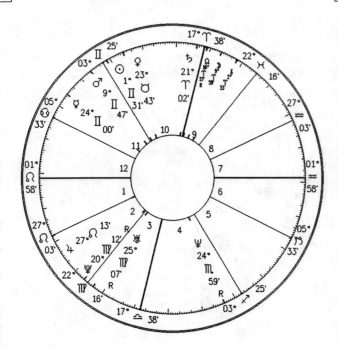

90. STEIN ROE SPECIAL-SRSPX
May 22, 1968   NYC   10:0:0 AM EDT
40N45'00"   1:05:02 ST   74W00'23"

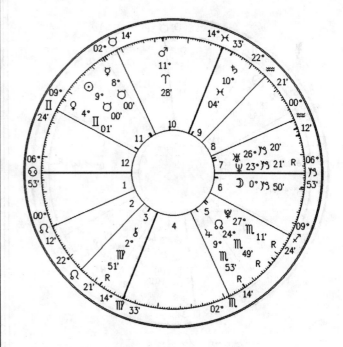

91. STEIN ROWE YOUNG-SRYIX
Apr. 29, 1994   NYC   9:30:0 AM EDT
40N45'00"   23:03:06 ST   74W00'23"

92. STRONG OPPORTUNITY-SOPFX
Dec. 31, 1985   NYC   9:30:0 AM EST
40N45'00"   16:13:51 ST   74W00'23"

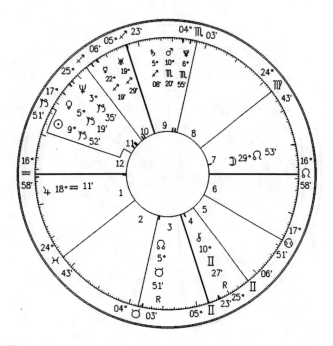

93. T. ROWE PR.SPECTRUM-PRSGX
June 29, 1990   NYC   9:30:0 AM EDT
40N45'00"   3:03:29 ST   74W00'23"

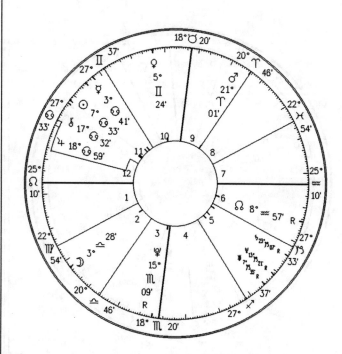

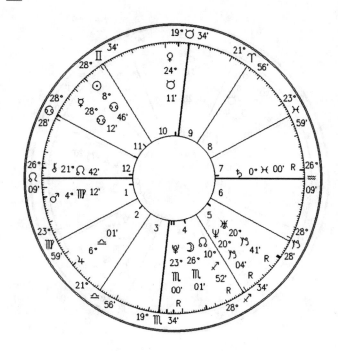

94. T. ROWE PRICE BLUE-TRBCX
June 30, 1993   NYC   9:30:0 AM EDT
40N45'00"   3:08:30 ST   74W00'23"

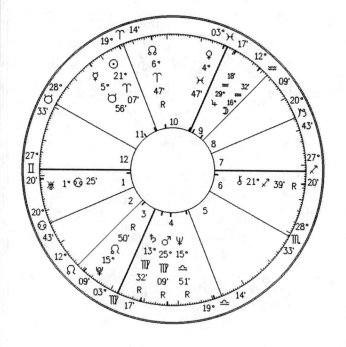

95. T. ROWE PRICE GROW.-PRGFX
Apr. 11, 1950   NYC   10:0:0 AM EDT
40N45'00"   22:20:52 ST   74W00'23"

96. UNITED VANGUARD A-UNVGX
Oct. 21, 1969   NYC   10:0:0 AM EDT
40N45'00"   11:03:21 ST   74W00'23"

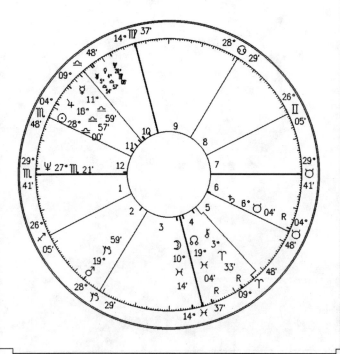

97. VALUE LINE-VLIFX
Mar. 1, 1950   NYC   10:0:0 AM EST
40N45'00"   20:39:23 ST   74W00'23"

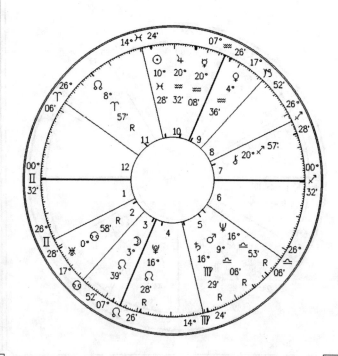

98. VANGUARD PRIMECAP-VPMCX
Nov. 1, 1984   NYC   10:0:0 AM EST
40N45'00"   12:48:20 ST   74W00'23"

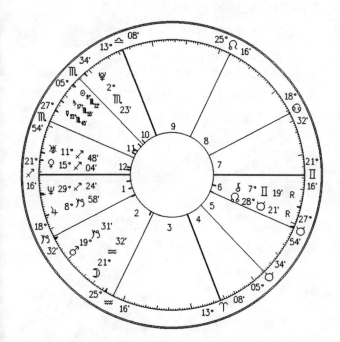

99. VANGUARD US GROWTH-VWUSX
Jan. 6, 1959   NYC   10:0:0 AM EST
40N45'00"   17:05:46 ST   74W00'23"

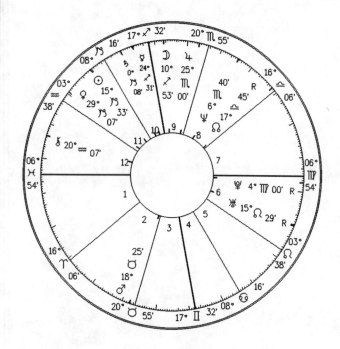

100. WASHINGTON MUTUAL-AWSHX
July 31, 1952   NYC   10:0:0 AM EDT
40N45'00"   5:40:31 ST   74W00'23"

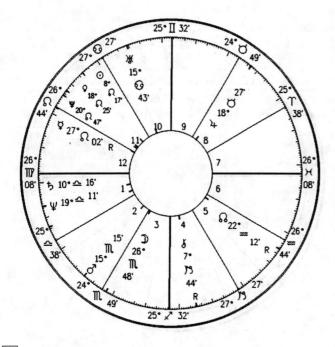

Foreign Funds

1. 1ST AUSTRALIA FUND-IAF
Dec. 12, 1985   NYC   9:30:0 AM EST
40N45'00"   14:58:57 ST   74W00'23"

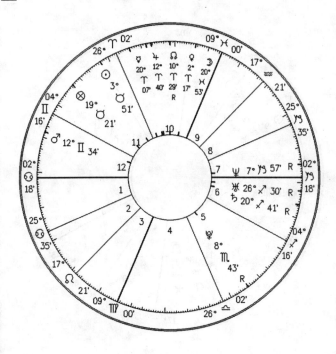

2. ASIA PACIFIC-APB
Apr. 24, 1987   NYC   9:30:0 AM EDT
40N45'00"   22:42:23 ST   74W00'23"

3. ASIA TIGERS FUND-GRR
Nov. 19, 1993   NYC   9:30:0 AM EST
40N45'00"   13:28:29 ST   74W00'23"

4. AUSTRIA FUND-OST
Dec. 22, 1989   NYC   10:0:0 AM EST
40N45'00"   16:08:46 ST   74W00'23"

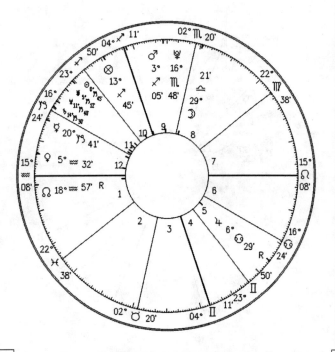

5. BRAZIL FUND-BZF
Mar. 31, 1988   NYC   9:30:0 AM EST
40N45'00"   22:10:55 ST   74W00'23"

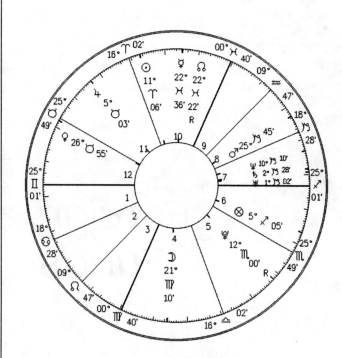

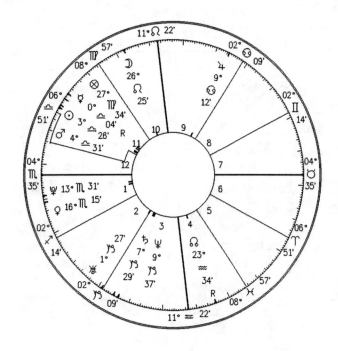

6. CHILE FUND-CH
Sep. 26, 1989   NYC   9:30:0 AM EDT
40N45'00"   8:55:19 ST   74W00'23"

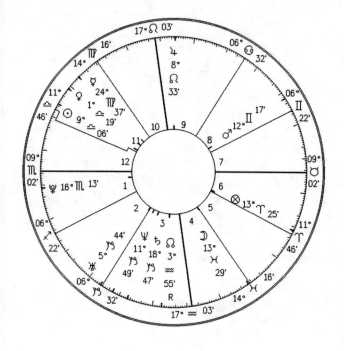

7. EMERGING MEXICO FUND-MEF
Oct. 2, 1990   NYC   9:30:0 AM EDT
40N45'00"   9:18:01 ST   74W00'23"

8. FRANCE FUND-FRF
May 11, 1990   NYC   9:30:0 AM EDT
40N45'00"   23:50:17 ST   74W00'23"

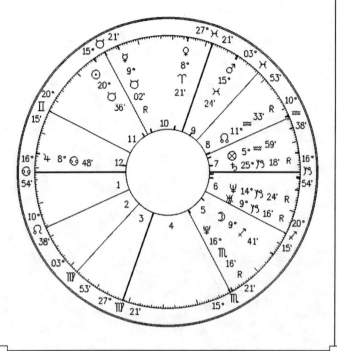

9. GERMANY FUND-GER
July 18, 1986   NYC   9:30:0 AM EDT
40N45'00"   4:18:28 ST   74W00'23"

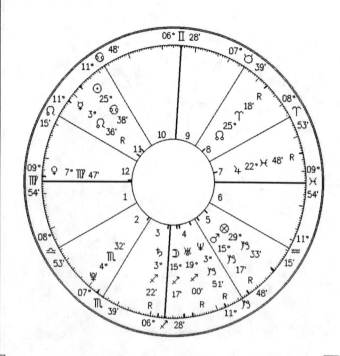

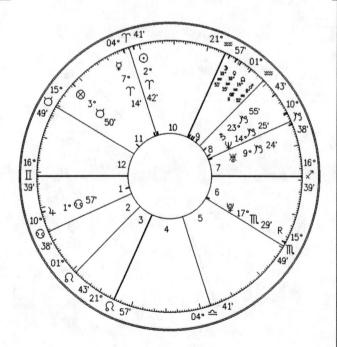

10. GT GREAT.EUROPE FUND-GTF
Mar. 23, 1990   NYC   9:30:0 AM EST
40N45'00"   21:37:16 ST   74W00'23"

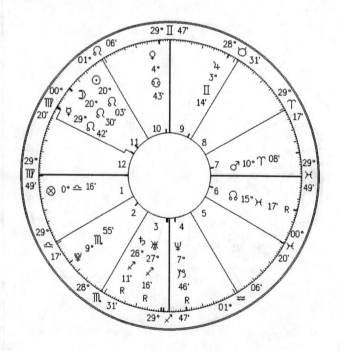

11. INDIA GROWTH FUND-IGF
Aug. 12, 1988   NYC   9:30:0 AM EDT
40N45'00"   5:59:04 ST   74W00'23"

12. INDONESIA FUND-IF
Mar. 1, 1990   NYC   9:30:0 AM EST
40N45'00"   20:10:30 ST   74W00'23"

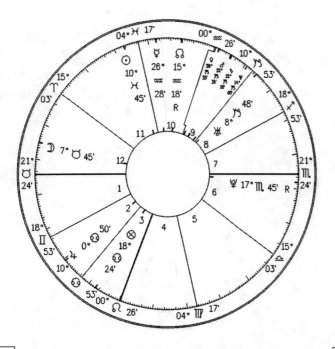

13. IRISH FUND-IRL
Mar. 30, 1990   NYC   9:30:0 AM EST
40N45'00"   22:04:52 ST   74W00'23"

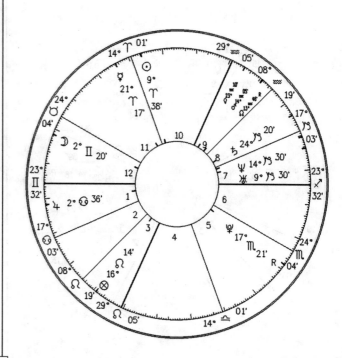

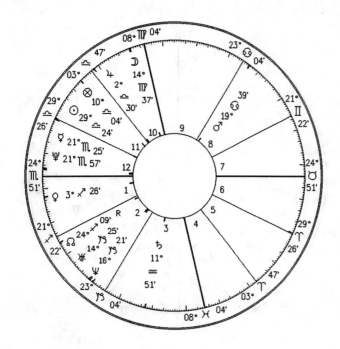

14. IST ISRAEL-ISL
Oct. 22, 1992   NYC   9:30:0 AM EDT
40N45'00"   10:38:53 ST   74W00'23"

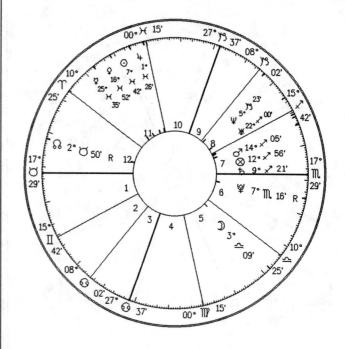

15. ITALY FUND-ITA
Feb. 26, 1986   NYC   9:30:0 AM EST
40N45'00"   19:58:47 ST   74W00'23"

16. JAPAN EQUITY FUND-JEQ
   Aug. 14, 1992   NYC   9:30:0 AM EDT
   40N45'00"   6:06:52 ST74W00'23"

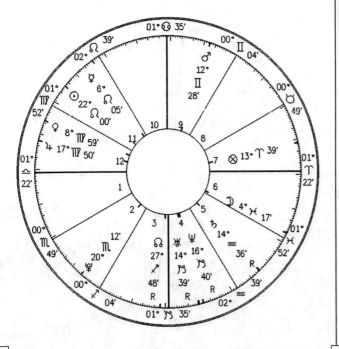

17. JAPAN OTC FUND-JOF
   Mar. 14, 1990   NYC   9:30:0 AM EST
   40N45'00"   21:01:47 ST   74W00'23"

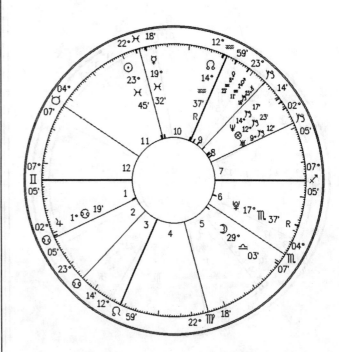

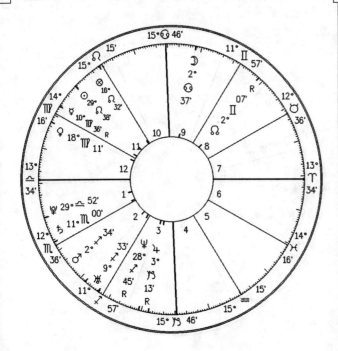

18. KOREA FUND-KF
   Aug. 22, 1984   NYC   10:0:0 AM EDT
   40N45'00"   7:08:27 ST   74W00'23"

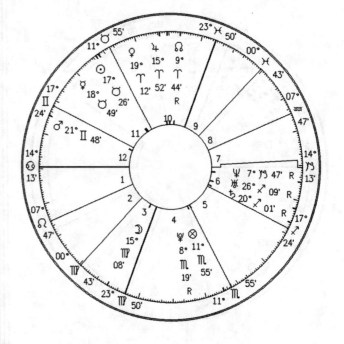

19. MALAYSIA FUND-MF
   May 8, 1987   NYC   9:30:0 AM EDT
   40N45'00"   23:37:23 ST   74W00'23"

20. MEXICO FUND-MXF
June 4, 1981 NYC 10:0:0 AM EDT
40N45'00" 1:55:42 ST 74W00'23"

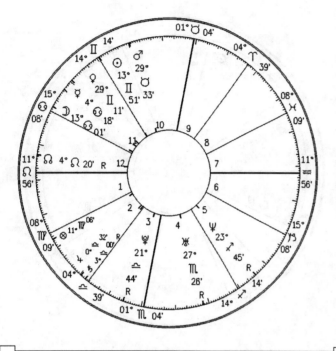

21. MORGAN STANL. RUSSIA-RNE
Sep. 25, 1996 NYC 9:30:0 AM EDT
40N45'00" 8:52:35 ST 74W00'23"

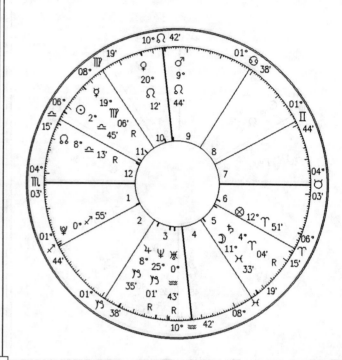

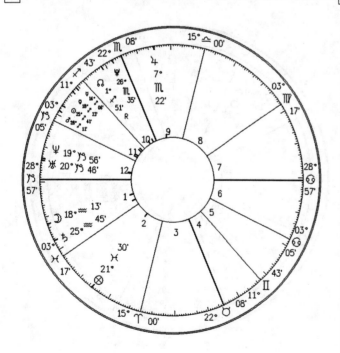

22. PAKISTAN FUND-PKF
Dec. 17, 1993 NYC 9:30:0 AM EST
40N45'00" 15:18:54 ST 74W00'23"

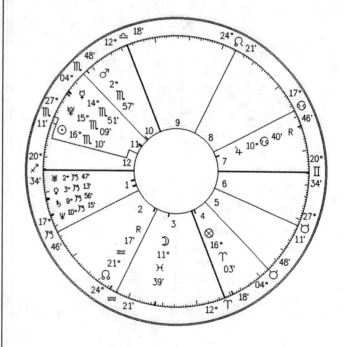

23. PHILLIPINE FUND-FPF
Nov. 8, 1989 NYC 9:30:0 AM EST
40N45'00" 12:45:13 ST 74W00'23"

24. PORTUGAL FUND—PGF
Nov. 1, 1989   NYC   9:30:0 AM EST
40N45'00"   12:17:37 ST   74W00'23"

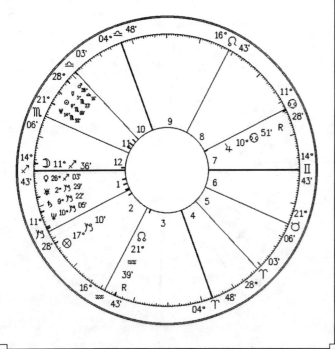

25. SCANDANAVIA FUND-SCF
June 17, 1986   NYC   9:30:0 AM EDT
40N45'00"   2:16:15 ST   74W00'23"

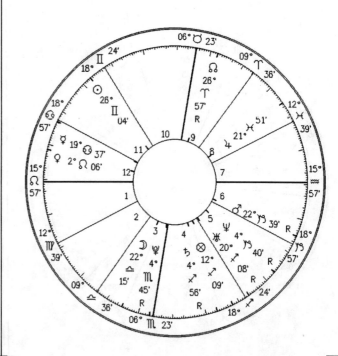

26. SPAIN FUND-SNF
June 21, 1988   NYC   9:30:0 AM EDT
40N45'00"   2:34:03 ST   74W00'23"

27. SWISS HELVETIA FUND-SWZ
Aug. 19, 1987   NYC   9:30:0 AM EDT
40N45'00"   6:23:28 ST   74W00'23"

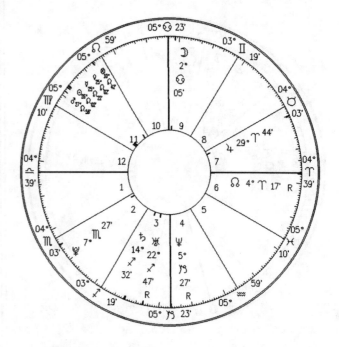

28. TAIWAN FUND-TWN
Dec. 1, 1988   NYC   9:30:0 AM EST
40N45'00"   14:16:51 ST   74W00'23"

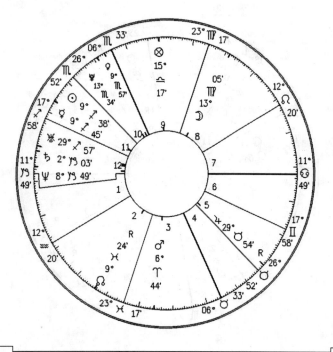

29. TEMPLETON CHINA-TCH
Sep. 9, 1993   NYC   9:30:0 AM EDT
40N45'00"   7:48:24 ST   74W00'23"

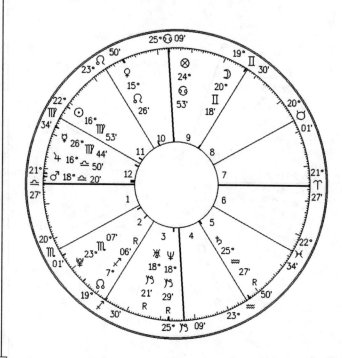

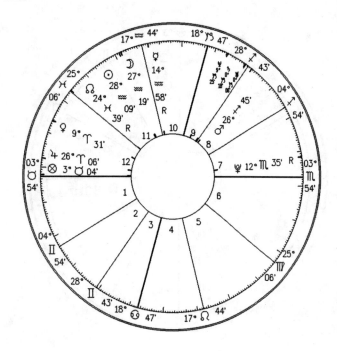

30. THAI FUNDS-TTF
Feb. 17, 1988   NYC   9:30:0 AM EST
40N45'00"   19:21:23 ST   74W00'23"

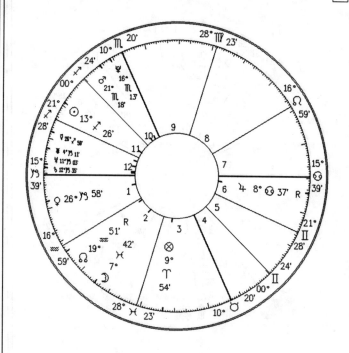

31. TURKISH FUND-TKF
Dec. 5, 1989   NYC   9:30:0 AM EST
40N45'00"   14:31:40 ST   74W00'23"

FINANCIAL INSTITUTION CHARTS

T he following section has been added to edition two. These horoscopes are set for the beginning of or for significant moments in the history of financial institutions, such as the New York Stock Exchange (NYSE).

1-NYSE (Leary):

William Leary claimed to be the only astrologer with a seat on the Exchange during the 1929 crash. Distressed that standard methods did not give a warning, he studied in earnest in subsequent years. Writing in the 1940s, he claimed that this was the first horoscope of the NYSE. Unfortunately, he kept the source a secret. I have not used it, but thought that it would be of interest.

2-NYSE (Lavoie):

This is the standard date given for the beginning of trading. Alphee Lavoie rectified the time to 11:22 PM.

3-NYSE Formed (Meridian):

On this date, thirteen brokers and seven firms met in New York City. They laid out a set of rules and chose a name, The New York Stock and Exchange Board. In fact, this original document was lost until discovered in an attic in Newark, N.J. in 1900. It was then presented to the Exchange. There is no exact time, but it is believed that the meeting took place in the morning.

4-NYSE Constitution:

The same gang that met on February 25 made this constitution official on this date.

5-NYSE (Hasbrouck):

The Exchange was reorganized on this date. This chart was originally used by Muriel Hasbrouck; the date was obtained from Harriett Higginson.

She originally set out to predict earthquakes, but her husband noticed that the market changed direction on her projected dates. She began a market timing service.

The U.S. government also noticed. In correspondence found in the files of the Foundation for the Study of Cycles, she corresponded with Ed Dewey.

The U.S. first offered to help her, but then simply shut her operation down. She believed that this action was taken because her dates coincided with the dates of the government's missile tests.

I have found this chart to be the most useful. If one wants an astro "reason" for the lates 1980s-1990s bull market, note that secondary progressed Jupiter was passing over the natal Sun of the chart. At the time of this writing, the orb is one minute of arc.

6- Dow Jones 1st Index:

The Dow Jones Industrial Average was first published by Charles Dow on this date.

7- NYSE (Sepharial):

This is the date that the Exchange opened in its current location. A New York Times article on the next day stated that officials spoke at 11 AM, after which trading began. So Sepharial's time of 11:20 is supported by fact.

8- Federal Reserve:

This is the date that President Wilson signed the Fed into existence, an act which he later regretted. The Fed booklet says that Wilson strode into the room at 6 PM and walked to the desk where he signed the bill. Another book said that the signing was done via live radio broadcast, one of the first from the White House.

At 6:02 PM, the President stated that he was signing the bill. Note that the Saturn station at zero Aries on December 4,1996, was followed in a few days by Fed Chairman Alan Greenspan's comments that he was concerned about the stock market's "exuberance." The Dow fell over 100 points on the next day. The symbolism of his comments coming after Saturn going direct on the chart's midheaven cannot be missed.

I did a detailed analysis of this chart in the *NCGR Journal* in 1983.

9- Fed Operations:

The Fed actually began to operate on this date. The selected time is arbitrary. I utilize both charts as an aid in determining Fed policy.

10- AMEX1-Moves Indoors:

The American Stock Exchange moved indoors on this date, according to their library. The time chosen is arbitrary.

11- AMEX2-Adopts Name:

The Exchange adopted its current title on this date.

12- NASDAQ Opens:

The over-the-counter market began trading on the NASDAQ on this date and at this time. The grouping of planets in Aquarius is appropriate due to the large number of technology stocks on this exchange. Today, it is the home of Microsoft, Intel, and Cisco. In fact, the 50 largest stocks account for most of the trading volume.

13- Bond Futures:

Futures contracts on bonds began trading on this date at this time in Chicago. This is a very useful chart. The Jupiter return of August 1,1989 coincided with the top to the day. In the Journal of the Astrological Association of Great Britain, I was able to predict the late 1993 top and the 1994 bear market in bonds, partially based upon this chart. The Saturn-Pluto square in late fixed signs hit the natal Sun.

Financial Institutions

1. NYSE (LEARY)
Mar. 21, 1792   NYC   10:0:0 AM LMT
40N45'00"   21:59:13 ST   74W00'23"

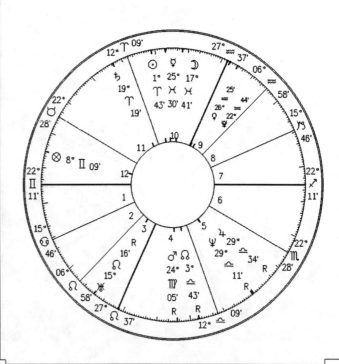

2. NYSE (LAVOIE)
May 17, 1792   NYC   11:22:00 AM LMT
40N45'00"   4:17:22 ST   74W00'23"

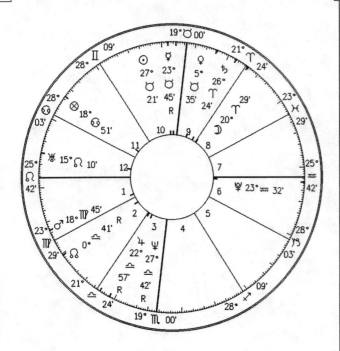

3. NYSE FORMED (MERIDIAN)
Feb. 25, 1817   NYC   10:0:0 AM LMT
40N45'00"   20:20:26 ST   74W00'23"

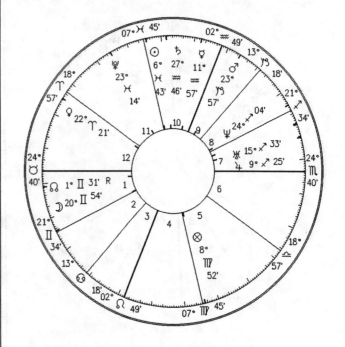

4. NYSE CONSTITUTION
Mar. 8, 1817   NYC   0:0:0 PM LMT
40N45'00"   23:04:08 ST   74W00'23"

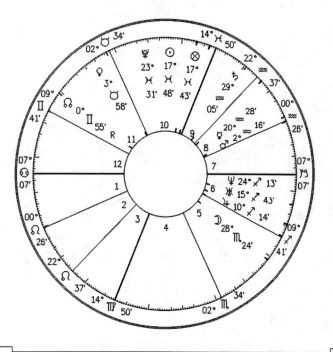

5. NYSE (HASBROUCK)
May 11, 1869   NYC   10:30:0 AM LMT
40N45'00"   1:47:49 ST   74W00'23"

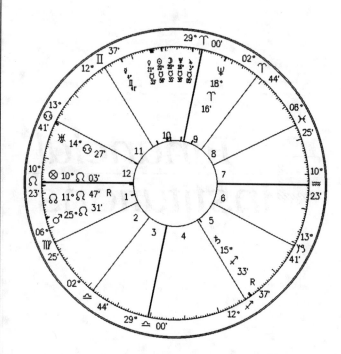

6. DOW JONES-1ST INDEX
July 3, 1884   NYC   10:0:0 AM LMT
40N45'00"   4:48:08 ST   74W00'23"

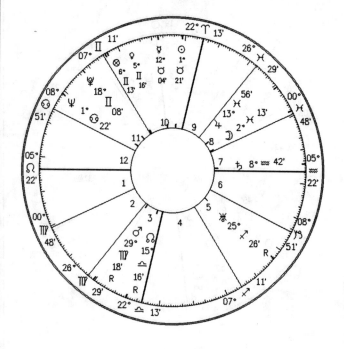

7. NYSE (SEPHARIAL)
Apr. 22, 1903   NYC   11:20:0 AM EST
40N45'00"   1:22:11 ST   74W00'23"

8. FEDERAL RESERVE
Dec. 23, 1913   WASHINGTON,DC   6:2:0 PM EST
38N53'00"   0:01:26 ST   77W01'00"

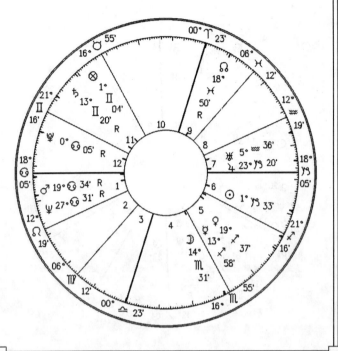

9. FED OPERATIONS
Nov. 16, 1914   NYC   9:0:0 AM EST
40N45'00"   12:43:23 ST   74W00'23"

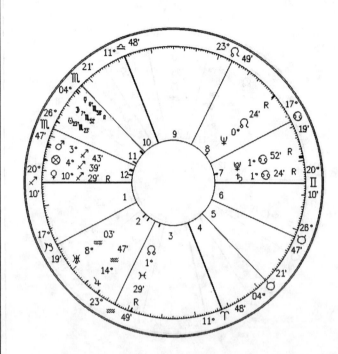

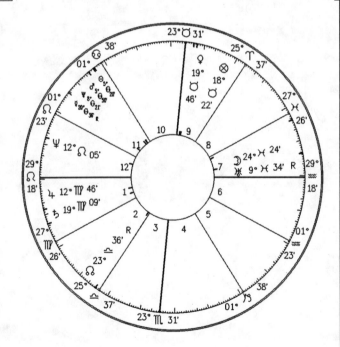

10. AMEX1-MOVES INDOORS
June 27, 1921   NYC   10:0:0 AM EDT
40N45'00"   3:24:32 ST   74W00'23"

11. AMEX2-ADOPTS NAME
Jan. 5, 1953   NYC   10:0:0 AM EST
40N45'00"   17:03:37 ST   74W00'23"

12. NASDAQ OPENS
Feb. 5, 1971   NYC   10:0:0 AM EST
40N45'00"   19:04:37 ST   74W00'23"

13. BOND FUTURES
Aug. 22, 1977   CHICAGO   8:0:0 AM CDT
41N53'00"   5:12:25 ST   87W37'00"

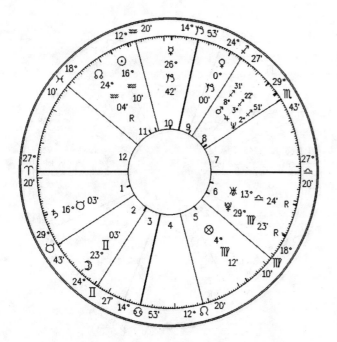

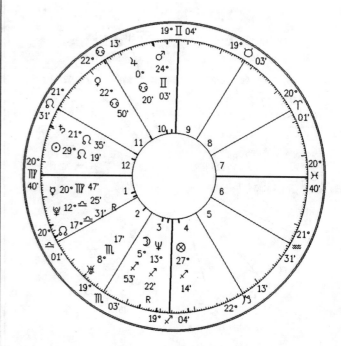

UK Stock Section

The following section includes some fifty first trade charts for the UK Stock Market, the vast majority of which are included in the UK FTSE 100 Index.

Researching the British financial markets has proven to be somewhat difficult, as many of the UK's blue chip stocks have been trading for several years and have been subject to mergers and takeovers since their early beginnings, some dating back over several hundred years. Consequently, deriving an absolute "birthtime" for many companies has been impossible. Many of the corporations have little history about their past, and this is also the case with the UK Stock Exchange. What follows is believed to be accurate but cannot be guaranteed. The bulk of this research has been conducted by communicating with relevant companies and even visiting them to check documents within their archives. More recent first trades have been noted from the financial media.

With regard to the FTSE 100 index, this commenced compilation on 3 January 1984 and an assumed time of 9.00 am has been given, based in London. This index superseded the previous UK equity barometer named "The All Share Index". It is worth noting that the constituent companies of the FTSE 100 undergo regular updating and so the homogeneity of the Index is not that pure. The UK Stock Exchange has undergone numerous changes over the last few years and perhaps the most important of these was known as "Big Bang" which took place on 27 October 1986, when equity trading moved from the floor into the dealing rooms. This date has been used as a turning point for first trade times. Shares with first trade dates prior to this have been given notional times of 9.00 am and thereafter 8.30 am. These are official dealing times and it should be noted that often with major flotations, dealings begin earlier on the unofficial "grey" market. On 20 October 1997 an order driven system of trading was introduced for 120 companies whereby buyers and sellers have been matched by computer. The official first trade time then changed by one minute to 8.31 am. This is known as "SETS" (Stock Exchange Electronic Trading Service). At the time of writing, UK traders are experiencing considerable difficulties with this system.

Research has shown that shares with a high volume of trading are the ones that will react with astrological synchronicity, and overall, there would, at this moment in time, appear to be slightly less astro "influence" with UK charts than with the US charts where higher volume trading takes place. Clearly, as stated by Bill Meridian, always trade with the trend and it is important that some degree of technical analysis is used with these charts.

Both Bill Meridian and Charles Jayne have written about common degrees of the zodiac showing up in related charts. This is prevalent in historic charts of some of our present day companies and these areas become "hot" when activated by eclipse, transit etc. It may also be noted that common degrees may be derived from comparisons of a first trade chart with that of the company's incorporation chart. A further observation has been that outer planets, especially Pluto, when transiting or aspecting the descendant of a first trade chart have frequently led to price movements associated with mergers/take-overs, etc.

Research into first trade charts in the UK is still in its infancy and the authors would be pleased to hear from anyone involved with similar projects.

Andy Pancholi
9 February 1998, Brockham, Surrey

Andy Pancholi has a BSc(Econ) honours degree in Economics and has also been studying Astrology for eighteen years.

The vast majority of his research has centred on examining correlations between the Stock Market, Economic Cycles and Planetary motion. Currently he lives in Surrey England and runs Cycles Analysis - a company specialising in supplying Astro and Gann software, books, courses and seminars, as well as providing a consultancy to corporate and private organisations.

He can be contacted by e-mail at:
cyclesanalysis@mcmail.com, or
info@cyclesanalysis.com.
His website is www.cyclesanalysis.com

British Airways —

The first trade took place 11 February 1987, and the incorporation was on 13 December 1983.

First Trade

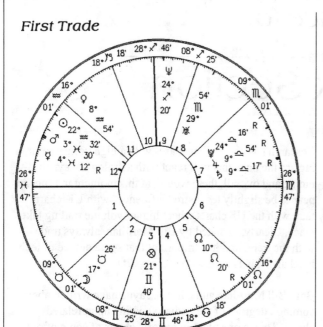

Incorporation

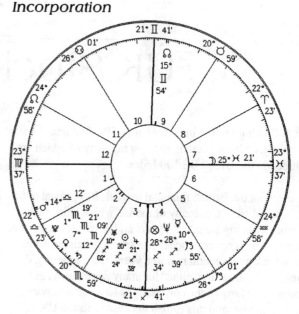

A lunar eclipse took place at 23 Pisces 56 on 16 September conjunct the first trade Ascendant (25 Pisces 43) and Jupiter of British Airways and squaring the natal Uranus. This triggered a large decline in the share price. Earlier on, when Mars transited the eclipse point prior to the lunation, a change in trend took place.

In keeping with Charles Jayne's and Bill Meridian's theories about zodiac degree chains, it is found that the incorporation chart for this company has an ascendant of 23 Virgo 48 and the Moon is at 25 Pisces 22 thus showing that 23 to 26 degrees of mutable signs is a critical area for this company. As an incidental note 4 to 6 degrees of Sagittarius is often associated with flight (see Mundane Astrology - Harvey, Campion and Baigent) and that Pluto has been transiting this degree of late. During this time, British Airways has been negotiating the world largest airline alliance with American Airlines. The rival STAR alliance has taken place involving several flag carrier airlines and Air-

bus Industrie has launched the design and building of the largest airliner yet to be made. Boeing considered and abandoned a similar project for a "Double Decker" jumbo. Globally, air travel is at its highest level ever.

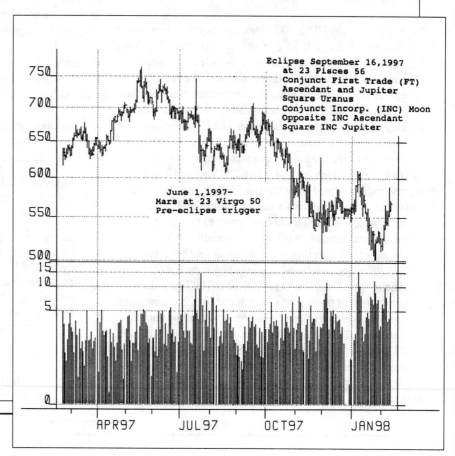

Eclipse September 16,1997
at 23 Pisces 56
Conjunct First Trade (FT)
Ascendant and Jupiter
Square Uranus
Conjunct Incorp. (INC) Moon
Opposite INC Ascendant
Square INC Jupiter

June 1,1997-
Mars at 23 Virgo 50
Pre-eclipse trigger

British Stocks
FTSE

Note: Due to erratic pricing caused by the SETS system, as of Monday 20th, July 1998 all UK equities began trading at 9:00 AM - 30 minutes later than previously.

1. 3I-3I   Investment Trusts
July 18, 1994   LONDON   8:30:0 AM CET
51N30'00"   3:12:51 ST   0W10'00"

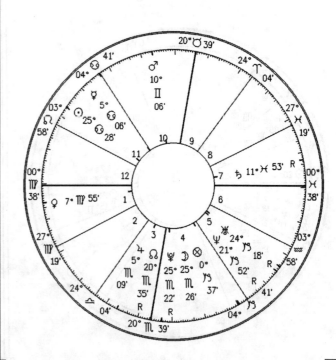

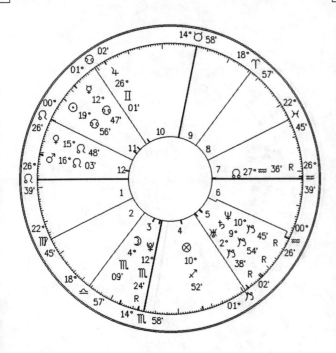

2. ABBEY NATIONAL-ANL   Banks, Retail
July 12, 1989   LONDON   8:30:0 AM CET
51N30'00"   2:50:02 ST   0W10'00"

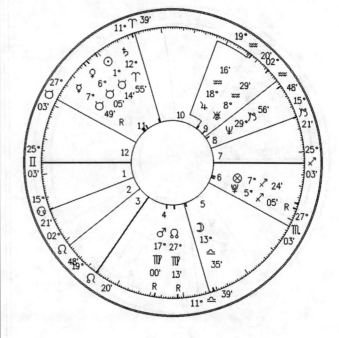

3. ALLIANCE & LEICESTER-AL   Banks, Retail
Apr. 21, 1997   LONDON   8:30:0 AM CET
51N30'00"   21:26:59 ST   0W10'00"

4. ANGLIAN WATER-AW   Water
Dec. 12, 1989   LONDON   8:30:0 AM GMT
51N30'00"   13:53:25 ST   0W10'00"

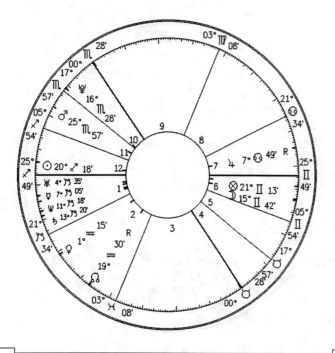

5. ASDA-ASSD   Retail - Food
Dec. 19, 1978   LONDON   9:0:0 AM GMT
51N30'00"   14:49:46 ST   0W10'00"

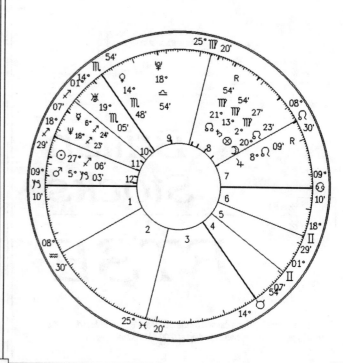

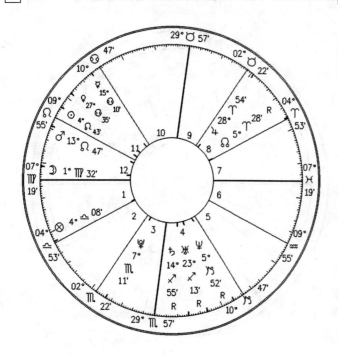

6. BAA-BAA   Transport
July 28, 1987   LONDON   8:30:0 AM CET
51N30'00"   3:51:05 ST   0W10'00"

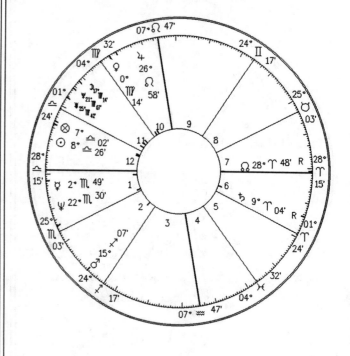

7. BASS-BASS   Brewers, Pubs & Restaurants
Oct. 2, 1967   LONDON   9:0:0 AM CET
51N30'00"   8:40:46 ST   0W10'00"

8. BILLITON-BLT *Extractive Industries*
July 28, 1997   LONDON   8:30:0 AM CET
51N30'00"   3:53:22 ST   0W10'00"

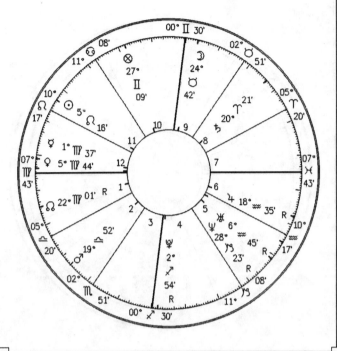

9. BOC GROUP-BOC *Chemicals*
Dec. 1, 1916   LONDON   9:0:0 AM GMT
51N30'00"   13:38:52 ST   0W10'00"

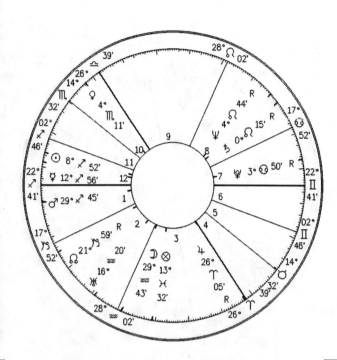

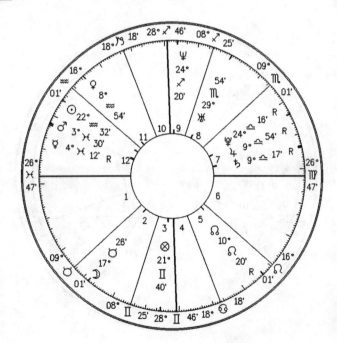

10. BRITISH AEROSPACE-BA *Engineering*
Feb. 11, 1981   LONDON   8:30:0 AM GMT
51N30'00"   17:54:37 ST   0W10'00"

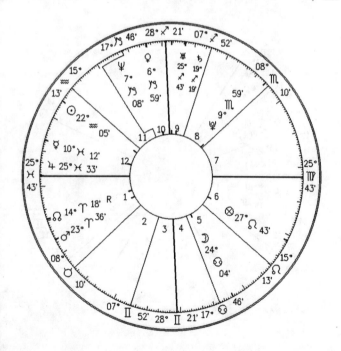

11. BRITISH AIRWAYS-BAY *Transport*
Feb. 11, 1987   LONDON   8:30:0 AM GMT
51N30'00"   17:52:50 ST   0W10'00"

12. BRITISH ENERGY-BGY   Electricity
July 15, 1996   LONDON   8:30:0 AM CET
51N30'00"   3:03:04 ST   0W10'00"

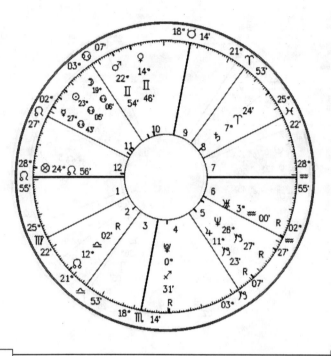

13. BRITISH GAS-GAS   Gas Distribution
Dec. 8, 1986   LONDON   8:30:0 AM GMT
51N30'00"   13:36:34 ST   0W10'00"

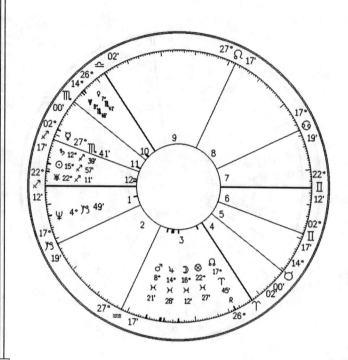

14. BRITISH STEEL-BS   Engineering
Dec. 5, 1988   LONDON   8:30:0 AM GMT
51N30'00"   13:26:46 ST   0W10'00"

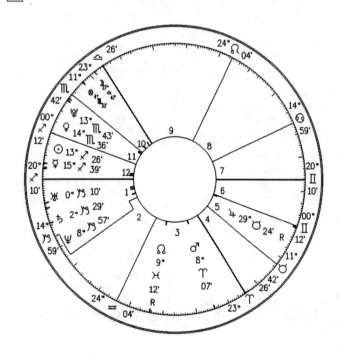

15. BRITISH TELECOM-BT.A   Telecommunications
Dec. 3, 1984   LONDON   9:0:0 AM GMT
51N30'00"   13:48:51 ST   0W10'00"

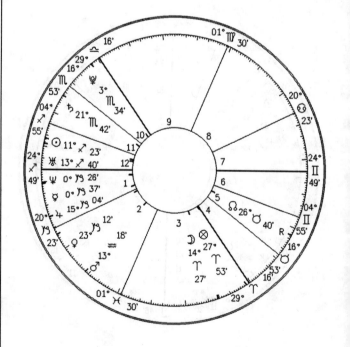

16. BTR-BTR *Engineering*
Nov. 12, 1951   LONDON   9:0:0 AM GMT
51N30'00"   12:22:05 ST   0W10'00"

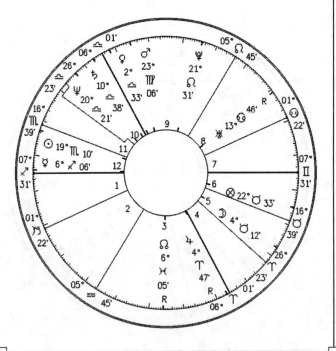

17. CABLE & WIRELESS-CW *Telecommunications*
Oct. 28, 1981   LONDON   9:0:0 AM GMT
51N30'00"   11:25:50 ST   0W10'00"

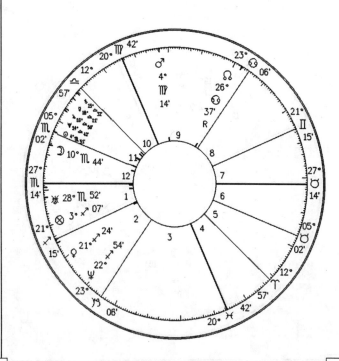

18. CARLTON COMMUN.-CCM *Media*
Feb. 25, 1983   LONDON   9:0:0 AM GMT
51N30'00"   19:17:59 ST   0W10'00"

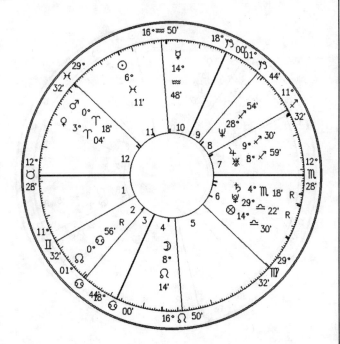

19. CENTRICA-CTR *Gas Distribution*
Feb. 17, 1997   LONDON   8:30:0 AM GMT
51N30'00"   18:18:46 ST   0W10'00"

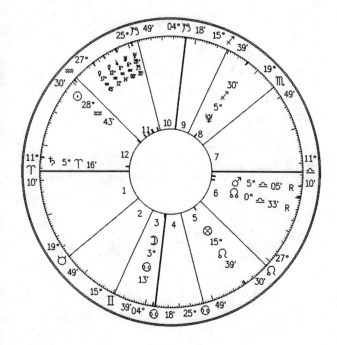

20. COMMERCIAL UNION-CUAC Insurance
June 4, 1990   LONDON   8:30:0 AM CET
51N30'00"   0:19:16 ST   0W10'00"

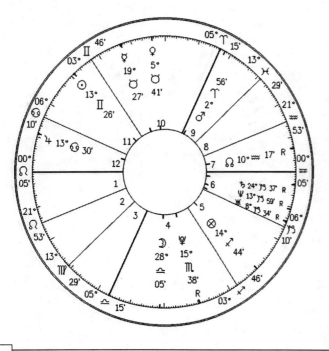

21. ENTERPRISE OIL-ETP Oil Exploration & Properties
June 27, 1984   LONDON   9:0:0 AM CET
51N30'00"   2:21:48 ST   0W10'00"

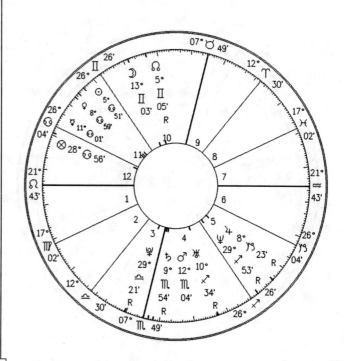

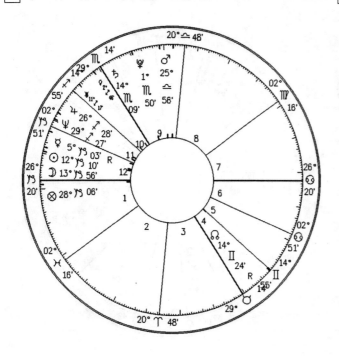

22. FTSE 100 INDEX
Jan. 3, 1984   LONDON   9:0:0 AM GMT
51N30'00"   15:48:05 ST   0W10'00"

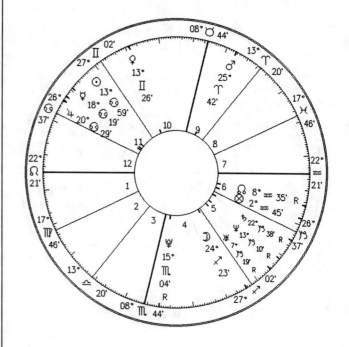

23. GENERAL ACCIDENT-GACC Insurance
July 6, 1990   LONDON   8:30:0 AM CET
51N30'00"   2:25:25 ST   0W10'00"

24. GUARDIAN ROYAL-GARD   *Insurance*
Nov. 12, 1984   LONDON   9:0:0 AM GMT
51N30'00"   12:26:03 ST   0W10'00"

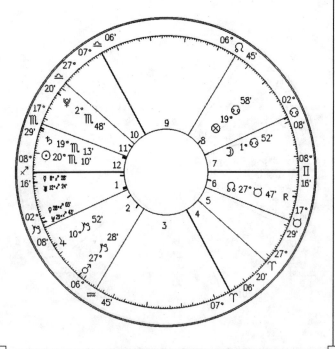

25. HALIFAX-HFX   *Banks Retail*
June 2, 1997   LONDON   8:30:0 AM CET
51N30'00"   0:12:35 ST   0W10'00"

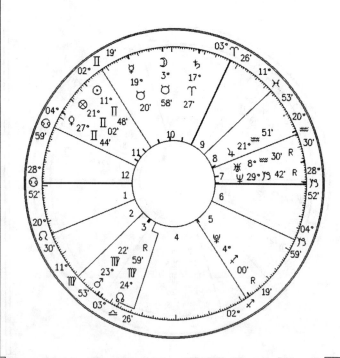

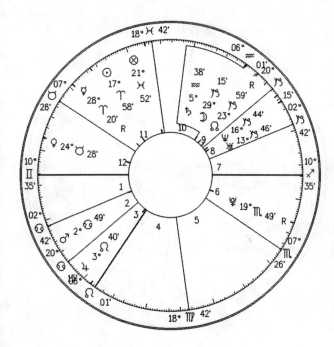

26. HSBC HOLDINGS-HSBA   *Banks, Retail*
Apr. 8, 1991   LONDON   8:30:0 AM CET
51N30'00"   20:33:35 ST   0W10'00"

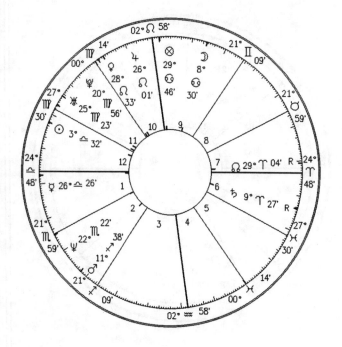

27. LADBROKE GROUP-LAD.B   *Leisure & Hotels*
Sep. 27, 1967   LONDON   9:0:0 AM CET
51N30'00"   8:21:03 ST   0W10'00"

28. MARKS & SPENCER-MKS General Retailers
June 17, 1926   LONDON   9:0:0 AM CET
51N30'00"   1:38:37 ST   0W10'00"

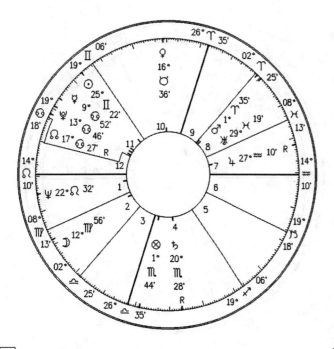

29. NATIONAL GRID-NGG   Electricity
Dec. 11, 1995   LONDON   8:30:0 AM GMT
51N30'00"   13:47:41 ST   0W10'00"

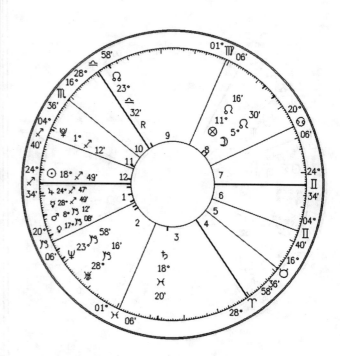

30. NATIONAL POWER-NPR   Electricity
Mar. 12, 1991   LONDON   8:30:0 AM GMT
51N30'00"   19:47:18 ST   0W10'00"

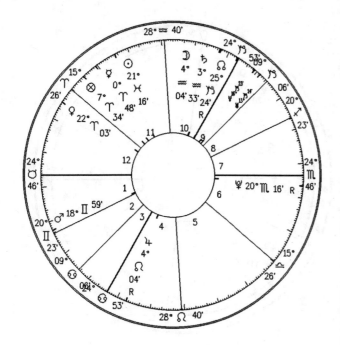

31. NORTHERN ROCK-NRK   Banks, Retail
Oct. 1, 1997   LONDON   8:30:0 AM CET
51N30'00"   8:09:38 ST   0W10'00"

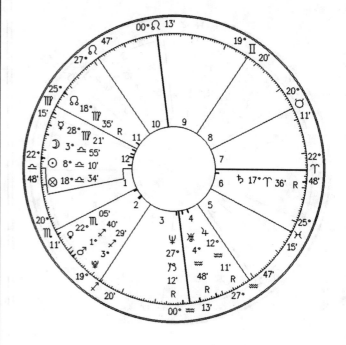

32. ORANGE-ORA   **Telecommunications**
Apr. 2, 1996   LONDON   8:30:0 AM CET
51N30'00"   20:13:02 ST   0W10'00"

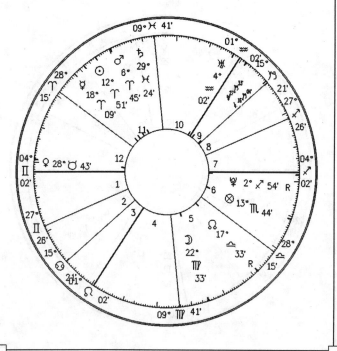

33. PEARSON-PSON   **Media**
Aug. 14, 1969   LONDON   9:0:0 AM CET
51N30'00"   5:29:36 ST   0W10'00"

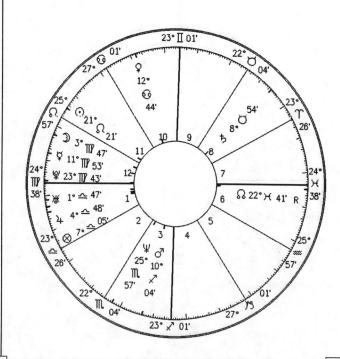

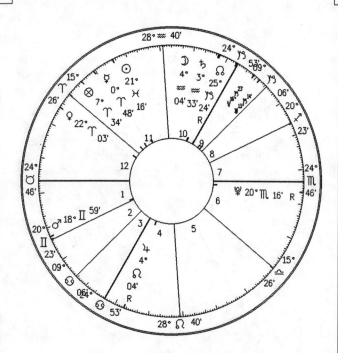

34. POWERGEN-PWG   **Electricity**
Mar. 12, 1991   LONDON   8:30:0 AM GMT
51N30'00"   19:47:18 ST   0W10'00"

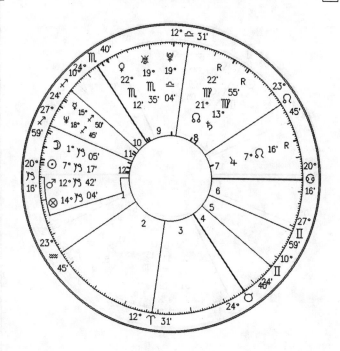

35. PRUDENTIAL-PRU   **Life Assurance**
Dec. 29, 1978   LONDON   9:0:0 AM GMT
51N30'00"   15:29:12 ST   0W10'00"

36. RAILTRACK-RTK   *Transport*
May 20, 1996   LONDON   8:30:0 AM CET
51N30'00"   23:22:17 ST   0W10'00"

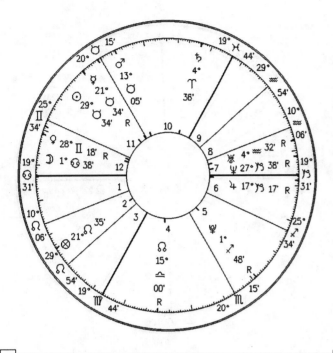

37. RANK GROUP-RNK   *Leisure & Hotels*
July 7, 1937   LONDON   9:0:0 AM CET
51N30'00"   2:58:48 ST   0W10'00"

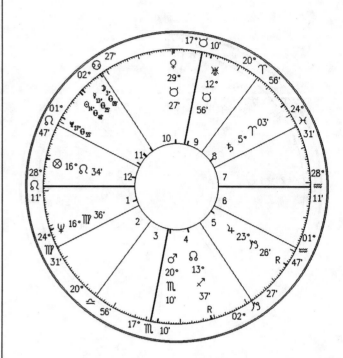

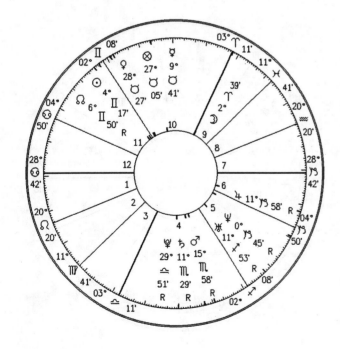

38. REUTERS-RTR   *Media*
May 25, 1984   LONDON   9:0:0 AM CET
51N30'00"   0:11:42 ST   0W10'00"

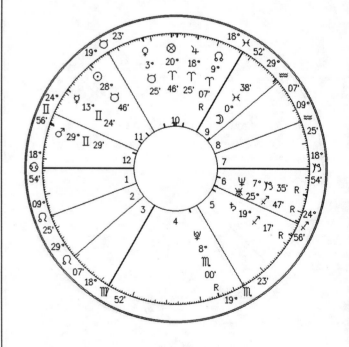

39. ROLLS ROYCE-RR   *Engineering*
May 20, 1987   LONDON   8:30:0 AM CET
51N30'00"   23:19:03 ST   0W10'00"

40. RTZ-RTZ   Extractive Industries
July 2, 1962   LONDON   9:0:0 AM CET
51N30'00"   2:38:52 ST   0W10'00"

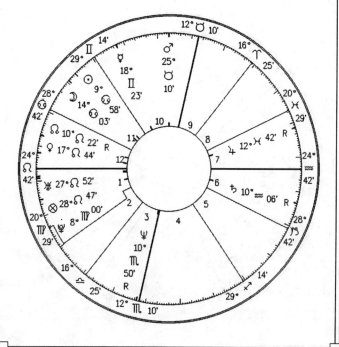

41. SAINSBURY-SBRY   Retailers, Food
Sep. 11, 1973   LONDON   9:0:0 AM CET
51N30'00"   7:20:07 ST   0W10'00"

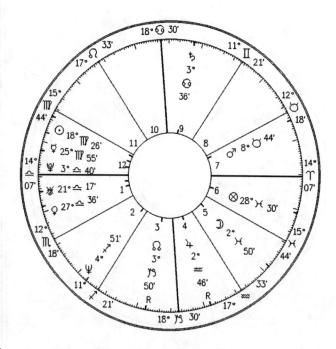

42. SCOTTISH POWER-SPW   Electricity
June 18, 1991   LONDON   8:30:0 AM CET
51N30'00"   1:13:30 ST   0W10'00"

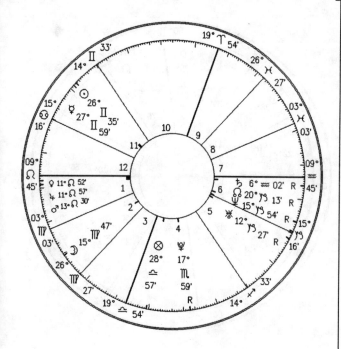

43. SEVERN TRENT-SVT   Water
Dec. 18, 1989   LONDON   8:30:0 AM GMT
51N30'00"   14:17:04 ST   0W10'00"

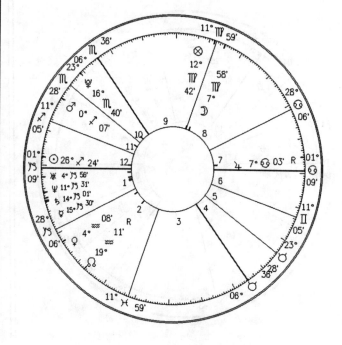

44. SOUTHERN ELECTRIC-SEL   *Electricity*
Dec. 11, 1990   LONDON   8:30:0 AM GMT
51N30'00"   13:48:31 ST   0W10'00"

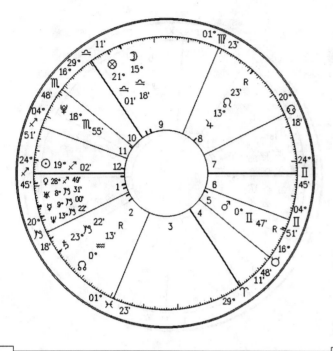

45. THAMES WATER-TW   *Water*
Dec. 12, 1989   LONDON   8:30:0 AM GMT
51N30'00"   13:53:25 ST   0W10'00"

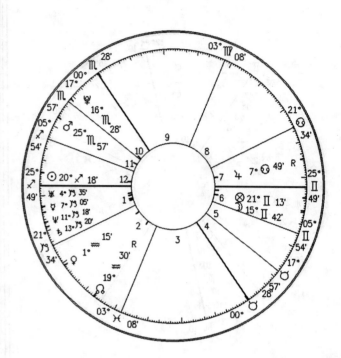

46. TOMKINS-TOMK   *Diversified Industrials*
Dec. 20, 1962   LONDON   9:0:0 AM GMT
51N30'00"   14:53:13 ST   0W10'00"

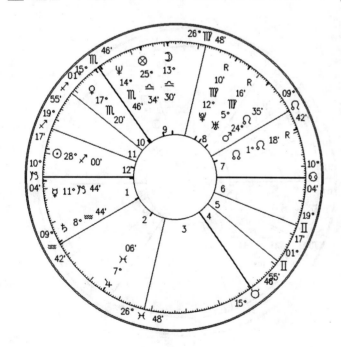

47. UNITED BISCUITS-UBIS   *Food Producers*
July 21, 1948   LONDON   9:0:0 AM CET
51N30'00"   3:55:19 ST   0W10'00"

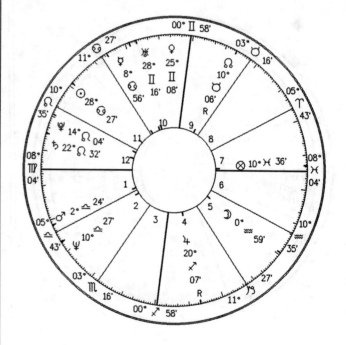

48. WOOLWICH-WWH   *Banks, Retail*

July 7, 1997   LONDON   8:30:0 AM CET
51N30'00"   2:30:34 ST   0W10'00"

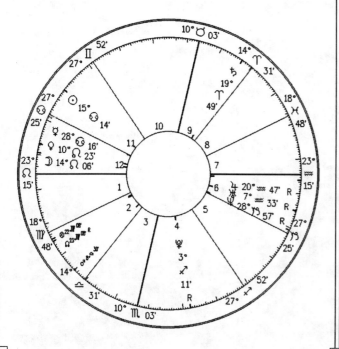

49. YORKSHIRE WATER-WY   *Water*

Dec. 12, 1989   LONDON   8:30:0 AM GMT
51N30'00"   13:53:25 ST   0W10'00"

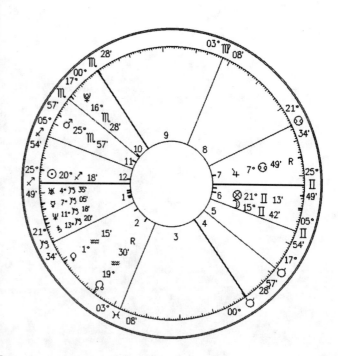

50. ZENECA-ZEN   *Pharmaceuticals*

June 1, 1993   LONDON   8:30:0 AM CET
51N30'00"   0:08:31 ST   0W10'00"

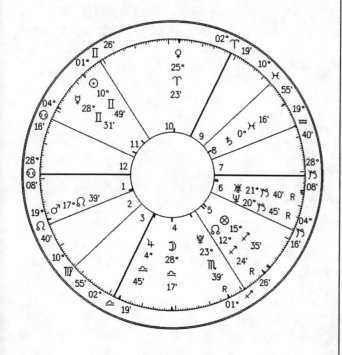

Other Chart Data

Illiquid Stocks from Edition one

ACE LTD.-ACL   Mar. 25, 1993
NYC   9:30:0 AM EST 40N45'00"
21:46:12 ST   74W00'23"

ALEXANDERS-ALX   Oct. 7, 1969
NYC   9:30:0 AM EDT 40N45'00"
9:38:16 ST   74W00'23"

ALLEGHANY CORP.-Y   Dec. 24, 1986
NYC   9:30:0 AM EST 40N45'00"
15:45:30 ST   74W00'23"

ALLIANT TECHSYSTEMS-ATK   Oct. 8, 1990
NYC   9:30:0 AM EDT 40N45'00"
9:41:53 ST   74W00'23"

AMBAC-ABK   July 11, 1991
NYC   9:30:0 AM EDT 40N45'00"
3:50:02 ST   74W00'23"

AMER. DENTAL LASER-ADLI   June 18, 1991
NYC   9:30:0 AM EDT 40N45'00"
2:19:21 ST   74W00'23"

AMERICA ONLINE-AMER   Mar. 19, 1992
NYC   9:30:0 AM EST 40N45'00"
21:23:44 ST   74W00'23"

AMLI RESOURCES-AML   Feb. 9, 1994
NYC   9:30:0 AM EST 40N45'00"
18:51:47 ST   74W00'23"

AMWAY ASIA-AAP Dec. 15, 1993
NYC   9:30:0 AM EST 40N45'00"
15:10:59 ST   74W00'23"

ANN TAYLOR-ANN May 17, 1991
NYC   9:30:0 AM EDT 40N45'00"
0:13:11 ST   74W00'23"

APPLIANCE RECYCLING-ARCI   Nov. 8, 1991
NYC   9:30:0 AM EST 40N45'00"
12:43:19 ST   74W00'23"

ARACRUZ CELULOSE-ARA   May 27, 1992
NYC   9:30:0 AM EDT 40N45'00"
0:55:36 ST   74W00'23"

ARMCO-AS   Jan. 2, 1946
NYC   10:0:0 AM EST 40N45'00"
16:50:47 ST   74W00'23"

AVALON PROP.-AVN   Nov. 12, 1993
NYC   9:30:0 AM EST 40N45'00"
13:00:53 ST   74W00'23"

BANCO COMM. PORTUGUE-BPC June 12, 1992
NYC   9:30:0 AM EDT 40N45'00"
1:58:41 ST   74W00'23"

BANCO FRANCES-BFR   Nov. 24, 1993
NYC   9:30:0 AM EST 40N45'00"
13:48:12 ST   74W00'23"

BASS PLC-BAS   Feb. 8, 1980
NYC   10:0:0 AM EST 40N45'00"
19:15:44 ST   74W00'23"

BELL IND.-BI   Oct. 31, 1979
NYC   10:0:0 AM EST 40N45'00"
12:41:15 ST   74W00'23"

BET HOLDINGS-BTV   Oct. 31, 1991
NYC   9:30:0 AM EST 40N45'00"
12:11:46 ST   74W00'23"

BIOSPECIFICS-BSTC   Nov. 15, 1991
NYC   9:30:0 AM EST 40N45'00"
13:10:54 ST   74W00'23"

BOCA RESEARCH-BOCI   Feb. 25, 1993
NYC   9:30:0 AM EST 40N45'00"
19:55:50 ST   74W00'23"

BOSTON CELTICS-BOS   Dec. 5, 1986
NYC   9:30:0 AM EST 40N45'00"
14:30:35 ST   74W00'23"

BRITISH AIRWAYS-BAB   Feb. 11, 1987
NYC   9:30:0 AM EST 40N45'00"
18:58:41 ST   74W00'23"

BRITISH GAS-BRG Dec. 8, 1987
NYC   9:30:0 AM EST 40N45'00"
14:41:28 ST   74W00'23"

BRITISH TELECOM-BTY   Dec. 3, 1984
NYC   10:0:0 AM EST 40N45'00"
14:54:42 ST   74W00'23"

BUCKEYE PARTNERS-BPL Dec. 16, 1987
NYC   9:30:0 AM EST 40N45'00"
15:13:00 ST   74W00'23"

CAMDEN PROP.-CPT   July 22, 1993
NYC   9:30:0 AM EDT 40N45'00"
4:35:13 ST   74W00'23"

CARR REALTY-CRE   Feb. 9, 1993
NYC   9:30:0 AM EST 40N45'00"
18:52:44 ST   74W00'23"

CASINET DATA-CSDS   Apr. 5, 1993
NYC   9:30:0 AM EDT 40N45'00"
21:29:25 ST   74W00'23"

CATALYST SEMI-CATS   May 11, 1993
NYC   9:30:0 AM EDT 40N45'00"
23:51:21 ST   74W00'23"

CATELLUS DEVELOPMENT-CDX Nov. 26, 1990
NYC   9:30:0 AM EST 40N45'00"
13:55:14 ST   74W00'23"

CELADON GROUP-CLDN Jan. 21, 1994
NYC   9:30:0 AM EST 40N45'00"
17:36:52 ST   74W00'23"

CHATEAU PROP.-CPJ   Nov. 17, 1993
NYC   9:30:0 AM EST 40N45'00"
13:20:36 ST   74W00'23"

CHINA TIRE-TIR July 15, 1993
NYC   9:30:0 AM EDT 40N45'00"
4:07:37 ST   74W00'23"

CITY NATIONAL-CYN   May 17, 1990
NYC   9:30:0 AM EDT 40N45'00"
0:14:09 ST   74W00'23"

CNA FINANCIAL-CNA   Feb. 3, 1969
NYC   10:0:0 AM EST 40N45'00"
18:58:39 ST   74W00'23"

COASTCAST-PAR Dec. 13, 1993
NYC   9:30:0 AM EST 40N45'00"
15:03:06 ST   74W00'23"

COLEMAN CO.-CLN   Oct. 22, 1981
NYC   10:0:0 AM EDT 40N45'00"
11:07:52 ST   74W00'23"

COMPREHENSIVE CARE-CMP   July 18, 1988
NYC   9:30:0 AM EDT 40N45'00"
4:20:30 ST   74W00'23"

CONE MILLS-COE June 19, 1992
NYC   9:30:0 AM EDT 40N45'00"
2:26:17 ST   74W00'23"

CORRPRO-CO   Oct. 1, 1993
NYC   9:30:0 AM EDT 40N45'00"
9:15:08 ST   74W00'23"

CURTISS WRIGHT-CW   Aug. 22, 1929
          NYC   10:0:0 AM EDT
40N45'00"   7:05:46 ST   74W00'23"

DAIMLER BENZ-DAI   Oct. 5, 1993
NYC   9:30:0 AM EDT 40N45'00"
9:30:54 ST   74W00'23"

DATAWARE TECH.-DWTI July 22, 1993
NYC   9:30:0 AM EDT 40N45'00"
4:35:13 ST   74W00'23"

DEFLECTA SHIELD-TRUX Jan. 21, 1994
NYC   9:30:0 AM EST 40N45'00"
17:36:52 ST   74W00'23"

DIAGNOSTIC PRODUCTS-DP   July 15, 1988
NYC   9:30:0 AM EDT 40N45'00"
4:08:40 ST   74W00'23"

DONALDSON-DCI Nov. 27, 1979
NYC   10:0:0 AM EST 40N45'00"
14:27:56 ST   74W00'23"

DUTY FREE-DFI Dec. 18, 1991
NYC   9:30:0 AM EST 40N45'00"
15:21:01 ST   74W00'23"

ELF AQUITAINE-ELF   June 14, 1991
NYC   9:30:0 AM EDT 40N45'00"
2:03:35 ST   74W00'23"

ETHAN ALLEN-ETH   Mar. 16, 1993
NYC   9:30:0 AM EST 40N45'00"
21:10:43 ST   74W00'23"

FAILURE GROUP-FAIL   Aug. 20, 1990
NYC   9:30:0 AM EDT 40N45'00"
6:28:42 ST   74W00'23"

FANSTEEL-FNL May 14, 1985
NYC   10:0:0 AM EDT 40N45'00"
0:33:14 ST   74W00'23"

FEDERAL HOME LOAN-FRE   July 7, 1987
NYC   9:30:0 AM EDT 40N45'00"
3:34:08 ST   74W00'23"

FEDERAL SIGNAL-FSS   Apr. 1, 1969
NYC   10:0:0 AM EST 40N45'00"
22:43:22 ST   74W00'23"

FISHER SCIENTIFIC-FSH Dec. 18, 1991
NYC   9:30:0 AM EST 40N45'00"
15:21:01 ST   74W00'23"

FUND AMERICA-FFC   Oct. 23, 1985
NYC   9:30:0 AM EDT 40N45'00"
10:41:51 ST   74W00'23"

G TECH HOLDINGS-GTK   July 22, 1992
NYC   9:30:0 AM EDT 40N45'00"
4:36:23 ST   74W00'23"

GABLES RESOURCES-GBP   Jan. 20, 1994
NYC   9:30:0 AM EST 40N45'00"
17:32:55 ST   74W00'23"

GAYLORD ENT.-GET   Oct. 24, 1991
NYC   9:30:0 AM EDT 40N45'00"
10:44:00 ST   74W00'23"

GENESCO-GCO   July 15, 1939
NYC   10:0:0 AM EDT 40N45'00"
4:34:05 ST   74W00'23"

GENUS-GGNS   Nov. 10, 1988
NYC   9:30:0 AM EST 40N45'00"
12:54:03 ST   74W00'23"

GIBSON GREETINGS-GIBG May 19, 1983
NYC   10:0:0 AM EDT 40N45'00"
0:50:55 ST   74W00'23"

GLENDALE BANK-GLBK   Jan. 11, 1994
NYC   9:30:0 AM EST 40N45'00"
16:57:26 ST   74W00'23"

GLIMCHER REALTY-GRT   Jan. 24, 1994
NYC   9:30:0 AM EST 40N45'00"
17:48:42 ST   74W00'23"

GOTTSCHALKS-GOT   Apr. 18, 1986
NYC   9:30:0 AM EDT 40N45'00"
22:19:41 ST   74W00'23"

GRAND METROPOLITAN-GRM   Mar. 13, 1991
NYC   9:30:0 AM EST 40N45'00"
20:57:05 ST   74W00'23"

GRUPO CASA-ATY Dec. 7, 1993
NYC   9:30:0 AM EST 40N45'00"
14:39:27 ST   74W00'23"

GRUPO FINANCIAL-SFN   Dec. 1, 1993
NYC   9:30:0 AM EST 40N45'00"
14:15:48 ST   74W00'23"

GRUPO TELEVISA-TV   Dec. 14, 1993
NYC   9:30:0 AM EST 40N45'00"
15:07:03 ST   74W00'23"

GRUPO TRIBASA-GTR   Sep. 22, 1993
NYC   9:30:0 AM EDT 40N45'00"
8:39:39 ST   74W00'23"

GUARANTY NATIONAL-GNC   Nov. 15, 1991
NYC   9:30:0 AM EST 40N45'00"
13:10:54 ST   74W00'23"

HARMAN IND.-HAR   Nov. 11, 1987
NYC   9:30:0 AM EST 40N45'00"
12:54:47 ST   74W00'23"

HARRISON BANK-HARS   Jan. 25, 1994
NYC   9:30:0 AM EST 40N45'00"
17:52:38 ST   74W00'23"

HEALTH CARE & RET.-HCR Oct. 18, 1991
NYC   9:30:0 AM EDT 40N45'00"
10:20:21 ST   74W00'23"

HILITE IND.-HILI   Jan. 21, 1994
NYC   9:30:0 AM EST 40N45'00"
17:36:52 ST   74W00'23"

HITACHI-HIT   Apr. 14, 1982
NYC   10:0:0 AM EST 40N45'00"
23:34:02 ST   74W00'23"

HONDA-HMC   Feb. 11, 1977
NYC   10:0:0 AM EST 40N45'00"
19:30:26 ST   74W00'23"

HORACE MANN EDUCAT-HMN   Nov. 15, 1991
NYC   9:30:0 AM EST 40N45'00"
13:10:54 ST   74W00'23"

HORIZON OUTLET-HGI   Nov. 2, 1993
NYC   9:30:0 AM EST 40N45'00"
12:21:28 ST   74W00'23"

HOSPITALITY FRANCH.-HFS   Dec. 10, 1992
NYC   9:30:0 AM EST 40N45'00"
14:52:14 ST   74W00'23"

HOUGHTON MIFFLIN-HTN Sep. 15, 1967
NYC   10:0:0 AM EDT 40N45'00"
8:39:35 ST   74W00'23"

HUGOTON ENERGY-HUGO Jan. 26, 1994
NYC   9:30:0 AM EST 40N45'00"
17:56:35 ST   74W00'23"

IBP, INC.-IBP   Oct. 1, 1987
NYC   9:30:0 AM EDT 40N45'00"
9:13:12 ST   74W00'23"

IND. SCIENTIFIC-ISCX   June 30, 1993
NYC   9:30:0 AM EDT 40N45'00"
3:08:28 ST   74W00'23"

INTER. GAME TECH.-IGT   Jan. 31, 1991
NYC   9:30:0 AM EST 40N45'00"
18:15:26 ST   74W00'23"

IONICS-ION   Oct. 25, 1990
NYC   9:30:0 AM EDT 40N45'00"
10:48:54 ST   74W00'23"

JONES APPAREL-JNY   May 17, 1991
NYC   9:30:0 AM EDT 40N45'00"
0:13:11 ST   74W00'23"

JP REALTY-JPR   Jan. 14, 1994
NYC   9:30:0 AM EST 40N45'00"
17:09:16 ST   74W00'23"

KEYSTONE CONSOL.-KES Feb. 25, 1936
NYC   10:0:0 AM EST 40N45'00"
20:21:24 ST   74W00'23"

KIMCO REALTY-KIM   Nov. 22, 1991
NYC   9:30:0 AM EST 40N45'00"
13:38:30 ST   74W00'23"

KOHLS-KSS   May 19, 1992
NYC   9:30:0 AM EDT 40N45'00"
0:24:04 ST   74W00'23"

LIDAK PHARMA.-LDAKA   May 9, 1990
NYC   9:30:0 AM EDT 40N45'00"
23:42:23 ST   74W00'23"

LINCOLN SNACKS-SNAX Jan. 14, 1994
NYC   9:30:0 AM EST 40N45'00"
17:09:16 ST   74W00'23"

LONE STAR-LCE   Oct. 16, 1936
NYC   10:0:0 AM EST 40N45'00"
11:43:58 ST   74W00'23"

LUBYS-LUB   Feb. 22, 1982
NYC   10:0:0 AM EST 40N45'00"
20:12:58 ST   74W00'23"

M.S. CARRIERS-MSCA   May 5, 1986
NYC   9:30:0 AM EDT 40N45'00"
23:26:43 ST   74W00'23"

MANUFACT. HOMES-MHC Mar. 26, 1993
NYC   9:30:0 AM EST 40N45'00"
21:50:09 ST   74W00'23"

MARK IV-IV   Oct. 11, 1987
NYC   9:30:0 AM EDT 40N45'00"
9:52:38 ST   74W00'23"

MARVEL ENTERTAIN.-MRV July 16, 1991
NYC   9:30:0 AM EDT 40N45'00"
4:09:45 ST   74W00'23"

MATSUSHITA-MC Dec. 13, 1971
NYC   10:0:0 AM EST 40N45'00"
15:30:46 ST   74W00'23"

MAXXAM-MXM   Aug. 11, 1958
NYC   10:0:0 AM EDT 40N45'00"
6:22:18 ST   74W00'23"

MITEL-MLT   May 18, 1981
NYC   10:0:0 AM EDT 40N45'00"
0:48:39 ST   74W00'23"

MONARCH MACHINE-MMO May 11, 1944
NYC   10:0:0 AM EWT 40N45'00"
0:21:08 ST   74W00'23"

MORGAN KEEGAN-MOR Nov. 4, 1985
NYC   9:30:0 AM EST 40N45'00"
12:29:19 ST   74W00'23"

MORTON INTER.-MII   July 5, 1989
NYC   9:30:0 AM EDT 40N45'00"
3:28:17 ST   74W00'23"

MYERS,L.E.-MYR June 2, 1971
NYC   10:0:0 AM EDT 40N45'00"
1:45:44 ST   74W00'23"

NACCO-NC   June 9, 1986
NYC   9:30:0 AM EDT 40N45'00"
1:44:42 ST   74W00'23"

NASHUA-NSH   Dec. 11, 1967
NYC   10:0:0 AM EST 40N45'00"
15:22:45 ST   74W00'23"

NETFRAME-NETF June 4, 1992
NYC   9:30:0 AM EDT 40N45'00"
1:26:55 ST   74W00'23"

NETWORK SOLUTIONS-NWSS Apr. 27, 1993
NYC   9:30:0 AM EDT 40N45'00"
22:56:09 ST   74W00'23"

NIEMAN MARCUS-NMG   Aug. 18, 1987
NYC   9:30:0 AM EDT 40N45'00"
6:19:44 ST   74W00'23"

NINE WEST-NIN   Feb. 3, 1993
NYC   9:30:0 AM EST   40N45'00"
18:29:05 ST   74W00'23"

NORTH BORDER PART.-NBP   Sep. 27, 1993
NYC   9:30:0 AM EDT 40N45'00"
8:59:22 ST   74W00'23"

NORTHGATE EXPLOR.-NGX   Feb. 3, 1970
NYC   10:0:0 AM EST 40N45'00"
18:57:41 ST   74W00'23"

OAKWOOD HOMES-OH   Sep. 30, 1986
NYC   9:30:0 AM EDT 40N45'00"
9:10:13 ST   74W00'23"

OEA,INC.-OEA   Jan. 4, 1991
NYC   9:30:0 AM EST   40N45'00"
16:28:59 ST   74W00'23"

ORBITAL ENGINEERING-OE   Dec. 5, 1991
NYC   9:30:0 AM EST   40N45'00"
14:29:45 ST   74W00'23"

O'SULLIVAN INDUST.-OSU Jan. 28, 1994
NYC   9:30:0 AM EST   40N45'00"
18:04:28 ST   74W00'23"

PACIFIC ENTERPRISES-PET   Apr. 22, 1948
NYC   10:0:0 AM EST 40N45'00"
0:06:17 ST   74W00'23"

PANAMERCIAN BEVS.-PB Sep. 22, 1993
NYC   9:30:0 AM EDT 40N45'00"
8:39:39 ST   74W00'23"

PARAGON TRADE-PTB   Jan. 28, 1993
NYC   9:30:0 AM EST   40N45'00"
18:05:25 ST   74W00'23"

PAYLESS CASHWAYS-PCS Mar. 9, 1993
NYC   9:30:0 AM EST   40N45'00"
20:43:07 ST   74W00'23"

PEOPLES BANCORP-PPLS Jan. 18, 1993
NYC   9:30:0 AM EST   40N45'00"
17:26:00 ST   74W00'23"

PEOPLES CHOICE-PCTV July 8, 1993
NYC   9:30:0 AM EDT 40N45'00"
3:40:01 ST   74W00'23"

PHILLIPS VAN HEUSEN-PVH   June 11, 1976
NYC   10:0:0 AM EDT 40N45'00"
2:24:20 ST   74W00'23"

PHYSICIAN CORP.-PCAM   Mar. 30, 1993
NYC   9:30:0 AM EST   40N45'00"
22:05:55 ST   74W00'23"

PINNACLE-PNCL July 1, 1993
NYC   9:30:0 AM EDT 40N45'00"
3:12:25 ST   74W00'23"

PLAYTEX-PYX   Jan. 27, 1994
NYC   9:30:0 AM EST   40N45'00"
18:00:31 ST   74W00'23"

POLYGRAM-PLG   Dec. 14, 1989
NYC   9:30:0 AM EST   40N45'00"
15:07:09 ST   74W00'23"

POST PROPERTY-PPS   July 16, 1993
NYC   9:30:0 AM EDT 40N45'00"
4:11:33 ST   74W00'23"

PREMARK-PMI   Oct. 31, 1987
NYC   9:30:0 AM EST   40N45'00"
12:11:39 ST   74W00'23"

PRESLEY COS.-PDC   Oct. 11, 1991
NYC   9:30:0 AM EDT 40N45'00"
9:52:45 ST   74W00'23"

R.P. SCHERER-SHR   Oct. 11, 1991
NYC   9:30:0 AM EDT 40N45'00"
9:52:45 ST   74W00'23"

REGENERON PHARM.-REGN   Apr. 2, 1991
NYC   9:30:0 AM EST   40N45'00"
22:15:56 ST   74W00'23"

RLI CORP.-RLI   May 8, 1987
NYC   9:30:0 AM EDT 40N45'00"
23:37:35 ST   74W00'23"

ROANOKE GAS-RGCO   Feb. 1, 1994
NYC   9:30:0 AM EST   40N45'00"
18:20:14 ST   74W00'23"

ROYAL APPLIANCE MFG.-RAM   July 1, 1992
NYC   9:30:0 AM EDT 40N45'00"
3:13:36 ST   74W00'23"

ROYAL CARIBBEAN-RCL Apr. 28, 1993
NYC   9:30:0 AM EDT 40N45'00"
23:00:05 ST   74W00'23"

SALANT-SLT   June 3, 1987
NYC   9:30:0 AM EDT 40N45'00"
1:20:06 ST   74W00'23"

SEAGULL ENERGY-SGO   Feb. 11, 1981
NYC   10:0:0 AM EST 40N45'00"
19:30:33 ST 74W00'23"

SEALED AIR-SEE May 31, 1979
NYC   10:0:0 AM EDT 40N45'00"
1:38:06 ST   74W00'23"

SHAMAN-SHMN   Jan. 27, 1993
NYC   9:30:0 AM EST 40N45'00"
18:01:29 ST 74W00'23"

SHAW INDUSTRIES-SHX   June 22, 1981
NYC   10:0:0 AM EDT 40N45'00"
3:06:52 ST   74W00'23"

SHONEYS-SHN   Apr. 5, 1989
NYC   9:30:0 AM EDT 40N45'00"
21:29:31 ST 74W00'23"

SIGNAL APPAREL-SIA   Sep. 4, 1946
NYC   10:0:0 AM EDT 40N45'00"
7:56:33 ST   74W00'23"

SIMON PROP.-SPG Dec. 14, 1993
NYC   9:30:0 AM EST 40N45'00"
15:07:03 ST 74W00'23"

SINGER-SEW   Aug. 2, 1991
NYC   9:30:0 AM EDT 40N45'00"
5:16:46 ST   74W00'23"

SOUTHWEST BANCSH.-SWBI   June 29, 1992
NYC   9:30:0 AM EDT 40N45'00"
3:05:43 ST   74W00'23"

SPARTA FEEDS-SPFO   Jan. 11, 1994
NYC   9:30:0 AM EST 40N45'00"
16:57:26 ST 74W00'23"

SPS TRANSACTION-PAY   Mar. 26, 1992
NYC   9:30:0 AM EST 40N45'00"
21:51:20 ST 74W00'23"

ST.JOHN'S KNITS-SJK   Mar. 11, 1993
NYC   9:30:0 AM EST 40N45'00"
20:51:01 ST 74W00'23"

STOKELY-STKY   Oct. 29, 1985
NYC   9:30:0 AM EST 40N45'00"
12:05:40 ST 74W00'23"

STONE CONTAINER-STO   Oct. 31, 1966
NYC   10:0:0 AM EST 40N45'00"
12:42:04 ST 74W00'23"

T.W.SERVICES-TW Jan. 8, 1987
NYC   9:30:0 AM EST 40N45'00"
16:44:38 ST 74W00'23"

TALBOTS-TLB   Nov. 19, 1993
NYC   9:30:0 AM EST 40N45'00"
13:28:29 ST 74W00'23"

TALLEY-TAL   Oct. 28, 1968
NYC   10:0:0 AM EST 40N45'00"
12:32:16 ST 74W00'23"

TANGER FACT. OUTLET-SKT   May 28, 1993
NYC   9:30:0 AM EDT 40N45'00"
0:58:22 ST   74W00'23"

T-CELL SCIENCE-TCEL   May 15, 1986
NYC   9:30:0 AM EDT 40N45'00"
0:06:08 ST   74W00'23"

TELECOM NZ-NZT July 17, 1991
NYC   9:30:0 AM EDT 40N45'00"
4:13:41 ST   74W00'23"

TELULAR-WRLS   Jan. 27, 1994
NYC   9:30:0 AM EST 40N45'00"
18:00:31 ST 74W00'23"

TEMTEX IND.-TMTX   Jan. 26, 1994
NYC   9:30:0 AM EST 40N45'00"
17:56:35 ST 74W00'23"

TEPPCO PARTNERS-TPP   Feb. 28, 1990
NYC   9:30:0 AM EST 40N45'00"
20:06:47 ST 74W00'23"

TETRA TECH-WATR   Dec. 19, 1991
NYC   9:30:0 AM EST 40N45'00"
15:24:57 ST 74W00'23"

TIMBERLAND-TBL June 10, 1991
NYC   9:30:0 AM EDT 40N45'00"
1:47:35 ST   74W00'23"

TIS MORTGAGE-TIS   Aug. 19, 1988
NYC   9:30:0 AM EDT 40N45'00"
6:26:40 ST   74W00'23"

TOWN & COUNTY TRUST-TCT   Aug. 17, 1993
NYC   9:30:0 AM EDT 40N45'00"
6:17:43 ST   74W00'23"

TRANSTECHNOLOGY-TT   Feb. 3, 1988
NYC   9:30:0 AM EST 40N45'00"
18:26:11 ST   74W00'23"

TRANS-WORLD MUSIC-TWMC   July 24, 1986
NYC   9:30:0 AM EDT 40N45'00"
4:42:07 ST   74W00'23"

TRM COPY CENTERS-TRMM   Dec. 20, 1991
NYC   9:30:0 AM EST 40N45'00"
15:28:54 ST   74W00'23"

TUFCO TECH.-TFCO   Jan. 21, 1994
NYC   9:30:0 AM EST 40N45'00"
17:36:52 ST   74W00'23"

TYLER CORP.TYL Mar. 24, 1969
NYC   10:0:0 AM EST 40N45'00"
22:11:50 ST   74W00'23"

URBAN SHOP. CENTERS-URB   Oct. 7, 1993
NYC   9:30:0 AM EDT 40N45'00"
9:38:47 ST   74W00'23"

VENTURE STORES-VEN   Oct. 8, 1990
NYC   9:30:0 AM EDT 40N45'00"
9:41:53 ST   74W00'23"

VITAL SIGNS-VITL Aug. 30, 1990
NYC   9:30:0 AM EDT 40N45'00"
7:08:07 ST   74W00'23"

VIVRA-V   Sep. 16, 1989
NYC   9:30:0 AM EDT 40N45'00"
8:16:06 ST   74W00'23"

VWR-VWRX   Feb. 28, 1986
NYC   9:30:0 AM EST 40N45'00"
20:06:40 ST   74W00'23"

WABASH NATIONAL-WNC Nov. 8, 1991
NYC   9:30:0 AM EST 40N45'00"
12:43:19 ST   74W00'23"

WELLSFORD RESIDENT.-WRP   Nov. 20, 1992
NYC   9:30:0 AM EST 40N45'00"
13:33:23 ST   74W00'23"

WELLS-GARDNER EL.-WGA   Nov. 23, 1981
NYC   10:0:0 AM EST 40N45'00"
14:14:12 ST   74W00'23"

WESTERFED FINAN.-WSTR Jan. 10, 1994
NYC   9:30:0 AM EST 40N45'00"
16:53:30 ST   74W00'23"

WHITTAKER CORP.-WKR   June 17, 1986
NYC   9:30:0 AM EDT 40N45'00"
2:16:15 ST   74W00'23"

WINDMERE-WND Mar. 1, 1989
NYC   9:30:0 AM EST 40N45'00"
20:11:41 ST   74W00'23"

WYNNS INTERNAT.-WN   Dec. 10, 1980
NYC   10:0:0 AM EST 40N45'00"
15:22:10 ST   74W00'23"

ZENECA GROUP-ZEN   June 1, 1993
NYC   9:30:0 AM EDT 40N45'00"
1:14:08 ST   74W00'23"

ZOLL MEDICAL-ZOLL   July 9, 1992
NYC   9:30:0 AM EDT 40N45'00"
3:45:08 ST   74W00'23"

Inactive Stocks from First Edition

This appendix contains earlier first-trade data for stocks in the book. For example, LSI first traded on the NASDAQ as LLSI. The LLSI date is in this section. The LSI date is in the NYSE section earlier in this volume. Other stocks changed names or symbols; the newer dates are used in the chart section of the book. These dates are included for those who wish to research them.

ACCUSTAFF-ATSF Aug. 17, 1994
NYC   9:30:0 AM EDT   40N45'00"
6:16:47 ST   74W00'23"

ACUSON CORP.-ACSN   Sep. 16, 1986
NYC   9:30:0 AM EDT   40N45'00"
8:15:01 ST   74W00'23"

AICORP-AICP   July 16, 1990
NYC   9:30:0 AM EDT   40N45'00"
4:10:42 ST   74W00'23"

AMERICA ONLINE-AMER   Mar 19, 1992
NYC   9:30:0 AM EST   40N45'00"
21:23:44 ST   74W00'23"

APPLIED MAGNETICS-AMAT   Oct. 12, 1972
NYC   10:0:0 AM EDT   40N45'00"
10:29:09 ST   74W00'23"

B.A.T. INDUSTRIES-BAT   Dec. 13, 1976
NYC   10:0:0 AM EST   40N45'00"
15:33:53 ST   74W00'23"

CERNER-CERN   Dec. 5, 1986
NYC   9:30:0 AM EST   40N45'00"
14:30:22 ST   74W00'23"

COTELLIGENT-COTL   Feb. 14, 1996
NYC   9:30:0 AM EST   40N45'00"
19:09:36 ST   74W00'23"

CYPRESS SEMICONDUCTOR   May 29, 1986
NYC   9:30:0 AM EDT   40N45'00"
1:01:20 ST   74W00'23"

DILLARD DEP. STORES-DDSA   Oct. 27, 1969
NYC   10:0:0 AM EST   40N45'00"
12:27:22 ST   74W00'23"

DYNATECH-DYTC Dec. 31, 1973
NYC   10:0:0 AM EST   40N45'00"
16:43:46 ST   74W00'23"

GATEWAY   Oct. 23, 1987
NYC   9:30:0 AM EDT   40N45'00"
10:39:56 ST   74W00'23"

GENERAL ELECTRIC   June 23, 1892
NYC   10:0:0 AM EST   40N45'00"
4:34:05 ST   74W00'23"

GENENTECH-OTC 1st TRADE   Sep. 26, 1980
NYC   10:0:0 AM EDT
40N45'00"   9:26:19 ST   74W00'23"

GLENAYRE1   Mar. 17, 1988
NYC   9:30:0 AM EST   40N45'00"
21:15:31 ST   74W00'23"

IBM1   Nov. 11, 1915
NYC   10:0:0 AM EST   40N45'00"
13:22:41 ST   74W00'23"

INT. HARVESTER (OLD NAV)   Oct. 2, 1918
NYC   1:0:0 AM EST
40N45'00"   1:44:46 ST   74W00'23"

IOMEGA-IOMG   July 7, 1983
NYC   10:0:0 AM EDT   40N45'00"
4:03:54 ST   74W00'23"

ITT (OLD)   Apr. 26, 1923
NYC   10:0:0 AM EST   40N45'00"
0:18:33 ST   74W00'23"

LEARNING CO.-LRNG   Apr. 29, 1992
NYC   9:30:0 AM EDT
40N45'00"   23:05:01 ST   74W00'23"

LIVE ENTERTAINMENT-LIVE   Aug. 30, 1988
NYC   9:30:0 AM EDT
40N45'00"   7:10:02 ST   74W00'23"

LIZ CLAIBORNE-LIZC   June 5, 1981
NYC   10:0:0 AM EDT
40N45'00"   1:59:51 ST   74W00'23"

LSI LOGIC-LLSI   May 13, 1983
NYC   10:0:0 AM EDT   40N45'00"
0:27:15 ST   74W00'23"

NEWBRIDGE NETWORKS-NNCXF July 28, 1989
NYC   9:30:0 AM EDT 40N42'51"
4:58:44 ST   74W00'23"

NIKE-NIKE   Nov. 28, 1980
NYC   10:0:0 AM EST 40N45'00"
14:34:52 ST   74W00'23"

SAFECARD SERVICES-SFCD   Nov. 23, 1977
NYC   10:0:0 AM EST 40N45'00"
14:14:04 ST   74W00'23

SEAGATE-SGAT   Oct. 22, 1981
NYC   10:0:0 AM EDT 40N45'00"
11:07:52 ST   74W00'23"

SENSORMATICS-SNSR   Dec. 1, 1970
NYC   10:0:0 AM EST 40N45'00"
14:44:25 ST   74W00'23"

SHARED MEDICAL-SMED June 22, 1976
NYC   10:0:0 AM EDT 40N45'00"
3:07:42 ST   74W00'23"

SILICON GRAPHICS-SGIC Oct. 29, 1986
NYC   9:30:0 AM EST 40N45'00"
12:04:43 ST   74W00'23"

SOFTKEY-SKEY   Feb. 4, 1994
NYC   9:30:0 AM EST 40N45'00"
18:32:05 ST   74W00'23"

ST. PAUL COS.-STPL   Dec. 1, 1970
NYC   10:0:0 AM EST 40N45'00"
14:44:25 ST   74W00'23"

STRATUS COMPUTER-STRA   Aug. 26, 1983
NYC   10:0:0 AM EDT 40N45'00"
7:21:14 ST   74W00'23"

SYMBOL TECH.-SMBL   June 1, 1979
NYC   10:0:0 AM EDT 40N45'00"
1:42:03 ST   74W00'23"

TCBY   May 10, 1984
NYC   10:0:0 AM EDT 40N45'00"
0:18:25 ST   74W00'23"

TRAVELERS-TIC Dec. 9, 1968
NYC   10:0:0 AM EST 40N45'00"
15:17:52 ST   74W00'23"

U.S. AIR   Oct. 29, 1979
NYC   10:0:0 AM EST 40N45'00"
12:33:36 ST   74W00'23"

U.S. STEEL-(OLD USX)   July 1, 1923
NYC   10:0:0 AM EDT 40N45'00"
3:38:36 ST   74W00'23"

WESTERN DIGITAL-WDC May 8, 1984
NYC   10:0:0 AM EDT 40N45'00"
0:10:32 ST   74W00'23"

ZILOG-ZLOG   Feb. 27, 1991
NYC   9:30:0 AM EST 40N45'00"
20:01:53 ST   74W00'23"

Appendix II

he following lists will allow you to find which stocks in this collection of first-trades are being affected by any given celestial event.

The first listing is an alphabetical sort of the companies in this book by ticker symbol and company name. The second sort covers each planet and angle, in ascending numerical order, preceded by its ticker symbol. Planetary positions are given in decimal notation.

Hot to use this Sorter

Example: If you want to see what companies were affected by the Saturn (1° Taurus) Neptune (1° Aquarius) squares of 1998, you would check the companies represented by ticker symbols at 30° and 300°.

Quick Converter:

Aries	0-29.99	Libra	180-209.99
Taurus	30-59.99	Scorpio	210-239.99
Gemini	60-89.99	Sagittarius	240-269.99
Cancer	90-119.99	Capricorn	270-299.99
Leo	120-149.99	Aquarius	300-329.99
Virgo	150-179.99	Pisces	330-359.99

Ticker Symbol — Company Name

All planets in the following section are listed in decimal notation and are preceded by the ticker symbol. Use the alphabetical ticker key below.

Ticker	Company	Ticker	Company	Ticker	Company
1AF –	1ST AUSTRALIA FUND	AMR –	AMR	BSC –	BEAR STERNS
COMS –	3 COM	APC –	ANADARKO PET.	BDX –	BECTON DICKINSON
THDO –	3DO	ADI –	ANALOG DEVICES	BSPT –	BELL SPORTS
MMM –	3M	ABCW –	ANCHOR BANCSHARES	BNL –	BENEFICIAL CORP.
ABAX –	ABAXIS	ANDW –	ANDREW CORP.	BBY –	BEST BUY
ABT –	ABBOTT LABS	NSTA –	ANESTA CORP.	BS –	BETHLEHEM STEEL
AKLM –	ACCLAIM	BUD –	ANHEUSER BUSCH	BEV –	BEVERLY ENTERPRISES
ACN –	ACUSON	APA –	APACHE	BGEN –	BIOGEN
ADPT –	ADAPTEC	AAPL –	APPLE COMP.	BMET –	BIOMET
ADBE –	ADOBE	APSO –	APPLE SOUTH	BDK –	BLACK & DECKER
ACCOB –	ADOLPH COORS	AMAT –	APPLIED MATERIALS	BMCS –	BMC SOFTWARE
AALR –	ADVANCED LOGIC RES.	ADM –	ARCHER DANIELS	BA –	BOEING
AMD –	ADVANCED MICRO DEV.	RCM –	ARCO CHEMICAL	BCC –	BOISE CASCADE
AADV –	ADVANTAGE BANCORP	ARRO –	ARROW IND.	BOST –	BOSTON CHICKEN
AET –	AETNA	ASA –	ASA	BSX –	BOSTON SCIENTIFIC
AHM –	AHMANSON	AR –	ASARCO	BZF –	BRAZIL FUND
APD –	AIR PRODUCTS	ASND –	ASCEND COMMUNS.	BGG –	BRIGGS & STRATTON
ABF –	AIRBORNE FREIGHT	ASH –	ASHLAND OIL	BMY –	BRISTOL MYERS
ALK –	ALASKA AIR	APB –	ASIA PACIFIC	BP –	BRITISH PETROLEUM
ALBK –	ALBANK FINANCIAL	GRR –	ASIA TIGERS FUND	BST –	BRITISH STEEL
ACV –	ALBERTO CULVER	ASTA –	AST RESEARCH	BROD –	BRODERBUND
ABS –	ALBERTSONS	ACAI –	ATLANTIC COAST AIR	BFI –	BROWNING FERRIS
AL –	ALCAN	ARC –	ATLANTIC RICHFIELD	BC –	BRUNSWICK
AA –	ALCOA	ATTn –	ATT (NEW)	BNI –	BURLINGTON NORTHERN
ALEX –	ALEXANDER & BALDWIN	ATTo –	ATT (OLD)	CWP –	CABLE & WIRELESS
AGN –	ALLERGAN	ATTr –	ATT (REORGANIZATION)	CS –	CABLETRON
ALD –	ALLIED SIGNAL	ASPX –	AUSPEX	CDN –	CADENCE DESIGN
ALL –	ALLSTATE	OST –	AUSTRIA FUND	CCC –	CALGON
AT –	ALLTEL	AUD –	AUTO. DATA PROCESS.	CBB –	CALIBER SYSTEMS
ALMI –	ALPHA MICRO SYSTEMS	AZO –	AUTOZONE	ELY –	CALLOWAY GOLF
ALTR –	ALTERA	AVY –	AVERY-DENNISON	CATP –	CAMBRIDGE TECH.
AMX –	ALUMAX	AVID –	AVID TECHNOLOGY	CCH –	CAMPBELL RED LAKE
AMZN –	AMAZON	AVT –	AVNET	CPB –	CAMPBELL SOUP
AHC –	AMERADA HESS	AVP –	AVON PRODUCTS	CAR –	CARTER WALLACE
ABX –	AMERICAN BARRICK	(BBells) –	BABY BELL COS.	CAT –	CATERPILLAR
AEP –	AMERICAN ELEC. POWER	BHI –	BAKER HUGHES	CESH –	CE SOFTWARE
AXP –	AMERICAN EXPRESS	BLL –	BALL CORP.	CTEA –	CELESTIAL SEASONS
AGC –	AMERICAN GENERAL	ONE –	BANC ONE	CENF –	CENFED FINANCIAL
AGREA –	AMERICAN GREETINGS	BKB –	BANK OF BOSTON	CTX –	CENTEX
AHP –	AMERICAN HOME PRODS.	BAC –	BANKAMERICA	CNTO –	CENTOCOR
AIG –	AMERICAN INT. GROUP	BT –	BANKERS TRUST	CTL –	CENTURY TELEPHONE
AOL –	AMERICAN ONLINE	BNYN –	BANYAN SYSTEMS	CEN –	CERIDIAN
APCC –	AMERICAN POWER CONV	BCR –	BARD	CHA –	CHAMPION INT.
ASC –	AMERICAN STORES	BKS –	BARNES & NOBLE	CHRS –	CHARMING SHOPS
AW –	AMERICAN WASTE SERV.	BBI –	BARNETT BANKS	CMB –	CHASE MANHATTAN
AMGN –	AMGEN	BSET –	BASSETT FURNITURE	CHKR –	CHECKERS DRIVE IN
AN –	AMOCO	BTIOF –	BATTERY TECH.	CKFR –	CHECKFREE
AMP –	AMP	BAX –	BAXTER TRAVENOL	CSK –	CHESAPEAKE

Ticker	Company	Ticker	Company
CHV –	CHEVRON	CUM –	CUMMINS ENGINE
CH –	CHILE FUND	CYCH –	CYBERCASH
CHPS –	CHIPS & TECHNOLOG.	CYBR –	CYBERMEDIA
CQB –	CHIQUITA BRANDS	CYGN –	CYGNUS
CHIR –	CHIRON	CY –	CYPRESS SEMICON.
C –	CHRYSLER	CYRX –	CYRIX
CB –	CHUBB	CYRK –	CYRK
CI –	CIGNA	DCN –	DANA
CMZ –	CINCINNATI MILACRON	DGN –	DATA GENERAL
CC –	CIRCUIT CITY	DRAI –	DATA RESEARCH
CIR –	CIRCUS CIRCUS	DH –	DAYTON HUDSON
CRUS –	CIRRUS LOGIC	DF –	DEAN FOODS
CSCO –	CISCO SYSTEMS	DE –	DEERE
CCI –	CITICORP	DLCH –	DELCHAMPS
CTZN –	CITIFED BANCORP	DELL –	DELL COMPUTER
CLE –	CLAIRES STORES	DAL –	DELTA
CMH –	CLAYTON HOMES	ENG –	DESTEC
CLX –	CLOROX	DEX –	DEXTER
CNF –	CNF TRANSP.	DEC –	DIGITAL EQUIPMENT
CCE –	COCA COLA ENT.	DLNK –	DIGITAL LINK
KO –	COCA COLA	DDS –	DILLARD DEPT. STORES
CGNX –	COGNEX	DIS –	DISNEY
CL –	COLGATE	DOW –	DOW CHEMICAL
CGEN –	COLLAGEN	DJ –	DOW JONES
COT –	COLTEC	DI –	DRESSER IND.
CG –	COLUMBIA GAS	DIGI –	DSC COMMUNICATIONS
CMCSA –	COMCAST CORP.	DSPC –	DSP COMMUNICATIONS
CMSB –	COMMONWEALTH BANK	DUK –	DUKE POWER
CPQ –	COMPAQ	DNB –	DUN & BRADSTREET
CA –	COMPUTER ASSOCIATES	DD –	DUPONT
CSC –	COMPUTER SCI.CORP.	EGRP –	E*TRADE
TSK –	COMPUTER TASK GROUP	ENM –	EASTMAN CHEMICAL
CQ –	COMSAT	EK –	EASTMAN KODAK
CAG –	CONAGRA	ECH –	ECHLIN
CNC –	CONSECO	EIX –	EDISON INTERNAT.
ED –	CONSOLIDATED EDISON	EGG –	EG&G
CNG –	CONSOLIDATED NAT.GAS	EPG –	EL PASO NAT. GAS
CBE –	COOPER IND.	EGLS –	ELECTROGLAS
CPLY –	COPLEY PHARM.	ERTS –	ELECTRONIC ARTS
CORR –	COR PHARMACEUTICALS	LLY –	ELI LILLY
GLW –	CORNING GLASS	EMC –	EMC CORP.
CCR –	COUNTRYWIDE CREDIT	MEF –	EMERGING MEXICO FUND
CPC –	CPC INTERNATINAL	EMR –	EMERSON ELECTRIC
CR –	CRANE	EC –	ENGELHARD
CREAF –	CREATIVE TECHNOL.	ENP –	ENRON LIQUID GAS
XCOM –	CROSSCOM	ENE –	ENRON
CCK –	CROWN CORK & SEAL	EQ –	EQUITABLE COS.
CSX –	CSX CORP.	XON –	EXXON

Ticker Symbol — Company Name

All planets in the following section are listed in decimal notation and are preceded by the ticker symbol. Use the alphabetical ticker key below.

FDO – FAMILY DOLLAR STORES
FDX – FEDERAL EXPRESS
FD – FEDERATED
FOE – FERRO
FINL – FINISH LINE
FBS – FIRST BANK SYSTEM
FDC – FIRST DATA
FSR – FIRSTAR
FLE – FLEETWOOD
FMC – FMC
F – FORD
FORE – FORE SYSTEMS
FO#1 – FORTUNE BRANDS #1 –
FO#2 – FORTUNE BRANDS #2
FWC – FOSTER WHEELER
FRF – FRANCE FUND
FCX – FREEPORT MCMORAN
GCI – GANNETT
GPS – GAP STORES
GTW – GATEWAY
GMT – GATX
GY – GENCORP
GNE – GENENTECH
GD – GENERAL DYNAMICS
GE – GENERAL ELECTRIC
GIC – GENERAL INSTRUMENT
GIS – GENERAL MILLS
GM – GENERAL MOTORS
GNCI – GENERAL NUTRITION
GHV – GENESIS HEALTH CARE
GPC – GENUINE PARTS
GGC – GEORGIA GULF
GP – GEORGIA PACIFIC
GER – GERMANY FUND
G – GILLETTE
GEMS – GLENAYRE
GLN – GLENFED
GLBL – GLOBAL IND.
GLM – GLOBAL MARINE
GR – GOODRICH
GT – GOODYEAR
GWW – GRAINGER
GAP – GREAT ATLANTIC & PA.
GLK – GREAT LAKES CHEMICAL
GTF – GT GREAT.EUROPE FUND
GTE – GTE
HAE – HAEMONETICS

HAL – HALLIBURTON
HDI – HARLEY DAVIDSON
HRS – HARRIS
HMSY – HEALTH MNGMT.
HNZ – HEINZ
HELE – HELEN OF TROY
HERB – HERBALIFE
HPC – HERCULES
HSY – HERSHEY
HWP – HEWLETT PACKARD
HLT – HILTON HOTELS
HLYW – HOLLYWOOD ENT.
HD – HOME DEPOT
HM – HOMESTAKE
HON – HONEYWELL
HI – HOUSEHOLD INTER.
HOU – HOUSTON INDUSTRIES
HUM – HUMANA
HTCH – HUTCHINSON TECH.
IBM – IBM
IDXX – IDEXX LABS
ITW – ILLINOIS TOOL WORKS
ICII – IMPERIAL CREDIT
INFS – IN FOCUS SYSTEMS
N – INCO
IGF – INDIA GROWTH FUND
IF – INDONESIA FUND
IFMX – INFORMIX
IR – INGERSOLL RAND
IAD – INLAND STEEL
IFF – INT. FLAVORS & FRAG.
ICST – INTEGRATED CIRCUITS
IDTI – INTEGRATED DEVICES
INTC – INTEL
INEL – INTELLIGENT ELEC.
INDQA – INTER. DAIRY QUEEN
INGR – INTERGRAPH
IK – INTERLAKE
IRF – INTERN. RECTIFIER
ITSI – INTERN. TOTALIZATOR
IP – INTERNATIONAL PAPER
INTV – INTERVOICE
INTU – INTUIT
IOM – IOMEGA
IRL – IRISH FUND
ISL – IST ISRAEL
ITA – ITALY FUND

ITT – ITT
JBHT – J.B. HUNT TRANSPORT
JCP – J.C. PENNEY
JPM – J.P. MORGAN
JTAX – JACKSON HEWITT
JEC – JACOBS ENGINEERING
JR – JAMES RIVER
JAMS – JAMESON INNS
JEQ – JAPAN EQUITY FUND
JOF – JAPAN OTC FUND
JP – JEFFERSON PILOT
FORMF – JETFORM
JNJ – JOHNSON & JOHNSON
JCI – JOHNSON CONTROLS
KSWS – K SWISS
KLU – KAISER ALUMINUM
KAB – KANEB SERVICES
KT – KATY IND.
KBH – KAUFMAN & BROAD
K – KELLOGG
KEYLA#1 – KELLY SERVICES #1 –
KELYA#2 – KELLY SERVICES #2
KEY – KEY CORP.
KMB – KIMBERLY CLARK
KWP – KING WORLD PROD.
KLAC – KLA INSTRUMENTS
KLM – KLM ROYAL DUTCH
KM – KMART
KMAG – KOMAG
KF – KOREA FUND
KR – KROGER
KURZ – KURZWEIL APP.INT.
LA – L.A. GEAR
LHP – LAKEHEAD PIPELINE
LRCX – LAM RESEARCH
LMS – LAMSON & SESSIONS
LSTR – LANDSTAR SYSTEM
LSCC – LATTICE SEMI
LEVL – LEVEL ONE COMMUN.
LIFE – LIFELINE SYSTEM2
LTD – LIMITED
LNCR – LINCARE
LLTC – LINEAR TECH.
LIT – LITTON IND.
LIZ – LIZ CLAIBORNE
LMT#1 – LOCKHEED MARTIN #1 –
LMT#2 – LOCKHEED MARTIN #2

LTR – LOEWS
LGN – LOGICON
LOJN – LO-JACK
STAR – LONE STAR STEAKHOU.
LOR – LORAL SPACE & COMM.
LPX – LOUISIANA PACIFIC
LOW – LOWES
LSI – LSI LOGIC
LTV – LTV
LU – LUCENT TECH.
LUNR – LUNAR CORP.
LCOS – LYCOS
MAIL – MAIL BOXES
MF – MALAYSIA FUND
MANU – MANGUISTICS
MDA – MAPCO
MAPS – MAPINFO
MAR – MARRIOTT INT.
MHS – MARRIOTT
MUS – MARTECH
MAS – MASCO
MSX – MASOTECH
MATH – MATHSOFT
MAT – MATTEL
MXIM – MAXIM
MYG – MAYTAG
KRB – MBNA CORP.
MCAF – MCAFEE ASSOCIATES
MDR – MCDERMOTT
MCD – MCDONALDS
MD – MCDONNELL DOUGLAS
MHP – MCGRAW HILL
MCIC – MCI COMMUNICATIONS
MEA – MEAD
MDT – MEDTRONIC
MEL – MELLON
MNTR – MENTOR CORP.
MST – MERCANTILE STORES
MRK – MERCK
MER – MERRILL LYNCH
MXP – MESA
MCLL – METROCALL
MXF – MEXICO FUND
MCHP – MICROCHIP
MU – MICRON TECH.
MSFT – MICROSOFT
MTSI – MICROTOUCH SYSTEMS

MWHS – MICROWAREHOUSE
MIL – MILLIPORE
MOB – MOBIL
MB – MOLECULAR BIOSYSTEMS
MOLXA – MOLEX
MTC – MONSANTO
RNE – MORGAN STANL. RUSSIA
IIF – MORGAN STANLEY INDIA
MS – MORGAN STANLEY
MOT – MOTOROLA
MYL – MYLAN LABS
NTAIF – NAM TAI ELECT.
NII – NAT. INTERGROUP
NME – NAT. MEDICAL ENTER.
NSM – NATIONAL SEMI.
NB – NATIONS BANK
NAV – NAVISTAR
NELL – NELLCOR
NSCP – NETSCAPE
NCDI – NETWORK COMP.DEVICE
NWK – NETWORK SYSTEMS
NN – NEWBRIDGE NETWORKS
NGC – NEWMONT GOLD
NEM – NEWMONT MINING
NWS – NEWS CORP.
NKE – NIKE
NOBE – NORDSTROM
NSC – NORFOLK & SOUTHERN
NFB – NORTH FORK BANCORP
NT – NORTHERN TELECOM
NOC – NORTHROP
NOB – NORWEST CORP.
NOVL – NOVELL
NVLS – NOVELLUS
NUE – NUCOR
OXY – OCCIDENTAL PETROL.
OII – OCEAN ENGINEERING
OLOG – OFFSHORE LOGISTICS
ONCS – ONCOGENE
ORCL – ORACLE SYSTEMS
ORBI – ORBITAL SCIENCES
OREM – OREGON METAL.
ORX – ORYX ENERGY
GOSHA – OSHGOSH B'GOSH
OM – OUTBOARD MARINE
OI – OWENS ILLINOIS
PCAR – PACCAR

Ticker Symbol — Company Name

All planets in the following section are listed in decimal notation and are preceded by the ticker symbol. Use the alphabetical ticker key below.

PAGE – PAGING NETWORK
PWJ – PAINE WEBBER
PKF – PAKISTAN FUND
PMTC – PARAMETRIC
PARQ – PARCPLACE
PH – PARKER HANNIFIN
PE – PECO ENERGY
PZL – PENNZOIL
PSFT – PEOPLESOFT
PEP – PEPSICO
PKN – PERKIN ELMER
PFE – PFIZER
PCG – PG & E CORP.
PNU – PHARMACIA UPJOHN
PD – PHELPS DODGE
MO – PHILIP MORRIS
FPF – PHILLIPINE FUND
P – PHILLIPS PETROLEUM
PFS – PIONEER FINAN.
PCO – PITTSTON
PHII – PLANET HOLLYWOOD
PLN – PLANT CORP.
PSQL – PLATINUM SOFTWARE
PCL – PLUM CREEK TIMBER
PPP – POGO PRODUCING
PRD – POLAROID
PMS – POLICY MANAGE.SYSTEM
PESC – POOL ENERGY SVCS.
PGF – PORTUGAL FUND
PCH – POTLATCH
PPG – PPG IND.
PX – PRAXAIR
PG – PROCTER & GAMBLE
PRGS – PROGRESS SOFTWARE
PEG – PUBLIC SERVICE ENT.
PURT – PURE TECH.
QLGC – QLOGIC
OAT – QUAKER OATS
QCOM – QUALCOMM
QNTM – QUANTUM
RNBO – RAINBOW TECH.
RAL – RALSTON PURINA
RTN – RAYTHEON
RDA – READERS DIGEST
RBK – REEBOK
RMDY – REMEDY
RGEN – REPLIGEN
RLM – REYNOLDS METALS

REY – REYNOLDS+REYNOLDS
RCHY – RICHEY ELECTRONICS
RAD – RITE AID
RN – RJR NABISCO
ROAD – ROADWAY SERVICES
RDC – ROWAN COS.
RD – ROYAL DUTCH
RBD – RUBBERMAID
RYAN – RYAN STEAK HOUSE
R – RYDER
SB – SALOMON BROS.
SANM – SANMINA
SFL – SANTA FE PACIFIC
SLE – SARA LEE
SCF – SCANDANAVIA FUND
SGP – SCHERING PLOUGH
SLB – SCHLUMBERGER
SCHL – SCHOLASTIC
SFA – SCIENTIFIC ATLANTA
SEG – SEAGATE TECHNOLOGY
VO – SEAGRAM
S – SEARS ROEBUCK
SDTI – SECURITY DYNAMICS
SEBL – SEIBEL SYSTENS
SEPC – SEILER POLLUTION
SRM – SENSORMATICS
SKO – SHOPKO
SGI – SILICON GRAPHICS
SKY – SKYLINE
SII – SMITH INTERNAT.
SNA – SNAP ON TOOLS
SSPE – SOFTWARE SPECTRUM
SO – SOUTHERN CO.
LUV – SOUTHWEST AIR
SNF – SPAIN FUND
SDII – SPECIAL DEVICE
FON – SPRINT
SPYG – SPYGLASS
SOTA – STATE OF THE ART
SSW – STERLING SOFTWARE
SSS – THREE-S
STK – STORAGE TECHNOLOGY
SRA – STRATUS COMPUTER
SUN – SUN CO.
SUNW – SUN MICROSYSTEMS
SNS – SUNDSTRAND
SWZ – SWISS HELVETIA FUND
SYBS – SYBASE

SYMC – SYMANTEC
SBL – SYMBOL TECHNOLOGY
SYMBA – SYMBOLLON
SYQT – SYQUEST TECHNOLOGY
TWN – TAIWAN FUND
TMB – TAMBRANDS
TDM – TANDEM
TAN – TANDY
TBY – TCBY
TEK – TEKTRONIX
TELC – TELCO SYSTEMS
LBTYA – TELECOM LIBERTY
TCOMA – TELECOMMUN. A
TMX – TELEPHONE DE MEXICO
TLAB – TELLABS
TIN – TEMPLE INLAND
TCH – TEMPLETON CHINA
TEN – TENNECO
TX – TEXACO
TXN – TEXAS INSTRUMENTS
TXU – TEXAS UTILITIES
TXT – TEXTRON
TTF – THAI FUNDS
TNB – THOMAS & BETTS
TIF – TIFFANY
TWX – TIME WARNER
TKR – TIMKEN
TJX – TJX COS.
TOL – TOLL BROS.
TR – TOOTSIE ROLL
TOS – TOSCO
TOT – TOTAL
TOY – TOYS R US
TRV – TRAVELERS
TRB – TRIBUNE
TRCD – TRICORD SYSTEMS
TRMB – TRIMBLE NAVIG.
OIL – TRITON ENERGY
TRW – TRW
TTX – TULTEX
TKF – TURKISH FUND
UH – U.S. HOME
USRX – U.S. ROBOTICS
USS – U.S. SURGICAL
USW – U.S. WEST
UAL – UAL CORP.
UTEK – ULTRATECH STEPPER
UCM – UNICOM CORP.

UCC – UNION CAMP
UK – UNION CARBIDE
UNP – UNION PACIFIC
UIS – UNISYS
U – UNITED AIR
UNH – UNITED HEALTH
UTX – UNITED TECHNOLOGIES
UFC – UNIVERSAL FOODS
UCL – UNOCAL
UNM – UNUM CORP.
USFC – US FREIGHTWAYS
USWI – US WATS
FG – USF&G
USG – USG CORP.
UST – UST
MRO – USX MARATHON
X – USX
VCI – VALASSIS COMMUN.
VJET – VALUJET
VAR – VARIAN
VENGF – VENGOLD
VTA – VESTA INSURANCE
GRA – W.R. GRACE
WBN – WABAN
WAG – WALGREEN
WALL – WALL DATA
WMT – WALMART
WAC – WARNACO
WLA – WARNER LAMBERT
WTEC – WARRANTECH
WMX – WASTE MANAGEMENT
WLP – WELLPOINT HEALTH
WFC – WELLS FARGO
WEN – WENDYS
WDC – WESTERN DIGITAL
WGR – WESTERN GAS RE-SOURCE
WX – WESTINGHOUSE
W – WESTVACO
WY – WEYERHAUSER
WHR – WHIRLPOOL
WMB – WILLIAMS COS.
DIXIE – WINN
WMS – WMS INDUSTRIES
WLV – WOLVERINE TUBE
WNDR – WONDERWARE
Z – WOOLWORTH
WTHG – WORTHINGTON IND.

WWY – WRIGLEY
XRX – XEROX
XLNX – XILINX
XIRC – XIRCOM
XTR – XTRA
YHOO – YAHOO
YELL – YELLOW FREIGHT
YSII – YOUTH SERVICES
ZBRA – ZEBRA TECHNOLOGIES
ZE – ZENITH ELECTRONICS
ZLG – ZILOG

Sun	Moon	Mercury	Venus	Mars	Jupiter	Saturn	Uranus	Neptune	Pluto	Node	Asc	MC
MS 0.68	GGC 0.48	GABAX 0.18	ALK 0.92	ORX 0.03	FON 1.55	YHOO 0.63	G 1.27	HM 37.00	HM 54.58	GGC 0.32	JAMS 0.23	TMX 0.37
COMS 1.18	HAE 1.08	SUNW 0.70	IBM 1.77	CCM 0.30	GT 3.28	IOM 1.03	GT 3.13	ATTo 91.23	ATTo 78.65	P 0.70	SBL 1.10	GTE 0.88
BGEN 1.42	CC 1.40	NPR 0.80	MATH 1.83	CY 0.67	BTR 4.78	PHII 1.43	N 3.50	EK 95.57	EK 79.97	RCM 1.80	NSTA 1.93	FBS 1.80
PURT 1.95	RTR 2.65	PWG 0.80	APB 2.28	ACN 1.13	AMR 5.10	CYBR 2.02	MHP 5.10	S 106.72	S 84.85	RNBO 3.07	OAT 3.83	AMZN 1.98
EMC 2.18	HON 3.53	ALBK 1.37	ASH 2.80	CTX 1.22	NEM 5.15	LOR 3.38	GIS 5.42	AR 120.73	AR 91.43	SKY 4.10	WLP 4.07	ASH 2.00
BP 2.57	N 4.33	CI 1.42	CCM 3.05	RAD 1.28	FMAGX 6.57	RNE 4.07	CAT 7.55	GM 124.38	GM 93.47	AL 4.13	OPTFX 5.00	ZEN 2.32
GTF 2.70	WFC 6.40	XIRC 2.07	FSNGX 3.77	MKS 1.58	DREVX 6.82	RTK 4.60	PCO 8.05	KM 124.70	BOC 93.83	SWZ 4.28	PCO 5.68	SRM 2.52
AADV 4.20	HWP 8.08	BP 2.58	FORMF 3.77	CUAC 2.93	BHI 8.38	AOL 4.75	TRW 8.90	BOC 124.73	KM 94.22	MOMGX 4.53	FO#1 6.32	INTV 2.62
COT 4.20	PRD 8.47	ASC 2.82	FDC 4.03	ADM 3.12	TDM 8.62	DOW 4.78	CCK 9.62	XON 128.90	XON 95.67	JHNGX 5.00	CYGN 6.70	PFS 2.72
XON 4.67	W 9.25	JPM 4.22	ORCL 4.32	BS 4.20	GABGX 9.35	RNK 5.05	KMB 9.62	ARC 129.78	ARC 95.90	RN 5.35	RN 8.42	ASND 2.77
SSW 7.65	SRSPX 9.98	BUD 5.90	SANM 5.03	FFIDX 4.53	WY 9.55	CTR 5.27	PD 9.62	FO#1 130.33	FO#1 96.22	BAA 5.47	DLNK 8.77	FSDAX 2.82
NTAIF 8.13	ORBI 10.17	MD 6.12	MSFT 5.57	KSWS 4.57	AA 9.83	AGWFX 5.67	HON 9.93	PEP 131.23	PEP 96.95	BBY 5.87	MAPS 8.77	RTR 3.18
FMCSX 8.67	RYOCX 10.83	CMZ 6.68	CATP 5.77	IK 6.50	WLA 10.83	GLM 5.73	PG 10.20	DD 133.43	DD 98.68	CSC 6.48	OM 9.62	CCK 3.22
DRTHX 9.02	MNTR 11.77	GTE 6.93	JAMRX 5.92	FTRNX 6.65	TEK 11.73	TEN 5.98	FWC 10.67	IAD 135.40	MO 99.10	HERB 6.57	CTR 11.17	KMB 3.22
BNI 9.48	AW 11.90	ENG 7.02	JAVLX 6.07	WX 6.72	APB 12.67	EGRP 6.73	BGG 11.33	MO 135.85	IAD 99.22	PRGFX 6.78	SGRFX 11.22	PD 3.22
IRL 9.63	AUD 12.10	GTF 7.23	THDO 6.32	TWN 6.73	SLE 13.75	FCYCF 6.90	HPC 11.37	IBM 136.48	IBM 100.53	HDI 6.88	RAD 11.32	CMZ 3.37
MD 10.15	SB 12.37	AADV 7.87	GOSHA 7.08	ORA 6.75	WIN 13.75	FNATF 6.90	FFIDX 12.95	TKR 137.35	IR 100.68	INEL 6.93	CBE 11.38	HFX 3.43
FKGRX 10.80	MDT 13.50	COT 7.87	GLBL 7.60	LCOS 6.98	RDC 14.85	BGY 7.40	FKREX 25.93	IBM 138.85	TKR 101.17	TJX 7.20	NEM 11.77	ZLG 3.57
NME 11.02	RYAN 13.72	PLN 8.52	CYCH 7.67	SII 7.25	TIF 15.18	LMS 7.93	MTC 25.93	C 140.95	BC 102.23	CCI 7.82	IGEN 12.15	TBY 5.02
ALTR 11.10	BT.A 14.45	FSNGX 8.65	FRF 8.35	LGN 7.43	UST 15.42	FCNTX 8.80	BMY 26.88	KO 141.65	ADM 102.68	WMB 8.42	SEPC 12.15	GD 5.03
BZF 11.10	VENGF 14.80	FORMF 8.65	LGN 8.85	BS 8.12	MF 15.87	BASS 9.07	DE 26.95	GE 141.90	UK 102.72	KMAG 8.68	YSII 12.15	CUAC 5.25
XIRC 11.13	ORCL 14.90	CCH 9.00	RLM 8.85	BST 8.22	BDX 16.13	LAD.B 9.45	BNL 27.38	ADM 142.35	S 103.13	VLIFX 8.95	KAB 13.93	WX 5.50
ZE 11.38	WWY 15.53	VCI 9.23	INTV 9.27	LU 8.52	NT 16.25	SII 10.70	UTX 31.12	MKS 142.53	GE 103.30	RR 9.12	MATH 14.25	NELL 5.70
CI 11.55	GWW 16.08	NME 9.85	TTF 9.52	TAN 8.77	CAG 16.58	TAN 10.93	AN 31.23	IK 142.72	KO 103.50	NELL 9.15	WDC 15.17	K 6.15
JPM 11.70	JAOLX 16.98	STAR 9.93	FMAGX 10.15	XLNX 8.92	NELL 18.25	DI 11.67	MEA 31.73	UK 142.95	MKS 103.77	AMRMX 9.38	LMS 15.50	BSX 6.55
PZL 11.95	PX 17.25	JAVLX 10.18	ASPX 10.38	NVLS 9.93	ACCOB 18.30	CHCLX 12.03	VO 32.17	GIS 146.40	IK 103.95	CLX 9.45	JR 15.65	ICII 6.55
ALBK 12.12	JP 17.90	GD 10.42	MAS 11.13	BMCS 10.13	RR 18.42	DEX 12.33	BS 32.52	TX 146.70	GIS 105.20	BCR 9.50	FD 16.42	NWS 7.03
AZO 12.35	BNL 18.07	EPG 10.48	MHP 12.07	IGF 10.13	STK 18.48	KT 12.45	KKTWX 35.13	MOB 146.97	MOB 105.42	MF 9.73	HMSY 16.72	GTW 9.48
ORA 12.85	VAR 19.53	LNCR 10.85	WWY 12.13	BSX 10.43	KAB 18.63	AL 12.92	BA 35.28	G 148.12	TX 105.92	AET 9.82	CCR 16.77	MRK 9.52
LCOS 13.13	PMTC 19.92	DRTHX 12.37	PFS 14.03	ICII 10.43	USS 19.82	PZL 14.93	OM 35.68	CCK 148.60	GT 106.17	UST 9.85	SGI 17.13	BAX 9.92
ADI 13.27	WGR 19.92	COMS 13.62	HD 14.48	SRYIX 11.47	MIL 19.88	AMZN 15.70	SGRFX 35.68	KMB 148.60	CCK 106.53	TIF 9.90	TOS 17.22	SOTA 9.97
ONCS 13.53	ABS 20.38	GOSHA 15.40	BT 15.35	SFL 11.50	KMAG 20.12	GTW 16.43	HI 35.93	PD 148.60	KMB 106.53	APB 10.48	U 20.95	BT 11.05
WWY 13.72	NME 20.88	RGEN 16.53	MS 15.57	WFC 11.58	FBGRX 20.22	HFX 17.45	ABT 36.53	BGG 149.43	PD 106.53	GABGX 11.22	LIFE 22.28	FORE 11.33
GY 13.80	SEG 20.88	BNI 16.78	TIF 15.57	ABS 12.32	IFF 20.67	NRK 17.60	BDK 37.18	HPC 149.60	MHP 106.57	MHS 11.37	LTR 22.53	FCNTX 11.52
KRAGX 14.38	EMR 21.72	GY 16.98	AXP 15.63	MB 13.95	OXY 20.88	JHNGX 18.72	CR 37.77	MHP 150.13	G 107.08	TDM 11.38	SLB 22.82	MER 12.15
LU 15.10	TXT 21.75	SSW 17.33	BAX 15.95	GLW 14.33	WMB 21.10	MOMGX 18.83	DOW 42.55	FFIDX 150.83	FFIDX 107.62	BHI 11.43	DREQX 25.27	HUM 12.67
BHI 16.22	FINL 21.97	ORA 18.15	BP 16.67	ACCOB 14.35	ABF 21.13	SKY 19.08	RNK 42.93	FWC 151.30	N 107.68	GPC 11.68	PARQ 25.32	AXP 13.25
TDM 17.20	LBTYA 23.23	CNF 18.47	UST 16.78	YHOO 14.65	GIS 22.30	CSC 19.25	CHCLX 43.50	N 151.32	BGG 107.78	CEN 11.73	GLBL 25.70	GCI 13.47
HSBA 17.97	AIG 23.82	LCOS 18.75	TTX 17.03	STK 14.75	GGC 22.70	WWH 19.82	DI 43.95	PG 151.82	TRW 107.83	TSK 13.50	ROAD 26.85	MOT 14.85
BSPT 19.95	WLP 24.40	PEG 19.73	WX 17.62	GRA 15.08	SBL 22.38	BLT 20.35	GTE 46.87	HON 152.07	HPC 107.95	ABX 13.55	YELL 26.95	KMAG 15.32
FON 20.02	MHP 24.87	APB 20.12	KM 18.10	AXP 16.05	GY 23.93	CCI 20.75	NEM 47.98	TRW 152.40	PCO 108.25	CCR 14.55	TCOMA 27.22	LLTC 15.52
GABGX 20.15	AMRMX 24.97	MRO 21.22	AHM 18.50	NEM 16.08	GWW 24.27	S 20.87	W 49.57	PCO 152.97	FWC 109.10	MAT 15.82	BSET 27.33	FINL 16.10
FDC 20.93	FOCPX 25.25	IRL 21.28	MCHP 18.63	BC 16.77	TJX 25.13	SRSPX 21.03	AMR 49.63	CAT 153.58	CAT 109.28	SRSPX 16.45	PCAR 27.33	GLW 16.17
CCH 20.95	CS 25.42	INTV 22.35	TRCD 18.63	SRFSX 17.03	GM 25.42	MAT 22.25	FOE 50.43	FKREX 157.45	PG 109.35	WTEC 16.78	USFC 27.68	EC 16.47
PRGFX 21.12	FSAVX 25.78	LU 22.87	MF 19.20	AVP 17.13	INEL 25.88	GTE 22.38	CHA 53.63	MTC 157.45	HON 109.45	GAS 16.80	MUS 28.05	TTX 16.50
EK 22.03	FSPFX 25.78	HAE 23.50	GD 19.27	FINL 17.25	HDI 26.02	CLX 23.17	IP 58.27	DE 157.85	FKREX 111.90	LA 17.75	LA 28.92	FMC 16.63
AALR 22.38	FSHCX 25.78	WX 24.47	LSTR 19.37	DEX 17.82	BOC 26.08	BCR 23.23	CSK 64.83	BNL 159.08	MTC 111.90	RBK 18.00	RYOCX 30.05	KLM 17.33
CATP 22.65	FSRBX 26.03	CHCLX 25.73	SIII 19.37	FDEQX 18.52	TTF 26.10	AET 23.67	CBE 64.83	BMY 160.13	DE 112.57	FDCAX 18.37	CYCH 30.83	SRSPX 17.63
YHOO 22.92	FBMPX 26.03	LRCX 26.35	WALL 19.47	KT 18.57	RCM 26.40	MHS 25.23	PFE 65.12	AN 161.92	BNL 113.67	AEP 18.55	GP 30.97	KM 17.80
MYL 24.37	FSNGX 26.65	FBS 26.47	AVID 19.98	BGEN 19.57	HERB 26.82	NEM 25.27	CNG 68.12	UTX 162.13	BMY 114.30	CCE 18.63	RDA 31.63	AHM 18.62
SANM 24.60	FORMF 26.65	FDLSX 26.65	INTU 19.98	PHII 20.02	BBY 28.27	GPC 25.40	WX 71.87	BA 164.20	AN 115.42	PZL 19.15	CSCO 33.17	DREVX 18.82
PESC 27.27	MSFT 27.18	FSDAX 26.67	GLW 20.97	KRAGX 20.03	MXIM 28.37	CEN 25.42	GLW 72.45	KKTWX 164.45	BS 115.48	UNM 19.43	WFC 33.88	CS 19.00
DAL 27.33	P 27.97	TBY 27.28	CCK 21.73	CCR 20.30	GNE 28.77	W 25.52	EMR 73.07		UTX 115.53	KT 20.20	TTF 33.90	SPW 19.90
IAD 27.55	HRS 29.80	TMX 27.33		FSDCX 21.02	RNBO 28.88	JPM 26.43	JNJ 73.12		ABT 116.80	DEX 20.25	ABS 35.38	DD 19.95

Sun	Moon	Mercury	Venus	Mars	Jupiter	Saturn	Uranus	Neptune	Pluto	Node	Asc	MC
BUD 28.72	JCI 29.85	HSBA 28.33	KMB 21.73	FSCPX 21.02	BAA 28.90	FOE 26.97	MMM 73.98	BS 165.60	BA 116.80	TAN 20.88	AR 35.52	WMB 20.55
HD 29.68	FLCSX 30.97	AZO 28.75	PD 21.73	PRSGX 21.02	GD 29.23	AMR 27.95	JCP 74.18	DOW 166.42	MEA 116.87	CHPS 20.97	IIF 36.12	GE 22.08
PHII 29.77	SSW 32.55	JAMRX 29.35	NPR 22.05	BBBY 23.25	SWZ 29.73	MAS 30.72	PPG 75.02	RNK 166.60	KKTWX 116.95	SII 21.00	WMS 37.02	ALL 22.18
AVP 30.55	KRB 33.17	ZE 29.40	PWG 22.05	NCDI 23.25	N 30.48	BT 32.07	CMZ 75.07	VO 166.68	SGRFX 117.17	PE 21.08	ARC 38.52	KEY 22.23
AL 31.23	OII 33.60	SRM 29.55	GRA 22.13	ASND 24.45	NME 31.20	PCH 32.40	MRK 76.15	MEA 166.77	OM 117.45	APC 21.33	LIZ 38.75	WEN 22.80
FSNGX 31.45	HFX 33.97	K 29.62	PLN 22.50	JANSX 24.67	AVP 32.02	RAD 32.53	MOT 76.43	ABT 167.78	DOW 117.47	FSHOX 21.45	LGN 38.88	HLT 24.35
FORMF 31.45	BTR 34.20	THDO 31.25	JPM 22.82	GACC 25.70	EMC 33.02	WFC 33.28	HLT 76.95	CR 168.13	RNK 117.63	FSCGX 21.45	INDQA 39.07	NCDI 24.53
GTE 31.58	IF 37.75	AMZN 31.25	GE 22.97	DREQX 26.07	NTAIF 34.37	ABS 33.35	MST 78.88	BDK 168.48	CHCLX 117.92	FSDPX 21.45	NAV 39.07	BBBY 24.58
ORBI 33.13	RNBO 38.15	HUM 31.40	GIS 23.37	ARRO 26.23	MHP 34.55	KBH 33.60	HNZ 80.38	CHCLX 168.57	HI 117.93	FSRFX 21.45	TXU 39.13	KBH 24.80
CMZ 33.82	SYMBA 38.45	FON 31.43	MXIM 23.37	ROAD 26.73	ALTR 35.05	CMB 34.37	TR 81.15	SGRFX 168.60	BDK 118.28	CNC 21.70	IBM 40.02	KSWS 25.10
APB 33.85	BMY 38.58	HD 33.98	KBH 23.90	YELL 26.73	BZF 35.05	JANSX 34.68	AHP 81.30	OM 168.62	CR 118.73	IFMX 21.70	TRW 40.80	AL 26.47
GD 35.33	MB 42.73	AXP 35.57	IFF 24.40	GIC 26.97	CHA 37.43	JP 34.78	ATTr 81.30	HI 168.97	GTE 118.75	CA 22.40	MHP 41.15	MKS 26.58
PLN 35.58	LTR 43.38	PRGFX 35.93	ABT 24.72	ABF 27.45	EK 37.98	UNP 35.87	PCG 81.50	AMR 170.57	AMR 119.23	KWP 22.40	CSK 41.67	CLE 27.02
UCL 35.77	MU 43.60	GTW 36.37	CLE 24.92	BLL 28.15	GMT 41.15	UNVGX 36.07	ENE 82.10	GTE 170.95	DI 119.92	LMS 22.48	ATTn 42.10	UIS 27.27
JAVLX 36.28	LIZ 43.88	GLW 36.53	BNI 25.32	PMS 28.60	GLK 41.15	AHC 36.13	FKGRX 82.55	DI 173.30	NEM 120.72	ADBE 23.93	TELC 42.10	FKREX 27.57
GLK 36.53	SDTI 44.53	GIS 36.57	ZEN 25.38	FORE 30.48	WAG 41.63	DRLEX 36.13	TXT 83.72	FOE 174.65	W 121.67	TEN 24.17	CCM 42.47	MTC 27.63
RGEN 38.93	BS 45.12	KM 36.67	OXY 25.55	DGN 31.38	FCX 43.30	BP 37.15	HSY 83.90	IP 175.00	FOE 122.83	GER 25.30	SCHL 44.12	DNB 27.95
SRYIX 39.00	BSC 45.52	MRK 36.93	GNE 25.68	WMX 31.43	TRV 44.73	BNI 37.97	ED 86.10	W 175.15	IP 122.92	TOL 25.42	IDTI 44.80	TMB 28.25
FFIDX 39.48	CHIR 46.30	EK 37.42	ENG 26.00	XCOM 32.87	DUK 45.10	UAL 38.62	DCN 86.57	NEM 175.27	CHA 123.00	AGWFX 25.45	WIN 45.93	CRUS 28.47
GIS 39.97	BKB 46.48	DREVX 37.52	FMCSX 26.05	PZL 33.42	GRA 45.45	DH 38.65	GP 86.60	CHA 177.42	CSK 124.22	GLM 25.45	TSK 47.15	ARRO 28.75
CHCLX 40.53	WX 46.77	AL 37.82	ALL 28.13	ABX 33.60	AT 45.52	PSON 38.90	UBIS 86.80	CNG 182.95	CBE 127.18	X 25.78	ITA 47.48	NSC 28.80
PEG 40.88	BA 47.43	PFS 37.92	DAL 28.13	LOR 33.62	UCM 46.22	CHA 39.42	HAL 88.27	EMR 183.20	PFE 127.85	FSAVX 26.27	ELY 48.22	BCC 28.92
CG 41.08	CPC 47.72	SRYIX 38.00	AL 28.85	REY 34.10	PH 46.27	SGP 45.70	VLIFX 90.40	CSK 183.82	WX 128.02	FSPFX 26.27	QLGC 50.13	PCL 29.12
FMAGX 41.45	MDR 48.08	YHOO 38.38	HWP 28.90	TSK 34.13	AWSHX 47.78	BKB 45.82	AMRMX 90.97	GLW 183.82	CNG 128.13	FSHCX 26.27	AMRMX 50.53	MAIL 29.22
NOB 41.60	FDO 48.58	IAD 38.45	CMB 29.58	MOB 34.58	RTN 48.45	LTR 45.95	PRGFX 91.05	CBE 183.88	EMR 128.72	FBMPX 26.27	MXIM 50.83	GIC 29.78
GOSHA 42.10	PHII 49.20	SOTA 38.70	F 29.68	PX 37.25	HOU 50.93	BSET 46.05	PFE 91.42	JNJ 183.93	CMZ 129.35	FSRBX 26.27	IF 51.40	MAT 30.23
JAMRX 43.12	USG 49.23	FRF 39.03	HUM 30.07	TRMB 38.20	XTR 51.18	PCAR 46.05	ASH 92.10	WX 183.95	MRK 129.43	NGC 26.58	ALK 51.40	ADPT 30.25
THDO 44.08	HLT 49.32	GCI 39.28	ZLG 30.72	MO 38.73	BAC 51.40	TCOMA 46.05	AL 92.43	PFE 184.22	MOT 129.57	SCF 26.95	GNE 53.42	MXF 31.07
LRCX 44.27	DD 49.52	RTR 39.68	ONCS 31.57	SBRY 39.20	CCK 51.62	ALEX 47.58	AEP 93.63	MST 185.90	HLT 129.62	ADPT 27.27	GABAX 53.95	XLNX 31.32
TIF 44.53	TR 49.80	KLM 40.47	NELL 32.52	MOLXA 41.60	KMB 52.07	AGREA 47.58	SO 94.35	HLT 185.93	JNJ 129.75	MAIL 27.32	FCYCF 54.37	NB 31.57
CNF 44.85	FSLEX 50.12	AVP 40.87	LRCX 32.92	MTSI 41.78	PD 52.07	DEC 47.58	TXU 95.00	MOT 186.05	MST 129.80	DCN 27.38	FNATF 54.37	NWK 31.57
MAS 44.88	CMSB 50.38	AALR 41.77	NSC 33.15	BP 42.23	HELE 53.17	ASC 48.57	OAT 95.77	MRK 186.12	MMM 130.47	FMC 27.95	NPR 54.77	CMB 32.05
FCX 45.27	JTAX 50.38	TTX 42.23	RR 33.42	PCG 42.32	SNF 54.10	FLE 48.98	CL 96.47	CMZ 186.55	JCP 131.02	LLTC 28.02	PWG 54.77	PCG 32.33
UST 45.50	USWI 50.38	TIF 42.33	BGEN 33.90	DRAI 43.08	AKLM 54.30	CQB 49.17	P 96.98	TR 186.87	PCG 131.15	NWS 28.43	APA 55.10	BABSX 34.47
MRO 46.50	TXU 51.40	GLK 43.40	CUAC 35.68	RTK 43.60	DELL 54.30	AUD 49.23	DREVX 97.40	ENE 188.03	PPG 131.40	BASS 28.80	SUNW 55.30	WBN 34.63
FBS 47.18	GD 51.52	CG 43.90	AL 36.08	TX 44.53	DJ 54.45	LLY 49.92	AA 97.47	PCG 188.08	ENE 131.55	LAD.B 29.07	ABX 55.78	ACCOB 35.67
LOR 47.27	FDEGX 51.98	UST 44.48	FBS 36.08	LA 45.17	CQ 56.07	FDESX 50.00	WLA 98.45	PPG 188.47	TR 131.62	PEG 29.43	SII 56.53	JP 36.13
ASH 47.40	PD 52.28	BSX 45.03	FDLSX 37.83	NB 45.45	CUM 56.07	IP 53.62	GR 98.87	MMM 188.62	CG 131.87	GP 29.45	LSTR 56.83	SCF 36.38
MF 47.43	PZL 52.50	ICII 45.03	FSDAX 37.87	UCL 45.45	REY 56.15	HUM 56.08	GY 99.38	JCP 188.62	FKGRX 132.57	RGEN 29.55	BS 57.47	AMR 36.40
INTV 47.92	ENE 52.97	AHM 45.83	KSWS 38.32	LUV 45.77	EIX 56.17	DREQX 59.60	SLE 100.18	AHP 189.47	ED 132.68	MYL 30.33	JANSX 58.32	STK 36.68
FDLSX 48.13	CCK 52.97	PESC 45.90	TBY 40.32	PWJ 46.37	APCC 56.37	ROAD 59.60	WIN 100.25	ATTr 189.47	AHP 133.28	ONCS 30.92	SNA 58.48	LTD 37.00
FSDAX 48.15	KMB 52.97	MOT 46.38	LTD 42.47	BNI 46.70	FDEQX 56.95	YELL 59.60	GD 100.55	HSY 190.00	ATTr 133.33	MS 31.60	GRA 58.55	AA 37.50
KMB 48.43	IAD 53.23	KEY 46.58	NOC 42.63	GAP 46.75	LA 57.08	CTX 60.62	BTR 103.77	ED 190.22	HNZ 133.33	MSFT 32.03	DSPC 58.70	SFA 37.73
PD 48.43	CTX 53.60	DAL 46.62	MD 42.97	ASA 47.53	GPS 57.20	BFI 61.47	GRA 104.67	HNZ 190.23	UBIS 133.33	ORCL 32.08	TAN 58.98	ETP 37.82
HAE 49.40	APSO 54.03	ORBI 47.52	UNP 43.37	MYG 48.42	SFL 58.40	UH 62.55	AWSHX 105.72	UBIS 190.45	HSY 134.07	SUNW 32.50	NFB 59.03	XCOM 37.95
TBY 50.08	CPLY 54.27	ASPX 47.57	KMAG 43.43	VWUSX 49.45	BST 59.37	DRTHX 62.57	GMT 106.12	CG 190.85	DCN 134.22	GABAX 32.57	CB 60.33	ACV 38.12
WX 50.50	BLT 54.70	UIS 48.27	EK 43.85	EC 49.55	TWN 59.40	OLOG 65.10	WAG 107.38	FKGRX 191.65	TXT 134.48	FFIDX 32.62	UK 60.40	PESPX 38.15
FRF 50.60	FLE 54.90	MF 48.82	OREM 44.27	ENE 49.55	VAR 59.90	NOBE 65.70	RTN 107.87	HAL 191.98	GP 134.67	ITA 32.83	VLIFX 60.53	MB 38.43
K 51.01	PCL 55.10	PHII 49.13	MYL 45.13	SFA 49.78	PURT 60.60	WTHG 66.38	UCM 108.47	PE 192.53	HAL 135.30	INDQA 33.15	ABT 60.80	GACC 38.73
ASPX 51.83	CAG 55.68	AL 49.25	XLNX 45.33	GWW 50.83	CNF 61.80	EVGRX 66.38	TXN 112.75	TXT 192.85	ASH 135.47	NAV 33.15	IFF 62.52	OREM 38.95
TMX 53.27	INGR 55.80	HFX 49.33	AHC 46.32	NOB 52.93	NVLS 62.93	SUN 66.50	RD 113.63	AEP 193.62	PRGFX 135.80	FO 35.73	S 62.62	ICST 39.15
MRK 54.12	KELYA#1 55.80	CUAC 49.45	DRLEX 46.32	LUNR 53.48	BMCS 63.12	FSR 66.50	CCH 113.63	DCN 194.25	FCNTX 135.83	GLN 35.73	RLM 62.77	WWH 40.05
	DSPC 56.83	TMB 49.80	MKS 46.60	ABCW	63.23	GCI 68.32	CPB 117.00	AL 194.75		SOPFX 35.85	OXY 63.68	CCC 40.22
		RTK 51.57		S		NSM 74.30		SO 194.78		FCNTX 36.08		IDXX 40.22

Sun	Moon	Mercury	Venus	Mars	Jupiter	Saturn	Uranus	Neptune	Pluto	Node	Asc	MC
BAX 54.48	CCR 57.55	KSWS 52.23	MSX 46.87	EQ 53.63	IGF 63.23	ITW 74.37	HRS 117.50	P 194.98	AL 136.03	TRW 36.58	ECH 63.87	CC 40.85
AMZN 54.75	BT 58.12	MER 53.17	CHV 47.18	WEN 53.80	ORX 63.82	OPPSX 74.47	F 118.57	GP 195.03	VLIFX 136.47	FSAIX 36.63	ORA 64.03	SNF 40.93
SRM 55.18	IIF 58.20	UCL 54.35	EMC 47.65	RTZ 55.17	BGG 65.07	CMCSA 75.12	SCDUX 120.88	ASH 195.17	AMRMX 136.63	FBIOX 36.63	VCI 64.27	FLCSX 41.18
PFS 55.42	PWJ 58.33	NOB 55.52	AZO 47.68	VJET 56.11	CY 65.25	NUE 75.23	WHR 121.00	PRGFX 195.85	AEP 136.90	FSESX 36.63	ORCL 64.87	AKLM 41.88
ASND 55.45	TMX 58.43	GE 55.85	FTRNX 47.85	FDEGX 57.85	ACN 65.45	LPX 75.62	UCC 121.88	SLE 196.78	DREVX 137.55	FSVLX 36.63	AVID 65.12	DELL 41.93
BT 55.52	CHCLX 58.93	NWS 56.22	DOW 48.85	BLUEX 58.27	HPC 66.30	WWY 75.78	DAL 122.88	WLA 196.78	P 137.63	FSPCX 36.63	INTU 65.13	RTZ 42.17
FCNTX 55.98	BBY 58.97	ASH 56.55	WMB 49.50	INFS 58.42	PCO 66.45	WMT 79.30	KLM 123.65	AA 196.83	SO 137.72	FSRPX 36.63	STAR 65.50	ENE 42.45
ZLG 56.18	ATTo 59.10	LOR 58.10	LUV 50.55	TWCGX 59.30	IP 66.47	CSK 79.70	LIT 127.28	VLIFX 196.88	AA 137.83	IAF 36.85	MSFT 65.92	SYMC 42.63
MER 56.52	OLOG 59.12	PCL 58.43	CNF 50.98	DDS 59.37	TRW 66.68	CBE 79.77	ZE 127.62	AMRMX 197.05	WLA 137.97	BRWIX 36.85	EPG 66.62	MSX 42.67
HUM 56.98	AR 59.25	CRUS 58.82	PCG 51.15	MXF 59.55	BCC 69.43	MER 80.43	FTRNX 129.17	DREVX 197.07	SLE 138.50	CPQ 36.95	JOF 67.08	DDS 42.70
AXP 57.50	MDA 59.67	CS 58.97	BSX 52.03	JAVLX 60.15	AXP 69.75	AMAT 80.50	SRFSX 129.93	GR 197.85	TXU 138.52	MXP 36.95	ENG 68.00	FTRNX 42.78
GCI 57.72	FBGRX 60.02	FFIDX 59.55	ICII 52.03	CCH 60.45	CAT 71.50	PFE 80.72	CAR 131.37	AWSHX 199.18	OAT 139.05	HAL 37.13	F 68.13	DUK 43.32
NELL 58.05	AGN 60.73	FMAGX 59.78	NB 52.52	BHI 60.58	ACV 71.53	DNB 82.33	PRD 131.60	TXU 199.38	GD 139.10	PCO 37.75	LMT 69.05	NGC 43.42
BSX 58.82	EMC 61.75	NWK 60.10	MB 53.57	KRB 60.58	FWC 74.25	CNG 86.35	DIS 131.65	CL 199.50	GY 139.27	BSC 39.18	WALL 69.58	AMGN 43.77
ICII 58.82	SYQT 61.90	XLNX 60.85	SRSPX 53.72	SEL 60.78	PG 75.55	PWJ 88.42	MD 132.40	OAT 199.53	CL 139.33	UBIS 40.50	RMDY 70.13	PX 43.97
MOT 58.93	FFIDX 62.05	BCC 60.88	NTAIF 53.88	Z 60.80	HON 76.00	DGN 90.80	K 132.45	GD 199.92	GR 139.75	CAT 40.50	HSBA 70.58	TJX 44.17
NWS 59.23	IRL 62.33	FCX 61.37	CMZ 54.10	TDM 61.27	CS 76.47	BLL 91.72	MYG 132.95	BTR 200.35	WIN 140.13	ALD 41.30	DEX 72.55	ALMI 44.25
RTK 59.57	AXP 62.55	CLE 61.62	TRBCX 54.18	DRTHX 61.60	PCL 76.93	SBRY 93.60	RLM 133.17	RTN 200.40	AWSHX 140.78	ED 41.68	MCHP 72.78	WLA 44.52
GLW 60.13	LA 62.90	WBN 62.02	HSBA 54.47	IAD 61.72	EGG 77.18	WMX 94.68	BABSX 133.27	GY 200.52	BTR 141.52	LQJN 42.73	TRCD 72.78	ANL 44.97
EC 60.42	GP 63.35	FCNTX 63.12	DRTHX 54.55	XRX 61.72	FFIDX 77.23	OREM 96.02	RBD 133.90	WIN 201.52	GRA 141.65	HTCH 43.15	LNCR 73.13	Z 45.35
TTX 60.45	LUNR 63.45	JP 63.47	IK 55.00	CPC 62.00	KM 78.45	WX 96.07	CPC 135.05	UCM 202.25	RTN 142.18	FSLBX 43.15	KT 73.60	ANDW 45.48
KLM 61.20	TWX 64.52	FINL 63.63	AMR 55.35	DREVX 62.08	CRUS 78.55	GLW 98.67	VWUSX 135.48	TXN 203.05	GMT 142.67	FSCHX 44.05	ITW 74.42	CORR 46.13
GTW 61.48	PPG 64.95	AA 64.05	FKGRX 55.90	TOY 62.50	LUV 79.00	EMR 98.80	GAP 136.12	RD 203.35	WAG 143.15	FDCPX 44.05	MS 74.57	SPYG 46.15
SRSPX 61.52	BAX 65.10	CMB 64.33	ALTR 56.92	ENP 62.55	NWK 79.25	JNJ 100.10	TWCGX 136.15	WAG 203.45	UCM 143.18	FSELX 44.05	BHI 75.17	NOC 46.25
KM 61.62	GTE 67.77	AMGN 64.47	BZF 56.92	CYGN 62.77	WBN 79.95	AR 100.30	ASA 136.23	GRA 203.58	RD 143.80	FDFAX 44.05	MO 75.57	UNP 47.12
SOTA 61.93	ERTS 67.88	HLT 65.25	BGG 57.52	RN 63.08	DDS 81.78	ACCOB 107.97	AMP 141.08	GMT 203.87	TXN 144.28	FSCSX 44.05	ASC 75.95	RNK 47.17
AHM 62.38	FIDSX 67.95	MAS 65.88	RTR 58.45	GABGX 63.27	SYMC 81.78	STK 108.08	BAX 141.40	HRS 205.47	CCH 144.45	CG 44.38	PURT 75.98	VJET 47.38
DREVX 62.60	FSUTX 67.95	LTD 67.03	ORA 58.72	MU 64.32	FSLEX 83.17	CMZ 109.07	HWP 142.42	WHR 206.62	HRS 145.32	HON 44.42	TDM 76.18	ED 48.13
FORE 63.15	SBL 69.65	UNP 67.12	LCOS 59.00	GOSHA 64.38	KRAGX 84.83	ABF 110.18	SB 142.92	CCH 207.03	SCDUX 146.68	PG 44.78	EMC 76.20	BGY 48.23
DD 63.55	KELYA 71.20	KBH 67.75	RNK 59.45	WDC 64.72	ANL 86.02	MRK 110.67	CHV 143.00	CPB 207.62	CPB 146.75	SNS 44.88	OPPSX 76.40	FSDCX 48.33
RTR 64.28	XON 72.83	CCK 68.93	SFA 59.80	HMSY 64.72	SNA 86.17	MOT 111.13	R 143.60	UCC 207.65	F 146.90	FWC 45.53	GTF 76.65	FSCPX 48.33
GE 65.52	ETP 73.05	KMB 68.93	FFIDX 60.08	PFE 65.20	TXN 86.17	MMM 111.23	LTV 143.80	SCDUX 207.68	UCC 147.10	FKGRX 46.02	AADV 78.25	PRSGX 48.33
KEY 65.72	AVT 73.23	PD 68.93	LU 60.92	CHCLX 65.38	CGNX 87.82	JCP 111.73	AVT 145.42	LIT 209.92	WHR 147.25	NOC 46.17	COT 78.25	RBD 48.52
WEN 66.18	MMM 74.03	AHC 69.65	CTEA 61.67	CREAF 65.90	AGN 89.28	HLT 112.03	PKN 145.73	F 210.08	KLM 147.97	CLE 47.18	HWP 78.40	FSLEX 48.57
KMAG 66.70	CNC 74.07	DRLEX 69.65	CHCLX 61.97	PURT 66.87	MCIC 89.77	PPG 113.42	RTZ 147.87	KLM 210.43	DAL 148.03	AHM 47.60	BSPT 78.98	INEL 49.08
LLTC 66.92	IFMX 74.07	BAX 69.73	CYRK 62.77	MUS 67.25	IF 90.83	GWW 114.30	XRX 148.33	DAL 211.33	LIT 149.38	TTX 47.70	GABGX 79.12	FSAVX 49.28
FINL 67.45	IBM 74.12	DDS 70.03	FINL 63.08	KEY 67.53	CSCO 90.90	MST 115.90	SLB 149.15	SRFSX 212.05	FTRNX 150.10	HPC 48.12	DCN 79.30	FSPFX 49.28
HLT 67.58	VCI 74.87	SYMC 70.03	ENE 63.27	CDN 67.57	RDA 90.93	NME 116.03	RAL 149.98	FTRNX 212.22	ZE 150.15	INTV 48.40	FDC 79.98	FSHCX 49.28
FMC 67.88	ACCOB 75.60	NSC 70.55	RGEN 63.38	BNYN 67.90	NFB 91.00	KAB 118.83	APD 150.32	CAR 212.22	SRFSX 150.40	BGG 48.45	AALR 81.43	FSRBX 49.28
KBH 68.02	AW 75.70	FLCSX 70.88	HPC 63.57	INTV 68.45	JCI 91.20	GM 119.28	FMAGX 151.17	MYG 212.38	K 151.67	GOSHA 48.72	SSW 81.60	TRBCX 49.57
AL 69.53	TW 75.70	TRV 71.23	SRYIX 64.02	ALMI 68.77	JOF 91.32	CAG 120.15	FON 151.52	PRD 212.70	BABSX 151.83	JAVLX 49.03	CATP 81.62	IP 49.85
CLE 70.05	WY 75.70	BT 71.95	FSDCX 65.40	SRSPX 69.78	SGI 91.35	BOC 120.25	ECH 152.82	DIS 213.00	CAR 151.87	MDA 50.92	YHOO 81.88	MTSI 49.87
CS 70.07	BUD 76.18	NELL 71.95	FSCPX 65.40	RLM 69.85	MNTR 91.77	RDC 121.93	TNB 152.97	CPC 213.55	MYG 151.87	TXT 51.32	NTAIF 82.15	DRLEX 50.00
UIS 70.28	DNB 76.52	ASND 72.80	PRSGX 65.40	LIZ 70.05	GTF 91.95	TR 122.13	HM 153.60	ZE 214.00	RBD 152.05	CCK 51.47	FMCSX 82.60	AHC 50.05
FKREX 70.60	LHP 76.63	DUK 72.87	SRFSX 65.45	3I 70.10	SSW 92.40	BAC 122.63	TOMK 155.27	RBD 214.33	MD 152.10	KMB 51.47	COMS 82.73	HDI 50.07
MTC 70.60	HLYW 76.87	MB 73.05	PEG 65.82	CBE 70.55	IRL 92.60	NT 122.95	AVP 156.15	BABSX 214.55	PRD 152.10	PD 51.47	BGEN 82.97	IK 50.47
ZEN 70.82	MCLL 76.87	RR 73.40	AMZN 65.97	FDSSX 71.23	AALR 94.13	HELE 123.62	DUK 156.43	TWCGX 214.63	DIS 152.20	MCD 52.82	IRL 83.53	3I 50.65
DNB 70.92	KMAG 77.17	SCDUX 73.52	UIS 66.13	CSK 71.88	MDT 94.83	DJ 124.50	Z 156.50	K 215.17	RLM 152.73	LGN 52.90	SANM 83.53	EIX 50.75
TMB 71.25	GEMS 77.65	LLTC 73.68	MER 66.43	MEF 72.28	PESC 94.83	PCG 125.33	BDX 157.33	ASA 215.97	CPC 153.20	NOVL 54.27	BP 83.98	DRAI 50.83
WMB 71.50	IP 77.77	SPYG 73.85	TMB 67.35	JEQ 72.47	ORBI 95.73	ENE 126.37	OXY 157.80	GAP 216.17	TWCGX 153.90	USG 55.07	ALTR 84.93	CHV 50.97
NSC 71.70	USFC 78.68	FKREX 75.32	YHOO 68.23	APB 72.57	OST 96.48	GPS 126.68	IFF 157.85	MD 216.27	VWUSX 154.00	FOCPX 55.17	XIRC 84.97	APCC 51.77
BCC 71.80		MTC 75.32	MAT 68.45	AW 72.73	SRA 96.75	AHP 128.57	TEK 159.78	VWUSX 216.67	GAP 154.22	BVALX 55.70	BZF 85.02	DOW 52.73
HFX 71.80		FMC 75.82	MCD 70.77	CESH 74.43	SVT 97.05	ATT(R) 128.57	WY 160.03	RLM 216.80	ASA 154.23	ASTA 55.75	AL 85.05	SCDUX 53.07
		ABF 75.97	KLM 71.22	AVY 74.48	JEC 97.40	HNZ 128.85		SB 217.05	BAX 155.55	CMH 55.80	ALBK 85.98	ABF 53.50

Sun	Moon	Mercury	Venus	Mars	Jupiter	Saturn	Uranus	Neptune	Pluto	Node	Asc	MC
PCL 72.00	TTX 79.18	ZLG 76.50	HLYW 71.53	NKE 74.48	AW 97.82	KM 129.30	CNF 160.77	R 217.38	CHV 155.92	MHP 55.90	XON 86.05	LUV 53.98
ALL 72.98	TCH 80.30	Z 76.92	MCLL 71.53	AA 74.68	TW 97.82	AXP 131.17	BCC 160.80	LTV 217.52	AMP 156.12	HSY 56.30	PESC 86.18	BAC 55.18
MAT 73.00	TIN 81.10	WLA 78.02	EC 72.02	KAB 75.10	WY 97.82	VAR 134.65	CQ 160.82	AMP 217.60	SB 156.22	BTA 56.67	AZO 86.20	TOY 55.45
CUAC 73.43	UIS 81.12	AKLM 78.37	BBBY 72.92	CAG 75.18	TWX 97.90	HOU 134.70	CUM 160.93	CHV 218.72	R 156.35	KRAGX 57.70	LCOS 86.87	DE 55.58
MXF 73.85	TWCGX 81.23	DELL 78.37	NCDI 72.92	TTX 77.33	PMTC 98.27	LUV 134.72	ACV 160.95	BAX 219.55	HWP 156.60	GARD 57.78	ONCS 87.25	HERB 55.87
NB 74.32	XTR 81.72	RTZ 78.38	GACC 73.43	MAT 78.05	WGR 98.27	XTR 135.67	EGG 161.73	LMT#1 220.22	LTV 156.73	VPMCX 58.35	PRGFX 87.33	CTEA 56.33
CMB 74.72	IRF 82.77	IR 78.48	BUD 73.82	AHM 78.68	ERTS 98.55	CG 135.93	AT 164.47	PKN 220.37	RTZ 158.00	N 58.87	PHII 88.47	FBMPX 56.65
PCG 75.02	BSET 83.05	FSLEX 78.58	APCC 74.00	NPR 78.98	TKF 98.62	FKGRX 136.00	PH 164.80	XRX 220.75	AVT 158.03	AIG 59.52	LU 88.70	IR 56.95
BBBY 75.12	PCAR 83.05	SNF 78.58	PHII 74.08	PWG 78.98	FRF 98.80	HSY 137.95	MCD 166.22	AVT 220.82	PKN 158.13	MEL 60.05	DRTHX 90.02	CYRK 57.28
NCDI 75.12	TCOMA 83.05	BAC 78.93	EIX 74.10	DAL 79.32	CH 99.20	ED 139.25	KRAGX 166.47	RTZ 220.83	XRX 158.22	ENE 61.33	FSNGX 90.03	MST 57.35
KSWS 75.58	MYL 83.22	STK 79.33	FLCSX 74.48	WLA 79.52	CWP 99.30	TXT 142.37	JCI 167.28	HWP 221.00	LMT#1 159.20	PCG 61.87	FORMF 90.03	SRFSX 57.40
BABSX 77.03	LRCX 84.53	ACCOB 79.90	GTW 74.55	TIF 79.83	GABVX 99.48	UBIS 142.53	MDA 167.98	APD 221.43	SLB 159.48	KF 62.12	BNI 90.53	CQB 57.53
ACCOB 78.12	BGG 84.73	EIX 79.90	BGY 74.77	UST 80.48	PFS 99.75	MNTR 142.72	FCNTX 170.33	TNB 221.83	FMAGX 159.63	S 62.50	MD 91.12	X 58.00
JP 78.53	MANU 84.88	ACV 80.18	CYRX 74.88	ENG 80.57	LSCC 100.63	SNA 146.20	SNS 174.07	RAL 223.17	APD 159.92	KELYA 63.65	ORBI 91.58	AGC 58.08
CRUS 78.68	WLV 84.88	APCC 80.47	UCL 75.32	MF 81.80	FPF 100.77	HAL 149.57	SRSPX 175.12	SLB 223.47	RAL 159.92	ETP 65.08	FKGRX 91.65	PMS 58.98
AMR 78.78	TJX 86.07	DOW 80.85	AVP 75.85	RDC 81.82	LSI 100.77	MCIC 150.13	LAD.B 175.38	BDX 223.87	FON 159.95	CC 65.40	NME 91.92	BAA 59.95
ARRO 78.95	RDC 86.23	BBBY 81.15	DIGI 76.32	CHRS 81.98	PGF 100.85	MDT 150.18	BASS 175.70	FMAGX 224.38	TNB 160.72	TMB 66.45	ZE 92.23	BLT 60.50
STK 79.08	JBHT 86.42	NCDI 81.15	TLAB 76.47	AMGN 82.07	RD 102.85	DCN 150.90	KT 177.40	TOMK 224.77	ECH 160.82	UIS 66.50	APB 92.30	KLU 60.65
LTD 79.37	MWHS 86.75	BGG 81.77	AGC 76.62	CNG 82.23	MCD 103.10	PE 153.75	DEX 177.45	FON 224.95	DUK 161.75	RTR 66.83	CI 92.40	SSPE 60.65
MAIL 79.38	DIGI 87.32	EC 82.20	AKLM 76.77	SB 82.63	CUAC 103.50	GP 153.90	CEN 177.55	Z 225.43	AVP 161.78	JCI 66.97	JPM 92.53	UBIS 60.97
AA 79.83	PPP 87.32	FTRNX 82.30	DELL 76.77	BGY 82.90	KSWS 103.98	XON 156.28	GPC 177.62	DUK 225.48	TOMK 161.85	TBY 67.62	PZL 92.75	BGG 61.27
GIC 79.90	SRM 88.32	NB 82.38	SNF 77.25	MHP 82.90	XLNX 105.25	NB 157.70	MHS 177.95	CQ 225.57	BDX 162.17	FSDAX 67.72	PLN 93.82	MCD 61.30
SFA 80.05	UCM 88.32	AMR 82.75	TJX 77.48	CLE 84.08	MB 106.77	SFA 158.00	TAN 177.95	ECH 225.60	OXY 162.62	FDLSX 67.72	ADI 93.85	UH 62.03
ADPT 80.33	STAR 88.65	BABSX 83.67	ARRO 77.83	MD 84.58	FSDCX 108.98	ADI 158.17	SII 178.03	CUM 225.62	IFF 162.93	FBS 67.78	WWY 94.32	EGG 62.47
ACV 80.42	FWC 88.77	SRSPX 84.00	ACAI 78.23	PE 84.82	FSCPX 108.98	TOY 159.22	GLM 178.63	WY 226.43	ACV 162.97	LRCX 67.93	GY 94.40	CHRS 62.58
OREM 81.22	STK 89.22	DNB 85.07	CMCSA 78.32	MCD 86.25	PRSGX 108.98	ARC 159.42	AGWFX 178.78	AVP 226.92	CNF 163.77	COMS 70.27	GLK 94.73	HELE 62.78
XLNX 81.32	MOMGX 89.57	FORE 85.15	NUE 78.43	FSENX 87.43	GACC 110.48	AEP 159.47	LMS 178.92	EGG 227.38	CQ 163.78	GIS 71.27	KRAGX 94.87	C 63.12
NWK 81.55	SPYG 90.28	DD 85.98	PMS 78.50	FSPHX 87.43	CCH 110.92	CTL 160.75	TEN 179.20	TEK 227.42	TEK 164.07	CB 71.37	HD 95.27	TOL 64.60
WBN 84.42	FOE 90.75	CHRS 86.72	GIC 79.07	FSPTX 87.43	MDA 111.07	FO#1 160.75	AET 179.75	OXY 227.78	CUM 164.08	HNZ 71.97	RGEN 96.88	HLYW 64.83
ENE 84.58	RTK 91.63	KMAG 87.62	WEN 79.37	NELL 88.98	PMS 111.43	PEP 161.65	CMB 179.87	ACV 227.80	EGG 164.13	IDTI 72.02	SRYIX 96.88	MCLL 64.83
FTRNX 84.92	GARD 91.87	SPW 87.98	WNDR 79.37	RR 89.20	TRMB 114.35	ASH 162.62	JP 179.87	IFF 227.80	WY 164.15	EGG 72.10	PEG 98.53	LLY 65.08
MKS 85.37	SWZ 92.08	CC 88.45	IR 79.53	MNTR 89.48	MOLXA 115.02	PPP 162.70	KBH 179.90	BCC 228.02	AT 164.20	ATTn 72.12	FON 99.85	ABCW 65.12
DUK 85.43	ONE 92.33	ZEN 88.52	MRK 79.65	AZO 89.75	CPB 118.78	AL 162.80	UNP 179.95	JCI 228.60	MCD 166.08	TELC 72.12	JAMRX 100.50	SLE 65.65
AMGN 85.82	KF 92.62	WEN 88.98	GLK 79.80	N 89.78	ADI 119.12	SO 163.53	AHC 179.98	PH 228.65	PH 166.20	LIFE 72.80	UCL 100.60	FDESX 65.97
SCF 86.07	RNK 93.15	HPC 89.57	SPYG 80.58	LTV 89.85	FCNTX 119.12	PRGFX 163.53	DRLEX 179.98	CNF 228.75	KRAGX 166.32	AHP 73.35	CCH 100.63	EQ 66.05
ALMI 86.27	CTR 93.22	ARRO 89.58	FKREX 81.48	NT 91.25	LUNR 119.20	ASSD 163.90	BT 180.13	MDA 229.43	MDA 166.47	ATTr 73.35	JAVLX 100.97	GER 66.47
WLA 86.53	ADI 94.42	HRS 89.97	MTC 81.48	HSBA 92.55	AZO 123.55	FDX 163.92	BCR 180.13	MCD 229.60	JCI 167.17	ACV 73.42	THDO 101.33	DIGI 66.55
SPW 86.58	TMB 94.57	XRX 90.43	RYAN 81.50	GCI 92.82	HSBA 123.67	PRU 163.92	CLX 180.18	AT 229.72	FCNTX 167.23	DGAGX 73.60	LRCX 101.48	HPC 66.88
Z 87.33	CEN 94.92	PESPX 90.72	EGLS 81.62	FDO 93.87	ENG 123.88	FDO 163.93	MAS 180.32	KRAGX 231.73	MAT 168.02	BCC 73.90	EK 101.58	XRX 66.88
ANDW 87.47	ECH 97.13	FSENX 91.47	TOY 81.72	SLE 93.98	NPR 124.07	VLIFX 166.48	UAL 181.17	LAD.B 232.37	SRSPX 170.18	CNF 74.05	TIF 101.78	CMCSA 67.42
XCOM 87.55	SGI 97.55	FSPHX 91.47	NOB 82.22	KMAG 94.45	PWG 124.07	AMRMX 167.10	JPM 181.55	BASS 232.50	SNS 170.20	FTSE 100 74.40	FCX 102.42	TLAB 67.43
PESPX 87.78	BGEN 98.23	FDPMX 91.47	ANDW 82.32	NME 94.85	SNS 124.27	P 167.60	PSON 181.98	SNS 232.58	LAD.B 170.53	USW 74.45	UST 102.62	CYRX 67.63
MB 88.02	LAD.B 98.50	FSPTX 91.47	UCC 82.50	NOC 96.00	MRO 125.70	ANDW 170.82	CCI 182.02	FCNTX 232.90	PZL 170.93	ITT 74.55	MRO 103.47	BBY 68.12
NOC 88.22	BSPT 98.78	GIC 91.63	INEL 83.58	HWP 96.75	LIZ 125.73	BUD 171.13	CSC 183.18	CEN 233.83	BASS 171.00	TIN 75.18	MYL 103.55	HRS 68.35
ICST 88.73	CNF 99.20	MAT 91.77	ASND 84.60	WMB 97.88	CDN 126.00	AMD 171.52	DH 183.22	GPC 233.88	KT 171.12	BAY 75.90	FFIDX 103.75	CGNX 68.53
UNP 89.05	MTSI 99.68	VJET 91.85	HDI 84.80	AVT 98.08	NB 126.00	AGC 171.53	JHNGX 183.90	MHS 233.88	DEX 171.53	TWCVX 76.45	LOR 104.07	RYAN 68.88
CCC 89.68	NSM 100.07	ALL 92.40	DNB 84.83	GLBL 98.68	HAE 126.03	DIGI 172.17	MOMGX 184.00	AET 234.43	CEN 171.55	DLCH 76.57	GIS 104.22	UCC 69.17
IDXX 89.68	BABSX 100.28	CQB 92.82	CS 84.92	MATH 98.75	HRS 126.33	TLAB 172.23	SKY 184.82	GLM 234.57	GPC 171.72	JBHT 76.62	MF 104.22	DJ 69.32
ED 90.07	DLCH 100.40	LUV 92.82	UBIS 85.13	WLP 99.40	TMX 126.52	UFC 174.65	CQB 184.82	BCR 234.58	TAN 171.75	TR 77.27	CHCLX 104.62	FSENX 69.98
CC 90.33	GR 100.43	ICST 92.90	BCC 85.38	LSTR 100.47	MUS 126.55	DREVX 175.55	LLY 184.98	CLX 234.62	SII 171.87	CIR 77.72	FDLSX 104.82	FSPHX 69.98
SNF 90.38	DI 100.53	ALMI 93.00	LOR 85.43	SIII 100.57	SRM 126.77	AA 175.68	FDESX 185.00	MAT 234.67	TRB 171.92	TRB 78.10	CG 105.17	FDPMX 69.98
RBD 90.40	JR 100.62	FSDCX 93.68	FCX 85.48	KLM 101.25	SFA 127.05	WLA 175.88	UNVGX 185.90	AGWFX 234.73	ONE 171.97	ONE 79.48	FMAGX 105.40	FSPTX 69.98
FLCSX 90.67	RCHY 100.72	FSCPX 93.68	CG 85.55		PRU 127.27	IRF 176.02		SRSPX 234.98	CMB 172.42	MST 79.87	NOB 105.58	ACAI 70.42
AKLM 91.33	TLAB 100.80	PRSGX 93.68	FSLBX 85.70		FDX 127.33	TOS 176.52		TEN 235.55			HAE 105.95	

Sun	Moon	Mercury	Venus	Mars	Jupiter	Saturn	Uranus	Neptune	Pluto	Node	Asc	MC
DELL 91.33	NOC 100.88	ED 93.97	FSCHX 85.70	GNCI 101.45	CTL 127.42	JR 176.55	BNI 186.63	CCI 235.63	JP 172.42	NII 80.33	GOSHA 106.02	PE 70.68
IP 91.68	FSR 102.28	HELE 94.02	FDCPX 85.70	AVID 102.17	HMSY 127.43	BBI 176.65	BP 186.93	PSON 235.95	KBH 172.42	AT 81.05	DAL 106.05	TRMB 71.13
AHC 91.92	ALK 102.33	MXF 94.30	FSELX 85.70	INTU 102.17	WDC 127.57	KR 176.68	JANSX 187.90	UAL 235.95	BT 172.48	HLT 81.62	IAD 106.25	WNDR 71.33
DRLEX 91.92	TOT 102.40	WMB 94.53	FDFAX 85.70	MCAF 102.78	SOTA 127.72	LOW 176.72	PCH 188.42	DH 236.22	UNP 172.50	MOT 82.08	FRF 106.90	EGLS 73.18
DDS 92.05	EPG 102.72	SFA 94.57	FSCSX 85.70	GHV 102.95	FDSSX 127.90	SLE 177.02	ABS 188.43	PZL 236.22	AHC 172.53	MRK 82.35	BUD 107.22	MOLXA 73.90
SYMC 92.05	MATH 102.72	CCC 95.05	MOT 85.70	WALL 103.25	RN 128.10	DD 178.08	WFC 188.45	LMS 236.30	DRLEX 172.53	CHIR 82.55	TRV 107.30	AGN 75.03
MSX 92.08	MXF 103.02	IDXX 95.05	PCL 87.40	INTC 103.50	ASSD 128.15	DD 180.87	RAD 188.70	AHC 236.43	LMS 172.55	G 82.60	ASPX 107.93	RD 75.13
IK 92.28	K 103.17	3I 95.10	HFX 87.73	MCHP 104.13	CYGN 128.23	TXU 181.43	UH 189.58	DRLEX 236.43	MAS 172.62	PH 83.17	CNF 108.27	FSTCX 76.40
NGC 92.75	INDQA 103.22	PCG 96.50	SCDUX 88.12	TRCD 104.13	XON 128.23	KLAC 182.12	HUM 189.80	DEX 236.48	GLM 172.67	CMZ 83.47	MAS 108.35	PRGS 77.33
CHV 92.80	NAV 103.22	CHV 97.27	UAL 88.15	EGRP 104.47	MEF 128.55	OAT 182.25	NOBE 190.62	KT 236.48	AGWFX 172.73	AMGN 84.98	AVP 108.73	ENP 78.02
PX 93.27	AHM 104.05	RYAN 97.27	TRV 88.27	PKN 105.00	AW 128.85	MXF 183.00	AUD 191.52	UNP 236.50	TEN 172.87	GT 85.52	RR 108.90	KELYA 79.45
TJX 93.47	RTZ 104.05	BBY 97.58	RTK 88.30	CPLY 106.40	PPP 128.93	WEN 183.07	FLE 191.68	SII 236.53	AET 173.02	KEY 86.10	TMX 109.20	BAY 81.68
DOW 94.52	ITW 105.47	MAIL 98.65	MRO 88.32	NN 108.18	KRB 129.30	ALMI 183.17	FSR 192.25	TAN 236.53	BCR 173.23	NOB 87.42	RTK 109.52	CREAF 82.57
SCDUX 94.92	CI 106.90	UBIS 98.92	NWS 88.80	K 108.47	TOY 130.50	EC 183.17	ALEX 192.45	CSC 236.57	CLX 173.27	UCL 87.73	GTE 109.60	PSON 83.02
ABF 95.30	JAVLX 107.00	HERB 98.93	XCOM 88.88	MRO 109.05	CESH 130.55	CHRS 183.82	AGREA 192.53	JP 236.77	JPM 173.30	CUM 87.93	FBS 110.27	PCAPX 83.22
CORR 95.42	GPC 107.17	RD 99.72	MXF 89.18	CQB 109.20	AVY 130.67	FSENX 184.27	DEC 192.53	CMB 236.87	UAL 173.32	CQ 88.03	AMZN 110.38	GWW 83.25
SPYG 95.45	BAC 108.62	MKS 99.78	Z 89.50	ISL 109.65	NKE 130.67	FSPHX 184.27	BSET 193.40	KBH 237.03	PSON 173.72	JCP 89.07	ASH 110.40	FSLBX 83.73
LUV 95.80	EK 108.62	PE 99.87	UH 89.60	PSQL 109.65	BLUEX 130.93	FDPMX 184.27	PCAR 193.40	UNVGX 237.35	CCI 174.28	BGEN 89.58	SRM 110.82	FSCHX 83.73
ETP 95.85	BHI 108.82	ADPT 100.58	DD 89.85	CS 110.05	ARC 131.77	FSPTX 184.27	LTR 193.45	BT 237.40	DH 174.58	MMM 89.87	INTV 110.88	FDCPX 83.73
VJET 96.62	BCC 109.08	ETP 101.02	DUK 90.73	MDA 110.25	SPW 131.95	CSX 185.15	BKB 193.50	JHNGX 237.55	CSC 174.85	PPG 90.23	PFS 110.93	FSELX 83.73
BAC 96.98	BGY 109.10	NOC 102.07	HAE 91.68	IR 110.68	PESPX 132.18	INTC 186.15	SGP 193.57	MAS 237.68	CQB 174.87	CCM 90.93	ASND 110.97	FDFAX 83.73
TOY 97.23	DIS 110.53	OREM 102.55	CC 91.90	CENF 110.77	FDEGX 132.28	AAPL 186.58	SUN 193.57	MOMGX 237.83	LLY 175.00	ALK 91.02	FSDAX 111.02	FSCSX 83.73
DE 97.35	OM 111.02	ANL 102.78	HERB 92.13	PCL 111.32	ICST 132.37	APA 188.62	CMCSA 194.37	SKY 238.05	FDESX 175.02	U 91.33	CCK 111.33	LIT 84.48
FSDCX 97.55	MAIL 112.08	HDI 103.25	K 92.20	FMILX 111.68	CCC 132.55	BA 189.28	NUE 194.38	FDESX 238.35	SKY 175.05	Z 92.38	KMB 111.33	GPS 84.83
FSCPX 97.55	FDC 112.78	RNK 103.42	GCI 93.38	TNB 112.05	IDXX 132.55	TKR 189.68	GCI 194.68	LLY 238.37	MOMGX 175.10	DUK 92.98	PD 111.33	BNYN 85.23
PRSGX 97.55	TOS 113.20	UCC 103.70	NVLS 93.85	SNA 112.33	INFS 132.77	OPTFX 189.77	WTHG 194.70	JPM 238.43	JHNGX 175.12	FDGRX 92.98	CMZ 111.45	SDII 85.52
FSLEX 97.77	SDII 113.98	INEL 103.83	TRMB 94.12	CHIR 112.78	SEL 133.38	AWSHX 190.27	WMT 195.93	CQB 238.52	BNI 175.70	BBELL 93.77	ZLG 111.58	SYBS 85.52
INEL 98.23	SYBS 113.98	BAA 105.17	PCAPX 94.15	TJX 112.88	MU 133.58	BTR 190.63	DRTHX 196.60	PCH 239.35	BP 175.88	BMET 94.67	TBY 112.67	AWSHX 85.53
FSAVX 98.47	BTIOF 114.20	IP 105.17	FORE 94.20	MMM 113.02	CORR 133.70	INGR 190.70	OLOG 197.08	AUD 240.15	UNVGX 176.13	QNTM 95.00	TBY 112.68	AWSHX 85.53
FSPFX 98.47	DRAI 114.55	TJX 106.10	IGF 94.72	CATP 113.02	FO#1 134.40	KELYA#1 190.70	BFI 197.63	FLE 240.27	JANSX 176.52	AVP 95.57	WX 113.03	GT 86.38
FSHCX 98.47	CCE 114.58	XCOM 106.63	ED 94.78	TMX 113.07	KLU 136.70	GY 191.45	CTX 198.02	NOBE 240.30	ABS 176.92	MDR 95.83	NELL 113.18	UAL 86.38
FSRBX 98.47	OAT 115.27	CORR 107.48	CRUS 95.93	HSY 113.20	SSPE 136.70	FG 192.28	ROAD 198.23	RAD 240.53	WFC 176.93	CNTO 95.83	K 113.52	NSCP 86.40
FBMPX 98.48	GY 117.47	EGLS 108.15	TMX 96.13	SANM 113.88	PEP 137.85	IR 193.53	YELL 198.25	FSR 240.58	HUM 177.08	BEV 97.97	BSX 113.82	CHIR 86.68
IR 98.70	TXN 118.02	GACC 108.32	PX 96.42	SRM 114.22	WHR 139.75	WIN 194.43	DREQX 198.75	UH 240.65	RAD 177.18	OXY 98.05	ICII 113.82	P 86.88
TRBCX 98.77	CYRX 118.05	WNDR 108.40	ACV 96.42	LLY 114.38	FDO 140.30	RTN 194.85	AMAT 198.75	BNI 240.68	UH 177.20	IFF 98.10	NWS 114.17	NVLS 88.73
MTSI 99.00	LSI 118.22	ACAI 108.65	HLT 96.57	FDESX 115.03	PRGS 140.50	CW 195.53	DNB 199.20	ABS 240.77	PCH 177.33	MOB 98.17	GTW 115.97	GT 89.25
MST 99.12	DGAGX 118.23	DJ 108.87	HRS 96.82	JCP 115.42	CSK 141.58	LTD 195.55	MER 199.60	WFC 240.77	NOBE 177.98	OIL 99.55	MRK 116.02	BMCS 89.73
HDI 99.20	PAGE 119.13	ENE 109.22	MOLXA 97.73	CRUS 115.65	CBE 142.12	NSC 195.70	SBRY 201.33	BP 240.78	ASC 178.47	TX 100.38	BAX 116.30	IGF 89.78
SRFSX 99.22	CMCSA 119.37	SCF 109.62	FCNTX 98.25	CQ 115.88	SDII 142.47	IAD 195.93	WWY 201.33	JANSX 240.88	AUD 178.97	TEK 100.85	SOTA 116.32	ADBE 90.22
AGC 99.32	KLU 120.58	TLAB 109.72	EGRP 98.27	GEMS 115.90	SYBS 142.47	RYAN 196.02	OPPSX 202.10	ALEX 240.93	FLE 179.03	GLW 101.37	BT 117.13	MANU 90.45
AGC 99.87	SSPE 120.58	CYRX 109.87	SRM 98.33	INEL 116.08	CNG 143.68	CGEN 196.15	ITW 202.17	AGREA 240.93	FSR 179.18	WX 101.90	FORE 117.33	WLV 90.45
EIX 99.92	TDM 120.72	LLY 110.12	LLTC 98.38	AEP 116.45	F 143.97	ITSI 198.45	LPX 202.62	DEC 240.93	BSET 179.38	WY 102.70	FCNTX 117.47	LUNR 91.15
DRAI 99.95	NFB 121.15	DIGI 110.35	ETP 98.98	MWHS 116.67	ZBRA 144.00	MO 198.47	NSM 203.02	EVGRX 240.97	PCAR 179.38	RYAN 102.93	MER 117.95	JEQ 91.58
RTZ 99.97	ASND 121.35	RBD 110.60	FMC 99.58	HDI 116.73	PFE 145.17	OIL 199.48	OREM 203.82	SUN 240.97	TCOMA 179.38	LTD 104.68	ZEN 118.13	ZBRA 91.80
APCC 100.87	JEC 122.17	ANDW 111.48	NWK 99.60	CCK 117.00	LAD.B 146.02	FIDSX 200.00	WMX 203.98	WTHG 241.48	ALEX 179.43	NSC 105.12	HUM 118.33	LBTYA 91.82
BGG 103.03	MS 123.63	HLYW 111.58	BAC 99.85	KMB 117.00	PZL 146.47	FSUTX 200.00	BLL 206.83	HUM 241.83	AGREA 179.43	BDX 106.52	RTR 118.70	INTC 91.88
MCD 103.08	VLIFX 123.65	MCLL 111.58	PSON 102.73	PD 117.02	BASS 146.97	DF 200.40	DGN 207.23	BKB 242.17	DEC 179.43	IK 107.07	AXP 118.77	NOBE 93.17
UH 103.85	ADPT 124.22	FDESX 112.23	WBN 103.27	PSFT 117.02	SRSPX 147.22	UCM 201.00	PWJ 207.77	SGP 242.48	GCI 179.43	MKS 107.45	HFX 118.87	EGRP 93.42
GACC 103.98	UTX 124.65	IK 112.82	MANU 103.42	CUM 117.13	SCDUX 148.03	OIL 201.23	ABF 208.38	WMT 242.52	LTR 179.43	CI 108.38	GCI 118.93	KURZ 94.07
EGG 104.27	USS 124.88	GT 113.62	WLV 103.42	NWK 117.50	KT 148.23	WMS 202.13	GWW 208.57	NUE 242.75	CMCSA 179.60	GE 108.55	MOT 119.95	BNL 94.27
HELE 104.62	SGRFX 125.08	SRFSX 113.75	MTSI 103.63	CCK 118.10	DEX 148.33	BEV 204.78	STK 208.65	CMCSA 242.77	NUE 179.62	WMS 110.98	CUAC 120.08	MDA 94.27
RNK 104.77	FBS 125.35	PCAPX 113.95	DRAI 104.87	KMB 118.10	MAT 148.45	WAG 205.15		LTR 242.80	SGP 179.63	UK 113.15	KMAG 120.28	SWZ 95.38
C 104.90	LSTR 125.37	AGC 114.75	ALMI 105.07	PD 118.10	TAN 149.80			BSET 242.85	BKB 179.70	JNJ 113.97	LLTC 120.42	LEVL 96.78
	SIII 125.37	MSX 115.78		SOTA 118.28	SII 150.07			PCAR 242.85	EVGRX 179.87	DF 114.05	FINL 120.83	FDO 97.77
												HTCH 99.12
												TR 102.25

Sun	Moon	Mercury	Venus	Mars	Jupiter	Saturn	Uranus	Neptune	Pluto	Node	Asc	MC
HERB 104.92	NGG 125.50	PX 116.23	DREVX 105.22	WBN 119.37	BUD 150.33	GRA 206.85	ACCOB 208.67	TCOMA 242.85	SUN 179.87	FMAGX 114.25	GLW 120.92	CEN 102.87
WWH 105.23	SNS 125.73	CYRK 116.48	HTCH 105.23	AN 120.00	UCC 151.07	GMT 206.92	DJ 213.03	OLOG 243.03	DRTHX 180.47	FIDSX 114.32	EC 121.13	MYG 103.30
CTEA 105.43	ATTn 126.15	CTEA 116.95	P 105.45	HERB 120.57	AMD 153.03	TXN 207.48	HELE 213.03	ASC 243.05	WTHG 180.52	FSUTX 114.32	TTX 121.15	GPC 103.83
CYRX 106.38	TELC 126.15	PMS 117.15	SOTA 105.93	CMZ 120.80	LMS 153.58	AMGN 207.88	BAC 213.10	AMAT 243.40	WMT 180.80	EMR 115.02	FMC 121.25	KF 105.77
LLY 106.93	X 126.30	BGY 117.72	WMT 106.67	HRS 121.42	PAGE 154.18	CHIR 208.57	GPS 213.20	BFI 243.55	DNB 181.70	ITSI 115.22	KLM 121.77	LOJN 106.42
X 107.05	CTL 126.88	NGC 118.03	BBY 108.07	PPG 122.12	ANDW 154.20	KEY 208.68	NT 213.75	CTX 244.00	OLOG 181.72	FON 115.42	SRSPX 121.97	WMT 108.45
SLE 107.50	MXIM 127.05	TRBCX 118.20	KURZ 108.10	OREM 122.17	PLN 154.67	CNTO 209.48	RDC 215.83	GCI 244.05	ROAD 181.77	CGEN 116.33	KM 122.12	SBRY 108.50
FDESX 107.90	BROD 127.13	WWH 118.27	IP 109.10	JAMRX 122.68	GLM 155.02	MDR 210.03	NME 216.12	SBRY 244.85	YELL 181.77	CW 116.62	AHM 122.72	MHS 109.33
PMS 108.03	JAMS 128.03	CGNX 120.40	HELE 109.68	FSLBX 122.87	BSX 155.17	NOB 210.30	VAR 216.12	DREQX 244.98	DREQX 181.78	ECH 117.37	DREVX 122.85	FWC 111.60
DIGI 108.43	CCM 128.23	UH 120.40	KEY 109.92	FSCHX 122.87	ICII 155.17	UCL 210.75	CAG 216.75	ROAD 245.00	MER 181.83	FG 118.03	CS 122.97	AN 112.33
HPC 108.75	NVLS 128.55	MDA 120.72	LEVL 111.62	FDCPX 122.87	FDC 155.25	QNTM 211.13	KAB 217.05	YELL 245.00	BFI 181.93	INGR 118.72	DD 123.70	MNTR 113.80
XRX 108.78	TIF 128.62	ADBE 121.77	DDS 113.02	FSELX 122.87	BSPT 155.32	KO 211.37	LUV 217.83	DRTHX 245.12	CTX 182.03	KELYA#1 118.72	GE 125.28	AEP 114.48
CMCSA 109.35	TWCVX 128.68	BNL 122.10	SYMC 113.02	FDFAX 122.87	AGWFX 155.33	BMET 211.68	MNTR 218.60	DNB 245.92	AMAT 182.57	INTC 120.93	ALL 125.32	TCH 115.15
TLAB 109.40	DH 129.15	GWW 122.65	MAIL 113.85	FSCSX 122.87	SKO 155.35	NII 211.82	AXP 219.00	WMX 245.92	WWY 182.78	TOMK 121.30	KEY 125.37	RNBO 116.57
KLU 109.72	CPB 129.38	TOY 122.67	MDA 113.98	THDO 123.18	UNH 155.72	IBM 212.32	XTR 220.98	LPX 246.10	OPPSX 183.30	FSENX 122.22	WEN 125.80	BA 116.77
SSPE 109.72	DEX 130.20	DE 122.98	LOJN 114.62	UTX 123.82	FINL 155.77	RD 212.80	HOU 221.42	MER 246.33	ITW 183.35	FSPHX 122.22	HLT 126.95	CA 116.78
ANL 109.93	GCI 130.20	FSAVX 123.17	ADPT 115.03	AOL 124.20	TEN 155.77	BBELL 213.25	MDT 222.33	NSM 246.73	SBRY 183.67	FDPMX 122.22	NCDI 127.07	KWP 116.78
NUE 110.30	ORX 131.38	FSPFX 123.17	DE 115.77	DDS 124.35	ALBK 155.90	BGEN 213.25	MCIC 225.33	WWY 247.27	OREM 184.07	FSPTX 122.22	BBBY 127.12	UTX 117.93
HRS 110.40	HTCH 131.90	FSHCX 123.17	BAA 117.58	SYMC 124.35	USRX 155.92	ONE 213.52	CTL 225.75	OPPSX 247.42	NSM 184.38	CHRS 122.63	KBH 127.28	EMR 118.48
RYAN 110.85	RTN 131.97	FSRBX 123.17	FWC 117.80	BABSX 124.48	WAC 155.92	FDGRX 213.85	SNA 226.37	ITW 247.43	LPX 184.40	ALMI 123.65	KSWS 127.50	NN 119.63
UCC 111.12	MST 132.12	FBMPX 123.18	DJ 118.28	BAX 125.00	XIRC 156.00	CCM 214.30	FDO 227.08	BLL 247.83	WMX 185.33	MXF 124.33	AL 128.52	NRK 120.22
DJ 111.28	OPPSX 133.13	C 123.28	FSTCX 119.80	ECH 126.27	AGC 156.13	ALK 214.33	TOY 227.22	OREM 247.88	STK 186.48	WEN 124.75	CLE 128.92	SB 120.50
FSENX 112.02	NUE 133.15	GER 123.60	FSLEX 120.32	C 127.08	BBBY 156.48	U 214.33	PPP 227.23	DGN 248.23	ACCOB 186.50	EC 125.07	UIS 129.10	BMY 121.00
FSPHX 112.02	AT 133.28	SLE 123.75	CQ 120.40	ASPX 127.20	NCDI 156.48	TRB 215.02	SFA 227.72	GWW 249.15	ABF 186.50	C 125.70	FKREX 129.33	DH 121.27
FDPMX 112.02	X 133.65	FDO 123.88	LUNR 120.78	FSLEX 128.08	AADV 156.67	CIR 216.57	NB 227.93	PWJ 249.20	PWJ 186.52	TNB 125.73	MTC 129.38	CQ 121.47
FSPTX 112.02	WWH 134.10	MTSI 124.33	BABSX 121.72	CMCSA 128.18	COT 156.67	C 217.63	ASSD 229.08	ABF 249.75	BLL 186.67	CSK 125.77	DNB 129.62	AOL 122.02
PE 112.72	FSHOX 134.37	TOL 124.70	SCF 122.10	FON 128.70	ARRO 156.90	KELYA 219.80	AMD 229.52	STK 250.17	DGN 186.68	CBE 125.98	SPW 129.75	CDN 122.50
BGY 113.08	FSCGX 134.37	MST 124.73	CUM 122.47	NUE 128.85	GIC 157.02	ETP 219.90	FDX 229.55	ACCOB 250.20	GWW 186.78	PFE 127.30	TMB 129.83	FFTYX 122.72
TOL 113.72	FSDPX 134.37	MANU 125.37	ACCOB 123.20	BBY 128.85	LNCR 157.22	JBHT 219.92	PRU 229.58	NT 250.65	BAC 186.97	APA 129.62	CRUS 130.00	LAD.B 122.97
HLYW 114.02	FSRFX 134.37	WLV 125.37	ABCW 123.30	MDT 128.87	DIGI 157.65	DLCH 220.00	ADI 230.38	GPS 251.33	HELE 188.95	XRX 129.87	ARRO 130.22	KKTWX 123.35
MCLL 114.02	BBBY 134.45	DRAI 125.53	MNTR 123.50	MCIC 128.90	UFC 157.68	CC 220.08	UFC 231.40	DJ 251.60	DJ 189.02	BA 130.33	NSC 130.25	CUM 123.38
ABCW 114.25	NCDI 134.45	JEQ 126.08	STK 124.22	CEN 128.93	TLAB 157.82	TWCVX 220.25	TLAB 231.65	HELE 251.75	GPS 189.10	RTZ 130.37	BCC 130.35	PG 124.80
EQ 115.20	NTAIF 135.20	X 126.42	EQ 124.53	GPC 129.58	EPG 157.93	KF 221.00	DIGI 231.67	VAR 251.77	NME 189.40	OPTFX 131.37	PCL 130.48	WHR 125.47
3I 115.47	WHR 135.47	TR 127.58	AA 124.58	RNE 129.73	XCOM 157.98	TMB 221.03	AGC 231.85	BAC 251.93	NT 190.32	CNG 131.65	MAIL 130.98	BKS 125.58
GER 115.63	WMB 136.83	BNYN 127.60	C 124.87	INGR 130.38	STAR 158.05	UIS 221.08	ANDW 232.20	RDC 252.05	LUV 190.55	BC 134.87	GIC 131.33	FSR 125.60
CYRX 116.88	MSX 137.08	FSTCX 127.67	MYG 125.52	KELYA#1 130.38	VCI 158.17	ADM 221.43	IRF 232.57	CAG 252.92	RDC 191.42	CSX 135.60	ADPT 131.33	ERTS 125.60
RD 117.30	ENP 138.27	EGG 127.72	EGG 126.92	MRK 130.78	TOS 158.33	RTR 221.48	BBI 233.32	KAB 253.37	KAB 191.50	ADM 136.03	MAT 131.33	NII 125.68
BBY 117.32	AVP 138.80	MCD 128.17	HAL 127.18	AMD 132.00	JR 158.45	BAY 222.15	KR 233.37	MNTR 253.38	AXP 191.65	KLAC 136.98	MXF 131.93	BASS 127.78
CGNX 117.80	FDLSX 139.05	CREAF 129.52	CHRS 128.22	RBD 132.92	EMR 158.45	TBY 222.53	LOW 233.42	NME 253.90	CAG 191.70	SLB 138.28	XLNX 132.13	OIL 127.85
UBIS 118.45	TRMB 139.32	INTC 132.03	AOL 130.13	MOT 133.33	PX 158.78	FSDAX 222.68	KLAC 233.50	LUV 254.18	VAR 191.70	RAL 139.50	NB 132.30	HAL 128.07
ACAI 119.75	FSDAX 139.33	KURZ 132.68	NGC 130.28	MHS 133.42	TOT 158.90	FDLSX 222.68	BUD 234.58	XTR 254.75	MNTR 191.75	KO 140.73	NWK 132.32	RTN 128.10
TRMB 120.45	ASSD 140.38	ENP 133.25	WWH 130.38	RMDY 133.47	IRF 159.48	FBS 222.75	CSX 234.98	HOU 255.20	XTR 192.72	TLAB 141.70	CMB 132.68	IFMX 129.15
WNDR 120.70	BMCS 140.50	KLU 133.40	AMGN 131.18	SPW 133.50	MTSI 159.67	TIN 222.82	JR 235.15	AXP 255.25	HOU 194.15	DIGI 141.75	PCG 132.88	CNC 129.20
EGLS 121.83	IGF 140.50	LOJN 133.40	NOBE 131.33	LMT 133.57	DRAI 159.82	LRCX 222.98	TOS 235.17	MDT 255.25	MDT 194.18	AGC 142.23	MKS 134.17	RNE 130.70
EQLS 122.62	UST 140.60	SSPE 133.67	WLA 131.73	BAA 133.78	ELY 159.87	BC 223.12	INTC 236.05	CTL 256.42	SNA 195.73	APD 142.58	BABSX 134.50	INGR 131.00
MOLXA 123.32	KURZ 141.18	WMT 134.13	SPW 131.87	HTCH 133.78	BBI 160.12	ITT 223.92	FSENX 236.23	MCIC 256.77	TOY 196.27	ANDW 142.92	WBN 134.63	KELYA#1 131.00
AGN 124.48	AMD 141.23	AGN 134.58	DH 132.45	PESPX 134.25	KR 160.13	USW 224.08	FSPHX 236.23	PPP 257.20	SFA 196.43	LMT#1 144.33	ACCOB 135.42	HSY 131.23
BAA 124.72	DF 141.70	HTCH 134.87	KELYA 132.50	ICST 134.85	LOW 160.17	HD 224.10	FDPMX 236.23	FDO 257.80	NB 196.48	BUD 146.15	JP 135.77	CH 131.37
BLT 125.27	NSTA 142.17	CMCSA 135.72	PESPX 133.02	DSPC 135.02	SCHL 160.25	FTSE100 224.15	FSPTX 236.23	SNA 258.20	MCIC 196.55	CHV 150.10	SCF 135.95	HON 131.58
GWW 125.83	KT 143.75	NUE 136.62	NSCP 133.37	CCC 135.45	CHKR 161.53	MEL 224.30	KELYA#1 236.92	AMD 258.30	FDO 196.60	TOS 150.33	AMR 135.97	ATTo 131.62
FSTCX 125.97	MAR 143.90	ABCW 136.98	ICST 133.92	IDXX 135.45	USFC 161.63	HRS 224.52	ALMI 236.95	ASSD 258.38	CTL 197.07	JR 150.38	STK 136.18	ALD 132.02
FSLBX 126.38	INEL 145.50	EQ 137.22	WLA 134.30	FMAGX 135.80	CEN 162.00	DGAGX 225.23	AAPL 237.37	TOY 258.62	ADI 197.17	BAX 152.22	LTD 136.42	R 132.07
FSCHX 126.38	BBELL 145.83	LEVL 138.55	CCC 134.82	ANL 136.05	GPC 162.20	AIG 225.38		FDX 258.72	PPP 197.98	LOW 152.55	AA 136.82	CWP 132.40
FDCPX 126.38	GRA 146.13	UAL 139.78	IDXX 134.82	SO 136.90	APSO 162.27	COMS 225.82		PRU 258.75	ASSD 198.05			CKFR 132.88
									LOW 198.90			

Sun	Moon	Mercury	Venus	Mars	Jupiter	Saturn	Uranus	Neptune	Pluto	Node	Asc	MC
FSELX 126.38	CH 146.42	TRMB 140.92	TCH 135.43	ZEN 137.65	ABCW 162.28	LIFE 225.97	MXF 237.43	SFA 259.10	AGC 198.97	KR 152.60	SFA 136.98	FDSSX 133.10
FDFAX 126.38	OIL 147.05	GPS 142.90	VJET 135.45	HLT 138.03	FD 162.43	ATTn 226.32	FG 237.45	UFC 259.22	ANDW 199.00	IBM 152.65	XCOM 137.15	ONE 133.83
FSCSX 126.38	FSTCX 148.07	FSLBX 145.22	AN 135.78	FKGRX 138.13	EQ 162.47	TELC 226.32	WEN 237.75	NB 259.25	DIGI 199.02	BBI 152.67	ACV 137.28	FSHOX 134.05
PRGS 126.90	WY 148.67	FSCHX 145.22	MST 135.78	FG 138.40	BROD 162.82	IDTI 226.35	EC 238.00	IRF 259.92	TLAB 199.02	IRF 153.35	PESPX 137.28	FSCGX 134.05
LIT 127.12	CYGN 149.27	FDCPX 145.22	RBD 135.78	ALL 138.87	JNJ 163.17	CB 226.37	CW 238.87	KLAC 260.30	FDX 199.05	UFC 154.35	MB 137.52	FSDPX 134.05
GPS 127.52	CRUS 149.50	FSELX 145.22	ANL 135.80	LOJN 138.90	MHS 163.48	CPB 226.53	CGEN 239.17	BBI 260.40	PRU 199.07	HWP 155.33	OREM 137.92	FSRFX 134.05
ENP 127.62	SOPFX 149.88	FDFAX 145.22	PE 136.57	CORR 139.07	OI 163.53	WHR 226.93	OPTFX 239.35	KR 260.43	AMD 199.25	AMD 156.00	ICST 138.05	GABVX 134.32
AWSHX 128.28	OPTFX 150.52	FSCSX 145.22	FSAVX 137.25	AR 139.43	ABAX 163.72	VPMCX 227.92	BA 239.90	ADI 260.47	BUD 200.17	EK 157.08	CCC 138.88	UTEK 134.35
UAL 129.13	UNP 150.57	SWZ 145.37	FSPFX 137.25	NII 139.73	CTZN 163.72	GARD 229.22	APA 240.08	LOW 260.48	UFC 200.43	FDO 159.28	IDXX 138.88	LTV 136.00
CHIR 129.72	FCNTX 150.65	MOLXA 145.67	FSHCX 137.25	CGNX 141.22	FKREX 164.02	CCH 229.82	ITSI 240.45	TLAB 260.55	IRF 201.03	AVT 159.42	CC 139.35	APC 136.08
P 131.62	GNE 150.68	AWSHX 147.03	FSRBX 137.25	CG 143.77	MTC 164.02	IK 230.12	RYAN 240.87	DIGI 260.57	BBI 201.35	PKN 160.32	SNF 139.43	PAGE 136.80
GT 132.15	BAA 151.53	NVLS 147.82	FBMPX 137.28	LIT 144.55	QCOM 164.15	MKS 230.47	OIL 241.17	AGC 260.78	KR 201.38	TOY 160.72	FLCSX 139.62	MEF 137.05
CREAF 132.40	BOST 153.37	KELYA 147.92	RTZ 137.73	TOMK 144.58	OII 164.33	FSLBX 231.48	FIDSX 241.48	CSX 260.97	LOW 201.40	SFA 162.67	AKLM 140.15	AET 137.07
PCAPX 133.13	PSON 153.78	NSCP 149.20	FSENX 137.92	BAC 144.97	SYQT 164.42	FSCHX 231.48	FSUTX 241.48	ANDW 261.13	KLAC 201.45	NB 162.98	DELL 140.20	BDX 137.27
INTC 134.97	TOY 153.78	BMCS 149.70	FSPHX 137.92	AGN 145.60	LHP 164.45	FDCPX 231.48	DF 241.78	JR 261.87	CHRS 201.55	LTV 164.62	ENE 140.58	JNJ 137.87
BNYN 135.28	FMAGX 153.98	IGF 149.70	FDPMX 137.92	CYBR 146.22	ENP 164.87	FSELX 231.48	LTD 241.92	TOS 261.90	FSENX 201.58	IR 164.73	SYMC 140.73	KO 138.72
SDII 135.52	KO 154.83	LIT 150.75	FSPTX 137.92	ZLG 146.47	CREAF 165.83	FDFAX 231.48	NSC 242.23	INGR 262.15	FSPHX 201.58	R 164.82	MSX 140.75	AW 139.10
SYBS 135.52	GLK 155.03	BLT 151.62	KO 137.98	BUD 146.75	BNYN 166.43	FSCSX 231.48	BEV 242.42	KELYA#1262.15	FDPMX 201.58	SB 165.45	DDS 140.78	TNB 139.52
NOBE 136.33	MAT 155.50	CHIR 151.80	FDO 138.20	CHV 147.42	DE 166.80	BT.A 231.70	WMS 244.42	INTC 261.92	FSPTX 201.58	ADI 166.32	FTRNX 140.85	RGM 139.83
NSCP 136.50	ZE 155.55	FSR 152.32	LBTYA 140.77	SWZ 147.93	WX 167.55	GE 231.82	CI 244.40	FG 262.28	ALMI 201.60	ADI 166.85	DUK 141.27	MCAF 141.58
BNL 137.47	AA 155.78	MYG 152.65	HON 142.67	UFC 148.05	GLW 167.60	HTCH 231.82	CNTO 244.72	AAPL 262.33	MXF 201.73	NRK 168.58	NGC 141.35	SKO 142.88
MDA 137.48	ANDW 156.18	PRGS 153.05	UTX 143.15	KLU 148.18	JEQ 167.83	LOJN 232.13	MDR 245.03	BUD 262.52	JR 201.77	IAD 168.65	AMGN 141.62	BCR 143.08
NVLS 139.08	IDTI 156.70	ZBRA 153.37	NII 143.28	SSPE 148.18	AET 169.75	NOC 232.48	CHIR 245.13	FSENX 262.72	TOS 201.77	MO 170.45	ETP 141.72	CHPS 143.10
BMCS 140.05	CDN 156.72	P 153.87	SWZ 145.15	ONE 149.73	BCR 171.03	CMH 233.50	NII 245.47	FSPHX 262.72	WEN 201.87	PRU 171.37	PX 141.77	MEL 143.22
IGF 140.05	AMZN 156.78	CUM 154.40	FFTYX 145.10	HELE 149.77	CLX 171.25	ASTA 233.60	QNTM 245.70	FDPMX 262.72	INTC 201.92	FDX 171.40	TJX 141.93	EVGRX 143.32
ADBE 140.50	GABGX 157.28	CQ 155.03	CGNX 145.78	SEG 150.02	KLM 171.85	CLE 233.67	ONE 245.98	FSPTX 262.72	EC 201.98	ASSD 171.90	ALMI 142.00	CPC 143.52
MANU 140.80	HDI 157.45	SDII 155.88	ONE 146.62	MSX 150.13	DAL 173.30	BVALX 233.70	BMET 246.07	CW 262.90	CSX 202.46	BLT 172.02	WLA 142.20	CLX 144.10
WLV 140.80	SVT 157.97	SYBS 155.88	LLY 146.65	SDTI 150.47	BNL 173.73	ALD 233.87	AMGN 246.32	CHRS 262.92	INGR 203.15	WWH 173.13	GACC 142.35	UNH 144.92
FDO 141.18	CWP 158.60	CEN 158.42	CREAF 146.68	BGG 150.72	BT 176.17	AHM 234.25	TRB 246.52	CGEN 263.05	KELYA#1203.15	PPP 173.58	Z 142.85	WAC 145.88
PSON 141.35	FDEQX 158.98	CDN 159.58	ALD 146.93	AET 151.77	KBH 176.17	TTX 234.40	BBELL 247.03	ALMI 263.40	FG 203.65	CTL 174.85	ANDW 142.95	USRX 145.93
LUNR 141.50	APC 160.10	LBTYA 159.67	PAGE 147.23	DJ 154.02	KLAC 176.37	FOCPX 234.70	CIR 247.17	ITSI 263.73	AAPL 203.77	HFX 174.98	WWH 143.25	CPLY 149.73
JEQ 142.00	R 160.33	NOBE 160.10	X 147.60	TRBCX 154.20	CMB 176.37	USG 234.88	KEY 247.17	MXF 263.75	APA 204.10	GTW 175.55	CORR 143.45	ACN 149.77
ZBRA 142.23	ACAI 161.67	GPC 160.20	FDESX 147.80	CW 154.23	JP 176.55	INTV 235.37	FDGRX 247.77	OPTFX 263.80	RYAN 204.15	AMZN 175.93	SPYG 143.47	CESH 151.33
LBTYA 142.27	FKREX 161.67	KF 160.60	XRX 148.45	HPC 154.33	MAS 176.58	GOSHA 235.80	NOB 248.15	WEN 263.97	BA 204.27	IP 176.98	NOC 143.57	KLAC 151.33
HTCH 142.68	MTC 161.67	AN 160.65	LAD.B 148.55	BCR 155.53	WEN 177.27	TX 235.85	UCL 248.35	EC 264.12	LTD 204.28	AL 177.22	UNP 144.23	VAR 151.35
EGRP 143.95	MKS 162.93	PSON 161.88	BKS 148.75	TXT 155.92	CCI 177.48	UK 236.07	JBHT 248.38	OIL 264.30	OPTFX 204.35	TKR 179.45	VJET 144.43	AVY 152.37
KURZ 144.65	TRW 163.00	BMY 162.30	BASS 150.23	ALD 156.05	AHC 177.52	NOVL 236.17	DLCH 248.78	BA 264.33	NSC 204.40	FCYCF 179.80	RTZ 144.70	NKE 152.37
TR 145.97	TWN 163.00	RTN 164.75	BNYN 150.37	CLX 156.15	DRLEX 177.52	JAVLX 236.22	ALK 248.85	FIDSX 264.37	CW 204.70	FNATF 179.80	ED 145.02	CY 152.87
SWZ 146.03	RN 163.30	JNJ 164.97	KLU 150.82	IRF 156.15	LIT 178.70	UCC 236.40	TWCVX 248.95	FSUTX 264.37	CGEN 204.92	CTR 180.55	FSDCX 145.17	AIG 153.48
CEN 146.63	NEM 163.58	KO 165.38	SSPE 150.82	MST 156.45	MCAF 179.15	SCDUX 237.07	CCM 248.97	DF 264.55	OIL 205.53	AMP 180.70	FSCPX 145.17	TKR 153.77
MYG 147.03	AMP 164.50	EMR 165.50	SKO 151.97	IOM 156.68	BMY 179.65	LGN 237.68	BGEN 248.98	APA 264.60	ITSI 205.68	IOM 185.72	PRSGX 145.17	LMT#1 154.03
LEVL 147.53	ISL 164.62	MNTR 166.88	SLE 151.97	WMT 156.70	JPM 179.78	BSC 237.85	KF 249.55	BEV 264.72	CI 205.95	DD 186.02	RBD 145.33	JCI 154.12
GPC 147.58	PSQL 164.62	ONE 168.20	UNH 152.62	GT 157.07	WEN 180.45	MOB 240.80	KELYA 249.78	RYAN 264.98	FIDSX 206.22	CYBR 186.73	FSLEX 145.37	TRB 154.78
KF 149.63	MF 165.13	FDSSX 168.42	USRX 153.38	CGEN 157.23	EC 180.50	GT 241.03	BAY 250.03	LTD 265.85	FSUTX 206.22	SNA 187.50	INEL 145.78	AMAT 155.42
LOJN 150.38	CHRS 165.47	ATTo 168.43	WAC 153.38	TRB 157.78	MXF 180.53	CPQ 242.78	MEL 250.33	CNTO 265.87	DF 206.35	CHA 187.93	FSAVX 145.92	G 156.63
WMT 152.45	SPW 165.78	LUNR 168.67	ZBRA 153.50	CTEA 158.32	CPLY 180.85	F 242.78	TIN 250.43	MDR 266.05	BEV 206.67	RNE 188.22	FSPFX 145.92	LSI 156.78
MHS 153.38	CBE 167.17	RNE 169.10	KLAC 154.18	CYRK 158.92	ALMI 181.10	MXP 242.78	ETP 250.57	NSC 266.07	AMGN 206.82	AOL 188.68	FSHCX 145.92	AMD 157.88
FWC 155.52	BASS 167.23	MHS 170.42		PRGS 159.30	CSX 181.58	IAF 243.02	AIG 250.72	QNTM 266.45	WMS 206.83	RBD 188.98	FSRBX 145.92	ISL 158.07
AN 156.50	TBY 167.95	EGRP 170.78		CNF 160.15	CSC 181.68	BRWIX 243.02	CC 250.77	NII 266.48	CHIR 206.92	BABSX 189.65	TRBCX 146.15	PSQL 158.07
MNTR 158.05	EGRP 168.67	UTX 171.60		BBI 160.57	ISL 182.50	ADBE 243.10	ITT 251.13	WMS 266.48	KEY 207.15	EGRP 190.33	IP 146.38	BEV 158.18
AEP 158.78	LMT 169.65	BDX 171.72		TXN 160.65	PSQL 182.50	G 243.35	USW 251.23	ONE 266.60	NOB 207.77	MCIC 190.52	MTSI 146.40	CYBR 159.15
BA 161.10	TNB 170.55	SB 171.80		KR 160.87	UAL 182.58	GER 243.37	FTSE100 251.28	BMET 266.68	UCL 207.93	K 191.08	DRLEX 146.50	SUN 159.15
ATTo 161.35	RAD 170.58	CA 173.73		WHR 160.93	CHRS 182.72	TOL 243.43	TMB 251.58	TRB 266.78	NII 207.95	BGY 192.03	AHC 146.55	TXN 159.53
UTX 162.30	SNF 170.87	KWP 173.73		LOW 161.15	CENF 183.10	FSAIX 243.48		CHIR 266.82	CNTO 208.22	MDT 192.70	HDI 146.55	FG 159.77
										MD 193.30		

Sun	Moon	Mercury	Venus	Mars	Jupiter	Saturn	Uranus	Neptune	Pluto	Node	Asc	MC
EMR 162.87	DUK 170.90	ALD 173.80	AGN 154.22	RNBO 162.58	FSENX 183.65	FBIOX 243.48	UIS 251.62	CI 267.05	MDR 208.38	RLM 194.78	ANL 146.65	CENF 161.28
SB 164.93	ALTR 171.17	NII 174.38	TRB 154.62	FKREX 162.95	FSPHX 183.65	FSESX 243.48	VPMCX 251.80	CIR 267.05	ONE 208.53	RTK 195.00	IK 146.87	WTHG 162.05
BMY 165.45	BZF 171.17	MEF 174.62	LIT 155.40	MTC 162.95	FDPMX 183.65	FSVLX 243.48	RTR 251.88	BBELL 267.32	QNTM 208.73	LOR 195.68	EIX 147.08	MAR 162.30
DH 165.73	DE 171.18	SBRY 175.92	TOL 155.53	HLYW 163.70	FSPTX 183.65	FSPCX 243.48	DGAGX 252.07	FDGRX 267.85	BGEN 208.87	PHII 196.63	DRAI 147.17	SO 162.62
CQ 165.93	LLY 172.03	AOL 175.93	BLT 155.73	MCLL 163.70	ZEN 184.75	FSRPX 243.48	GARD 252.40	JBHT 267.90	BMET 208.90	YHOO 197.00	CHV 147.27	UNVGX 164.62
TCH 166.88	ORA 172.55	TCH 176.73	SDII 156.33	FLCSX 163.80	ALL 184.77	X 243.70	TBY 252.45	AMGN 267.92	TRB 209.03	MNTR 197.03	APCC 147.92	CAR 165.63
CUM 167.88	AMGN 172.70	GABVX 177.40	SYBS 156.33	TOS 164.00	PSON 184.80	CA 244.07	FSDAX 252.53	DLCH 267.93	BBELL 209.27	LUO 197.43	RNK 148.18	CTL 167.68
KKTWX 167.90	GIS 173.08	VAR 177.55	PRGS 157.25	JR 164.18	JHNGX 184.93	KWP 244.07	FDLSX 252.53	TWCVX 268.02	ETP 209.35	LCOS 197.53	DOW 148.67	CIR 168.52
RNBO 168.28	HPC 173.30	AW 177.98	GER 157.78	GPS 164.47	ASPX 185.32	FBMPX 244.13	FBS 252.57	U 268.33	CCM 209.37	ORA 197.55	BGY 148.92	WMX 168.92
SBRY 168.43	GPS 173.35	NRK 178.35	3I 157.92	SDII 164.93	MSX 185.50	FSAVX 244.15	LRCX 252.67	KEY 268.47	ALK 209.38	VWUSX 197.75	SCDUX 148.93	CNG 170.27
CA 168.52	ABAX 174.53	CWP 179.08	RD 158.27	SYBS 164.93	MOMGX 185.55	FSPFX 244.15	LIFE 252.70	BAY 268.65	KELYA 209.38	GAP 198.92	ABF 149.28	CW 170.70
KWP 168.52	CTZN 174.53	FWC 179.08	AMAT 158.33	CYRX 165.50	THDO 185.87	FSHCX 244.15	ATTo 252.95	KF 268.75	CC 209.40	ASA 199.28	LUV 149.68	TOT 179.98
PG 169.32	ENM 174.70	MEL 179.58	G 158.98	CIR 165.73	SKY 185.90	FSRBX 244.15	HD 253.13	MEL 268.78	FDGRX 209.47	CYCH 200.02	3I 150.63	BSC 181.48
WHR 170.00	LIT 174.92	ENM 179.84	JEQ 158.98	ED 165.85	JAMRX 185.95	NGC 244.48	TELC 253.13	ALK 268.87	U 209.53	LUV 200.48	BAC 150.65	PGF 184.80
FSR 170.12	CSX 175.30	CH 180.07	TXN 159.08	PH 165.97	TRBCX 186.02	CNC 244.90	IDTI 253.18	CCM 268.90	CIR 209.57	TWCGX 201.30	TOY 150.85	ORX 185.07
NII 170.22	PSFT 175.52	BA 181.80	CHIR 159.47	SPYG 166.48	GEMS 186.58	IFMX 244.90	CB 253.43	TIN 268.90	TMB 209.70	JAOLX 202.57	DE 150.97	GGC 185.32
NN 171.50	WNDR 176.27	EVGRX 182.18	OIL 159.52	AL 167.00	CTEA 186.67	SCF 244.93	COMS 253.57	AIG 268.92	UIS 209.72	AXP 202.60	HERB 151.18	BTR 186.02
OIL 172.40	LCOS 176.28	SUN 182.25	UTEK 159.73	ACAI 167.33	CYRK 186.77	SOPFX 245.13	BT.A 253.67	NOB 268.98	RTR 209.85	CPC 202.90	CTEA 151.57	CR 186.37
HAL 172.62	FDCAX 176.43	BEV 184.07	GWW 160.65	WNDR 167.93	FSNGX 186.77	FSHOX 245.27	LOJN 253.97	UCL 269.07	KF 209.87	NGG 203.53	FBMPX 151.82	PNU 186.40
RTN 172.65	FO 176.47	CPC 184.78	ACN 161.67	KM 168.10	FORMF 187.10	FSCGX 245.27	HTCH 253.98	BGEN 269.22	TBY 210.20	CBB 204.15	IR 152.07	GARD 187.10
AOL 173.95	GLN 176.47	AEP 184.93	CDN 162.65	BCC 168.22	INTC 187.20	FSDPX 245.27	FSLBX 254.20	KELYA 269.22	FSDAX 210.25	NEM 204.15	CYRK 152.33	TX 187.90
CDN 174.40	BC 176.52	TRB 185.95	KKTWX 162.78	ANDW 168.30	AAPL 187.60	FSRFX 245.27	FSCHX 254.20	ITT 269.35	FDLSX 210.25	MYG 205.12	MST 152.40	UNM 189.87
FFTYX 174.67	JPM 177.18	RNBO 186.33	CEN 163.15	CE 168.52	HLYW 187.65	FO 245.33	FDCPX 254.20	VPMCX 269.40	FBS 210.28	PNU 205.53	SRFSX 152.42	GR 191.30
INGR 175.55	BDK 177.38	ERTS 186.40	GPC 164.38	AMZN 168.55	MCLL 187.65	GLN 245.33	FSELX 254.20	USW 269.42	LRCX 210.37	CKFR 207.43	CQB 152.53	TWCGX 191.32
KELYA# 175.55	SLE 177.82	PAGE 187.98	CY 165.20	ITSI 168.77	PSFT 187.83	ADPT 245.35	FDFAX 254.20	FTSE100 269.45	JBHT 210.65	W 207.63	X 152.92	FOE 192.02
HSY 175.78	REY 178.77	SO 189.38	CIR 165.45	EGLS 169.15	SANM 187.90	MAIL 245.42	FSCSX 254.20	GARD 269.72	DLCH 210.68	SRFSX 207.77	AGC 152.98	BOST 192.27
HON 176.13	CESH 178.98	FFTYX 190.03	BNL 166.83	ZBRA 169.35	CYRX 188.03	APC 245.43	ALD 254.28	ETP 269.88	TWCVX 210.75	FTRNX 208.57	PMS 153.72	FPF 192.30
ALD 176.57	MOLXA 179.05	KKTWX 191.72	INTC 166.87	GTW 170.15	CATP 188.13	CHPS 246.02	CMH 254.65	DGAGX 270.00	HD 210.78	FOE 208.75	KLU 155.08	AHP 192.33
R 176.62	GLW 179.65	DH 191.98	BA 167.07	ACV 171.88	ACAI 188.42	FMC 246.30	ASTA 254.72	CC 270.05	MEL 211.10	HOU 209.25	SSPE 155.08	ATTrr 192.33
ERTS 177.57	MCIC 180.25	UNVGX 191.98	KF 168.18	ASH 172.15	WNDR 188.55	LLTC 246.37	BVALX 254.77	BT.A 270.43	BAY 211.32	XTR 209.75	BGG 155.58	CCI 193.05
BKS 177.60	UK 181.48	R 192.03	TOT 168.23	BTR 173.10	EGLS 188.83	NWS 246.97	FOCPX 255.35	LIFE 270.57	AIG 211.50	NSCP 210.08	MCD 155.62	VPMCX 193.13
LTV 180.53	PESPX 182.45	CY 192.30	CNG 168.38	HFX 173.37	APA 188.92	LIT 247.80	NOC 255.47	TMB 270.60	TIN 211.55	FSTCX 210.67	UH 156.23	LSCC 193.35
CNC 181.20	GABVX 182.62	HSY 192.52	GT 171.18	AGC 175.02	DD 189.17	PEG 248.27	USG 255.82	UIS 270.75	COMS 211.78	SPYG 212.37	EGG 156.58	CGEN 193.97
IFMX 181.20	KRAGX 182.70	ACN 194.52	MHS 171.78	PRGFX 175.15	DH 189.75	RGEN 248.38	BSC 255.88	RTR 270.83	ITT 211.78	ZE 212.58	CHRS 156.67	CSX 195.28
AET 181.57	AKLM 182.77	BKS 194.73	LMT#1 171.93	CCI 175.35	BA 189.90	UNM 248.95	CLE 256.23	ATTn 270.83	FTSE100 211.83	FLCSX 212.63	HELE 156.83	VTA 195.47
BDX 181.78	DELL 182.77	LSI 194.92	CYBR 172.88	PCAPX 175.35	OPTFX 190.47	INDQA 249.10	NOVL 256.42	TELC 270.83	USW 211.83	VAR 214.35	C 157.12	IOM 195.75
JNJ 182.37	U 183.07	NN 195.08	WHR 173.33	DE 176.12	PCAPX 190.47	NAV 249.10	AHM 256.57	ALD 270.87	CB 211.95	ZLG 214.53	BAA 157.32	PRD 195.88
TKR 182.73	ITA 183.15	CNC 195.73	RNBO 173.55	AL 176.32	MWHS 191.10	MYL 249.15	TTX 256.63	IDTI 270.88	FSLBX 212.02	AMR 216.38	BLT 157.72	GEMS 196.78
RKO 182.75	FSDCX 183.47	WHR 195.73	MAR 174.55	BDK 177.00	MCHP 191.18	ITA 249.35	INTV 257.12	LOJN 270.95	FSCHX 212.02	RMDY 217.77	UBIS 158.07	UCM 197.12
KO 183.18	FSCPX 183.47	PG 196.00	FSR 174.70	AT 177.42	TRCD 191.18	GABAX 249.50	GOSHA 257.32	CMH 271.03	FDCPX 212.02	LMT 217.82	TOL 158.35	CHKR 199.22
CH 183.43	PRSGX 183.47	OIL 196.78	FDSSX 176.33	FIDSX 177.42	WALL 191.53	ONCS 249.52	LGN 257.35	HTCH 271.05	FSELX 212.02	GPS 218.07	HLYW 158.53	BDK 201.27
LAD.B 183.53	RMDY 183.63	HAL 197.00	CPC 177.33	FSUTX 177.42	MANU 191.78	SUNW 249.52	JAVLX 257.48	TBY 271.05	FDFAX 212.02	DSPC 218.28	MCLL 158.53	AMX 201.80
TNB 183.98	NRK 183.92	AIG 197.35	HSY 180.12	RCM 177.93	WLV 191.78	ORCL 249.67	CPQ 258.22	ASTA 271.07	FSCSX 212.02	DJ 218.87	LLY 158.75	NT 201.85
CWP 184.42	FDESX 183.98	CKFR 197.93	NT 181.08	SNS 179.25	AVID 192.02	MSFT 249.68	MXP 258.22	BVALX 271.10	DGAGX 212.07	GTE 218.97	ABCW 158.77	AUD 202.07
CKFR 184.95	PURT 183.98	LTV 198.23	MEF 181.32	DF 179.82	INTU 192.02	MS 249.70	IAF 258.35	FSDAX 271.10	NOC 212.07	HELE 219.33	SLE 159.22	BS 203.43
FDSX 185.17	BEV 184.32	CW 198.35	EMR 182.10	DIGI 179.92	KURZ 192.47	CCE 250.67	BRWIX 258.35	FDLSX 271.10	IDTI 212.08	BAC 219.75	FDESX 159.47	GRR 203.90
G 185.47	WMS 184.37	SKO 198.40	BTR 182.55	TLAB 180.48	LSTR 192.77	FDCAX 251.25	ADBE 258.45	FBS 271.12	ATTn 212.10	DIS 220.00	EQ 159.55	PSFT 204.22
ONE 185.83	UCC 185.20	CR 198.83	ORX 183.18	ERTS 180.63	SIII 192.77	CAR 251.48	CA 258.45	LRCX 271.12	TELC 212.10	PRD 220.42	GER 159.90	DIS 204.32
FSHOX 186.12	UFC 185.35	CESH 198.97	AW 183.82	MANU 180.95	S 192.90	KLM 251.77	KWP 258.45	FSLBX 271.13	LIFE 212.10	CAR 221.12	DIGI 159.97	FLE 205.22
FSCGX 186.12	SRA 185.37	AVY 200.68	UNVGX 184.95	WLV 180.95	LEVL 193.00	RBK 252.08	FSAIX 258.58	FSCHX 271.35	HTCH 212.13	SDTI 222.68	HPC 160.25	APD 205.40
FSDPX 186.12	NWK 185.42	NKE 200.68	CSX 185.05	BSC 181.25	FMILX 193.18	GAS 252.65	FBIOX 258.58	FDCPX 271.35	CLE 212.38	SEG 222.78	XRX 160.25	APSO 205.50
FSRFX 186.12	SOTA 185.60	CCI 200.82	SB 185.88	FCYCF 181.75	GLBL 194.40	PRD 252.82	FSESX 258.58	FSELX 271.35	VPMCX 212.38	NME 224.47	CMCSA 160.70	CCE 205.73
GABVX 186.38	MHS 185.87	TNB 201.07	ADBE 186.00	FNATF 181.75	GHV 194.58	DIS 253.70	FSVLX 258.58	FDFAX 271.35	LOJN 212.43		TLAB 160.70	GAS 206.03
UTEK 186.42	LEVL 186.17	INGR 201.25	CHKR 186.73	UBIS 182.40	MATH 194.62	DAL 253.82			AHM 212.57	DI 224.63	CYRX 160.87	BOC 206.65

Sun	Moon	Mercury	Venus	Mars	Jupiter	Saturn	Uranus	Neptune	Pluto	Node	Asc	MC
BCR 187.47	BLL 186.65	KELYA#1 201.25	BDX 188.95	JBHT 182.47	GNCI 194.67	SWZ 254.53	FSPCX 258.58	FSCSX 271.35	TTX 212.60	LIT 225.57	BBY 161.27	UFC 207.10
MEL 187.58	DRTHX 186.68	HON 201.48	TR 191.08	DLCH 183.05	WLP 194.68	WTEC 254.78	FSRPX 258.58	HD 271.35	GARD 212.80	ATTo 226.77	NUE 161.47	NGG 208.97
EVGRX 187.73	JAMRX 187.50	CGEN 201.50	APSO 193.32	NSC 183.13	INGR 195.27	BAA 254.97	CNC 258.68	COMS 271.40	INTV 212.95	NN 227.50	HRS 161.57	SEL 209.18
SUN 187.78	AHC 188.02	UNH 201.77	JBHT 194.13	KURZ 183.48	KELYA#1 195.27	RNBO 254.97	IFMX 258.68	BSC 271.45	GOSHA 213.10	KAB 227.80	CGNX 161.62	BT.A 209.27
CPC 187.88	DRLEX 188.02	ORX 202.45	AEP 194.43	EGG 183.87	CAR 195.80	BBY 255.22	FSHOX 258.82	FOCPX 271.48	ALD 213.22	XON 227.90	RYAN 161.92	PPP 209.43
APC 188.07	LPX 188.13	USRX 203.43	ATTo 194.60	TWCVX 184.22	TCH 196.83	HERB 255.90	FSCGX 258.82	USG 271.57	JAVLX 213.27	CAG 228.65	UCC 162.15	AW 210.47
TXN 188.13	SKY 188.42	WAC 203.43	RTN 195.07	CH 184.52	HLT 197.85	RCM 256.28	FSDPX 258.82	NOVL 272.10	BT.A 213.57	KLM 229.22	DJ 162.28	TW 210.47
NRK 188.17	BP 188.82	FSHOX 203.45	DLCH 195.23	FSTCX 184.87	MST 197.88	HDI 256.28	FSRFX 258.82	NOC 272.35	CMH 214.07	RDC 229.97	FSENX 162.85	WY 210.47
FG 188.33	KLAC 189.63	FSCGX 203.45	CKFR 195.37	EMR 184.90	FG 198.05	INEL 256.35	APC 259.00	CPQ 272.80	ASTA 214.10	ARC 230.07	FSPHX 162.85	BROD 210.68
BASS 188.43	GOSHA 190.32	FSDPX 203.45	AMP 195.48	FWC 184.93	MOT 198.40	TJX 256.68	GER 259.07	MXP 272.80	BVALX 214.12	3I 230.58	FDPMX 162.85	FDCAX 210.85
CLX 188.45	LNCR 190.65	FSRFX 203.45	IOM 195.93	CTR 185.08	FFTYX 198.47	GIS 258.28	TOL 259.10	CLE 272.85	FOCPX 214.37	DAL 231.07	FSPTX 162.85	CBB 213.75
PAGE 188.85	ARRO 190.88	CYBR 204.13	BSC 196.23	CWP 185.17	PRD 198.55	WMB 258.35	X 259.28	IAF 272.87	USG 214.40	FO#1 231.13	ACAI 163.20	MDT 213.78
MEF 189.10	AVY 191.53	CNG 204.32	BEV 196.90	LTD 185.32	MRK 198.78	GGC 258.72	SOPFX 259.48	BRWIX 272.87	GER 214.53	VJET 231.63	PE 163.43	W 214.00
SO 191.05	NKE 191.53	G 204.68	EVGRX 197.10	LEVL 185.38	UNVGX 198.95	KMAG 258.72	FO 259.60	LGN 272.92	TOL 214.53	NT 231.98	TRMB 163.82	JBHT 214.35
AW 191.05	NWS 193.35	TXN 205.47	SUN 197.15	TR 186.35	BKS 199.08	CCR 258.97	GLN 259.60	FSAIX 273.02	X 214.55	PEP 233.08	WNDR 163.98	MU 215.03
RCM 191.78	TOMK 193.50	APC 206.43	TWCVX 197.45	GABVX 186.47	DIS 200.18	MYG 259.10	FSAVX 259.62	FBIOX 273.02	FSAVX 214.60	FORE 233.48	EGLS 165.53	DLCH 215.37
MCAF 193.55	AL 193.58	LAD.B 206.43	CESH 198.82	AMAT 187.52	UTEK 200.98	RR 259.28	FSPFX 259.62	FSESX 273.02	FSPFX 214.60	ASND 233.92	MOLXA 166.15	ITSI 215.80
SKO 194.77	NB 193.67	AET 207.45	BROD 198.90	WWH 188.50	CMZ 201.02	NELL 259.33	FSHCX 259.62	FSVLX 273.02	FSHCX 214.60	SRYIX 234.82	AGN 167.12	AMP 216.18
CHPS 194.97	DREQX 193.98	CAR 207.87	AVY 200.00	VLIFX 189.10	AN 201.63	MF 260.02	FBMPX 259.62	FSRPX 273.02	FBMPX 214.60	FMCSX 236.45	RD 167.20	TWN 216.55
VAR 195.42	PFE 194.83	UTEK 207.92	NKE 200.07	PEP 189.75	FTRNX 201.77	UST 260.13	FSRBX 259.62	AHM 273.03	NOVL 214.63	GWW 237.50	FSTCX 168.28	SVT 216.60
KLAC 195.43	FFTYX 195.10	JCI 207.95	R 200.63	CI 189.90	SRFSX 201.98	TIF 260.17	NGC 259.85	CA 273.05	NGC 214.65	CHCLX 237.82	PRGS 169.08	CNTO 216.63
UNH 196.75	QLGC 195.13	TKR 207.98	GLM 201.27	AMRMX 190.47	UTX 202.73	ABX 260.23	SCF 260.13	KWP 273.05	LGN 214.73	QLGC 237.98	ENP 169.68	TWCVX 217.35
AIG 197.43	SEL 195.30	CIR 208.22	BMY 201.63	CSC 190.50	PPG 202.90	CPC 260.27	UNM 260.37	CNC 273.07	BSC 214.75	IIF 238.52	KELYA 170.90	RBK 218.05
USRX 197.73	CNG 195.37	MCAF 208.68	VO 203.40	NSCP 191.60	TR 203.23	TSK 260.28	ADPT 260.38	IFMX 273.07	SCF 214.75	RYOCX 238.73	CREAF 173.58	OI 218.83
WAC 197.73	ICST 195.38	GGC 208.72	TX 203.42	G 192.42	TKR 203.50	APB 260.68	MAIL 260.42	TTX 273.08	ADBE 214.78	PARQ 238.88	BAY 173.62	CSC 219.05
LMT#1 198.03	SGP 195.38	PNU 208.77	LTV 205.55	AUD 193.45	MAR 203.58	GABGX 261.07	FMC 260.90	FSHOX 273.10	ADPT 214.83	ABF 239.18	PCAPX 174.13	HNZ 219.37
JCI 198.28	Z 196.30	BCR 210.78	JNJ 206.23	PG 194.05	CW 203.83	BHI 261.13	LLTC 260.95	FSCGX 273.10	MAIL 214.87	IGEN 239.32	GWW 174.17	TKF 220.33
MAR 198.28	VTA 197.20	CLX 211.05	AGWFX 206.88	BAY 194.20	CGEN 204.97	SRFSX 261.15	CCE 261.18	FSDPX 273.10	FMC 215.10	SEPC 239.32	FSLBX 174.58	BST 220.58
TRB 198.67	PKN 197.60	FG 212.67	AET 207.42	FLE 195.35	JCP 205.65	FTRNX 262.22	NWS 261.25	FSRFX 273.10	LLTC 215.12	YSII 239.32	FSCHX 174.58	CHA 220.83
AMAT 199.33	DLNK 199.72	BASS 212.82	SBRY 207.60	LBTYA 195.35	CQB 206.17	N 262.38	FDCAX 261.47	APC 273.12	NWS 215.32	DLNK 239.42	FDCPX 174.58	GLM 221.30
NKE 201.42	MAPS 199.72	WTHG 212.98	OI 208.03	FCNTX 195.52	MMM 206.20	TWCGX 262.63	INDOA 261.85	CHPS 273.20	KWP 215.47	MAPS 239.42	FSELX 174.58	MDR 221.67
CPLY 201.45	CAR 200.45	PGF 213.38	TX 208.45	GGC 196.00	LLY 206.47	USS 262.83	NAV 261.85	ADBE 273.32	PEG 215.83	NSTA 239.63	FDFAX 174.58	OLOG 223.32
AMD 201.62	SCF 202.25	APD 213.52	BOST 209.40	TIN 197.90	FDESX 206.47	FWC 263.90	PEG 261.87	INTV 273.33	RGEN 215.88	JAMS 239.68	FSCSX 174.58	PMTC 223.33
BEV 201.88	THDO 202.33	AMAT 214.77	CHA 212.58	JNJ 198.02	MYG 207.02	PG 264.07	RBK 261.88	GOSHA 273.42	CNC 215.90	BTIOF 239.73	PSON 174.63	WGR 223.33
CESH 202.93	LU 202.47	CHPS 216.40	APD 213.00	TCH 198.33	ZE 208.73	HON 264.27	RGEN 261.92	JAVLX 273.50	IFMX 215.90	RCHY 239.78	LIT 175.23	ALEX 223.52
AVY 203.92	SKO 203.05	NT 216.85	VTA 213.15	CAR 198.53	ITSI 209.32	MIL 264.48	ITA 262.00	SOPFX 273.58	FSHOX 216.07	CMSB 240.00	GPS 175.53	AGREA 223.57
NKE 203.92	EGG 203.70	GR 216.93	CA 213.52	HON 198.67	BOST 209.63	FBGRX 265.12	GABAX 262.12	FO 273.67	FSCGX 216.07	JTAX 240.00	BNYN 175.88	DEC 223.57
CY 204.40	QNTM 204.38	AMX 217.03	CLX 216.00	WMS 198.68	PCH 209.83	HPC 265.62	SUNW 262.15	GLN 273.67	FSDPX 216.07	USWI 240.05	SDII 176.12	USS 223.82
WTHG 205.53	GIC 204.45	RCM 217.27	MEL 216.33	RYAN 198.83	VTA 210.27	ZE 265.70	GAS 262.18	UNM 273.78	FSRFX 216.07	SYMBA 240.05	SYBS 176.12	VO 224.03
UNVGX 208.00	EGLS 205.00	VTA 217.80	INGR 216.58	HI 199.30	RYAN 210.82	BGG 266.02	MYL 262.23	GER 273.85	APC 216.15	STK 240.08	AWSHX 176.13	CAT 224.48
LSI 208.13	WMX 205.47	LMT#1 218.00	KELYA#1 216.58	BLT 199.87	LTD 210.88	BMCS 266.18	ORCL 262.27	TOL 273.90	MYL 216.30	ACCOB 240.13	UAL 176.87	SNS 224.52
CAR 208.90	ROAD 205.90	GRR 218.13	BAY 217.35	BNL 200.12	NSC 211.38	IGF 266.18	MSFT 262.28	X 274.08	CPQ 216.33	VENGF 240.17	NSCP 176.88	ASSD 224.90
ISL 209.40	YELL 205.90	KLAC 220.37	GAS 217.68	PAGE 200.47	AMX 211.53	NVLS 266.52	MS 262.35	CCE 274.32	MXP 216.33	ENM 240.95	CHIR 177.30	CPQ 225.28
PSQL 209.40	NSC 206.30	CPLY 220.52	QCOM 218.52	LSI 200.92	GRR 211.95	ASA 266.72	ONCS 262.35	FSAVX 274.32	IAF 216.36	PKF 241.85	P 178.90	MXP 225.28
CYBR 210.42	GLBL 207.12	BOST 220.63		FFTYX 203.62	FIDSX 212.57	ACN 267.55	RNBO 262.77	FSPFX 274.32	BRWIX 216.36	GRR 243.33	NVLS 179.03	MWHS 225.52
CTL 210.80	UCL 207.12	CSX 220.83		ITT 204.47	FSUTX 212.57	GAP 267.55	SWZ 262.78	FSHCX 274.32	CHPS 216.40	AMX 243.45	GT 179.35	TOMK 225.77
CIR 211.58	MEA 207.45	BDK 221.77		SKO 204.47	DF 213.47	CY 267.75	RCM 263.20	FBMPX 274.32	FSAIX 216.52	VTA 243.77	BMCS 179.77	AGWFX 226.20
WMX 212.02	BS 207.78	AMD 222.15		USW 205.53	BNI 213.75	MHP 268.22	BAA 263.22	FSRBX 274.32	FBIOX 216.52	BOST 243.92	IGF 179.82	TWX 226.30
CENF 212.38	CCC 208.02	MAR 223.02		BKS 205.62	BP 214.45	APCC 268.37	WTEC 263.28	FDCAX 274.40	FSESX 216.52	MAR 245.40	ADBE 180.20	IRF 226.35
CR 213.02	IDXX 208.02	CCE 223.15		UNH 205.82	CPC 214.72	EIX 268.43	BBY 263.45	NGC 274.48	FSVLX 216.52	UCC 245.78	MANU 180.38	SEG 227.02
CNG 213.28	CUAC 208.08	FDCAX 224.57		FTSE100 205.93	VJET 214.78	SBL 268.48	HERB 263.88	RBK 274.65	FSPCX 216.52	UTEK 246.03	WLV 180.38	IAF 227.20
TX 214.43	WTHG 208.27	FPF 224.85		P 206.38	RAD 215.07	ORX 268.98	HDI 264.12	SCF 274.67	FSRPX 216.52	BKS 246.52	LUNR 181.00	BRWIX 227.27
TOT 214.67	ZEN 208.28	CTL 225.98		USRX 206.48	3I 215.15	AKLM 269.08	INEL 264.17	GAS 274.82		FFTYX 246.68	JEQ 181.37	QCOM 227.73
CW 214.85		CHA 226.22		WAC 206.48	WFC 215.80					SCDUX 246.68	ZBRA 181.55	WY 228.20

Sun	Moon	Mercury	Venus	Mars	Jupiter	Saturn	Uranus	Neptune	Pluto	Node	Asc	MC
BSC 216.12	CENF 208.47	LSCC 226.47	SEG 218.77	ALEX 206.78	ABS 215.83	DELL 269.08	GGC 264.28	ADPT 274.83	ONCS 216.60	TCH 247.10	LBTYA 181.58	SFL 228.50
GR 217.62	ITSI 208.70	PRD 228.98	ERTS 219.35	AGREA 206.78	JANSX 215.88	SNF 269.17	TJX 264.35	MAIL 274.85	MS 216.90	LEVL 248.15	INTC 181.63	SDTI 228.98
TWCGX 217.68	JOF 209.05	SNS 229.80	WTHG 219.53	DEC 206.78	FORE 216.90	CCK 269.82	WMB 265.28	FMC 275.15	SOPFX 216.92	KURZ 248.32	NOBE 182.75	JEC 230.22
FOE 218.28	OST 209.35	TOT 230.10	PPP 219.77	JHNGX 206.97	PKF 217.37	KMB 269.82	KMAG 265.48	LLTC 275.17	FO 216.95	MANU 248.53	EGRP 182.95	ASA 230.35
AHP 218.58	AET 209.62	GLM 231.02	ALEX 219.78	FO#1 207.15	ASND 217.77	PD 269.82	CCR 265.52	RNBO 275.23	GLN 216.95	WLV 248.53	KURZ 183.52	MOB 231.08
ATTr 218.58	ABT 209.82	ISL 231.42	AGREA 219.78	PRD 207.17	AHP 217.97	VVUSX 270.13	RR 265.78	INDQA 275.25	MSFT 217.05	PCAPX 248.95	BNL 183.68	FSAIX 231.12
PGF 219.15	IFF 210.57	PSQL 231.45	DEC 219.78	CPQ 207.42	ATTr 217.97	CAT 270.28	NELL 265.80	NAV 275.25	ORCL 217.07	EGLS 249.53	MDA 183.68	FBIOX 231.12
CCI 219.27	BST 210.85	RBK 231.70	TWN 219.95	MXP 207.42	CI 218.37	TTF 270.30	MF 266.15	RCM 275.33	BBY 217.15	WNDR 249.63	SWZ 184.65	FSESX 231.12
VPMCX 219.37	CREAF 211.27	IRF 231.70	SDTI 220.02	PGF 208.27	OIL 218.65	MXIM 271.17	ABX 266.22	NWS 275.35	BAA 217.18	ACAI 249.70	LEVL 185.87	FSVLX 231.12
ORX 219.38	WTEC 211.97	ITSI 231.73	PEP 220.60	IAF 208.65	IR 219.12	GNE 271.30	UST 266.22	ITA 275.38	HERB 217.18	CYRX 249.85	FDO 186.70	FSPCX 231.12
GGC 219.63	GM 212.30	HNZ 232.30	AMX 220.68	BRWIX 208.65	SRYIX 219.88	TRV 271.82	TSK 266.23	SWZ 275.45	SUNW 217.20	HLYW 250.02	HTCH 187.87	FSRPX 231.12
CGEN 220.10	LTV 212.65	GM 232.75	UNM 221.57	VAR 209.83	WMS 220.08	TWN 272.05	TIF 266.23	GABAX 275.48	GABAX 217.22	MCLL 250.02	TR 190.57	OII 231.63
PNU 220.70	ASC 212.75	VPMCX 233.52	CNC 223.03	FSAIX 211.13	ENM 220.15	FCX 272.07	USS 266.32	SUNW 275.50	HDI 217.22	CYRK 250.43	CEN 191.08	PH 231.85
CSX 221.35	RDA 212.95	TWCGX 234.03	IFMX 223.03	FBIOX 211.13	TWCGX 221.15	EMC 272.25	APB 266.50	WTEC 275.50	INEL 217.23	CTEA 250.48	MYG 191.45	PKF 232.13
PRD 221.93	ZBRA 213.18	WMX 235.17	GRR 223.18	FSESX 211.13	NN 222.03	GLK 272.35	GABGX 266.68	ORCL 275.63	ITA 217.27	TRBCX 250.87	GPC 191.90	QNTM 232.47
UCM 223.15	SNA 213.67	CENF 235.20	OII 223.23	FSVLX 211.13	VENGF 222.15	NTAIF 272.40	TDM 266.70	MSFT 275.65	TJX 217.28	MSX 251.23	KF 193.57	FIDSX 232.67
UNM 223.88	ANL 214.15	IOM 235.20	RDC 223.50	FSPCX 211.13	SYMBA 222.38	ALTR 272.47	BHI 266.72	PEG 275.67	INDQA 217.32	ALL 252.28	LOJN 194.12	FSUTX 232.67
FPF 226.17	CLE 214.25	AUD 236.27	MEA 223.65	FSRPX 211.13	CMSB 222.50	BZF 272.47	MIL 266.77	RGEN 275.68	NAV 217.32	ZEN 252.40	SBRY 194.12	SYQT 233.62
BOST 226.20	KM 214.73	MOB 236.53	MCAF 223.95	UTEK 211.67	JTAX 222.50	BS 272.48	BMCS 267.27	MS 275.73	SWZ 217.45	F 252.57	WMT 195.83	LHP 234.53
BDK 227.03	WDC 215.40	TX 236.53	MDT 224.37	MOMGX 212.12	USWI 222.50	BST 272.50	IGF 267.27	MYL 275.80	UNM 217.57	ASPX 253.45	MHS 196.58	PRU 234.67
LSCC 227.17	AOL 215.43	BSC 237.30	BS 224.60	DIS 212.52	RCHY 222.92	SFL 273.43	NVLS 267.28	GGC 275.82	WMB 217.68	RNK 253.62	FWC 198.48	AAPL 234.87
NT 227.60	CSK 215.98	GAS 237.68	ASSD 224.80	ATTo 212.53	BTIOF 223.02	RBD 274.03	FBGRX 267.65	ONCS 275.82	KMAG 217.80	THDO 253.88	AN 199.10	SRA 235.05
AUD 227.80	XRX 216.55	UNM 237.75	BST 224.98	FPF 212.95	JAMS 223.10	BABSX 275.03	ACN 267.68	BAA 275.87	RNBO 218.00	JAMRX 253.93	MNTR 200.33	CPB 235.15
BTR 229.17	FON 217.32	MWHS 238.05	TIN 225.15	LSCC 213.62	NSTA 223.20	FDEQX 275.20	CY 267.78	BBY 276.05	RR 218.00	DOW 254.18	AEP 200.90	PKN 235.68
VTA 229.22	GLM 217.95	AGWFX 238.57	VAR 225.18	DGAGX 213.80	FMCSX 223.37	AMP 275.22	ORX 268.38	HERB 276.38	NELL 218.03	FSNGX 254.57	TCH 201.45	INFS 236.73
IOM 229.48	LMT#1 218.82	CSC 238.58	FLE 225.57	ARC 214.22	DLNK 223.53	RLM 275.52	APCC 268.55	HDI 276.55	CCE 218.17	FORMF 254.57	RNBO 202.62	BFI 236.95
DIS 229.97	FMCSX 218.93	CPQ 239.15	SYQT 225.60	CHA 215.22	MAPS 223.53	PCO 276.32	EIX 268.58	INEL 276.58	MF 218.32	SANM 254.93	BA 202.80	GAP 237.10
GARD 230.17	HELE 219.15	MXP 239.15	CPB 225.82	SKY 216.60	HNZ 223.60	K 276.53	AKLM 268.95	TJX 276.72	FDCAX 218.35	CATP 255.05	CA 202.80	PCH 237.42
GEMS 230.47	APA 219.45	IAF 240.08	FSHOX 225.88	LMT#1 216.65	IGEN 223.70	MD 276.85	DELL 268.95	USS 276.97	UST 218.38	MCHP 256.32	KWP 202.80	MIL 237.43
FLE 230.82	GT 220.28	BRWIX 240.08	FSCGX 225.88	HAL 218.00	SEPC 223.70	ERTS 277.37	SNF 269.00	CCR 276.98	TIF 218.40	TRCD 256.32	NRK 202.80	DF 237.47
APD 231.00	CHV 220.53	FOE 240.42	FSDPX 225.88	TOT 218.05	YSII 223.70	CH 277.48	SBL 269.20	WMB 277.30	RBK 218.60	WALL 256.47	UTX 203.75	BMET 238.23
UFC 232.65	KBH 220.68	FLE 240.88	FSRFX 225.88	XON 218.42	PARQ 224.20	CWP 277.52	TWN 269.95	KMAG 277.42	APB 218.72	AVID 256.68	EMR 204.20	WAG 238.48
CHKR 232.73	CW 220.73	AMP 241.17	CH 226.25	BMY 218.73	RYOCX 224.35	GABVX 277.57	TTF 270.10	MIL 277.48	GAS 218.77	INTU 256.68	LAD.B 204.80	BBI 238.92
PPP 234.92	MYG 220.82	DIS 241.35	LHP 226.80	BDX 218.90	IIF 224.50	REY 278.53	BST 270.17	ABX 277.50	RCM 218.80	LSTR 257.05	NN 205.15	PPG 239.15
AMX 235.27	WBN 221.20	AHP 242.15	APC 226.87	MAR 219.88	BEV 224.58	TRW 278.57	BS 270.17	TSK 277.52	GABGX 219.10	SIII 257.05	SB 205.85	FTSE100 239.23
GRR 237.28	CUM 221.32	ATTr 242.15	TNB 227.27	USS 220.15	QLGC 224.65	LSI 278.60	TRV 270.50	RR 277.58	TDM 219.18	GLBL 258.22	BMY 206.27	HI 239.32
PSFT 237.52	HM 221.45	UFC 242.87	TOMK 227.33	SOPFX 220.33	IAD 226.17	AGN 278.87	MXIM 270.52	ACN 277.60	BHI 219.20	MATH 258.58	DH 206.48	BLL 239.35
JBHT 239.73	INTC 222.48	PSFT 242.95	AUD 227.38	OM 220.35	AUD 226.78	CGNX 279.32	GNE 270.57	NELL 277.60	WTEC 219.33	WLP 258.90	CQ 206.65	PEP 239.43
DLCH 240.75	OXY 222.72	FSAIX 243.28	CWP 227.40	SGRFX 220.85	FLE 227.43	PGF 279.37	FCX 270.65	CY 277.65	APCC 219.83	GNCI 259.12	AOL 207.10	RDC 239.83
ITSI 241.23	PEP 224.32	FBIOX 243.28	PH 228.00	LIFE 220.98	BA 227.62	ATTo 279.87	SFL 270.65	BMCS 277.77	EIX 219.85	OREM 259.32	CDN 207.48	KR 239.87
AMP 241.58	CSCO 224.83	FSESX 243.28	AIG 228.25	FO 221.55	KKTWX 228.65	ANL 279.90	GLK 270.85	IGF 277.77	TSK 219.90	GHV 259.38	FFTYX 207.67	WTEC 240.50
CNTO 242.00	G 225.72	FSVLX 243.28	TKR 228.55	GLN 221.55	MO 228.78	FPF 279.93	EMC 270.97	FBGRX 277.77	GGC 219.90	ABT 260.38	KKTWX 208.18	LOW 240.82
TWCVX 242.77	LUV 225.82	FSPCX 243.28	CHPS 229.43	CC 221.72	ENE 228.97	LSCC 280.03	NTAIF 271.02	MF 277.78	NVLS 219.90	FMILX 260.60	CUM 208.20	TIN 240.85
BROD 243.83	TOL 226.13	FSRPX 243.28	HNZ 229.48	WIN 221.90	ASA 229.38	LA 280.38	ALTR 271.03	NVLS 277.78	ABX 219.92	MWHS 261.55	BASS 208.25	MEA 241.43
FDCAX 244.03	ASA 226.95	WAG 243.33	WTEC 229.48	ETP 222.07	PCG 229.92	FSLEX 280.83	BZF 271.03	UST 277.80	BMCS 219.92	WHR 261.88	PG 209.33	CMH 241.57
CSC 244.43	FG 227.12	PEP 244.33	GABVX 229.68	GD 222.55	GAP 230.82	DDS 281.27	ERTS 271.38	TIF 277.82	SNF 219.97	SGRFX 262.18	WHR 209.88	GM 242.00
HNZ 244.77	HMSY 227.58	CNTO 244.77	FDX 231.58	TMB 223.92	ALEX 231.37	SYMC 281.27	CH 271.45	CH 277.83	CCR 219.97	OM 262.23	BKS 209.98	N 242.08
CHA 246.25	IGEN 228.00	VO 245.25	FG 231.62	UIS 224.17	AGREA 231.37	FFIDX 281.82	CWP 271.50	APB 277.95	DELL 219.98	PSFT 262.67	ERTS 209.98	FDEGX 242.37
GLM 246.70	SEPC 228.00	UCM 245.50	CTL 231.98	CKFR 224.35	DEC 231.37	R 281.83	GABVX 271.55	ORX 277.95	AKLM 219.97	GEMS 263.03	FSR 209.98	ASTA 242.50
CBB 246.90	YSII 228.00	BTR 246.10	NRK 232.08	AWSHX 225.25	RBD 233.27	WBN 281.83	FDEQX 271.55	BHI 278.00	ISL 221.07	KM 263.48	NII 210.05	FDEQX 242.83
	MRK 228.28	ASSD 246.40	PRU 232.20	DI 225.37	CNTO 233.32	LTV 281.87	LSI 272.05	GABGX 278.00	PSQL 221.32	CENF 263.98	OIL 211.78	FMILX 242.87
	AALR 228.98	BBI 246.78	AAPL 233.00	RTR 225.97	HSY 233.55	SB 281.88	AGN 272.10	TDM 278.00	GLK 221.32	ISL 264.15	HAL 211.97	JAOLX 243.12
	UNH 229.25	PPG 246.88	FOE 233.12	ATTn 226.58	MDR 234.42	NWK 282.05	CGNX 272.33	APCC 278.75	USS 221.32	PSQL 264.15	RTN 211.98	BVALX 243.40
	AVID 230.20	OII 247.97	SO 233.32	TELC 226.58	BABSX 234.62	CRUS 282.23	PGF 272.48	EIX 278.78	HI 264.30	HI 264.30	IFMX 212.83	TXT 243.40
		SYQT 248.02						SBL 278.80				

Sun	Moon	Mercury	Venus	Mars	Jupiter	Saturn	Uranus	Neptune	Pluto	Node	Asc	MC
MDR 247.07	INTU 230.20	KR 248.18	CPLY 233.70	IDTI 227.38	VWUSX 235.00	TKF 282.58	ANL 272.63	TWN 278.82	ACN 221.67	CPLY 264.57	CNC 212.87	OST 244.18
MU 248.12	JANSX 230.25	GEMS 248.27	CAT 234.15	GY 227.92	QNTM 236.80	PCL 282.67	FPF 272.78	BST 278.95	MIL 221.77	MCAF 265.00	RNE 214.05	FBGRX 244.93
OLOG 248.77	CMH 230.53	LHP 248.27	SFL 234.85	KELYA 228.88	NOBE 236.98	CS 282.78	LSCC 272.83	BS 278.95	CY 221.78	HRS 265.17	INGR 214.28	SOPFX 245.38
BOC 248.87	DCN 230.92	GARD 248.47	TEN 234.85	MIL 229.37	UH 237.10	PMTC 282.92	FSLEX 273.15	AKLM 279.02	FBGRX 221.98	PWJ 266.25	KELYA#1 214.28	ADM 245.82
ALEX 249.02	AZO 231.10	PKN 248.87	GM 237.90	DOW 229.52	K 237.92	WGR 282.92	REY 273.22	DELL 279.02	ALTR 222.00	BDK 266.32	HSY 214.47	JHNGX 246.08
AGREA 249.02	BLUEX 231.30	USS 249.42	GGC 238.32	BKB 229.62	BMET 238.07	PURT 283.07	DDS 273.38	SNF 279.05	BZF 222.00	CR 267.05	CH 214.58	FO 247.25
DEC 249.02	ACV 232.15	LOW 249.60	ITT 239.47	RNK 230.17	BKB 238.63	TWX 283.13	SYMC 273.38	SFL 279.23	NTAIF 222.07	JEQ 267.80	HON 214.75	GLN 247.30
VO 249.52	BA 233.32	TWN 249.75	BKB 239.63	CHKR 230.50	FSR 240.27	AW 283.25	WBN 273.72	TTF 279.42	EMC 222.20	DGN 268.10	ATTo 214.77	ENM 248.23
TWN 249.63	OI 234.28	QCOM 250.02	PNU 240.23	TBY 231.10	SEG 240.68	TW 283.33	NWK 273.83	CWP 279.62	AGN 222.37	BNYN 268.17	ALD 215.08	LPX 248.95
CAT 249.97	CKFR 234.68	AAPL 250.43	DI 240.52	TKF 231.30	SGP 240.72	WY 283.33	CRUS 273.95	CH 279.62	CGNX 222.37	CREAF 268.33	R 215.12	TEN 249.10
SNS 249.98	KSWS 234.80	CBB 250.47	USW 241.87	CB 231.75	CHIR 241.10	JEC 283.70	LA 274.08	ERTS 279.62	ORX 222.38	ENP 268.60	CWP 215.38	CTX 249.17
RBK 251.13	FORE 234.85	GAP 251.15	AHP 242.05	FSDAX 231.82	SDTI 241.50	SVT 284.02	TKF 274.22	GABVX 279.63	ANL 222.40	BLL 268.68	CKFR 215.78	FDX 249.45
BT.A 251.38	IOM 234.87	W 252.50	ATTr 242.10	FDLSX 231.82	BBELL 241.63	SRA 284.27	PCL 274.22	MXIM 279.72	GNE 222.50	EQ 269.28	FDSSX 215.95	DGN 249.65
AGWFX 251.77	HERB 234.90	MDR 252.60	JCI 242.15	BA 232.08	RLM 241.63	OST 284.50	EK 274.23	GNE 279.77	SBL 222.50	ABCW 269.33	ONE 216.52	AVT 251.58
IRF 251.87	3I 235.43	JBHT 252.62	FTSE100 242.77	FBS 232.17	MD 241.75	PKN 287.48	CS 274.28	FDEQX 279.80	FSLEX 222.52	CCH 270.08	FSHOX 216.70	ITT 252.03
OI 251.93	PCO 235.45	CAT 252.78	ISL 243.43	LRCX 233.18	HUM 242.20	CDN 288.73	PMTC 274.37	LSI 279.87	MXIM 222.52	DRAI 270.13	FSCGX 216.70	FOCPX 252.68
BS 253.43	HSY 235.90	BOC 252.93	PSQL 243.43	PMTC 233.37	LTR 242.97	FDSSX 288.73	WGR 274.37	TRV 279.95	TTF 222.58	MTSI 270.18	FSDPX 216.70	MCIC 253.37
TKF 253.43	TRBCX 236.02	BLL 253.03	ADM 243.48	WGR 233.37	EVGRX 243.02	MEF 288.82	TWX 274.53	FCX 280.08	DDS 222.60	PX 270.50	FSRFX 216.70	USW 253.87
BST 253.68	CHA 236.12	DLCH 253.13	CR 244.18	AMP 233.57	SUN 243.03	AW 288.82	AW 274.58	EMC 280.08	SYMC 222.60	XCOM 270.82	GABVX 216.90	BBELL 254.08
WY 253.77	ADBE 236.60	CTX 254.23	CENF 247.08	CTL 233.97	BSET 243.37	CESH 289.15	TW 274.58	PGF 280.13	WBN 222.73	GIC 271.25	UTEK 216.92	MOMGX 254.40
GAS 255.95	AWSHX 236.80	CPB 254.50	CNTO 247.13	EK 234.48	PCAR 243.37	AVY 289.20	WY 274.58	GLK 280.15	NWK 222.80	ARRO 271.30	LTV 218.20	BLUEX 254.43
ASA 256.02	SCHL 236.88	CHKR 254.65	CPQ 248.90	FBGRX 234.67	TCOMA 243.37	NKE 289.20	JEC 274.77	NTAIF 280.17	CRUS 222.85	WMX 271.48	APC 218.27	USG 254.55
PMTC 256.48	WIN 237.32	FDX 254.93	MXP 248.90	APSO 234.72	AMGN 243.57	AVT 289.43	SVT 274.93	ALTR 280.17	PCL 223.02	BBBY 271.52	PAGE 218.83	XTR 255.42
WGR 256.48	LGN 237.62	BVALX 255.30	LPX 251.05	TWX 235.43	NII 243.97	SGI 289.85	SRA 275.07	BZF 280.17	CS 223.02	NCDI 271.52	AET 219.02	DI 256.52
MOB 256.80	BFI 238.15	BS 255.65	SGP 251.05	AW 235.95	FDGRX 244.27	LUNR 289.90	OST 275.20	FPF 280.25	ERTS 223.33	FINL 271.93	MEF 219.03	VWUSX 257.53
USS 256.97	CPQ 238.28	PRU 255.83	IAF 251.42	TW 235.95	VO 245.23	RDA 290.80	PURT 275.23	LSCC 280.27	CH 223.52	BSX 272.42	BDX 219.18	BKB 257.65
PH 257.58	MXP 238.28	ASTA 255.92	BRWIX 251.42	WY 235.95	FSTCX 245.57	CSCO 290.92	CDN 275.60	AGN 280.35	CWP 223.55	ICII 272.42	JNJ 219.65	JCP 259.53
QNTM 258.23	COMS 238.47	BST 256.03	CAG 253.42	ABT 236.02	NSCP 245.60	MOLXA 291.15	FDSSX 275.68	CGNX 280.53	TWN 223.57	PLN 273.68	KO 220.30	CL 260.25
CPQ 258.48	BKS 239.18	PKF 256.10	MDR 253.42	AHP 236.33	LBTYA 245.78	TRMB 291.37	MEF 275.73	ANL 280.75	GABVX 223.62	SBRY 273.83	AW 220.60	TEK 261.02
FIDSX 258.48	ALL 240.28	BFI 256.52	FDEQX 253.87	ATTr 236.33	KEY 246.32	IF 292.28	AW 275.73	REY 280.87	BST 223.72	FDC 274.48	TNB 220.92	RAL 261.47
FSUTX 258.48	MER 240.65	CMH 256.72	PCH 253.87	KKTWX 236.68	WTHG 246.32	MU 292.28	LUNR 275.98	TKF 281.05	BS 223.72	BSPT 274.53	RCM 221.15	SKY 261.73
MXP 258.48	TEN 241.75	TWCVX 257.12	UFC 253.87	OIL 236.97	ASC 246.37	PMS 292.32	CESH 276.02	FSLEX 281.08	SFL 224.00	ALBK 274.95	MCAF 222.50	VENGF 261.98
MWHS 258.80	USRX 241.83	PPP 257.28	CCI 253.90	COMS 237.07	ONE 246.45	GACC 292.63	AVY 276.05	PMTC 281.17	LSI 224.43	XIRC 275.00	SKO 223.48	CAG 262.92
NGG 258.82	WAC 241.83	MDT 257.43	CAR 254.18	HD 237.10	U 246.67	NFB 292.70	NKE 276.05	WGR 281.17	FDEQX 224.47	AADV 275.37	BCR 223.65	SYMBA 263.78
SEL 259.03	ALD 241.98	FOCPX 257.67	LSI 254.27	SGP 237.20	SPYG 247.43	FSDCX 293.12	MOLXA 276.55	DDS 281.25	PURT 224.85	COT 275.37	CHPS 223.73	GHV 264.00
TWX 259.53	TEK 242.55	LPX 258.28	PPG 254.55	KLAC 237.40	FLCSX 247.87	FSCPX 293.12	TRMB 276.65	SYMC 281.25	PGF 224.87	LNCR 275.63	MEL 223.73	CMSB 264.68
AW 260.30	ACN 242.92	FIDSX 258.50	VPMCX 255.07	LPX 237.93	TRB 248.67	PRSGX 293.12	PMS 277.15	TWX 281.27	MOLXA 224.97	EPG 275.95	EVGRX 223.83	JTAX 264.68
TW 260.30	BBI 243.52	FSUTX 258.50	MU 255.32	JEC 238.20	NOB 249.05	JOF 293.27	GACC 277.32	AW 281.30	TRMB 224.97	STAR 276.02	CPC 223.97	USWI 264.68
WY 260.30	GTW 243.70	USG 259.45	SNS 255.82	BROD 238.25	MEA 249.22	SEL 293.37	FSDCX 277.58	TW 281.30	PMS 225.03	VCI 276.07	CLX 224.42	MMM 264.93
SEG 260.33	S 244.40	SEG 259.50	FSAIX 256.45	BOST 239.57	ALK 249.35	LMT#1 293.40	FSCPX 277.58	WY 281.30	REY 225.05	CPB 276.40	UNH 225.03	BC 265.95
BAY 260.40	ASTA 244.73	ASA 259.65	FBIOX 256.45	APD 239.82	CCM 249.50	MB 293.78	PRSGX 277.58	JEC 281.42	GACC 225.07	ELY 276.75	WAC 225.77	HM 266.02
IAF 260.52	LOJN 245.50	APSO 260.82	FSESX 256.45	SVT 240.12	UCL 249.62	GTF 293.92	SGI 277.58	LA 281.45	LUNR 225.07	SCHL 276.92	USRX 225.80	ABAX 266.03
BRWIX 260.52	GE 246.67	OI 261.10	FSVLX 256.45	NRK 241.67	CKFR 250.10	XLNX 294.20	MU 277.92	WBN 281.47	FSDCX 225.15	FD 277.87	ACN 228.67	CTZN 266.08
AAPL 260.77	DAL 247.38	MCIC 261.18	FSPCX 256.45	SRA 241.68	AMP 250.38	SSW 294.22	MB 278.00	SVT 281.52	FSCPX 225.15	ABAX 278.60	CPLY 228.67	GMT 266.12
CPB 261.08	CCH 249.02	DI 261.75	FSRPX 256.45	VTA 241.72	BGEN 250.88	IRL 294.33	RDA 278.23	NWK 281.53	FPF 225.15	CTZN 278.60	CESH 229.83	KRB 266.30
QCOM 261.08	ITT 249.30	SOPFX 262.32	PFE 257.28	KF 242.57	CIR 251.13	KSWS 294.50	XLNX 278.27	CRUS 281.60	PRSGX 225.15	USFC 278.92	KLAC 229.85	PFE 267.22
PKN 261.62	FRF 249.68	FMILX 262.45	UCM 257.60	OST 243.08	ZLG 252.37	INFS 294.60	CSCO 278.28	SRA 281.60	LA 225.18	DNB 279.22	VAR 229.85	PWJ 267.65
SFL 261.82	BNYN 250.27	SDTI 262.65	WMX 258.12	AHC 243.18	TXT 253.12	CUAC 294.62	KSWS 278.48	OST 281.67	LSCC 225.20	BS 279.87	AVY 230.62	FDGRX 267.68
SDTI 262.37	AL 250.30	TXT 263.22	PKF 258.38	DRLEX 243.18	KO 253.73	AALR 294.93	SEL 278.52	PCL 281.77	MB 225.32	MER 280.02	NKE 230.62	HOU 268.08
BFI 262.98	ADM 250.73	BROD 263.85	W 259.32	UNP 243.83	DSPC 254.43	APD 295.00	CUAC 278.57	CDN 281.80	XLNX 225.45	LHP 280.40	CY 230.98	NSM 268.10
GAP 263.15	VWUSX 250.88	VWUSX 264.52	MOB 261.23	OI 243.93	LMT 254.98	PESC 295.08	IF 278.80	FDSSX 281.80	KSWS 225.53	SYQT 280.45	AIG 231.45	NOVL 268.18
PCH 263.48	PGF 251.60	WTEC 264.80	DGAGX 261.27	JCI 245.18	RMDY 255.03	ORBI 295.23	NFB 279.00	PX 281.82	CUAC 225.63	OII 280.57	TKR 231.67	RCHY 268.32
DF 263.57	ARC 252.60	FO 265.22	BDK 261.30	UAL 245.53	OLOG 255.52	PFS 295.23	PFS 279.15	MEF 281.82	CDN 225.75	QCOM 280.78	LMT#1 231.87	DGAGX 268.37
JEC 263.60	WLA 253.00	GLN 265.22	CW 261.40	AMX 246.05	IBM 256.05	FDEGX 295.27	INFS 279.17	AW 281.83	FDSSX 226.1	OI 281.25	JCI 231.92	GNCI 268.53

Sun	Moon	Mercury	Venus	Mars	Jupiter	Saturn	Uranus	Neptune	Pluto	Node	Asc	MC
BMET 264.33	GABAX 253.92	DF 266.37	ASA 262.68	LTR 246.63	PNU 256.55	FRF 295.30	JOF 279.20	AVY 281.95	PFS 226.13	BROD 281.68	TRB 232.42	SGP 268.55
FSAIX 264.58	NII 254.28	BLUEX 266.65	FO#1 264.13	JP 247.00	JBHT 257.05	BLUEX 296.80	FRF 279.27	CESH 281.95	MEF 226.22	APSO 281.93	AMAT 232.90	BA 268.77
FBIOX 264.58	NOVL 254.43	FDEGX 266.83	PGF 266.05	GRR 247.50	DLCH 257.27	HWP 297.67	GTF 279.40	NKE 281.95	TKF 226.22	CHKR 282.25	G 233.80	AT 268.95
FSESX 264.58	KEY 255.02	TKF 266.98	LTR 266.73	CMB 248.33	TWCVX 257.72	CHV 298.28	SSW 279.47	LUNR 282.20	FRF 226.27	WWY 282.35	LSI 233.90	BTIOF 269.22
FSVLX 264.58	IK 255.13	ALEX 267.53	CGEN 266.98	BSET 248.52	BFI 258.68	KRB 298.33	IRL 279.50	PURT 282.25	AW 226.27	TOT 283.22	AMD 234.72	REY 269.45
FSPCX 264.58	GER 255.28	AGREA 267.53	QNTM 267.23	PCAR 248.52	UBIS 260.12	CYGN 299.28	FDEGX 279.53	MOLXA 282.63	PMTC 226.30	OPPSX 283.35	ISL 234.85	JAMS 270.12
FSRPX 264.58	TKR 256.55	DEC 267.53	ABAX 267.93	TCOMA 248.52	HAL 260.53	RN 299.40	ORBI 279.55	TRMB 282.70	WGR 226.33	ITW 283.45	PSQL 234.85	SBL 270.58
WAG 264.62	AMAT 256.78	BKB 268.00	CTZN 267.93	PNU 249.93	CTX 261.60	BAX 299.83	AALR 279.58	MU 283.00	TWX 226.43	MEA 283.52	BEV 234.92	NSTA 271.02
BBI 265.07	KR 256.92	OLOG 268.08	GARD 268.05	PSON 250.07	BAY 261.63	WDC 299.87	PESC 279.58	PMS 283.05	AW 226.47	USRX 284.12	SUN 235.63	OAT 272.02
OII 265.15	AADV 257.47	SFL 268.23	PRD 268.53	CAT 250.17	BS 261.68	HMSY 299.98	PAGE 279.90	GACC 283.17	TW 226.47	WAC 284.12	CYBR 235.67	WLP 272.15
PPG 265.53	COT 257.47	JCP 268.60	SEL 268.82	QCOM 250.48	CBB 262.13	PAGE 300.20	SKO 279.98	FSDCX 283.35	WY 226.47	RD 284.13	TXN 235.92	OPTFX 272.63
BLL 265.53	CHPS 258.43	NGG 268.65	GEMS 268.88	INDQA 250.68	CR 262.43	SKO 300.20	UNH 280.02	FSCPX 283.35	JEC 226.67	UNH 284.17	FG 236.08	PCO 273.00
HI 265.53	WAG 258.57	QNTM 268.82	BSET 270.00	NAV 250.68	TIN 263.13	UNH 300.22	USRX 280.03	SGI 283.37	SVT 226.73	SKO 284.27	CENF 237.22	FO#1 273.33
PEP 265.65	BVALX 258.80	N 269.68	PCAR 270.00	KBH 250.70	ED 263.28	USRX 300.23	WAC 280.03	PRSGX 283.35	CESH 226.73	VO 284.47	CW 237.23	CYGN 273.55
PKF 265.68	HD 259.48	DGN 269.72	TCOMA 270.00	PPP 251.32	SB 264.28	WAC 300.23	BLUEX 280.30	SEL 283.62	SRA 226.77	PAGE 284.58	WTHG 237.77	CTR 274.30
RDC 266.07	FDX 259.90	WY 270.60	BC 270.87	LAD.B 251.63	NGG 264.78	TOT 300.65	ZBRA 280.32	MB 283.67	AVY 226.77	NSM 286.37	MAR 237.98	RN 274.45
KR 266.06	UH 260.53	BT.A 270.62	GAP 271.48	RTN 251.77	BDK 265.15	MUS 300.78	TOT 280.48	RDA 283.63	NKE 226.77	ZBRA 287.13	SO 238.20	DLNK 274.65
SVT 266.40	MEL 261.45	BC 271.12	CCR 271.65	NSM 252.27	R 265.15	RAL 300.82	SDII 280.52	CSCO 283.67	ORBI 226.77	LPX 287.48	UNVGX 239.68	MAPS 274.65
ASSD 267.10	CA 261.73	MIL 271.38	CBB 272.55	JPM 253.10	LTV 265.53	LIZ 301.55	SYBS 280.52	INFS 283.77	OST 226.80	SDII 287.50	CAR 240.42	OM 275.08
LOW 267.10	KWP 261.73	PMTC 271.52	KAB 272.90	OII 253.30	ITT 265.85	CHKR 301.60	PRGS 280.80	XLINX 283.78	PESC 226.93	SYBS 287.50	CTL 241.92	SGRFX 275.95
TIN 267.13	FSENX 262.22	WGR 271.52	OLOG 273.13	SBL 253.33	USW 266.28	APSO 302.02	KRB 281.07	KSWS 283.93	AALR 227.05	PRGS 287.98	CIR 242.55	RAD 276.00
SYQT 267.18	FSPHX 262.22	HM 272.17	FPF 273.23	ITA 254.08	FTSE100 266.47	ZBRA 302.40	CHKR 281.17	CUAC 283.98	IRL 227.35	KKTWX 288.82	WMX 242.85	CBE 276.03
MEA 267.82	FDPMX 262.22	CL 272.62	LMS 273.55	BT 254.48	WMT 268.48	BROD 302.40	APSO 281.45	FDEGX 284.00	SSW 227.38	KLU 288.93	CNG 243.85	NEM 276.25
CMH 267.90	FSPTX 262.22	MEA 273.62	LSCC 274.22	SYQT 254.75	CG 268.53	SDII 302.58	KLU 281.48	IF 284.00	GTF 227.48	SSPE 288.93	BTR 247.52	IGEN 276.45
TOMK 268.00	GACC 264.38	DGAGX 273.80	BMET 274.77	BASS 255.12	FKGRX 268.62	SYBS 302.58	SSPE 281.48	PAGE 284.00	PRGS 227.55	BA 289.18	GARD 248.27	SEPC 276.45
LHP 268.20	ALMI 265.77	SGP 273.58	SOPFX 275.32	HNZ 255.20	JAOLX 268.95	OI 303.08	CYGN 281.50	SKO 284.03	SDII 227.58	CORR 289.73	TOT 251.07	YSII 276.45
GM 268.43	CAT 266.22	INFS 274.53	MCIC 275.93	LHP 255.47	DREQX 269.60	PRGS 303.23	RN 281.55	USRX 284.05	SYBS 227.58	CCC 290.05	BSC 252.23	KAB 277.40
N 268.52	BDX 266.85	PH 274.88	DIS 277.02	HM 256.20	ROAD 269.78	SLB 303.23	BROD 281.70	UNH 284.05	JOF 227.63	IDXX 290.05	PGF 254.72	MATH 277.58
SRA 268.68	SUNW 268.00	FTSE100 275.05	NSM 277.28	CSX 256.23	YELL 269.78	NPR 303.55	WDC 281.77	WAC 284.05	KLU 227.63	ICST 290.10	ORX 254.92	WDC 278.07
ASTA 268.92	FCYCF 268.18	AVT 275.25	PSFT 277.28	MAS 256.35	DGAGX 269.80	PWG 303.55	HMSY 281.82	NFB 284.15	SSPE 227.63	PESPX 290.15	GGC 255.12	LMS 278.25
BVALX 269.93	FNATF 268.18	USW 275.97	IRF 277.50	IBM 256.55	NUE 271.27	ENG 303.85	CORR 282.08	JOF 284.28	ZBRA 227.65	SPW 290.22	CR 255.93	JR 278.33
TXT 269.93	IAF 268.45	TWX 275.98	FO 277.83	GABAX 256.90	CMCSA 271.37	QCOM 303.92	OI 282.12	TOT 284.28	NFB 227.70	GM 290.97	PNU 255.98	FD 278.77
INFS 270.48	BRWIX 268.45	TEN 276.00	GLN 277.83	SUNW 257.45	ADM 271.48	OII 304.32	MUS 282.17	PFS 284.33	SGI 227.73	AMAT 291.50	TX 257.10	HMSY 278.93
OST 270.75	EC 268.83	TEK 276.33	AT 277.83	BEV 257.98	AMAT 271.95	SYQT 304.52	CCC 282.33	FRF 284.40	IF 227.75	SOTA 291.58	UNM 258.65	CCR 278.95
MIL 271.22	FCX 269.77	RDC 277.00	WY 278.70	ORCL 261.83	LIFE 272.92	KLU 304.55	IDXX 282.33	GTF 284.43	CSCO 227.78	SRM 291.95	GR 259.78	SGI 279.15
ADM 272.57	ED 270.60	AT 277.03	LIFE 279.62	MSFT 262.38	KF 273.22	SSPE 304.55	ICST 282.37	ZBRA 284.43	RDA 227.78	BOC 291.98	TWCGX 259.82	TOS 279.20
JHNGX 272.88	LOW 270.63	AW 277.08	ENM 279.78	DH 262.52	ATTo 273.27	LHP 304.63	PESPX 282.40	BLUEX 284.48	CORR 227.82	TMX 292.05	BS 260.17	U 281.27
WTEC 274.52	SRYIX 270.83	TW 277.08	JCP 282.02	DD 263.40	HI 273.45	TNB 304.88	SPW 282.45	PESC 284.48	CCC 227.92	HAE 292.27	FOE 260.33	LIFE 282.00
LPX 275.98	AEP 271.07	WY 277.08	INFS 282.95	GR 265.78	MEL 274.68	AZO 305.27	LIZ 282.48	SDII 284.57	IDXX 227.92	MRO 292.43	BOST 260.57	LTR 282.15
TEN 276.18	PRU 271.08	HOU 277.10	CSC 284.13	RD 266.12	KELYA 275.12	CORR 305.53	QCOM 282.48	SYBS 284.57	ICST 227.95	HSBA 293.98	FPF 260.57	SLB 282.30
CTX 276.22	ICII 272.72	MMM 277.30	OPTFX 284.20	MS 266.63	ATTn 275.40	HSBA 305.63	OII 282.83	IRL 284.50	PESPX 227.97	WMT 294.05	AHP 260.60	DREQX 283.70
FDX 276.52	JNJ 273.32	OAT 277.37	USS 284.32	TTF 266.75	TELC 275.40	CCC 305.87	SYQT 282.95	AALR 284.57	SPW 227.98	AZO 294.28	ATTr 260.60	PARQ 283.73
DGN 276.75	ELY 273.43	NOVL 277.98	FD 285.12	MEL 266.80	AIG 275.75	IDXX 305.92	LHP 283.02	ORBI 284.57	MU 228.52	ENG 295.23	CCI 261.17	GLBL 283.95
FDEQX 277.08	ZLG 274.30	ITT 278.63	RAL 285.90	PKF 268.18	IDTI 275.77	ICST 305.97	NPR 283.23	PRGS 284.67	SOTA 228.60	NPR 295.40	VPMCX 261.27	ROAD 284.62
FMILX 277.12	SFA 274.57	BMET 278.93	NGG 287.13	CBB 269.27	CB 276.48	SPW 306.00	PWG 283.23	CHKR 284.67	PAGE 228.72	PWG 295.40	LSCC 261.42	YELL 284.67
PRU 277.28	USW 274.63	ADM 278.97	CBE 287.63	BOC 269.75	DRTHX 277.25	MRO 306.77	SOTA 283.33	APSO 284.78	SRM 228.80	NUE 296.38	CGEN 261.90	TCOMA 284.83
JAOLX 277.40	TRB 274.88	SEL 279.00	ITSI 287.70	WY 270.95	GCI 277.47	HAE 306.80	ENG 283.33	KRB 284.83	TMX 228.85	CMCSA 296.43	GAS 262.20	BSET 284.88
AVT 278.93	GHV 276.12	PFE 279.05	ARC 288.37	ASC 271.93	CB 277.80	SOTA 306.80	SRM 283.48	BROD 284.97	SKO 228.92	LIZ 296.45	BOC 262.68	PCAR 284.88
FBGRX 279.37	KAB 276.38	PCH 279.25	MMM 289.57	XTR 271.95	AOL 278.10	SRM 306.83	TMX 283.53	OI 284.98	SEL 228.92	MUS 296.82	CSX 262.97	USFC 285.10
ITT 279.37		BAY 280.92	REY 289.85	ONCS 273.22	EGRP 278.33	TMX 306.83	HAE 283.60	CYGN 285.23	HAE 228.97	HMSY 297.18	VTA 263.13	MUS 285.32
SOPFX 279.87		KRB 280.97	FDEGX 290.47	AIG 273.70	ETP 278.38	ABAX 308.48	MRO 283.65	KLU 285.25	UNH 229.00	WDC 297.25	IOM 263.37	LA 285.82
FOCPX 280.13		HI 281.25	BFI 290.53	MXIM 274.83	RNE 278.97	CTZN 308.48	AZO 283.77	SSPE 285.25	USRX 229.03	RN 297.45	PRD 263.45	RYOCX 286.48
MCIC 280.85		TOMK 281.73	SGI 290.98	ASSD 275.05	VPMCX 278.97	TOMK 308.73	HSBA 283.77	RN 285.28	WAC 229.03	CYGN 297.52	GEMS 264.22	CYCH 286.97
			RDA 291.93	F 275.12	CC 279.12		MCAF 284.12		MRO 229.05	KRB 297.93	UCM 264.48	GP 287.02

Sun	Moon	Mercury	Venus	Mars	Jupiter	Saturn	Uranus	Neptune	Pluto	Node	Asc	MC
USW 281.40	FSLBX 276.78	JEC 281.75	CSCO 292.22	SGI 275.80	CYCH 279.17	XRX 309.52	CPLY 284.23	WDC 285.43	INFS 229.30	BLUEX 298.62	NGG 264.57	RDA 287.42
BBELL 281.65	FSCHX 276.78	JHNGX 282.80	CSK 292.58	GNE 276.18	PKN 279.88	RTZ 310.10	ISL 284.42	HMSY 285.47	FDEGX 229.48	GCI 299.28	SEL 264.75	CCM 288.00
FO 281.90	FDCPX 276.78	ENM 282.85	BT.A 293.20	TKR 277.58	COMS 280.67	FD 310.17	PSQL 284.42	QCOM 285.55	TOT 229.67	FDEGX 299.32	BT.A 264.82	CSCO 288.35
GLN 281.90	FSELX 276.78	GM 282.97	ABX 293.37	NGG 278.20	GARD 280.87	BMY 310.75	CENF 284.48	CORR 285.65	HSBA 229.82	TXN 299.58	AW 265.82	TTF 288.78
MOMGX 282.07	FDFAX 276.78	GMT 283.75	WMS 293.38	MYL 278.38	TMB 281.35	USFC 310.98	JEQ 284.65	MUS 285.68	BLUEX 229.85	INFS 299.63	TW 265.82	WFC 288.78
FTSE100 282.17	FSCSX 276.78	RAD 284.10	BBI 293.63	ABAX 280.62	BGY 281.38	CPLY 311.82	BNYN 284.87	OII 285.68	AZO 229.93	SEL 300.22	WY 265.82	ABS 289.70
USG 282.17	PG 277.03	FBGRX 284.22	USFC 293.73	CTZN 280.62	UIS 281.45	ISL 311.85	CREAF 284.97	SYQT 285.77	KRB 230.12	MU 300.78	CHKR 266.18	AR 289.77
ENM 282.98	BMET 277.78	SGRFX 285.43	TSK 294.50	ENM 281.07	CYBR 281.55	PSQL 311.85	ABAX 285.02	LHP 285.80	ENP 230.13	DRTHX 301.93	BDK 267.92	IIF 290.17
XTR 283.13	CATP 278.12	OM 285.47	KR 294.88	ADBE 281.43	RTR 281.97	CENF 311.90	CTZN 285.02	CCC 285.82	CREAF 230.15	AVY 303.12	AMX 268.40	WMS 290.72
DI 284.38	RBK 278.25	SVT 285.50	ATTn 295.60	FDX 282.12	OM 282.37	MCAF 311.90	GEMS 285.10	IDXX 285.82	BNYN 230.17	NKE 303.12	NT 268.42	ARC 291.65
VWUSX 285.55	CYCH 279.18	TIN 286.17	TELC 295.60	RDA 282.33	SGRFX 282.58	SCHL 312.27	ENP 285.13	ICST 285.83	EQ 230.18	CDN 303.18	AUD 268.60	LIZ 291.82
BKB 285.65	INTV 279.27	U 287.98	BBELL 296.10	HOU 282.50	HD 282.80	GEMS 312.45	PSFT 285.40	PESPX 285.87	ABCW 230.20	AW 303.82	GRR 270.20	LGN 291.90
JCP 287.75	CORR 280.17	SRA 288.35	LOW 296.12	PRU 282.70	TBY 282.80	ELY 312.60	EQ 285.63	LIZ 285.90	JEQ 230.20	MEF 303.92	PSFT 270.43	INDQA 292.02
CL 288.55	SLB 280.55	XTR 289.37	WIN 296.85	RAL 282.82	FSDAX 282.85	BNL 312.68	ABCW 285.67	SPW 285.90	CYGN 230.23	FDSSX 304.13	DIS 270.53	NAV 292.02
TEK 289.40	BNI 281.62	ABAX 290.07	TKF 296.97	CSCO 283.07	FDLSX 282.85	PSFT 312.82	FD 285.80	MCAF 286.20	ENG 230.23	HM 304.48	SVT 271.15	TXU 292.07
BLUEX 289.85	LOR 281.87	CTZN 290.07	TXT 297.32	GM 284.48	FBS 282.88	VCI 314.00	USFC 286.15	CPLY 286.27	RN 230.25	CDN 304.72	FLE 271.32	IBM 292.62
RAL 289.90	CY 282.07	NSM 290.20	IDTI 298.07	RGEN 284.55	LRCX 282.93	STAR 314.10	DRAI 286.28	ENG 286.35	NPR 230.27	YELL 304.75	APD 271.47	TRW 293.12
SKY 290.90	MD 282.22	OST 290.68	IF 298.00	UK 284.55	AVT 283.78	EPG 314.22	MTSI 286.28	ISL 286.35	PWG 230.27	DREQX 304.80	APSO 271.57	MHP 293.35
CAG 291.53	WALL 282.52	LIFE 290.90	PWJ 298.62	GER 285.28	IOM 284.60	JEQ 314.60	MWHS 286.45	NPR 286.38	WDC 230.28	ROAD 305.17	CCE 271.77	CSK 293.68
MMM 293.87	CGEN 282.98	CYGN 292.08	VENGF 298.65	PEG 285.30	BT.A 285.07	LNCR 314.80	PX 286.55	PWG 286.38	HMSY 230.30	LUNR 306.52	UFC 272.98	ATTn 293.98
BC 294.98	SRFSX 283.40	FDEOX 292.22	PMTC 299.00	AAPL 285.77	ORA 286.07	BNYN 315.12	SCHL 286.67	CENF 286.40	MUS 230.35	CTX 306.80	PPP 275.08	TELC 293.98
GMT 295.18	NOB 283.57	LTR 292.40	WGR 299.00	TOL 285.85	LCOS 286.10	AADV 315.27	XCOM 286.78	SOTA 286.45	DRAI 230.37	BFI 307.50	BROD 276.23	NPR 294.88
HM 296.17	ALEX 283.83	SGI 293.00	VWUSX 299.12	GTE 286.95	LU 286.28	COT 315.27	ELY 286.80	SRM 286.57	LIZ 230.37	MOLGX 307.52	FDCAX 276.42	PWG 294.88
PFE 296.93	AGREA 283.83	FDGRX 293.48	PCO 299.52	CA 287.27	LPX 286.82	CREAF 315.35	GIC 287.07	TMX 286.58	CHKR 230.38	AR 307.55	CBB 279.13	SCHL 295.32
FDGRX 296.93	DEC 283.85	RN 293.53	ECH 300.17	KWP 287.27	YHOO 286.92	DE 315.50	ARRO 287.10	HAE 286.63	MTSI 230.38	TRMB 307.68	MDT 279.15	IDTI 295.80
NSM 297.38	UNM 283.85	FO#1 295.20	TWX 300.83	UCM 287.82	RTK 287.28	ENP 315.72	BBBY 287.23	JEQ 286.67	PX 230.48	OLOG 308.23	ASSD 279.17	WIN 296.55
HOU 297.40	FTSE100 283.93	WFC 295.23	SYMBA 301.17	X 287.87	PHII 287.30	XIRC 315.90	NCDI 287.23	MRO 286.67	XCOM 230.60	PMS 308.37	W 279.33	TSK 297.38
NOVL 297.45	AMX 284.23	KAB 296.10	FIDSX 301.18	CNTO 287.93	LOR 287.65	ALBK 315.98	VCI 287.30	VCI 286.68	APSO 230.63	UTX 308.47	JBHT 279.68	ITA 297.62
DGAGX 297.87	PCG 285.38	JAOLX 296.40	FSUTX 301.25	PCO 289.10	C 288.00	FMILX 316.00	STAR 287.33	AZO 286.68	GIC 230.78	GACC 308.58	TOMK 280.07	ELY 298.13
SGP 297.87	HNZ 286.88	ABS 296.40	AW 301.25	VPMCX 289.52	CMH 288.63	FKREX 316.35	EPG 287.37	HSBA 286.75	ARRO 230.80	AN 308.78	AN 280.35	QLGC 299.52
VENGF 298.28	MOT 287.58	BSET 296.70	TW 301.25	EMC 289.68	ASTA 288.87	MTC 316.35	FMILX 287.47	GEMS 286.82	BROD 230.83	FSDCX 308.95	DLCH 280.67	AMRMX 299.78
AT 298.33	NN 288.10	PCAR 296.70	GP 301.57	UNVGX 289.98	GP 288.93	BSPT 316.60	FINL 287.47	BNYN 286.90	BBBY 230.90	FSCPX 308.95	ITSI 281.12	MXIM 300.00
SYMBA 300.32	RGEN 288.53	TCOMA 296.70	MIL 301.67	FSAVX 290.32	BVALX 289.08	EQ 316.63	LNCR 287.55	CREAF 286.93	NCDI 230.90	PRSGX 308.95	AMP 281.47	IF 300.43
GHV 300.55	PESC 288.88	MOMGX 297.10	MWHS 302.18	FSPFX 290.32	ABT 289.57	FDC 316.67	AADV 287.67	PSFT 287.02	FINL 231.10	MB 309.48	TWN 281.82	ORA 301.03
CMSB 301.33	DREVX 289.85	GHV 298.55	CL 302.20	FSHCX 290.32	FOCPX 291.72	ABCW 316.70	COT 287.67	ENP 287.02	OI 231.15	XLNX 309.85	CNTO 281.90	ALK 301.73
JTAX 301.33	F 290.90	CBE 298.65	CMSB 302.42	FBMPX 290.32	NSM 291.72	BDX 317.02	BSX 287.70	ABAX 287.07	BSX 231.35	KSWS 310.17	TWCVX 282.65	GNE 301.90
USWI 301.33	FDSSX 291.55	TRW 299.00	JTAX 302.42	FSRBX 290.32	USG 291.85	ECH 317.25	ICII 287.70	CTZN 287.07	ICII 231.35	CUAC 310.28	RBK 283.32	GABAX 302.30
OAT 301.78	AGWFX 291.92	LA 299.12	USWI 302.42	ITW 290.63	SO 292.75	DRAI 317.58	XIRC 287.82	EQ 287.35	MCAF 231.37	WTHG 310.52	OI 284.12	FCYCF 302.63
OPTFX 302.52	RBD 294.60	PCO 299.23	NFB 302.77	NWS 290.90	AEP 292.82	PLN 317.62	ALBK 287.83	ABCW 287.38	QCOM 231.48	GRA 311.02	CSC 284.32	FNATF 302.63
ABAX 302.83	BCR 295.28	WDC 299.52	JEC 302.93	FD 291.18	RNK 293.43	MTSI 317.63	BSPT 287.95	FD 287.57	OII 231.62	PFS 311.28	HNZ 284.65	APA 303.15
CTZN 302.83	GMT 295.68	CYCH 300.57	AMRMX 303.12	NGC 291.62	DOW 294.73	PX 317.90	FDC 287.95	MWHS 287.58	CPLY 231.65	SUN 311.47	TKF 285.65	SUNW 303.30
PCO 302.90	APD 296.52	IBM 300.65	PKN 303.88	MDR 291.78	NOVL 295.37	XCOM 318.13	PLN 288.22	DRAI 287.77	SYQT 231.68	FRF 311.55	BST 285.90	ABX 303.68
KRB 303.08	HSBA 299.25	BBELL 300.85	SVT 304.13	OPPSX 292.05	DCN 296.50	WY 318.20	UTEK 288.22	MTSI 287.80	LHP 231.72	GMT 312.38	CHA 286.17	SII 304.25
FO#1 303.35	NSCP 300.02	HMSY 301.03	DF 304.17	JAOLX 292.30	LMT#1 297.85	GIC 318.35	BKS 288.25	USFC 287.80	ISL 231.95	FSR 312.42	GLM 286.65	LSTR 304.50
OM 305.25	UBIS 300.98	REY 302.97	VLIFX 304.60	LLTC 292.32	PE 297.88	ARRO 318.37	FFTYX 288.27	PX 287.97	PSQL 231.95	ORBI 312.50	MDR 287.03	SIII 304.50
RCHY 305.40	LTD 301.92	WMS 303.10	SRA 304.95	FMC 292.45	HWP 300.42	BSX 318.42	MAR 288.30	XCOM 288.12	PLN 232.02	PESC 312.82	OLOG 288.80	BS 304.97
GNCI 305.65	AHP 302.22	NEM 303.68	DSPC 305.52	IF 292.58	APD 301.30	ICII 318.42	TCH 288.33	SCHL 288.13	CENF 232.07	AALR 313.08	PMTC 288.82	JANSX 305.67
RAD 306.25	ATTr 302.22	CSK 304.23	OST 305.53	VENGF 292.60	LGN 301.38	BBBY 318.43	LEVL 288.78	ELY 288.23	FDC 232.38	EVGRX 313.17	WGR 288.82	SNA 305.77
SGRFX 306.27	SANM 303.00	RAL 304.82	HM 306.18	SCF 292.65	SBRY 302.77	NCDI 318.43	GHV 288.83	FMILX 288.32	BSPT 232.40	IRL 313.77	ALEX 289.03	GRA 305.82
BTIOF 306.42	ABX 303.60	RDA 304.93	BLL 306.38	CNC 292.67	WMX 303.47	FINL 318.48	KURZ 288.88	GIC 288.33	ALBK 232.57	SSW 313.87	AGREA 289.07	DSPC 305.97
NEM 306.53	CMZ 303.67	TXU 305.77	CTX 306.63	IFMX 292.67	ITW 303.70	GHV 318.55	BOST 288.97	ARRO 288.38	XIRC 232.58	GTF 314.13	DEC 289.07	HSBA 306.02
REY 306.63	EIX 303.68	DREOX 305.90	BS 306.68	ADPT 293.00	OPPSX 304.08	GNCI 319.13	MANU 289.00	UTEK 288.40	ABAX 232.65	NOBE 314.28	USS 289.33	TAN 306.18
JAMS 307.43	NPR 304.07	CSCO 306.35	RAD 306.68	MAIL 293.10	CHV 305.80	WLP 319.60	WLV 289.00	BKS 288.40	CTZN 232.65	JOF 314.62	VO 289.57	NFB 306.22
KAB 307.82	PWG 304.07	GNCI 306.98		NTAIF 293.73	CTR 306.23		VTA 289.07	BBBY 288.42	AADV 232.72	WAG 314.88	CAT 290.05	CB 307.27

Sun	Moon	Mercury	Venus	Mars	Jupiter	Saturn	Uranus	Neptune	Pluto	Node	Asc	MC
SBL 307.88	DOW 304.22	ROAD 307.55	BLUEX 306.77	SYMBA 294.15	BAX 307.00	MATH 320.33	GNCI 289.12	FFTYX 288.42	COT 232.72	NFB 314.98	SNS 290.10	UK 307.30
NSTA 308.45	C 304.53	YELL 307.55	WAG 306.95	CMSB 294.92	WWY 307.35	FON 320.87	PCAPX 289.27	MAR 288.42	PCAPX 232.72	IF 315.30	PRU 290.27	VLIFX 307.43
LMS 308.78	XCOM 305.07	VENGF 307.77	HI 307.30	JTAX 294.92	ALD 307.45	GLBL 321.17	AMX 289.30	NCDI 288.42	EGLS 232.73	CSCO 315.98	CPQ 290.95	ABT 307.63
JR 308.87	ONCS 306.40	GP 308.05	SCHL 307.45	USWI 294.92	BSC 308.25	TEK 321.43	WLP 289.35	TCH 288.48	ACAI 232.75	RDA 316.05	MXP 290.95	IFF 309.05
WLP 309.72	NGC 306.52	AR 308.50	RCHY 307.45	FSHOX 295.07	FCYCF 309.38	FMAGX 322.30	GRR 289.38	VCI 288.53	MANU 232.75	UH 316.08	MWHS 291.25	S 309.12
TOS 309.88	XLNX 307.45	AMRMX 308.65	SII 307.92	FSCGX 295.07	FNATF 309.38	UTX 323.48	EGLS 289.68	STAR 288.55	WLV 232.75	SGI 316.52	AGWFX 292.00	RLM 309.25
CYGN 311.22	HI 307.68	SKY 308.70	JOF 308.38	FSDPX 295.07	LQJN 309.67	BOST 323.75	MATH 289.68	EPG 288.57	WNDR 232.75	UCM 317.07	TWX 292.08	OXY 310.02
U 312.18	LMS 307.98	CAG 309.05	BTIOF 308.70	FSRFX 295.07	HTCH 310.62	LSTR 323.78	WNDR 289.77	FINL 288.57	CYRX 232.77	HUM 318.67	IRF 292.13	ECH 310.20
RN 312.33	CLX 309.03	ATTn 309.93	BA 308.90	ALTR 295.75	BLL 311.40	SIII 323.82	ACAI 289.80	LNCR 288.58	GEMS 232.77	OST 318.95	SEG 292.93	VCI 310.53
PWJ 312.33	GRR 309.93	TELC 309.93	JAOLX 309.68	BZF 295.75	MER 311.85	VTA 323.82	CYRX 289.92	BSX 288.68	KURZ 232.78	SRA 319.07	IAF 293.13	ORCL 311.03
DLNK 312.50	PFS 310.43	MHP 310.42	JAMS 309.95	APC 296.07	DNB 312.13	MAR 323.87	HLYW 290.03	ICII 288.73	LNCR 232.78	SVT 319.18	BRWIX 293.13	AVID 311.28
MAPS 312.50	MIL 310.65	BS 311.05	N 310.23	VO 296.47	NRK 312.18	AN 323.92	MCLL 290.03	AADV 288.73	HLYW 232.80	JEC 319.33	QCOM 293.73	INTU 311.28
LTR 312.95	SCDUX 311.15	SYMBA 311.17	TAN 310.38	USFC 296.52	RAL 312.65	AMX 324.00	GLBL 290.07	COT 288.77	LEVL 232.80	AW 319.50	WY 294.23	STAR 311.57
LTR 313.12	ASPX 311.20	MUS 312.10	UK 310.38	NFB 297.00	UK 312.75	GRR 324.07	CYRK 290.40	BOST 288.77	MCLL 232.80	TW 319.50	SFL 294.58	MSFT 311.97
SLB 313.30	MUS 311.40	CTR 312.20	MO 310.72	GARD 297.47	FSLBX 312.80	UTEK 324.30	CTEA 290.40	LEVL 288.80	EPG 232.85	WY 319.50	SDTI 295.18	EPG 312.55
IGEN 314.53	MOB 312.00	ALK 312.27	DGN 310.73	TEK 297.95	FSCHX 312.80	AVID 324.57	TRBCX 290.68	KURZ 288.80	FD 232.85	TWX 319.53	FTSE100296.33	JOF 312.98
SEPC 314.53	LLTC 312.12	FD 312.83	ELY 311.00	RCHY 298.02	FDCPX 312.80	INTU 324.57	PKF 290.77	XIRC 288.85	STAR 232.87	PMTC 319.70	JEC 296.60	ENG 313.78
YSII 314.53	PLN 312.75	CMSB 312.87	NSTA 311.22	GLM 298.30	FSELX 312.80	BKS 324.77	MSX 290.95	ALBK 288.85	CYRK 232.88	WGR 319.70	ASA 296.77	F 313.88
DREQX 314.90	CL 313.00	JTAX 312.87	FBGRX 311.53	BTIOF 298.80	FDFAX 312.80	FFTYX 324.93	LSTR 291.08	VTA 288.87	VCI 232.88	RTN 319.77	MOB 297.63	LMT 314.75
MATH 315.80	ASH 313.12	USWI 312.87	CMH 312.25	JAMS 299.57	FSCSX 312.80	WALL 325.02	SIII 291.08	BSPT 288.87	CTEA 232.90	TKF 319.85	FSAIX 297.70	WALL 315.22
ROAD 315.92	ABCW 313.60	IDTI 313.08	LA 312.38	CHPS 299.75	DGN 313.68	MCHP 325.33	AVID 291.35	FDC 288.92	USFC 232.92	LSCC 321.23	FBIOX 297.70	RMDY 315.73
YELL 315.92	YHOO 313.82	WLP 313.90	CB 312.87	QNTM 300.30	CPQ 314.02	TRCD 325.33	INTU 291.35	MANU 288.93	ELY 232.95	FPF 321.28	FSESX 297.70	DEX 317.95
BSET 316.17	MCD 314.63	MXIM 314.42	ASTA 313.40	NSTA 300.35	MXP 314.02	TCH 325.45	WALL 291.50	WLV 288.93	SCHL 232.95	PGF 321.65	FSVLX 297.70	MCHP 318.20
PCAR 316.17	CG 315.27	JR 314.65	ASC 313.48	SLB 300.53	HM 314.07	PKF 325.75	MCHP 291.58	PLN 288.93	TRBCX 233.00	ASC 322.05	FSPCX 297.70	TRCD 318.20
TCOMA 316.17	NT 316.03	CCM 314.80	BVALX 314.55	AGWFX 302.15	IAF 314.38	LEVL 326.90	TRCD 291.58	AMX 288.95	PSFT 233.05	AWSHX 322.20	FSRPX 297.70	LNCR 318.50
WDC 316.28	MCAF 316.12	TTF 314.97	SLB 314.80	JOF 302.18	BRWIX 314.38	KURZ 327.13	ALL 291.62	GRR 289.02	TCH 233.13	LSI 322.23	OII 298.33	KT 318.93
FD 317.05	PEG 316.18	GNE 315.68	FDGRX 314.90	DLNK 303.47	JAVLX 314.63	ENM 327.27	ZEN 291.67	GHV 289.07	MSX 233.13	GABVX 323.40	PH 298.57	AL 319.33
CCR 317.27	PRGFX 316.53	TOS 316.40	S 315.17	MAPS 303.47	FSAIX 315.13	MANU 327.43	ENM 291.73	PCAPX 289.10	FFTYX 233.30	CWP 323.52	PKF 298.95	ITW 319.73
HMSY 317.30	DJ 316.73	OPTFX 316.72	LMT 316.17	AMR 303.80	FBIOX 315.13	WLV 327.43	ASPX 292.08	GNCI 289.12	BKS 233.37	CH 323.57	QNTM 299.33	MS 319.90
SGI 317.55	CB 316.88	TAN 317.10	DLNK 316.23	SCHL 304.93	FSESX 315.13	IFF 327.57	CATP 292.10	EGLS 289.28	ALL 233.60	ERTS 323.88	FIDSX 299.58	BHI 320.45
GP 318.53	SII 317.10	SII 317.27	MAPS 316.23	BMET 304.98	FSVLX 315.13	CATP 327.67	SANM 292.15	WLP 289.40	UTEK 233.65	BSET 324.07	FSUTX 299.58	MO 320.85
WFC 320.45	PMS 317.10	S 317.93	GTF 316.42	IGEN 305.02	FSPCX 315.13	OXY 327.68	THDO 292.15	WNDR 289.43	ZEN 233.65	PCAR 324.07	SYQT 300.77	ASC 321.22
ABS 321.47	IR 317.40	LGN 318.72	JHNGX 317.20	SEPC 305.02	FSRPX 315.13	SANM 327.83	JAMRX 292.17	ACAI 289.45	MWHS 233.87	TCOMA 324.07	LHP 301.93	PURT 321.23
AR 321.57	SFL 317.50	RCHY 319.57	RMDY 317.35	YSII 305.02	GOSHA 315.27	PCAPX 328.02	FSNGX 292.18	CYRX 289.48	MAR 234.02	LTR 324.23	AAPL 302.33	TDM 321.47
CBE 321.73	PH 317.88	SLB 319.58	CTR 317.75	WWY 305.50	INTV 315.82	FSNGX 328.38	FORMF 292.18	HLYW 289.57	ASPX 234.20	SGP 325.02	SRA 302.57	EMC 321.48
BA 322.53	TSK 318.03	JANSX 319.58	OAT 318.48	TRW 306.10	NOC 316.63	FORMF 328.38	NN 292.50	MCLL 289.63	THDO 234.42	BKB 325.67	CPB 302.70	OPPSX 321.70
WMS 322.53	PKF 318.75	VLIFX 320.13	IGEN 318.75	ELY 307.23	TTX 316.65	EGLS 328.77	VENGF 292.62	MATH 289.63	JAMRX 234.45	ALEX 326.80	PKN 303.37	GTF 321.95
PARQ 322.63	APCC 318.78	DSPC 320.30	SEPC 318.75	HUM 307.25	AHM 316.73	VENGF 328.83	SYMBA 292.73	CYRK 289.65	FMILX 234.45	AGN 326.80	INFS 304.75	AADV 323.53
GLBL 322.88	MCHP 318.78	BTIOF 321.20	YSII 318.75	GTF 308.87	CLE 316.95	WNDR 328.88	CMSB 292.80	CTEA 289.85	FSNGX 234.50	CGNX 327.17	BFI 305.05	COT 323.53
ARC 323.63	TRCD 318.78	APA 321.72	SSW 321.20	MEA 310.47	TX 317.67	ACAI 328.95	JTAX 292.80	GLBL 289.88	FORMF 234.75	GD 327.33	GAP 305.23	HWP 323.67
LGN 323.85	GTF 319.88	ABT 322.03	TEK 322.03	ZE 311.25	SLB 318.07	SYMBA 329.05	USWI 292.80	PKF 289.88	SANM 234.92	AGREA 327.57	PCH 305.65	BSPT 324.28
TXU 324.10	LIFE 319.90	JAMS 322.82	FMILX 322.88	PARQ 311.28	SOPFX 318.18	CYRX 329.13	RCHY 293.03	TRBCX 289.93	CATP 234.97	DEC 327.57	MIL 305.67	GABGX 324.45
USFC 324.15	DGN 319.92	ECH 322.83	KRB 323.03	FSR 312.00	AL 318.27	CMSB 329.17	BTIOF 293.08	MSX 290.07	BOST 235.07	ANL 327.63	DF 305.73	DCN 324.60
MUS 324.38	AAPL 319.93	DEX 323.63	IRL 323.17	SSW 312.58	BLT 318.58	JTAX 329.17	JAMS 293.15	LSTR 290.25	GHV 235.12	BMY 327.63	BMET 306.73	FDC 325.30
IBM 324.67	NELL 320.13	QLGC 323.83	AVT 323.72	GLK 313.15	FO 318.62	USWI 329.17	NSTA 293.20	SIII 290.53	VTA 235.18	FSLEX 328.28	WAG 307.08	AALR 326.82
LA 324.88	ABF 320.18	LIZ 323.85	WFC 324.27	BTA 313.30	GLN 318.62	JAMRX 329.18	DLNK 293.43	ENM 290.57	GNCI 235.22	GY 328.50	BBI 307.68	CATP 327.03
TRW 325.22	AGC 320.77	F 324.32	CI 325.13	RYOCX 313.63	AMRMX 318.67	THDO 329.25	MAPS 293.43	NN 290.67	WLP 235.28	FLE 328.52	PPG 307.97	SSW 327.03
MHP 325.45	CGNX 321.40	NSTA 324.40	DEX 325.15	IRL 314.08	VLIFX 320.53	HLYW 329.30	IGEN 293.55	AVID 290.67	3I 235.37	DDS 328.60	HI 308.20	YHOO 327.33
RYOCX 325.67	VPMCX 321.53	MATH 324.53	ZE 325.23	EVGRX 315.02	WWH 320.78	MCLL 329.30	SEPC 293.55	INTU 290.68	MATH 235.37	SYMC 328.68	BLL 308.27	NTAIF 327.58
CSK 325.82	HAL 321.87	KT 324.58	APA 325.48	SUN 315.03	AMZN 320.93	PH 329.57	YSII 293.55	ALL 290.68	MCHP 235.38	AUD 328.68	PEP 308.35	FMCSX 328.08
ATTn 326.12	MRO 322.47	USFC 325.12	ABS 325.52	IIF 316.77	GTW 321.40	RCHY 329.62	S 293.88	ZEN 290.75	TRCD 235.42	WBN 329.02	RDC 308.93	COMS 328.20
TELC 326.12	CMB 324.62	WIN 326.12	FOCPX 325.93	UNM 317.13	PWJ 321.68	ASPX 329.67	PARQ 293.98	WALL 290.77	AMX 235.42	BNL 329.17	KR 308.98	BGEN 328.45
CYCH 326.18	DDS 325.33	SBL 326.17	KT 326.38	NOBE 317.18	HFX 321.85	CYRK 329.68	RYOCX 294.15	MCHP 290.83	WALL 235.45	NWK 329.18	WTEC 309.87	IRL 329.08
RDA 326.65	SYMC 325.33	IF 326.47	VCI 327.05	VCI 317.25	MOB 322.23	BTIOF 329.73	3I 294.30	TRCD 290.83	AVID 235.45	CRUS 329.33	LOW 310.30	SANM 329.10

Sun	Moon	Mercury	Venus	Mars	Jupiter	Saturn	Uranus	Neptune	Pluto	Node	Asc	MC
CSCO 327.65	FSAIX 325.40	LMS 327.03	TRW 327.13	OPTFX 317.90	GE 326.57	CTEA 329.73	IIF 294.35	ASPX 291.05	GLBL 235.45	PCL 329.70	TIN 310.33	BP 329.57
IDTI 328.13	FBIOX 325.40	PWJ 327.87	MOMGX 327.50	STAR 318.03	IK 327.07	JAMS 329.85	SEG 294.42	THDO 291.12	INTU 235.45	CS 329.82	MEA 311.15	ALTR 330.62
TTF 328.15	FSESX 325.40	HWP 329.32	KRAGX 328.02	BBELL 318.30	MKS 327.17	EK 329.95	SDTI 294.52	CATP 291.12	GRR 235.50	WIN 330.88	CMH 311.35	XIRC 330.65
CTR 328.72	FSVLX 325.40	ARC 329.73	USG 328.18	EPG 318.80	GR 327.68	NSTA 329.97	QLGC 294.83	JAMRX 291.12	LSTR 235.50	DE 331.40	GM 311.97	BZF 330.67
WIN 328.92	FSPCX 325.40	DLNK 330.23	STAR 328.28	FOE 318.98	CHCLX 329.30	TRBCX 330.00	VJET 295.08	SANM 291.13	SIII 235.65	FKREX 332.88	N 312.08	ALBK 331.73
IIF 329.72	FSRPX 325.40	MAPS 330.23	PARQ 328.78	WAG 319.00	PRGFX 329.30	MSX 330.18	FMCSX 295.90	VENGF 291.13	VJET 235.72	MTC 332.88	FDEGX 312.53	XON 331.80
LIZ 331.45	EQ 325.45	LMT 332.47	XTR 328.97	FCX 319.12	INDQA 330.00	ZEN 330.27	FORE 296.12	FSNGX 291.15	NN 235.72	PURT 333.52	ASTA 312.68	PESC 331.97
INDQA 331.67	FMC 325.85	IGEN 332.72	EPG 329.52	CL 319.83	NAV 330.00	ALL 330.30	ASND 296.23	FORMF 291.15	FORE 236.50	FDESX 335.20	FDEQX 313.18	AZO 331.98
NAV 331.67	GAP 326.17	SEPC 332.72	RYOCX 332.53	TEN 320.80	DI 331.35	CUM 330.43	SRYIX 296.33	SYMBA 291.20	PKF 236.58	LLY 335.25	FMILX 313.23	LCOS 332.75
AMRMX 332.42	EVGRX 326.60	YSII 332.72	CYGN 333.00	WTHG 321.40	ITA 331.43	DLNK 330.43	CKFR 296.55	CMSB 291.25	ASND 236.72	LA 335.48	JAOLX 313.60	ONCS 333.18
ALK 334.43	CTEA 327.12	IFF 332.92	U 333.63	UH 321.82	GABAX 332.63	MAPS 330.43	PNU 296.85	PNU 291.25	ENM 237.15	CQB 335.67	BVALX 313.60	PRGFX 333.28
SCHL 335.23	SUN 327.20	IIF 333.32	RN 334.25	TRV 323.05	SUNW 332.87	CQ 330.57	LBTYA 297.53	JTAX 291.25	SRYIX 237.18	BTR 336.08	TXT 314.00	PHII 334.57
APA 335.92	TTF 327.32	CB 333.33	PRGFX 334.78	LNCR 323.45	ASH 333.80	IGEN 330.67	CBB 297.72	USWI 291.25	VENGF 237.57	REY 336.43	OST 315.13	LU 334.83
CCM 336.18	FMILX 328.53	MO 333.88	FCYCF 335.55	AALR 323.75	TNB 334.47	SEPC 330.67	NSCP 297.75	RCHY 291.40	SYMBA 237.60	SFL 337.97	FBGRX 316.28	DRTHX 336.35
ABX 336.47	BOC 329.72	CCR 333.92	FNATF 335.55	QLGC 324.62	ORCL 334.77	YSII 330.67	FSTCX 298.17	BTIOF 291.43	CMSB 237.63	BST 338.77	SOPFX 316.97	FSNGX 336.37
SII 337.08	KKTWX 329.85	RMDY 333.95	AALR 336.43	KO 325.45	MSFT 335.00	PARQ 331.62	NGG 298.27	JAMS 291.47	JTAX 237.63	BS 339.18	ADM 317.57	FORMF 336.37
TSK 337.45	CSC 330.07	BA 334.20	SKY 336.45	CMH 325.68	P 335.18	RYOCX 331.98	DSPC 299.10	NSTA 291.50	USWI 237.63	TWN 339.20	JHNGX 318.02	BNI 336.90
ITA 337.70	INFS 330.37	OXY 334.70	ADI 336.57	ASTA 326.45	AL 336.37	IIF 332.47	JAOLX 299.22	DLNK 291.65	RCHY 237.63	BNI 339.40	FO 319.80	MD 337.60
BS 337.87	VO 330.57	FCYCF 336.10	LNCR 336.93	GP 326.75	CL 336.37	AVP 332.63	SPYG 299.42	MAPS 291.65	BTIOF 237.72	BP 340.60	GLN 319.85	ORBI 338.17
ELY 338.25	RR 330.63	FNATF 336.10	IIF 337.55	CCE 326.98	MS 336.87	AT 333.07	LMT 299.47	IGEN 291.72	JAMS 237.73	ORX 340.97	ENM 321.33	FKGRX 338.25
JANSX 338.60	SBRY 332.83	DCN 336.28	XON 338.57	BVALX 327.22	TOMK 337.10	QLGC 333.68	RMDY 299.50	SEPC 291.72	NSTA 237.75	CY 340.98	LPX 322.45	NME 338.53
SNA 338.67	MO 332.97	RYOCX 336.63	COMS 338.78	AADV 327.32	OAT 339.08	VO 334.03	FLCSX 299.58	YSII 291.72	NSCP 237.77	ACN 341.78	TEN 322.70	ZE 338.90
GRA 338.73	FDGRX 333.98	NFB 336.72	WDC 339.23	COT 327.32	ONCS 339.78	Z 335.03	ZLG 300.40	3I 291.87	DLNK 237.82	JANSX 341.93	CTX 322.80	APB 339.00
TAN 339.10	CHKR 334.03	GLBL 336.87	INDQA 339.37	PESC 327.48	MYL 342.15	DUK 335.05	RNE 300.72	SEG 291.88	FMCSX 237.63	SLE 342.23	FDX 323.25	CI 339.10
QLGC 339.77	PARQ 334.25	PARQ 337.57	NAV 339.37	PCH 330.03	XRX 342.57	MEA 335.07	AOL 300.87	SDTI 291.95	FSTCX 237.63	ABS 342.70	DGN 323.57	JPM 339.27
CB 340.22	JEQ 334.28	EMC 338.52	HMSY 340.47	OAT 330.07	RTZ 342.70	KKTWX 335.97	IOM 301.08	PARQ 292.00	MAPS 237.63	WFC 343.13	AVT 326.72	PZL 339.52
MXIM 340.23	HUM 336.65	SNA 339.12	BHI 340.63	FDGRX 330.08	UNM 342.98	BA 336.50	EGRP 301.73	RYOCX 292.10	ABS 237.63	WLA 343.18	ITT 327.45	PLN 340.83
UK 340.28	GNCI 336.80	TSK 339.78	NEM 341.08	CYCH 330.10	CCE 343.27	SEG 336.63	CYCH 301.98	IIF 292.23	LBTYA 237.63	RAD 343.85	FOCPX 328.55	ADI 340.87
ABT 340.63	TKF 337.70	MCHP 340.73	GMT 341.58	FDCAX 330.10	FDCAX 343.53	SDTI 336.75	BGY 303.00	VJET 292.38	IGEN 237.83	AA 343.93	MCIC 329.68	WWY 341.40
IF 340.75	JHNGX 339.13	TRCD 340.73	PESC 341.77	W 331.88	RBK 344.03	FMCSX 337.07	ORA 304.03	QLGC 292.53	SEPC 237.83	DREVX 344.23	USW 330.53	GY 341.50
IFF 342.07	CYRK 339.25	ABX 340.75	TDM 341.83	ORBI 331.97	TXU 344.08	NN 338.03	LCOS 304.05	CKFR 292.78	YSII 237.87	BMCS 345.18	BBELL 330.90	GLK 341.92
S 342.17	UNVGX 340.23	WALL 342.10	AADV 343.10	XIRC 332.73	GAS 344.47	SRYIX 340.07	LU 304.10	PNU 293.02	PARQ 237.87	IGF 345.28	MOMGX 331.45	KRAGX 342.08
GNE 342.23	KLM 340.73	FMCSX 343.18	COT 343.10	BA 333.50	CHPS 344.53	ASND 341.27	YHOO 304.30	FORE 293.13	RYOCX 237.97	NVLS 345.28	BLUEX 331.52	HD 342.55
RLM 342.28	CNTO 340.90	AVID 345.23	FON 343.80	ALBK 333.52	RGEN 345.10	JCI 341.43	PHII 304.43	FMCSX 293.15	IIF 238.00	PCH 345.33	USG 331.72	RGEN 344.55
GABAX 342.72	CBB 341.08	INTU 345.23	HOU 344.27	FOCPX 334.85	APC 345.27	FORE 341.70	RTK 304.53	ASND 293.23	QLGC 238.03	APCC 346.15	XTR 333.18	SRYIX 344.55
FCYCF 343.05	VJET 341.08	SCHL 345.47	CCH 344.43	RBK 335.08	PEG 345.47	3I 341.88	LOR 304.58	SRYIX 293.35	SPYG 238.07	EIX 347.45	DI 335.10	PEG 346.62
FNATF 343.05	XIRC 341.17	INDQA 346.72	NOVL 344.43	USG 336.38	FSHOX 345.50	BS 342.22	NRK 304.80	LBTYA 293.40	FLCSX 238.27	AKLM 347.50	VWUSX 336.90	FON 348.23
OXY 343.07	RNE 341.55	NAV 346.72	GABGX 345.43	CPB 336.62	FSCGX 345.50	VJET 342.38	CTR 306.00	NSCP 293.55	CKFR 238.37	DELL 347.98	BKB 337.12	RR 348.87
ECH 343.32	FPF 341.65	PURT 349.78	SBL 345.72	MER 336.62	FSDPX 345.50	CNF 344.97	BLT 306.75	CBB 293.60	SEG 238.53	ZLG 347.98	JCP 340.47	JAMRX 349.07
SUNW 343.72	QCOM 342.15	BHI 350.77	TXU 345.93	GAS 338.35	FSRFX 345.50	DSPC 345.22	FCYCF 306.75	FSTCX 293.83	SDTI 238.83	SNF 348.03	CL 341.77	UCL 349.18
LSTR 345.03	CR 342.17	ELY 350.77	ITW 345.93	IFF 338.95	CNC 346.10	BDK 346.75	FNATF 306.75	NGG 293.97	ZLG 238.92	PNU 348.03	TEK 343.18	CCH 349.23
SIII 345.03	TAN 343.07	PZL 351.03	JR 346.38	BSPT 339.68	IFMX 346.10	CR 346.27	WWH 307.55	JAOLX 294.60	PNU 239.30	TRV 349.07	RAL 343.98	EK 350.42
DSPC 346.55	WMT 343.07	OPPSX 351.40	JANSX 346.78	OXY 339.73	WTEC 346.70	LMT 346.32	AL 308.48	SPYG 294.80	EGRP 239.72	TXU 350.20	SKY 344.48	TIF 350.68
NFB 346.77	FO#1 343.22	MS 351.60	ITA 346.87	FDC 340.47	OREM 346.87	RMDY 346.43	HFX 308.50	FLCSX 294.85	BGY 240.33	FCX 350.47	VENGF 344.95	FCX 351.50
F 347.03	MEF 343.48	LSTR 351.83	SNA 347.47	U 341.83	CA 347.77	HI 346.48	GTW 308.63	DSPC 295.02	LMT 240.52	GLK 350.52	CAG 346.68	UST 351.75
DEX 351.12	SO 343.90	SIII 351.83	TOS 347.60	SCDUX 341.92	KWP 347.77	BCC 346.70	AMZN 308.67	RNE 295.07	FCX 240.55	DH 351.00	SYMBA 348.30	MRO 352.85
NPR 351.27	WEN 345.08	UK 352.00	GHV 347.62	GMT 342.12	NWS 348.63	ACV 346.67	AR 316.02	CYBR 295.07	DSPC 240.55	OAT 351.35	GHV 349.23	MYL 352.97
PWG 351.27	ENG 345.40	TDM 352.15	ORBI 348.27	APA 343.97	LLTC 349.75	EGG 347.17	BOC 316.33	LMT 295.07	AOL 240.60	CL 351.63	CMSB 349.98	FFIDX 353.23
VCI 351.28	OREM 345.70	ALTR 352.60	OPPSX 348.52	OLOG 344.30	FMC 349.88	CBB 348.05	GM 317.03	AOL 295.08	CBB 240.72	ALTR 352.33	JTAX 349.98	LOR 353.65
ORCL 351.72	RAL 345.88		MUS 349.17	FRF 345.40	MAIL 351.23	PNU 348.28	KM 327.67	RMDY 295.08	RNE 240.75	BZF 352.37	USWI 349.98	GIS 353.82
AVID 352.03	GAS 346.20		QLGC 350.03	LMS 345.73	ADBE 351.27	NGG 348.33	PEP 328.47	IOM 295.33	NGG 240.92	NTAIF 352.53	MMM 350.42	
INTU 352.03	PCAPX 347.50		DCN 350.23	DNB 347.02	ADPT 351.33	JAOLX 349.25	FO#1 330.10	ZLG 295.45	CYBR 241.20	PSON 352.68	BC 352.35	
KT 352.10	FD 347.90		NME 350.45	GE 347.12	SCF 351.85	OM 349.48	ARC 331.22	EGRP 295.62	RTK 241.77	EMC 353....	HM 352.47	
	PCH 348.12		IAD 350.57	TXU 347.33	NGC 352.33	SGRFX 349.58		CYCH 296.37	JAOLX 241.80	UAL 353.35	ABAX 352.50	
								BGY 296.45	LOR 241.87			
									UAL 242.13			

Sun	Moon	Mercury	Venus	Mars	Jupiter	Saturn	Uranus	Neptune	Pluto	Node	Asc	MC
STAR 352.27	JCP 349.20	BZF 352.60	PZL 351.03	FMCSX 347.42	FSAVX 352.62	CKFR 350.28	XON 333.50	NRK 297.20	IOM 242.47	GNE 353.90	CTZN 352.60	MF 353.83
MSFT 352.72	PRGS 349.57	KRAGX 352.75	XIRC 351.73	GIS 347.62	FSPFX 352.62	ZLG 352.77	TKR 340.77	ORA 297.55	PHII 242.58	MXIM 354.02	GMT 352.65	CHCLX 354.37
ITW 352.90	RCM 350.40	ITW 353.32	OM 351.75	NOVL 347.82	FSHCX 352.62	KRAGX 352.88	DD 343.37	LCOS 297.57	YHOO 242.72	TTF 354.65	KRB 353.02	FDLSX 354.62
EPG 353.27	APB 350.88	XON 354.87	GY 352.20	SNF 348.42	FBMPX 352.62	SNS 352.95	MO 344.15	LU 297.58	LU 242.87	AHC 355.42	PFE 354.73	CG 355.05
JOF 353.75	CYBR 350.92	ITA 355.58	GNCI 352.58	UCC 348.68	FSRBX 352.62	ABT 353.43	IAD 345.93	RTK 297.63	BLT 242.90	DRLEX 355.42	PWJ 355.55	FMAGX 355.38
MO 354.02	UTEK 353.08	CATP 355.95	SGRFX 352.83	AKLM 348.98	ECH 352.65	LBTYA 353.48	IBM 346.23	YHOO 297.68	LCOS 242.90	UNP 355.58	FDGRX 355.60	NOB 355.62
ASC 354.38	AMR 353.35	ADI 356.33	ALBK 352.97	DELL 348.98	GER 352.80	CYCH 353.72	IR 347.53	LOR 297.73	ORA 242.90	SBL 355.70	HOU 356.37	HAE 356.08
ENG 354.50	ALBK 353.47	GRA 356.47	DREQX 353.07	PFS 349.12	TOL 352.83	NSCP 353.82	ADM 347.92	PHII 297.73	CYCH 243.00	GR 356.03	NSM 356.42	GOSHA 356.17
OPPSX 354.90	PE 353.70	GABGX 356.52	GABAX 353.10	WTEC 350.98	X 352.85	FSTCX 354.32	BC 348.62	BLT 298.38	WWH 243.18	JP 356.17	NOVL 356.57	DAL 356.22
LMT 355.53	TRV 354.15	MYL 356.83	ROAD 354.27	PLN 352.05	CCR 354.50	FLCSX 354.60	KO 348.98	CTR 298.58	NRK 243.48	CMB 356.37	BA 356.78	IAD 356.47
WALL 356.02	NOBE 354.20	RLM 356.87	YELL 354.27	BFI 352.93	GTE 356.07	SPYG 354.68	UK 354.57	WWH 298.95	HFX 244.00	KBH 356.75	RCHY 356.80	FRF 357.35
RMDY 356.53	RD 355.23	BGEN 357.65	SUNW 354.35	EIX 353.92	G 357.57	HM 358.13	C 355.47	FCYCF 299.03	GTW 244.30	FBGRX 357.18	DGAGX 356.90	BUD 357.75
HWP 356.78	BAY 355.35	SANM 358.55	WLP 356.40	APCC 354.43	ABX 358.80	MDA 358.95	MOB 355.53	FNATF 299.03	AMZN 244.50	BT 357.43	GNCI 357.22	TRV 357.87
DCN 357.68	LSCC 355.97	MSFT 358.72	GTE 356.45	IP 354.87	W 358.88	ORA 359.40	TX 356.10	HFX 299.70	AL 245.08	MIL 357.62	SGP 357.23	ASPX 358.72
MCHP 359.00	UAL 356.58	BSPT 358.73	AR 357.57	ADI 357.33	TSK 359.03	LCOS 359.43	GE 358.87	GTW 299.85	CTR 245.50	MAS 358.02	AT 358.02	CNF 359.17
TRCD 359.00	PNU 357.37	FDC 358.80	LIZ 357.82	DCN 357.45	FOE 359.78	MCD 359.67	MKS 359.32	AMZN 299.92	FCYCF 245.60	USS 358.35	BTIOF 358.52	MAS 359.25
LNCR 359.25	CCI 359.03	ORCL 359.45	PURT 358.55	ALK 358.95	AR 359.87	LU 359.68	IK 359.40	AL 299.93	FNATF 245.60	JPM 359.82	REY 358.97	AVP 359.75

Stay in Touch

If you bought this book directly from Cycles Research, then you are on our mailing list and will receive updates about new books, software, and seminars.

If you purchased this book elsewhere, send your name and address to Cycles Research, 666 5th Ave.No. 402, New York City, NY 10103 —and we will let you know what's new and what's coming.